Solving the Problem of "Agriculture, Farmer and Rural Area" by Rule of Law

DING Guomin

TRANSLATED BY GAO JIANXUN AND LIU YUN

Hamilton Books

Lanham • Boulder • New York • Toronto • Plymouth, UK

4501 Forbes Boulevard, Suite 200, Lanham, Maryland 20706
Hamilton Books Acquisitions Department (301) 459-3366

Unit A, Whitacre Mews, 26-34 Stannary Street,
London SE11 4AB, United Kingdom

Printed in the United States of America
British Library Cataloguing in Publication Information Available

Library of Congress Control Number: 2017938899
ISBN: 978-0-7618-6920-7 (cloth : alk. paper)—ISBN: 978-0-7618-6921-4 (electronic)

Contents

Preface

The works of Dr. DING Guomin *Solving the Problem of "Agriculture, Farmer and Rural Area" by Rule of Law*, from analyzing the present situation of the three agriculture issues and the causes hereof, puts the countryside of China under the spotlight of rule of law, and proposes the fundamental solution to the problem, that is, the completion of rule of law in the rural area.

"Three Agriculture-related problems" is a social problem of public concern in China since its reform and opening up program. There have been great achievements in the economic and sociological circles, but the research in legal field is relatively weak. Nowadays, people from all circles of life have realized the seriousness of the problem, the urgency of solving the problem and the great significance of solving the problem to the deepening of socialist economic market. However, in search for methods and approaches for solutions, many researches did not go inside and just stopped where the problems arise. How to solve the "three agriculture-related problems" fundamentally, a more insightful research shall be made from a higher perspective. Therefore, it is of great significance to discuss the topic of "three agriculture-related problems" from the perspective of rule of law.

It seems that "three agriculture-related problems" and "rule of law" are two topics independent from each other. However, they are closely related. On the one side, if China is deemed to realize rule of law in the whole country, it shall include rule of law in the rural area, which shall not be isolated to be a vacuumed area. If rule of law is to be realized in rural area, then "three agriculture-related problems" must be solved, otherwise rule of law will become empty talk. On the other side, although there is not only one means or approach to solve the "three agriculture-related problems", the ultimate solution lies at the system level, which will guarantee the enforcement of the various approaches and measures. Today, while we are constructing a socialist country, rule of law shall take priority in solving of "three agriculture-related problems". Seen from the dual urban-rural structure of China, the legal enthusiasm and consciousness of citizens as well as the legal resources of urban area are much better than that in rural area. It is no exaggeration to say that the key to realize rule of law in China lies in the farmers, rural area and agriculture, i.e., the solving of "three agriculture-related problems".

The author of the book has been engaged in the teaching and research of economic law and has accumulated rich experience in the subject. While pursuing his doctorate degree he focused on the topic of rule of law in rural area, he collected great amount of data and carried out lots of surveys, which have constituted the basis of theoretical and practical analysis of this book. The main body of the book is the doctorate degree dissemination of the author. However, after graduation, the author gave up the chance to have the book published right away and continue to revise the book. During the period, he conducted more investigations into and researches on the grass-root masses in rural area and obtained abundant first-hand information and data, including the source of constitutionalism in rural area, CPC village committee election, land system, rural cooperative, agricultural industrialism, rural social security as well as the protection of rights of immigrant workers. This kind of research attitude is worth encouraging. It is believed that the publication of the works will produce beneficial social influence.

—QI Duojun
September 2007 Yuelu Mountain

Chapter One

Introduction

1.1 QUESTIONS

Since the topic of this book is "Solving the Problem of 'Agriculture, Farmer and Rural Area' by Rule of Law", it is necessary to explain what is rule of law, what is "agriculture, farmer and rural area" and the relationship between them. China is now in a special period of developing in depth, yet people's understandings of rule of law in the market economy are not consistent; and the problem of "agriculture, farmer and rural area" (hereinafter referred to as "Three Agriculture-related Problems"), as the special social problem in special historical period of China, is not known to the world.

1.1.1 What Is Rule of Law

For this question, relevant words used in China mainly include "rule the nation by existing law", "rule the nation by law", "a country under the rule of law", "a society under the rule of law", etc.; the extended concepts include "rule the factory by (existing) law", "rule the school by (existing) law", "rule the village by (existing) law", etc. In September 1997, Jiang Zemin proposed in the report of 15th Central Committee of CPC that "ruling the nation by existing laws refers to that the broad masses of the people manage the national affairs, economic and cultural undertakings and social affairs by all means and forms in accordance with the provisions of the constitution and laws under the leadership of the Communist Party of China (CPC), to ensure all works of the nation proceed in accordance with existing laws, to realize the systemization and legalization of socialist democracy, to make sure this kind of systems and laws will not change with the change of leaders, or with the change of opinion and attention of the leaders". This illustration basically represents the mainstream of current thoughts of rule of law in China. The rule of law and democratic politics are closely connected with each other, and can even be considered as two sides of a coin.

In contemporary Chinese language, "rule of law" is always confused with "rule by means of law", which also indicates that the convention of rule of man is deep-seated in China. The differences between rule of law and rule of man are self-explanatory; however, to accurately understand the connotations of the loanword, rule of law, we have to find answers in western languages, for "rule of law" in modern sense is translated from western languages. There are five expressions in English countries: Rule of Law, Rule by Law, Rule according to Law, Government by Law, and Government through Law.[1] All five expressions have the same meanings and reflect the principles of supremacy of law in national politics, economic and social life. Professor Dai Yisheng's illustration helps us accurately understand the connotations of rule of law by the distinction between Rule by Law and Rule of Law:

Rule of Law refers to the supremacy of law; it is the explicit limitations and regulations on the national powers. It requires that all powers must be subject to the applicable law. All people, including the persons holding the supreme powers, should be subject to the supervision of law instead of overriding it. All people shall have fair and full opportunities to know all provisions of the law, to understand the clear scopes of the penalties imposed by the government. Since the enforcements of law are compulsive, and the government would always hinder the enforcements of substantive laws and procedural laws which limit the power of government, therefore, only with the implementation of the cardinal principle of rule of law, can the individual's freedoms be well guaranteed. The concepts of rule of law were improved and developed in history by many ideologists including Plato, Socrates and Locke et al, and sometimes were realized only by continuous fights of the people against the autocratic privileges in history. The aim of rule of law is to safeguard individual freedoms so it strictly forbids any politic organizations or groups to impose their will on the people, and prohibit any political group to wrest political power illegally by going against the will of the people or by misrepresentations of law. The principle of rule of law is that "the government is composed of a set of laws and not of a group of men".[2]

It can be said that rule of law is an inexorable trend of democratic politics of human society. More developed human society and higher degree of civilization will lead to more individual freedom and more respect of individual rights , which could only be fully realized and guaranteed in a society under rule of law.

However, China is a country with a long history of rule of man, in which, people were tamed into docile lambs under the regulations of feudal conventions and ethnics laws. The emperor, the bureaucrat, the clansman, the eldership and the man formed a complicated power network, and the broad masses of people had no other choice but to obey. Freedom and right were highly luxurious things; the obligation orientation became the sole standard in the ideology of that age. After the founding of new China, the people should have broken from the feudal thoughts. However, the wrong guidance of the leadership just made the masses get out of the feudalism obligation orientation into the socialism obligation orientation. Personal cult and selflessness made the individual citizen completely lose the self-ego. "Individuals must be subordinated to the collective" and "national interests are the highest", etc. sound right. However, the unreasonable strengthening of the guiding ideology unconsciously covers up personal values, and the personal freedoms are severely limited.[3] Under such social background, the rule of law became a redundant or even "reactionary" word.

China's reform and opening up program is all round, involving not only economic field, but also the political or even cultural field. The proposing of the concept of rule of law may be the most important and also the first trumpet call of political reform and opening up in China in its true sense so far. Looking back at the constitutionalism history since China's reform and opening up, one decade has passed since the proposing of reform and opening up in the beginning of 1980s till the entry of "ruling the nation by law and constructing the socialist rule-of-law state" into the constitution at the end of 20th century. The progress made during the past decade in rule of law equals to that was made during the 80-year journey since the May Fourth Movement. If we say that the pursuing of democracy and rule of law in the May Fourth Movement "has a strong romantic color",[4] each step of China's rule of law construction since the reform and opening up is clear and down to earth. China's rule of law is far from perfect now, but it can be said that the shift from rule of man to rule of law is an irreversible historical trend in China.

China needs rule of law. Behind the strong call, we need seriously consider this question: which kind of rule of law does China need? In recent years, the hot debate over "good law and bad law" in the legal circle makes people ponder over the existing legal systems of China, and the theory of "bad law is also law" is denounced unprecedentedly. However, what is good law? What is bad law? What are the standards to distinguish them? These can be traced back to the question of legislation and judicial review. The legislation activities are closely connected with the social, political, economic and cultural objective factors of that time. Moreover, there are many subjective factors influencing the establishment of law principles by the law makers, including various personal subjective factors, quality and cultivation of the law makers themselves and overall legislation mechanism of the country, wherein the legislation concepts of the law makers are the most important. The legal concepts of law makers directly influence their understanding and judgment on what legal principles shall be established.[5] When interviewed by PKU

News Network, Professor Zhou Wangsheng, a famous legislative expert from China, also said that good law is closely connected with the law makers. Then what constitutes a qualified law maker? First, he must have modern legal sense, and know that the purpose of legislation is to protect civil rights and maintain good social order. If a law maker doesn't have this concept of rule of law and takes it for granted that legislation is to "manage the people", he is not a qualified law maker, for he does not know for what the legislation is at all. Second, the law maker must have good command of legislative skills and systematic theoretic knowledge. Third, the law makers must know the national conditions, local conditions and customs. They should be acquainted with the particular cultures, the service recipients of the legislation work, and whether the legislation can solve problems in actual situations. Since 1970s, we have formulated lots of laws, but most of them are of poor quality and failed to protect the legal rights that should have been protected. "The differences between rule of law and rule of man, in fact, are not whether the law is needed, but what the law aims at. One key standard of good law is protecting the people's rights, pushing the society forward towards a more civilized direction.[6] Since ruling the nation by law is established as China's basic strategy of running a country, it is often confused with rule of law. In fact, ruling the nation by law is only an incomplete proposition of rule-of-law, and only ruling the nation by law is insufficient to become a rule-of-law country. Pursuant to the classical explanations made by Aristotle, rule of law shall have two meanings: established laws have been universally abided by; meanwhile, the laws abided by the public shall be those well formulated. Ruling the nation by law can only cover the first meaning defined by Aristotle, but cannot ensure the established law is well formulated.[7]

Generally speaking, the laws required by rule of law shall have the following elements. First, the law shall be universal. The universality demands that the provisions of law shall be targeted at all persons governed by the law, rather than one or some persons. It shall become the code of conduct for all persons, and all persons shall be regulated by the law without exception. All people are equal before the law, and no privilege is allowed. Moreover, the universality of law requires that legal rules shall be explicit. Without the universality and explicitness of the law, the arbitrariness and randomicity of the governmental activities would be expanded, while the citizens could not make plans or decisions on their own activities in accordance with the law. Second, the law must be followable. The law must not be far away from practical life. It needs to play a role in social life, and must be dependable and followable in people's real life; the law must be human oriented, serve the people, and bring benefits and interests to the people. No oppressive or unequal law shall be formulated since it will not be observed and supported by the people. Third, the law must be stable and shall not be changed frequently. Stable laws and rules are reliable and expectable, which is a kind of guarantee of people's lives. Only with stable rules, can people predict the legal consequences of their conducts, and can orders become the guarantee of people's life. Fourth, the law shall be permissive. The laws required by rule of law must have permissive spirit and democratic sense; the laws should be able to distinguish the different motives of illegal acts, and deal with different illegal acts according to general requirements of morality and customs. The illegal acts out of evil motives must be punished severely to maintain social orders; whereas the illegal acts out of safeguarding public orders and good customs, and some illegal acts resulting from dramatic changes of the society must be forgiven and pardoned. Although the law is the supreme authority of the rule-of-law society, it is not the sole authority. Besides the law, there are other authorities, including ethic rules, religious disciplines or even "folk laws". They all play different constraint roles to the people in different circles. It should be admitted that the law has loopholes and defects even in the rule-of-law society, thus to govern the whole country with harsh and cold laws is against the good will of rule of law.

In exploring what kind of law is needed, we must consider this question: how is the law "formulated"? What laws do we need? How to make a law? The question of whether the law can be spread to , rooted and blossom in the marginalized rural area are very important and critical. Legislation, i.e., making laws, has been described appropriately as one of the greatest human's inventions that contain the gravest consequences, and its influences can be even more profound than the discovery of fire and the invention of ammunition. There are many problems to be settled in the formulation process of China's laws. In China, the formulation and amendment of some laws show strong "bureaucratic law" color. "Laws are hidden in the government, with inscrutable stateliness" is the inherent work style of China's bureaucratic system for several thousands of years, which depends more on and reflect more opinions and attitudes of relevant governing bodies in the process of formulation and amendment. Although the opinions of some other "neighboring" institutions can sometimes play certain role, they only influence the minor details of the law, rather than deciding or changing overall pattern of the law. Obviously, the development of this condition will turn the power of formulating and amending law into monopoly power of some departments to gain interests, thus turning rule by law into ruling the people by law. It is no wonder some scholars propose that we must be vigilant against "legislation corruption". The corruptive law is not the product of a deed, but the result of certain department's "April Fool's Day prank" caused by divorcing themselves from the masses and reality and acting blindly. Such kind of law becomes "teeterboard", which is convenient for the government but inconvenient for the ordinary people. It will certainly not be appreciated and cannot have satisfactory effect after coming into effect. Some may say that, China is contemporarily underdeveloped in productivity, many people have to work for living and have no time to care for democracy and rights, and the ordinary people are of poor cultural quality due to limitation of economic conditions, so more attentions should be paid to the opinions of jurist in the legislation. Of course, legislation by experts has certain benefits, that is, the experts can stand on a relatively detached position and consider the law rationally and objectively. Seen from the development trend, the role of experts in legislation shall be strengthened. However, we must also understand that some problems and shortages still exist in legislation by experts. The laws drafted by experts are usually too heavy in scholar's style due to the limitations of their own role definition and living experiences, with idealist feeling more or less, and therefore deviated from ordinary people's concrete practices and life.

In recent years, some democratic attempts are made in legislation in China. In 2001, the Ministry of Land and Resources (MLR) declared to solicit for the public opinions when formulating *Measures for Announcement of Land Requisitions* (Draft). The leader of Policy and Regulations Department of MLR expressed that "We look forward to the voice from the masses, especially the farmer, there is no forbidden area and so-called unified propaganda during the whole process of supervision, the opinions may be publicized in newspaper at any time." Gan Cangchun, Director of the Policy and Regulations Department, holds that the administrator only paid attention to the law abiding education to the farmer in the past to tell them how to do, but always neglected what the farmer care for and be afraid of indeed. While in fact, most farmers appealing to the higher authorities for help hold the Land Law at hand, showing that they will file a suit if we do not work in accordance with the law. Farmers' degree of concern and understanding of the land legislation may be even higher or better than some cadres including the cadres in land management system. When making a law, the change from divorcing oneself from the masses and reality to seeking advices from them is a directional change from legislation for administrative management to legislation for protecting the interests of the ordinary people. The change of this legislation may be considered as a good beginning of China's legislation history. The opening of legislation procedures is in itself a good law popularization opportunity. The legislation in nature is the distribution of rights and interests, and the law is the product of quarrel and compromise. Without the participation of ordinary people to the largest extent during the distribution process, this distribution in itself could hardly be fair. We do not deny the role of legislation by experts, and admit that the participation by all people may increase the costs and reduce the efficiency. However, it is dangerous and undemocratic for any law to exclude the regulated objects from the legislation process, which may turn the law into the autocracy tool. The legislation shall follow the mass line, that is, "everything is from the people, to the people, by the people and for the people". This is a good tradition in

China. The democratic participation and procedural justice in law making process increase the fairness, transparency and democracy so that the law may be deeply rooted in the fertile soil of social reality and possess high reliability and applicable vitality.

It is easy to discuss but difficult to implement the rule of law. Currently, China has entered a benign development circulation of rule of law track as a whole, but is far from a real rule-of-law state. One reason is that China's legal construction begins too late, some critical factors also need a progressive process, including national economy, overall education degree of nationals and conventional concepts of governing a state. Moreover, if the problem of judicial fairness cannot be well settled, all rule-of-law dreams will be disillusioned.

1.1.2 What Is "Three Agriculture-related Problems"

"Three Agriculture-related Problems" is the abbreviation for the problems related with the agriculture, farmer and rural area in Chinese language, which was first mentioned in 1990s. The Central Committee of CPC held a special conference to study agricultural problem in 1993, forming the "Agricultural Development Outline of China in 1990s". This document first abbreviated the problems of agriculture, farmer and rural area into "Three Agriculture-related Problems", thus forming a proper noun.[8] Originally, the three terms of agriculture, farmer and rural area were put together with no special meaning; later, they were combined into "Three Agriculture-related Problems" and taken as a focal issue from the Central government to local governments, the educational circle as well as all circles of society. The major reason is the severe imbalance between the economic development of urban area and that of rural area and a series of social problems arising therefrom. This problem, summarized by Li Changping, the former township Secretary of the Party Committee of Jianli County, Hubei Province, who once sent a letter to then Prime Minister Zhu Rongji, is "the farmers are really hard, the rural areas are really poor and the agriculture is really dangerous".[9]

Seen from the eyes of some urban residents, the rural areas are picturesque, with fresh air; the farmers go out to work at sunrise and come back home at sunset; the smoke curls up from kitchens, chickens and ducks are in groups. What a leisure fictitious land of peace! Some people catch a glimpse of many western style buildings along the roads of rural areas from the train, with grains piled like a hill. What a harvest and abundant scene! Of course, the existence of this image in their minds is very ordinary. What we often listen to and see in official media are mostly the "representative" and "image project", which are the excellent "political achievements" of some officers. Chinese officers always report only good news instead of bad news and are boastful, which have been changed to certain extent in recent years, but the bad habits and their nature have not been changed. What on earth do Chinese rural areas look like in general? The signs can be seen from the anxiety of two prime ministers who are honest to a great extent. What Li Changping described in the letter to Prime Minister Zhu in 2000 was the countryside picture in plain region of Hubei Province "Here in my hometown, almost all farmers left in early spring". For more than twenty days, Dongfeng trucks (people cannot afford passenger car) carried the farmers outside to work in the cities all over China day and night. Our township has 40,000 persons, including 18,000 labors. Now 25,000 have left, including 15,000 labors. There are new characteristics of personnel outflow in this year when compared with past years: the first is that there are many unemployed migrant people. In the past, the outflow was goal directed, while in this year, farmers go out with the frame of mind of not to be a farmer for the rest lifetime and take chances and stay in the city until death. The second is that the number of total persons and labor force is large. In the past, those went out for work are mainly girls and some surplus labor force, but now people of all ages go out for work in cities. The third is that many people abandon the paddy fields and farming. People used to go out for work after their fields are contracted to others, but now they just leave home with the field unattended. The number of outflow persons is still rising. It is estimated that the area of fields abandoned will reach 35,000*mu* (1mu = 666 $^2/_3$ m^2), accounting for 65% of the total area of the township. It is predicted that, even if we spare no effort to do contracting work for the fields, the fields abandoned in this year will still reach over 20,000*mu*." Just think about it, who wants to be migrant people if not driven by poverty? Who would abandon the fields that were loved by them generation after generation for a work if farming could bring them money? Hubei used to be a region where the cultivation of rice and the breeding of fish flourish, with Jingzhou as the representative. Even though the plain region with good agricultural basis is like this, you can imagine the conditions in other places. CCTV Legal Report of Feb. 24, 2004 covers a case that, five farmers of Leibo County, Sichuan Province wrongly killed a panda by mistake. The off-screen voice of the reporter "Leibo County is a national poverty-stricken county, the annual income of common farmer household is only two to three hundred Yuan, and 45% of the population of the whole county are ethnic minority, most of whom do not know Chinese language, which bring certain difficulty for the introduction of advanced production technology. The poor life makes the people living in the mountain for generations develop a hunting habit so as to supplement the need for daily life…Huang Changxi, the criminal of this case, even felt rather satisfactory when talking about his life in the prison. He said he could not have enough to eat at home, but in the prison, meals are guaranteed, and what's more, he could eat some meat or fish each month." In the face of the farmers' terrible poverty, it is high time for those holding the high-profile view of "a good situation in China" to go to the countryside to have a look.

Historically, the influences of Chinese farmers on the history development process of China were the largest and the most lasting. In a sense, it is no exaggeration to say that, the Chinese history after Qin and Han dynasties can be summarized into a countryside development history, the Chinese society of several thousands of years in nature is the society dominated by folk countryside. The most important riot, turmoil, uprising and revolution in the history all originated from the countryside. The world-shaking Chinese socialist revolution was the result of "encircling the cities from the countryside"; the household contract responsibility system emerged in the beginning of 1980s and a series of reforms initiated in China with this as the turning point also started from the countryside; the "democratic direct election" which will become the majority of China also selected the countryside that lacked a democratic sense as the starting point and "test field". So far, China is still a backward agricultural country with 900 million farmers, we still have 80% of population living in the countryside, and this is the basic national conditions and status quo of rural China. The agriculture, farmer and rural area are still the most important force in the shaping of China's reality and future.[10]

Today, when we hail about the achievements obtained by the reform and opening up, do we ever consider what situations the farmers are in? Do they also keep pace with the reform and opening up? Do they also enjoy the sweet fruit of the reform and opening up? China's economic development level has been listed by international organization in the top ten; moreover, some international organizations predicted that China will enter the top three of the world in respect of growth potential in the near future. However, China is a society of dual-structure, and anyone who have an opportunity to visit the rural areas will find that the rural areas are poor and backward. The situations in costal developed regions are different, but it should be said that most traditional agricultural regions cannot keep pace with the overall progress of rapid development and modernization of the state. Therefore, more and more people pay their attention to rural area problem. Especially in recent years, people begin to accept the concept that China's problem is not just the problem of agriculture, but "Three Agriculture-related Problems", i.e., the problems of "agriculture, farmer and rural area".

The striking feature of "Three Agriculture-related Problems" is the severe imbalance between the urban area and the rural area, and the dramatic contrast between farmers and citizens arising therefrom. The way to form city oriented policy is the policy of so-called "scissors difference", that is, the product prices and production factor prices are contorted by the government, creating a policy environment going against the agriculture, farmer and rural area, and agricultural surplus is reaped to supplement the industrialization.

The city oriented policy in China was directly rooted in the heavy industry oriented strategy beginning in 1950s. The above measures of contorting urban and rural relationship adopted in developing countries for the city-oriented policy can also be found in China. However, the policy and measures with the most Chinese characteristics are a series of system arrangements hindering the labor flowing.[11]

"Three Agriculture-related Problems" is not the problem in single respect of agriculture, farmer or rural area, but a comprehensive problem. The problem remains unsolved for a long time, with the contradiction being sharpened day after day, thus attracting the large concerns from the society. Since 1996, the agriculture has entered a hard time and the income gap between farmers and urban citizens has become larger and larger. In March 2000, Li Changping, former Secretary of the Party Committee of Qipan Township, Jianli County, Hubei Province, listed the striking crisis in rural area in the letter to Prime Minister Zhu: unemployed migrant people looks like "flood", the burdens like "Mount Tai", the debts like "Mount Qomolangma", cadres like "locusts", responsibility system like "fetters", policies like "lies", and lies like "truth". The letter of Li Changping created a nationwide stir, and the crises of "Three Agriculture-related Problems" are exposed to the public immediately.

"Three Agriculture-related Problems" becomes the social concern mainly because it has constituted substantially powerful threaten to the social stability of China. First, the farmer is overburdened and the situation is increasingly deteriorated. According to the spot sampling survey of 11 ministries and commissions including National Bureau of Statistics of the People's Republic of China (NBS), the average number of institutions in each town and township Party Committee and government is 16, with 158 personnel in average, exceeding the scheduled staffing scale by 2 to 3 times; the average number of subordinated units of each town and township is 19, with over 290 personnel.[12] The severely overstaffing personnel impose heavy burden to the farmers, some government organs heavily in debt cannot make ends meet, and this financial conditions is one of the very root of overcharging in rural areas. Furthermore, the report of NBS shows that, the rural Gini coefficient increased from 0.2124 in 1978 to 0.3361 in 2003, which is far larger than the growth rate of urban Gini coefficient (0.16-0.295).[13] The income gap between urban and rural citizens reached 3.3 times in 2006, and the Gini coefficient of income gap between urban and rural residents has reached 0.496.[14] Second, the spirit of revolt is growing stronger day by day. From the late 1980s, with the deterioration of rural development situations, the farmer rebels more and more frequently and in larger and larger scale, with the rebellion forms aggravating day by day, and with violence orientation sometimes. "Three Agriculture-related Problems", if not settled, will destroy the social stability in the long term, and hinder the sustainable and stable development of national economy for the short run. Third, the labor force is in surplus, with high employment pressure. It is estimated that Chinese land needs 100 million of agricultural labor force at most, while currently labor force in rural area totals 550 million, if another 120 million will be absorbed, there will be still about 300 million labor forces in surplus. Based on current population growth rate and newly generated employment opportunities, China will still confront severe labor force surplus within at least 40 years. Many labor forces cannot be absorbed in rural area and can only turn to urban area. How to settle the employment problem of 300 million people becomes the huge difficulty of China during the economic development process. The more problems are exposed, the tenser will be the suppression system of the local governments, and the stronger will be the revolting spirit of farmers. This forms a vicious circle, which finally further deepen the accumulated rancor between the farmers and local government. Therefore, over the time, the farmers have formed a relatively fixed thinking model that, only the Party Central Committee and the State Council could attend to their difficulties and injustices. Consequently, the phenomena of collective appeal, skipping appeal and appeal to Beijing occur frequently. If it is said that, among the consecutive 6 No. 1 Documents of the Central Party Committee of CPC after the founding of new China, the first five are targeted at the consolidation of delightful achievements in the reform of rural reform, while the sixth, nearly 20 years later, was the forced response of the Central Party Committee to the increasingly severe crisis of "agriculture, farmer and rural area".

The problems of agriculture, farmer and rural area are not separated from and irrelevant with each other, they are an overall problem. The agricultural production modes are extensive, with low efficiency, the countryside infrastructures are backward, and the inputs are severely insufficient, which result in the low income of farmers. Moreover, local governments increase the burdens of farmers impractically, the farmers, especially those in backward areas cannot rely on agricultural production to maintain their existence now. The helpless farmers have to leave their hometown for cities, only to confront various kinds of discriminations in the cities. All unhappy problems that the farmers have to confront are the negative chain effects at the system level. Seen from the internal relationship of "Three Agriculture-related Problems", insufficient agricultural input → backward agriculture → low income of farmer → more unwarranted agricultural input → poorer conditions of the whole rural area, has formed a typical vicious circle. Seen from the external relationship of "Three Agriculture-related Problems", China's industrialization is a way of developing the industry at the cost of the agriculture. The plunder of cities and industry aggravated the poverty of rural areas, and widened the income gap between urban and rural areas, while the poverty of farmer and the shrinkage of rural market in turn affect the development of cities. When attending the "Century Forum", Dr. Wen Tiejun translated

"Three Agriculture-related Problems" into "three dimensional rural issues". He considered the rural problem in three dimensions, put "Three Agriculture-related Problems" into the background of national urbanization and industrialization, and opposed to the deliberation on "Three Agriculture-related Problems" from only one dimension of agricultural input & output and supply & demand.

"Three Agriculture-related Problems" are a comprehensive problem. Chinese state-owned enterprises also have many problems, including low efficiency, huge losses, large number of laid-off workers, workers' poverty and insufficient social security, etc. However, we will not combine the problem of state-owned enterprise, the problem of state-owned staff and the problem of community of state-owned staff into the "problems of state-owned enterprise, worker and community"; likewise, if the coal mining industry have some problems, we will not call it as "problems of coal industry, coal enterprise and coal worker", call the problem of iron and steel industry as "problems of iron and steel industry, iron and steel enterprise and iron and steel worker" ; if problems arise in the banking industry, we will not call it "problems of banking industry, banking enterprise, and banking employee". China has farmers divided as per blood lineage, but has no coal workers or iron and steel workers with blood lineage shifting; has scattered and isolated villages, but has no artificially isolated coal worker or iron and steel worker community; has the agriculture controlled by the mufti-layer national institutions to make contributions without proper rewards, but other industries may either have more freedoms or receive more aids. The combination of problems of "agriculture, farmer and rural area" into one problem has its reasons, but the settlement methods of the problem should never be confined inside the combined problems, in which no way out can be found. It is unrealistic to attempt to develop the agriculture vigorously only by the structure adjustment, and by science and education, so as to change the backward conditions of rural area and the fate of farmer. Even though China's agriculture creates the impossible miracle, it is obvious that the farmer which accounts for 70% of total population cannot bring forward the all-round, well-off and common prosperity by supplying foods, fruits and vegetables to the other 30% of population. The agriculture is agriculture, the farmer is the farmer, and they are not the same thing. The rising of agriculture does not necessarily mean the "liberation" of farmers, and vice versa, the "liberation" of farmer does not always result in the rising of agriculture. The relationships between the problem of rural area and the problem of agriculture and the problems of farmer are likewise. [15]

The core of current problems of "agriculture, farmer and rural area" in China is the problem of farmer, that is, the problem caused by the ignorance, trampling and infringement of farmers' rights. Who ignore, trample on and infringe the rights of farmers? The problems between farmers are not tough questions since they can always be solved and regulated by mature civil and commercial law, criminal law, etc., and the relationship in this regard is now in an orderly status; the Gordian Knot is not the one between the farmers and urban citizens or other common civil subjects, and so far, there is no direct confrontation and conflict of such groups or population, if any, it can be easily regulated and coordinated. The real issue is between the grass-root government and the farmers, which is still aggravating today. The governments of various periods have been aware of and very worried about this problem, but no good tactics can be found so far, or the implementation of such good tactics is impossible, with no proper conditions or no good effect. Some may ask, since there is a management relationship between the government and the farmers, how can it be aggravated into an unsolvable problem? To answer this question, we have to clarify the following questions: Who possess the land right of the farmers? Who have the decision-making rights on the burdens of the farmers? Who shall be responsible for the supply of such public products as education, pension, remedy and infrastructure construction, etc.? These all point to one subject – the government. And the main contents of current problem of farmers are the above problems. The nature of problem is the poor role positioning of the grass-root governments, who have not properly changed from the "regulation" government under planned economy into the "service" government under market economy.

Why "Three Agriculture-related Problems" has emerged long before but been ignored for nearly 20 years? Only when the emergence of large number of urban laid-off workers caused social panic, did the government understand that the root of problem of cities lies in the rural area, why? The problems of "agriculture, farmer and rural area" is proposed and attracted great attentions only after the problems of cities occurred, which more clearly proved that the rights of farmer have been ignored for long. In this regard, the problem of "Three Agriculture-related Problems" is not only the problem of agriculture, farmer and rural area, but also a social problem involving the whole society. China will never get out of trouble before proper settlement of "Three Agriculture-related Problems".

1.1.3 Relationship between Rule-of-Law and "Three Agriculture-related Problems"

"Three Agriculture-related Problems" and the rule of law seem to be quite different things, but in fact, they are closely connected with each other. On one hand, to realize all-round rule of law, the rural area shall also be ruled by law, and shall not become the vacuum zone beyond the rule of law; while "Three Agriculture-related Problems" must be solved for the realization of rule of law in rural area, otherwise everything of rule of law is nonsense. On the other hand, there may be more than one solution to "Three Agriculture-related Problems", but in the final analysis, the implementation of all programs and measures must be guaranteed by rule of law to solve the problem in social systems. Today, when China is building the socialist rule-of-law state, the settlement of "Three Agriculture-related Problems" must follow the steps of rule of law.

Seen from the dual structures between urban and rural areas of China, to realize rule of law in urban area is far better than in rural area no matter from the rule-of-law enthusiasm of the citizens or from the rational value judgment or from the available legal resources in urban area. It can be said that, the key to rule-of-law in China is the rural area. "Three Agriculture-related Problems" must be settled for realizing rule-of-law in rural area. However, this problem has become the "forever pain of the heart" of Chinese government since it remains unsolved for a long time.[16] All circles of the society, especially the economics and sociology circles have paid great attention to the solution of "Three Agriculture-related Problems" since the end of 1980s, publishing many articles; the government also took pains to hold the conferences for agriculture-related problems every year, with the agriculture-related preferential policies being issued every year, but the "Three Agriculture-related Problems" remains unsolved. If the key to realize rule of law is rural area, where is the breakthrough point for settlement of "Three Agriculture-related Problems"? It is still the rule of law in rural area. This is one of the conclusions that I draw from the pondering over rule of law and the "Three Agriculture-related Problems".

1.2 SIGNIFICANCE OF THE TOPIC

1.2.1 Significance in Practice

Building a well-off society in all-round way has become an overall objective for current social development of China. Speaking from the aspect of rule of law, a well-off society shall be a rule-of-law society respecting the laws and with developed legal services. Today, when we are heading to an all-round well-off society, we shall pay equal attentions to economic construction and legal construction, with one point to be emphasized that legal construction shall be, just like the economic construction, all-round rather than local. Under current situations, the key to realize the target of all-round well-off society lies in the rural area. The well-off society is the one in full sense only after the rural area realizes all-round well-off; likewise, China is a rule-of-law society in full sense only after the rule-of-law is realized in the rural area. Therefore, rural area is also the emphasis and key to realize ruling of law in China. However, the status quo of rule of law in rural area is unsatisfactory, or rather, in disorder, so the research on the topic is very urgent.

Seen from the practical conditions of China, the biggest barrier to rule of law in rural area lies in not only the lack of democracy ideology and the legal systems, but also the lack of effective supervision, where law enforcement corruption arises. During the process of legal construction, there exists a pair of universal contradictions: on one hand, the legal consciousness of farmer increases continuously, on the other hand, the law enforcement in rural area is weak and corruptive. The law enforcement here is the general understanding, i.e., the activities of national administrative organs, judicial authorities and the organizations with legal authorization and their working personnel in implementing and applying the laws. We often hear that the farmers protest the law enforcement with violence, which give us the first impression that Chinese farmers are unruly. Of course, China has but very little unruly farmers. In fact, Chinese farmers are the most honest group. If we can completely clarify the ins and outs of each event in the rural area, maybe we will sympathize with Chinese farmers deeply. To be frank, the law enforcement in rural areas are ill-formed, with severe enforcement corruption problems. To their superiors, the law enforcers will abide by the laws, but to the farmers, they will do whatever they say. "Why your officials do not follow the laws?" This is often heard from the "anti-law" farmers. However, the law enforcers rarely listened to the farmers. They still do things in their own way. How can these conditions not thrill the farmers? How can the farmers believe in the authoritativeness of laws?

There was such a report from Phoenix TV on Dec. 8, 2003 that: the petition letter tide of this year is the consequence accumulated by many years of reform and development, which is a great challenge, and also rare opportunity for the new leaders dedicated to innovation and reform. The petition army coming from all over China forms the cold current in the capital Beijing, which flow amongst the Petition Bureau of the Office of Standing Committee of National People's Congress, State Bureau for Petitions and Calls, CPC Central Commission for Discipline Inspection, Ministry of Land and Resources, Ministry of Public Security, the Supreme People's Court, the Supreme People's Procuratorate and other authoritative departments. For the guards of all these organs, the miserable images and helpless faces of some petitioners are very common for them. However, the petition tide occurred in July 2003 was rare in these organs. Zhou Zhanshun, the Director of National Bureau for Petitions and Calls, when interviewed by *China Comment* of Xinhua News Agency in November, admitted that "total number of petitions from ordinary people has been rising since the beginning of this year". Zhou Zhanshun particularly pointed out that, during recent period, the number of collective petitions of ordinary people, repeat petitions and petitions of ordinary people to Beijing rise rapidly, which are characterized by large number of persons, larger scale, long duration and violent behaviors, resulting in chain reactions in some places and industries, and severely influencing the social stability of Beijing and local regions. The authority classified the problems complained by the petitioners into eight aspects, wherein the problems of agriculture, farmer and rural area are particularly serious. They mainly reflect that the rural taxes and fees reform in some places are not fully implemented, the burden of farmer was not obviously mitigated; the financial managements in some villages and groups are in chaos, the election at expiration of office terms in some villagers committees are non-standard; the lands are requisitioned and occupied and traded illegally in some places, and the land compensation is in low standard and withheld by governments at various levels, and the farmers losing lands have not been properly relocated; the actions of grass-root cadres are rude and brutal, the contradictions between cadres and common people are prominent, and so on.[17]

This report reminds me of one thing. When I went to Beijing by train, I saw a large catch phrase on the wall along the railroad line in Jiaozuo, Henan Province, reading: "Skipping appeal is strictly prohibited! Crack down the petitioners coming to Beijing!" The white and large lime words are extremely striking on the walls. Based on this condition, we can at least draw the following conclusions: 1. Chinese farmers have suffered too much wrong and injustice; 2. Nowhere can the wrong and injustice be complained; 3. The broad farmers are disappointed about self-remedy and judicial remedy; 4. The farmers believe that only the Party Central Committee and the State Council will adhere to the principles and uphold the justice for them. All these problems summed up, we can see that the legal conditions in Chinese rural area are poor, the legal consciousness of farmers are weak, and the legal sources in rural area are severely insufficient. In a rule-of-law state, general problems of the people shall be addressed by self remedy and common judicial remedy permitted by the law, and the dialog with the government and the parade and demonstration occur only when public interests are involved or in political games. However, China is different, especially in rural area, the old thoughts that "please Your Excellency uphold the justice for me" has not been changed after the baptism of modern civilization. Current legislation is extensive and backward; the authority of law fails to be manifested in judicial practices; and pan administration further intensifies the rule-of-man color.

"Three Agriculture-related Problems" may be the social problems most concerned about currently by the whole people in China, and was the core topic of the 16th CPC National Congress, the 10th National People's Congress and the 10th Political Consultative Conference etc. The CPC Central Committee and the State Council held the rural work conferences for many times in recent years to discuss the countermeasures of "Three Agriculture-related Problems", for which Prime Minister Wen Jiabao is also called as "Farmer Prime Minister". How to address the problems such as low agricultural production efficiency, backward agricultural production manner and rural poverty has become the primary work of Chinese government. People realized more and more clearly that, without solving the "Three Agriculture-related Problems", the targets of industrialization, modernization, striving for well-off, becoming a moderately developed country and the like will be hard to be realized and even become empty words. The mainstream of the world has entered post-industrial phase, while the industrialization degree of China is still rather low. To accelerate the industrialization progress, narrow the gap between China and developed countries, and to catch up with and even exceed the economic development level of developed countries, we must first solve the "Three Agriculture-related Problems". Without solving the "Three Agriculture-related Problems", China's industrialization will lack of strong support. The key to solve the "Three Agriculture-related Problems" is to realize the modernization of agriculture, urbanization of rural area and the civilization of farmers, which shall be pioneered by advanced technologies, based on scientific management means and guaranteed by standard legal systems.

Over the years, all circles of the society have proposed many good advices from different perspectives for the "Three Agriculture-related Problems", the government also increased the input to rural economic development, system construction and education and science & culture construction and other fields, but why "Three Agriculture-related Problems" is still a great "problem"? There is one Chinese old saying describes the non-fundamental measure for addressing the problem, which is "treat the head when the head aches and treat the foot when the foot hurts". If we only consider the matter as it stands for rural problem, to treat one problem when it occurs, it just verifies this old saying. Besides, to timely address the problems discovered is only an ideal, many problems cannot be solved in time due to the interference of various factors. That is to say, for the "Three Agriculture-related Problems", we should not only consider the solutions to the problems from existing specific problems. What's more important is to think of and settle the "Three Agriculture-related Problems" fundamentally. So what's the root causes of "Three Agriculture-related Problems"? Poor economic basis, backward agriculture and the like are still the phenomena and concrete representations. Why is the economic basis poor? Why is the agriculture backward? How to change these conditions? To explore it by following these problems, we should be able to master the root causes of the "Three Agriculture-related Problems". Of course, the "Three Agriculture-related Problems" are formed by many factors, including those hard to change, such as historical reasons, objective material basis and resource endowment. Some of them can be and must be changed, and they are just the regulating ideology and model for the "Three Agriculture-related Problems". To select Solving the Problem of "Agriculture, Farmer and Rural Area" (hereinafter referred to as "Three Agriculture-related Problems") as the topic of this book is to analyze "Three

Agriculture-related Problems" from legal perspective, to find out the crucial reasons of "Three Agriculture-related Problems" and put forward some suggestions to settle the "Three Agriculture-related Problems". This is of great practical significance for solving the "Three Agriculture-related Problems" that afflicting current overall development of national economy of China.

1.2.2 Significance in Theory

The topic intends to find out the legal and policy breakthroughs at present stage through the analysis of legal condition jurisprudence for the "Three Agriculture-related Problems", so as to provide legislation advices and policy references for effective settlement of the "Three Agriculture-related Problems" afflicting the economic and social development in China.

Since the reform and opening up, great changes happened in the ideological sphere of China, a country with strong tradition of rule of man. Many civil right legislations involving people's livelihood, caring for folk customs and reflecting public will are spreading rapidly, which become the living reality from "rights on paper"; "administration according to law and administration for the people" is no longer an empty slogan, but just with specific measures and complete implementation; the State is unprecedentedly active and earnest about the protection and remedy of private rights; the civil consciousness's in execution and assertion of rights are emerging and increasingly rising. These reforms are not so vigorous and heart-stirring as Reform Movement in 1898 led by Kang Youwei and Liang Qichao, the Revolution of 1911 led by Sun Yat-sen and the May 4th Movement, but all these reforms are just like the wind sneaked into the night, moistening all things silently, pushing the whole society evolve towards the enlightened government, clear politics, well-developed civil rights and civilized laws. All these provide new chance for the difficult progress of rule of law in China, bringing new hope.[18] Especially since 1990s, "ruling the nation by law" was written into the Constitution, and the concept of market economy and rule-of-law economy were deeply rooted into the heart of the people. The legal lectures attended by the top leaders in the turn of the century indicated the resolution and confidence of Chinese government in rule-of-law. In the environment of accelerating the construction of a rule-of-law state, many problems need our in-depth research, heated discussion and debate, and serious speculation and consideration. During the research, discussions and speculations, a series of valuable theoretical and practice literature rose in response to the proper time and conditions. The flourishing of jurisprudence in these years is inseparable from current age of reform and opening up.

The study on jurisprudence is one subject, most closely connected with the reality since empty and mechanical jurisprudence, will lose its vitality. It should be said that, during recent years, rich achievements have been obtained in both theoretical jurisprudence and applied jurisprudence in Chinese jurisprudence circle. But at the same time, we also discover a worrying phenomenon, that is, to establish a complete jurisprudence system, too much of our time and energy have been spent on the discussions on the boundary of branch law and on how to divide the branches of law. Even now, these problems hardly have any explicit answer even today. One more important problem is that, the excessive pursuit of the formats of jurisprudence system often restrains the hands and feet of the scholars. For example, people feel uncomfortable about criminal law scholars studying civil law problems or economic law scholars studying procedural law problems etc., some even deny the research results of others on the cause that "he is not the person studying this domain". In this respect, Professor Qi Duojun, a Chinese famous economic law scholar, has such a statement that worth our thinking, "The scholars at different times and in different countries have had many discussions on the relationships between rights and powers, and their understandings were quite different. In recent years, quite a few scholars in China picked up this topic again. I also have some thoughts, but I was mainly dedicated to the study of branch law in previous years and have not stepped into in the field of jurisprudence. Just as Richard Allen Posner says, 'Jurisprudence shall not be a domain solely occupied by a few legal scholars good at it.' The scholars mainly engaging in the research of various branch laws, including me, may certainly and shall pay attentions to the jurisprudence problems."[19] It is a shame that, the "Three Agriculture-related Problems" has afflicted the economic and social development of China for so many years, with great attentions being paid by the economics circle and sociological circles, but what is the response from the jurisprudence circle? When mentioning the experts of "Three Agriculture-related Problems", we will go far back to Liang Shuming and Fei Xiaotong, then naturally Wen Tiejun, Chen Xiwen, Xu Yong, Qin Hui et al in recent years, and Yu Jianrong, He Xuefeng, Li Changping et al in more recent years. When mentioning the experts from jurisprudence circle, it seems that it is difficult to find a scholar really and systematically researching "Three Agriculture-related Problems". If it is said that the results of Professor Tian Chengyou and his students are relatively systematic, they are only tentative researches, and many things should be done for further research. Of course, in recent years, many scholars in jurisprudence circle focused on the researches of "Three Agriculture-related Problems", including Professor Liang Zhiping, Professor Su Li, Professor Zheng Yongliu, Professor Wang Taixian, et al. However, when compared with the researches from sociological circle and economics circle, the concerns about "Three Agriculture-related Problems" coming from jurisprudence circle are too little and shallow. People often consider that the law is one of the superstructures, so jurisprudence research is something that must be looked upward. In recent years, however, the concerns about "Three Agriculture-related Problems" from jurisprudence circle indicate that, the research of these experts on legal problems is in downward angle of view. It is a good thing to have a downward angle of view, but the legal problems about "Three Agriculture-related Problems" will never be thoroughly researched without putting the heart and soul into it, including going across mud road, eating with and talking with farmer family by only looking downward.

We got the complete perceptual and rational understandings on China's "Three Agriculture-related Problems" from the analysis of model and series of numbers of the economics circle and the phenomenon perspective of sociological circle. However, the solutions to several problems seem hard to touch the roots, thus are impossible to settle the "Three Agriculture-related Problems" fundamentally. The settlement of "Three Agriculture-related Problems" is a huge systematic engineering, which require us to master the overall situation and start from the root causes. Paying more attentions from jurisprudence aspect to "Three Agriculture-related Problems" has become a pressing matter of the moment for trying to build a rule-of-law state.

The topic discusses the "Three Agriculture-related Problems" from the legal perspective, which will provide supplements for the governance mode of "Three Agriculture-related Problems". During recent years, the researches on "Three Agriculture-related Problems" of economics and sociological circles made in-depth, detailed slice analysis on the rural traditions and status quo from such respects as villager autonomy, urbanization construction and income burden.[20] As a whole, the problems are fully exposed, all of them are the specific expressions of the "Three Agriculture-related Problems", which directly give the basic conditions of Chinese rural areas to the governmental officials, academic personnel and all circles of society who have no or little chance to go deep into rural lives. The attentions paid by the State to agriculture-related problems are inseparable from the hard work of these scholars. Meanwhile, we must clearly see its shortage, i.e., this research method is not macroscopic, global and systematic. Through these researches, we can know that the "Three Agriculture-related Problems" objectively exist and have to be settled, although their settlement method and the targets and effects need our further consideration. About this, current relevant research remains focusing on specific solution for specific problem. For example, most people know if real villager autonomy is to be realized the relationship between villagers committee and Party committee of the village shall be made clear, while the next step for solving the problem thoroughly is often omitted. This reminds me of the problem of novelists, they can meticulously observe the social reality, but are limited to raise the problems but fail to or reluctant to find out solutions. This kind of people are said to be slippery fellows, for the raising of questions generally will not cause dispute, while the solutions there of often bring troubles or become the target of public attack. We do not mean to disparage the people from all walks of life that make contributions to the discovery of "Three Agriculture-related Problems", instead, they are respectable. Without their hard work, maybe the "Three Agriculture-related Problems" will not draw great attentions from all circles of the society. Here I just want to say that, today, too few people have ever delved into the root causes of the existence of "Three Agriculture-related Problems" and make the solutions. The jurisprudence circle ought to have shouldered these responsibilities in the days of building rule-of-law in China. The topic intends to dissect and find the breakthrough for the "Three Agriculture-related Problems" from jurisprudence perspective. From this sense, I suppose the topic is of significant academic research value.

1.2.3 Significance in History

We must acknowledge this reality: the existence of "Three Agriculture-related Problems" is a historical course or a phenomenon in a historical development phase. The phenomenon objectively exists and should not be avoided and surprised at. Meanwhile, we should never take them lightly and disregard them. Only by facing up to this phenomenon and finding out the historical origin can the "Three Agriculture-related Problems" be settled precisely.

Seen from the world scope, large scale colonial expansion accumulated rich resources for the industrialization progress of Western Europe. However, the "Enclosure Movement" was the typical example for pushing the industrialization by sacrificing the interests of farmers. "Three Agriculture-related Problems" also can be found in the capitalist industrialization process of Western Europe, and their settlement also experienced a long period. It took nearly one hundred years to solve the "Three Agriculture-related Problems" in Britain, over seventy years in USA and the period of near two generations in Japan. The settlement of "Three Agriculture-related Problems" in China will not jump out of this law, and maybe the time needed will be even longer. At the beginning of modern history of China, the people with lofty ideals always took "Three Agriculture-related Problems" as the big obstacle that must be confronted on the way to a great power, but no good solution is found yet in the industrialization process. The trouble has been brewing for quite some time. The serious and numerous "Three Agriculture-related Problems" in China are not accumulated in a day. They are results of long term and abnormal non-agricultural strategy. Non-agricultural strategy refers to the industrialization with the cities as the priority, which needed huge funds and resources, and for which finance and resources became the greatest problem. Historically, the funds and resources for industrialization came from two channels. One is the industrialization road taken by Western European countries including Britain, France and Spain. They raised funds by plundering foreign countries. The other road is the injection of foreign funds, for example, the industrialization in South Korea, Japan and Taiwan of China. After the founding of new China, to smash the blockade and sanction of Western Countries led by USA, we must establish our own industrial system and rapidly realize industrialization. So large quantity of funds is needed, while both financing channels for the industrialization in the history were not applicable, therefore the problem could only be solved by ourselves; we had to sacrifice the agriculture, farmer and rural area, which are to take the "surplus" of farmers as the fund source for reproduction of industries. The reason was that, the "cake" was only such size, if more funds and resources were used in one industry; it would inevitably result in fewer funds for other industries. The non-agriculturization development strategy was to accelerate the development of industry by limited funds and resources through administrative means. This policy ensures the need of industrial development, while the agriculture, farmer and rural area have to pay the huge price, which is the economic basis and development background that have not been experienced by any other industrialized countries.[21] Chen Xiwen, Deputy Director of Development Research Center of the State Council, said in CCTV "Dialog" program on Mar. 24, 2003 that, "To my understanding, though there exist some differences due to different methods and standards, a widely accepted concept is that, the contributions made by farmers were 600 billion to 800 billion Yuan from about 1953 when agricultural products were purchased and marketed by the State in a unified way for the first time till 1985 when the unified purchase and marketing of agricultural products were cancelled". This fact of course stimulates the educational circle to voice their sympathy to the farmers.

When thinking carefully, we can find that Chinese farmers rarely lived well since the late Qing Dynasty. Chinese farmers had paid severe price for the development of capitalism in modern times and were always in the bottom level of the society; they finally met the savior Mao Zedong, who led the workers and farmers to become the master of the state, and the farmers could stand up and straight, but the following Sino-Soviet Split and the cold war trapped China into the predicament of military readiness industrialization. The military readiness industrialization road is at the price of sacrificing the agriculture, which made Chinese farmers "meet the trouble before turning over to be the master"; now that, the reform and opening up begins and the land is contracted, the farmers begin to lead a good life by hard work. However, for the improvement of market economy and acceleration of industrialization, the farmers' interests have to be sacrificed once again. The condition that "Three Agriculture-related Problems" continue for so long is only found in China, and some people predict that they will continue for even longer. Mr. Deng Dacai describes in his work *Basic Characteristics of Chinese "Three Agriculture-related Problems*" the difficulty in the solution of Chinese "Three Agriculture-related Problems", demonstrating the long duration (transfer of surplus labor force, accumulation of capitals including human capital, organization and system innovations), complexity (entanglement with the reform, globalization; encountering the information technology and new economy; out-sync between non-agriculturization and industrialization and urbanization), political nature ("Three Agriculture-related Problems" are ideological problems, the route problem and democracy problem of the reform) and specificity (special historical background, resource conditions and village administrative management system). However, we should not be pessimistic for that. After all, the existence of "Three Agriculture-related Problems" is a historical period, even though the period may be either long or short, depending on the efforts made by us. The existence of "Three Agriculture-related Problems" is undoubted, and their gravity also attracts the attentions from all circles of life. The key is how to find out the breakthrough to thoroughly settle "Three Agriculture-related Problems". The fundamental settlement of "Three Agriculture-related Problems" is of historical significance for realizing the target of modern construction of China and making China stand in the powers of the world.

The previous researches also proposed different solutions to the "Three Agriculture-related Problems" from economics or sociological perspective, for example, the "Tenant Farmer Economy" Theory of Mr. Zhang Wuchang, "Small-farmer Economy" Theory of Mr. Wen Tiejun, and the "Manor Economy" Theory that was bubbling with noise in 1990s. These theories aimed at solving specific problems, or proposing some assumptions for certain entry point of the problem, or doubting about current mainstream reform proposal. Anyhow, these theories are very helpful for us to completely and objectively understand and settle the "Three Agriculture-related Problems". However, to find out the reasons and propose radical solutions for these problems are strategies that need further consideration. The topic tries to make a historical attempt and breakthrough, to propose the conclusive proposition that solving the problem of "Agriculture, Farmer and Rural Area" by rule of law is the radical measures on the basis of tentative analysis of root causes of "Three Agriculture-related Problems". It is hoped that more scholars will join in this research.

1.3 PRESENT STATUS OF RESEARCH DOMESTICALLY AND ABOARD

Most researches of domestic scholars on "Three Agriculture-related Problems" list the features and corresponding countermeasures on the basis of analyzing the causes of "Three Agriculture-related Problems". For the convenience of narration and structural arrangement, relevant results of experts and scholars will be discussed in the next chapters, which will not be unfolded in details here.

1.3.1 Research from Economic Perspective

Maybe the economics, especially property economics and system economics are the first to pursue the root causes of "Three Agriculture-related Problems". Perhaps this is decided by the characteristics of so-called economic imperialism. The attempt in this respect began from the doctoral dissertation of Mr. Zhang Wuchang in 1960s— *The Theory of Share Tenancy*, which created the precedence using economics theories in the analysis of agriculture. It broke away from the ceaseless theoretical quarrels caused from land problem by such economists as Adam Smith and Alfred Marshall, and demonstrated from the existing agricultural phenomena whether existing agricultural phenomena are reasonable and what were their reasonability, thus opening up the broad application of empirical economics in agriculture. This theory started from the basic assumptions of economists, they supposed people are rational and would pursue the maximization of personal interests under rational guidance, considered the property right relationship as the fundamental factors affecting economic development and social progress. While the greatest key fact of property right evolution lies in the amount of transaction cost, or in whether the hitchhike phenomenon can be effectively limited. China has no explicit private property rights under the public ownership system in the past, but the ambiguous property rights beyond public ownership system, which initiated the low efficiency and hitchhike phenomena etc. and severely hindered the social economic development. Therefore, explicit ownership seems to be unalterable principles from the view of point of the economists, and the ambiguous ownership is the root of "Three Agriculture-related Problems".

However, after land contract system was implemented in rural area, especially after the regulation on land was further loosened, Chinese rural economy experienced only a temporary flourish in 1980s, and then got into trouble again in 1990s. Why? Obviously, it is impossible to make satisfactory explanation again by borrowing traditional property right economics without any change, for existing rural land system has legally provided the property rights of agricultural lands, which in certain degree may be deemed as the property right contract with clear provisions. This urges the economists to re-speculate the status quo of China, to improve their theoretical system. Mr. Zhou Qiren supposed in the series of articles including "Farmer Incomes Are A Series of Events" written for "21st Century Economic Report" that, the root causes of rural reform are not only limited to the property right problems about lands, but originated from a more magnificent field of vision—the nationwide economic situation. Starting from this field of vision, Mr. Zhou considered that the ongoing rural reform as the second reform after 1978, which is also a land reform "delayed by over a decade". For the land reform in the end of 1970s, Mr. Zhou considered that, the land contract system partially transferred the property rights of lands to the farmers in legal form, which was hardly possible in the times when public ownership prevailed in the whole nation. The reason was that ten years of Great Cultural Revolution and subsequent economic bankruptcy not only drove the broad farmers to actively or even risk their lives to create a living way, but also compelled the nation to push forward the rural reform. Now, with the economic development in rural areas, the original driving force of reform has been vanished. The rise of one rural reform "dormant for ten years" was caused by the decisive factors of "great bottom of market", more specifically, due to the progressive decrease of farmer incomes since 1990s and subsequent insufficient purchase power of farmers, which affected the domestic demands. "The standstill of farmer incomes smuggled the national economy", which in turn resulted in slow growth and influenced the strategic deployment of the nation. Mr. Zhou basically held the point of view of property right economics, except that the emphasized point of view was no longer simple transaction costs, but the whole "Three Agriculture-related Problems" in details from income-property perspective from the height of the whole nation. Maybe this is the explanation height that can be reached by property right economics.[22]

Wen Tiejun, the researcher of Research Center of Rural Economy of Ministry of Agriculture, has written quite a few high quality articles and works on the "Three Agriculture-related Problems" on the basis of broad investigations. His works analyzed the causes of, and put forward countermeasures and advices for, the "Three Agriculture-related Problems". However, his prediction that "small-farmer economy" would exist in China for a long term is pessimistic.

Mr. Lin Yifu (Justin Yifu Lin) not only dissected the causes of Chinese "Three Agriculture-related Problems" from macro-economic angle, but also proposed practical solutions for government decision making to new village movements.

1.3.2 Research from Sociological Perspective

Sociological points of view believe that the "Three Agriculture-related Problems" rises from the social aspect of the whole nation. They believe that, the household register system implemented since the founding of new China split the country into two distinct societies— one is the city enjoying various kinds of special benefits, while the other is the ignored broad rural areas. This urban-rural barrier restrains the rural development, results in the second-rate citizen identification of the farmers, and finally drives the whole farmers into a terrible "lock-in effect". So they proposed tit for tat the opinion that "the root causes of Three Agriculture-related Problems are the restraint of urban-rural structure system". While the countermeasure is getting rid of urban-rural barrier and giving the national treatment to the farmers.

Mr. Xu Qianxi from Beijing Contemporary Chinese Institute supposes that current agriculture-related problems in China are too pressing and serious to be solved by vulgar economic ethics and policies, and thus are calling for a "sober and tough" political leadership. Mr. Xu is particularly opposed to vulgar economic ethics practitioners and those belief practitioners. He is opposed to the former "always selling off a soft eudemonism view, without perceiving the overall political thoughts and moral integrity of the nation", and opposed to the latter "establishing their own disclosure system simply out of 'the principle of conscience', out of 'unlimited confidence to their subjective belief', for the overall existence of the State and nation" and "floating on the uncertain opinions of chaotic worshippers". For politics, it must first face a sharp question—what position does the political system place the people to? The political philosophies and historical lessons of all ages and all countries all reveal such a truth: the people are the judges de facto. Therefore, it is certainly that the political system shall be people oriented. While the people-oriented political system must certainly "give national treatment to the farmer". This is logically consistent. "Giving national treatment to the farmer" never takes the marginal effect maximization discussed in the economics as the code, it is "the problem about what places does the political powers lie in". He believes that, it is "the common people at the bottom level, especially the farmers who snatch the social consciousness of several generations", which is inconsistent with the political nature, thus requiring objectively "the politicians and their assistants must learn to perceive the huge sense of historical responsibility and sense of national responsibility, distinguish the true requirements of political principles and execute the justice".[23]

Doctor Fei Xiaotong was well known for his "Economy of Jiangchun Village" and "Folk China" in his early period, who first researched Chinese rural area problems from sociological perspective. In current academic circle, many experts, including Xu Jingyong of Xiamen University, Xu Yong of Central China Normal University, Wang Sibin of Peking University and other professors, and Han Jun of CAAS, Chen Xiwen of the State Council and other experts, have published many works about the "Three Agriculture-related Problems", most of which analyzed Chinese "Three Agriculture-related Problems" from political, sociological and economic perspectives, attempting to find out the crucial reasons and countermeasures for the problems, including some constructive opinions.

Li Changping, the news figure once known for "I tell Truth to the Prime Minister", after working in the office of "China Reform" journal, successively published many articles about "Three Agriculture-related Problems". His articles analyzed various problems existing in rural areas very meticulously, concretely and practically, almost all of them are first hand data. He has been served as the town leader, fully understood the actual conditions, and obtained information from both the folk and official sources, which endowed him with acute insights to some sharp problems. However, he rarely proposed the solutions while discovering many problems, and his theories are not systematic.

Lu Xueyi analyzed the influences of urban-rural dual structure on the "Three Agriculture-related Problems", holding the opinion that the system of "separately administering the urban and rural areas in one country by two policies" was gradually formed under the centralized planned economy system, was applicable to the shortage economy at that time, it sacrificed the interests of farmers, confining the farmers within the rural areas, and the consequences are the restraint of activity of farmers, hindering the development of agricultural production for a long term, "foods are insufficient while 800 million farmers engaging in agriculture", which further aggravated the situation of shortage economy, and the system of "separately administering the urban and rural areas in one country by two policies" was therefore intensified due to shortage of materials, forming a vicious circle. It is suggested that the urban-rural relationship should be strategically adjusted, and the pattern of "separately administering the urban and rural areas in one country by two policies" be changed gradually. We must build a unified large market for over one billion population, not to continue two markets separating the urban and rural areas and excluding 900 million farmers from the cities. The present household registration system must be reformed to open the city and town gates, broaden the employment channels of farmers, and liberate the farmers once more. Of course, this kind of change or transition needs the promulgation and step-by-step implementation of a series of supporting laws, regulations and policies. Anyway, administering the urban and rural areas separately without any change is infeasible.

Zhang Xiaoshan proposed the root cause of "Three Agriculture-related Problems" is contorted national income distribution pattern. For a long time, there existed great disparity in taxation and re-distribution of national incomes between urban and rural areas in China. Before the reform and opening up, to complete the leapfrog development of heavy industry and realize the industrialization, the distribution pattern of national incomes in China mainly supported the heavy industry; after the reform and opening up, to accelerate the modernization of cities, the distribution pattern of national incomes in China mainly supported the cities. This is a contorted distribution pattern of national incomes, which is discriminatory and unfair for the agriculture, farmer and rural area.

1.3.3 Research from Jurisprudence Perspective

We cannot tell which one is better to classify "Three Agriculture-related Problems" as economic problems or political problems. However, we can easily discover a common point from the comparison of them, and they both attribute the final problems to the nature of role of human. The former emphasizes the great role of farmers in the game process between the State and the farmer, while the latter emphasizes the body politic shall be human oriented, both of them achieve the same purpose. This kind of analysis takes human as the focus. From the point of view of French writer Michel Foucault, both belong to the "Anthropology" disclosure system. All the conditions are similar to the status quo of China in many aspects— both can be attributed to a constitutional expectation generated due to the improvement of self-position of human for the increase of human value. Therefore, one reform way out for present China's "Three Agriculture-related Problems" is to push constitutional reform as early as possible, to continuously satisfy the expectations of farmer, and thus finally to believe and show confidence in the farmer.[24]

Professor Qin Hui, Chinese famous scholar, said at a lecture in Peking University that: "the so-called 'Three Agriculture-related Problems' is in fact the farmer problem. There is no agricultural problem, the agriculture, i.e., the supply problem of agricultural products is no longer a problem after the beginning of reform and opening up in 1980s. Once we have heard the words of "rice bag" and "vegetable basket", but now agricultural products are excessively supplied. The farmer problem, if any, will never be caused in rural area but in urban area. The subject of agricultural problems is embodied in the contradiction between the farmers coming to the cities and the original system. The farmer problem may be either rather complex or quite simple. It is unlike the farmer problem of western countries which was mainly the protection of rights. The contradiction of farmer problem in China is very sharp, but the direction is rather clear, it is the problem during the reform process, while in western countries, it was the problem after modernization. In short, two major problems that cannot be bypassed during the agricultural modernization process are the improvement of rights and the decrease of agricultural population. The improvement of rights is what Mr. Du Run said "giving national treatment to the farmer". The farmer problem of China includes many aspects, all of which are related with the problem of shifting from farmer to citizen, or endowing the citizen rights even though the farmer does not become the citizen. If the observation of farmer problem is not carried out for the purpose of improving farmer rights and interests, it may cause many problems.[25]

The articles such as "Spread Law to the Countryside" of Professor Su Li of Peking University, "Law and Order in Rural Society" of Liang Zhiping of Chinese National Academy of Arts and "National Law and Folk Law in Rural Society" of Tian Chengyou of Yunnan University tried to dissect the problems confronted by the rural development in China from constitutional level. Most of these scholars consider the problems confronted by rural area from the angle of the conflict between existing laws and rural behaviors and traditional cultures, with the trend of merging national laws with rural resources. I supposed that the merge is improper, the penetration of national laws into rural society must have a process, during which the rural behaviors should be respected as far as possible, but finally the authority of national laws must be set up in the rural area. As for the introspection of rule of law in rural area, the trend of "local rule of law" must be alerted. Rule of law in rural area shall focus on the research and absorption of local resources, but it is absolutely prohibited to exaggerate the role of "local resources", otherwise it may result in pulling out of the mud into quagmire.

"Basic Problems for Chinese Rural Economic Laws" written by Wang Cunxue, Luo Yousheng et al of CAAS systematically introduces the history and status quo of rural legal construction in China, and provides some advices for borrowing foreign experiences. However, this book is only limited to the description of phenomena and the structural unification in form, while the analysis and solutions of the problem are not deep enough.

1.3.4 Research Abroad

There is no the concept of "Three Agriculture-related Problems" abroad, but the treatment of agricultural, farmer and rural area problems were also not so smooth. The "Three Agriculture-related Problems" brought by original capitalist industrialization were far more tragic than in China. We must be at least very familiar to the "Sheep Eating People" phenomenon described by Marxist classical writer. However, it was not until the beginning of 20th century that the educational circles of western developed countries officially took "Three Agriculture-related Problems" as the major concern to influence the governmental decision making. Taking USA as the example, in 1930s, USA Professor Hadlow W. Hanna's discussion in the article "Law and Agriculture" on the generation and role of agricultural law arose enormous responses in jurisprudence circle. After that, a lot of economic and jurisprudent personnel engage in researches on farm operation and leasing problems. Professor Nil E. Haar wrote an agricultural works as huge as 15 volumes in 1980s. Moreover, "Agricultural Law Center" and "Center of Agricultural Laws" etc. were set up successively. Nil Hamilton, the president of American Agricultural Association, believed that one of the reasons that USA agriculture realized the success and historical development was that legal system played important role in agricultural production and operation.[26] Now USA has formed the agricultural law system consisting of near 100 agricultural laws with Agricultural Adjustment Act as the base and core.

Japan always looked up to Chinese ancient physiography as the standard in 20th century. Nitobe Inazo, the figure on JPY 5000-bill, was the outstanding physiography representative. Seen from the practices, it was from the middle and later 1920s that Japanese government invested in large scale into agriculture and rural area, when Japanese economy recessed severely, the society was turbulent, and the national economy nearly collapsed. However, Japanese government created the macroscopic control means through issuing national debts by open market businesses under the guidance of physiography, and invested the financed funds into the rural area and agriculture in large scale, which rapidly improved the incomes of farmer and expanded rural market, and changed the backward conditions of traditional countryside. The correct settlement of "Three Agriculture-related Problems" has helped Japan not only get through the global crisis, but also accumulate the comprehensive national power for invading China.[27]

By making an overall view on the legislative and academic researches of developed countries on "Three Agriculture-related Problems", it can be seen that most of them focus on the agricultural protection of the government, for the purpose of facilitating the farm owners to effectively engage in agricultural production, so as to satisfy the agricultural demands for national consumption and exports and for implementing domestic and overseas relief program. The expressions of foreign "Three Agriculture-related Problems" are widely different from that in China, so foreign experiences should never be indiscriminately imitated, but be borrowed on the basis that consistent with Chinese practices.

1.4 LOGIC STRUCTURE AND MAIN CONTENTS OF THE BOOK

The logic structure of the whole book is: 18 chapters in total, the former 10 chapters are general information mainly discussing basic theoretical problems of solving the problem of "agriculture, farmer and rural area" by rule of law; the latter 8 chapters mainly discuss the specific problems of rule of law in rural area, for example, rural constitutionalism, villagers committee election, rural land, rural cooperative, agricultural industrialization, rural social security and protection of migrant workers' rights and interests, etc.

Chapter 1, Introduction. It mainly raises the questions, explains the basic meanings of rule of law and that of solving the problems of "agriculture, farmer and rural area"; demonstrates the purposes and meanings of the topic; generally describes domestic and overseas research results.

Chapter 2, Causes of "Three Agriculture-related Problems". The author holds that government administrative ideology constitutes the root cause of "Three Agriculture-related Problems". Based on this judgment, four specific causes for "Three Agriculture-related Problems" are analyzed, including rural land property rights, urban-rural dual-structure, conditions of farmer right and rule of law.

Chapter 3, Choice of Mode for Solving "Three Agriculture-related Problems". Through the analysis of democratic politics construction (in politics aspect), property right system reform (in economics aspect), urban-rural overall development (in sociological aspect) and administration and safeguard of individual right (in jurisprudence aspect) and other governance models, the ideology of comprehensive regulation of "Three Agriculture-related Problems" with priority of rule of law is put forwarded.

Chapter 4, Necessity and Urgency of Solving "Three Agriculture-related Problems". Smooth development of all undertakings of the State has close relationships with the "Three Agriculture-related Problems" whose thorough settlement can only rely on rule of law so as to advance the smooth progress of all undertakings.

Chapter 5, Feasibility of Solving "Three Agriculture-related Problems" by Rule of Law. The feasibility of solving "Three Agriculture-related Problems" by rule of law is demonstrated through the national rule-of-law consensus, rule-of-law experience accumulation in rural area, the benign interaction between state laws and rural society and the experience borrowed from aboard.

Chapter 6, The Target, Principle, Step and Content System of Solving "Three Agriculture-related Problems" by Rule of Law. It includes the following contents: the targets of solving "Three Agriculture-related Problems", i.e., securing stability of rural area and agricultural industrialization operation, integrated development of urban-rural areas and safeguarding of rights; the principles of safeguarding national legal authority, securing the equal rights of farmers, and protecting the rights of action of farmers and comprehensive regulation; the basic framework system of implementing strategy step-by-step for solving "Three Agriculture-related Problems" by rule of law.

Chapter 7, Modes and Approaches for Solving "Three Agriculture-related Problems" by Rule of Law. The driving mode of solving the problem of "agriculture, farmer and rural area" combining governmental initiation and social promotion is proposed; the problem of "agriculture, farmer and rural area" is solved through such channels as improvement of legislation, fair justice, enhancement of legal consciousness of the public and strengthening of supply of rural legal resources.

Chapter 8, Legislative Drawbacks of "Three Agriculture-related Problems" and Corresponding Strategies. The drawbacks are pointed out and countermeasures are proposed through the analysis of the status quo of "Three Agriculture-related Problems".

Chapter 9, Judicial Drawbacks of "Three Agriculture-related Problems" and Corresponding Strategies. The drawbacks are expounded and countermeasures are suggested through the analysis of the judicial status quo of "Three Agriculture-related Problems".

Chapter 10, Solving "Three Agriculture-related Problems" by Rule of Law and Legal Consciousness of Relative Subjects. Through the analysis of status quo of legal consciousness of the farmers and rural cadres, the author is of the opinion that the legal consciousness will have a strong influence on solving "Three Agriculture-related Problems" by rule of law, and accordingly, the cultivation path of legal consciousness of relative subjects is put forwarded.

Chapter 11, Solving "Three Agriculture-related Problems" by Rule of Law and Constitutionality in Rural Area. The feasibility and specific path for realizing rural constitutionalism are discussed based on the analysis of origin, main connotations and practical significance of rural constitutionalism.

Chapter 12, Solving "Three Agriculture-related Problems" by Rule of Law and Improvement of Villagers Committee Election System. Some thoughts for improvement of Chinese villagers committee election system are conceived through the analysis of the characteristics, existing drawbacks and influencing factors etc. of villagers committee election.

Chapter 13, Solving "Three Agriculture-related Problems" by Rule of Law and Improvement of Land System in Rural Areas. Some suggestions on the improvement of use right circulation system and requisition system of rural land in China are made through the analysis of drawbacks of existing rural land property right system of China.

Chapter 14, Solving "Three Agriculture-related Problems" by Rule of Law and Improvement of Rural Cooperative System. The theoretical and practice bases for the establishment of legal system of Chinese rural cooperative are discussed based on the analysis of the functions, characteristics and legal system fundamental principles of domestic and overseas rural cooperatives; the basic conceptions for setting up the legal system of the cooperative applicable to practical conditions of rural area in China are proposed based on the necessity and feasibility analysis for the establishment of legal system for rural cooperative in China.

Chapter 15, Solving "Three Agriculture-related Problems" by Rule of Law and Improvement of Agricultural Industrialization System. Governmental activity codes and specific legal problems during the agricultural industrialization operation, including problems in rural operation contract and manor economy, are discussed based on the analysis of fundamental principles of agricultural industrialization legal system.

Chapter 16, Solving "Three Agriculture-related Problems" by Rule of Law and Improvement of Social Security System in Rural Areas. The "Three Agriculture-related Problems" exposes the severe drawbacks of social security in rural area of China. While the building of harmonious socialist society is closely associated with the social security system of rural areas, this chapter focuses on the discussion of the system of subsistence allowances of rural residents.

Chapter 17, Solving "Three Agriculture-related Problems" by Rule of Law and Protection of Rights of Migrant Workers. The system defects in the protection of labor interest, cultural and educational interest, family life interest etc. of migrant workers are analyzed based on the analysis of status quo of interest protection system of migrant workers, and basic countermeasures for the improvement of system are proposed.

Chapter 18, Summary, Prospect and Acknowledgment. The limitations of the book and the thoughts for further research are pointed out.

The logic structure of the book follows the simple thoughts of: discovery of problem – settlement of problem, that is, what is solving "Three Agriculture-related Problems" by rule of law? Why solving "Three Agriculture-related Problems" by rule of law is needed and how to realize solving "Three Agriculture-related Problems" by rule of law. The whole book is in the structure style of generalization and specificity. Chapter 1-10 are the general survey and Chapter 11-18 are the specific description.

NOTES

1. Wang Taixian, Ai Ming, *Concepts and Strategies of Rule of Law*, China Procuratorial Press, Version of Aug. 2001; P14.
2. *The Philosophy of Law –An Encyclopedia*, Gerland Publishing, 1999, Translated from Dai Yisheng, *Confusion about Rule of Law*, Recorded in *Teahouse for Jurists* (2nd issue), Shandong People's Press, 2003 Edition, and P154.
3. Ding Guomin, *Legal Problems in Institutional Restructuring of Township Enterprises*, Science of Law of Hebei, 2003.6.
4. Zhang Hao, *Criticism and Affirmation of May 4 th Movement*, Shanxi People's Publishing House, 1989 Edition, P54.
5. Qi Duojun, *Fundamental Theory of Economic Law*, Wuhan University Press, 2000 Edition (3rd Edition), P170-171.
6. Zhang Di, *Interview to Zhou Wangsheng—One of the Top-10 Good Teachers*: Spread Benefits to the People with "Good Laws", http://pkunews.pku.edu.cn, Sep. 16, 2003.
7. Liu Taigang, *Background of "Good Law" of Rule-of-Law State*, http://www.tyfw.net, Jun. 22, 2002.
8. Wen Tiejun, *The Problem of "Agriculture, Farmer and Rural Area" at the Turn of the Century*, Century Forum of Phoenix Satellite TV, 27thIssue, Jul. 31, 2001.
9. Li Changping, *I Tell Prime Minister the Truth*, Journal of Reform, 1stIssue, 2002.
10. Tian Chengyou, *Focus on Rural Rule-of-Law*, http://www.nongyou.org, Dec. 3, 2003.
11. Cai Fang, *Income Gap between Urban and Rural Areas and Critical Point of System Reform*, *Theoretical Economics*, 2ndIssue, 2004.
12. Shen Yansheng, *Retrospect and Prospect of Chinese Rural Governance*, *Strategy and Management*, 1st issue, 2003.
13. National Bureau of Statistics: *China Statistical Yearbook*, China Statistics Press, 2003 edition.
14. Shan Feng, *Analysis and Prediction of Chinese Social Situation for 2006-2007*, *Chinese Academy of Social Sciences Review*, Dec. 29, 2006.
15. Yang Guang, *Analysis on Three Agriculture-Related Problems*, Transferred from *Chinese Sociology Network*, accessed March 23, 2003, http://www.sociology.cass.net.cn.
16. The Former Prime Minister Zhu Rongji always felt heartache and hard to fall into sleep when mentioning the "three agriculture-related problems". The current Prime Minister Wen

Jiabao is called as "Farmer Prime Minister", but he is also very worried about the "three agriculture-related problems".

17. Hu Kui and Jiang Shu, "China Encounters Petition Flood in 2003, New Leaders Confront New Challenge," *Oriental Outlook*, Dec. 30, 2003.

18. Gao Hongjun et al, "Start Point of Approach to Rule of Law – Glance Back to Development of Civil Rights in 2003", Legal Thoughts Network, accessed December 25, 2003, http://www.law-thinker.com.

19. Qi Duojun, "On Power," *Chinese Journal of Law* 1(2001).

20. The slice analysis here refers to the research methods for the "three agriculture-related problems" of the educational circle in recent years. For example, Mr. Fei Xiaotong's "Economy of Jiangchun Village", Yu Jianrong's "Politics of Yuechun Village", Cao Jinqing's "China beside Yellow River", Ma Yinlu's "A Secretary of Country Party Committee: Diary for Resident in the Village" etc., Most of them do representative analysis for a specific village or a local area, for the purpose to see the whole picture. This slice analysis method has the greatest advantages of detailed and in-depth analysis, but it is also inevitably one-sided.

21. Deng Dacai, "Basic Characteristics of Chinese "Three Agriculture-related Problems," *Journal of Agricultural Science and Technology* 12(2002).

22. Chen Wenlong, *Three Agriculture-Related Problems under Modern Context, China Studies*http://www.nows.com/c, Aug. 29, 2003.

23. Xu Qianxi, *Farmer Problems as Political Problems, Strategy and Management*, 1stIssue, 2002.

24. Chen Wenlong, *Three Agriculture-Related Problems under Modern Context, China Studies*http://www.nows.com/c, Aug. 29, 2003.

25. Qin Hui, *Chinese Farmer Problems*,http://newyouth.beida-online.com, Mar. 23, 2003.

26. Wang Cunxue and Luo Yousheng, *Basic Problems for Chinese Rural Economic Laws*, Law Press Mar. 1998 Edition, P33.

27. Xu Xianglin, *What are the Focuses for Solving Three Agriculture-Related Problems*, Journal of Dushu (Reading), 10th issue, 2002.

Chapter Two

Causes of "Three Agriculture-related Problems"

The three agriculture-related problems mainly focus on the issue of farmers. However, the poverty of the farmers is not borne by nature. Over the years, the concern from all circles of life gives us a sketch of the poverty of the farmers: which is thought-provoking. What are the causes of the poverty of today's farmers ? Only after we get the answer to the question can we find the solution to problem.

The expert of agricultural issues Wen Tiejun unveiled the sources of poverty from the expounding of modernization, "Modernization is a wonderful picture, which people dream of and rush into recklessly, even if it is a picture on the wall, which makes your head knocking and bleeding, you will still insist on knocking on it. If you don't decompose the modernization movement, you are not likely to let people understand the reasons for rural construction. Why does industrialization bring about the rural construction movement? That is because the industrialization will accelerate the introverted accumulation, introverted deprivation, because China could not go out, to plunder, she does not have the 'gunboats', nor the iron paw, thus she could not get things from other country, but only from her own country. From whom? From the farmers. Just as written in history, the 'golden ten years of high speed growth is the ten years' deprivation of farmers, with the rapid growth of agricultural commercialization rate, also accompanied by what we call agricultural industrialization (regional planting, specialized production). With the industry and commerce capital flood into agricultural, with financial capital flush into agriculture, exploitation of the traditional small-scale farmer economy has become more serious, which is a kind of aggravated deprivation. As is proved by the history, it is one of the most important reasons for the collapse of the rural area and bankruptcy of farmers. Of course, it also brings the biggest difference from the traditional small-scale production, that is, once the specialization and regionalization is completed, the risk is greatly increased, and no one, whether government or company, will provide necessary protection against this increased risks, which, of course, inevitably fall on the small farmers who have already been knocked down and bleeding all over, then these small farmers will put all the eggs into one basket and make this society gangland."[1]

An exploration into the causes for the "three agriculture-related problems" from the historical perspective will help us gain a deep insight into the current "three agriculture-related problems". The "Century Reflection" put forwarded by Professor Wen Tiejun again clears the venation of the historical causes for us. Since the end of the Qing Dynasty, there have been four movements of industrialization initiated by the governments. The first two movements are the "Westernization Movement" and the industrialization led by the government of the Republic of China in 1920-40's, both resulting in the intensification of social contradictions or even the outbreak of the revolution owing to excessive extraction of surplus of the smallholders. The other two movements happened in the two stages of socialist China: one is the industrialization initiated by central government in the name of the socialist countries and the whole people in 1950-70s, with a relatively successful completion of the primitive accumulation of capital; since the reform and opening up, in the pursuit of high growth target by the Central government, the local government launched the movement of "local industrialization", which accelerated the economic growth, enhanced the comprehensive national strength on the one side, but also caused serious problems of resources and environment on the other side. As far as the system arrangement is concerned, objectively it still depends on how to solve the problem of resources control by the government, and the problem of transaction cost in the extraction of agricultural surplus from farmers. When People's Republic of China was founded, the western countries have completed the pattern of resources distribution through two world wars, and there was indeed no room for adjustment, and surrounding geopolitical environment was very arduous. If China were to stand up among the nations of the world, primitive accumulation of capital must be completed through industrialization. However, the primitive accumulation will not be completed under the smallholder economy with low commodity rate. For the first 3 years after the founding of new China, there was no problem with 400 million farmers providing 50 million of urban population with agricultural products. During the "First Five-year Plan" period, 2 million of rural labor forces rush into the city to support industrial construction, which means a sudden increase of 40-50% grain consumer population, and a shortage of supply of agricultural products. Moreover, under the smallholder economy of labor force surplus, the farmer's way of accumulation is inputting labor force instead of capital investment, which makes it hard for the urban industrial products to enter the rural market, and the exchange between the agriculture and industry cannot be realized. Therefore, the Chinese people had to face an unprecedented self-deprivation under the highly centralized power: in rural areas, two interdependent systems of "unified purchase and sale" and "the people's commune" are implemented; in the city, the redeployment plan and bureaucratic system are adopted. Through the second distribution of surplus in the central fiscal, the surplus value of the workers and farmers are appropriated into the heavy industry for reproduction expansion. In the meantime, the government transformed the "new democracy" development strategy which contains a variety of economy composition including private capitalism and state capitalism, to a single public ownership of "the general line of socialist under the transitional period". In addition, vigorously developing heavy industry would inevitably bring about the phenomenon of "labor force being expelled by intensified capital", which will consequently produce "a dual-structure of confrontation between urban and rural areas" which restrict the migrant worker from entering the urban areas. Although we have thousands of farmers died at the stage of industrial capital accumulation of the state, we finally in the shortest time got over the stage, and formed the industry base for maintenance of national independence.[2] China's rural economic reform originated in 1970s, not only greatly promoted the development of rural economy in China, but also greatly promoted China's economic reform and the high growth in the 80's. However, in the 1990s, especially in the second half of 1990s, the agriculture, farmers and rural issues were becoming increasingly prominent, and have become the biggest obstacle to China's economy stable and healthy development. If we were to analyze the causes of the low growth rate of agriculture, rural and farmer income, we should first look to the reasons of high growth rate in the past years, and then consider what kind of change happened and whether any new factors arouse.

Farmers in China suffered great sacrifice at the Chinese socialist revolution and construction period, yet under the market economy period, it is still the farmers to scarify, which is clearly unfair. We rely on the farmers to get the world, and let the farmers swallow humiliation and bear a heavy load to help us to stabilize the society, but how much have we given to the farmers? When the state suffered misfortune, it was the farmer who assumed the heavy burden. When the city encountered difficulties, we always let the farmers to make sacrifices. In 1950s, scissors difference in prices between industrial goods and agricultural products seized over 8000 hundred million from farmers, since the reform and opening up, the city land acquisition took away another over 2 billion from farmers, but how much did the farmers get? For a decade since the reform and opening up, the life of the farmers did improve , but their relative living conditions are declining. Before the reform and opening up, the per capita income of urban residents is 316 yuan, per capita net income of farmers is 133 yuan, the gap between the two is 2.37:1. Nevertheless, for the past 20 years, the income gap has not been narrowed, but enlarged to 3:1. In fact, the figures far cannot summarize the widening gap between urban and rural areas. City residents have unemployment insurance, medical insurance, retirement pension, and welfare housing or housing provident fund loans preferential, but farmers almost do not enjoy any welfare of the country. If a farmer had a serious illness, he would have to dissipate all his fortune; although the state law provides the nine years of compulsory education, the financial support for rural compulsory education are mainly from levies of farmer, the education of children in countryside is basically the duty of the farmers themselves. Urban residents are entitled to the welfare house and loan at preferential interest rate of provident fund loans, but farmers can only borrow money for themselves to build their houses.[3]

The poor fate of the farmers not only comes from the exploitation from several sides, they also encounter the discrimination treatments both personally and economically in the market economy society of today. We need not trace back too far in history by just mentioning the long-term planned economy after the founding of the PRC. At that time, the "movement of selfless" spread all over the country, and the farmers were not waived. In addition, they also bear the heavy burden of for "Military Industrialization". At the beginning of reform and opening up, the farmers themselves create the system of fixing of farm output quotas for each household, which was ratified by the government, the production enthusiasm of the farmer was brought into forth unprecedentedly, the rural productivity is greatly upgraded, and the life of the farmers improved immediately. While the majority of farmers were celebrating with other walks of life the great achievement of "China feeds one quarter of world's population with only 7% of the world's land" (however, nobody mentions it is the world's 40% farmers are feeding 22% of the population), and moving on with a full stomach towards the well-off life, the heavy burden imposed on the farmers from all sides. Originally, the farmers' just need to pay tax after the grain is harvested. Nowadays, the various levies and tolls from the county to the township to the village committee are imposed on the farmers, just like locusts. First comes the "3 withholds and 5 levies (3 withholds, the public accumulated fund, public welfare fund and administrative fee; 5 levies, education surtax, family planning fee, civil military training fee, civil administrative alimony and civil transportation construction fee) , Next comes the fund raising of the township enterprises, then is the education fund collection, and the last is the fees and expenditure for village committee affairs...A multitude of names. How much grain can be produced by each household with the small parcel of land of 2 *mu* of land? After deducting the costly inputs and necessary expenditures of the farmers themselves, the farmers eventually get an "IOU" from the government. How can the farmers bear so heavy burden? Consequently, various kinds of "coercive measures" have come in handy, including borrowing money from the bank to pay tax, taking away the ox of the household or demolishing the house of farmers, or shutting the farmers up to force them to pay tax etc. Instead of enjoying their happiness, the farmers got a blow, then is the suffering fate again for over 20 years. Think carefully, "non-national treatment" of the farmers is the cause of lack of protection of the farmer rights. Compared with the urban residents, the farmers' right to receive education, the right of free migration, the right to work and the minimum medical care standard, minimum living standard and other social welfares are not guaranteed, which is a serious inequality.

As far as the identity of the farmer is concerned, farming for a living is the most remarkable characteristic. However, for a long period, the farmers could not make their ends meet. Isn't the living in the cities better? In order to survive, the farmers left their homes to work for the urban residents and got some small salary. There is an old saying in China, "house leakage to meet even the rainy days, ship breaking to meet the huge wave". After they are sucked blood and sweat in the land, the Chinese farmers have again been hurt badly in the cities. Originally, it would have been a good thing for the farmers to work in the city, which is good for the development of the city. However, the existing system prevents the farmers from entering into the city. Even though they entered the city, a variety of discriminatory treatments were waiting for them.

First, the rigid household registration system makes no room for the farmers to merge into the city. For a long term, a large portion of funds are invested in urban construction and social welfare, whereas the vast rural areas got only small investment, and this in turn enlarges the gap between urban area and rural area. Some local household registration departments took advantages of the demands of farmers to get into the city, charge them a large sum in the household registration, thus further widening the gap between rural area and urban area. In the first half of 1992, *hukou* (household) for urban residents was sold in almost every province in the country. According to an incomplete statistics of the Ministry of Public Security of the 950 cities (counties) in 17 provinces or autonomous regions, a total of 2,480,000 people purchased the non-agricultural *hukou*, with the price of each *hukou* ranging from 2,000 yuan to 20,000 yuan, the revenue from selling *hukou* in 1992 amounts to far more than 10 billion to nearly 20 billion yuan. It is safe to say that the non-budget revenue is downright deprivation over farmers.[4]

Second, the very inhumane "shelter and repatriation system" was putting the migrant farmers on tenterhooks all day, even the basic human rights cannot be guaranteed, not to mention earning money. After the farmers got into the city, they could hardly find a place to settle down, let alone enjoying the same treatment as urban residents. This is no exaggeration. We can just see it from the movement of cracking down "blind migration" in cities. What is the "blind migration"? It is the migrant farmers. If this is not discrimination, then what is it? If there was no Sun Zhigang Case, and the three doctors had not signed the petition, we are sure many more farmer worker would be persecuted by "Measures for Detention and Repatriation of Vagrants and Beggars in Cities". If it were not owing to the series of social problems caused by the great increase of laid-off workers in urban area, we would not know when the government and society would shift their attention to the farmers in the "hot water".

Sun Dawu, a farmer entrepreneur from Hebei Province who has a close attention to farmer problem, observes that the "national treatment" to migrant farmer workers, is, the same treatment as to the urban residents. The urban residents enjoy the social welfare, i.e., the minimum living standard, the medical care, and the free education. Can they be given to the farmers? Can the government afford this? How could the government find the fund source? The government had goodwill in put forward such a slogan, but it is just a lip service. We will just forget the "national treatment" to farmers. The Compulsory Education Law has been in force for 10 years. Do the farmers enjoy the right to free education now? Can the surtax to education and the fund raising for education in countryside be discharged? If the farmers are discharged of the obligation, then who can afford the salary of the teachers? The fund of government allocation accounts for only a small proportion of the teacher's salary. Even though the compulsory education law cannot take effect, how can we realize the "national treatment" to the farmer? In my opinion, it is just a wish, a dream. It is not based on the real situation of China. Whoever the Chairman of the State is, whichever Party is in power, the "national treatment" to farmers could not be realized.[5] Mr. Sun has a keen sight on the current situation of farmers in China today and has a good understanding of the gap between urban area and rural areas. However, his conclusion is wrong. Theoretically, giving the farmers "national treatment" is not a difficult thing. Nevertheless, if the existing systems continue to exist without reforming, it would prove the rightness of the conclusion of Mr. Sun. The question is how long this kind of unfair system hindering the progress of society can exist? A consoling thing worthy of our comfort is the fact that the major direction of our economic system reform and political system reform is not wrong, but the pace is too slow, and there have been too many twists and turns. As long as we speed up the pace and rhythm of reform, and the Party and the government is determined to conform to the historical trend, to combat the corruption, the prospects for China, and the future of farmers are optimistic. Some people would argue, it is easier said than done, but how to speed up the pace and rhythm? How can we make up our mind to combat corruption? In fact, although there are a lot of problems in China's economic system reform, it is successful on the whole. There are still many problems in the reform of the economic system, but the reason for the problem is not the reform of the economic system itself, but the reform of political system, which has been seriously lagged behind. The problem of farmer, the gap between the urban area and rural area all lie in the political system reform. Rule of law has been written in our constitution as a national strategy, and the current constitution has established the protection of human rights and private property as a constitutional basic principle. These have provided fundamental basis for farmers to enjoy "national treatment". The eradication of existing discriminatory treatment to farmers, and according them the "national treatment" is the irresistible trend of the times.

It is not objective to say the governments do not attach importance to the "three agriculture-related problems". It has been 26 years since the rural reform beginning in 1978. During this period, aiming at the problems and obstacles encountered in different periods, the Party Central Committee issued 6 "No. 1 Documents". In January 1, 1982, the Party Central Committee issued the "No. 1 Documents", which summarized to the rural reform quickly thrust are, and made specific deployment for the rural reform and agricultural development of the year and the next period. Afterwards, the next 4 No. 1 Documents all focus on the policies in the rural area. The five "No. 1 Documents" were then called "Five No. 1 Documents" in the history of rural reform in China. The No. 1 Documents in 1982 makes some breakthroughs in the system framework of "three-layer public ownership of commune, production brigade, and production team, with production team as the basic unit", and clearly points out that Fixing of farm output quotas for each household, work contracted to households or "Dabaogan" both falls into the "socialist production responsibility system". In January, 1983, the second "No. 1 Documents" of Party Central Committee *Several Issues of Economic Policies in Current Rural Areas* was formally promulgated, which theoretically expounds that the household contract responsibility system is a great creation of Chinese farmer under the leadership of CCP. It is a new development of Marxism agricultural cooperative in China practice". On January 1, 1984, the Party Central Committee issued the third No. 1 Document *Announcement of Agriculture Work in 1984*, which stresses that the household contract responsibility system should be continually consolidated and completed, and the land contracting period shall be extended. With a view to encouraging farmer's input in the land, the document stipulates that the contracting period of the land shall be generally over 15 years, and for the project with long production period, the contracting period shall be longer. In January, 1985, the Party Central Committee promulgated *Ten Measures for Activating Rural Economy*, the fourth No. 1 Documents. The main theme of the documents is to adjust the industry structure in the rural area, annul the system of unified and fixed state purchase of agricultural and sideline products which had been in force in China for over 30 years and adopts a new policy of government plan and purchase according to contract concerning the major product of grain and cotton, and the change the payment form of agriculture tax from goods to cash. On January 1, 1986, the Party Central Committee and the State Council promulgated the *Deployment of Agriculture Work in 1986*, the fifth No. 1 Documents, which confirm the correctness of the guideline and policy of rural reform, which shall be stressed and carried through. Regarding the phenomenon and tendency of agriculture stagnation and slackness, the document emphasizes that the status of agriculture shall be adjusted. In the years to come, with the slow growth of farmer's net income and the widening gap between the farmers and urban residents, on February 9, 2004, the Party Central Committee issued the Proposal of Party Central Committee and the State Council on Several Measures for Raising Farmer's Income, which was the sixth No. 1 Documents of the CCP after reforming and opening up. The six No. 1 documents include a series of policies addressing the different problems in the rural areas in different periods, which shows the great concern from the Central Party Committee and the government for the agriculture issues, which exerts great influence to the whole national economy and social stability. However, the stopgap and piecemeal solutions of treating the head when the head aches and treating the foot when the foot hurts could only make the acute disease evolve into chronic disease, or eventually cancer. The problem of the current rural China is close to the "cancer". If we do not remove "cancer cells" fundamentally, we could not completely solve the problem. And this "cancer cell" is the drawbacks of the system, the "brain tumor" in the government administrative guiding ideology.

The mention of "three agriculture-related problems" will easily remind us of industrialization. Some people will naturally hold the views that farmers shall make some sacrifice in the process of industrialization, which is a "glorious" thing. There is one way to get such persons wake up. That is, they shall not work as scholars and not work in office, and shall not earn money by means of paper work, but let them labor on the farm, hand in the grain to the government as some kind of tax, and pay the tolls etc. ... The impact of industrialization on rural society is inevitable, even the history of western developed countries was also accompanied with the suffering of the farmers. If we are to realize industrialization, we will need to establish factory; if we are to construct the factory, we will need to occupy the land, which means the loss of farmland and reemployment of farmers; if the farmers could not be re-employed, they would be just "bought out". When the farmers are bought out, they have nothing to do and just wander around. However, the government would not let them wander away, and then the farmers had no other choice but join the factory as cheap labor force, and make contribution for the accelerated development of industry... This whole process seems quite natural, step by step, toward the completion of the expected industrialization. Seen from the surface, the farmers are also victims, and also made sacrifices. However, compared to China's industrialization process, there is a very significant difference, that is, during the whole process; the farmers have the right to say. When their land was levied for construction of factories, the farmers enjoyed the right to bargain with the levying parties; the raw material and raw agriculture products needed for development of industry were provided by the farmers at the market price in accordance with the supply-demand relationship. The transaction itself is relatively fair and meets the requirements of market economy. However, the situation in China is different. According to Dr. Wen Tiejun, as the transaction cost for the raw material and primary agriculture product needed for industrial development were too high at the industrialization stage, so that the government had to adopt the policy of state monopolization for purchase and sale of agricultural products, so as to realize the goal of industrialization. This is a historical fact, but it does not mean it is normal and reasonable, as it was an unfair transaction. If it was justifiable for the government to force the farmers to make sacrifice during the period of military industrialization for national survival, it is unreasonable for the government, after the reform and opening up, keeps control over, domination and exploitation of farmers for so long a time. Therefore, the government should seriously reflect on responsibility for the "three agriculture-related problems", and carry out a thorough transformation from the administrative ideology. Since 2004, the government began to increase agricultural support, and there have been drastic policies almost every year. Remarkable achievements have been made in the field from the abolition of agricultural tax, tax for special agricultural products, to the adoption of direct subsidies to grain farmers, and to the exemption of tuition and other fees during the rural compulsory education period. However, the "three agriculture-related problems" still exist. It can be seen that, apart from the administrative forms and ideology, the direct causes for the "three agriculture-related problems" involves the system, which can be summarized into the following 4 aspects:

2.1 VAGUENESS OF PROPERTY RIGHT OF THE AGRICULTURE LAND

While discussing the causes and countermeasures of "three agriculture-related problems", most domestic scholars will consider the applicable land property right system as the culprit, which should be the object for reform. The representative point of view holds that, the allocation of land resources in rural areas in the past were mainly for the substance for living, thus the principle of fairness is of overriding significance. This is also the corollary of Chinese historical development. Take the family as the basic unit of agricultural production and operation and the market main body status is also decided by the productivity development level in most rural areas. However, with justice as the starting point, relying on administrative means to the allocate land resources mean will hardly produce the ideal productivity and the impetus for modernization. Since the land is used for free with no time limit, it is not conducive to the flow of production factors and their combination, nor is it in compliance with the principle of value maintenance and growth of the assets. Under the condition of market economy, land as a factor of production, as plant and machine in industry, also possesses the property of commodity, which shall participate in the circulation and exchange. Therefore, the free flow of land use right at the fair market price, not only can induce the land flowing from inefficient operators to efficient operators, effectively promote the rural surplus population to non-agricultural industries, but also will be conducive to the reform of agricultural technology.[6]

Dr. Wen Tiejun considered the "three agriculture-related problems" in the twentieth Century as the problem of farmers' land, and the "three agriculture-related problems" in the twenty-first Century as the problem of farmer employment.[7] However, it cannot be inferred that the land problem of Chinese farmer has been solved. On the contrary, fundamentally speaking, although the rural land property right is clear on the surface, it is not clear in practice, which can also be called as the incomplete property rights. The standard expression at present is that the land in the countryside and at the suburb belongs to the collective. Collective ownership equals to public ownership, but who is the rural collective? Is it the community, or the collective economic organizations? Is it the cooperatives, or the local government? We don't know. For the farmers, the land cultivators, when they contracted the land, they became the operators, but not the land owners. They are the operators of collective land. The right of operation includes the right to occupy, to use and to get benefits from the land, but they could not dispose the land, that is, the land could not flow freely in accordance with the wishes of the individual operators. Since the ownership determines the right of operation, land transfer could not be carried without the permit of the land owner. Fundamentally speaking, the owner has the right to contract the land to you, they also have the right not to contract the land to you, or they can also find someone else to farm the land. At the present stage, we stipulate that the land contracting will remain unchanged for 30 years, what will be the case 30 years later? Will there be another 30 years? Or two 30 years of contracting period? Nobody knows. As the operators of arable land are not the land owners, they do not know what will happen to the land in the future. Therefore, they will not have long-term, permanent investment in the land, but most likely operate the land in a predatory way.[8] The *"Rural Land Contract Law"* implemented in March 2003 is a paradox in the guiding ideology: on the one hand, the basic pattern of land property right is still the collective ownership, on the other hand, it tries to create on the land a new right of free circulation by the land users.

Dr. Wen Tiejun absolutely denied the land private ownership. There are two main reasons: one is that China is a shortage of land resources, consequently the system costs of privatization would be too high, the other is China's agricultural land has the function of social security, and social security cannot be privatized. Dr. Wen further reflects his previous "property - circulation - scale" theory, 'as a tester in the grass-root rural area, I finally understand that, this theory seems logical and integral, is actually ambiguous.' he pointed. Dr. Wen thinks those who still emphasize the property right to farmland are "theorist without practical experience who just advocates the out-of-date slogans".[9] However, we need to think, what is the reason for the farmers to cling to the land even though they get into debt from the land? Who delegate with the local government to levy tax and fees from the farmers even though they get negative output from the land? What are the reasons for the desertion of large number of farmland? Why does the farmer could not get rid of the primitive mode of farming with human and animal power? Eventually we found the answer to the questions. That is the farmland contract right, which is a concept of uncertainty and ambiguity. Even though the stipulation of 30 years or even 70 years also contains uncertainty. Anyway, the farmers have only the right to use, and they have to act at the will of the owner. In addition, the land collective ownership is also uncertain, as the government is the real subject of ownership. Given the fact that the property right is unclear, 30 years is only a kind of heavy chains, placing the farmers in something of a dilemma, they could not leave the land. however, if they choose to stay, they were in a worse situation. Professor Qin Hui precisely pointed out the problems existing in current system of property rights to land in rural areas. He said, the view that the land embodies the social security function and thus can not be privatization is in essence an obligation of farmers as against the right of the state, which is totally different from the social security in general sense.

The fact that the government enjoys the rights on the land whereas the farmers perform obligations cannot be said to be social security for the farmers. On the contrary, the farmers are treated as fools. Farmers will not necessarily sell the land once they get the land. In addition, the land does not guarantee the farmers' life, but it is sheer obligation for farmers.

We can clearly see the root of the problem: unless the farmers get the right to say with their farming land, the situation of high cost and low income or even negative income in the use of rural land will not be changed radically.

2.2 DUAL STRUCTURE BETWEEN URBAN AREA AND RURAL AREA

Dr. Wen Tiejun wrote a series of articles and books on “three agriculture-related problems”, and has keen insight to the causes and countermeasures for the “three agriculture-related problems”. However, his assertion that “farmer economy” will exist in China for a long time is somewhat pessimistic. In his view, two basic contradictions have restrained the solving of “three agriculture-related problems” in China: one is the contradiction relationship between people and land, which is the basic situation in China; the other is the system of contradiction of urban-rural dual-structure, which is the system problem.

We will not understand the essence of “three agriculture-related problems” without analyzing the above two contradictions. Meanwhile, if we want to solve the “three agriculture-related problems”, we must have a profound understanding of the two contradictions. Only the policies which more or less mitigate these two contradictions will have some effect.[10]

In the 2002 annual conference of China Society of Economic Reform, Zhang Haoruo, Deputy Director of the Environmental Resources Committee of the NPC, pointed out, “three agriculture-related problems” cannot be solved by local and temporary measures. The fundamental route is to develop the productive forces, solve the dual-structure contradictions, accelerate city construction, and vigorously develop the rural economy.

China has made great achievements in the reform towards market economy in cities. However, the fundamental problem of “three agriculture-related problems” has not yet been solved. The “three agriculture-related problems” in China is not simply a question relates to agriculture and the rural economy or farmers’ income, but the overall problems for China’s economy and social development. China rural population accounts for nearly 70% of the national population. If the majority of farmers cannot live a well-off life, it is difficult to achieve the strategic goal of building a well-off society. Farmer income growth is slow, making the rural consumption at a low level. The per capita consumption of rural population only accounts for 1/3 of that of city population. The rural population accounts for nearly 70% of the total population in China, while the consumption amount is only 39% of the total national consumption. The income and consumption gap between urban area and rural area is not narrowing but continue to be enlarged, which form a gap between total supply and total demand which is difficult to fill in the short time.

The crux of “three agriculture-related problems” in China is the contradiction between the rural area and urban area. The core of contradiction of the dual-structure is the rapid industrialization and the lagging of city urbanization. To promote the coordinated development of urban and rural areas, we shall accelerate the pace of rural industrialization and urbanization. This is a summary of the successful experiences of foreign industrialization. In the process of industrialization, the economic structure change trajectory of different countries has followed the same basic rules. According to the standard structure table of Simon Kuznets (Table 1, Table 2)[11] the acute transformation phase of industrial and agricultural output value structure of in China has passed, and the industrialization has entered the stage of growth, but the economic structure is obviously lagging behind, with the third industry lagging behind the second industry, and the employment structure seriously accumulating in the first industry. According to the standard comparison table, the employment structure evolution situation in China in 1995 is similar with country of $150 level. This shows that the Chinese economy has entered the period which "objectively" demands the rapid transformation of dual-structure, which requires the pace of urbanization and the development of the third industry macroeconomic strategy be accelerated, the rural industry be included into the system of urban industry.

At present, the dual-structure contradictions do not tend to ease, but tend to aggravate. This shows that the "three agriculture-related" problems will be more serious. We cannot rely on the partial and temporary measures to solve the problem, but shall introduce a series of major initiatives, including guiding the productive elements to flow to the rural area and the rural population to move to the cities, so as to develop the rural economy and speed up the process of urbanization. If we want to eliminate the "dual-structures" contradictions, it is important to eliminate the barriers between the city and the countryside. Only by vigorously develop the non-agricultural industries (especially the service industry), will the surplus rural population gradually moved to the towns, and will the rural land be relatively concentrated for implementation of intensive operation. Otherwise it will be impossible to fundamentally ease the sharp contradictions of the dual-structure.

After Mr. Du Runsheng proposed giving "national treatment" to farmers, Li Changping, with a large number of data, stressed that the "non-national treatment to farmers" of the government is the indifference to and infringement of the farmers' right. National treatment is one of the principles of international law, which requires giving the citizens of member state the same treatment as that to its own citizens. Here we just borrow the term to show that the scarcity of right and interest enjoyed by the Chinese farmers. Just think about it, we shall give the same treatment to even the foreigner. Why are the urban citizens and rural citizens treated differently? If we are to resume the "national treatment" to farmers, we shall, except for the stipulations in the constitution that urban residents and rural residents should be equal in right and obligations, a series of integrated policies covering education, medical, employment, social security, market access and other aspects

Table 2.1. Share (%) of each industry sector of the great power (population over 100,000,000) in per capita GDP of each datum point value (dollars price in 1958)

Industry classification	Benchmark value (USD)				
	70	150	300	500（China 1995）	1000（China 2000）
First industry	45.8	36.1	26.5	19.4（20.6）	10.9（15.9）
Second industry	21.0	28.4	36.9	42.5（48.4）	48.4（50.9）
Third industry	33.2	35.5	36.6	38.1（31.1）	40.7（33.2）
Percentage decreased in first industry with per capita GDP increase of every $10	1.215	0.64	0.355	0.17	

Data sources: (United States) Simon Kuznets. Economic Growth of Different Countries. Beijing: The Commercial Press, 1985; China's Statistics Bureau. China Statistical Yearbook. Beijing: China Statistics Press, 1996, 2001.

of public expenditure shall be gradually promoted, aiming at realizing the integration of urban area and rural areas finally.[12]

Economist Hu Angang believes that only when the problem of long-term opposition and separation between urban area and rural area are solved, can the "three agriculture-related problems"be solved in China. The largest obstacle is the current system which hinders the flow and transfer of rural labor. We will make hundreds of millions of rural surplus labor force leave the rural area to become urban residents, which is known as the "third liberation "of the China farmers. We shall provide farmers with equal opportunity as urban residents.[13] However, the current household registration system is an invisible wall, which the migrant farmers could never breakthrough. While recruiting staff, many employers would add a restrictive condition: the urban residents. The farmers are thus seemed inferior to the urban residents, and most of them engage in the trade with low incomes, poor working environment and high intensity of labor. The old pension, medical care, social insurance for the urban residents were also barred to the migrant workers. Children of immigrant workers were excluded from the local education system. If they want to study in the local school, they have to pay additional costs. As a result, even some farmers work in the city for 10 years, 8 years, they cannot be integrated into the city, they cannot take the city as their home, but only choose to live temporarily, with their home at the hometown; they will save money on food and expenses and send most of their income back to home. Consequently, the consumption demand which should belong to the city also leaves the city. The household registration system not only makes the farm-

Table 2.2. per capita GDP benchmark level (US dollar in 1958) calculation of the labor department share (%)

Industry classification	Benchmark value (USD)				
	70	150	300	500（China 1995）	1000（China 2000）
First industry	80.5	63.3	46.1	31.4（52.9）	17.0（48.7）
Second industry	9.6	17.0	26.8	36.0（23.0）	45.6（23.0）
Third industry	9.9	19.7	27.1	32.6（24.1）	37.4（28.3）

Data sources: the same as in Table 2.1.

ers stay in the city reluctantly, but also greatly reduces the industry chain effect of city.

2.3 NEGLIGENCE OF FARMER'S RIGHTS

The issue of farmer's rights is actually connected with the above two problems together. The problem of land can be said to be the most important and the most direct property rights of farmers. Unclear property right is not a guarantee even infringement of property rights; the different kinds of discriminatory treatment can be said to be closely related with the identity right of farmers, which is a violation of the farmers' basic rights of equality and human rights and freedom of a citizen as stipulated in the *Constitution.* Essayist Jiao Guobiao once challenged the difference treatment between urban and rural workers: if a worker is cut off the finger by the machine, we call it industrial accident; if a cadre is injured in a car accident on business, we call it work-related injury, and both enjoys work compensation,; then if a farmer is injured in harvesting or is poisoned or even died in spraying the pesticide, why we do not compensate them? The primary and secondary schools in cities can obtain a large number of national financial subsidies, while rural schools get very little subsidies, yet the farmers still need to raise fund for the school. As for the education of the children of migrant workers, its hardness is already known. Urban residents enjoy pensions, unemployment insurance and so on; these are of course elusive for farmers. Can farmers retire? No. When the farmers are too old to move, they will retire to rest in bed. However, that means they will have to lead a bitter life, as the sky won't drop old pension to them (not only that, when the farmers lose labor ability and do not have social security, they still have to hand in the "tolls"). The dual-structure between urban area and rural areas has existed for over half a century, and it will remain unchanged in the near future. Under the dual-structure system, the labor market could not be integrated, even if farmers have more chance to work in the cities, they do not enjoy equal employment, fair income and the same social security of "citizens". If they were to stay in the countryside, the situation will be worse. You know, the farmers' labor is not "labor". What the labor and social security departments referred to as "labor", "labor" as stipulated in *Labor Law*, and "physical labor and mental workers" mentioned in *Trade Union Law* all have nothing to do with the farmers.[14]

There are both the institutional reasons and the working style of the grassroots cadres for the rising of "Three agriculture-related problems". The two reasons summed up into one point, the rights of farmers were not respected. After the founding of the PRC, with the implementation of the household registration system, the cities and countryside have been completely separated. In history, through the price scissors between the industry and agriculture, the countryside gave the city a blood transfusion of six hundred to eight hundred billion yuan. At present stage, the current rural consumption level and the level of investment is greatly lower than that in the city, resulting in the insufficient demand in our country, which eventually lead to the bottleneck of economic development. Although the fiscal expenditure increased substantially in recent years, the proportion of agricultural expenditure decreases. When we are addressing the problems of relative poverty of farmers, first of all we shall focus on the social unfairness, it can be said that the urban-oriented income distribution system is the deep-seated institutional reasons of farmers' heavy burden. Its price is the long-term stagnation of development and socio-economic conflicts between the urban area and the rural area. At the same time, under the WTO framework, grain production in China has lost its comparative advantage. According to some expert analysis, for agricultural products import of 100 million each, 200 thousand agricultural employment opportunities will be lost. Notwithstanding, the scattered management model of farmers makes it impossible for the farmers to obtain equal right in negotiation either politically or economically. At present, with a view to solving the "three agriculture-related problems", the first thing for us to do is to respect the rights of farmers.[15]

2.4 ABSENCE OF RULE OF LAW IN RURAL AREA

From the above analysis, we can basically grasp that the fundamental source of "three agriculture-related problems", that is, the rights of farmers have long been neglected or infringed. It is still the case today. Why farmers' rights are not guaranteed? The answer is very clear, the lack of rule of law. A sound legal system together with the fair and transparent law enforcement environment is the guarantee of farmers' rights. It is safe to say that the change of strategy in ruling of the country cannot be delayed! But how to do change it? Talking about the strategy of ruling the country, it cannot be summarized in a word. However, for anyone who is somewhat interested in politics, he should understand the basic differences of the two opposing concepts, that is, the rule of man and the rule of law. Jiang Zemin put forward the "rule of virtue" at the end of twentieth Century, which aroused "the century hot discussion" of the strategy of governing the country, and the results were self-evident. In modern civilization, the rule of man is having less and less space, "rule of virtue" as a strategy of ruling the country apparently lacks feasibility, the rule of law has already become the main theme of modern civilized society. Since China's reform and opening up, China has been in the right direction of statecraft, which is witnessed by the fact that the rule of law is written into the current constitution. Given the fact, why does the countryside lack the rule of law? We will need to conduct a historical research on the countryside in China.

Some people analyzed the roots of backwardness of rule of law in countryside through the production style, the interpersonal relationship, the traditional rural governance, and the mode of village governance, and concluded that the traditional China is the rural society formed on the basis of the farming economy. The farmers lived on land. Law isn't the sole means of social control and not even the most important way. Customs, habits, patriarchal clan rules and moral is the important means of social control for a long-term. People show more respected to customs and habits than to the law. Law has not been chosen as the main means of social control, the reasons include: first, China is a typical agricultural society, with 90% of the population living in rural areas, and family as the basic production unit. In this closed economy system and simple social mode, self-sufficiency results in the single interpersonal relationship and people were familiar with each other. Second, agriculture society, agricultural production activities naturally require a stable environment and a stable environment is easy to limit the pioneering and enterprising spirit of individuals as producers. The farmers will easily fall into the conservative and conformist personality. The farmers' families are weak, with narrow vision and conservative consciousness. They are isolated from each other and cannot form a unified force to safeguard their own interests. The dependence on land often forces them to succumb to the rule of land, and further succumb to the rule of land owners. The result is that the legal consciousness of the legal subject is totally lost, the ideology of the equality and freedom contract find no way to exist. Third, agricultural production cycle is long and the technology is complex. It's very easy to make the elders in a superior position. As a result, the senior person as a symbol of skills and experience naturally has the highest position and the greatest authority in rural society in China. Under such circumstance, following the experience and obeying the customs is the logical matter. In addition, the patriarchal clan system is combined with the *Baojia system* (neighborhood administrative system), making the kinship and geopolitical relationship complement each other. All these finally developed into the folk culture, local practice, customs, habit, clan rules and family law which controls local Chinese farmers' behavior strictly and becomes binding rules on every member of the family member.[16]

In studying the causes for the prosperity of "Cun Xue Xiang Xue" in rural area and its repelling of state law, if we cannot jump out of the rural society, we cannot find the root of the problem. The fundamental causes for the rural society to drift away outside the state law does not lie in the production and life style in rural area, but in the abatement and ablation of the national law in rural society; it's not in the confrontation between the rural society and the laws of the state, but in its compromise and concession of state law; it's not because of the strongness of the rural social etiquette habit, but of the "weakness" of the state law.

Let us have a look at the strong infiltration of the state law into the rural society in contemporary times. After the Chinese Communists Party came to power with the guideline of seizing the power from the countryside by using armed force, the people's government first implemented the absolute land reform in rural areas, and ended the reign of landlords in the countryside, and then gradually implemented and improved the degree of cooperation and socialization. With a view to realizing socialist in the whole country, the Communist Party, placed the integration of rural society in a very important position. Land reforms, cooperative movement, as well as the introduction of the people's commune have strongly impacted the rural basic organization and control mode. Especially the commune movement, it has affected every field of social life in rural areas and farmers' way of life and production for generations. Commune movements brought a top-to-down network of economic and administrative control, making the control and infiltration of state power over and to the rural society reached the scale and depth of the hitherto[17] unknown. Here we will not comment whether the measures were good or bad, but just analyze its basis for successful infiltration. At that time, the famers were not in a picture of how the new socialist China they were heading to would be like. Therefore, the Communist put forward the slogan of "letting the farmers become the masters", the downfall of the local tyrants and distribution of their land were indeed the happiest things for the farmers who had longed for the rights and freedoms for decades. Will the farmer not welcome this kind of penetration of state power in the rural area?

We can never think too highly of ourselves and underestimate the farmers, who also have strong desire for new things, especially law and justice. If our system binds the farmers on the land, so that they cannot breathe "the air of freedom from the city", the problem lies in our system itself. A person like Zhou Guangli is not uncommon in the countryside. If the scholars would walk out of the reading room and the office, to take a walk in the countryside to have a talk with the farmers, they will find that they were totally wring to think that farmers are ignorance of and indifference to law.

In fact, the enthusiasm of farmers for rule of law is so high that we feel deeply ashamed. When Ma Yinlu left Qixiu Village, he was puzzled by the eight questions of farmers: Why the problem of heavy taxes has not been mitigated according to the principle of seeking truth from facts? When we will stop paying tax with loan? Why do the prices of agricultural products fell in a straight line, while the prices of pesticide, chemical fertilizer, and farming tools are rising constantly? No clear answers were given to these questions in Mr. Ma's *Notes in the Village*. It is not the farmers do not know the answer. Maybe it is our government officials do not want to, dare not or feel inconvenience to give the answer. In mid-March 2004, I encountered several farmers from Quanzhou, Guilin, and Guangxi Province. When talking about the problems of farmers' burden, I told them that Premier Wen said in his report that, five years after the abolition of tax for agricultural special product and reduction of agricultural tax, the latter would be totally abolished. A farmer said excitedly: "Don't mention it, don't mention it! The more attention is paid by the center government to the agriculture, the bitter is our life". I asked why? He replied that the agricultural tax and tax for special agricultural product only accounted for about 5% of the whole burden on the farmers, can it solve any problem even though they are abolished? I asked him what the other kinds of burden were. He gave me a list, including "3 withholds and 5 levies", education fund, fees for water and power, expenditure for pesticide and fertilizer etc. I asked, pesticide and fertilizer, and water and power are normal input and expenditure, why they were counted as burden? He said I was outsider, and there was great secret inside, persons in charge of water and power are the relatives of the town officials, and the amount of water and power fees are decided by them; the seller of pesticide and fertilizer are not company, but the government. Last year the price of urea was only 54. Now when the governments call for the reduction of farmers' burden, the price of urea suddenly rose to RMB 89. Blackmail! I said, under the market economy, the price is decided by the market. It is normal. He said: "you do not know ah! If it were true market economy, it would be good. The price of urea in the neighboring province is RMB 54 dollars, but it cannot be sold here. Nobody dared to carry it here. There are inspectors here and there. Once it is found here, it will be confiscated. If we pick up the urea by ourselves in the other province, the transportation fee would be too high for us. In addition, it is also not allowed by the local government. There are over 20 staff that is fed on the financial budget in our town. However, in fact, over 200 people receive salaries from the township but do not work. Still, this does not include some of the 'temporary worker'. These parasites are all to be fed by us. We had no choice, as they are the kinship of the cadres. Hearing this, I thought of what is written in Li Changping's letter to the prime minister, *the burden of farmers is as heavy as Mountain Tai, the debt is as high as "Mount Everest", and the cadres are just like "locusts"*. I felt guilt that I did not do a good job in conducting surveys in countryside. At the same time, I am consoled that the farmers have this kind of understanding. After all, they are no longer those who are described by some of our scholars as knowing nothing. In fact, they see clearly in many problems. They are eager to enjoy rights; they have strong desire for freedom and equality. The only things are the channels are too narrow for them to realize the dream, and they meet so many difficulties that they become indifferent. Once this desire has been excited, they still have very high enthusiasm of the rule of law.

In the process of rural social transformation, we see that although the human relationships in rural areas is decided by kinship, the social significance of blood relationship has disappeared; the social rank based on the kinship and class has been broken, and the social class and status of people are decided by economy and law; with nearly 20 years continuous legal education and the impact of the commodity economy in rural area, the status of law have risen in rural area, and that of traditional customs and habits have declined; with the change of external environment and the rise of education quality of farmers, these all have some impact on the rural society, and have changed the trend of development of rural China. Rule of law is coming to the rural area.

NOTES

1. Wen Tiejun, *China Mainland Rural Construction*, Edited by Wu Ming, *Open Era* 2(2003).
2. Wen Tiejun, "Reflection on the 'Three Agriculture-related Problems' Over the Century", *Reading* 12(1999).
3. Zhang Xiantang, "In the Face of Farmers, We Should Confess", *China Economic Times*, December 22, 2002.
4. Zhou Qiming, "The Legal Guarantee of Equal Rights of Farmers", *Studies in Law and Business*, 2(2000).
5. Sun Daniu, "Expounding Three Agriculture-related Problems - Predicting the Future of China," accessed March, 2003, http://www.sinoliberal.com.
6. Song Yaping, "The Fundamental Way out for Three agriculture-related problems Lies in the Modernization", *Xinhua Digest* 12(2000).
7. Wen Tiejun, "The Problem of 'Agriculture, Farmer and Rural Area' at the Turn of the Century." Century Forum of Phoenix Satellite TV, 27th Issue, Jul. 31, 2001.
8. Xiao Liang, "Analyze 'The Three Agriculture-Related Problems' from A Strategic Perspective," *Theory Frontier* 7(2001).
9. Wen Tiejun, "Market Failure" and "Government Failure" - "Three Agriculture-related Problems" in Double Predicament", *Reading* 10(2001).
10. Wen Tiejun, "Reflection on the 'Three Agriculture-related Problems' Over the Century, *Reading* 12(1999).
11. Zhang Gaiqing, "Causes of 'Three Agriculture-related Problems' and Solutions," *Study on Agriculture Modernization* 1 (2003).

12. Guo Shutian and Lu Xueyi, "Ten Suggestions to Solve 'Three agriculture-related problems'", *China Economic Times*, March 26, 2003.
13. Xia Aiming, "'Three Agriculture Issues' is A Problem Faced by China at Currently Economic Development," accessed November 24, 2002, http://www.secretchina.com.
14. Xu Xunlei, "The Most Difficult Problem is the 'Three Rural Problems'," *China Rural Studies*, accessed February 28, 2004, http://www.ccrs.org.cn.
15. Dong Shaoguang, "Three Agriculture Issues: Start from the Respect for Farmers' Right," *Economic Reference News*, August 20, 2003.
16. Wang Xin, "The Practice of the Rule of Law in the Countryside during Social Transformation Period", Yunnan Xinming Lawyers Network, accessed June 12, 2003, http://www.yn148.com.
17. Wang Mingming, *The Local Social Order, Justice and Authority* (Beijing: China University of Political Science and Law Press, 1997), 418.

Chapter Three

Choice of Mode for Solving "Three Agriculture-related Problems"

Through the analysis of the causes of "Three Agriculture-related Problems", we can deal with the problems in a pertinent way. So far, various suggestions have been put forward from the different perspectives.

3.1 POLITICAL REFORM IN RURAL AREA WITH PEOPLE AT THE CORE

Scholars will not overlook the importance of political reform in rural area when they are pondering over the solutions to "Three Agriculture-related Problems". In the article *China along the Yellow River: Observation and Thought of Rural Society from the Perspective of a Scholar*, the author Cao Jinqing, through an anthropological investigation into some poor and backward areas in Henan province, holds that the modernization of agriculture, countryside and farmers has been troubled by the problem of tillage method, cultural tradition and the burden of farmers, and it is inadequate to solve the poverty and development problem only rely on the autonomy of villagers and the election system. In the article *Tell the truth to the Prime Minister*, the author Li Changping revealed the serious poverty problem of farmers caused by the heavy burden he experienced in Jianli County, Hubei Province… He thought "the government black hole" is the system root of the problem. Based on a two-year field investigation in Hengyang Area, Hunan Province, Yu Jianrong analyzes the political reasons of the problem from the perspective of rural politics in his book *Yue Village Politics: Changes in Rural Political Structure in Transitional China*, he thinks that organized "peasant revolt" has seriously affected the political stability in rural areas. Rural political reform must begin from the following aspects:

3.1.1 Shift of Government Function and Change of Government Structure in Rural Area

Regarding problems with farmers in China, many people think government should give farmers the national treatment. Indeed, this is the key point. However, it is not the problem of allocation of happiness-resource in economic utilitarian calculus, but the implementation of political rights. Aristotle had pointed out: the so-called "king ship", in a sense, exists in any kind of political system, as the essential issues of any kind of political system is the implementation of the central authority. A so-called "sovereignty over sovereignty" is never allowed in political arrangement of the constitution and the rule of law, and the citizens in a state are not allowed to be divided on levels of fundamental rights. In other words, the basic unit of modern political society can only be the individual citizen and this is the popular-sovereignty principle which is well known by politicians. This principle also means the political ties between the individual citizen and the central authority must be direct, which is not allowed to be intercepted by any local community or divided population. The concept of citizens in itself preinstalls the concept of nationality: citizens are citizens of a country, not a person of local community or population community. The ultimate goal of China's political reform does not allow the political ties between the individual citizen and the central authority to be cut off in any way, and these ties should be made highly fortitude and democratic, otherwise the country will not be able to withstand any sorts of impact or shock.

"Three agriculture-related problems" is not a simple economic issue; it is directly related to the reform of political system. The fundamental cause of excessive burden on farmer lies in the overstaff of county and township grass-roots government personnel. The huge expenditure makes it hard for the government to make both ends meet, which are finally apportioned to farmers. At present stage, with the graveness of three agriculture-related problems and the deterioration of financial budget of county governments in the central and western regions, it is no use for the Central government to just give orders to ban apportion. While the huge county township cadres need money, however, the fiscal income at the corresponding level is not adequate and the Central government was reluctant to make subsidies. Inevitably they turn to the farmers to maintain their life consumption level. For example, most township government leaders living in the city now, the expenditures on buying and taking care of cars, drivers, gasoline for them to commute between their homes and the government amount to hundreds of billion yuan. The current primary budget is simply impossible to cover this huge expenditure. Finally, more than half of it was passed onto the farmers in various names. Therefore, neither the order nor the reform of "replacement of administrative fees with taxes" can solve the problem ultimately. To completely alleviate the unreasonable heavy burden on farmers, we must reduce the number of grass-roots cadres and their expenditures. Some scholars proposed revocation of the organizations of township and villages and adopting the system of farmer autonomy by election of head of township and head of villages. This advice is a drastic approach. Indeed, only by reducing the huge number of grass-roots cadres in the rural area who are feed by apportion and carrying out the democratic election for cadres above the township levels, can the problems be solved fundamentally. This involves a completely political reform in the rural area. If we call the cancellation of three levels of ownership in the people's commune and adoption of household contracting of land in early 1980s a major "revolution", then cutting off the number of cadres in rural area and carrying out democratic elections for cadres above the township levels is the second "revolution" which will liberate the farmers since the rural reform. The second "revolution" is more profound than the first "revolution" of land contracting and canceling the commune system, as it has to touch the fundamental interests of grassroots cadres. At the contradiction of the safeguarding the interests of farmers or the interests of the grassroots cadres, the government is difficult to make a choice. The second "revolution" is also related with the question of changing the management system of rural political society which has been in force for a long time. The size, number and function of basic level government shall be based on the farmers' needs and affordability, which is totally different from what it has been for the latest 20 years, which is, setting the number and function of cadres according to the need of higher levels of government and forcing the farmers to pay to feed them. The conversion of functions and the change of structure of rural grassroots government, means the major changes in rural political system in the whole nation. The cost of maintaining the existing political and social management system in rural areas has greatly exceeded what the Central government and farmers can bear. If we continue to maintain the system, it will inevitably cause the further depression of rural society, and social contradictions will become increasingly intensified. Therefore, the reform of this system means a contest between 900 million farmers and tens of millions of grassroots cadres.[1]

The goal of functions conversion and structure change of rural grassroots government is to convert the control-oriented government to a service-oriented government; to transform the bloated government to a streamlined and efficient government. For this reason, it was proposed that the government shall procure services, and this proposal has been in experiment in some regions. In the rural areas, government procurement of services is especially needed. This is because, on the one hand, the farmers urgently need the government to provide more and better services, including services in the production, services in life, as well as culture, education and other services; on the other hand, the service facilities in the large rural areas are small in number and poor in quality, if the government continues to do everything by itself on its own expense, the limited resource of the government cannot play a big role, and the farmers will not get the proper services. On the whole, government procurement of services in rural areas will have at least the following three main functions. First, it will help the government to streamline the organization and improve efficiency. In the past, governments at all levels have always played the role of a strong government, having control over everything and do everything personally. Consequently, not only the administrative departments have expanded greatly, but also various institutions are also increasing. If the government carries out the purchase of services, various service activities of government can be entrusted to social service agencies, which allows the government to get out from the tedious affairs, and creates conditions for government agencies to streamline and improve efficiency. Second, it helps the government to improve the practical effect of public spending. In the past, with the government doing everything in its expense, a substantial part of the government fund which could had been used on farmers were used to feed a large number of the government-affiliated agency personnel, and it easily led to arbitrary charges and increased the burden on farmers. After the government carries out the purchase of services, large amount of fund which was used to feed the government agencies and personnel could be saved and used efficiently in the purchase of services. On the other hand, it will be beneficial for these government agencies and personnel to participate in the market activities and bring their intelligence into full play. Third, it helps promote the formation and development of the rural tertiary industry. Tertiary industry itself is the service industry. If the government carries out the purchase of services, the demand for services will rapidly increase, forming huge service consumption, thereby creating opportunities for the development of and laying a good foundation and conditions for tertiary industry in rural areas. It will also absorb more rural labor force, thereby increasing farmers' income and further revitalizing rural economy and developing rural social undertakings.

3.1.2 Building Up of a Bridge between Representative of Farmer Interest and the Government on an Equal Foot

While interviewed by Zhang Xingjian, the chief reporter of the *China Reform (Rural Column)*, Dr. Yu Jianrong says: the question is, for a long time people's attention to "three agriculture-related problems" mainly focus on the economic aspects, their focus of research is land system, farmer's income, transfer of rural labor force etc.; while few people study the causes of

China "three agriculture-related problems" and the solution to the problems from the political perspective. However, facts have proved that the historical process of the rural political situation not only decides the national political stability and modernization, but also decides and restricts the final solution to the "three agriculture-related" problems. China is a country with long history of power concentration, with a striking feature of social development dominated by the state power. Especially compared to the traditional rural society, economic benefits are always concealed in various means. The most direct manifestation is that the allocation of economic resources is determined by the allocation of political power, and its cultural form is only the propaganda of dominant power. From the "centralized rural mobilization system" established after Communist Party seized the power, to the household contract responsibility system in the new period, then to establishment of township and village political system with "village self-governance" as the core, all belongs to the development pattern of urban society guiding the rural society under the background of state power. That is to say, the mode of social system change in rural area during the transitional period is mainly a mandatory system supply, and the national authority is the most fundamental iconic arrangement of rural society. In other words, the farmers have never really enjoyed the right to say in the process of social development in rural area. The lack of political expression for the interests of farmers in a true sense is the main reason that Chinese village gradually declined and the farmers became vulnerable groups.

Theoretically, the way of expression of the interests of vulnerable groups can be generally divided into two forms: in-system expression and anti-system expression. The peasant movements in modern history of China and events of farmers protesting against the grassroots party organization at present stage, all belong to anti-system expression, whereby their own interests are sought from outside of the system. When the interests of farmers are not expressed from the legitimate political way, it will be particularly difficult to achieve the stability of social order and coordinated development of various parties of the society. In this sense, we can say, to solve the "three agriculture-related problems" and strive for farmers' "national treatment" in China, we cannot stay on the breakthrough of the dual-structure social system; it should be a more important task to fight for the right to say in social development. Once the farmers obtained such right, they will obtain the right of dialogue with the social strong stratum. The key is to carry out the farmers "organization innovation". The peasant movement history from modern China shows that, the farmers' organization, as a political party's tool for political mobilization, cannot represent the peasants ultimately, the fundamental reason is externalization of organization function. Now the villagers' autonomous organization is the organization form which allows the farmers to speak, but the range of this organization is just in the community of village, and it is restricted by the rural grass-roots political power of the country. The community autonomy at township level is a target for social development. In addition to these community organizations, the establishment of political associations of farmers is also a viable option.[2]

3.1.3 Eradication of the Officialdom in Rural Society Management

In some relatively backward areas, township cadres spent most time on curettage (abortion) and taxes collection, and did not put the main focus to the development of economy. Consequently, it is of prior importance to improve the rural cadre selection and assessment mechanism without delay. Family planning is a basic policy of the State. However, in some regions, in order to complete the so-called "goals", the working method of family planning is just like the soccer playing, with the skills of "looting", "attacking" and "surrounding" to treat the people violating family planning, resulting in the consumption of large amount of manpower and resources, and creating tensions between cadres and the masses. A few cadres even on adopts a Laissez -Faire policy, the more children the farmers give birth to, the more penalty fees they collect; the more penalty fees they collect, the more children will be borne by the farmers, resulting in a vicious cycle. Reform of family planning and assessment methods shall be carried out to impose a certain working pressure to township Party and government cadres instead of setting mandatory target.

In addition, some grassroots cadres just became machines for tax collection. First, the tax burden is too heavy owing to exaggerated performance by the local government. Let's look at how these outrageous tasks are assigned? When the taxation task is assigned to the township government, the township government, in order to circumvent the inspection of the superior authority, will assign the task to the village committee in oral form rather than by means of written documents, then the village committee will pass on a heavier burden to the lower level organization of villager team, which will finally be borne by the farmers altogether. The ways of task assignment are diversified. Tax on agricultural and forestry products is usually collected on the acreage of the forest (regardless of whether there is any forest products), or on the acreage of the arable land (where there is no forest or few forest), or according to the proportion of the forest and land, or collected according to family members. Secondly, let's look at how these outrageous tasks are completed. Usually, it is the tax authorities to carry out the duties. However, in practice, the tax authority is just like an exhibit. Since the responsibility system of each level of government was implemented for the taxation task, the township government must assume the overall and final responsibility for the task at the township level. That is to say, at the township level, the township government must guarantee the accomplishment of the task of the tax authority. Meanwhile, the tax authority will take a backseat and just play a consultative and supporting role (be responsible for things like calculation, accountant settlement and summarization). As a matter of fact, the township and village cadres became the main executor for the collection of rural taxes and the collection of rural taxes also became the most important work for the township and village cadres. Although they do not possess the law enforcement power of tax collection, they had to undertake the main task of tax collection; on the contrary, the tax staff with the power did not necessarily need to execute the task of tax collection. This was probably one feature of the rural tax administration and collection system with Chinese characteristics. The specific collection measure was mostly that the township and village cadres withheld the tax at the Grain Supply Center (the operation was of course flexible). For those villagers whose grains withheld were not enough for the tax or whose produced grains were simply insufficient, the village cadres will usually collect the tax from door to door. In case the village cadres meet any difficulty or hindrance, the township cadres would provide assistance for the door-to-door collection. This involves the issue of mandatory measures to the farmers[3] .

All this exposes a very serious problem—the grass-roots cadres' selection, assessment, practical work etc. are all governed by a set of downright officialdom ideas and operation procedures. This led to a misgovernment system of officers bullying the masses and the superior oppressing the lower levels. To eradicate such phenomenon, China will need to reform its upper level of government besides improving its democratic politics construction at grassroots level. It needs to reform and improve the appointment and dismissal assessment mechanism of administrative officers of the whole country. First, it should be guaranteed that the election of the people's congresses at all levels be carried out without any administrative intervention so that the whole election procedure could be democratic and the elected representatives in conformity with the will of the people; second, it should be guaranteed that the representatives of the people have full freedom and necessary conditions to exercise their rights; third, the transparency of government affairs should be promoted not only at the grassroots level but also at all levels so that the acts of government could be under the supervision of the general public (unless otherwise specified by law).

3.2 PROPERTY RIGHT REFORM WITH AGRICULTURE LAND AT THE CORE

3.2.1 Privatization of Land Ownership

Some people are against privatization of land. The main reason is that privatization will lead to annexation of land, resulting in a large number of farmers lost land, thus causing the social instability, or even triggering the peasant war. However, a general survey will help us understand that the land annexation in China at current stage is nothing less than in the countries of land privatization. The annexation of land is realized by the government in the form of enclosure. However, the land contracting fees do not go to the farmers but to the government. Originally, the real estate company should negotiate and sign agreements with the farmers regarding land acquisition. Nowadays, the government makes the decision for the farmers, and the phenomena of the old society emerges "the government is bribed to find fault with the farmers, who had no choice but sell the land". It would be an impossible thing to acquire such a large land through free trading of market if without the interference of the government. After privatization, will the land become conglomerated? To what extent will it become conglomerated? Now the land annexation happening in China is just because the farmers do not possess the property rights. It is clearly stipulated in the *Law of the People's Republic of China on the Contracting of Rural Land* that the farmers enjoy the *right in rem* but not the *right in personam*, which implies the relationship between the farmers and the land is not the tenant relationship, the fees paid by the farmers to the collective does not belong to the rent, and the behavior of delaying in payment does not constitutes the reason for taking back the land (on the contrary, in the case of *right in personam*, if it is regarded as a tenant relationship, then rent shall be paid before the occupation of land, and the landlord enjoys the right to retrieve the land in case of default payment of the rent). This stipulation essentially strengthened the property rights of the farmers. However, the problem remains to be solved.

Endowing the farmers with the land ownership seems to be the trend of the times which is essential to solve the problem of the efficiency concerning the land in rural area. First of all, if the farmers have the ownership of land, they get the right to fight against the unreasonable burden on the land. Secondly, if the land is possessed by the farmers, the production efficiency on the land will be improved, as in the sphere permitted by the laws and regulations, how the farmers use the land will directly connect with their immediate interests. Thirdly, if the farmers enjoy the land ownership right, there will be the complete property right based on the ownership, including the ground right, easement, the rights above and below the land. In addition, only when the farmers have the land ownership right, can the efficient scale operation in the true meaning be realized. The relationship between the scale operator and the land owner will be based on equal consultation in the market, with the pros and cons of the transaction being fully considered, and thus the utility of land being brought to full play. However, in the scale operation initiated by the government, the situations of power rent-seeking, corruption, land speculation for profits, or land abandoning will happen easily.

3.2.2 Access to Property Right to Public Utilities in Rural Area

It seems natural that the public facilities in rural areas, such as water, electricity, flood control, irrigation and other facilities all belong to the State. However, the drawbacks emerged with the nationalization are adequate to deny its reasonableness. If we have a look at the burdens imposed on farmers for these utilities, and the threats posed to the farmers. To complete the tax collection task, the local governments rack their brains in raising the rate of public utilities. The high charges for water and power makes the farmers would not use electricity except watching television; the irrigation water is as expensive as oil; the charge for flood control becomes a fixed financial resource of local governments. For the farmers, these facilities are not welfare, but heavy burden of the State. Originally, these facilities belong to a part of the State investment in the rural areas, which shall belong to the farmers. Of course, it does not mean that the property rights of these facilities shall be granted to the farmers. They are just the common properties of the farmers. It is precisely because the property rights of these utilities are not handled correctly, so that their efficiencies are very low and the damages rates are extremely high.

Vesting the farmers with the property rights to the public facilities is of great significance to solve the "three agriculture-related problems". First, it can make these facilities exert the maximized utility, thus solving the problem of great waste with the facilities. Secondly, it can block the channel for arbitrary fee collection; thirdly, these facilities are not likely to suffer intentional damages.

3.3 INTEGRATED DEVELOPMENT OF URBAN AREA AND RURAL AREA WITH SOLVING THE PROBLEM OF URBAN-RURAL DUAL STRUCTURE AS THE CORE

After the assembly of the Sixteenth National Congress of the Communist Party of China, the Party proposed to solve the problem of agriculture, farmer and rural area from the perspective of integrated development of urban and rural areas. For which, we need to not only construct a modern agriculture, but also further stimulate the development of rural economy and increase farmers' income. To solve these problems, we need to integrate the urban and rural areas rather than seclude the rural areas from the outside world. This also requires us to accelerate our urbanization, transfer more agricultural population to the urban area for non-agricultural industries and therefore form an integrated development pattern of urban and rural areas so as to gradually find a new solution and bright future for solving Chinese problem of agriculture, farmer and rural area. Many schools have provided strong evidence and demonstration for this.

Chen Xiwen points out that our existing economic dual structure of urban and rural areas hasn't changed yet. With such economic dual structure, it would be no doubt that our urban and rural areas would develop in a segmented manner which is quite unfavorable for rural development. However, after entering into the stage of overall construction of moderately prosperous society, it would be very difficult to actually construct such a society if we cannot break the thinking featuring division of urban and rural areas or if we fail to gradually reflect the integration of urban and rural areas from the systems and policies. Therefore, we can say that the concept of urban and rural integration actually includes such two aspects of economy and society. Just as mentioned in the report of the Sixteenth Congress, it is necessary to realize urban and rural integration in all three areas of material, political and spiritual civilization construction.

Xu Jingyong thinks that it would be impossible for us to finally solve the social and economic issues of rural area if we keep and develop a relatively independent social and economic sector of rural area for a long time. Only by changing the traditional pattern of social division of labor in urban and rural areas and gradually expanding the non-agricultural industries that concentrated in urban area in the past to rural area, can we allocate the production factors in a more reasonable manner, thus fundamentally solve and overcome the series of contradictions caused by the relatively independent urban area and rural area and usher in a broad prospect for coordinated develop of our whole social and economic system.

Lu Xueyi suggests strategically adjusting urban and rural relationship and gradually changing the pattern of "separated regulation of urban and rural areas and different policies in one country". What we need to construct is a unified big market for billions of people rather than two separated markets for urban and rural areas. In other words, we cannot block up the nine million farmers outside the urban area. We must reform the existing household registration system, open the door to urban area and provide more employment opportunities for farmers so as to liberate farmers again. Of course, such a big change or conversion would need a series of supported regulations and policies which need to be implemented by steps.

Zhou Pigai holds that the implementation of "three orientations of agriculture, farmers and rural area" represents an effective way to reform the dual system—the big obstacle for development of "agriculture, farmers and rural area". The "three orientations of agriculture, farmers and rural area" refer to the industry orientation of agriculture, citizen orientation of farmers and urban orientation of rural area. The "three orientations of agriculture, farmers and rural area" and dual system represent two different forces, namely the driving force and restraining force for development of "agriculture, farmers and rural area" which are also a pair of direct contradictions. Promoting the "three orientations of agriculture, farmers and rural area" can fundamentally reform and weaken the dual system.

Guo Shuqing thinks that, of the existing structure of national economy, the output structure is unreasonable on one hand, and conversion of employment structure lags behind that of output structure on the other hand. Such situation has considerable defects which are in urgent need of great adjustment. The "three agriculture-related problems" at current stage are just an epitome of the whole unreasonable structure of our national economy. Therefore, as a matter of fact, the "three agriculture-related problems" are not just pure problems related with the agriculture, rural area and farmers. To solve the "three agriculture-related problems", it would be necessary to adjust the big industrial structure of our national economy. To promote the adjustment of agricultural and rural economic structure and increase farmers' income, it would be necessary to improve and optimize the overall economic structure and vigorously develop the tertiary industry.

For overall planning of urban and rural areas, it is necessary to avoid several kinds of misunderstanding: the first is that overall planning means no planning. The planning without any priority or focus means no planning at all. We need to understand the concept of overall planning under the context of solving the severe "three agriculture-related problems". In face of such acute problems as insufficient agricultural input, backward rural infrastructure and heavy farmers' burden, our national finance shall provide more preference to the rural area. The second is that overall planning means high concentration. The market economy needs to provide maximum freedom to the market subjects. Overall planning of urban and rural areas mainly refers to the aspects of governmental strategy for administration and macro control and regulation. Therefore, it is necessary to direct our overall planning of urban and rural areas into the orbit of constitution as well as ensure law-based administration and absence of ultra vires or abuse of power. Overmuch emphasis on overall planning may bring about actual concentration of power by the government under the excuse of overall planning and may direct our national development of economy and society to the old path of planned economy.

Overall and integrated development of urban and rural areas would inevitably raise the requirement of institutional innovation for the existing "three agriculture-related problems", especially the requirement of fundamental reform to the three systems featuring discrimination to farmers:

3.3.1 Urbanization of Agriculture Population

The existing household registration in China adopts a separate management of "agricultural population" and "non-agricultural population" and administrative examination and approval system, by which the relationship between the population and the land and local administration is fixated, thus increasing the cost for migration and reducing the efficiency of resource allocation. The small-town development strategy promoted in recent days is a kind of wrong choice of strategy and outdated notion. It, in nature, promotes "leaving the land instead of the rural area" and, in fact, intends to prevent the farmer from entering the city. Free migration of population serves as an important driving force of rapid development of the economy and society. There will be a period in the future in China which features not only rapid rise of economy but also major migration of population and great adjustment of population distribution. To adapt to the trend of population mobility, it is necessity to endow the citizens with the right of free migration. China needs to amend its constitution and relevant laws as soon as possible, formulate the *Law for Free Migration of Population*, revolutionize its household registration system and improve its resident identification card system so as to form a legal system that supports the population to migrate from the mountainous area to the plain, from the plain to the city and from the hinterland to the coastal area, thus realizing optimal distribution of population resources in urban and rural areas as well as in the eastern and western areas in accordance with the principle of efficiency, and promoting efficient utilization of our geographic space resources. Fundamentally, it is necessary to rely on the "two major migrations" of pupation (i.e., to increase the migration of population from the rural area to the urban areas and the migration of population from the western area to the eastern area) to narrow the "two great gaps" (i.e., the gap between the urban area and rural area and the gap between the eastern area and western area). The "two major migrations" of population can help fundamentally solve the issues of rural overpopulation, and overlarge ecological stress in western area, realize efficient allocation of overall land and population resources and achieve long-term prosperity and political stability of China.[4]

3.3.2 Capitalization of Agriculture Land

China implements separate administration of the rural and urban areas and agricultural and industrial land and has no unified and coordinated land market for the urban and rural areas. The farmers' collective-owned land has no access to the industrial and urban land market. Chinese industrialization and urbanization have badly damaged the farmers' interests of land. They are the system root of "land-lost farmers" and "village-in-city" problems in the urbanization district. Since the land is the farmers' "subsistence allowances" and largest "family belongings", the farmers should receive the benefits brought by land appreciation. We used to inveigh against the bloody "sheep-eating-people" enclosure system in Britain at the initial stage of industrialization. However, shouldn't we rethink the social inequity of existing land system of "transforming from agricultural land to non-agricultural land"? Just take a look at the large quantity of good field and land that has been swallowed by the city each year and the large sum of lost funds that may have been used for rural development! The State has extracted huge stocks of rural resources in its industrialization and urbanization, but rejects the rural labor force entering the city, leading to the decrease of farmers' share of possessive resources and wealth, shrinking of living space and deterioration of economic and social conditions. It is necessary to start a new round of land system revolution and accelerating the capitalization of farmers' collective-owned land as far as possible. China needs to learn from the international experience and formulate the *Law for Fair Trade of Land* complying with general requirements of market economy so as to legally support free circulation of rural land in accordance with the principle of market efficiency and ensure that the farmers can obtain reasonable economic benefits from the industrialization and urbanization of land.

3.3.3 Simplification of Taxes and Fees Collection Process

When Premier Wen announced the cancellation of tax on agricultural specialty products (excluding the tobacco) and further cancellation of agricultural tax, and implementation of direct subsidy for the grain farmers on Mar. 5, 2004, there were great excitement among the farmers. Some people began to blame that the farmers are numbed and indifferent to their own businesses and lack the right consciousness. However, if these people knew that 12,000 copies of Manual for Alleviating Farmers' Burdens were sold out to farmers in Jiangxi within half a month, they would not express such opinions on Chinese farmers. The reason for the farmers' indifference to the cancellation of agricultural tax lies in that, compared to the whole burden of the farmers, such tax is just a drop in the bucket. Moreover, according to most farmers, the tax on agricultural specialty products is reasonable and shall not be cancelled, whereas the vast majority of those unjustifiable taxes still weigh down on them heavily like Chinese Mountain Tai. How could the farmers express their "gratitude" to our fatherly Premier Wen under such circumstance?

The reform of rural taxation system implemented currently gives expression to simplification, alleviation and standardization in terms of policy design. Although progress has been achieved in reform of taxation, the unreasonable and discriminative nature of agricultural tax system itself has not been changed. Moreover, there have emerged some new problems after the reform of taxation. China is one of the few countries in the world that levy agricultural tax. The agricultural tax and tax on agricultural specialty products have not only some insurmountable defects of tax system, but also many accumulative contradictions because of undersize tax base, scattered tax source and over-high taxation cost. It is inevitable to pay higher economic, social and political costs to continue to maintain the existing system of agricultural taxes and fees, which is unsuitable for the political stability of rural areas. In consideration of the small gross amount of agricultural tax and the substantial financial resources in China, it is quite acceptable to consider cancelling the agricultural tax and the tax on agricultural specialty products. In accordance with the principle of integration development of urban and rural areas, after the cancellation of the agricultural tax and the tax on agricultural specialty products, individual income tax will be collected in a unified way in both urban and rural areas. The cancellation of agricultural tax and tax on agricultural specialty products means alleviation of the burden to the farmers; which is a thing totally feasible in terms of financial resources and the best means of subsidy to the agriculture after entering into WTO. As far as the local government is concerned, it can avoid many troubles, reduce conflict of interests with the farmers, spend more energy on public services, accelerate development of regional economy and promote the relationship with the farmers.[5] The "one-tax system" anticipated by Chinese farmers for a long time may be realized under the guidance of the thinking of urban-rural integration development.

3.4 CREATING AND SAFEGUARDING RIGHT AS THE CORE IN SOLVING "THREE AGRICULTURE-RELATED PROBLEMS" BY RULE OF LAW

It is a simple truth that the taxpayer pays for the government on the condition that the government will fulfill their wishes; the taxpayer has the right to know where the tax has been used, whether it should be used, who has the power to use it, etc. Of course, the will won't be exercised by each individual alone. It must be the real and comprehensive representation of the will of all taxpayers. The existing issue lies in the difficulty for generating such a representative due to the lack of "soil" for such generation. Ding Zuoming, Zhang Guiyu, Zhang Hongzhuan, Zhang Guimao etc. in the writings of Chen Guidi paid their life for alleviating the farmers' burden; only few can still embrace a good ending after much torment like Wang Junbin, Wang Xiangdong and Wang Hongchao, while many others have been annihilated in bud.[6] The reason lies in the absence of rule of law. Therefore, it is very urgent for the rural areas to exert operative constraint on the executive power of the local government in accordance with the law and safeguard the legal interests of the vast farmers.

3.4.1 Creating Rights According to Law

The creation of rights according to law mentioned hereunder is based on the expansion of executive power. All power of the government shall only be used for seeking happiness for the society, and therefore shall be exercised in accordance with existing promulgated laws instead of arbitrary decision and impulse.[7] Creating rights according to law mainly consists of three aspects:

1. Define the scope of executive power according to the law. According to some realistic cases, the strong inertia of rule of man still makes some grass-roots staff rely more on executive power instead of the law to solve the agriculture-related problems today. It leaves to the farmers the impression of strong power rather than holy law. In Mar. 2003, some villagers from a village in Chengbei District, Nanning, Guangxi attempted to inherit all land owned by their landlord grandfather before liberation by enclosure with bounding wall. The village judicial official responsible for handling the event and the other staff take sides on the issue at first because of their kindred with the villagers. However, other villagers who had obtained the right to use the land and whose traffic had been disrupted by the enclosure refused to obey and forcibly removed the bounding wall as they think the land has been processed after liberation and the right to use the land has changed, leading to violent clashes of group scuffle. The township government had to make order to remove the bounding wall and recover the land at last.[8] The claim to inherit the land of landlord is no doubt absurd and exposes the lack of legal awareness in some farmers. However, the different attitudes of the township government on handling the event show that it is of the same urgency to improve the legal quality of village and township grass-roots staff and the legal awareness of farmers. In fact, the law has explicit stipulation on such kind of problems which can be solved in accordance with the regulations on property right and right of adjacent in *General Principles of Civil Law* and the official reply on relevant problems from the Supreme People's Court in 1955. However, the township government staff failed to explicitly present the legal basis of their decision. The parties involved only knew that they had no other choice but obeyed the decision of the government and had no channel to know relevant legal basis.

In case of disputes, whether large or small, the villagers are accustomed to go to the village committee or township government for solutions, and the village committee or township government are also willing to make "authoritative decision" for such dispute as a "local magistrate". Such phenomenon is caused by long-term influence of the "administrative boss" thought. The thinking of "the Party and government call the shots for the people" leads to the extremity of rapid power expansion of local government. Under such circumstance, the public security organs, procuratorial organs and people's courts become the government "footmen", and the government hides the truth from the masses and acts on its own will.

To define the scope of executive power according to the law, it is necessary to, first, define the function and nature of the government and introduce the idea that the government and the public are of a contractual relationship, based on which, the public pays the tax to purchase services from the government and the government shall, after collecting the money, handle affairs in accordance with the public's will, provide good services to the public and transform its function from administration to service-providing; second, define the prohibitions of government in accordance with the governmental function stipulated in the constitution; and third, define the behavioral pattern, measure and means of the government in accordance with the law, and particularly prevent abuse of coercive measures in administrative acts.

2. The judiciary shall conduct independent adjudication on the legality of executive power according to the law.

The exercise of rural grass-roots executive power becomes very complicated owing to human factors. In the "first case in China concerning the villagers suing the village committee" accepted by Nanchang Intermediate People's Court, the court session was finally opened on the condition that the farmers made a compromise to change the defendant. The simple cause of action lies in that the farmers don't agree to the resettlement standard for land acquisition of the village committee.[9] The judicial and educational circles haggled over whether the village committee could be a defendant of administrative litigation. In fact, there is no need for such argument. The village committee can definitely be sued since it is implementing the executive functions. As to the question of qualification of the village committee as an independent status, the court shall initiatively or advise the plaintiff to add the "superior" township government of the committee as the joint defendant. The issue rose by some people that the village committee is the farmers' voluntary association is the key and substantive one. Since the organizing and function of the village committee are subject to the township government, the village committee has become a proxy of the government rather than a spokesperson of the villagers. This has made village self-governance a fraud. If the village self-governance is real, the resettlement compensation plan would immediately become invalid upon the villagers' disapproval, and there would be no need for going to court or appealing to other third party for solutions. The reality plays jokes on the farmers. On the one hand, the village self-governance is declared; on the other hand, the villagers simply have no means to decide their own business by themselves. In practice, the one who abuses executive power usually evades the legislation on purpose and asks those temporary organizations "without the qualification of legal status" and governmental "temporary worker" to carry out the ultra vires. Therefore, the people's court, after filing of the case, shall break out of the frame of mechanism doctrine and hear the case matter-of-factly to judge the legality of the administrative act.

To accept the case is one thing, the trial is more important and significant. In reality, it would be difficult to obtain an outcome of real justice in administrative litigation if the pattern of the judicial being subject to the administrative is not broken. The judicial independence usually referred to by the public mainly means that the judicial shall be independent of the administrative. Only in this way, can it be assured that the judiciary will take a neutral position while hearing an administrative lawsuit and judge the legality of the administrative act objectively.

3. Safeguard the public's effective supervision on the act of government

Who will check and supervise the administrative act of the government? The constitution appoints the National People's Congress to undertake the task besides the legal supervision of the People's Procuratorate. In practice, the two kinds of supervision stipulated by the constitution exist in name only and the really effective supervision comes from the media. The malfeasant and lawless official who plays the tyrant in a locality fear the journalists' interview the most. The supervision with single channel is abnormal, especially in China where the media is usually under the control of the administrative and becomes the main and key mouthpiece of the government. That means the government completely calls the shots for what can and cannot be publicized by the media. No wonder people say that the exposure of greedy officials we see in daily life is mostly for the governmental propaganda and the outcome of internal political struggle.

How to safeguard the public's effective supervision on the act of government? The first is to urge the government to make government affairs public. Some may think the idea is naive since it is difficult enough to make the village affairs public, not to mention making government affairs public. However, there is no need for too much disappointment. Our government has, after all, made some efforts though with small steps and frequent changes. The second is to create some groups or organizations that are actually appointed and removed by the public, independent from the government and capable of contending against the government so that they may accuse any unlawful act of the government and its staff on behalf of the public. The third is to create a third party not subject to the government to make neutral judgment on the petition made by the representative of the public on the government.

3.4.2 Safeguarding Rights According to Law

There is no other age in which Chinese farmers need more right-safeguarding. The root of the "three agriculture-related problems" lies in the absence of guarantee for farmers' rights. It has become the hardest nut to crack for the Party Central Committee and State Council to seek methods for safeguarding the rights of farmers—the largest vulnerable group of Chinese society. The farmers have no other choice but appeal for help and sometimes even go to the capital city to appeal for help since their rights cannot be safeguarded and they cannot find better remedy channel. This has increased many unstable factors for Beijing and generated great shock on the work of the Party Central Committee and the State Council. Therefore, the Party Central Committee and State Council are also eager to safeguard the farmers' rights. The problem should be easily solved since both the leader and the farmers have the same wish. However, the problem is far from being easy. So many obstacles lie on the road of safeguarding farmers' right! What are the obstacles?

First, it is a question who shall define the farmers' rights. The main and common cases in which the farmers' rights are infringed by the government include overcharge, excessive fines and apportion, illegal land acquisition and coercive and unified production and marketing. The farmers are usually confused by the government's infringement. They know that the infringement is not right but have no idea of what the bases are. This is also the reason that 12,000 copies of *Manual for Alleviating Farmers' Burdens* were sold out to farmers in Jiangxi within half a month. What the farmers are eager for is the "effective weapon"! Therefore, the first step to safeguard rights is to clearly define the farmers' rights in the law. China already has many protective laws for the vulnerable groups, including the *Law on the Protection of Disabled Persons*, *Law on the Protection of Woman's Rights*, *Law on the Protection of the Minors*, *Law on the Protection of Consumer Rights and Interests*, etc. Why not introduce the *Law on the Protection of Farmers' Rights and Interests*? If there is a law of such kind that defines the farmers' rights endowed by the constitution and law in detail, the farmers would have their "effective weapon" for safeguarding their rights.

Second, who will decide whether the infringement exists? In case of a governmental infringement, who will the farmers resort to for claiming of rights? The government? In practice, there is the stipulation that in case of any infringement of the local government, the farmers may appeal to the higher authorities of government. The stipulation is practicable under general condition. But can the farmers with their rights infringed get effective remedy when the integrated interests of the government itself are involved? The next is the administrative litigation. Look at the "end" of Zhou Guangli. Look at the weakness and absolute obedience of the court in front of the government. You will know what obstacles lay on the road. Therefore, the farmers' rights won't be practically safeguarded unless the judicial is independent.

Third, who will provide legal aid for safeguarding farmers' rights? To change the farmers into legal experts is as impractical as to change a chicken into a golden phoenix. Wang Ying becomes a legal "expert" and alcohol "expert" because of tenacious pursuit of litigation after his husband's death from alcoholism. But how many people like her do we have in reality? Moreover, the resources for rural education and publicity are limited. Compared with any other groups in our society, the farmers need the most legal aid. However, the existing legal aid mechanism in China is far from being completed and relevant financial input of the government is limited. The tree of legal aid hasn't taken root or bloom on the land of village, not to mention borne any fruit. It is necessary to vigorously promote the legal aid project in rural areas to effectively safeguard farmers' rights. First, special funds must be established for the capital for legal aid in rural areas from the financial department and shall not be controlled by local government. Otherwise the funds will be withheld or embezzled. Second, we shall mobilize all social forces to provide funds for legal aid in rural areas. It is a good try for the "Protection Center for the Vulnerable" in some colleges and universities in Beijing, Wu Han and other cities to utilize the grant from aboard. Third, we shall strengthen the popularization of the law so that the farmers can correctly deal with some simple law-related issues.

In the countries of industrialization and under industrialization, the agriculture is the weak industry and farmers are the vulnerable group. Many countries (especially USA EU and Japan) have corresponding protective policies for the agriculture and farmers. The US *Farm Security and Rural Investment Act of 2002* specifies that, in the future six years, total agricultural subsidy of the government will be as high as 80 billion dollars. In the negotiation for access to WTO, China lists the trade subsidy for agricultural products as one important item and finally decides a rate of subsidization no more than 8.5%. Since China is one of the two countries in the world that levy agricultural tax, its subsidy to the farmers are far less than that of the European countries and US, sometimes even goes to minus. It shows that Chinese protection for the agriculture and farmers is far from being enough.[10]

Creating and safeguarding rights according to law is just the core of the rule of law for the "three agriculture-related problems". The wide range of contents of the "three agriculture-related problems" also includes the agriculture-related legislation, judiciary, legal supervision and services and many other aspects. All in all, it is necessary to include all activities of the rural local government and organization and vast farmers into the orbit of the rule of law, to act by law and strictly prohibit such phenomena as privileges beyond the law, power-treading-law or people-treading-law.

3.5 COMPREHENSIVE REGULATION OF "THREE AGRICULTURE-RELATED PROBLEMS"

The regulation of "three agriculture-related problems" is a systematic project. None of the democratic politics construction, property right reform for the land, urban-rural integration development and rule of law can be successful alone in rural areas. They must work in coordination and require a combination of measures. In practice, the "three agriculture-related problems" are comprehensive and one problem may involve different governance models. For example, the issue of increasing income and alleviating burden for farmers and the issue of tax reform are usually considered as the key issues of the "three agriculture-related problems" and respective solutions are proposed. As a matter of fact, both issues are the same as other specific issues, which embodies the great diversity of "three agriculture-related problems". We need to classify these specific problems and find and solve the fundamental problems that affect the overall importance of "three agriculture-related problems".

Increasing the income and alleviating the burden for the farmers involves the issue of democratic politics construction in rural areas. The strong control of the local government over the rural areas makes village self-governance a mere formality and the village committee a proxy of local government. The local government and village committee "cooperate" to exploit the farmers. The second aspect involved is the issue of land property right. It is the unclear property right of agricultural land that enables the administrative to rudely intervene in the farmers' production and sales. The farmers lack the sense of security in terms of good anticipation of the land output after investment. The short-term act, sometimes even predatory exploitation, is prevalent. All these have direct influence on farmers' income-increasing. The third aspect involved is the issue of urban-rural integration development. The urban-rural dual structure enables the "price scissors" to cut the farmers' earnings step by step to naught. Since it becomes impossible for the farmers to increase their income through the single channel of agricultural land, to work in cities becomes a good way to increase their income. However, the discriminatory treatment to farmers in cities deeply hurts the farmers too. The fourth aspect involved is the issue of rule of law. The root causes of the difficulty for the farmers to increase income and alleviate burden lie in the absence of guarantee for farmers' rights. In face of the price drop of agricultural products and price rise of the industrial products, the farmers know that the phenomenon is the outcome of administrative intervention rather than functioning of natural law of market economy. However, they have no right to say no. In face of the countless tax and fee burdens that are entirely groundless, the farmers can do nothing but carry silent resentment. In face of varied discriminatory treatment, the farmers have no way to appeal. The absence of rule of law makes the farmers' income-increasing and burden-alleviating lack of the most basic guarantee.

Similarly, the reform of taxation expenses alone cannot fundamentally solve the "three agriculture-related problems". It is usually closely associated with the democratic politics construction; land system, urban-rural integration development and others issues in rural areas. What are the bases and conditions for implementing "one-tax system"? Why do we implement "one-tax system"? Why do we need to reform the existing tax and fee system?

What do we need to change? There would be no complete and reasonable answer to these questions if we break away from the reality of village self-governance, village land system and urban-rural structure relationship.

The democratic politics construction, land system reformation, urban-rural integration development and rule of law constitute a basic frame of governance for solving the "three agriculture-related problems" in rural areas. Of which, the democratic politics construction in rural areas is the fundamental. If the farmers cannot decide their own businesses, and if their production, management and even personal freedom are controlled by others, they are bound to suffer poverty and bully. The farmers can only be manipulated by others if they have no qualification to have equal dialogue with the government. Therefore, the democratic politics construction in rural areas is the basic issue that affects the solution of the "three agriculture-related problems". Only after real realization of village self-governance, can all measures of rural reform be smoothly implemented. Of course, when we emphasize the fundamental role of village self-governance in solving the "three agriculture-related problems", we do not mean that village self-governance is all-powerful. As some people said, you farmers want village self-governance. OK, the state will stay out of it entirely. Let's see how you will govern yourselves! No absolute things can avoid the end of negation. If the village self-governance is the fundamental solution for solving the "three agriculture-related problems", the reform of agricultural land would be the basis. The agricultural land is the most important and direct properties of the farmers and also the most important and direct source of farmers' income. Without solving the problem of agricultural land, the farmers will not have the guarantee for even the basic material life and other rights of self-governance and equality will lose their material basis. The unclear property right of agricultural land is also the root of unstable factors of our society and the contradictions and conflicts among the villagers, between the villagers and village committee, between the villagers and township government and between the villagers and land acquisition unit. To clearly define the property right of agricultural land doesn't mean to make the right a "David's deer", just as the stipulation of the *Rural Land Contract Law*. On the contrary, it means to clearly define the farmers' sole ownership to the land. Only in this way, can the farmers' basic property right be considered as complete and the solution to "three agriculture-related problems" be provided with the most basic material resources. The urban-rural integration development is the essential means for solving the "three agriculture-related problems" which is closely connected with each other rather than an absolute issue.

Except for the dozens of millions of poverty-stricken populations who have no guarantee for even the most basic food and clothing, the issue for the vast majority of rural areas lies in the sharp contrast with the cities in terms of infrastructure construction, daily consumption, channels for information and educational conditions. All these make the farmers feel frustrated, vexed and worthless. When people are violently lashing Chinese "deep-rooted bad habit" of "not worry about poverty, but rather about the uneven distribution of wealth", have they ever thought of that the most basic pursuit of modern civilization is nothing but equity? Although absolute equity is unachievable, overall and relative equality shall become a basic starting point of today's social governance model. As to the "three agriculture-related problems", the urban-rural integration is the solution to the disadvantages of dual structure system and achieve overall well-off and equity of the society. The rule of law serves as the core and basic guarantee for solving the "three agriculture-related problems". Only after stepping into the orbit of rule of law, can the democratic politics construction in rural areas, reform of agricultural land and urban-rural integration development be provided with reliable system guarantee so that they won't be aborted halfway or destroyed in one day because of the change of view or assumption of duty of some people. One important aspect of rule of is to provide a unified and most basic standard for each behavior of people in social practices, and to safeguard the individuals' rights and freedom to the utmost while regulating people's behaviors. A basic function of rule of law is to determine and balance the relationship of rights and obligations among all social subjects. The core of the "three agriculture-related problems" lies in the farmers' right issue. The democratic politics construction in rural areas, property right reform of agricultural land, urban-rural integration development and other treatment measures all closely connected with the guarantee of farmers' rights as well as the restriction and prohibition of the infringement by the government and other parties on farmers' rights. The core of the "three agriculture-related problems" lies in the issue of farmers' rights, therefore the core of solution to the problems also lies in the rule of law for the purpose of determining and protecting farmers' rights.

On the macro level, the concept and strategy of governance of human society feature a step-by-step evolution process in history. It is a qualitative leap of human society to change from governance by the nature (human cannot master their own destiny which is dependent on the choice of nature) to governance by the God (human has possessed initial capability to conquer the nature, but has to seek help from the strength of the "God" in face of some unrecognizable and uncontrollable influence or phenomenon that determines the survival of mankind. The age of governance by the God comes when the "strength of the God" extends to become the general guidelines for judging and determining people's acts). It is a symbol of society progress to change from the governance by the God to governance by people. Nevertheless, the boundary defining such change is blurry. The personification of god and deification of people lead to the consequence that human society has been in an authoritarian era that features hierarchical control and concentration of power in individuals because of blind worship. It is a milestone for full realization of human self-liberation to change from governance by people to governance by law. The governance by law abolishes the myth of absolute authority in individuals and breaks the authoritarian system of hierarchical control so that each social individual may obtain full and equal rights and freedom. It is the best choice of concept and strategy of governance in modern civilization.

The governance of the "three agriculture-related problems" serves as an important part of overall national and social governance. It is a fundamental guiding thought for effective governance of "three agriculture-related problems" to grasp the rule of law, i.e., the general orientation and main theme of our age, while taking specific governance measures in specific aspects of the "three agriculture-related problems". This requires the government, i.e., the direct responsible body for addressing the "three agriculture-related problems", to timely change their concepts and update their ideas to include each measure for governing "three agriculture-related problems" into the orbit of rule of law.

NOTES

1. Chen Xiaonong, "Three Agricultural Issues Triggered Political Reform," *Reform Pioneer* 4(2001).
2. Zhang Hangjian, "*Yu Jianrong: Rural Political Reform --the Key to Solve the 'Three agriculture-related problems*," *Social Science*, August 8, 2002.
3. Li Ming, "Perspective on Farmers' Burdens," Forum on Making the Country Prosperous, accessed Aug. 15, 2003, http://www.people.com.cn.
4. Dang Shuangren, *"Urban-Rural Integration Development Promotes Ten Major Institutional Innovations," Research and Decision-Making* 12(2003).
5. Dang Shuangren, *Urban-Rural Integration Development Promotes Ten Major Institutional Innovations*, *Research and Decision-Making*, Dec. 9, 2003
6. Chen Guidi and Chun Tao, *Survey on Chinese Farmers* (Beijing: People's Literature Publishing House, 2004), 47.
7. (British) Locke: *Two Treatises of Government* (Beijing: The Commercial Press, 1964), 86.
8. Lu Mingwei, "On the Construction of Legal Aid Institution in Rural Areas," Chinese Reform Forum, accessed Aug. 4th, 2003, http://www.chinareform.org.cn/.
9. Li Jingying, "Court Session Opened Ten Months after the Prosecution of the First Case in China where the Villager Sues the Village Committee," *China Youth News*, Jan. 19, 2004.
10. Xu Peiying, "Zhang Haoruo: Overall Well-off Can Be Achieved Only after Solving the 'Three Agriculture-related Problems'," *Economic Information Daily*, Dec. 12, 2002.

Chapter Four

Necessity and Urgency of Solving "Three Agriculture-related Problems" by Rule of Law

4.1 SOLVING "THREE AGRICULTURE-RELATED PROBLEMS" BY RULE OF LAW IS NECESSARY FOR SPEEDING UP INDUSTRIALIZATION

4.1.1 The "Three Agriculture-related Problems" Cannot be Neglected in the Process of Industrialization

As the global economy is rolling on the fast track of post-industrialization and informization, China is yet still in the process of industrial revolution. China needs to speed up the process of industrialization so as to catch up with the developed countries in the world in the shortest possible time. Although China's modernization is regarded by many people to be a trap, or rather pseudoscience,[1] it is indeed a matter of understanding on modernization from different perspectives. If we conceive modernization as a process of learning and introducing from the West the advanced experience and technologies, including those systems proven to be accordant with the trend of historical development, such modernization is undoubtedly helpful for making the country powerful and the people rich. In this sense, industrialization is a vital part of modernization and acceleration of industrialization is an irresistible trend of history. Meanwhile, we need to avoid lopsided development in the process of industrialization. Industry, agriculture, commerce and service industry constitute four integral parts of national economy. If without any of them, the national economy would become lopsided and cannot develop soundly and rapidly. At present stage, an extremely acute problem has come to the surface in the process of China's industrialization, i.e. the problem of "agriculture, farmer and rural area".

By analyzing the development history of world economy, we can find that most countries have experienced the following three stages during economic structure evolution and industrialization: 1) dominance of traditional agricultural economy; 2) coexistence of traditional agricultural economy and modern industrial economy; and 3) dominance of modern industrial industry. The structure of existence of traditional agricultural economy and modern industrial economy is what economists call "dual economy structure". In this stage, driven by modern technologies, management and policies, the modern industrial economy that navigates the development of advanced productivity grows steadily and has its position entrenched gradually. However, there's little doubt that the concepts of traditional agricultural economy are so deep-seated that the outdated mode of agricultural production are still widely practiced at this stage and the quantitatively indexed output, population and number of employees of agriculture are almost the same with those of industry. Therefore, to establish and strengthen the influence of modern industrial economy becomes the top priority and an inevitable task of industrialization and modernization for all countries to develop national economy. However, according to the basic laws of industrial structure evolution for an industrial country, special attention should be given to the development of agriculture and light textile industry so that it would provide financial and technical support for the development of modern industry and improvement of industrial structure. Meanwhile, the development of modern industrial economy is good nourishment needed by agriculture in terms of technology improvement and surplus labor shifting. This pattern of making their respective advantages complementary to each other results in the status of agriculture and industry coexistence, which is then gradually replaced by the structure featured by dominance of modern industrial economy. Thus, firstly, communicating the cyclic relation between agriculture and industry constitutes the essence of eliminating the dual economy structure. A significant and practical policy implication of this conclusion is to establish mutual supporting development strategies based on harmonious development and mutual benefit of agriculture and industry so as to satisfy the requirements of "balancing urban and rural development". Secondly, if a country's agricultural development is lagging behind, it should attach special importance to the financial, technical and manpower input to agriculture when eliminating the dual economy structure. Any practice of neglecting agriculture and promoting industrialization alone without considering agriculture could consolidate rather than eliminating the dual economy structure, thereby intensifying the conflict between agriculture and industry and eventually impeding the process of industrialization.[2]

China's industrialization is a process different from early industrialization in some developed countries. It is not only a matter of times having changed and circumstances having changed. China's industrialization cannot be achieved without successfully coordinating and solving the "three agriculture-related problems". When it comes to modernization and industrialization, we always refer to the case of Britain while ignoring the times when Britain implemented industrialization. Britain's industrialization is accompanied by territorial expansion and colonization, so the "three agriculture-related problems" are less significant and the industrial revolution could embrace its triumph in a short period. With its current national strength and amidst the present international situation, China can never grow into a great power by aggressing and plundering other countries, let alone wide territorial expansion and colonization. Such being the case, what can we do? Farmers pay a heavy price for that. Are farmers ought to be victims of industrialization? Certainly not. Here let us make a study on the ways in which other countries somehow similar to China attempted to solve the "three agriculture-related problems" in the process of industrialization.

France experienced a series of political and economic reforms and wide civil and foreign wars in the 18th century, forming a severe hit to the traditional agricultural society and farmers. One of radical changes among them lies in land laws and decrees. Specifically, overthrowing the rule of feudalism and recognition of individualism contributed to the spreading of private ownership. Consequently, the number of dependent small landowners was on the rise, and the social constitution and class relations of farmers were remarkably changed since then.

Land ownership was a priority issue back then. In fact, the leaders of French Revolution became aware of the necessity to destroy the old land ownership from the start in the violent mass uprisings organized by farmers against the government. The French government promulgated the August Decrees, whereby all feudal powers were abolished and all dues related to land were declared redeemable. In Mar. 1790, the Constituent Assembly adopted the regulations governing redemption of feudal duties. In Aug. 1792, the Legislative Assembly further issued the decrees regarding distribution of countryside public lands and important land policies stipulating, among others, that all redeemable feudal powers should be abolished and feudal lords should restitute the public lands in their possession to farmers. In Sep. 1792, the Legislative Assembly expropriated lands from the fled nobles and split the same into small parcels which were then rent out to farmers for an indefinite duration by installment rent payment or land purchase. All these decrees changed the nature of land ownership radically. Shortly thereafter, the National Convention confiscated and sold the properties owned by the fled nobles and the Church in accordance with the decrees launched on Jun. 3, 1793. Such measures as distributing public lands equally on a per capita basis stipulated in the Decrees dated Jun. 11 sated most farmers' appetite for lands to some extent. According to statistics, there were approximately 15%-60% state properties purchased by farmers in different regions of other provinces across the country. There were more and more farmers owning lands, and it was even possible for some farmhands to possess a few of lands of their own in the revolution. Some owner-farmers with mere one or two hectares on their hands in the past owned 5-10 hectares of land after land purchase, thus forming a class of well-off petty bourgeois in the countryside. This radical reform of land ownership created a new situation totally different from that in the 18th century when 2/3 lands were occupied by the French royal family, nobles and monks. In a period spanning one and a half centuries, the French Revolution helped to cement the small-scale farmer management system established on the basis of self-sufficiency and extensive employment of household labor force. As a result of such changes in the countryside, namely the changes to land distribution, the number of landowners were on the rise and the lands became more fragmented. As revealed by the statistics of the year 1826, all the lands of France were then divided into over 100 million shares. With every 10 shares being owned by 6 persons, a total of 6 million farmers possessed lands back then. However, the taxes paid by about 80% of farmers are just below ₣20. These farmers formed a majority of farmers across the country, but each of them owned a small area of lands, accounting for 17% of agricultural income in total. While the landowners paying tax of more than ₣1,000 accounted for 0.13% of all farmers across the country but accounted for 9% agricultural income in total. The above gives us a general view of land fragmentation and small-scale farmer economy specific to France. Such land fragmentation continued till 1850s. All the lands in the country were divided into 11.5 million shares in 1842 and 13 million shares in 1858. There are two major roots underlying the phenomenon of land fragmentation: on the one hand, following the end of the French Revolution, the Constituent Assembly promulgated the decrees on Mar. 15, 1790 to abolish primogeniture and make family property distribution and right of succession equally available to all successors, thus creating a great potential for land fragmentation; later in Jun. 1793, the French National Convention issued decrees to confiscate lands from the fled nobles and sell them to poor farmers in small parcels; in addition, the *Code Napoleon* promulgated in 1804 further safeguarded the farmers' land ownership in the revolution; furthermore, even Louis XVIII acknowledged the outcomes of revolution in the Charter 1814 in his times of Restoration by promising that the property rights of those having purchased state properties were protected by law. The legislative regulations established in different historic stages all operated to protect the fragmented lands gained by farmers in the French Revolution and in turn consolidate the ownership of lands owned by small-scale farmers. It coincides with the thought proposed by the Economist Caron, F. stating: legislations established in the revolution not only reinforced the farmers' individualistic tendency but also strengthened their dogged determination to possess the lands. Therefore, over the long period, French took on a new look of agricultural economy different from Britain featured by land centralization. On the other hand, by digging into the specific reasons, we can find that some large landowners migrated between urban and rural areas and gradually left their lands with the development of industrialization and urbanization, leaving the lands an object of trading in shares and thus making them fragmented.

In general, the above changes to the land ownership occurring in early 19th century in France shaped the social relations, production mode and economic position in the countryside and the farmers' political attitudes. Though villages in a region differed from those in other regions, the French rural society was typically comprised of large landowners, rural bourgeois, small landowners and rural proletarians. Among them, large landowners and rural proletarians each took up a small proportion, while small landowners formed the majority. Large landowners, though small in number, occupy a great many of properties (according to incomplete statistics, in 1842, the large landowners earning income of ₣300 or more accounted for 1% of all farmers owning lands but possessed 1/4 of fortunes). They can be further divided into three groups: (1) the landowners who own plenty of lands by way of either inheritance or investment, but they migrate from the villages where they were born and grew up to settle in the urban area and hire others to manage the farm properties on their behalf. In this sense, they are not farmers anymore and have nothing to do with agricultural production and countryside except collection of rent. (2) the landowners like landadels in the old times who become well-off by inheriting family properties from their ancestors or purchasing state properties or make fortune by serving as civil or military officials during the times of the First Empire and later return to their hometown. They live in houses as spacious and gorgeous as castles in the countryside, manage farming for the whole year by themselves, and go out for hunting for a few months. However, they would hire tenant farmers for farming on the lands instead of farming by themselves. In the cold winter, these landowners return to a winter resort in the urban area and socialize with people there. They remain closely related with the countryside by leading such life characterized by migration between urban and rural areas. (3) the farmers in the true sense who are closely tied up lands and agriculture. The landowners of this group own vast lands, rich and educated. Subsisting on agricultural production, they follow agricultural development with interest or are even interested in agricultural experiments. They employ seasonal laborers or tenant farmers for farming and manage farming by themselves. What's more, while leaving in the castle-like houses, they socialize frequently with villagers in their neighborhood and enjoy a high reputation among them. The term “cultivator” we typically use to describe farmers is not completely applicable for them since they’ve actually changed into agricultural producers engaging in agriculture. The agricultural societies and institutes that emerged in the 18th century become gathering places where they socialize with others for exchange of experience and ideas. These landowners are regarded as forerunners who later founded the federation of agriculture, advanced the agricultural production reform and took the initiative to carve out the road to agricultural modernization. Apart from large landowners, there are petty bourgeois who engage in agricultural work. Though small in number, they enjoy a prestige comparable with large landowners. They are mostly natives, owning properties and lands in the villages and towns and generate income substantially out of lands. They are educated, well-informed, well-addressed and polite. They take up a variety of occupations in the countryside ranging from notary, magistrate, store and inn owner to doctor and pharmacist, etc. In consideration of their personal morality, they are seen as notables in the villages but are the notables who form a part of the village regime without the slightest stateliness. The ways the bourgeois lead a life and socialize with others have a significant impact on the countryside. The middle bourgeoisie, though scattered in villages and towns, are still closely tied up with the lands and constitute the bridge for communication between farmers and ruling cities. Apart from the above two strata, there are also quite a few small landowners. They are truly what we call “cultivators” who make a living by farming on their own small parcels of land (accounting for 4/5 of total population in the rural society but occupying only 1/5 properties). These small landowners can be further classified by family income into four groups: (1) the well-off petty farmers who make a living by farming on their own lands, self-supporting and typically owning a kind of farm tools at least. They acquire more and more wealth through hard working and get satisfaction out of that. (2) the less well-off petty farmers who subsist substantially on farming but usually leave home for working as a daily or seasonal laborer for a short period whenever possible so as to boost their family income since the farming income alone is not enough to cover the family expenditure. In some cases, they may also do paid farm work in rich farmer families or engage in cottage crafts. (3) the farm workers or craftsmen who own tiny parcels of land that could not support the whole family, so they have no choice but to take up other jobs to make ends meet. These impoverished petty farmers are widely distributed in mountainous areas. (4) mass rural laborers who generate limited income from farming on their tiny parcels and planting vegetables and fruits, so they have to serve as paid stewards or tenant farmers for large landowners who do not participate in agricultural production by themselves. Acting as manager of all farmhouse affairs, stewards do not perform physical labor in person; while tenant farmers without means of production have no choice but to work with instruments of labor, seeds and livestock provided by the large landowners. They are mostly employed by large landowners on an annual basis subject to a verbal agreement which may be renewed year after year or even generation after generation. The last stratum rural proletarians are made up of poverty-stricken farmers from the underclass in villages. With little lands or properties, they live in misery and have to support the family by either farming on rented lands or working in cottage handicraft workshops. For those living in a big family, they usually leave home to find a job as a seasonal laborer or servant with the help of their parents (mostly farther) to make a living or wander here and there. On the one hand, they form the least stable group of the rural society; on the other hand, they later become a part of the reserve army of labor in the process of industrialization and of the immigrant group in the process of urbanization.

In a word, the French Revolution buffeted French rural areas in early 19th century. Consequently, the feudal land system was radically changed and all feudal rights and duties were abolished, creating an opportunity for the development of an agricultural society dominated by petty farmers farming on their own lands. All these determined the development trend of French rural areas took a different road of agricultural modernization compared with other countries like Britain. The society is complicatedly composed with a wide gap between the rich and the poor, but to be sure, those of the two extreme classes of the society represent a small fraction of total population. Between these two extremes are the middle classes who are rather representative in both population and land area. After breaking away from the tie of feudal society, privatization of property was regarded as the bedrock of agricultural development, and the role played by the majority of ordinary petty farmers in possession of private land properties was exactly the same as the role played by the bourgeois agricultural producers in the course of agricultural development. [3] All these measures would not have been practiced successfully if without the regulation of law. The fairness of laws is fully manifested here. In addition, legal regulation does not hamper the society's pursuit for economic efficiency. Fairness and efficiency are two contradictory but also coherent concepts. If they are well coordinated, the society will develop rapidly with few barriers. If not, the society will develop slowly under the influence of internal friction and various obstacles.

China is now struggling with such a pressing problem. As state-owned assets in urban areas are disposed of and privatization is springing up in waves, many entrepreneurs stand out and enterprises that are dying or have been declared dead are vitalized one after another by privatization. "Private" is not a taboo subject any more, and people are no longer worried about social unrest brought about by state-owned enterprise reform. The Chinese government can take it calmly when seeing more and more laid-off workers in urban areas and carry forward the state-owned enterprise reform without hesitation. However, in rural areas, you'll witness a totally different scene.

Farmers only have the right to use the lands and they have to grow gains in the face of foreseeable loss, to pay taxes even if they do not grow gains, and to bear all sorts of unreasonable burdens even if they need to turn to banking institutions for loaning. It is such a sharp contrast that has driven rural economy to the edge of death. Someone says China cannot acquire the resources required for industrialization by plundering other countries like what Britain did during the period of industrialization, so it has no choice but to plunder the resources from its people, especially from the farmers. It seems that farmers are born to be victims of industrialization. By probing into the rural reform measures taken by France in the process of industrialization, we can find that industrialization is an irresistible trend of history, but it is not necessarily to be accomplished at the expense of farmers' interests. In the process of industrialization, we should reasonably solve the problem of farmers and stabilize the rural area so that industrialization can advance without any burden. On the contrary, endless and relentless exploitation will lead only to civil conflicts, and rural unrest is bound to become a threat to the industrialization.

4.1.2 Solving "Three Agriculture-related Problems" by Rule of Law Is Guarantee of Smooth Promotion of Industrialization in China

The industrialization process will be held back if the "three agriculture-related problems" is not solved properly. Therefore, if industrialization were to accelerated, the agriculture should also develop stably. However, it would not happen naturally. That means an impetus will be required. In China, the impetus has long been exerted by the Party and the government, evidenced by the countless meetings and official or unofficial documents regarding the "three agriculture-related problems" convened and published by the Party and the government over the past few years. However, in the opinions of farmers, the more the government values the farmers, the poorer the farmers become. Why so? Many experts and scholars living in cities feel puzzled with this paradox, but farmers understand it well. The problems of farmers can never be solved by mere concern without getting into action or addressing the existing concrete issues only. Instead, the problems will be solved only with a forward-looking vision and by focusing on the fundamental issues. Solving the "three agriculture-related problems" and promotion of the industrialization process would never come under sound interaction in the absence of rule of law. Solving the "three agriculture-related problems" by rule of law is a guarantee of smooth promotion of industrialization in China.

The practicing of planned economy in China makes us believe that: (1) the policy designed to absorb agricultural surplus by virtue of price scissors between industrial and agricultural products frustrated the farmers in agricultural production and adversely impacted the state's supply of agricultural products which were in shortage back then. As a consequence, agricultural products were not sufficiently supplied until the reform and opening up policy became remarkably fruitful (in 1984). (2) Though an array of factories were established with expropriated farming funds, these factories had no accumulation ability and were even underperformed in self-transformation and renovation. (3) Industry failed to absorb rural surplus labor. Even worse, some emerging labor forces (urban workers lay off during the period of Great Leap Forward Movement, especially the so-called movement of encouraging the educated youth to work in the countryside and in mountainous areas) that cannot be accommodated by urban industry were released to the countryside. It is evident that China's economy in the era of planned economy is characterized by its falling into the "Ricardo trap". The only difference between China's economy and the typical pattern of "Ricardo trap" lies in low income. Most workers in businesses under ownership by the whole people and collective ownership get low pay which remains unchanged in a dozen years. It is called a "trap of planned economy".

Some scholars, though acknowledging that deprivation of agricultural resources has reduced the supply of agricultural products, indulge in elaborating on the argument that this policy contributes to accumulation of construction funds for industrialization and thus regard it a great achievement. Frankly speaking, this viewpoint reveals that some Chinese experts in economics are somewhat ignorant of general economic knowledge. Even a beginner in economics knows that capital is a monetary expression of the values of resources (wealth) required in business activities conducted by way of exchange. The essence of capital is useful resource but not money since the latter is only a statutory symbol serving as a means of exchange and a measurement of value. Money is nothing but a piece of paper or some data if the useful resources do not function as it is intended. Thus, cutting the supply of agricultural products which are already in shortage is actually an act of reducing capitals. If we acknowledge that this common sense of economics must be observed when studying economic issues, it is against the common sense of economics to hold that the policy of agricultural resources deprivation contributes to accumulation of construction funds for industrialization. In addition, by examining the actual supply of agricultural products by rural areas to urban areas and non-agricultural industries in the era of planned economy, we can find that the agricultural products, serving as either food or industrial raw materials, were then in critical shortage. In such circumstance, the government could only seek to balance the gap between demand and supply by issuing coupons and quota. It would cost much higher than the planned price for urban residents or enterprises to get agricultural products exceeding the quota. The economists regard such situation a boost to build up construction funds for industrialization. This assertion amounts to saying that short supply is beneficial to industrialization or shortage economy is an ideal or consequent development pattern of early industrialization.[4] It is surely a fallacy. Given the status quo of industrialization in China, the industrialization process would be held back and even the past achievements would be cast to the winds if the "three agriculture-related problems" are not solved satisfactorily. But how to solve the problem? Rule of law is the final answer.

Many people do not believe agricultural products are in shortage. On the contrary, they think agricultural products are in surplus. Moreover, they suggest empowering farmers to use existing arable lands for non-agricultural purposes based on the "surplus theory".[5] In my opinion, it is a good reform thinking to entitle farmers to use their own lands out of free will provided that the mandatory laws regarding, among other, environmental protection are complied with. However, those who deny the fact that those agricultural products are in shortage merely scratch the surface but not the root of the problem. Superficially, farmers couldn't sell the grains, thus resulting in surplus. But why the country imports grains in quantities every year? It is a contradiction. But what is the root of this contradiction? Because imported grains are cheaper and have a higher quality. Then why can't we produce high quality and cheap grains? Is it because of technical flaws? Certainly not, the Father of Hybrid Rice is born in China. The underlying reason lies in that the current system has driven the cost of grain growing to an extremely high level. However, the current system could only be broken by rule of law. Wanton exploitation on farmers can be curbed only by regulating agricultural input, agricultural technology transfer and agricultural product trading markets by laws, so that farmers are able to start production and laboring from the same scratch line with other social classes. Chinese central government proposed on the 2nd Session of the Tenth National People's Congress that grain farmers should be given direct subsidy in addition to their entitlement to reduction or exemption of agricultural tax and agricultural special duty. It is a good news for farmers as they are not only relieved more or less from tax obligation but also compensated by the state. But yet, it is not the fundamental solution to stimulating farmers' initiative in growing grains. First of all, we need to figure out the underlying reasons why farmers cannot grow grains.

Firstly, agricultural production is a costly task due to high land cost and high prices of seeds, fertilizers, pesticides and farm tools. Notwithstanding, the production and marketing departments of seeds and fertilizers would also declare that they do not earn a penny. This is true actually. A great many of seed, fertilizer, pesticide and farm tool producers are currently operating at a loss and soon going to close down. When accident is factored out, output should be a natural outcome of production. But the fact is that agricultural products are produced at a loss throughout the channel from input to output. Then what are the reasons behind the loss? It can be figured out easily by visiting and consulting with the competent authorities. Now let us have a discussion about the problem of rural land use, namely, what to grow on the land. The case of land being raked forcibly reported in Lianhe Village, Longmiao Town, Shuyang County, Jiangsu Province [6] can be found elsewhere across China. Farmers' production activities are neither determined by the market nor carried out of their free will. Instead, the decision rests with the government, especially a group or a person in the government. Their acts are akin to seeking private and group gains in the disguise of "fighting for the interests of farmers". Under such circumstance, it is not difficult to understand why agricultural is a highly costly task. The second problem is that farmers have no title to the lands, making them seek for instant benefit rather than long-term investment. The land contracted by a farmer today may be transferred to others tomorrow at the order of the local government with a thousand excuses. The central government has been stressing the importance of stabilizing land contract over the years by specifying a fixed term like 15, 30, 50 or 70 years. But what's the use? Illegal encroachment of farmlands can be seen everywhere in China. Then who are encroaching the farmlands? Exactly the government or government-backed agencies. The laws become a mere scrap of paper here. Then let us have a look at farm-oriented industrial goods. Take fertilizers for example, the production and marketing of fertilizers are interfered by the government in all aspects. But what for? For gains surely. Don't be naive enough to think the government does that for the interests of enterprises. Administrative departments tend to request enterprises to cover the cost for recreational activities, but enterprise is not a cornucopia. Then what should we do? The government has the solution. Supposing the unit price of fertilizer is 46 yuan, the government would manage to raise it to 64 yuan or even 96 yuan if desired. But how does the government do that? By power. Administrative market monopoly is a useful weapon. That being the case, you farmers should determine whether to buy the fertilizer at such a high price of 96 yuan. If you do not buy it from the enterprises, you're unable to get the fertilizer from any other sources, thus making farming impossible. Even so, you're still obliged to pay taxes. It is not too much to state that some local governments have absolutely no respect for the law.

Secondly, the efficiency of agricultural output is too low. By output efficiency, we mean not only the productivity but also the overall return. It is an unarguable fact that China has an extremely low agricultural productivity. Compared with advanced countries, China's agricultural productivity has dropped to the floor level. For example, in 1995, China produced 111 kg soybeans per mu on average, while Italy produced 236 kg, which is 2.13 times the yield of the former. In Israel, the yield of tomato per mu reaches 30t, which is 6-10 times the yield of tomato per mu in China (3-5t). The yield of mango per mu is 1,000 kg in Taiwan but is merely 100 kg on the most fertile lands in Hainan. Nowadays in Western Europe, U.S., Japan and Israel, plenty of vegetables are produced in factories. The yield of tomato per square meter is 35 kg, which is 8-10 times the yield of tomato grown in conventional ways. As to the breeding industry, the annual production of dairy cow is 1,529 kg fresh milk on average, however, the figure in Denmark and Netherlands is nearly 10,000 kg; the average carcass weight of a beef is 130 kg in China but 392 kg in Japan; the average carcass weight of a pig is 76 kg in China but 140 kg in developed countries. In terms of the forestry and fruit industry, China produces 15-20 kg Chinese chestnuts per mu on average, while Japan produces 150 kg, which is 7-10 times the yield of the former. [7] The Father of Hybrid Rice is born in China, but the yield of rice per mu remains at a low level. Agricultural input features a much lower overall return than agricultural production. One factor contributing to the low return on agricultural input is that the price of farm-oriented industrial good is on the rise while that of agricultural products is on the fall. We need to find out the root cause behind such contrast. Is it because of market? We can do little for that if it is caused by market force. Nonetheless, the fact is such situation is attributed to human behaviors in most cases. Objectively, Chinese agricultural products are not well received on the global market, which is one of the most adverse consequences of China's accession to WTO. To solve the problem, Chinese government should intensify macro-control and offer more supports and subsidies to agriculture. However, in fact it is quite the opposite. In local governments, some cadres try all means available to impose administrative monopoly on the price of farm-oriented agricultural good in pursuit of personal gains; the subsidies are not granted to farmers as prescribed, and even the fiscal transfer payments and remedies granted by the Central government are withheld and embezzled by them; apart from that, there are a variety of tax and fee burdens imposed on farmers. Thus, the agricultural production is now proceeding with input overdrawn. How would it generate returns in such case? Therefore, it is a top priority for China to regulate market order by law, especially to effectively restrain acts of the government by law so as to procure the positive effect of agricultural output.

When the agricultural development comes to a standstill, there is no need to worry about the mass surplus labors required for industrial development any longer. In this sense, is it true that it would contribute to promoting the industrialization process? Certainly not. Quite on the contrary, industrialization can absorb plenty of surplus labors only if the industrialization itself is advancing rapidly while accommodating market demand. The reality is that the industrialization process is severely impeded by the "three agriculture-related problems". The huge market which is a must for industrialization would never take into shape if the "three agriculture-related problems" are not solved radically. In such case, a great many of industrial goods don't sell as planned. And most of these unsalable goods have to be digested by the domestic market as we cannot appeal to foreign plundering and invasion like

Western capitalist countries did in the past. Maldigestion of these goods leads to industrial crisis, which in turn greatly hinders the process of industrialization. Consequently, many urban workers lose their jobs. Urban areas themselves cannot absorb urban surplus labor and have to release the same back to rural areas, let alone absorption of rural surplus labor. It is proven that industrialization cannot march ahead alone. Instead, it should advance in coordination with agriculture and commerce including education and technology, etc. Facing the increasingly prominent "three agriculture-related problems", only by delegating rights to the people and administering by law can the government escape from the disasters brought by rule of man. And only in this way can the rural economy develop with a steady pace and the industrialization forges ahead without any burden.

4.2 SOLVING "THREE AGRICULTURE-RELATED PROBLEMS" BY RULE OF LAW IS A WAY TO CONSOLIDATE THE STATUS OF AGRICULTURE IN THE NATIONAL ECONOMY

Chinese government has been stressing the foundational status of agriculture for decades. It is a correct policy itself. Here the problem is that agriculture's foundational status is not given due substantive weight. People tend to keep saying "agriculture is the foundation of the national economy" over and over, but most of them have forgotten the connotation of this sentence. Foundation means the root affecting the overall situation. If the foundation of a building is not firmly erected, the whole building may collapse at any time. Likewise, agriculture is the foundation of the national economy, so the decline of agriculture may bring the national economy (including industry and commerce, etc.) to a standstill. Chinese government, local government in particular, is barely aware of this crisis or such sense of crisis has been weakened or even eliminated by the growing departmental and personal interests. What a terrible thing it is! To consolidate the foundational status of agriculture, we need to procure the ample supply of agricultural resources. Some people will say that agricultural products in China are in surplus, in surplus as early as the late 1990s. According to statistics, as of the end of Jun. 1999, China's grain storage had amounted to 226,750 million kg, which was more than half of the country's total grain output; in 1998, China's cotton storage reached around 3.5 million tons, presenting an extreme oversupply; the supply of non-staple foods such as meat, poultry, egg, vegetables, aquatic products and fruits is growing much faster than the demand of the same. [8] However, we must be soberly aware that we only have a few agricultural products that are up to the average consumption and the current oversupply of agricultural products is relative, provisional, impermanent and structural. The deep-seated problems present in agriculture remain unresolved and are even magnified. For example, agricultural products are featured by low quality, few varieties, inter-regional overlapped input and serious waste of resources; with a low technological content, agricultural products are not competitive in the global market; ecological agricultural resources are destroyed and the sustainable development of China is threatened, which in turn undermine the foundational status of agriculture.

Over the years, Chinese government has been managing agriculture with administrative means, while developed market economy countries mainly resort to legal means for agricultural adjustment. All the economic means and administrative measures employed by the latter were recognized by law and were practiced within the scope of law. To secure the foundational status of agriculture in the national economy, the government should not only increase inputs and fiscal & financial banking supports but also appeal to the rule of law. Only by incorporating the guidelines and policies regarding agricultural development into legislation can agriculture develop reliably and steadily. On the whole, the *Agriculture Law of the People's Republic of China ("Agriculture Law")* in effect can effectively consolidate the foundational status of agriculture. The key point now is to implement the law. We should take the following major actions to guarantee the foundational status of agriculture in the national economy.

4.2.1 To Adjust the Agriculture Construction According to Law

China makes improper adjustments to the agricultural structure, and it's undeniably true that China has an extremely low agricultural productivity. We have been emphasizing the structural adjustment of agriculture every year in the past, only to find that the adjustment is ineffective. The fundamental causes lie in absence of rule of law and expansion of rule of man. In addition, the adjustment is performed subjectively and randomly, resulting in low sustainable stability. Due to pursuit of immediate interests brought by local finance and exercise of administrative powers without due constraints, the structural adjustment of agriculture has ended up as a fantasy and the law has become a matter of tokenism or is even distorted and trampled by some people. To adjust the structures of agriculture and rural economy by law, first of all, the governments at or above the county level should frame their policies and allocate funds as stipulated in the *Agriculture Law* to guide and support the structural adjustment of agriculture, develop and implement agricultural development plans, bring the regional superiorities into full play and adjust and optimize the structure of agricultural production. Meanwhile, the state shall guide and support farmers and agricultural production and operation organizations in their efforts to adjust and optimize the structure of agricultural production in light of market demand, to coordinate the development of farming, forestry, animal husbandry and fishery, and to develop an agriculture with high quality, high yields and good returns in order to enhance the competitiveness of agricultural products in the global market. Moreover, the state shall also support the development of farming and food industries, increase the added value of agricultural products, give aid to the development of rural secondary and tertiary industries and townlets, optimize the structure of rural economy, boost the all-round development of rural economy and gradually eliminate the differences between the rural and urban areas. Furthermore, in order to safeguard farmers' interests in the structural adjustment, the state should grant ample subsidies in grain for green projects, put more efforts in construction of agricultural and rural infrastructures, create better agricultural production conditions and maintain and improve the comprehensive agricultural productivity.

4.2.2 To Safeguard the Industrialized Operation According to Law

The *Agriculture Law* only has abstract and general provisions on the industrialization of agriculture. Pursuant to the law, the government shall encourage and support farmers and agricultural production and operation organizations in their efforts to develop integrated operation of production, processing and marketing and take measures to develop industrial management of agriculture in various forms; guide and support the enterprises, research institutes and other organizations specialized in production, processing and circulation of agricultural products in their efforts to cooperate with farmers or rural specialized cooperative economic organizations in forming interests communities that jointly share profits and undertake risks in order to give impetus to the development of agriculture; assist the rural specialized cooperative economic organizations and township enterprises in agricultural product processing and comprehensive development and exploitation; carry forward the construction of agricultural product marketing system, encourage and support the organization of a variety of agricultural product marketing campaigns, seek to guarantee the unblocked transportation of agricultural products and construct green transport channels for agricultural products. If the above provisions are enforced properly as intended, agricultural industrialization would be substantially achieved. However, on the one hand, these provisions are non-specific and hard to implement; on the other hand, all others would become fantasy and hard to achieve if the fundamental problems of system are not resolved. For example, the business pattern referred to as "company plus farmer" that used to be frequently discussed in economics is nothing but an attempt to work behind closed doors on a whim. It is inoperable in practice. Even it is implemented; the only consequence is that farmers will be exploited again without cause.

4.2.3 To Ensure the Quality and Safety of Agriculture Products

Nowadays, the quality and safety of agricultural products are outstanding and have become the public concern. The revised *Agriculture Law* sets out the following provisions on the quality and safety of agricultural products: the state shall take measures to enhance the quality of agricultural products, establish a sound system for quality standards of agricultural products and supervisory system for quality inspection and testing, formulate mandatory standards of agricultural products for the purpose of guaranteeing the consumption safety of agricultural products and ecotope, prohibit production or operation of agricultural products incompliant with the said mandatory standards; the state shall support the establishment of a sound certification and mark system for quality agricultural products and give an aid to the production of pollution-free agricultural products; for quality agricultural products that are up to the standards prescribed by the state, an application may be made for the use of green food and OTAP marks; the state shall also establish sound quality standards of products processed out of agricultural food to protect food safety; establish a sound system of animal and plant epidemic prevention and quarantine, strengthen the monitoring, early warning and prevention and control of animal epidemic diseases and plant diseases, set up a rapid elimination mechanism for major animal epidemic diseases, plant diseases and insect pests; take measures to protect the agroecological environment and prevent contamination of agricultural products in the course of production; apply the system of registration or license in respect of the production and operation of the means of agricultural production which may endanger the safety of human beings and livestock. All these regulations shall be implemented and put into practice by the competent authorities.

4.2.4 To Procure the Grain Safety According to Law

As a populous country, China should rely on its own strength to put enough food on the table, and food safety remains the fundamental guarantee for a stable nation and prosperous economy. In order to procure the stable productivity of grain and realize the goal of balance between gain supply and demand, the *Agriculture Law* provides that the state shall take measures to protect the grain productivity, establish the system of protection for arable land, and give major assistance in terms of policy, fund and technology to the staple producing areas in order to build up stable bases for the production of commodity grains; the state may decide to introduce the protective price system for some varieties of grain; the state shall establish an early warning system to guarantee grain safety and a system for the regulation of grain storage at different levels, and establish a risk fund for grain.

4.2.5 To Strengthen the Input in Agriculture

Pursuant to the *Agriculture Law*, the state shall gradually increase the overall input to agriculture; set up special agricultural funds according to law, enhance supervision and auditing of financial and credit funds used in agriculture, encourage and guide farmers and agricultural production and operation organizations to increase their inputs to agriculture, encourage investment of social funds in agriculture, and promote increased use of foreign funds in agriculture; specify the measures intended to protect import of agricultural products and promote export of agricultural products by following WTO rules; encourage and support the provision of information services to agriculture and commercialized services before, during and after the process of agricultural production; establish a sound rural financial network; establish a sound insurance system for agriculture, develop a sound policy-related insurance system for agriculture progressively, encourage operation of insurance business in agriculture, and assist in operation of cooperative agricultural insurance; and do a good job of preventing and fighting against disasters and providing disaster relief.[9] All these policies and regulations shall be further implemented.

The rules and regulations concerning guaranteeing the foundational status of agriculture in *Agriculture Law* shall be further improved by other supporting regulations. However, this is not the solution. The key point lies in law enforcement and supervision. The "sixteen-character guideline" stating that "there must be laws to go by, the laws must be observed and strictly enforced, and lawbreakers must be prosecuted" which has been practicing in China for long basically summarizes the fundamental requirements of rule of law. It is utterly groundless for some people, especially some leading cadres, to insist on rule of man on the ground that rule of law is not fully operative. Though Chinese laws are somewhat imperfect, a country ruled by law will be substantially established if the existing laws can be effectively implemented and put into practice. In a word, the key to guarantee the foundational status of agriculture lies in law enforcement and supervision.

4.3 SOLVING "THREE AGRICULTURE-RELATED PROBLEMS" BY RULE OF LAW IS NECESSARY FOR DEMOCRATIC POLITICS AND SOCIAL STABILITY

4.3.1 The Democratic Politics in Rural Area Develops Slowly

The rural democratic construction in China has long come into a standstill due to deep-rooted feudal autocracy and clansman remnant. After steeping in modern capitalism thoughts and liberation of thoughts during the reform and opening-up period, urban residents acquire a profound consciousness of democracy and rule of law, which creates favorable external conditions for the development of rural constitutionalism. The government stresses the importance of democratic construction every year. Even so, the age-old problems remain unresolved. All these political slogans are of little use as long as the fundamental problems are not solved. As a Chinese saying goes, "a crying cat never catches a rat." That means once you're determined to do something, take immediate action instead of indulging in empty talk. As to the corruption problem, corruption runs wild exactly when the central government frequently stresses fighting against corruption. After the sloganeering quietens down for a period, the cull of corrupt officials one after another makes the mass believe that the government wants to play hardball, and other corrupt officials will then haul out. This is also true with rural democratic construction. Village self-governance is a great creation of farmers following the tide of the times, just like "fixing farm output quotas for each household". It is recognized and promoted by the state, which is the concrete embodiment of China's democratic politics progress in the countryside. Yet in practice, village self-governance is executed unsatisfactorily and even distorted and destroyed in some places.

On Feb. 2, 2004, the CCTV program "Law Today" broadcast a case discovered in Bayi Town, Changzhi County, Shanxi Province, in which the Election Steering Group exerted an illegal intervention with the Bayi Village Committee in election. This case uncovers the fundamental problems presenting in democratic construction of local governments. In the election organized by Bayi Village, 2,451 ballots were issued, among which 2,448 were handed in. The candidates Ding Jianguo and Zhao Bin received 1,225 and 1,109 votes respectively. Subject to the rule, the candidate who received a majority of votes shall be elected. Nevertheless, after waiting for more than half of a day, the villagers were told that the Village Election Committee was ordered by the Election Steering Group of Bayi Town to delay announcement of the election result. The Election Steering Group asserted that the total ballots issued should be 2,451 and half of the ballots should be 1,226. Therefore, Ding Jianguo failed in the election by one vote. For more than 4 months thereafter, Bayi Village was running in a chaos without officials. Later, Ding Jianguo seized the leadership without authorization and was chopped in a conflict with Zhao Bin. Thus, Bayi Village was thrown into chaos again.

This case unveils a prominent problem before us: administrative intervention is the greatest barrier to rural democratic construction. Village self-government will end in vain in the presence of administrative intervention. The key to the problem is how to guide the local governments to carry out rural work orderly. Thus, the following two relations must be properly addressed in coping with the problem in practice:

1. The relation between Party leadership and democratic construction in local governments. It is actually the relation between village committee and Party branch. During the period of People's Commune Movement, government administration was integrated with commune management and people were under centralized Party leadership. At these times, a village's political power rested with the Party branch and a production brigade is merely a single production management organization. After collapse of the People's Commune System, government administration was separated from commune management and village self-government was implemented. At these times, village committee was set up at the village level apart from Party branch. Two village management bodies of different natures, i.e. Party branch and village committee, coexisted in Chinese villages practicing self-governance. Theoretically, they are two organizations of different natures and functions. As stipulated in the constitution, laws and Party constitution, village committee is a self-governing mass organization composed of farmers, elected directly by villagers for the purpose of self-management, education and service. Party branch is the Party's basic-level organization in village, elected by Party members among villagers and being responsible for political leadership of the village. Being the core of leadership, Party branch is endowed with the leadership to other village organizations including village committee. These two organizations coexisting in a village usually create various conflicts because of different opinions and visions. The Party's political leadership to village organizations of all levels is determined by the nature and position of the Party. Village self-governance and village committee's work cannot be accomplished alone without Party leadership. Nonetheless, on the other hand, the principles of "separating functions of the Party from those of the government" and "practicing mass-governance in the local government" are designed to reshape the state's power relation, whereby power is delegated to the government and the people. These principles are consistent with China's basic state policy to push ahead the construction of socialist democracy and rule of law in the country. The most important thing is to abide by the fundamental principles prescribed by the *Constitution* and laws to properly address the relation between village Party branch and village committee.

2. The relation between township government and village committee. In the era of planned economy, all the township affairs, regardless of their respective importance, were brought under administration, thus forming an administrative hierarchy composed of commune, production brigade and production team. This pattern of management is helpful for political mobilization and social control, but it frustrates the members of the society and hinders the development of economy. The People's Commune System gives birth to a top-down network of economic control and administrative control, thus enhancing the state power's penetration into and control over villages.[10] After the household contract responsibility system with remuneration linked

to output was launched in China, farmers were freed from the highly-centralized control and gradually grew into an independent subject. This system arouses farmers' initiative and creativity and in turn boosts the development of rural economy. Village self-governance system emerged at the historic moment when the rural economic and social relations were radically reshaped. Village committee is a self-governing mass organization at the basic level and not a political organization of the state at the grass-roots level, a primary-level government or a representative body of the government. Therefore, the relation between township government and village committee cannot be addressed by simply copying the experience in dealing with the relation of governments at higher and lower levels. However, in practice, township government tends to give orders in respect of all kinds of work to the village committee and the village committee would lose its bearings if without directions by the township government, making village self-governance a mere formality. Village committee is a regional self-governance mass organization organized according to the *Constitution*, not an economic organization or a state organ. It is a continuation of administration at the gross-roots level. Collective economic organization is typically managed by village committee, but it's often the case that the two establishments are managed by the same group of officers. Besides, village committee often has a subordinate economical production committee. It is rarely the case that a collective economic organization is established by itself. In fact, it is the result of long-term planned economy, which is referred to as "integration of government administration with enterprise or social organization" in rural areas. The primary task of the village committee is to execute the tasks assigned by the township government. For this purpose, the village committee will resort to violent means to break down all barriers ahead like "tartars". The village committees in some regions are even controlled by scandals. How would such a village committee practice village self-governance? How could it perform the intended functions as a collective economic organization? Robert A. Dahl asserts in his work *Modern Political Analysis* that a person may be discouraged in political involvement if he is not confident in his political efficiency. Likewise, a person's political involvement will seem unnecessary if we have a high degree of trust on the justification, legitimacy, stability and fairness of the decisions made by a political system.[11] A village committee that is absolutely obedient to the township government is actually incapable of "self-governance". Therefore, I suggest uprooting the organizational system of village committee so that the township government may reclaim its designed powers and functions. Meanwhile, farmers in each village may set up a collective economic organization having the same functions as the villagers' cooperative economic organization without any administrative function. It is of great significance to promote the implementation of the *Law of the People's Republic of China on Land Contract*, thus effectively curbing malpractices and corruption in land contract, guaranteeing fairness and efficiency in land contract, and realizing village self-government in the real sense. The township government should set up a specialized organization for giving specific instructions to the village committee in respect of democratic election, decision-making, management and supervision which are common concerns expressed by the villagers and also the key links of village self-governance, so that every task of self-governance is executed by following the established legal procedures and to the villagers' satisfaction. The township government should never attempt to control over or intervene with the election and replacement of the head of village committee or to directly interfere with the affairs within the scope of village self-governance. Furthermore, the township government should recognize its powers and functions clearly and learn to delegate powers to lower levels and villagers.

At present stage, the village self-governance was constrained by the applicable mode of rural governance. As the self-governance of scattered single villages and democratic election organizations could not affect the state's decisions on policy-making, thus it is hard to restrain the behaviors of local governments and in turn change the farmers' weak position in the pattern of social interest distribution. The village self-governance and grass-root election cannot change the government's policy of "differential treatment" on agriculture, farmer and rural area, thus the pattern of the state's control and governance of rural society through grass-roots administrative organs substantially remains unchanged. As a result, transformation of China's rural governance from People's Commune System to village self-governance and villagers' democratic election system cannot help agriculture, farmer and rural area out of the dilemma confronted in the process of modernization and marketization.

To this end, some scholars come up with a series of solutions and conceptions concerning rural management system. For example, some suggest shifting township government to a representative body of county development so that the country and township fiscal difficulties can be settled by streamlining the governmental management hierarchy and innovating the fiscal system; or the township government may be removed to realize self-governance. In the county and township management hierarchy, the township government acts as both the supplier of village public goods on one hand and an incentive to increase farmers' burden on the other hand. If the self-governance is elevated to the level of township government based on village self-governance, and township chief election is practiced and popularized step by step, so that farmers can implement "democratic election, decision-making, management and supervision" within the jurisdiction of villages and towns, then the current mode of rural governance will have certain progress in structural change.[12]

The core of village self-governance lies in democratic election, management and supervision as well as transparent village management. No link can function well without villagers' extensive involvement. In the practices of village self-governance over 20 years, villagers are most widely involved in the link of democratic election. Every villager or villager's representative will vote for his favorite candidate after hearing of the candidates' speeches. After a village committee is elected, villager involvement is liable to become a mere formality because of traditional customs, individual educational level, moral integrity and other factors. The democratic construction centering on democracy and transparency gives full play to socialist democracy and reflects the fundamental principles of "democratic election, decision-making, management and supervision". In addition, it also reveals the fundamental principles of democracy, including popular sovereignty, civil liberty, equality, majority rule and minority liberty, public supervision and procedural legalization. Village self-governance is regarded as a real practice of democracy in modern Chinese history, and there is no reason to have it snuffed out and distorted. With further development of rural undertakings and spreading of rural education, rural population will increase gradually and farmers will develop higher democratic quality. In such context, to carry forward and improve the village self-governance is beyond doubt a great project to practice democracy. The Party and government representing the interests of the masses are liable and obligatory to procure farmers' enthusiasm and capacity in political involvement in a favorable environment. In a word, practicing of extensive village self-governance and pure democracy in rural areas not only enriches and safeguards numerous farmers' democratic rights that would in turn promote the overall development of rural society but also contributes to construction of stable countryside and national. We believe that as the village self-governance pushes forward progressively, Chinese democracy will be constructed in a more comprehensive and thorough way.[13]

4.3.2 Rule of Law Is the Powerful Safeguard of Democratic Politics in Rural Area

Since China's reform and opening up, village democratic construction has made unprecedented achievements. After the village self-governance system highlighting villager's self-governance and self-education is executed, the democratic construction featured by "democratic election, decision-making, management and supervision" springs up and is under continuous development and improvement. Nonetheless, the development of democratic construction varies in different regions as China is a country with a large population and vast lands, in addition to the historic, natural environmental and economic and cultural factors. To build a well-off society in an all-round way, China must firstly realize the important goal of developing socialist democratic construction and socialist political civilization, thus setting higher standards for rural democratic construction. Democracy is inseparable from rule of law. Democracy must be constructed by following the rule of law and the form of democracy must be embodied in the procedures of rule of law.[14] The village self-governance initially proposed in the 1980s is considered as a great creation of the Party in leading the numerous farmers to construct socialist democracy with Chinese characteristics. It is characterized in that all rural affairs are brought under legalized, standardized and procedural administration in order to develop a complete set of systems integrating democratic election, decision-making, management and supervision together with an operation mechanism, establish systems by law and administer villages by systems, and accelerate the institutionalization and legalization of democracy at the grass-roots level.[15]

To enforce and improve the institutionalization of democratic election system in the context of village self-governance is an important means and way to safeguard farmers' democratic rights. In order to establish and execute a sound democratic election system based on the principles of popular, equal, differential and secret voting, we shall:

1. Procure that the village Party branch must lead and direct villagers to act by law. Though village self-governance has been practicing for years in some places, some leading cadres still do not grasp the point and have a weak legal sense; they think farmers are under-educated and lacking a profound awareness of democracy, so the implementation of direct democratic election system is a practice against China's actual situations; some cadres even consider democratic election and rural stability a pair of conflicting terms, asserting that failure in direct democratic election may impair rural stability and economic development; and others worry that the newly elected cadres may be disobedient and inexperienced in rural management, which may exert adverse impacts on the implementation of rural policies. For this reason, some leaders, especially township leaders, do not attach due attention to the general election of village committee and are underperformed in playing leadership role. Leaders in some regions choose to take a wait-and-see attitude and delay the election in the excuse of complicated village conditions. Although these problems are rare cases, they severely hindered the implementation of direct democratic election in rural areas. In order to implement the direct election system of village committee, we should, first of all, seek to correct the thoughts and understandings of the leaders of all levels, especially township leaders. And the Party should put more leadership efforts in this regard.

2. Regulate the procedures and measures of democratic election by law. Rural democratic election system is the foundation and prerequisite of the four essential elements of village self-governance, i.e. "democratic election,

decision-making, management and supervision". Specifically, we should govern villages by law and improve the rural democratic election system.

3. Regulate farmers' democratic rights by law. Village self-governance will end up with a formality without villagers' involvement. Therefore, it is important for us to carry out more publicity and education activities concerning the new governance mode of village self-governance, so that they'll understand the link of their interests to political involvement and develop a sense of political involvement; to enhance their capacities in participating in political activities and direct them to play an active role in democratic construction in all aspects so that they'll take the initiative to participate in political activities. Only in this way can we facilitate the institutionalization and legalization of rural democratic construction in local governments.

4. Cope with the patriarchal clan influence on democratic election when practicing village self-governance by law. Patriarchal clan influence remains a prominent problem in some rural areas in China, which will be inevitably and fully revealed in democratic election. Since village committee members are given some powers and authorities in village self-governance, patriarchal clan representatives always fight intensely for a presence in the village committee so as to procure political and economic powers. Consequently, different patriarchal clans fight each other with open and secret means, undermine each other's work and canvass for their own; even worse, some clans may resort to bribery for election and the election may be manipulated by powerful forces, resulting in intensified conflicts and even vicious events such as beating voters, disturbing election venues, smashing ballot boxes, tearing up ballots, etc. All these make election a difficult task. In other cases, some clans refuse to participate in the election out of fear that the candidates representing the clans may fail the election. As a consequence, the election cannot be carried out smoothly as the necessary quorum cannot be reached. At present, there are many factors underlying the problems existing in rural democratic election, among which the most serious is the intervention from patriarchal clans, which should be given great attention.

5. Create more opportunities for education on rule of law for villagers. We should exert more efforts in guiding village committees to organize publicizing and education activities of laws and regulations in rural areas so that farmers may develop a sense of rule of law, understand and abide by laws. In addition, it is of great necessity to enhance the masses' democratic awareness, direct farmers to exercise their democratic rights properly, get rid of the influence and control from patriarchal clans and act by law so as to gradually construct villages in which farmers could master their own affairs. Moreover, we should instruct farmers to properly deal with the relation between giving full play to democracy and acting by law. To this end, in the course of general election of village committees, we should not only instruct farmers to enhance their democratic awareness and exercise their democratic

rights properly but also educate them to develop a deeper sense of rule of law and act by law instead of acting for the interests of patriarchal clans. Otherwise, village self-governance cannot move forward smoothly. Rural democratic election system is the foundation and essential prerequisite of village self-governance. Practicing direct democratic election in villages is the only way to ensure villagers can directly exercise their democratic rights. Elections must be conducted on the basis of democracy, competition and by following legal procedures. The principles of fairness, equality and transparency must be followed throughout the election process from registration of voters and announcement of candidates so as to ensure the villagers can fully exercise their democratic rights according to law. It has been proven that the successful implementation of villagers' democratic election system will create favorable conditions for "democratic election, decision-making, management and supervision" and thus lay a solid foundation for village self-governance.[16]

4.3.3 The Stability in Rural Area Cannot Be Achieved without Rule of Law

Rule of law is an important prerequisite to the stability in rural areas. At present, China is facing a grim situation in respect of rural public security, which has adversely affected farmers' wish to live and work in peace and contentment. Therefore, we need to restore rural order by law and reinforce public security control with the intention to create a favorable social environment for rural reform and development. The sharp changes in agriculture and rural area have diversified the subjects of rural market and greatly increased the conflicts and collisions among different interest subjects, including the state, collective and individual, which manifests as legal conflicts in legal relation and interest. According to statistics, 70% of the complaint letters and petitions made by the masses are concerned with legal problems. Apparently, in order to settle the social problem and conflicts present in rural areas and protect rural stability in the new era, we should resort to not only the vehicles of administration, economy and ideological education but also legal means by taking advantage of the regulation, standardization, punishment and protection functions of law.

To protect rural stability is not only a concern of the Party and the government but also a demand of numerous farmers. In Dec. 2000, Zhengzhou Guidance Center of Agricultural Economy Management conducted a questionnaire survey targeting at 1,623 farmers in 12 counties across the city. The results of this survey involving 12 issues with respect to rural policies or hot spots are summarized below: 1. Among the listed 7 issues that matter most for them, the top issues are listed below in order (3 alternatives at most for each question): village finance 57% (representing the percentage of farmers expressing their concerns on this issue to the total respondents, same below), rural public security 54%, farmers' burden 40%, the Party's execution of rural policies 34%, birth control 29%, general election 25% and homestead 17%. 2. The major reasons behind the tension between cadres and the masses and rural unrest (3 alternatives at most for each question): village finance mismanagement 43%, farmers' heavy burden 41%, cadres' style of work 41%, rural public security problems 41%, village cadres' abuse of power for personal gains 27% and village cadres' acceptance of bribe 27%.[17] It is wrong to look down upon farmers as to their political consciousness. Farmers are best qualified to speak on what kinds of basic production and living environment they desire and what problems exists in the current environment. The results of the above survey suggest that absence of transparency in village management is the top issue that bothers farmers and a stable society is one of their greatest wishes. These two conclusions are in a cause-and-effect relation in that absence of transparency in village management is one of the key factors and also the root cause of rural unrest. Of course, absence of transparency in village management is also attributed to some other deep-seated factors, i.e. drawbacks of the current system. Apart from the absence of transparency in village management, the rampant rural vicious power resulting from drawbacks of the current system is probably the most direct cause of rural unrest.

It is terrible to see that vicious powers in many places were operating in collusion with local governments in recent years. If the vicious powers are not uprooted, there will be no peace in the countryside and even in the country. In order to squeeze profits from farmers and build wealth, township officials indulge these vicious powers and attempt to legalize them in the disguise of "enforcement team" and "working team" in disregard of the state's long-term stability. These vicious powers turn a blind eye to the laws and regulations and do all sorts of evils and run roughshod over the masses. They commit one or more of the following crimes: controlling the market and trade using coercion; practicing blackmail to get an unearned income; creating troubles and fight with others; persecuting the innocent heartless; threatening the government and acting against the law. They do whatever they want. Even worse, some even penetrate in the rural grass-roots authorities by all means and thus become a part of the rural regime. Backed by the grass-roots authorities and beaters, they become dominators who can openly challenge the authorities of national laws. As a consequence, villagers are boiling with resentment, endangering the state's stability. Just as described in the novel of the five martial arts sects fighting for supremacy, nowadays there are five overlords wrecking the villages in China. Li Xiuwen from Liuzhuang Village, Weishan County, Shandong Province who ever served as Party Branch Secretary and Deputy Director of Village Economic Committee is known as the "Eastern Overlord". Under the cover of these powers and formal authorities, Li gathered a group of scandals and restructured the village construction company into a base composed of dozens of beaters. Later, they forcibly occupied lakes and lands covering over 1,000 *mu*, dozens of fishponds, a large shipyard, a brickyard and a dock. Zhao Xiuguo from Xianfeng Village, Yuhu District, and Xiangtan City, Hunan Province is called the "Southern Overlord". He got elected as the village head by unlawful means. Later, Zhao formed cliques for personal interests and excluded outsiders by all means. Since then, five party branch secretaries of the village had been coerced to resign, driving the village's primary party organization into a paralyzed state. Wu Guoyan from Qilidian Village, Weidu District, and Xuchang City, Hunan Province is known as the "Western Overlord". He had frequent interactions with gang leaders after released from the labor camp. After being elected as the Party Branch Secretary, Wu secured the villagers' belongings by force or trickery in collusion with gangs and hired gangs to hurt others. Liu Jingshan from Hongtoushan District in the east of Fushun City who ever acted as the Party Branch Secretary and Chief of the district is known as the "Northern Overlord". Liu organized and led a reactionary gang called "The Thirteens" to back his malpractices such as usurping, corruption and control of mines and to intervene with the affairs of mines and government. He Changli from Limin Town, Yuxian County, and Henan Province who ever acted as the Deputy Chief of Limin Town is known as the "Central Overlord". 5 out of 7 party branch secretaries and 7 out of 10 township business owners worked for him, thus turning the village into a typical fortified castle dominated by vicious powers.

The presence of these village overlords is assertive evidence that village vicious powers have penetrated into the grass-roots authorities. This problem has aroused a wide concern from superior governments and even the Central government. Over the past few years, we've made some achievements in the action of cracking down the underworld force. However, Chinese rulers and scholars have not realized the root cause of the problem lie in the degradation of the regime. Therefore, most regulation measures are just temporary reliefs. The existence of rampant vicious power could be attributed to the following deep-rooted political and economic causes: (1) Township leaders' indulgent. Township leaders always tolerate and even connive at vicious powers' abuse of "legitimate authority", which is one of the most prominent features of vicious powers' invasion to rural political realm. (2) Democratic election under forced control. Vicious powers make use of the self-claimed "democratic election" of village committee to manipulate rural grass-roots authorities, which is another feature of vicious powers' invasion to rural political realm. (3) Seduction by benefits from the rich. Vicious powers manage to manipulate the rural grass-roots authorities by temptation of money, which is an essential means for them to invade the rural political realm. (4) Political elites' transformation. Some village cadres have transformed from political elites to vicious powers, which is another reason behind vicious powers' invasion to rural political realm.

Given that vicious powers have run wild in Chinese villages, it is of urgent need for us to find out their roots and take corresponding countermeasures. Just as the saying goes, "To draw lessons from history, one knows why dynasties changed." Prasenjit Duara, a renowned American historian, ever discovered during research on the rural political status in the Republican period that as local squires released themselves from the traditional village self-governance regime, there was a void in the rural political realm, creating an opportunity for local vicious powers to invade the rural regime. Local villains, bullies, ruffians, rascals and other bad men came into alliance with local governmental officials. On the one hand, they helped local governments to exploit farmers and extort resources, which seemed to have strengthened the state's power. On the other hand, while in alliance with the governments, they also took brides, ran amuck and ran roughshod over the masses in the name of tax levy for the state, leading to the loss of national political and economic resources. They had an extensive corrosive effect on the governmental officials. As a result, many local governmental officials abandoned their political roles and have transformed into vicious powers dressed in robes. What they do now is not to serve and manage villagers as they should have done but to exploit them. Such contradictory phenomenon that the state's power gets reinforced seemingly but degraded in fact was referred to as "involution" by Prasenjit Duara, i.e. degradation of the state. In the process of "involution", the Central government receives plenty of taxes in the short run, giving us a false impression that the state has a greater ability to grab resources. But in fact, the Central government is running without foundations and has lost its control over local governments along with its effective control over rural tax funds and eventually its control over the rural society. As a consequence, it would arouse widespread discontent in the rural society.

As to the topic of how to crack down rural vicious powers and guarantee rural stability, Yu Jianrong proposed the thought of "weakening governmental powers and reinforcing democratic rights, consolidating rule of law and correcting official morality".[18] All the above solutions are intended to practice governance by rule of law except "correcting official morality" that emphasizes self-discipline construction of the Party and government. The core of rule of law lies in delegation of rights to the masses, abolition of privileges, legislation of all governmental behaviors, reinforcement of supervision and regulation mechanism and enhancement of punishment on unlawful acts. We can teach from the lessons of regime change that ruler he who is reluctant to change by following the tide of the times would get submerged eventually. The entire body would decay if one does not cut away the dead muscular tissues.

4.4 SOLVING "THREE AGRICULTURE-RELATED PROBLEMS" BY RULE OF LAW IS THE DEMAND OF SPIRITUAL CIVILIZATION IN RURAL AREAS

Spiritual civilization remains one of the fundamental guidelines for the Chinese Communist Party and the government to construct socialism for the long run. The contents of spiritual civilization vary in different historical periods. In the era of planned economy, affected by extreme thoughts, the government emphasized uniform ideology, rejected foreign thoughts and gained an absolute control over individual minds and spirits by stultification. Since reform and opening up, Chinese government has been stressing the importance of freeing our minds and opening to the outside world while upholding the four fundamental principles. As a result, foreign thoughts streamed out from the outside world, having a significant impact on Chinese ideological sphere. China has undergone the times when the ideological sphere was in a mess with morals collapsed. The alarm bell of spiritual degeneration kept ringing back then. In this context, the men of insight were actively exploring the root causes of this problem and its countermeasures. As such, spiritual civilization was again identified as a key strategy of nation building. In fact, such ideological chaos is a normal phenomenon when the old morals and values are severely impacted to a state of near-collapse while the new ones are yet to be developed. However, two decades have passed, we are still not clear what kinds of morals and values we shall pursue, this will adversely affect the process of socialist modernization. Therefore, the government restated the strategic significance of spiritual civilization. The theory of "ruling by morality" initiated by Jiang Zemin is probably intended to emphasize the importance of spiritual civilization.

Spiritual civilization consists of two parts: 1) ideological and ethical cultivation; and 2) education and scientific & cultural development. Rule of law is the foundation for both two parts of spiritual civilization in rural areas.

4.4.1 The Ideological and Moral Construction in Rural Area Cannot Be Achieved without Rule of Law

For a long time, when discussing about ideological and moral construction, we have been stressing the importance to have a socialist orientation under guidance of Marxism-Leninism, Mao Zedong Thought, Deng Xiaoping's theory of establishing socialism with Chinese characteristics and the theory of "Three Represents" and to arm people with scientific theories, provide them with correct media guidance, imbue them with lofty ideals, and inspire them with excellent works of literature and art. There is nothing to be said against this general orientation. However, too much slogans are just like empty talk. Moreover, forcible indoctrination is an outmoded practice now.

The pursuit of material benefits in the era of market economic system gives rise to expansion of selfish desire and moral disorder, such as money worship, hedonism, disregarding moral principles in pursuit of profit, venality, utilitarianism, corruption and other negative phenomenon. How to treat these phenomena properly? And what kinds of outlook on life and values should be developed? The past uniform values and ethics prevailing under the planned economic system are no longer suitable for the market economy. Some are worried that it is dangerous to let people's thoughts flow freely while abandoning ideological indoctrination and unification. Indeed, it is a pure groundless worry. In the context of market economy, we highlight the awareness of individual right, protection of individual freedom and fair-and-square legal order. Law represents the minimum restraint of morals. Law is linked to morals, but we shouldn't confuse the two. A person could be of high or low morality, and a law could be good or evil. A person with moral integrity must be of high morality. Nevertheless, not every law is a good law, and law must be the minimum requirement of morals. Rule of law is the foundation for moral construction in a modern civilized society. In a country lacking democracy and legal order, moral construction is bound to be accomplished in an autocratic, pressing and distorted way. Development of basic awareness of democracy and rule of law is of great importance to establish new moral and value systems, and also a precondition for cultivation of morality.

4.4.2 Rule of Law is Needed in Education, Science and Culture Construction

Education, science and culture construction consists of the following parts:

1. Developing educational undertaking. "Education is the foundation for scientific and technological development." It is a truth proven by developed countries. For example, after the World War II, Japan increased the state's educational expenditure to 20% of the government's aggregate administrative expenses despite of fiscal difficulties. During the period from 1950s to 1970s, Japan increased educational expenditure by 10 times. Education in Japan is spread in a wide, high-level and high-tone manner, thus creating miracles in the process of modernization which is advancing at a peerless speed and standard. There is no doubt that inter-state competition of economic strength is substantially the competition of technology materialized in commodity economy, competition of technology, culture and level of intelligence, and in the final analysis, the competition of talents. Therefore, we should place considerable value on education by investing more in education, paying more efforts in education, diversifying contents of education and building more schools so as to ensure that the education of varied levels and types is readily available to all members of the society depending on their

demands. Only by doing this can we improve the nation's scientific and cultural level and provide powerful human resources for building well-off society in an all-round way.

2. Spreading and improving science & technology. "Science and technology are the primary productive forces." Given the soaring development of world's science and technology, China should keep in pace with the global development, have itself geared to the international practices and advance with the times in order to have an influential presence in the world and grow into a mighty power. Apart from that, China should also develop high-tech of its own so as to find a place in the global high-tech fields.

3. Laying equal stress on carrying forward outstanding national culture and absorbing excellent foreign culture. Chinese social members are characterized by a moderate cultural quality owing to historical reasons and a large and unevenly distributed population. Improvement of the national's cultural quality is an important intelligence support for building well-off society in an all-round way. [19]

It is imperative to accomplish spiritual civilization in rural areas for the following reasons:

1. There is an appetite for backward and decadent culture in rural areas, and belief quandary can also be found with farmers. Remnants of feudal ideology and obsolete custom find their shelters in the vast rural areas due to under-developed science and technology and poor schooling. The masses' minds and souls are corroded by some false and foul thoughts present in market forces. As a consequence, some temples are worshiped widely and farmers are confused with the practice of combining feudal superstitions with modern superstitions. In a state of belief quandary, some farmers worship whichever temple they encounter. Farmers are no longer satisfied with dull cultural life in spare time and are badly in need of enriched and diversified cultural life. Especially, owing to wide coverage and low consolidation rate of rural spiritual civilization, farmers' ideological root of correct faith is apt to be destroyed in case of special circumstances and during special periods, thus leading to belief quandary in rural areas. For example, during the SARS period, people in fear of death worshiped the Buddha and God to bless them, with firecrackers setting off everywhere. All these revealed the weakness of rural spiritual civilization.

2. Farmers have only a shallow understanding on spiritual civilization and weak self-driven spiritual strength. Because of poor schooling and under-developed technology in rural areas, farmers cannot understand the connotation and requirements of spiritual civilization or the significance of advanced culture development. They even haven't learned about systematic spiritual civilization, thus lacking enthusiasm and initiative in spiritual civilization. In addition, rural spiritual civilization is typically organized and arranged by governmental leaders focusing on local economic development. Farmers par-

ticipate in the campaign passively and follow the leaders' orders blindly without subject consciousness, which has diminished the effect of spiritual civilization. No wonder some farmers are complaining that, "there is much said but little done about spiritual civilization, not alone implementation in real earnest."

3. The socialist ideological and ethical system in rural areas is vulnerable and civil moral education is progressing slowly. Over the past few years, a variety of rural economic interests have emerged. The resultant differentiation of rural interests is accompanied by diversification of ideology, which in turn causes progressive differentiation of farmers' moral idea. Negative social effects such as profit-grabbing, money-driven action and power-for-money deal destroy the mental balance of some farmers. As a result, they question about the applicability of reform and open-up policy and socialism. Further, they are unable to distinguish right from wrong and develop correct values, spiritual pursuit and code of conduct. Some are even trapped in the world of distorted ideology and ethics. In a word, there is still a spiritual desert in ideological and ethic system of farmers.

4. Cadres of villages and towns have not fully understood spiritual civilization or paid enough attention to it. They do not implement this campaign in real earnest. On the one hand, governments at all levels keep emphasizing the importance of economic development and subordination of spiritual civilization to economic development. On the other hand, they are apt to lay particular stress on material progress construction while neglecting spiritual civilization. They put too much weight on noticeable quantified achievements while regarding spiritual civilization icing on the cake, leading to the phenomenon that spiritual civilization lags behind economic development in rural areas. Some villages even never broadcast public information about spiritual civilization, which greatly hinders the progress of spiritual civilization.

To solve this problem, people come up with a lot of ideas and programs, mostly in the traditional forms and modes. For example, some suggest enriching the forms of spiritual civilization: 1. to spread the essence of spiritual civilization to every town, village and household through radio, television and "cultural yard". 2. to organize mass spiritual civilization activities like "civilized household", "civilized village" and "civilized town". 3. to improve farmer's spiritual and cultural cognition in the process of town construction.[20] These common solutions could be effective in practice. But we should implement them properly in a heuristic rather than compulsive way. The conventional way of forcibly achieving ideological unification is unworkable in modern society. With the development of human society and civilization, individual rights and freedom are valued more than ever before. As a result, some people consider it is meaningless to implement spiritual civilization. That is incorrect. In fact, spiritual civilization should be enhanced nowadays, provided that its scope and method should be rethought and changed. To respect the rights and freedoms of others, care for and help vulnerable groups and cultivate patriotism are still the main contents of ideological and moral construction; and the conventional forcible indoctrination used in spiritual civilization should be replaced by heuristics. Therefore, the mission is even tougher and more efforts should be paid today. Since the traditional "hard" tactics should be replaced by "soft" ones, then other more reasonable and supportive measures should be taken to facilitate the sound development of spiritual civilization, that is the rule of law. Only by enhancing governance by law could the government develop common code of conducts for people of varied ideologies. With this common code of conducts, people could pursue healthy and upright spirit, respect other's human rights and get rid of bad habits and social evils. For example, persuasion, civilized demonstration and mobilization are far from enough to wipe out bad habits like gambling. Instead, laws must be employed for that purpose.

On Dec. 19, 2002, *Southern Weekly* reported the following event. In the 25 villages in Dizhuang Town, Xupu County, Hunan Province, there are nearly a thousand "*Jitou* (pimps)". Among them, the largest one is Mr. Chen, director of a village committee. He has more than one hundred "*Jitou*" working for him and is directing the local farmers toward a "well-off" life. "*Jitou*" here refer to those who kidnap women and force them into prostitution. These "*Jitou*" have greatly changed the minds of farmers in all villages of Dizhuang Town in the past few years. There are several factors behind it. First, the indulgence of the government and administrative authorities. It is reported that, When Gu Yuerui (alias name), a farmer from Yangxing Village, Dizhuang Town, hears that his daughter is kidnapped by a "*Jitou*" Gong Haijian, he runs to Gong's father, demanding him to release his daughter. However, Gong's father says: "You want to call the police? My son has kidnapped many women and has been doing this for a long time. Have you ever heard any police catching him? There are so many "Jitous" in Dizhuang, have you ever heard of any of them caught by the police? "Consequently, Gu Yuerui calls the police. But the policemen ask for 1,500 yuan to find his daughter, or they will do nothing about the case. The policemen say they are short of management funding. However, 1,500 yuan is a large sum of money for ordinary farmers and some could not afford it. Therefore, the policemen's behavior of demanding money indulges the crimes of kidnapping women, which makes crimes run wild. Second, victims worry their reputation and integrity will be ruined and are afraid of revenge, which makes the "*Jitou*" more unscrupulous. When villagers turn to superior towns, cities and provinces for help, they could never get quick and effective feedback. On the contrary, they are exposed to greater potential risks. Zhang Xisheng, a villager who joined a protest group in which some radical actions were taken, was seized by the police and sentenced to the prison for 9 years for the alleged crime of assembling crowds to attack state organs. Though the old man has assisted the local police to crack more than 300 criminal cases, he is ended up in prison at last. Seeing this "model", may other farmers become desperate, dumb, and even start to accept the fact about "*Jitou*". Having recognized the police have disguised protection and farmers' helpless, "*Jitou*" grasp the opportunity and lead local farmers to become rich by forcing women into prostitution. Third, the "economic base determines superstructure" and "some people laugh at poverty but not prostitution". It is said that there is a widow who turns her two daughters to prostitutes in Fujian. After two years, they build a new modern house and the girls become very beautiful and fashionable. Seeing their change, other neighbors change their minds thoroughly. They care nothing but money. As the families become richer after women are forced into prostitution by "*Jitou*", some members of the families start to say good words about "*Jitous*" and are even grateful to them. Then, people's view of procreation is changed. For some people, one daughter is much better than 10 sons. Then the view of choosing spouse also changes. When a man is looking for a mate, he cares about the girl's appearance rather than character. Men, especially the young ones, get used to encouraging their wives or girlfriends into prostitution when money is tight.[21]

This is a strong irony and mock to spiritual civilization in China. The civilization plans proposed by the scholars in research institutions are totally ineffective and meaningless in this situation. Publicity, education and implementation of rich and colorful actives become "games in the kindergarten". Only by finding the root cause could we solve the problem effectively. The root is the absence of rule of law. Since the deterrence of law is not strong enough, the policemen dare to misconduct with the excuse of shortage of funding; since there are no powerful regulation mechanisms for law-executor, the policemen illegally ask farmers for money; since laws are only effective for the weakness, farmers could not get help and even suffer revenge. If laws are just decorations and even national law enforcement agencies themselves regard it as a trifle, how could farmers respect laws? Law is the lowest level of morality. It is no surprise that moral is declining when laws lose their binding force. To develop spiritual civilization, the authoritativeness of laws must be established and secured first.

4.5 SOLVING "THREE AGRICULTURE-RELATED PROBLEMS" BY RULE OF LAW IS NECESSARY FOR CHINA TO CATCH UP WITH INTERNATIONAL PRACTICE AFTER ITS JOINING INTO WTO

Accession to WTO suggests that China's reform and opening up has ushered in a new era. Comparing with GATT, WTO Agreement on Agriculture is most characterized in that a set of new trade rules are established and reforms are made on agricultural trading systems relating to market entry, domestic support and export subsidy. The new rules advocate improving market entry, reducing domestic support and exporting subsidy through tariffication of trade measures and tariff concession, so as to build a fair, just and market-oriented agricultural trading system. Besides, the new rules specify basic rules regarding equipment safety, animal and plant health standards and environment protection. Specifically, the Agreement provides producer supporting policy and export subsidy policy to all countries, stipulates certain restrictive provisions on execution mechanisms and allowed numbers of policies, and endows relatively large freedom for the governments to decide its reduction of tariff of different commodities. Governments could meet the demands of average tariff reduction by greatly cut trade volumes or cut the tariff of sensitive departments. Although the Agricultural Agreement made at the Uruguay Round contains a lot of contents and reaches agreement on a series of long-debating and contradictory questions, due to the differences of economic status and interests, countries of different type will still come across complex questions when completing the agreement.

In fact, the whole Uruguay Round is conducted by developed countries, so the Agreement mainly manifests the opinions and demands of them, while at the same time realizes the interests of the developing countries to some extent and seeks to achieve a balance of interests between developing and developed countries. On the one hand, developed countries, which are led by EU and Keynes Group, disagree with each other for their own interests, and are hard to reach a compromise on issues like domestic support, market entry and export subsidies. On the other hand, along with the development of developing countries and global economic integration, developed countries could not totally neglect the interests of the developing countries and have to make some concessions. For example, developing countries could enjoy many preferential treatments under the Agreement on tariff reduction and market entry etc. therefore, to some extent, the Agricultural Agreement is the results of balance of interests between the developing and developed countries.

The Agreement has improved market entry conditions by cutting import barriers. It has improved trading environment, reduced subsidies to agricultural products which directly or indirectly affect agriculture trade. It has decreased the twist and constraint of technical barriers like sanitary and phytosanitary measures on trade, which weakens trade protectionism and helps build a more open and free international trade system. These are all the progress of the Agreement. However, the Agreement also has many limitations. As it has been said before, in reduction of tariff, the Agreement limits the countries on the one hand, and endows the countries freedom to decide their own reduction of tariff, which cannot ensure every country strictly practice reduction of tariff. Besides, in Uruguay Round, the negotiation result that are concluded by countries closely involved in some trades are unconditional applicable to all WTO members, thus the weakness of bilateral trade negotiation of one single commodity will be brought into multilateral trade negotiation, which result in the developing countries lacking bargaining ability become the weak side of the negotiation, which is adverse to correcting the policy distortion in some countries.[22]

China's decision on signing WTO Agreement on Agriculture signifies that the Chinese government actively accepts the international economic regulation in international agricultural products trade.[23] International regulation is an important regulating mechanism of international market, which regulates the structure and operation of international social economy together with market regulation and national regulation of every country. The international regulation, represented by WTO, deeply affects China's national regulation and economic legislation.[24] As an important part of international regulation, WTO Agreement on Agriculture will greatly influence China's agricultural economy legislation in many aspects, such as legislation principles and value orientation.

Since China's reform and opening up, household contract management, which is spontaneously created by farmers, is designed to break the framework of planned economy. This creative measure brought great changes to the vast rural areas in China, and triggered the reform of economic system from rural areas to urban areas. For more than 20 years, the reform of China's urban economic system has been in full swing and basic framework of market economy has been gradually established. In contrast, the reform of rural areas, where market economy firstly emerged, is faltering. For these two years, China has taken many measures to speed up agricultural legislations to make economy of rural areas become more market-oriented, with a view to catching up with the international trend. For example, China has revised *Agricultural Law*, amended *Grassland Law*, introduced *Rural Land Contract Law*, completed agriculture-related credit laws and regulations, organized training of migrant worker and formulated *The Import Tariff Quotas of Agricultural Products*. However, we must face up to the fact that rural marketization still has a long way to go. Except the long-existed planned economy, the mismatch between rural traditional culture and market economy is another obstacle in the way. Poor economy, backward development, small land with large population, extensive farming, poor circulation of products all make problems of "agriculture, farmer and rural Area" prominent, hindering the economic development of the whole country. China's government has paid great attention on these rural issues and could not find efficient method these years. Undoubtedly, rule by law will effectively solve these problems. Although China temporally scarifies some interests by making accessions in WTO Agreement on Agriculture, it will promote the establishment, revision and repeal of laws, which is helpful for the modernization of China's agriculture in the long term.

From the existing agricultural legislation, the reform is still slow and the conception of lawmakers should be further updated. Professor Qi Duojun, a famous expert in economic law, in analyzing the guiding ideology in current legislation, points out that with the rapid development of globalization and China's accession to WTO, the concept of "Chinese cultures as basis, western cultures as subsidiary" should be rethought.[25] People often say that China's legal system is not complete and a lot of things have no legal basis. This view is impartial. In fact, the current legal system in China is relatively complete. Further complement is important. But what is more important is to adapt existing laws to the trend of times. Many countries have successfully handled the challenge brought by WTO Agreement on Agriculture. For example, Japan, Brazil and Australia's green agriculture policy and legislation has helped these countries successfully break down the tariff and quotas barriers in the trade with America. These are closely associated with the fact that these countries thoroughly carry out WTO Agreement on Agriculture in agricultural economic legislation. For example, in 1999, Japan passed *Food, Agriculture and Rural Areas Basic Act*, and advocated to establish a sustainable agriculture that makes contributions to environment protection. In 2001, Japan passed the "agricultural management policy" and determined the three key objectives of future agricultural production, namely, to improve the price competitiveness of domestic agricultural products, and select 40,000 farmers and support their mass production; to promote no-fertilizer agriculture through reform of 3 to 4 years; to improve the sales and circulation of agricultural products. According to the survey, 20% of Japan's 3.12 million farmers have realized organic agricultural production. One third farmers in Hokkaido have engaged in green agriculture. They actively produce green products to ensure their competitiveness in international market.[26] Why do we not directly borrow these legislative experiences, digest and complete them in practice?

WTO Agreement on Agriculture is made for eliminating international trade barriers brought by agriculture protection policies of some countries. However, for a long time, the agriculture protection policy of China is not the same as prevailing agriculture protection policy in the world. As for China alone, the negative agriculture protection of China has made China's problem of "agriculture, farmer and rural area" become increasingly prominent. Generally, agriculture protection policy indicates that a country has good economic condition to ensure self-supply of food and the proportion of its agricultural labor force is reduced to low enough to ensure a larger proportion of population can provide subsidiary for a smaller proportion of population. Nevertheless, the statistical data for January-August 2002 published by the National Bureau of Statistics show that the proportion of rural population accounts for 62.3% and the proportion of agricultural labor force is still up to 56%. Consequently, China does not meet the conditions for comprehensive agriculture protection.[27] The agriculture protection of China shall has its special policy implication: the limited agriculture protection is based on the development of domestic agricultural market, the income of farmers is increased through price support of agricultural products or other direct subsidiaries, significant development of agriculture is ensured and more and more competitive agricultural product production sectors are gradually found out through the implementation of a certain industrial policy, thereby preventing great policy price which is likely to occur under protection, that is, on one hand, the prices of agricultural products of China exceed international level; on the other hand, prices cannot meet the need of support for which agricultural producers seek.[28] After China joins WTO, agriculture faces a brand-new overseas environment. In view of dual influences of WTO on the agriculture of China, it is imperative for China to adjust agricultural legislation.

4.5.1 The Legislative Adjustment to the Circulation System of Agricultural Products

The provision on the circulation of agricultural products in the *Agriculture Law* issued in 1993 and amended in December 2002 mainly includes the following content: the purchase and sale of agricultural products shall stick to the principle of combination of market adjustment and national adjustment; an unified, open, competitive and orderly agricultural product market system shall be established; the development of agricultural product exchange activities in various forms shall be encouraged and supported; the development of agricultural product processing industry and food industry shall be supported and the added value of agricultural products shall be increased; China shall encourage the development of agricultural product import and export, etc.

After joining WTO, according to the objective need of the internationalization of agricultural product circulation, the current legal system for agricultural product circulation still has a large space for improvement. That is, the legal adjustment of agricultural product circulation is not only the adjustment of market itself, but also involves national adjustment and even international adjustment. These three kinds of adjustments coexist in the international market. This is the concrete manifestation of "Three Three Theory"[29] on economic law proposed by Professor Qi Duojun in the field of agricultural product circulation. International adjustment mentioned here refers to WTO Agreement on Agriculture and it is the further adjustment of agricultural product adjustment measures of each country. Therefore, the provision on agricultural product circulation of the *Agriculture Law* should respect WTO

Agreement on Agriculture, based on which the adjustment of agricultural product circulation is made by China.

The *Agriculture Law* basically provides the principles for the nature of agricultural product circulation system and relevant systems. Since the reform of agricultural product circulation system is under the process of exploration through continuous practicing and experience summarizing and many systems are immature, the specific legal system for agricultural product circulation has not been systematically established. At present, the legal adjustment of agricultural product circulation facing market internationalization should not only rely on the support of stipulation on legal principle, but also the specific legal system. Currently, about 100,000 agricultural product purchase and sale organizations in rural and urban areas are overstaffed with low efficiency and suffer serious loss; there are many barriers between higher and lower levels or between different departments and regions in different provinces and cities, agricultural product circulation requires a lot of circulation links and high cost, thus seriously hindering the efficient circulation of agricultural products. It is also important for the reform of Chinese agricultural product circulation system to establish an efficient circulation system, shorten procedure, reduce intermediate cost, build the image of Chinese products and strengthen international agricultural product promotion activities. In this case, economic operation thinking for market economy should be also included in the framework of agriculture legislation so as to solve the problem of agricultural product circulation.

4.5.2 The Legislative Adjustment to Agriculture Input and Protection

Facing fierce competition of international markets, China should facilitate the establishment of agriculture support and protection system. After joining WTO, China should fully apply WTO's Green Subsidy Policy and increase the government's input in agriculture. WTO Agreement on Agriculture eliminates 12 domestic supporting measures, of which 6 measures are still in blank in China and other support measures are also limited. It is necessary to increase spending in general services for farmers and continue to increase the input in infrastructure construction, scientific research and education and technology promotion. The support of WTO's yellow subsidiary policy should be adjusted and increased. In the negotiation on China's accession to WTO, it has been determined that yellow subsidiary should not exceed 8.5% of gross output value of agricultural products, whereas at present, our subsidiary is less than 2% of gross output value of agricultural products.[30] Based on current output value of agricultural products and subsidiary, there is still about RMB 150 billion which can be used as yellow subsidiary. In addition, the original subsidiary structure can be adjusted, with most of subsidiary being spent in production link and farmers instead of circulation link.

The expansionary policy which should be implemented by China should tilt toward agriculture, build agricultural product export bases for earning foreign exchange, focus on supporting infrastructure construction and environmental protection, encourage enterprises of diversified ownership forms to invest in and develop export-oriented agriculture, give self-operating import and export rights to all enterprises meeting requirements for operating agricultural product export trade and support agricultural product export enterprises meeting relevant conditions to enter into the stock markets at home and abroad to issue stocks and expand their scales, thus improving the international competitive power of agricultural products of China. At the same time, China should facilitate the establishment of a perfect agricultural insurance system. China should set up disaster insurance compensation to provide insurance subsidiary for income loss, loss due to natural disaster and the like of farmers, protect the interests and production enthusiasm of farmers, found an agricultural structural adjustment fund specially used for supporting farmers to adjust structure, develop livestock, aquatic and agricultural product processing industries and allow farmers to benefit from structural adjustment, also establish an interest compensation system for compensating farmers who suffer losses due to structural adjustment and actively help farmers to find out employment opportunities. China should also, in accordance with the requirements of WTO Agreement on Agriculture, adjust agricultural product export tax policy as fast as possible, properly raise tax refund rate for agricultural product export and give refund in time, implement tax reduction or exemption policy on production materials such as production and processing equipment and seeds imported by agricultural product export enterprises, exempt tax on exported agricultural specialty products and reduce or exempt the inspection and quarantine expenses of agricultural product export enterprises.

Fund input in agriculture is the fundamental guarantee for sustainable and stable development of agriculture. At present, China's control of fund input in agriculture is mainly based on the policies of the Communist Party and government. The *Agriculture Law* only provides the principles for fund input in agriculture, namely, "The State gradually increases the overall input to agriculture. The annual overall input to agriculture by the Central Government and the local governments at or above the county level shall be increased by a broader margin than their regular revenues respectively." Due to the laggardness of legislation, in China, the fund input in agriculture has not realized legalization and standardization yet. Since the investment of China in agriculture aims to improve agricultural production capacity after China joins WTO, our thought for legislative improvement should be raising fund for agriculture from multiple channels while ensuring the stable growth of investment in agriculture. Firstly, China should greatly strengthen the support of national finance in agriculture. Financial expenditure should focus on cross-regional agricultural infrastructure construction, basic research of important agricultural science and promotion of agricultural science, agro-industries, important agricultural development projects and the like; secondly, it is necessary to exert the effect of policy-based financial institutions and increase the input of credit funds in agriculture; thirdly, China should, according to the practices of foreign countries, set up a national agricultural construction protection fund, with the funds from transfer fee of state-owned land use right, adjustment tax on of fixed assets investment, farmland conversion tax, groups and individuals directly benefiting from the ecological benefits and foreign preferential loans and donation; fourthly, farmers should be instructed to use a proportion of accumulated fund for the fund input in agricultural construction.

4.5.3 The Legislative Adjustment to Agriculture Resources

Paragraph 12 of Annex 2 (Domestic Support: Basis for Exemption from the Reduction Commitments) to WTO Agreement on Agriculture has two provisions on the payment under environmental protection plan: a. eligibility for such payments shall be determined as part of a clearly-defined government environmental or conservation programme and be dependent on the fulfillment of specific conditions under the government programme, including conditions related to production methods or inputs. b. The amount of payment shall be limited to the extra costs or loss of income involved in complying with the government programme. It can be seen that the support of China in environmental protection belongs to domestic support measure of exemption from the reduction commitments. We should fully utilize this rule to properly solve the environmental problem and effectively provide strong support for the sustainable development of agriculture.

As a general view, Chinese agricultural environment and resource protection legislation develops rapidly. However, we must also be aware that the law and regulation system of agricultural environment and resource protection in China initially takes shape, with much incompleteness and unsoundness. Furthermore, China is now cracking the international agricultural products market. Therefore, it is extremely urgent for us to further improve and perfect our agricultural resource protection legislation. First of all, we should establish and implement the principles of sustainable development. As we know, protecting agricultural resource and ecological environment is the basis of agriculture protection. Hence, we should increase the development potential of agriculture by enhancing the protection and control of natural environment, including land, river, forest and grassland, etc. Secondly, we should formulate new agricultural environment and resource protection laws and regulations with respect to key fields, such as prevention and control of desertification, agricultural environmental protection in ecologically vulnerable areas, green food, agricultural water conservation and promotion of environmental protection industry. Thirdly, we should improve the existing agricultural environment and resource protection laws and regulations: establish the rules of law that are beneficial for agricultural environment and resource protection; take appropriate measures to coordinate agricultural environmental protection and agricultural resource protection; enhance the operability and enforceability of agricultural environment and resource protection laws, emphasize legal liabilities in laws and direct township enterprises to reasonably utilize the resources and prevent and control environmental pollution.

4.5.4 The Legislative Adjustment to Agriculture Education and Science

Since joining WTO, China has suffered from increasing "green trade barrier" in export of agricultural products (such as livestock), which has seriously impact on the export. Currently, the export of agricultural products in developed regions of China has been seriously affected. From January to March 2002, 896 batches of products in coastal areas were detained by United States Food and Drug Administration, occupying 78.6% of the total detained products. In the first four months of 2002, the export volume and trade value of frozen chicken in Shenzhen Port were both decreased by 40% compared with the same period of 2001. In 2001, the value of the export commodities affected by the "green trade barrier" was up to USD 7 billion. According to the estimation, in 2002, the foreign technological barrier, especially the "green barrier" resulted in more than USD 10 billion of direct and indirect losses in agricultural product export of China. It should be noted that the annual export sales of aquatic products, animal by-products and fruits & vegetables of China were only USD 10 billion in the past year. However, there is a contrary case which has ever been widely reported by the media, that is, "Shandong farmer wins over the United States in an anti-dumping case". [31] The details of the case are as follows: Oriental Juice (Group) Co., Ltd., engaged in processing of apple juice concentrate, mainly exports its products to the USA, Europe, Japan and the like. By 1999, its annual production capacity of apple juice had reached 20,000t. In June 1999, some American enterprises applied to the United States Department of Commerce for charging anti-dumping duties on the apple juice from China at the rate of 91.84%. After a series of investigation on more than 300 issues, United States Department of Commerce preliminarily determined, in November 1999, that the ten Chinese enterprises, including Oriental Juice, won the lawsuit. The reasons include the pass rate of the export products of Oriental

Juice always remained at 100%; Oriental Juice had successively passed the inspection of FDA and the largest fruit juice importer of Japan—Mitsui; in 1997, it got the certificates of KOSHER (US) and SGF (German); in July 1999, it became the sole Chinese enterprise obtaining HACCP Certificate which is the strictest one in the international food industry. It can be seen that how important agriculture science and education is in international agricultural trade.

The legislation of agricultural science and technology in China has begun to take shape. However, compared with the developed countries, our agricultural science and technology is less developed, the education of agricultural science and technology is far from being universal and the legislation of agriculture education and science is lagging behind. The present legislation of agriculture education and science cannot meet the requirements for entering the international agricultural market and developing high-yield, high-quality and good-benefit modernized agriculture. Joining WTO has brought severe challenges to the improvement of our agriculture education and science legislation. Facing these challenges, we should further improve the *Law on the Popularization of Agricultural Technology* published in 1993 and enhance the incentives in the respects of agricultural research team building and agricultural science and technology input, so as to standardize the agricultural scientific research institutions, increase input in agriculture science and education, protect the legal interests of agriculture science and education practitioners, standardize the agricultural technology market and promote the transformation of scientific and technological achievements in agriculture. Besides, we should also improve the training of the practitioners and professionals to make it standardized, normal and legislative. This is the basis and precondition for developing agriculture through science and education.[32]

China's accession to WTO has brought a huge impact on both agricultural production and agricultural products circulation of China. Backward production mode, poor product quality, lack of circulation channel and information and undeveloped transportation make it difficult for China to make a figure in the international agricultural market. The national economy will be seriously affected if we do not implement feasible agricultural policies to promote the development of agriculture. When China signed the WTO Agreement, it was publicly declared that China joined WTO at the expense of decreased agricultural benefits, which means that WTO rules are detrimental to China's agriculture (temporarily at least). But complaint makes no sense. It is urgent for us to accelerate the development of agricultural legislation so as to reach the international level. Solving the problem of "agriculture, farmer and rural area" by rule of law is a common method adopted by most developed countries to protect and develop agriculture and guarantee benign development of national economy. Most countries attach much importance to protect and develop agriculture by legislation. At present, the USA has published more than 80 laws and Japan has published more than 200 laws related to agriculture. In addition, many other countries, such as Vietnam and France, have also incorporated agricultural reform and protection of farmers' interests into legislation. It has been proved that the practices of these countries have greatly promoted the development of their national economy.

NOTES

1. As said by Wen Tiejun, an expert in agricultural problem, modernization is probably neither a dream nor a reality for the Chinese. Instead, it is pseudoscience and a mirage placed ahead by westerners. Western modernization is a pseudo-problem for China, thus all the self-claimed "science" supporting such western modernization should be restudied for us Chinese. Please see Wen Tiejun. Rural Development in Mainland China [J]. *Open Times*, 2003 (2).
2. Hu Lijun and ChenJing, "Communication of Cyclic Relation between Agriculture and Industry", *Hubei Daily*, December 25, 2003.
3. Mei Duanmu, et.al, *Social Problems in French Modernization Process* (Beijing: China Social Science Press, 2001), 33-36.
4. Xu Xianglin, "Criticism and Alternatives of the Theory of 'Three Stages of Industry-Agriculture Relation'," accessed January 15, 2004, http://www.ccrs.org.cn.
5. Sun Dawu, "On the Problem of 'Agriculture, Farmer, Rural Area' and the Hope of China," accessed March, 2003, www.sinoliberal.com.
6. CCIV, *Law Today*, May 22, 2003.
7. Dai Xiongwu, "Comparison of China with Developed Countries in Terms of Agricultural Productivity," *Economic Theory and Business Management* 1(1999).
8. HanJun, "Safeguarding and Promoting Rural Reform, Development and Stability According to Law," *CPC Central Committee's Collection of Lectures on Legal Institution (1998-2000)* (Beijing: Law Press, 2001), 114.
9. Kun Wu, "Amendment to the Agricultural Law: to Consolidate Agriculture's Foundational Status and Increase Rural Income," *Legal Daily*, June 27, 2002.
10. Huang Zongzhi, *The Peasant Family and Rural Development in the Yangtze River Delta* (Beijing: Zhonghua Book Company, 1992), 167.
11. Robert A. Dahl, *Modern Political Analysis* (Shanghai: Shanghai Translation Publishing House, 1987), 136.
12. Xu Xianglin, "Reform to Rural Governance Structure is Requisite for Solving 'three agriculture-related problems'," *Social Science Weekly*, July 17, 2003.
13. Li Jidong and Wang Lixin, "On Village Self-Governance and Rural Democratic Construction," *Journal of Ningxia University* 3(2003).
14. Yang Lixi, "Keys to Develop Rural Democratic Construction," *Creation*, 4 (2003).
15. Li Changqi, "Safeguarding and Promoting Rural Reform and Stability,". *CPC Central Committee's Collection of Lectures on Legal Institution* (Beijing: Law Press, 2001).
16. Chen Chunzhu, "Study on Legislation of Democratic Election, Decision-Making, Management and Supervision Forming Four Elements of Village Self-Governance," *Social Science Research*, 3 (2003).
17. "Zhengzhou Guidance Center of Agricultural Economy Management. Summary and Analysis of Questionnaire Survey on Rural Problems in Zhengzhou," accessed February 12, 2001, http://www.sdnw.gov.cn/.
18. Yu Jianrong, "Rural Vicious Powers and Decline of Grass-Roots Authority," *Strategy and Management*, 5(2003).
19. Liu Libo, "Relation between Building Well-off Society in an All-Round Way and Spiritual Civilization," *Journal of Dalian University* 1 (2003).
20. Zhang Suhuan, "Advancing Rural Spiritual Civilization under the Guidance of Decisions Made at the 16th CPC National Congress," *Qian Yan*, 10 (2003).

21. Qing Feng, "'Jitous' Lead Farmers to Wealthy," accessed December 26, 2002, http://www.southcn.com.
22. Ye Haitao, "The Impact of WTO Agreement on Agriculture on China and Its Solutions," *International Business Research* 1(2004).
23. For International Regulation and International Economic Law, Please See The Synchronous Evolution of Market, Regulating Mechanism and Law in Qi Duojun *Economic Law Review* (Volume I) [C]. Beijing: China Fangzheng Press, 1999.
24. Qi Duojun, "New Stage of WTO Market Internationalization and International Regulation –and the Influence of China's Accession to WTO on China's National Regulation and Economic Law," *Journal of Central South University* 4(2003).
25. Qi Duojun "New Stage of WTO Market Internationalization and International Regulation –and the Influence of China's Accession to WTO on China's National Regulation and Economic Law," *Journal of Central South University* 4(2003).
26. Zeng Qinghua and An Yuli, "Implication of Japan's and Australia's Response to Influence of Accession to WTO," *Shandong Agriculture (Rural Economy)* 6(2002).
27. Zhao Xiao, "Discussion on Adjustment of Macro Policy Orientation: from 'Promoting Growth' to 'Full Employment'," *China Economic Times*, September 11, 2002.
28. Chen Zhiyuan, "Influence of the U.S.—China WTO Market Access Agreement on Agricultural Product Trade in China," Chinese Rural Economy, 5(2000).
29. For "State Regulation Theory" on Economic Law Proposed by Professor Qi Duojun, Please See Qi Duojun, The Basic Theory of Economic Law (Wuhan: Wuhan University Press, 2000); and Qi Duojun, Economic Law Forum (Beijing: China Fangzheng Press, 1999).
30. Guomin Ding, "Influence of WTO Agreement on Agriculture on Agricultural and Economic Legislation of China," Economic Law Forum (Volume 1). Beijing: China Fangzheng Press, 2004-5: 330.
31. "A Shandong Farmer Won over the US in An Anti-Dumping Case," Farmers' Daily, September 10, 2003.
32. Song Bingbin, "WTO Agreement on Agriculture and Agricultural Protection Legislation of China," Research of Agricultural Modernization 6(2001).

Chapter Five

Feasibility of Solving "Three Agriculture-related Problems" by Rule of Law

5.1 A SHIFT FROM RULE OF MAN TO RULE OF LAW HAS BECOME COMMON SENSE OF THE NATION

The rule of man and rule of law represent a pair of categories. From the perspective of epistemology, the rule of man falls into the empirical category while the rule of law the normative category. The rule of man, i.e., the rule of officer, is related with the "rule of rites" and "rule of virtue". From the perspective of modern political science, the rule of man represents a kind of rule with distinct mark of feudalism which realizes rule and governance through the ruler's personal talent, virtue and the like. Corresponding with the rule of man, the rule of law refers to the "governance of law", that is to implement rule and governance through the law reflecting the common will and interests of the ruling class. Under the rule of law, the law occupies the dominant position of a country and society with supreme authority.

The rule of law to advocated by the ancient legalism in China is not equal to the rule of law in modern sense, i.e., the rule of law implemented under the framework of the society with rule of law or the rule of law that advocates the concept of "all people are equal before the law". Chinese legalists after Qin Dynasty proposed to implement a kind of rule-of-law thought with the purpose of monarch centralization and had ever had some practices of political reform. However, in general, their rule of law is a kind of "rule of law under the rule of man". With the development of the society, the rule of man becomes more and more unsuitable for political civilization development and therefore should gradually be replaced by the principle of rule of law. It represents a kind of criticism and reform of the thought of rule of man and rule tradition promoted by the persons of virtue following Yao and Shun as well as the doctrine of Confucius and Mencius. For ruling the country by law, the "ruling the country" should focus on "ruling power" which involves the issues of who to administer whom, namely the subject and object of the "ruling power". Therefore, the "ruling power" has a broad sense and narrow sense. Cicero put great emphasis on the role of ruling a country by law in his *Laws*: a praetor's duty lies in ruling the people by law and offering proper and useful guidance. Since the law rules the praetor and the praetor rules the people, the praetor becomes the talking law and the law becomes the speechless praetor. Despite the historical and class limitation, Cicero has answered the question of "ruling power" from one perspective. In China, people are the master of the country and the Constitution and laws a concentrated reflection of the will of the majority of Chinese people. The so-called "ruling power" in a broad sense is represented on one hand by that people rule the country and the country's officials (namely the "government officials") in accordance with the Constitution and laws ("rule the officials" by law); and on the other hand by that the government agencies and officials rule the country, society and all citizens in accordance with the Constitution and laws ("officials rule" by law). The two aspects are unified and indivisible in the process of rule of law. While the "ruling power" in a narrow sense may refers to any side of that in a broad sense. The doctrine that everything has two aspects usually entails the doctrine that everything has a key aspect. From the perspective of modern country, especially the people nature of our country, the key aspect should lie in that people rule the state machinery and government officials by law. There is a saying which goes like this, in order to rule a country, one should rule the country's officials first. However, judging by the tendency of administering orientation and representative system of state sovereignty, the key aspect should lie in that the state agencies and officials, namely the "government officials" rule the country, society and people in accordance with the law (i.e., "officials rule" by law). Sun Yat-sen pointed out that the goal of "ruling power" mainly covers such "five kinds of power" as the executive power, legislative power, judicial power, examination power and supervision power. To sum up, as to the relation of the two aspects of "ruling power", only ruling the government officials by law can guarantee the integrity of the government officials' ruling and only the integrity of the government officials' ruling can realize good ruling of a state and the world as a whole. Therefore, in order to build a society with rule of law, it is necessary to emphasize that the legislation should represent the fundamental interests for the masses, and to realize "all people are equal before the law" in its true sense under the premise. Without legislative justice and true equality for everyone before the law, there will be no real country under the rule of law or ruling a country by law in real sense. Without the justice of modern sense or the country under the rule of law founded on the interests of the broad masses of the people, the rule of law can only be deemed as another expression of the rule of man. It is the most fundamental guarantee condition for people to judge and supervise the legislative, judicial and law enforcement justice.[1]

Although we cannot ignore or deny the critical role of the leaders, especially the top leaders of party and government administration for advancing the overall working, nor can we deny or ignore the special role of "rule of man" under special environment and conditions, our goal, expectation and ideal is to implement democracy and rule of law and to administer state affairs well, ensure national security and promote the development of different undertakings through rule of law. Therefore, it is the route we must take to change from "rule of man" to rule of law in order to establish the democracy and legal system of China. The experience of "Ruling of Changzhi"[2] shows us that only the path of rule of law can enable the press supervision to get rid of the restriction and influence of personal factors, realize systematization and standardization, confine the press supervision within the scope of laws, standardize different kinds of actions and phenomena from the press supervision, impose legal sanction to those obstruct and suppress the press supervision and implement legal protection for those carry out press supervision. In this way, the press supervision will not be affected because of personal factor of certain leader. To Changzhi, regardless of whether Lv Rizhou will stay in Changzhi or what change would happen to Lv Rizhou, the press supervision of Changzhi City will continue in accordance with due procedures and along the right path as long as there is relevant laws and regulations for guarantee. This is the key to solve the systematization and standardization issue of press supervision fundamentally. Otherwise, once Lv Rizhou leaves Changzhi or something happens to Lv Rizhou, the press supervision of Changzhi will be impacted and shocked. The many times of rebound occurred during the press supervision of Changzhi represent the good lessons. It is learned that Lv Rizhou mainly go to the most extreme lengths and suppress interference to promote the news criticism and press supervision through his personal courage and charisma. In many cases, to ensure little interference and smooth implementation of press supervision, he often needs to have the final say alone. So, there comes another question, i.e., "who will take charge of supervising Lv's personal power". The consequence will be quite dangerous once there is no supervision for personal power. Furthermore, how should Lv deal with his relationship with the leading group of the municipal party committee, or the relation of press supervision, inner-party supervision, administrative supervision, the People's Congress supervision and much other supervision? These questions all need to be solved through certain systems, laws and regulations.[3]

Theoretical knowledge needs the test of practice. Theories have fully demonstrated that, superior to the rule of man, the rule of law has become the inevitable requirement of modern democratic and civilized society. Historical lessons have made people acutely aware of the serious drawbacks of rule of man. The deceit to the common people in the era of rule of man naturally makes people start to yearn for the era of rule of law. China has made great achievement in the promoting of rule of law and opposing rule of man from top to bottom since the reform and opening up. Over the years, our central leading cadres have deeply realized the importance of learning and understanding the law as well as ruling the country by law. Our top leaders have squeezed out time from their tight schedules to attend the legal experts' legal lectures, laying solid foundation for the Chinese government to promote the rule of law. Although there still exists great disadvantage in our existing system which needs bold and resolute reform from the bottom, the Party and the government have realized the importance of and been actively promoting the concept of ruling the country by law. This shows a good momentum. Meanwhile, we should also realize that it is far from enough for the law to be used and utilized only by the leading cadres. What is more important is to make the law become the standard of behavior and highest authority of all people in social life. The behavior of the people and departments with power, in particular, should be put under the supervision of the general public. The power of these people and departments must be checked and supervised by another parallel party without direct interest relationship with them. We need to adhere to the leadership of the Communist Party of China (CPC) rather than just copy the "separation of the three powers" of the western countries. However, it really constitutes an important subject for us to research how to effectively check and supervise our Party itself. Those who take the principles of "CPC is the vanguard of Chinese working class" and "CPC is the political party that serves the people whole-heartedly" as the excuses for the argument that the party needs only self-discipline and self-supervision and no check and supervision from another parallel party are either extremely selfish dictators or schemers with an ulterior motive. Such misconception will ultimately lead CPC to a bottomless chasm. The good news is that our Party has realized the great harm of power without check and supervision and is now actively constructing and improving effective check and supervision mechanism of power.

At present stage, although the legal accomplishment of the common people still needs further improvement, the enthusiasm for the rule of law is prevalent. To each stratum of today's Chinese society, the rule of law is not just a kind of thinking and exploration, but also a type of ideological trend and strong passion. From the clear proposal of "ruling the country by law" to the active response of "ruling the city by law" and even "ruling the village by law"; from the legal system course led by the Central government, to the legal training course led by local government and to the opening of the citizens' hot line for ruling of law; from the law-based administration of government to the operation of March 15; from successive capture of corrupt officials to the straight climb of the number of citizen suit...All these not only signify that the project for ruling of law is quietly launching on Chinese land by particular means, but also represent that a strong passion for the rule of law is prevalent on Chinese land from the inner part of our country and society.[4] Only after entering into the orbit of comprehensive rule of law as quickly as possible, can we maintain the strong enthusiasm and passion for rule of law and push forward the process of ruling the country by law.

5.2 CHINA HAS ACCUMULATED PLENTY OF EXPERIENCE IN RULE OF LAW

The practice of village self-governance has aroused the consciousness of right among the general farmers and fostered the farmers' legal awareness. After the founding of the new socialist PRC, although the general farmers have turned into their own master and begun to have a decisive say in business management, they have not personally experienced much the feeling of being a master except for some outlets for emotions during the campaign of fighting landlords. Actually, the occasional campaign or revolution used to leave the general farmers completely at a loss. Chinese farmers, who always struggles at low-income level are quite unfamiliar with, even do not dare to claim, the concept of individual rights. The village self-governance finally enables the general farmers get the chance to make the decision for their own businesses. This actually means that the country has returned the villagers' rights to the villagers. Nevertheless, the villagers' enthusiasm for self-governance is still very high. In Ma Yinlu's book, people from Qixiu Village have the tradition of "bombing a meeting". However, we cannot regard the Qixiu villagers as a group of unruly people. As a matter of fact, the tradition is none other than a representation of stronger consciousness of rights from the farmers. Why would they "bomb a meeting"? The reason is that they are dissatisfied with the meeting. If the meeting really give full expression to the general farmers' will rather than just deliver the mind from the upper level, will the farmers "bomb a meeting"? This is an understandable style of unbosoming for the farmers to fight for their own rights.

There are two typical cases from He Xuefeng's investigation of "villages administered by good persons":

One is Yucun Village from Hubei, a suburb village. According to the nomination of the mass-election before the 1999 election, Bao and Li became the two official candidates of the villagers committee. The incumbent leader Bao was a valiant, selfish and capable villain, and the incumbent deputy leader Li, a widely-recognized good person. The villagers were required to make a choice between Bao and Li. From the aspect of emotion, all the villagers were partial to Li. However, according to the analysis of several reasonable villagers, Yucun Village was a suburb village and Li would not dare to offend any villager or superior owing to his good-person character if he was to be elected as the village leader. This might lead the village miss a good opportunity for development; whereas Bao, in spite of his bad character and inevitable embezzlement, couldn't go so far as to earn less than his corrupted part of money after being elected as the village leader by virtue of his toughness and capability. The rational analysis became a major topic of villagers' discussion before the election. Finally, under the assistance of the election guidance group from the county government that stationed in Yucun Village, Li adjusted his strategy and emphasized that his lack of boldness was caused by his position as a deputy and that he would definitely act with courage and determination if elected. As a result, Li won the election by a narrow margin.

The other is Xinghuo Village from Ruian, Zhejiang, also a suburb village. For a long time, the upper level government had planned to construct a vegetable market in Xinghuo Village. It is a favorable thing to both the town and village as Xinghuo Village is located at the center of the built-up area of the town. After constructing the market, the people from the town could enjoy much convenience, the villagers committee could collect more than 1,000,000 of booth rental from the market each year and the villagers could enjoy higher rental for their houses because of the land appreciation brought by the market construction. The thing that was beneficial to all parties had been discussed for many years among the leading cadres and on the village representative assembly, but bogged down due to the difficulty to balance the compensation for some villagers' houses to be destroyed for the market. Some villagers thought their compensation standards were too low and asked for higher standards. However, after the raise of compensation standard for one household's, more households would ask for higher standards too. The village cadres couldn't solve the complex issue and the villagers blamed the cadres for their incapability to deal with such petty thing. The thing had been left unsolved for more than five years. In the general election of the villagers committee of 1999, Zhou, a valiant villain who took drugs, indulged in gambling and had some connections with the vicious power, participated in the election for the village leader. He advocated that he could handle the issue of the vegetable market once he became the village leader. The villagers also believed that a valiant like Zhou could solve the complex issue of compensation as the villagers were all afraid of him. The town government disagreed Zhou's participation as the formal candidate because of his notorious record. However, Zhou managed to win the election by more votes than the educated, capable and righteous former village officer by means of "other candidate to recommend" in the ballot tickets. Most of the eight investigated villages from the town where Xinghuo Village is located had the phenomenon of valiant being elected as the village cadre.[5]

The two typical cases show us the following extra information:

1. The farmers' consciousness of rights has been awakened;
2. New view of value is gradually forming in rural areas;
3. The farmers have certain hope on the rule of law.

Being submissive and swallowing insult represents the nature of the farmers that is domesticated and nurtured during thousands of years. These farmers will only release all of their suppressed and accumulated power of rebellion by irresistible trend when things become beyond endurance which is usually the time for regime change. The ideology of obligation standard makes the farmers seldom think of what kinds of rights they exactly have. After the reform and opening-up, owing to the strong impact of foreign value on the vast rural area of China, Chinese farmers also have the gut to say "NO" too. The emergence of contract with remuneration linked to output and village self-governance has reflected the awakening of the farmers' consciousness of rights to some extent. Their thinking of "what am I required to do?" and "what should I do?" begins to be added with such elements as "what do I want to do?" and "what I can do?". Rights, freedom, equality, democracy and the like are no longer unfamiliar words to the farmers. The farmers have learned to consider some issues from another viewpoint. For example, the issue of legality has become a major train of thought for modern farmers in analyzing an issue. During my career as a lawyer, I have contacted many farmers involved in different cases and I was surprised to find that the "rural China" described by Fei Xiaotong is gradually vanishing and the "new rural China" depicted by He Xuefeng gradually maturing. We can also say that the reform and opening-up, land contract and village self-governance have triggered huge and strong vigor and enthusiasm in rural area and the farmers' passion for rule of law is gradually increasing. Although different kinds of existing problems of "Agriculture, Farmer and Rural Area" usually throw head-on blows on the farmers' enthusiasm for rule of law, to rule the country by law has become the general trend and all resisting power are only temporary.

It is an irresistible trend of times and gradual process to change from rule of man to rule of law. At the beginning of the founding of PRC, the successful challenge launched by rule of law against feudal autocracy and wide spread of humanity liberation and free thought laid solid foundation for establishing the public awareness of law. Although the rule of law has suffered from trample and nearly catastrophic explosion, the seeds of humanity liberation and freedom have been deeply buried in people's mind. In rural area, especially in the marriage and family aspects of the rural area, Chinese awareness of freedom and equality have gone through unprecedented improvement, thus making good preparation for the realization of rule of law.

In rural China, the clan force and traditional sense of family have always been a strong spirit weapon that dominate farmers' production and life, which are now fading off at high speed. Their intermittent repetition cannot resist the farmers' eagerness to the rights, freedom, equality and democracy.

5.3 A CONDUCIVE MECHANISM OF STATE LAWS PENETRATING SUCCESSFULLY INTO RURAL SOCIETY AND RURAL SOCIETY BEING RESPONSIVE TO STATE LAWS HAS BEEN ESTABLISHED

In today's rural China, the compulsive top-down doctrine, i.e., the progression patterns adopted by the government for the spirit of rule of law have basically realized its goal. In particular, years of popularization of laws has provided the farmers with basic knowledge about the social functions and stakes of laws. The farmers' eagerness and expectation for the rule of law have entered a stage of sound progress. These farmers have deeply realized the great advantage of utilizing the law to safeguard their own rights and interests and solve disputes through legal means over the traditional way of solving disputes. Meanwhile, such "new things" as the laws are definitely worthy of pursuing and promoting for the farmers with strong thirst for knowledge. Of course, the farmers' belief in the law and the social environment of rule of law are inseparable. In a social environment where the authority of law is well maintained, people will have high expectation to law and respect law. Otherwise, people will regard the law as just "toilet paper". The "white wine logo lawsuit" insisted by Wang Ying, a rural female from Henan Province, filled me with deep esteem in terms of the Chinese farmers' awareness of law. It has shown the farmers' strong passion for laws and the successful permeation of state laws to the rural area.

On June 20, 2001 when the Ministry of Land and Resources solicited advice from the public for formulating the *Measures for Land Acquisition Announcement (Draft)*, Gan Cangchun, the Director of the Department of Policies and Laws said that, in the past, we only focused on the farmers' "education to abide by the law", i.e., what should one do, and ignored the farmers' actual concerns and worries. As a matter of fact, "when applying for an audience with the higher authorities to appeal for help in today's world, most of the farmers would take the *Land Law* with them. They would sue the officers if the officers did not comply with any stipulation of the Law. The farmers' concern for and understanding of the land law are sometimes higher than the cadres, including the cadres of the land management system."[6] As to whether the farmers' expectation to the law is high or low, we can see a dialogue from an interview among Gui Xiaoqi, the former Deputy Director of *Rural Development Forum*; Cao Zhengjie, a farmer from Jiangxi; and

Chen Dahui, the journalist of Half-Hour Economy after the ban of *Hand book for Alleviating Farmers' Burdens*:

Chen Dahui: When did you realize your heavy burden?

Cao Zhengjie: It begins from this year. We had no idea of those taxes before this year.

Chen Dahui: Why this year?

Cao Zhengjie: Because I read the book *Handbook for Alleviating Farmers' Burdens* this year and I started to know the inside information. The book has described clearly relevant documents and regulations of the Central government.

Chen Dahui: Can you give us an example? Can you name a thing that you got to know after you read the book?

Cao Zhengjie: Yes. For example, the butchery tax. One has to pay twelve yuan for each pig and twenty-four for two. As to those pigs that are slaughtered mainly for self-consumption during some major festivals, the tax will be one half. In our village, one person has to pay the tax for a pig. It doesn't matter whether or not you have pigs. You just have to pay the tax for certain number of pigs and the certain number equals the number of your family members.

Chen Dahui: When and under what circumstances the town governments will publicize some policies and spirits for alleviating the farmers' burdens from the State Council, central or provincial Party Committee?

Cao Zhengjie: I have never heard of the publicity about the policies of central Party Committee or participated in a conference since the household responsibility system of 1982.

Chen Dahui: Do you have any idea about the use of the tax?

Cao Zhengjie: The use of the tax? I think the money has been turned over to the higher authority but we know nothing about it.

Chen Dahui: If your family doesn't have the money and couldn't pay the charge or tax, what would happen?

Cao Zhengjie: They would take away whatever I have.

Chen Dahui: Take away whatever you have? According to the handbook, you farmers actually have many rights. In face of unreasonable tax, you may boycott, report, apply for administrative review, file a suit in a court or send a petition letter. Which of these means would you choose in case of any unreasonableness?

Cao Zhengjie: I may have some choices. I already have the faith. In face of the unreasonable, I will file a suit. I will make my request to the government.

Chen Dahui: You mean you would choose...

Cao Zhengjie: Go to the law.[7]

The ordinary conversation reflects the change of farmers' concept and idea which is worthy of our serious consideration. Why the farmers have to pay different kinds of taxes but have no idea of why should they pay the taxes, where the taxes have been to, what the taxes have been used for and how much should they pay? The one who collects the taxes is always right. The reason lies in that the farmers' rights have been greatly ignored for a long time. The top-down operation for constructing a socialist country ruled by law launched after the reform and opening-up, especially after the establishment of the market economic system. The several consecutive five-year plans for popularizing the laws have at least provided the farmers the opportunity to know about Chinese laws in form. Varied media like the radio, newspaper and TV also conveyed various kinds of information to the countryside and even outlying mountain villages. Large number of farmers flooded into the city for employment. They listened to and heard of varied legal phenomena and personally experienced the power of rule of law. The awakening of the farmers' legal awareness has stimulated strong enthusiasm for the rule of law. Cao Zhengjie's words like "I already have the faith. In face of the unreasonable, I will file a suit" have showed the voice of farmers. In face of different kinds of unreasonable treatment, they will fight to "have a say" through any fighting channel they could find rather than willingly choose submission to humiliation. Meanwhile, we are surprised to find that the farmers' sensitivity to the law has gone far beyond our imagination. For this, we need to ponder over how on earth we should formulate the law, what kind of law we should formulate, and how the formulated law can be well implemented. Practices have proved that a good law that can meet the farmers' actual needs, once been known by the farmers, could immediately become powerful weapon for the farmers to safeguard their rights. This is a good momentum. To maintain such good momentum, we need the support from all sectors of society, especially greater efforts for system reform from the government. It has become imperative for us to reform the legislative system, judicial system and supervision of law enforcement.

With the progress of the society ruled by law, juridical practice in rural areas and spread of rule-of-law thought by the media, the farmers' expectation and aspiration are gradually enhancing. The law has begun to occupy more and more important position in farmers' life. Meanwhile, the legalization of the whole country has entered into a stage of unprecedented development after 1980s which is mainly manifested by people's increasing enthusiasm for rule of law. We not only have more lawsuits now but also give full expression to people's willingness in the lawsuits. Typical cases include one-penny lawsuit, claim for compensation for mental impairment, etc. The trend will definitely spread to the rural areas with backward legalization and push the rural areas towards comprehensive rule of law.

5.4 THE SUCCESSFUL EXPERIENCE IN FOREIGN COUNTRIES IN SOLVING "THREE AGRICULTURE-RELATED PROBLEMS" BY RULE OF LAW HAS SET UP GOOD EXAMPLES

To Chinese reform and opening-up, it is a very important guiding ideology to learn the advanced technology and successful experience from the foreign countries. It is no exception to the task of solving the problem of "agriculture, farmer and rural area". Since the successful foreign experience for solving the problem of "agriculture, farmer and rural area" has provided reference and example for us, we have no reason to abandon and ignore such experience to wade the river totally by groping for stones. To sum up, the successful experience for solving the problem of agriculture, farmer and rural area" from foreign countries mainly covers the following aspects:

5.4.1 To Establish Complete Legislative System Concerning Agriculture

In foreign countries, especially in the developed countries, the legislation system for agriculture is complete and comprehensive. Of all the agriculture-related laws and regulations, the comprehensive basic laws and special laws are well matched, consecutive, well-joined, mutually coordinated and complementary with high level of legislation, strict procedure, high authority, specific articles and good operability.

For example, the US congress has passed large amount of agricultural laws during the period of over 160 years. The agricultural legislation of the congress represents a debate and repeating negotiation procedure as well as a process in which different interest groups make compromise. The legislation is the base for the government to formulate agricultural policies and implement agricultural plans. The congress has formulated about one hundred agricultural laws, including the *Homestead Act*, *Agricultural Law*, *Food Agricultural Resources and Trade Act*, *Agricultural Credit Act*, *Federal Crop Insurance Act*, *Disaster Relief Act*, *Agricultural Products Sales Agreement Act*, etc. The purpose of the laws is to guarantee the profit for the farmers, ensure reliable supply for the consumers and safeguard the rights and interests of America in foreign trade.

Since the establishment of the Ministry of Agriculture, Forestry and Fishery in 1881, Japanese congress has passed 54 agricultural laws, including 33 passed after the war (of which, 18 are related with agriculture, 9 forestry and 6 fishery). The government regards agricultural legislation as the motive power for agricultural development and names the *Basic Agricultural Law* as the "agricultural constitution". Relevant laws include the *Basic Agricultural Law*, *Food Administration Law*, *Farmland Law*, *Cultivated Land Improvement Law*, *Agricultural Improvement and Facilitation Law*, *Agriculture and Forestry Central Treasury Law*, *Agriculture, Forestry, Fishery Finance Corporation Law*, *Fund Subsidy Law for Agricultural Improvement*, *Agricultural Products Wholesale Market Law*, *Agricultural Products Price Stability Law*, *Agricultural Disaster Compensation Law*, *Fertilizer Management Law*, *Agricultural Mechanization Law*, *Farm Chemical Management Law*, *Seeds and Seedlings Law*, *Fruit Tree Prospering Law*, *Dairy Farmer Prospering Law*, *Chicken-raising Prospering Law*, *Livestock Improvement and Multiplication Law*, *Beverage Safety and Quality Law*, *Veterinarian Law*, etc.

France successively promulgated the *Agricultural Guidance Law* and its auxiliary laws during 1960-1962 to emphasize the protection of agricultural products price, increase the country's investment to agriculture, encourage the development of agricultural mutual assistance and cooperation and attach importance to agricultural R&D, education and technology promotion. UK promulgated the first *Agricultural Law* in 1947 to implement the policy of guaranteeing the price and market supply for the food necessities and other livestock products, to provide proper subsidy and certain living conditions for the farmers and agricultural operators and to offer generous profit to agricultural investors so as to strive for self-sufficient livestock products and food. It also successively formulated the policies to provide financial subsidy for agricultural infrastructure construction, offer subsidy and bonus to the farmers and implement the lowest guaranteed price after 1947. The country also formulated the *Agricultural Products Tariff Law* in 1974 for trade protection of many agricultural products and the *Agricultural Credit Law* for guaranteeing agricultural input.

Germany formulated the *Cooperative Law* in 1867 and series of laws and regulations after the war to safeguard agricultural production and protect farmers' interests. It also enacted the agricultural law in 1955 to give permission to land free trading and renting and stimulate the expansion of farms. The country implemented the *Land Reclamation Law* to connect the land and improve the farmers' living and ecological environment in mid 1950s. It also put into effect the *Land Consolidation Law*, *Seed Law* and *Forest Law* (according to which, the cutting amount of woods shall not exceed the annual increment and the forest area shall not be decreased; the cutting amount shall at least equal the planting amount for the private forest while the planting amount must exceed the cutting amount for the state-owned forest; cutting trees in districts with little forest shall seek permission first and implement complementary planting later; protection forest belt is promoted and encouraged, etc.). The country's *Agricultural Machinery Law* stipulates that the agricultural machinery supplier must guarantee the machinery quality as well as supply of the spare and accessory parts and will otherwise be held responsible. The country also promulgated the *Plant Protection and Farm Chemical Law*, *Environmental Protection Law*, and *Land Planning Regulations*, etc.

South Korea issued the *Village Prospering Law* in 1960 and *Agricultural Products Circulation and Price Stability Law* later. It also formulated in 1972 the *Land Utilization and Management Law*, *Farmland Protection and Utilization Law*, *Special Measures Law for Agricultural and Fishing Village Development*, *Agricultural and Fishing Village Planning Law*, *Agricultural and Fishing Village Reorganization Law*, *Agricultural Management Law for Restricting Environmental Pollution of Agriculture*, etc. The purpose of the laws is to improve the agricultural production rate by technology and operation capability and carry out agricultural development aiming at improving competitiveness.

Mexico, with sound agricultural law system, has recently revised relevant laws and regulations like the *Phytosanitary Law*, *Water Law*, *Forest Law*, *Seed Law*, *Fertilizer Law*, *Official Quality Standard*, etc. Other countries like Australia, New Zealand, Hungary, Malaysia, Egypt, Thailand and Brazil have all promulgated different laws and regulations for managing agriculture.

To ensure the stability and flexibility of agricultural legislation, most of the countries stipulate that agricultural laws and regulations should be formulated and revised at proper time in accordance with their own economic and social development. Relevant laws should be passed or approved through certain legal procedures and published through the standards and patterns of authoritative institution. Each agricultural law has its concept explanation, definition of rights and obligations, responsible organ, object scope, pursuit of goals, implementation measures, reward and punishment rules, required supplementary articles, etc. Attention should be paid to the combination of stability and flexibility of the laws.[8]

5.4.2 To Establish Three-dimension Legal Enforcement System Concerning Agriculture

The enforcement of agriculture-related laws in foreign countries mostly combine the economic, administrative and legal means to form an organic integrity for combined action and effective realization of regulation goal.

President Roosevelt's government in 1930s carried out economic intervention to the agriculture and adopted effective price protection and financial support policies so as to realize the agricultural law. Until now, American macro-control has kept three features: the first one is setting functional organization (commodity credit corporation) and establishing enormous and flexible federal reserve system; the second is providing sufficient financial support (the expenditure that the federal government used for agricultural support is about US$ 10 billion, over US$ 25 billion for the highest); the third is putting into practice the farmers' "voluntary" agricultural plan and providing close cooperation through such means as price, credit and subsidy. American Ministry of Agriculture carry out unified management to agricultural production, processing, transportation and sale, foreign trade, agricultural R&D and education promotion through well-positioned law and stable organization with clearly-defined functions. It has to not only safeguard the producers' and consumers' interests, but also ensure fair competition within the law.

The UK governments provide more than 200 million pounds for the price subsidy of agricultural products each year. To encourage the farm to develop towards large scale, the decree regulates that those small farms willing to merge may get 50% of relevant expenses. The government also provides 60% of relevant expenses for land reclamation as subsidy, 15%-25% of relevant expenses for land improvement, construction and equipment purchasing for horticultural enterprise as subsidy, and financial aid for the mountainous area with poor land conditions. The farmers who intend to enhance the reproduction capability may utilize the short-term or long-term loan.

While enforcing the law, the German government utilizes such economic means as loan and subsidy to promote agricultural development. The government regulated in 1965 that all farmers selling their land can obtain some bonus or loan to help the farmers transfer to the non-agricultural sector, which greatly promoted the free flow of land and expand the farm scale. The government allocated 4.2 billion Mark for land reclamation during 1950-1971.

In Australia, the laws stipulate that the country will strengthen its financial support to the agriculture by providing concessional loan or grant to farms, subsidy to agricultural fertilizer and petroleum, 18% of the cost for infrastructure construction of farms and concessions to agricultural tax. The country legally and officially established Wheat Board in 1939 to manage in a unified way the international and domestic market sales which is a monopoly organization of service. However, since 1989, the country has canceled the method of utilizing Wheat Board as a unified platform for sales and settlement and started to treat the Board as an equal operator and competitor on the market and let the domestic sale price to be determined by the market. The state-owned land of the country accounts for 87% which is usually leased to the rancher and forestry company. The country guarantees the consistency between its private land and national policies by its land administrative organization.

The Canadian congress passed its *Cereal Purchase and Quality Inspection Law* in 1912 to regulate that the protein content of exported wheat shall reach 136% and that the country will provide support for the price of the exported wheat. It also passed its *Prairie Farm Revitalization Law* in 1935 to provide technical assistance for improving the land and water-conservancy projects of the prairies. For this, the country has specially established its Wheat Board and Prairie Farm Revitalization Authority to take charge of actual implementation of relevant tasks.

Malaysia promulgated its *Law of Cooperative Society* in 1948 and established its farmers' organization and Management Authority as well as Fisherman Organization and Management Authority in 1975 to provide management talents, financial assistance and comprehensive service for farmers' production and life. The cooperative society can enjoy a tax preference of 20% less than that for the private companies. The two authorities merged in 1982 and were transferred to the national cooperative society to become and self-development organization. The country provides supervision and guidance to the cooperative society by legal and policy means so that varied cooperative societies can have faster development and the farmers more employment opportunities.[9]

NOTES

1. Zheng Hengfeng, "Significant Symbol of Political Civilization Development: From Rule of Man to Rule of Law in Modern Sense," *Journal of Guangxi College of Education* 1(2003).
2. Refer to the report by Zhong Weizhi et al, "Ruling of Changzhi", *The Economic Observer*, August 19, 2002.
3. Zheng Baowei, "'Rule of Man' —Rule of Law—Changzhi—Analyze the Development Path of Chinese Press Supervision from the Experience of Changzhi," *Exploration Longitude and Latitude* 10(2002).
4. Wang Taixian and Ai Ming, *Concept and Strategy of Rule of Law* (Beijing: China Procuratorate Press, 2001), 2.
5. He Xuefeng, "Rural China in the 21st Century," accessed Sep. 11, 2003, http://www.ccrs.org.cn/big.
6. Tian Chengyou, "Conditions and Guarantee for State Laws to Succeed in Rural Society," accessed Aug. 30, 2001, http://www.pen123.net.cn.

7. Chen Dahui, et al, "Why the Handbook for Alleviating Farmers' Burdens is Banned?" CCTV-2 Half-Hour Economy, accessed Nov. 28, 2001. The written materials come from http://news.xinhuanet.com. Nov. 29, 2001.

8. Zhu Pirong, "International Experience of Solving Agriculture-Related Problems by Rule of Law," *World Agriculture* 1(2000).

9. ——— "International Experience of Solving Agriculture-Related Problems by Rule of Law," *World Agriculture* 1(2000).

Chapter Six

The Target, Principle, Step and Content System of Solving "Three Agriculture-related Problems" by Rule of Law

6.1 TARGET OF SOLVING "THREE AGRICULTURE-RELATED PROBLEMS" BY RULE OF LAW

The "three agriculture-related problems" are so severe that it is of great necessity to solve them as soon as possible so as to protect the farmers' rights and realize common progress of the whole society. This is also the specific target for solving the "three agriculture-related problems" which is consistent with the target of rule of law. What is the target of rule of law? The proposal of modern ideology for rule of law originates from the campaign against feudal autocracy with freedom, equality and fraternity as its goals. "Most western ideologists set their goal as constructing a society in which every individual, with a minimum dependence on discretionary authority of his rulers, would enjoy the privileges and responsibility of determining his own conduct within a previously defined framework of rights and duties." argues Friedrich Hayek.[1] John Rawls also says that there is obviously close connection between rule of law and freedom.[2] We have for a long time regarded Marxism as the only domination of the ideological sphere. However, we haven't understood or correctly understood the essence of Marxist theory about "people's freedom and social comprehensive development". It is not until after the reform and opening-up that the communist supervisor's theoretical essence is correctly understood. The theory itself contains the development goal of modern civilized society which should be a society ruled by law, and the direct goal of rule of law is to guarantee individuals' rights and freedom and promote social equality.

The goal of solving the problem of "agriculture, farmer and rural area" by rule of law is a branch from the goal of rule of law and concrete expression of the goal of rule of law on the "three agriculture-related problems". The overall goal of social development, the goal of rule of law, the administration goal for "three agriculture-related problems" and the goal of solving the problem of "agriculture, farmer and rural area" by rule of law share the relationship of "four points on a line". They are of generalization and individuality relationship, including and being-included relationship but always on the same line which represents safeguarding individuals' rights and freedom and promoting overall balance and development of the society. Specifically, the main targets for solving the "three agriculture-related problems" include:

6.1.1 To Keep Stable of the Rural Society and Maintain Good Social Order

It has always been a goal actively pursued by the rulers and incumbent Chinese government to safeguard social stability and order. To the vast urban and rural people, social stability and good order are the guarantee for their living and working in peace and contentment, and therefore a goal actively pursued by them. From the perspective, whether to the ruler or the ruled, social stability and good order are the choice of consistent benefits. However, the issue is not so simple. In history, the ruler wanted the civilians to be obedient and create no trouble on one hand but victimized the civilians to the greatest extent on the other hand. They hardly realized that they were confronted with a pair of irreconcilable contractions. Therefore, the circulation of social stability-upheaval-revolution-stability in history has fully reflected the operation law of the pair of contradictions. When a new dynasty is established, as a result of starting from revolution, the rulers know deeply the civilians' sweetness, bitterness and power that cannot be ignored. Just like the saying goes, while water can carry a boat, it can also overturn it. The civilians are the water for the boat of the government. Also, the rulers need to honor their promise from the revolution period. Therefore, during this period, there are usually clear and bright politics as well as strict enforcement of orders and prohibitions to ensure the civilians living and working in peace and contentment and the society stable and prosperous. However, beautiful scenery usually does not last long. The process to maintain the operation of the ruler's autocracy always entails the potential factors of social turmoil caused by daily-increasing cost for the rule which usually leads to the issue of daily-increasing burden on the civilians. When the civilians' burden reaches a critical point, turmoil would begin. With the aggravation of the civilians' burden, the turmoil factors accumulated intensifies and finally leads to another revolution without doubt. The success of the revolution would generate a new generation of open-minded rulers. Such circulation represents a typical characteristic of autocratic society. Therefore, the rulers' goal for stability and the civilians' target for stability are different in the autocratic age. The social stability required by the rulers is the civilians' obedience without making any trouble while the stability pursued by the common people is the guarantee and safeguard of their rights and interests. Under the social background of civilization and democracy, as the rulers' function changes from regulating or controlling the people to serving the people and with more effective constraints over the rulers' power by the principle of contract, the targets for social stability from the rulers and the ruled become more and more consistent in terms of contents. In any event, social stability is a unanimous choice between the rulers and the ruled.

Although today's China cannot be deemed as an autocratic society, it still has a great distance from the basic requirements of modern democracy and civilization. This is especially true in rural areas of China where the residue of feudal autocracy still has certain living space. Therefore, we need to define the stability goal of solving the "three agriculture-related problems" by rule of law. Modern civilized society should undoubtedly be a society featuring supreme civil rights, and the government an institution serving the people and governing the society as entrusted by the people in accordance with the principle of contract. The trouble is that the role definition of government hasn't been well dealt with in real life and the strained relation between the government and civilians usually become a factor leading to instability. Therefore, in today's rural China, there mainly exist two factors leading to instability: the first includes such criminal activities as theft and robbery that affect the public social order; the second is the sharpening contradiction between the government and the farmers that causes political instability. Both of them would bring about negative effect on the social development of rural China and therefore need the regulation and coordination of the laws for radical cure of the problems. Therefore, to safeguard the social stability of rural areas in accordance with the law means to strengthen comprehensive treatment of social security issues in rural areas, and to prevent and fight crimes, especially the crimes of vicious power on the one hand; and regulate the government acts in accordance with the law, effectively constraint the government power and guarantee that the government power is put under efficient supervision of the people on the other hand. Only in this way, can the lowest level of value goal and order pursued by rule of law be realized in the rural society.

6.1.2 To Ensure the Smooth and Rapid Development of Rural Economy and Realize Social Efficiency

As a significant value goal of law, effectiveness should also be a value goal for solving the "three agriculture-related problems" by rule of law. Since economic base determines the superstructure, without sustainable and rapid development of rural economy, the solving of "three agriculture-related problems" by rule of law will lose solid material base. Moreover, the backward economy of rural areas is in itself an aspect of the "three agriculture-related problems". To safeguard sustainable and rapid development of rural society and economy by law means to safeguard effective implementation of agricultural industrialization and modernization as well as the strategy of promoting agriculture by applying scientific and technological advances through legal means. Industrialized operation of agriculture has been frequently emphasized by the economic circle but reaped little effect, and even gone to the extreme of moving towards the reverse side of its original intention. The model of "company plus farmer household" added another slaughter scar by the industry and commerce on the farmers' body already full of wound scars. It also plays a trick with the romantic hypothesis and model of economics. Then where is the issue? Is there any issue with the design of economics? It is also not right to be so assertive. We should let the fact speak for itself. Currently, our low level of agricultural industrialization is mainly represented by the following aspects: weak comprehensive competitiveness of the operating organization for industrialization; short production and manufacturing chain of agricultural products; and low level of farmers' system orientation. Therefore, in face of the existing characteristics from our farmer household like small scale, high level of decentralization, weak investment ability, backward operating means and methods, large population but few land in rural areas and the model of family operating as the main body, we mainly need to undertake the following tasks to safeguard agriculture industrialized operation in accordance with the law:

1. To establish rational administrative operating system by law. Firstly, we should construct the macro system, including the village self-governance system, rural economic development system and the like, especially the social security system. It is the key of agricultural industrialization and macro system orientation to ponder over how to guarantee the change of these systems from theory into reality, and therefore govern and affect the farmers' life at macro level. Secondly, we should build the micro system, including the system orientation of the government acts, the improvement of farmers' legal awareness and institutionalization of farmers' activities, especially the system orientation for constructing the associations. We need to comprehensively push forward the construction of micro system orientation of agricul-

tural industrialization based on the coordination and communication of all factors.

Our agriculture industrialized development has many problems caused by incomplete system. One good example is that the contradiction between the land circulating system and scale operation has not been effectively solved. The household contract responsibility system with remuneration linked to output represents a long-term basic policy of China for rural areas. The vast farmers have recognized and got used to such organization method of "small production". However, such method has serious conflicts with the scale economy of industrialized operation. One way to solve the issue is to learn from the principle of separation of two rights of the industrial development process, i.e., to transfer the operating right and overcome the inherent disadvantages of small production by concentration of operating rights in accordance with the principles of legality, willingness and compensation and based on zero change to the contracting right. However, we have encountered numerous difficulties and certain problems in actual operation. Therefore, it is of great necessity to explore a type of system and mechanism that can keep the farmers from trouble through which scale operation can be realized.

2. To safeguard the policy support in accordance with the law. In today's villages, most leading companies are in desperate need of financial assistance, for example, the preferential policies like support of credit funds, high line of credit and loan with low interest from Agricultural Development Bank. They also cry for national solutions for trans-regional operating. Since trans-province operating has such issues as multiple profit levels, complex operating procedures and huge market risk, relevant policies are required for corresponding support and coordination. Such support and coordination policies need legalization and standardization so that the policies won't be inconstant, the coordination of varied relations could be unified and such domestically regional barrier as "regional protectionism" that severely affects the sound operation of market economy could finally be eliminated.

3. To safeguard farmers' practical profits by law. In most places of China, the profit distribution mechanism of agriculture industrialized operation is inconsistent with the farmers' urgent need for becoming rich. Therefore, the farmers' profit cannot be guaranteed and the fundamental objective of agriculture industrialized operation is violated. During the operation under the "company plus farmer household", farmers have actually been thrown to the market unilaterally. Most of the farmers, especially those in the backward districts, feature blocking of information, low quality and weak risk-resisting ability. Therefore, they have no initiative in the industrialized operation since the prices of most agricultural products are actually determined by the company. The farmers can only swallow the "inarticulate misery" and cannot avoid being bullied in face of such circumstances as price gap (between the low price of agricultural products and high price of the pesticide and chemi-

cal fertilizer) and unfair competition. The issue of no guarantee for farmers' profit represents an important factor for the slow development and low quality of industrialized operation and unsmooth relationship between the company and farmers in some districts. It is a key link to actively develop the agriculture industrialized operation to establish scientific and reasonable profit distribution mechanism in accordance with the law. The development and maturity of agriculture industrialized operation will finally be dependent on the improvement and completion of its profit distribution mechanism.

4. To safeguard the establishment of varied specialized cooperative economy organizations in accordance with the law. Currently, the farmers' specialized cooperative economy organization remains at its initial stage owing to small cooperative scale, low level of production and management and lack of corresponding supporting policies from the government. The national policies for supporting the leading enterprises should also be vested to the farmers' specialized cooperative economy organization. The associations represent a transition and buffering zone between the government and the farmers and their activities are the indispensable links of varied rural undertakings. Through varied means like supervision and intermediary service, the associations can effectively coordinate the relationship between the government and the farmers and that between the farmers and the market so that the governmental policies can be implemented and farmers' enthusiasm be triggered. Especially when the existing governmental force is insufficient to guarantee the farmers' ability to take risks, the associations can form economic entities of certain scale, prevent and resist risks, supervise the government acts and have equal dialogue with the vendors.

5. To safeguard the construction of such soft environment as rural infrastructure hardware, education and technology by law. Infrastructure construction is indispensable for rapid development of rural economy. The construction of the infrastructure of road traffic, irrigation and water conservancy, warehousing and deposition, electric communication and the like cannot reap effect quickly by the farmers' own force. There must be input of financial resources. Besides, education and technology development falls into the category of public welfare establishments and therefore belongs to important tasks that should be undertaken by the government. To guarantee reasonable input of rural hardware and software construction, it is of great necessity to make laws for regulation and standardization so that the input method, scope and intensity of the government to rural areas as well as regional balance can be standardized and systemized, that the disadvantages of contrived unfairness and insufficient investment caused by government arbitrary acts can be decreased and rural economy can develop rapidly.

6.1.3 To Secure Coordinated Development and Realize Social Equality

To safeguard coordinated development between urban and rural areas, we should first increase the government input to rural areas. The transitional plunder of cities to villages caused by the long-term industrialization has led to shortage of due material base for varied aspects of rural infrastructure and economic development. Therefore, the government should increase its investment intensity to the village. It is passive and of no guarantee to depend on the government mood or repentance for more input to rural areas. There must be corresponding laws for guarantee.

The unbalance of urban and rural tax and fee burden has increased the difference between urban and rural areas and deteriorated rural contradictions. We are in urgent need of planning as a whole the urban and rural taxes by law. For a long time, the increase speed of agricultural tax is higher than that of farmers' income as shown in Table 3. During 1990-1996, the national fiscal revenue has increased by 144%, including the increase of 285% from the revenue of national agriculture tax. While the proportion of agricultural output in gross national output is continuously decreasing, the proportions of national agriculture revenue in national fiscal revenue and tax revenue are climbing constantly. A comparison example is that our national rural per capita net income is RMB 686.31 in 1990 and RMB 1,926.07 in 1996, with an increase of 180.64%. The increase is also lower than that of 285% of agricultural tax. Therefore, an overhaul is necessary for tax legislation.

In 2004, Premiere Wen Jiabao promised to cancel the tax on agricultural specialty products and gradually decrease and cancel the agricultural tax in

Table 6.1. Proportions of Agricultural Tax in National Revenue Tax and Fiscal Revenue (Unit: RMB 100 million)

Year	National Revenue Tax	Agricultural Tax	Proportion of Agricultural Tax in National Revenue Tax (%)	Proportion of Agricultural Tax in National Fiscal Revenue (%)
1990	2821.86	87.86	3.11	2.7
1991	2990.17	90.65	3.03	2.5
1992	3296.91	119.17	2.88	2.9
1993	4255.30	125.74	2.27	2.5
1994	5126.88	231.49	4.06	4.4
1995	6038.04	278.09	4.60	4.4
1996	6901.35	338.76	4.91	5.2

Data source: *China Rural Statistical Yearbook (1997)*, P39.

five years. This is just a primary goal. The final goal for planning and coordinating urban and rural taxes is to establish the single-tax system with only individual income tax. The existing tax collection and management laws and regulations need to be integrated to guarantee the realization of this goal. The realization of single-tax system represents a key link to promote coordinated development between urban and rural areas and to realize social fairness.

Besides the urban and rural inequality of government input and tax and fees burden, rural laborers' social treatments increasingly become a serious social issue in real life. It starts to show not only unfairness to rural laborer but also disadvantage to overall development of the country. The issue has greatly hindered rural labors' normal flowing and integrating to the urban society and suppressed rural laborers' enthusiasm to improve their own ability. Currently, the number of rural labors has exceeded that of urban workers. The rural labors have become the main body of workers. If we fail to solve the issue of their social treatment, the worker group will not only have difficulty in becoming the "leading stratum" domestically, but also losing due competitiveness internationally. From the perspective of "three agriculture-related problems", if we cannot find good solution to the issue of rural labors' social treatment, we cannot find fundamental solution to the "three agriculture-related problems". Since the rural labors cannot receive their due social treatment in cities, they can only continually contribute their youth and reap low remuneration which is sufficient only for their expenditures of family life and production in villages without much left for developing their own career.[3]

To safeguard coordinated development between urban and rural areas by law represents a precondition for promoting the whole society to form a positive operation mechanism. Practice has proved that the expansion of difference between urban and rural areas will have certain help to speed up urban development in short period, but will have more obvious side effect in long period which would greatly delay the rapid development of the whole society. One of the goal to solve "three agriculture-related problems" by law is to coordinate urban and rural development and try our best to avoid artificial widening of the gap so as to realize overall fairness of the society.

6.1.4 To Safeguard the Right and Freedom of the Farmers and Realize Social Justice

The discussion about the standard for justice should share a common knowledge whether in typical capitalist country or socialist China which is "human's freedom and all-round development of society". Of this, the guarantee of human's freedom is the most fundamental and all-round development of society the idealist. The core of Chinese "three agriculture-related problems" is the farmers, with the issue of guaranteeing farmers' rights as the priority.

We are currently facing the reality of great worries for farmers' freedom and rights. For this, only by guaranteeing farmers' rights and freedom by law, can we realize social fairness in real sense.

1. Safeguard Farmers' Personal Rights and Freedom by Law

In defending themselves against the allegation for violating farmers' rights, the governments at the grassroots level usually take the incomplete legal system as shield. As a matter of fact, although our legislation does have many loopholes and need further improvement, the *Constitution* has already given specific stipulations on farmers' basic rights. The issue is that the grassroots-level governments always fail to treat farmers as the citizens or the subject of social relationship. Instead, they treat farmers as the object of social relationship and of control and regulation. Therefore, farmers' act to fight for their rights and freedom is naturally deemed as the act by "unruly people". To solve the "three agriculture-related problems", we must first eliminate such power consciousness of "theory of farmers as object" and the leading cadres at different levels should establish the thought of people orientation. Otherwise, the farmers' rights and freedom would not be guaranteed and the goal of solving "three agriculture-related problems" by law could not be realized. This involves an issue of relationship between the managing power and safeguarding power. The managing power means the managing officials' power. We should clearly define the scope, method, duty, supervision etc. of administrative power so that it can be exercised in accordance with the law and people's willingness and abuse of power and corruption can be prevented. Safeguarding power means the power for safeguarding the people, especially the weak group of farmers. The society, including the government, should provide more support and assistance to farmers. The managing power represents the means and measures while the safeguarding power represents the target and result.

To safeguard farmers' rights and freedom is not a luxury goal of solving the "three agriculture-related problems" by law but one of the most basic goals and the bottom requirement of a society under rule of law. We should specially define the following contents at present stage:

(1) Farmers' right of personal liberty.

No guarantee for farmers' right of personal liberty is both an expression and consequence of the "three agriculture-related problems". Currently, attention should be paid to one thing that most of the acts violating farmers' personal rights originate from direct conflict between the grassroots-level government and farmers. Farmers are beat, scolded, put in confinement or illegally interrogated due to failure to pay the tax and fee as required. They are also hit and taken revenge on because of their report about farmers' heavy burden, disclosure of corruption from the grassroots-level government.

Sometimes the grassroots-level governments even join hands with the vicious power to bully and oppress the common people. All these cry for greater intensity of managing power and safeguarding power. The managing power means the managing officials' power. The administrative power of local governments must be exercised within the scope of law and the law must clearly define the contents, methods and procedures of government acts. To those without clear authorization by the law, local governments cannot have any act involving violation to farmers' personal rights and freedom at will. In practice, serious violation to farmers' personal rights caused by farmers' breach of family planning occurs frequently and originates from incorrect concept of political achievements and weak legal awareness from local governments.

(2) Farmers' right of free migration.

This is one of the most basic rights to liberate the farmers. The key is to reform the household system so that the farmers can enter into cities and have the same treatment as the citizens. Pilot projects for farmers to become citizens after entering into cities have already achieved success in some places. Free migration is not just an issue for farmers entering into cities. In rural areas, farmers migrating from one place to another place have to deal with the household system and social security issues, and the essence of the issue lies not in migrating or not, but in the right safeguarding issue caused by migration. For the case of claiming for compensation for land acquisition by Zhou Yuanlan from Guixi, Jiangxi, the court actually gave the final judgment of no support for the plaintiff's request for the reason that the land compensation allocation plan formulated by the defendant, Xiangshan villagers committee, goes against the national land administrative law and relevant enforcement regulations and therefore should be deemed as invalid, and the reason that the plaintiff's request for the defendant to allocate the due land compensation is inconsistent with relevant regulations of national land administrative law. It happens that there is a similar case. Jiang Ling (alias) from another group of the same village who was unmarried was awarded with the judgment by the court that she was divorced and would be deprived of the right to the land compensation. The reason for her final judgment is the same as that for Zhou Yuanlan. Now that "the land compensation allocation plan formulated by the defendant, Xiangshan Villagers Committee, goes against the national land administrative law and relevant enforcement regulations and therefore should be deemed as invalid."[4] Why do not instruct relevant people to amend it? Does it mean that the "unlawful act" will succeed under the excuse of "beyond the scope of this case"? Will you just leave the legitimate right unprotected? To vest the farmers with free right to migrate, we should practically implement measures for relevant living security for the farmers.

(3) Farmers' valid right of relief.

How rare the channels for farmers to seek for relief! People always attribute the lack of protection for farmers' rights to the farmers' little legal awareness and habit of seeking for relief outside the scope of law. It cannot be denied that such attribution has certain base. But once the farmers awaken and resort to legal channel or other "official" channel, what would the result be? Being rebuffed repeatedly has undoubtedly given a head-on blow on the legal awareness that is just awakened. The first is the judicial remedy. Without independent justice, such relief channel for farmers would impossibly be smooth. The second is the administrative relief. Mr. Sun Dawu from Dawu Group has keenly felt the pain, "Dawu Group has occupied over 100 hectares of land for plants, the right to use of which was obtained in 1985. After constructing a pig farm and chicken farm, the town government demanded RMB 10,000. Dawu didn't pay the money and reported it to the county government. The county government demanded RMB 50,000. Dawu didn't pay the money again and reported it to the Land Administration Bureau of Baoding City. The Land Administration Bureau of Baoding City demanded 100,000 and claimed to bulldoze Dawu Group otherwise." The channel is blocked. One channel may lead to encirclement, pursuit, obstruction, interception or even fatal disaster, but provides one ray of hope. That is to appeal for help in Beijing (Do not get me wrong. My original intention is not instigating farmers for petitioning in Beijing, which I set myself against). The authorities in many places have the habit of dealing with affairs in accordance with the official reply from the higher authority rather than the law. Therefore, the rare relief channels for farmers constitute one of the main reasons that farmers choose non-legal channel for relief.

To guarantee farmers' right to seek for effective relief channel represents a procedural requirement to guarantee each of the farmers' rights. The realization of farmers' substantial rights and guarantee of their procedural rights complement each other. Without the regulations for substantial rights, safeguarding farmer's right would become water without source; and without the safeguarding of procedural rights, the regulations of substantial rights would become a mere scrap of paper. It is of great necessity to provide corresponding legislation to punish those who retaliate, illegally disturb or shift responsibility onto others in case of farmers' relief so as to guarantee unblocked channel for the farmers to seek for relief.

2. Safeguard Farmers' Property Right and Freedom

(1) Complete property right

The farmers' property right is not complete. What property can farmers have? Their property includes nothing but the land, house and agricultural products. Most farmers have measly share of other properties. The first is the land. Since the farmers have no ownership, their land property right is incomplete. The second is the house. Farmers have the ownership of the house but no proprietorship to the house site. It is like a castle in the air. Now that the law stipulates that when farmers transfer their houses, they would transfer the proprietorship of their house sites at the same time. Why not just provide farmers with complete property right? It is so troublesome. Therefore, it is of great importance for the legislation to endow farmers with property right to their contracted land and house sites.

(2) Right to know about their obligations

No right to know about their obligations or no channel for dialogue leads to disappearance of farmers' assets without good reason. It is an important measure for safeguarding farmers' property right to safeguard farmers' right to know about their own obligations and to request hearing for those taxes and fees in doubt.

(3) Right of freedom for economic activities

Farmers' freedom of economic activities is faced with the risk of being violated. How to develop rural economy fast has also become a heart disease of the government because of the low efficiency of rural economy, heavy burdens for farmers and increasingly sharp contradiction between the officers and farmers. Therefore, some local governments, out of kindness, forced the farmers to implement unified production plan at large scale in accordance with the development plan for rural economy formulated by the governments themselves. The result is that good deed reaps no good outcome and on the contrary aggravates the contradiction between officers and farmers.

Farmers have the right to freely engage in some producing and operating activities which shall not be deprived or violated. The government influence exerted on rural economy based on macro control can only adjust, but not violently interfere with farmers' production and operating by legally applying such economic leverages as finance, tax, banking and price etc. Farmer's right of production and operating shall be guaranteed by the *Constitution*. In the citizens' basic rights and obligations, there should be the right to participate in economic activities. Corresponding laws and regulations to safeguard farmers' rights and interest should clearly specify the farmer's decision-making right for their production and operating.

3. Farmers' right of equality

"In accordance with the principle of fairness, it is impossible to undertake obligations for unjust system, or at least impossible for the system of injustice beyond people's tolerance (there hasn't been any regulation about it yet). It is especially impossible to undertake obligations for autocratic government system."[5] To safeguard farmers' right of equality is to change farmers from the long-term role as subject of obligation to the role as subject of right so that farmers can enjoy the rights and freedom equivalent with those of urban resident and the right to confront illegal administration of the government.

(1) Equal right in market transaction

It can be said that the current market transaction rules still contain discrimination against the farmers. As China needs to develop the industry and realize industrialization, the investments to the industry and agriculture are obviously unequal and unfair. Greater investment to the industry always accompanies greater deprivation from the agriculture. Originally, the agriculture should be endowed with national subsidy. However, in practice, our subsidy to the agriculture is of negative value as the subsidy is far less than the deprivation. The price of industrial products is far higher than the price of agricultural products with the same labor. The natural law of market is acceptable but the artificial inequality must be corrected. The unified purchase and sales of agricultural products mean protection and subsidy when the purchase price is higher than the market price. Otherwise they mean exploitation and deprivation, which is the artificial unfairness caused by government acts. Regional protectionism also means tread on the equal right of market transaction. Today's regional protectionism in the agriculture-related area is reflected by the local governments controlling the price of farm inputs and domestic "foreign trade" (trans-regional trade). The trade involving agriculture and other industries should be controlled and regulated by corresponding legislation so as to block the back door of local protectionism and monopoly of administrative inappropriateness and therefore guarantee fair trade.

(2) Equal right to social security

The social security here is of broad sense. It includes the government investment to the agriculture, compensation to the unavoidable loss caused by such factors as natural disaster, as well as the construction and improvement of such security items as rural education, medical care and pension. For a long time, there are many reasons for the failure of constructing a legal system for social security in rural areas. This is inseparable from the deviation of the government guiding thoughts which hold that farmer's life could be guaranteed with the right to use the land and social security is unnecessary. As a matter of fact, farmers are the one with the least security. To construct rural social security system by law means significant guarantee for farmer's living and working in peace and contentment, rural stability and efficient development of agriculture.

6.2 PRINCIPLES OF SOLVING "THREE AGRICULTURE-RELATED PROBLEMS" BY RULE OF LAW

To realize the goal of solving the "three agriculture-related problems" by rule of law and deal with relevant issues, the following principles must be followed:

6.2.1 Principle of Supreme and Absolute Authority of State Law

The authority of state laws is emphasized here mainly for the fever for research of "folk laws"[6] in recent years from the educational circle, especially the educational circle of law. The "folk law" of rural society exists and plays certain role without doubt. The social function believers advocating "folk laws" think that, from the perspective of legal principle, the village regulation and non-governmental agreement embedded deeply in the rural society order fall into the category of folk customary law corresponding with the national law. The law undoubtedly represents regulations that the whole society should observe. The law as social regulations should be interpreted as the law of broad sense and therefore should include both the official law and the effective customary laws like the village regulation and non-governmental agreement, customs and common practices from the folk.[7] For example, as to the illicit cohabitation phenomenon of "having a concubine" that is increasingly serious and almost going to out of control, "folk laws" embark upon a political venture and seem to have played certain role. As reported by *Southern Daily* on May 31, 2000, to punish the husband "having a concubine" and safeguard the legitimate rights and interests for women, some villages in Baiyun District of Guangzhou formulated the village regulation and non-governmental agreement that all villagers with bigamy or illicit cohabitation acts divorcing their ligatured spouses will have their share transferred to their original spouse. Such village regulation and non-governmental agreement basically belongs to a kind of folk customary laws with the binding force of morality and public opinion rather than legal binding force and nature of punishment. That is to say, such village regulation and non-governmental agreement can be adopted as admitted evidence when the parties involved are negotiating or the court is mediating a divorce. However, when making a judgment for divorce, the court in principle cannot adopt such village regulation as the base for application of law. As a matter of fact, while dividing the joint assets, the judge usually shows more care to the female party without fault.

Today when we are accelerating the legal construction, we cannot entirely deny the value of "folk laws". Nor can we raise their position to the equal level of "state laws". The reasons are quite simple. The first is the procedural issue. The state laws of modern civilized society should be formed in accordance with the concept and procedure of democracy and republicanism, and therefore embody the common willingness from the overwhelming majority of people of a country and have the characteristic of universality. Any act or rule that denies their universality should go through corresponding procedures. That is to say, if the state laws have an issue or are disjointed with practices and the application of certain "folk law" is more consistent with the spirit of rule of law, we should revise the existing law through legal procedures. There is no need for multiple departments to issue different laws which would lead to people's confusion. The second is the issue of legal effect. The state laws are safeguarded by coercive force of the state and recognized by the overwhelming majority of the people from one country. While the folk law represents the common knowledge of just a small scope of people without any coercive force or just the coerce from individual force. The danger is that there might be confusion of standards. As a result, either the people become more closed or the whole society shows serious unfairness and disorder. Therefore, while handling the relationship between state laws and "folk laws", it is necessary to emphasize the absolute authority of state laws. When the "folk laws" do not conflict with the national mandatory law and the parties involved do not resort to the state laws for judgment, it would not be a bad thing to let "folk laws" play certain role and realize the positive effect of complementing the shortage of state laws. Otherwise, the "folk laws" should abdicate for the sake of state laws.

To solve the "three agriculture-related problems" by law, it is particularly important to emphasize and stick to the principle as the main battlefield of "folk laws" is the rural areas, especially the poor and backward rural areas. Too much emphasis on the role of "folk laws" means only retrogress and would be unfavorable for the social and economic development as well as the improvement of farmers' cultural quality in rural areas. It may also lead to the failure of solving the "three agriculture-related problems".

Moreover, the absolute authority of state laws is emphasized also for the administrative order, measure and enforcement. In rural areas, today's administrative order shows the trend of replacing the law. A meeting of the Central government, a notice from the provincial government, a call from the county government, a town government officer stationed in the village—these have basically become a fixed model for current administration. On the administrative chain, we cannot see the any involvement of the law. The Central government will deliver the "spirit" to the provincial government, the latter, after receiving the "spirit", will issue a notice to the city or county. The city and county governments are the final recipient of administrative paper order, as they will not forward the paper documents to the lower government. Instead, they will give instruction by call to the township government, and the later will implement the order. But how? A call to the village government won't play much role. Moreover, the orders are usually "dead orders" that need to be "handled under supervision" immediately. The town government officers will have to station at the village. Under special circumstance, the county or provincial government officers will also need to station at the village. The whole administrative system is disassociated with rule of law. The inside supervision is powerless and outside supervision out of the question. It is natural for the policies to shrink and deform, and sometimes become totally different, during the process. In countries with high level of democracy and legalization, the issuance of government decree usually need deliberation or re-deliberation by the congress or parliament so as to ensure that the decree is in consistent with the *Constitution* and people's willingness. China seems to have the deliberation process too since the NPC regular meeting of each year needs to review the work report of all main bodies of the country. However, most of the process is just going through the motions. We haven't seen any not-passed report yet. This doesn't mean that our political decrees are much better than that of other countries. Instead, it just means that we do not have the organization check and supervision that can say "No". For the deregulation for administration, it is very important to emphasize the authority and role of state laws in the agriculture-related administration. All political decrees must pass legal procedures by the organ of authority before their implementation. Moreover, the whole process of implementation must be carried out within the scope of the law and under the supervision of the public.

6.2.2 Principle of Safeguarding the Equal Right of the Farmers

It is a fundamental principle for a country under rule of law that all people are equal before the law. It is also the so-called basic principle of law. It is of great practical significance, rather than just simple repetition, to propose the guarantee of farmers' right of equality as a basic principle for solving the "three agriculture-related problems" by law. On the whole, farmers' rights at present are still defective and incomplete. Compared with other subjects of the society, farmers are more in shortage of the right of equality. The lack of farmers' right of equality has become a great barrier for villages and farmers to walk into the market economy. Therefore, utilizing the law to guarantee farmers' right of equality can not only show the care of modern democratic society to farmers, but also represent the basic requirement to construct a socialist country under rule of law.

The first is the legal safeguard issue concerning farmers' political right of equality. Our farmers have huge difference with urban citizens in terms of the occupation of actual political rights and interest-expressing mechanism. Such difference can be seen from the laws too. Of all previous NPC members, the share of farmers is quite out of proportion in terms of the fact that farmers take up over 80% of the whole population. Even based on the "861" theoretical model design, the hypothesis that rural population accounts for 80% and urban population 20%, the rural representative should take up 33.3%, which is also very different from the actual number. If taking into account the fact that the non-farmer representative can also represent the farmers' interests, the phenomenon would seem to be understandable. However, in this way, it would be of no significance to specify the different numbers of population represented by each rural and urban representative.[8] Under the market economy, we should gradually abolish the laws and regulations showing inequality of farmer's political rights. Although farmers may not have the ability to fully exercise their democratic rights for such factors as disposing capacity, no law shall contain any article of inequality for such factor.

The second is the legal safeguard issue of farmer's economic right of equality. Since the implementation of market economic system, the urban and rural income gap shows the trend of continuous expansion. Undoubtedly there are many aspects of reasons for the income gap. However, the lack of farmers' economic right of equality represents an important aspect without doubt. After the founding of PRC, our national investment to the agriculture is decreasing year by year. It was 10% of all national investment during the "sixth five-year plan" period, 5% during the "seventh five-year plan" period, 2.2% in 1993 and 1.9% in 1994, which was only about 13% of the investment to real estate from the state-owned enterprise during the same period. Most of the agricultural investment for water conservancy was used for solving the issue of urban and industrial water.[9] At present when we are implementing the system of socialist market economy, we should overweight the village and farmer in terms of macro distribution of resources to return the great contribution that farmers made to socialist construction and support the congenitally deficient farmers to participate in the market competition.

The third is the equal right to social security. The urban residents have always enjoyed "high employment rate, good welfare and high subsidy", and the State has provided urban citizens with varied kinds of social security valuing at tens to hundreds of billion Yuan. Urban citizens can enjoy various kinds of social welfare like retirement insurance and the lowest living security. However, in rural areas, only small numbers of poor people enjoy slender social relief.

If the vast farmers cannot enjoy de facto right of equality like the urban residents in political, economic, social and cultural life. The "special civics" will definitely have the sense of inequality as time passes. This will affect their identification with the government and even creates estrangement and contradiction which would be unfavorable for social stability and development. The urban and rural gap is caused by history, but it is after all an important goal of socialism to narrow and even eliminate the gap. Given the long-term "blood drawing" by the city from the village, the condition that the village has been more backward than the city for a long time and the fact that it is impossible to change the backwardness of the village and realize farmers' right of equality only through the natural development of the village, we must politically support farmers to actively participate in national life, economically support the farmers and legally affirm farmers' right of equality.

6.2.3 Principle of Assuring the Litigation Rights of the Farmers

The most important part for the goal of solving the "three agriculture-related problems" lies in safeguarding farmer's rights. When farmer's right is infringed, it becomes a key for realizing the goal of solving the "three agriculture-related problems" by law to find way to ensure that farmers can effectively exercise their litigation right. It is of great practical significance to put forward farmer's full exercise of their litigation right as a basic principle.

After examining the status quo of the "three agriculture-related problems", we will find that the fundamental issue of "three agriculture-related problems" lies in serious infringement of farmer's right and lack of channel for appealing after the infringement, which leads to exacerbation of the problems. The people applying for an audience with the higher authorities may directly go to Beijing. This shows that the people with the farmers as the main body have suffered too much unjust treatment and that farmers lack the channel for appealing. According to the textbook, the relief channels for people's rights are of wide range, including self-relief methods like negotiation and compromise among parties involved; folk relief measures like mediation by such a third party as the clan leader, village head and other people with high prestige; administrative relief measures like asking for assistance for solving issues from relevant administrative organizations; and judicial remedy measures like lawsuit. The textbook also tells us clearly that the judicial remedy is the most effective and the final relief of all channels. All the theory from the textbook should endure the test of practices. Currently, in China, no channel for relief of farmers' right is smooth. This is especially true when there emerges the contraction between the government and farmers and the dispute of government infringing farmers' rights and interests. Under such circumstance, there is nothing but two kinds of effective relief methods: administrative relief and judicial remedy. The administrative relief usually means to resort to the superior level of the administrative organization for solutions. In the land utilizing right case for Dawu Group from Hebei, the increase of fee collection step by step by the three levels of administrative organizations ranging from the village land office to the city land board represents undoubtedly a kind of colluded and consistent door-closing for the channel of farmers' administrative relief. Since the judicial remedy is the most effective and the final relief, the farmers may file a lawsuit directly. However, the reality is cruel. The judicial system is subject to the administrative system and the farmers are just "putting their necks into the noose". Wang Junbin, Wang Xiangdong and Wang Hongchao's bitter experience as described by Chen Guidi, i.e., suffering from judicial persecution after seeking for judicial remedy, is suffice to terrify farmers who want to seek for judicial remedy.[10] Therefore, it is undoubtedly of great significance for solving the "three agriculture-related problems" through relief channels to stick to the principle of safeguarding farmers' full exercise of the litigation right. How to ensure that? The answer is that the judicial is really independent and under efficient supervision of the public.

6.2.4 Principle of Comprehensive Management

The emphasis on solving the "three agriculture-related problems" by rule of law doesn't mean the exclusion of other management measures. On the contrary, solving the "three agriculture-related problems" by rule of law is a measure of comprehensive management. In the whole project system of solving the "three agriculture-related problems" by law, the key is to constraint and standardize the administrative acts of the government. This is also the key of rule of law as the proposal of the thought of rule of law aims at restricting the government power and safeguarding the right of civil liberty.[11] The governmental power is entrusted by the public rather than "charismatic" or inherent. People's rights are not congenital either, but from the social life and required by peaceful coexistence and continuous progress for humans. Di Ji commented on "man's natural right" as follows: Rousseau's social contract theory is just a set of sophistry covered with beautiful coat of language at best. People cannot naturally obtain some natural right for the reason that they are just a social being. If people enjoy some rights, the rights can only come from the social environment that they live in. They cannot turn upside down to have their own rights override the society. He also makes wonderful discussion about the government power as follows: to the economic organization of modern society, what a country needs is no longer just the right to give order, but to fulfill the required obligations. The power of a country has a limit which is the minimum value required for them to fulfill obligations. The functions that they must fulfill constitute the government affairs on the whole.[12] By this token, rights are determined by the society. However, rights involve the issue of corruption. The public of a society and the persons in power shall have check and balance for power themselves.[13] What channels can the public of a society and the persons in power adopted for realizing check and balance of power? The rule of law can naturally undertake the task in the most appropriate way. It can have the government power within the scope of the constitution, laws and regulations to avoid act beyond one's authority or abuse of power. It can also define the rights of the public in the form of law and specify the liability for tort so that the rights of the public can be safeguarded. While limiting the government power and safeguarding the rights of the public, we will comprehensively utilize the civil, criminal, economic, administrative and other adjustment and regulation methods to form a three-dimensional network of managing power and safeguarding power.

In modern society, things won't work without rule of law, but the rule of law is also not all-powerful. To ensure the realization of the goal of solving the "three agriculture-related problems" by law, we need the cooperation from other measures and standard modes. For example, we can use the power of traditional morality to regulate social activities in rural areas. However, just like the law distinguishes the good and evil, the morality also makes a distinction between the high and low morality. Edifying people with high morality can make the world more orderly and the implementation of rule of law more effective. Utilizing scientific means of economy and management to promote rapid development of rural economy and increase farmers' income will also lay solid material foundation for solving the "three agriculture-related problems" by law.

It is necessary and urgent to develop education and promote technology in terms of both the farmers' own master of knowledge, search for new path to fortune and the economic development of the village and the country as a whole in the long term. The improvement of farmers' quality is essential to the effect of solving the "three agriculture-related problems" by law. People always say that the law is made by people and to be observed and enforced by people. Such words have been used by some people advocating rule of man with ulterior motives. However, they make sense to a certain extent. "People first" is a basic requirement for rule of law. The popularization of law and promotion of rule of law are in themselves a project to improve people's quality.

6.3 STEPS OF SOLVING "THREE AGRICULTURE-RELATED PROBLEMS" BY RULE OF LAW

Currently the cultural background and reality of backwardness in rural areas have all determined that the development of rule of law in rural areas cannot be synchronized with city. In accordance with the blueprint for overall construction of a moderately prosperous society, rule of law in rural areas needs to be implemented by stages and steps.

6.3.1 Stage of Separated Regulation in Urban Area and Rural Area

The separated regulation here doesn't mean to isolate the connection of rule-of-law between the urban and rural areas. On the contrary, the uniformity of rule of law determines that it is impossible to implement different legal systems and ideas of rule of law in the urban and rural areas. The separated regulation here mainly emphasizes that in face of the shortage of existing rule-of-law resources, we need to increase our input to rural areas in terms of specific administration measures, especially the supply of resources. The task is mainly for governmental macroeconomic regulation and control. It means that the government should increase its inclination to rural areas in terms of the allocation of rule-of-law resources at the stage.

Given the economically separated regulation for urban and rural areas and the reality of urban and rural gap, we need a long time to promote cultural education, economic development, social security and legal remedy through governmental input, policy guidance and legal safeguard so as to really enhance farmers' legal status and consciousness of right, farmers' overall cultural quality, organizational degree and self-governance capability. At the present stage, we need to lay emphasis on the publication and transplant of western rule-of-law culture, and fully exploit and creatively transform the beneficial resources of the traditional culture from the villages themselves. For example, we can improve the system of self-governance of villagers so that the villagers committee can really become the organization representing farmers' interests and featuring villagers' self-governance and self-service. We need to impact, disorganize and replace the traditional ethnic with modern legal systems. Of course, the stage will also be a stage when Chinese rural economy entirely walks into market orientation and internationalization. We also need to improve corresponding agriculture economic and legal systems. Special attention should be paid to improve the legislation for such matters as agriculture economic macro-control, agricultural product trade, utilization of foreign investment for agriculture, rural market access, agriculture technical information and social security in rural areas.

6.3.2 Stage of Coordinated Development in Urban Area and Rural Area

At this stage, the urbanization development of rural areas will enter into climax and the pattern of separated regulation for urban and rural areas will be broken. The rural population will flow into cities at large amount. Correspondingly, in terms of rule-of-law, we need to provide legal safeguard for the urbanization development and ecological environment protection in rural areas and try best to eliminate the obstacle for urbanization development. Coordinated development of urban and rural rule-of-law is still based on separated regulation for urban and rural areas. The development of rule of law needs to take into consideration both urban and rural requirements, and gradually narrow urban and rural gap so as to pave the way for the urbanization development in rural areas.

6.3.3 Stage of Integrated Development in Urban Area and Rural Area

At this stage, there will be no gap between the urban and rural areas. Rural rule-of-law no longer has its particularity except for its special industrial distinction and geological environment. Of course, the village, agriculture and farmers will continuously exist and rural rule-of-law will also play greater role for promoting rural development and prosperity and safeguarding farmers' rights and interests.[14]

6.4 CONTENT SYSTEM OF SOLVING "THREE AGRICULTURE-RELATED PROBLEMS" BY RULE OF LAW

Solving the "three agriculture-related problems" by law represents a systematic project, the main contents of which include:

6.4.1 Legislation for "Three Agriculture-related Problems"

We need to improve the legislative system for the "three agriculture-related problems", including the legislative subject and procedures, legal form and content hierarchy to reflect people's willingness.

The first is the legislative subject. In broad sense, the legislative subject is the public. However, to enable the public individual become actual legislative subject, we need to start with the link of introducing the bill. Who has the right to introduce the bill? The *Legislative Law* specifies that the basic laws shall be deliberated and passed by NPC (National People's Congress). Those that can be directly submitted to NPC for deliberation are the bills of act from the presidium. The bills of act from the Standing Committee of NPC, the State Council, the Central Military Commission, the Supreme Judicial Court, the Supreme People's Procuratorate and each special committee of NPC will be listed on the conference agenda after the decision by the presidium. The bill of act proposed by a delegation or jointly by over thirty representatives will be determined whether to be included on the conference agenda by the presidium; or be submitted to relevant special committee for deliberation and determined whether to be included on the conference agenda after the proposal of opinion about whether to be included on the conference agenda. The proposal, deliberation and voting procedures for the bills of act for the regulations of local governments, rules and regulations of the State Council departments, autonomous regulations and specific regulations, local laws and regulations, administrative regulations and laws to be deliberated by the Standing Committee of NPC shall follow the above-mentioned regulations. Due to the lack of flexibility, many obsolete laws cannot be abolished or modified timely and the legislation pace is slow. The abolishing of *Meas-*

ures for Taking in and Sending Back Urban Tramps and Beggars features the fastest response. However, it has also suffered from numerous twists and turns and caused great influence before it was finally submitted to relevant department for deliberation and abolishing. The channels for proposing the bill shall be smooth so that the legislative institutions can practically master and timely show feedback for the legislation suggestions and requirements of the public. The legislation for the "three agriculture-related problems" shall directly summarize the suggestions and requirements of the vast farmers.

The second is the legislative procedure. The key for determining whether a law has fully reflected people's willingness lies in the whole process ranging from proposing the bill of act, from forming the draft of law to the passing of deliberation. Of the whole process, the discussion and modification of the draft is the most important. The substantial content of law shall be determined by the public and the technical content checked by legal experts. The whole process should resolutely remove the old situation in which an individual or some individuals from the government or other organs of political power has or have the say or even hides or hide the truth from the masses so as to really return the legislative power to people. The draft for the legislation of "three agriculture-related problems" should be fully discussed by the farmers rather than just go through formalities. As to the link of legislative procedure, it is quite urgent to establish a constitutional review system with material meaning. The constitutionality of each law and regulation shall all be specially reviewed before the law and regulation takes effect.

The manifestation for the legislation of "three agriculture-related problems" shall be an in-depth and comprehensive one: 1. The *Constitution* should fully reflect the care for farmers' interests. The Constitution revised in 2004 involves farmers' interests in such aspects as land system, private property protection, status of private economy and human right protection and has certain innovation. However, it always gives people a feeling of dodge evasion, fails to fully reflect real willingness of the people, and especially fails to fundamentally solve the issue of farmland ownership. 2. The basic laws should contain special basic laws for the "three agriculture-related problems" to specify each farmer's right rather than simply repeat the existing empty laws and regulations. For example, the issues of farmland ownership, village self-governance, agricultural input, farmers' burden, farmers' social security, relief channels for farmers' right and the like need special regulations for protection. 3. The administrative laws and regulations related with "three agriculture-related problems" need trimming and neatening. The numerous administrative rules and regulations related with agriculture need trimming and neatening to avoid repetition, chaos and different regulations for the same thing from different departments. 4. Local and self-government laws and regulations related with agriculture need to lay emphasis on real effect. Our existing condition is that one law corresponds to one local regulation, and there are regulations for each level ranging from the province to the city, the county and township. Most of them are mechanical and repeated and only few shows real effect. There is no need for local regulations at all for those have been clearly specified by the law. Concision and pertinence are also required for the amendment to the regulations in accordance with local reality.

The manifestation for the above-mentioned legislation shows a distribution of pyramid. The pyramid spire features the highest efficiency and least amount of contents. It seems like that people usually have a thinking set. They usually think that constitution is the basic law of a country and should therefore be more principle-oriented. Those laws of lower levels will involve specific implementation and therefore have more contents. As a matter of fact, such kind of thinking set has no scientific bases. Be it the constitution and local regulations, the number of articles doesn't represent the level of efficiency. If the constitution of a country cannot even cover the most basic rights of people, what kind of constitution can it be named as? Such constitution would become furnishing and decoration. It will just provide a disguise for the expansion of administrative right. It is the purpose of the constitution to specify the basic civil rights. Some scholars propose that our constitution should at least extend the following ten civil rights: the right to exist, property right, environmental right, and right of development, right to know, right of privacy, freedom to economy, freedom to migration, right of equality and right to a fair trial.[15] Why cannot these practical suggestions from the people be included in the policy making procedures? The contents of constitution are usually divided into two parts: the first is to standardize and limit the power of the state; and the second is to protect the basic rights for civics.[16] However, we can hardly see the way that the constitution revision adopted to limit the power of the country. Instead, what we see is the "shyness" on the protection of basic rights for civics. The origin of the "three agriculture-related problems" can be traced back to the unsound constitution in China.

6.4.2 Judicial Enforcement of "Three Agriculture-related Problems"

The miscarriage of justice is especially serious in rural areas and the miscarriage of justice in rural areas is reflected in a concentrated way in the dispute between farmers and government. The abuse of power and ultra vires of executive law enforcement related with "three agriculture-related problems" have reached a limit in recent years. Often only when the Central government "gets angry", will the relevant authority intensify the management for a while. However, things may immediately become more serious later. Take the farmers' burden as an example. Each time when the Central government made the decision to decrease the burden, the farmers' burden would become heavier. Premier Wen call it the "strange cycle of Huang Zongxi". What once seemed bewildering will no longer be so. As the root cause of illness is not eliminated, once the patient's condition repeats, the disease would go beyond cure. Things are the same to the abuse of power and ultra vires of executive law enforcement related with "three agriculture-related problems". Every time when the contradiction between rural governments and farmers is intensified to deadly results, the superior government would take "powerful measures" to remove the title of the county and township governments' officials. However, the failure to eliminate the root cause will only make the corruption of the newly-appointed officials more technical, which entails higher costs. People only know that the high cost of corruption can restrict the multiplication of corruption, but they do not know that, on the hotbed of corruption, high cost can only bring about more serious corruption.

What is the prescription for standardizing the executive law enforcement of "three agriculture-related problems"? Besides improving relevant legislation, we need to ensure the judicial independence and judicial fairness to check the administrative power and safeguard the rights and interests of the farmers.

6.4.3 Legal Service Market in Rural Areas

The serious inadequacy of rural legal service market constitutes a key factor to restrict the realization of the goal of rule of law in rural areas. We have to start with the following aspects to improve the rural legal service market: 1. The government puts investments to establish and improve the legal aid system in rural areas. Currently, the legal aid in rural areas is basically blank. As the vulnerable group, farmers can better safeguard their legitimate rights only after receiving effective and timely legal aid. 2. The government improves the rural infrastructure so that more legal service personnel can provide legal service for farmers conveniently. To the legal service personnel, the unwillingness to go to rural areas also has some relations with the backwardness of such infrastructure as the transportation and the poor life conditions in rural areas. Many legal talents would rather be in idle than go to exploit the rural market, and the reason is inseparable with the hostile environment in rural areas. 3. The government cultivates and supports farmers' legal service talents. There are farmers' lawyers like Zhou Guangli who are willing to study the agriculture-related laws and provide legal assistance to farmers without consideration of salary. What a rare legal resource they are! If we encourage and support, rather than attack and retaliate, such kind of enthusiastic persons, there will be dozens of, hundreds of or even millions of Zhou Guangli in future, and the resource shortage of legal service market in rural areas will be greatly relieved.

6.4.4 Legal Consciousness of Farmers and Rural Cadres

To strengthen the farmers', especially the rural cadres' legal consciousness constitutes important contents for solving the "three agriculture-related problems" through rule of law. The safeguarding of farmers' rights is finally determined by the awakening and strengthening of farmers' awareness of right. How to strengthen farmers' legal awareness? 1. Undoubtedly, the State shall assume the responsibility of popularization of law. Popularization of law cannot just go through the motions. To spread law to the countryside, we have to pass on legal solutions to farmers for the issues of their concern. In terms of the laws, regulations and legal ideas related with the farmers' immediate interests s, we need to awaken the farmers through popularization and education, rather than force the farmers to buy one law popularization book to cover the pickle jar. 2. Demonstration effect of judicial justice. The demonstration effect of judicial justice is unimaginable to the urban citizens. The individuals' independent living pattern featuring complete isolation from each other all their lives can be compensated for by the extensive information acquisition channels like radio and television, newspapers and network. However, the scenario is quite different in rural areas. Farmers are quite sensitive to their surrounding things and would therefore show the response of "better to believe the worst, and be pleasantly surprised, than to be optimistic and learn the worst" to the gossip and hearsay. Fair judicial precedent will spread rapidly from mouth to mouth among farmers. With the high praise to the judicial reputation from the farmers, there would be no need to worry about the improvement of legal awareness. 3. The orientation of rule of law published by the media is also quite important. Mr. Zhang Yang gave powerful attack on today's films and television programs that promote the individualistic heroism of rule of man.[17] Such attack has fully demonstrated the influence of the media, especially the widely-spreading literary and artistic works, on the society under rule of law. With the popularization of TV in rural areas, the orientation of rule of law for media popularization will have direct influence on the forming and improvement of farmers' legal awareness.

NOTES

1. (British) Friedrich Hayek, *The Constitution of Liberty (I)* (Beijing: SDX Joint Publishing House, 1997), 4.

2. (USA) John Rawls, *A Theory of Justice* (Beijing: China Social Sciences Publishing House, 1988), 225.

3. Wang Chunguang, "Promoting the Solution of 'Three Agriculture-related Problems' with Social Treatment as the Base Point," accessed March 23, 2003, http://www.sociology.cass.net.cn.

4. This assertion represents an expression of ignoring farmers' rights. There are many judgments of this kind in China. The main idea of this assertion is: instead of being allocated to

villagers, the land acquisition money can only be controlled by the villagers committee "for the development of agricultural production" as the land is owned by the collective. In real life, the large sum of land acquisition money is usually used for other purposes, squandered or corrupted by the villagers' committee and town government. After acquiring farmers' life-supporting land, why cannot allocate the land acquisition money to farmers? Isn't it stark-naked plunder for farmers? The root lies in the disadvantage of property right of farmland. In the name of justice, after acquiring farmland, the compensation money should not only be allocated directly to farmers, but also paid at full. This would involve the issue of fairness. The farmers are so poor. Although the standard for acquiring land is so low, the price is still higher than farmers' harvest from the land (the difference of price scissors is evident). Farmers earnestly wish that all land could be acquired and paid with corresponding land acquisition money. In this way, the farmers from the same group whose land isn't acquired would feel unfair. It is understandable. To this, our country should introduce a coordinate scheme in principle for the farmers' reference so as to implement the balance measures rather than just collect the land for the ownership of the collective or let land-losing farmers suffer from one disaster after another.

5. (USA) John Rawls, *Theory of Justice* (Beijing: China Social Sciences Publishing House, 1988), 67.

6. The educational circle is very cautious about the definition of "folk laws". People from the circle either quote the opinion from others without taking a stand or beat about the bush as to the definition. However, most of them think that the folk law is another set of regulations in contrast with the state law and that the folk law plays the role of regulating people's behavior in real life, especially the rural society. Refer to Liang Zhiping, *Customary Law in Qing Dynasty: Society and State*, China University of Political Science and Law Press, 1996; Xie Hui and Chen Jinzhao: *Customary Law(Vol.1)*, Shandong People's Publishing House, 2002 for relevant research.

7. Liu Wujun, "To Do Something by 'Folk Laws' and Not To Do Everything by 'State Laws'," *Jurisprudence Daily*, October 19, 2000.

8. Zhou Qiming, "Legal Safeguard Issue of Farmers' Right of Equality," *Law Quotient Research* 2 (2000).

9. Guo Shutian, "Re-discussion about Today's Farmers' Issue," *Agricultural Economy Issue* 10(1995).

10. Chen Guidi and Chun Tao, *The Survey of Chinese Peasants* (Beijing: People's Literature Publishing House, 2004), 47.

11. Wang Taixian and Ai Ming, *The Concept and Strategy of Rule of Law* (Beijing: China Procurate Press, 2001), 16.

12. (France) Duguit, *Changes of Public Law · Law and State* (Shenyang: Liaohai Publishing House & Chunfeng Literature and Art Publishing House, 1999), 12-13.

13. Qi Duojun, *" On Power"*, *Chinese Journal of Law* 1 (2001).

14. Xue Gangling and Wang Wenying, "Reflection on Rural Rule-of-law Development," *Hunan Social Sciences* 5 (2003).

15. Xu Xianming, "Ten Rights Should Be Fixed by the Constitution," *Southern Weekly*, March 14, 2002.

16. Liang Zhiping et al, "Thoughts on Modifying the Constitution," Shanghai Law and Economics Research, accessed July 12, 2003, http://www.sile.org.cn..

17. Zhang Yang, "*Literary & Artistic Creation and 'Rule of Man',*" recorded Gong Ben Xin: *Teahouse for the Jurisconsult (II)* (Jinan: Shandong People's Publishing House, 2003), 130.

Chapter Seven

Modes and Approaches for Solving "Three Agriculture-related Problems" by Rule of Law

7.1 MODES FOR SOLVING "THREE AGRICULTURE-RELATED PROBLEMS" BY RULE OF LAW

As China has gone through the feudal society of over two thousands of years and the big government and small community of planed economy period, the rule of man has left deep imprint on the countryside. The feudal rule by rites, customs as well as town schools of long standing have made Chinese farmers habitually choose the pattern of rule of man to realize the village order. Currently, to realize the goal of ruling the country by law, we would inevitably face different contradictions like those between internationalization and localization, between the traditional and the modern as well as between fairness and efficiency. A concentrated reflection of these contradictions lies in that Chinese implementation of rule of law is advanced by the government or social evolution.

None of the historical accumulation, realistic practice, international environment and self-requirements of Chinese rule of law allows too much time for China to abrogate the old traditions and accumulate new experience to push forward the modernization of rule of law. First, the practice to modernize Chinese rule of law is always confronted with external pressure and internal crisis. The comparative pressure constituted by the combined action of both internal and external forces Chinese government to care about the time cost and therefore takes the modernization path with economic advancement as the core, and the path of legal change with the government as the main impetus. Second, Chinese modernization lacks the civil society base of western countries. The civil society is a community of people and organizations independent of the country. Its status and resultant force are enough to contend against the State. It is not only the hotbed of western democratic constitutionalism, but also the place for accumulating modern knowledge. However, the two thousand years of feudal history of China has made Chinese society a stable and enclosed body in which the civil society is very narrow and vulnerable. It has no force to contend against with the State at all. Indeed, in a sense, China has no typical civil society and Chinese traditional society is a big family with hierarchical structure. The country and society are included by the big family and the boundary between the two obliterated. Therefore, Chinese modernization of rule of law would inevitably adopt the path featuring the main impetus of government, which is quite different from the western countries. Such top-down artificial and even compulsory completion of the change from traditional society to modern society under rule of law has certain advantages, the largest one of which is the response to the urgency of time. If a simple path were to taken with rule of law evolving along the social change, the precondition of high time cost will be needed for the accumulation of knowledge, summarization of rules and learning of experience.[1]

However, we must be acutely aware of the disadvantages of rule of law advanced by the government. Let's deconstruct the government first. General scientific theory of the western society believes that, under the market economy conditions, the government should be a night watchman and subject of macro-control. However, since 1840 when it opened the door to the outside world, China has begun to realize the necessity "to learn the advantage from the foreign invader first and then defeat them". Later, China realizes that it needs not only "the weapons", but also "the systems". The government has realized this early. Even Empress Dowager Cixi herself realized that China needed to learn from western countries. However, there is one point that she didn't and had no plan to learn. That is to leave the government totally independent of the economy. Most of the developing countries like Brazil and Latin America have completed their capital accumulation by the government and their governments become the economic subject at the initial stage when the government enters into industrialization. Since the government is the economic subject, the government could not undertake the responsibilities of controller and night watchman. It will firstly serve its own function of profit maximization. Under whatever circumstances, if we count on it to become a government totally independent of market and detached with the economy, we would still need a very long period.[2] One disadvantage of the rule of law advanced by the government also a lie in that modern rule of law is mainly to restrict the government acts. "Since all the government power (function and power) are just for pursuing happiness for the society, they should not be arbitrary or just for temporary happiness. On the contrary, they should be exercised in accordance with the existing and published laws."[3] On one side, in today's society, the safeguarding of human rights and realization of personal freedom are all related with the efforts and achievements for providing such elements as the politics, economy, society and culture. On the other side, the increase of a country's control over social resources, especially the rapid expansion of administrative power, may become a threat to rule of law. In China, people encounter similar but more serious problems because of different causes. Therefore, how to decrease the common citizens' dependence on the state, standardize the administrative power through the law and establish a limited government based on the principle of rule of law? These questions may be more urgent and important than the active and effective requirements raised to the government.[4]

Since construction of rule of law still takes the path featuring the main impetus of government, the rule of law advanced by the government has provided for the progress of rule of law for our society with the possibility of system arrangement. We need to make historical analysis for evaluating the rule-of-law pattern advanced by the government. After the founding of the new socialist China, our country got bogged down in the mire of rule of man or "random ruling" and the rule of law suffered from destructive damage after temporary boom of rule of law. We call it destructive damage mainly because, to the people as the subject of rule of law, the awareness of civic rights or legal consciousness has nearly been destructed completely. For a long time, people were afraid of mentioning rule of law and saying no to the then political rulers. They can only show their grace to the political rulers and worship to their leaders. "It is better for the doer to undo what he has done". In today's world of market economy, only when the government actively promote rule of law, can we rapidly restore some basic conditions of rule of law, including the people's knowledge about as well as practice and belief of the laws. Without the active impetus for rule of law from the government, god knows when we can realize the path of rule-of-law reform from bottom to top with hopes pinned on automatic awakening of the people and emergence of enough force for confronting the government by the people. Therefore, it is the historical decision of our construction of rule-of-law to adopt the pattern of main impetus from the government. However, we should also see that the duration of government impetus would not last too long. The dynamics of such impetus would also become weaker, disappear or even go over to the opposite side to become strong resistance to rule-of-law along with the change of the original motivation. The active impetus from the government to rule-of-law at the beginning was for self-rescue through change and reform. However, the fundamental element of rule-of-law is to administer the government rather than the people, and to restrict the rulers to avoid abuse of power. Under the condition of market economy, instead of deifying the political rulers, we need to include the acts of the rulers into the orbit of rule of law. Constraint and counter-constraint are natural phenomena. The constraint to government acts by rule-of-law would inevitably bring out the counter-constraint acts from the government which would become the barriers for rule-of-law. To decrease and eliminate such barriers, the social impetus for rule-of-law needs to develop quickly. The game between rule-of-man and rule-of-law is of long-term kind. Even in the countries with developed modern rule-of-law, the sign of rule-of-man would "glitter" from time to time. Therefore, our realization pattern of rule-of-law should adjust its emphases in accordance with the change of time. Professor Wang Taixian thinks that our path of rule-of-law should adopt "the pattern featuring interaction between the government and society" and divides the pattern into three stages: government launch, social self-governance boosted by the government as well as benign interaction between the government and society.[5] This is a kind of ideal pattern, although the three stages have no clear boundary. The principal line of government driving—social response—interaction between government and society should be a practical pattern choice for realizing rule-of-law consistent with our national conditions.

In the rural areas, current rule-of-law progress still belongs to one of the three stages comprehensively. However, in retrospect, our government has launched rule-of-law for over twenty years which can be counted as a long period. Nevertheless, we see just low response voice of social self-governance. We need an analysis. What makes the response voice of the society to rule-of-law construction so low and weak? Is it the rejection from the society? The inefficiency of government? The difficult in enforcement? Or is it not commenced at all? This requires our government to carry out concrete analysis on the launch of rule-of-law in rural areas.

7.1.1 Government Promoting Mode and its Operation Mechanism

1. The facilitation role of government boosting pattern to realization of rule-of-law in rural areas

The launch of rule-of-law in rural areas is promoted by the national power. Such situation seems to be natural in China. The reason for such saying is not that Chinese legalization in rural areas can be launched only by the government, but that the active government launch of rule-of-law in rural areas complies with not only the requirements of the country development but also the general trend. At the point when planned economy is walking towards dead end, we have different social contradictions piled up like a mountain. If the government doesn't seek for change itself, "great revolution" would arrive when varied contradictions are intensified to such extent that the government cannot operate normally. Will a modern and smart government wait for such moment? In rural areas, since the reform and opening-up policy, the rule-of-law boosted by government has achieved certain effect in general, which is mainly reflected by:

(1) The continual improvement of national legislation has laid solid foundation for rural rule-of-law

Since the reform and opening-up policy, the agriculture-related legislation has developed rapidly. If searched by the key word of "agriculture", 2,121 sets of laws and regulations could be found from Chinalawinfo.com on October 28, 2003 and the figure was 2,342 on April 2, 2004. Be it the total number or the speed of agriculture-related legislation, the legislation related with "three agriculture-related problems" shows surprising results. Besides the temporary order, specific reply, notice and judicial interpretation, the basic agriculture-related law system itself has been constructed to considerable scale. In recent years, China has established an agriculture-related legislation system with *Agriculture Law* as the base and *Land Management Law, Rural Land Contract Law, Grassland Law, Forest Law, Fishery Industry Law, Water Law, Villagers Committee Organization Law, Agricultural Technology Promotion Law, Town Enterprise Law* and the like as the main contents. Although these laws and regulations need to be amended and improved in accordance with the social development requirements, they have played very important role for establishing the leading position of agriculture, standardizing rural market and protecting farmers' rights.

(2) Rural justice and government legal aid has expanded the legal relief channel

The poverty and backwardness of the countryside has determined that if they want to obtain the justice of judicature, the weak group of farmers especially need legal assistance, but the assistance force from different walks of the society is limited and not guaranteed. This requires the government to take full advantage of its control, regulation and service functions and help farmers obtain impartial judicial relief in terms of both legal and financial support.

The *Legal Aid Regulations* formulated and issued for enforcement in 2003 represents the first administrative regulations for legal aid in China. It has established the basic framework of Chinese legal aid system and specified the scope of civics' right for legal aid service. By the end of 2003, we have 2,774 legal aid institutions, 9,457 legal aid employees and 166,433 legal aid cases processed. The people's court has further strengthened the legal aid work. To those parties involved who have financial difficulty, the court has in a whole year decreased the legal cost for 4,860 cases, exempted the legal cost for 16,926 cases and extended the legal cost payment time for 206,496 cases. In total, it has in the year decreased and exempted RMB 141 million of legal cost and extended the payment time for RMB 916 million.

This has guaranteed that the people whose legitimate rights and interests have been infringed or violated and whose financial capability is weak can afford to file a lawsuit.[6]

(3) State laws popularization has strengthened farmers' legal awareness

Farmers' legal awareness won't be generated by itself. Currently farmers have very limited channels to obtain rule-of-law resources, especially in those backward areas. Therefore, it is of great significance to deliver the laws to the countryside. For this, we have to deliver law in an all-around way, including the legal ideas, documents, instruments and justice. In recent two decades, the government has successively implemented several five-year plans of state laws popularization. The law popularization penetrating to rural areas has played important role for the forming of farmers' legal awareness.

2. Restrictive acts in the process of government boosting of rural rule-of-law

Under the market economy, the government role of "night watchman" needs to be emphasized in many circumstances. In China, the long-term planned economy makes the government take on everything, including individuals' personal life. Such role of "parent-like officers" is still quite popular in today's rural areas. The town government and the villagers' committee with the nature of agency of the town government always deem the villagers as the objects that can be controlled at will. From the perspective of the government officers, the farmers are stupid and they should be the master of the farmers. The farmers should handle matters totally in accordance with the government officers' will. Otherwise, the farmers would be classified as "unruly people". However, the market economy means the rule-of-law economy. Everything has to take the law as the criterion so as to protect each individual's rights and freedom to the maximum extent. Instead of just being the master of the people who take the responsibility for the people, the government should also be the "servant" who provides service for the people. The government cannot do whatever it wants to do. In order to solve the "three agriculture-related problems" through rule-of-law, we must restrict the government acts.

(1) To change the administrative control into administrative service

To solve the "three agriculture-related problems" through rule-of-law, the government should ensure the legality of all its acts, i.e., the government must administer in accordance with the law. The law-based administration of government is especially important in rural areas. The attitude of the government towards rural work should change from the original administrative control to administrative service. The lesson taught by the disadvantage and hazard of administrative control is profound. The over-staffing in organizations, superfluous staff, bullying and oppression to people and tyrannizing in rural areas area all evil consequences of administrative control.

In those countries with developed modern market economy, as the objects of government control, the economic activities involve the whole process of economic circulation including the production, exchange, distribution and consumption, as well as such elements as the finance and transport related with the process. Some people sitting in a study take it for granted that the control of our government to the economy is far from enough and needs to be strengthened. They hardly realize that the economic theory for such large amount of government control is the blind development without order in the economy and social unfairness brought about by market failure. After the industrial revolution, the western countries pursue the system principle of free market. People believe that an "invisible hand" will correctly guide the economic operation and everyone pursues their own interest so that the optimum of the whole society, namely the so-called "Pareto Optimum" will be realized. To the economic organization of today's society, what a country requires is no longer the power to give order, but the obligation to fulfill demands. The power of a country has a limit which is the minimum power required for fulfilling its obligations. The functions that a country has to accomplish constitute the government affairs as a whole.[7] Only when the market fails, the monopoly aggravates and the defects hindering normal operation of market increases, would the government come forward to intervene so as to realize fair competition and overall balance of the society and economy. While reviewing the situation of China, the market economy is still at its rudimentary stage. What we need is to form a real fair and free market as soon as possible rather than to strengthen the government intervention and control of economy. Under our current background, it is urgent for us to weaken the economic function of the government so as to change the situation formed under long-term planned economic system in which the government has the final say for everything as soon as possible.

If the urban enterprise reform in recent years is walking towards the market economy (although there are many imperfections in the process, including the issues of no guarantee for employees' interests and loss of state-owned property during the sales, transfer and lease of state-owned and collectively-owned enterprises, the general direction is right), the reform of rural economic system would be timid and overcautious. Why cannot the farmers own the property right of the land? Why does the government have the final say for which types of plants be cultivated by the farmers? Why is the farmers' burden always a black hole whose bottom can never be seen? Why does the village self-governance need to be led and controlled by the town government? All these problems have fully exposed the serious disjointing between the existing political and economic systems in rural areas and the existing market economy and rule-of-law construction in China. If we don't change the administrative system in rural areas, the market economy and rule-of-law construction would become empty talk. But how to change? We need to change the administrative control into administrative service. The government would do what the rural market or the farmer needs the government to do, and not the other way around.

Some local governments also talk about the change of functions and emphasize the administrative service. But let's see what kind of administrative service they have provided. Jinyun Town Government of Zhejiang issued an order and 4,000 *mu* fertile farmland was immediately taken over for use as land for industrial development area. Without notifying the villagers, the village Party branch secretaries and heads of villagers' committee of each village have successively offered their signatures in two days. Villagers' protest followed. After two times of appeal in Beijing and the approval from the Ministry of Land and Resources to invalidate the land acquisition order, the land acquisition activities in those places have been accelerated rather than stopped. On November 24, 2003, 1,000 villagers from several villages had a collision with over 600 armed polices, joint defenses, militiamen and cadres. Over 30 villagers were hurt.[8] In the incident, relevant people in charge from Jinyun County Government asserted eloquently that their aim was to help local farmers become rich as soon as possible. However, anyone with discerning eyes knows that they just want to feather their own nests under the flag of serving for farmers. The administrative service needs to be provided in accordance with the market requirement and farmers' will, rather than the administrative persons' interest.

(2) Power delegation is the core of the goal of solving "three agriculture-related problems" by rule-of-law

Today, there has been little substantial change to the low efficiency for handling affairs in rural areas. The interests-oriented administrative enforcement has severely damaged the vast farmers' interests. Power delegation means to untie the farmers, streamline the organization and improve the efficiency of administrative approval. All of these are basic project for solving "three agriculture-related problems" through rule-of-law.

The democracies at the grassroots level and village self-governance are mostly carried out under the promotion of the county and township Party committee and government. The county and township Party committee and government play a leading role in the village-level democratic system construction, which represents the basic characteristic of village self-governance construction in China. However, it is also the resistance for realizing village self-governance of real sense. The power subject of county and township governments as the direct promoter of democratic system construction at the grassroots level has its advantages. However, it may easily lead to the direct infringement of villagers' right of self-governance by the traditional top-down administrative order, taking on what ought to be done by others and many other habits. All the blood case emerged during the villager election in different areas of the country have something to do with the wanton interference of the county and township governments. Only when the county and township governments completely delegate their power to the lower level, can we realize the village self-governance in real sense. The hegemony people from the county and township governments always take such excuses as "stabilizing the social order of rural areas" and "preventing the election from being utilized by ax-grinders or manipulated by vicious power" to directly intervene in the villager election and therefore lead to disastrous results. Some also take such excuses as "the county and township governments supervise the villager election, safeguard the expression of villagers' willingness and have the right to investigate and deal with the illegal activities reported by the villagers in accordance with the law" to wantonly intervene in the villager election. According to a report from the web edition *Jurisprudence Daily*, from 1999 to May of 2002 in one city, of the 329 heads of villagers' committee generated from election, 187 were replaced by the town organization or because of personal violation of rules, which takes up 57% of the total. Meanwhile, 432 deputy heads and members of villagers' committee generated from election were replaced. After the 619 heads, deputy heads and members of villagers committee were illegally replaced, none of their successors are legally elected by the villagers.[9]

The phenomenon that the town government is unwilling to hand state power back to the people have deep-rooted economic causes. The town government represents a level of governmental organization with the most direct relationship with the village and villagers. Therefore, the village becomes important resource bases of the town government. Under the circumstances of scale and function expansion of town governments, imperfect construction of township finance, limited source of finance and difficulty to form a virtuous cycle of self-finance, when the increase of town finance cannot catch up with the increase of organizations and expenditures, even when there exists large amount of non-normal expenditures, the town government would turn to the village and villagers for the funds requirement of the town. Then the order and control from the Central government to the town government, from the town government to the village and the villagers' committee would become inevitable. With the major adjustment and reform of Chinese rural management system, the rural finance system, especially the county and township finance system, has increasingly become the "barrier" for village self-governance progress. The contradiction and conflict of rural relations not only have certain internal link with the political management system in rural areas, but also directly have close relationship with the county and township finance system. If we do not study the county and township finance system, we would not be able to really interpret the varied contradictions of today's rural relations and realistic difficulty of village governance. After careful and in-depth research on special topics related with the village organizations and their financial position, a scholar proposed the thought of "passive administration".[10] Such "passive administration" is to delegate the power, i.e., no administration for those who shouldn't be administered and good administration for those who should be administered. There is a standard for the matters that should be administered and that shouldn't be administered just like the standard for measuring a qualified communist. The standard for delegating power is to see whether the government act or negative act complies with the villagers' willingness and interests based on the constitution and laws of a country.

3. The legality of administrative law enforcement right is the key for promoting rural rule-of-law

Currently, there are numerous law enforcement teams in the rural area in China. As to the law enforcement, the subjects are mostly do-nothing bludgers, and the objects are the farmers without exception. The contents of the law enforcement are mostly plundering people's property under various sorts of pretexts, and the procedures usually include threat, beating, scolding and robbing to the farmers. Chen Guidi surveyed thoroughly over fifty counties (cities) in Anhui Province and made an inventory of farmers' burdens, including:

Funds raising: funds raised for constructing the office building, teaching building, science and technology network, out-patient department, CPC members service center, propaganda station for family planning, broadcasting station, movie theater and enterprise of the town; funds for transforming the town environment; budget subsidy for cracking down on crimes, etc.

Expenditures of the village cadres and non-production employees: subsidies of fixed quotas for the party Branch secretary, villagers committee head and accountant; subsidies for work compensation of the militia commander, public security committee member, league branch secretary, woman director and village group leader; subsidies for the veterinarian, agricultural technician, broadcaster, forest ranger, slope protection personnel, newspaper deliveryman and health officers; subsidies for the electrician, plumber, carpenter, bricklayer and all odd-job-men arranged for the village, etc.

Education expenditures: salaries for teachers from civilian-run schools; subsidies for teachers from state-run schools; construction and transformation cost for school buildings; normal administrative expenses of schools; costs for newspapers, books and reference materials, expenditures for teaching apparatuses as well as recreational and sports equipment and facilities, etc.

Family planning expenditures: health subsidies for sole child; nutrition fees for contraceptive operation, subsidies for family planning committee members, subsidies for family planning team, etc.

Militia training expenditures: living subsidies for militia training, subsidies for work compensation caused by militia training, duty-performing subsidies for guarding the ammunition, etc.

Expenditures for public welfare establishments as well as preferential treatment compensation and comfort; subsidies for the seniors' home servicemen; cooperative medical care construction; subsidies for rural medical staff; preferential treatment for the families of servicemen and martyrs, disabled army-man, families of the compulsory serviceman on active duty as well as the old, weak, sick and disabled veterans; care for the rural labor with occupational injury, family in financial or material difficulties and households enjoying the Five Guarantees, etc.

Others fees and expenditures, including: the voluntary labor service subsidies for transport construction; employment subsidies for civilized village construction; expenditures for maintaining street and constructing collectively-repaired road, homestead planning and approval for house construction; seed quarantine fees, poultry guard fees, livestock manager fees, electric wire erection fees and unified deratization fees; the expenditure for purchasing the walkie-talkies and motorcycles for the police, and for purchasing the clothes for the judicial officials.

In some places, there are sponsorship fee, counseling fee, examination paper fee, material fee and broom fee for town schools; and live pig tax, slaughter tax, value added tax, income tax and urban construction tax for pig raising. Many villages and towns would levy the pig head tax in accordance with the number of family members, no matter there is a pig or not.

In addition, almost all agriculture-related departments, including those included in the governmental organization list and those not included in the governmental organization list but undertook the governmental function, especially such departments as the food, supply &marketing and financial departments, have showed the integration of government and enterprise and distinct inclination of transformation to enterprises and been equipped with the double functions of implementing policies and increasing profits with the deepening of reform and opening-up. They always ignore the state laws & regulations and the rules & policies, and forcibly or passingly collect fees for some activities that should not collect money for.

Some towns even collect 14 items of fees for just one item of marriage registration. Besides the production cost of marriage certificate, there are recommendation letter fees, marriage notarization fees, premarital check-up fees, motherhood and child protection fees, one child guarantee fund, wedding party consumption fees, pig butchering fees, wedding afforestation fees, constructing preparation fees for children playground, family planning guarantee, late childbirth guarantee, conjugal affection guarantee, golden wedding guarantee, etc.[11]

As a matter of fact, the legality of administrative law enforcement right has already got some laws to follow. First, the items of taxes that farmers should pay are very clear and the farmers have the right to decline the additional expenditures or burden that failed to pass the villager meeting. Second, the *Administrative Penalties Law* has specified the subject, jurisdiction, procedures and the like of administrative law enforcement. Why there still emerge so much illegal law enforcement subjects or contents? Chen Guidi's remarks pointed out frankly the truth. "Since the issuance of *Environmental Protection Law*, some places actually took the smoke from farmers' kitchen chimney as 'environmental pollution' and collected 'pollution emission fees' door by door. The farmers who dare to have a say asked for reasons and explanations for the cadres collecting the fees and were actually levied with another item of 'attitude fees'. The cadres also brought out a theory that was popular during the 'cultural revolution' period: 'what's important is not the seriousness of the issue, but the 'attitude', and the number of fees to be collected is determined by the 'attitude'. Some cadres are very straightforward. They just collect money without any pretext and immediately come to blows to those who dare to say no. All in all, to administer is to collect fees. This has become a kind of persistent ailment for many departments."[12] It seems like that the issue lies not in the legislation or the judicial, but in the legal supervision. In rural areas, who has enough power to contend against the government? In face of the abuse of power by the government, who can provide effective supervision? None. Therefore, farmers put their hope on the interview from the CCTV "Topics in Focus", and on the 'Imperial Sword' received from appeal in Beijing. However, we all know that one cannot be in two places at once, and the "Topics in Focus" could only take care of few issues of this kind.

How to ensure the legality of administrative law enforcement right? The key lies in the judicial independence, without which, the court would not be able to carry out effective investigation to the illegal acts of the government. The occurrence of the incident on the public trial by Linquan Court of Anhui Province for the fact that Wang Xiangdong and Wang Hongchao "illegally taking into custody public security officers" shows the issue that the judiciary authorities are seriously enslaved or subordinated to the government. The working team of the county Party Committee described the event with the words of "criminal activity of illegally taking into custody public security officers". The *Notice for Urging Wang Junbin and Other Criminal Offenders to Surrender Themselves to Justice* posted up by the county Public Security Bureau described the event with the words of "beating, smashing and looting" and even the remark of "recklessly carry out reactionary propaganda". The Commission for Discipline Inspection of the CPC at county level also clearly described the event as "constituted the crime of robbery" in the *Decision on Dismissing Wang Junbin's Party Membership.* Obviously, the working team of the Party Committee, Public Security Bureau and Commission for Discipline Inspection of the county have all determined the nature of "criminal offender" respectively before official trial of the county court. This constitutes a kind of unlawful act ignoring the laws.[13] However, in face of the unlawful act of the Party committee and government, the court has no power to make investigation or correction, but could only let it be. Without judicial independence, the executive power would be abused in an imposing manner and unscrupulously.

3. The positive acts of rural rule-of-law boosted by the government

The government under market economy undertakes the function of providing social public goods and plays significant role in promoting rural rule-of-law.

(1) The government should strengthen its support and protecting for rural economy

It is the main function of the government to strengthen the macro-control of rural economy and even the national economy as a whole, and the goal of such function is to safeguard the realization of fairness and efficiency and coordinate the development of the whole national economy. For this, we need to accelerate the legislation of economic law and take full advantage of such economic leverages as planning, finance, tax and price for macro-control.

According to the practices of China and the conditions of each developed country, the support and protection of a country to agriculture are mainly reflected by helping agriculture enhance its competitiveness and decrease its risks. Specifically speaking, the first is to incline to agriculture in the secondary allocation of national revenue, increase agricultural input, support agriculture to improve agricultural production conditions (water conservancy construction of farmland, promotion of agricultural science and technology, farm machinery and equipment, agricultural means of production, etc.), and increase the subsidies for natural disaster insurance of agriculture at the same time so as to improve the agricultural production level and capability to resist natural disaster. The second is to establish and improve the risk funds system and reserve regulation system of main agricultural products so as to decrease the agricultural market risks. The third is to implement the "light tax burden" policy and industry policy favorable for agricultural development so as to increase the agricultural self-accumulation and self-development and absorb the social resources towards agriculture. To protect agriculture for increasing agricultural competitiveness and decreasing agricultural risks is in essence to protect the farmers, especially the farmers' enthusiasm for production.[14]

(2) To stimulate industrialization operation of agriculture by law

The industrial operation of agriculture represents the correct thought for current development of agriculture. The government undertakes heavy responsibility and should speed up the pace. In the meantime, the government should carry out all businesses in accordance with the laws. All compulsive acts without legal ground not only would fail to help the situation, but also may easily lead to irretrievable regret. After the exposure of the event that Longmiao Town, Shuyang County, Jiangsu Province adjusted its structure and forcibly harrowed and destroyed 800-mu corn field and sublease the field to the county Party Committee office for contracting project of developing and planting flowers, the Party Secretary of Shuyang County said that it was a good thing to adjust the planting structure and develop the speciality industry. However, in terms of the issue related with farmers' land transfer, it is necessary to stick to the principles of willingness, legality and compensation, and the farmers cannot be forced to do things against their will.[15] It is wished that our government had the most basic common knowledge of law like this before the exposure of similar event. The promotion of agricultural industrialization must be carried out in accordance with the law.

(3) To vigorously support and promote the transformation of agricultural science and technology into productivity

The government is incumbent on the promotion of agricultural science and technology and the specific measures, including encouraging the scientific and technical personnel to go to rural areas, accelerating scientific and technological transformation, increasing investment, providing necessary fiscal and financial support and protecting agricultural IPR through legislation. Xinhua News Agency published news on March 30, 2004 that, in order to implement the Central No. 1 Document and the spirit of the "Report on the Work of the Government" passed on the Second Session of the Tenth NPC and to promote grain yield and farmers' income, the State Council decided to adopt nine measures that are more direct, powerful and decisive so as to further arouse farmers' enthusiasm and vigorously develop grain production. Of the nine measures, the seventh has the most profound meaning and aims to promote advanced and applicable technologies, vigorously promote high-quality and high-yield grain varieties and further increase the unified seeds supplying rate and coverage rate of high-quality seeds. According to such measures, the government would organize agricultural scientific and technological personnel to go to the front line of rural areas to carry out technical guidance and training and help farmers solve technical problems emerged during production.[16] We need to provide most of the agricultural scientific and technological personnel in China with favorable position for the use of their skills and do well the research and promotion of agricultural science and technology so that the production of agricultural products can enter into virtuous development stage of high-yield, high-quality and high-efficiency. However, China hasn't established a system and mechanism for most of the agricultural scientific and technological personnel to boldly carry out agricultural scientific and technological research and technological promotion. The main reason is still the issue of system. The *Agriculture Technological Promotion Law* is slapdash at first and its encouraging measures failed to be implemented. Therefore, the promotion of agricultural technology got into trouble. The government has much work to do for stimulating agricultural technology promotion in accordance with the law, of which, the main work include the implementation of encouraging measures and safeguarding of investment for agricultural technology promotion.

(4) To accomplish the protection and coordination of agriculture on the increasingly competitive international market

In face of the globalization trend of today's world economy, all countries are seeking for channels to establish unified international market on one hand, and ransacking their brains for more protection for their own economic development on the other hand. After access to WTO, agriculture becomes one of the industries that endured the strongest shock. The government should strive for Chinese agricultural interests internationally and enhance the protection and subsidy intensity of such basic agricultural production as grain production domestically.

(5) To safeguard and stimulate agriculture to pursue sustainable development path

The government must intervene in order to guarantee the synchronization between agricultural development and environmental protection. There should be not only prohibitive regulations but also encouraging and compensatory regulations in terms of legislation so that the farmers' loss for environmental protection and sustainable development can be compensated in time. The 40th International Agriculture Expo. in France chose one of its themes as to "develop rational agriculture", which means the competitive agriculture with overall consideration for the producers' economic interests, consumer demands and environmental protection, and its goal is to guarantee farmers' income, improve the quality of agricultural products and create favorable conditions for environmental construction. Rational agriculture is regarded as the most reliable and vital sustainable development form of agriculture. First, the government has formulated a series of agricultural production reference standards endured the test of practice. The farmers who have tasted the sweetness of rational agriculture started to consider the implementation of rational agriculture as self-conscious pursuit. Some fashion-conscious farmers have affixed the label of rational agriculture to their exhibits. The Normandy districts even establish the development committee of rational agriculture and organizations to issue relevant certificates. These organizations execute contracts with farmers, provide funding support for constructing the water conservancy projects for avoiding water and soil loss as well as soil erosion, guide the raisers to construct livestock raising buildings consistent with relevant regulations and environmental protection requirements, ask the personnel working on agricultural and livestock raising to obtaining relevant professional qualification certificates or receive special training of relevant knowledge, management regulations and latest technologies.[17] French success has told us that the government formulation of regulations to encourage and support farmers to take sustainable development path in accordance with the law is much more effective than any coercive measures.

(6) To establish and improve social security mechanism in rural areas

The establishment of social security mechanism in rural areas won't show obvious effect without the government interference. Some said that those died in hospitals in rural areas and those died at homes in urban areas are all rare cases. This on one hand reflects the urban and rural differences, and on the other hand shows the backwardness of the social security system in rural areas, especially the medical insurance. The change of such backwardness needs the government acts.

Currently, family supporting remains the base for social provision for the aged in rural areas. The minimum living security system in rural areas represents the social relief system established by the country and society for safeguarding the living for the poor rural people who cannot maintain the most basic life. The rural "Five Guarantees" is impossible to be replaced by other forms for a relatively long period. The emerging rural medical insurance system mainly solves such risks as poverty caused by diseases in rural areas, while the traditional cooperative medical services mainly solves the problems of shortage of doctors and medicines. According to a research analysis to 2,972 farmer households in 10 national poverty counties in China, the basic requirement for farmers from poor areas is RMB 733, which is close to RMB 750, per capita net income of the respondents.[18] Under such conditions, establishing social security system in rural China lacks necessary conditions in accordance with the traditional ideology. It is widely recognized to stick to the principles of "personal payment as the main source, collective subsidy as the secondary source and national policy as the support". To operate social security through the means of commercial insurance has exceeded the economic development level of rural areas. The government should, in accordance with the reality of rural society, increase the investment. To help farmers overcome poverty and achieve prosperity represents the precondition for establishing complete social security mechanism in rural areas.

7.1.2 Society Promoting Mode and Its Realizing Conditions

Rural rule-of-law launched by the government has its inevitable limitation. During such construction process of rule-of-law, the laws are not coming up just for restricting the exercise of national power. Instead, they are coming up as a tool to strengthen the force of national political power to social reform.[19] The government plays double role in promoting rule-of-law reform and reform transformation. It is both the promoter and object of the reform. This is also the challenge of Chinese reform issue.[20] Therefore, after accomplishing the short-term task of government launched rule-of-law, there should be follow-up relay runners. Otherwise, the rule-of-law progress may come to a premature end. Who would be the relay runner? The society.

After the course of over two decades, rural rule-of-law has changed from passive acceptance to active absorption. It has become undisputed facts that farmers' legal awareness has achieved substantial and considerable progress, although the progress shows a little reluctance at the beginning. The improvement of farmers' legal awareness can of course be attributed to the following factors: the first is over one decade of large-scale law popularization campaign in China; the cultural poverty alleviation activity of delivering the law to the countryside has improved farmers' legal awareness to certain extent. Although it fails to achieve its expected effect, it has played certain role objectively. Farmers have walked out of the blind worship and started to learn and accept the laws. Although currently, many farmers don't know the specific stipulation of the law most of the time. They regard the "legal knowledge" obtained indirectly as the criterion of law. We still think this situation is a kind of improvement of legal awareness. The second is that reform and opening-up has enhanced population mobility, especially the mobility of rural population to the urban area. Since the rule-of-law level in urban China is relatively high, the mobility process of rural population to cities is also beneficial for improving farmers' legal awareness, especially farmers' experience of legal authority. The third is that the developed radio and television in rural areas has provided farmers with convenient channels to know about the laws. Today's radio and television have introduced many programs concerning legal issues, including many programs involving cases in rural areas. This has stimulated the improvement of farmers' legal awareness to a great extent. What's more, thanks to the popularization of education in today's world, there are more and more literate people in rural areas. Under the influence of the tradition that Chinese people usually pay respect to the literate people, the literate people have exerted relatively huge influence on the legal concept of the people surrounding them to a certain extent. The improvement of farmers' legal awareness represents an inevitable result and undeniable fact.[21] The change of such concept represents a prerequisite for the society to promote rule-of-law. As Friedrich Hayek puts it, the reason that people can form a society with the ability to formulate laws lies in that they have long since enjoyed some common beliefs. It is because of these common beliefs that they get the possibility to discuss with and persuade each other. Moreover, in order to be recognized as compliant with the law, the explicit regulations also need to comply with these beliefs.[22] The cultivation of legal awareness has exerted fundamental influence on the rule-of-law process.

The awareness of democracy and right has been awakened in rural areas. The practices of the county and township government showing no respect to people's will and infringing villagers' democratic rights urge farmers to rise to contend and actively maintain their own democratic and self-governance rights. For example, the villagers from a village in Sichuan requested to dispose the two official cars for many times. After their request being ignored, the villager representative assembly made the decision finally and actually auctioned the two official cars, Santana 2000 and Alto. Two villages from Hunan Province elected and reported the nominees of their village secretaries. However, their superior town government issued a notice and designated in the notice other nominees, none of whom are members of the Villagers committee. The notice has aroused the villagers' dissatisfaction and the villagers immediately reported the whole thing to relevant superior governmental organization and people's congress. However, the town government paid no attention to the written instructions from relevant superior authorities and persisted in their old ways. Therefore, the Villagers committees from the two villages filed administrative lawsuits to the court. Loudi Intermediate People's Court, after trial, ruled that the specific administrative acts of the town government to designate the village secretaries are illegal and invalidated the document.[23]

After the rule-of-law process driven by the society possesses the most basic conditions, we must have a primary design for the pattern of rule-of-law process for its sustainable development:

1. To generally legalize the organizations that really and directly represent farmers' will and interests

By far, there haven't been any organizations that really and directly represent farmers' will and interests have been recognized by the law. Therefore, the social driving force has been greatly reduced. Some would ask, aren't the villagers committee and county and township people's congress the organizations directly represent farmers' will and interests? Then let's investigate the villagers committee and county and township people's congress to see whether they can represent farmers' interests well.

The *Villagers Committee Organization Law* issued for implementation in 1987 and revised in 1998 has defined the nature and position of Villagers committee. Article 1 stipulates that "This Law is enacted in accordance with the *Constitution* with a view to ensuring self-government by the villagers in the countryside, who will administer their own affairs according to law, developing democracy at the grassroots level in the countryside, and promoting the building of a socialist countryside which is materially and ethically advanced." The article makes clear the purpose from the very beginning to formulate the law in order to safeguard village self-governance. The follow-up Article 2 goes "The villagers committee is the primary mass organization of self-government, in which the villagers manage their own affairs, educate themselves and serve their own needs and in which election is conducted, decision adopted, administration maintained and supervision exercised by democratic means. The villagers committee shall manage the public affairs and public welfare undertakings of the village, mediate disputes among the villagers, help maintain public order, and convey the villagers' opinions and demands and make suggestions to the people's government." The article further expounds the main contents of village self-governance in Article 3, "The primary organization of the Communist Party of China in the countryside shall carry out its work in accordance with the Constitution of the Communist Party of China, playing its role as a leading nucleus; and, in accordance with the *Constitution* and laws, support the villagers and ensure that they carry out self-government activities and exercise their democratic rights directly". The article emphasizes the support and safeguard to village self-governance from the grassroots-level party organizations. Article 4: "The people's government of a township, a nationality township or a town shall guide, support and help the villagers committees in their work, but may not interfere with the affairs that lawfully fall within the scope of the villagers' self-government. The villagers committees, on their part, shall assist the said people's government in its work." The article points out that the relationship between the Villagers committees and the town governments is guidance, support but without intervention. This is just my personal interpretation of the regulations. Perhaps the overwhelming majority of people would interpret the regulations in this way. However, the county and township governments and the Villagers do not interpret the regulations in this way. Typical demonstrations include the contradiction between villager election and government designation, government's forcible intervention to villager election and village cadres' joint corruption and bullying to farmers in varied places in recent years. Why there emerged such universal phenomena of government violation of law? Besides the information dissymmetry and power unbalance, there are also the cause of the laws and regulations themselves. First, the vast farmers have narrow channels to understand and be acquainted with the *Villagers Committee Organization Law* because of the limitation of educational level and lack of effective propaganda. Second, farmers' force is far from enough to contend against with the power of the grassroots-level government and there exists no third party force to form effective check concerning abuse of governmental power. What is the issue of the law itself? We might as well modify the last sentence of Article 2 "reflect villagers' opinions and requests, and provide suggestions to people's governments" into "to carry out on behalf of the villagers between the villagers and people's governments on equal foot and settle the issues related with villagers' interests through consultation", and in Article 4, delete the "guidance", "but" and "The villagers committee provide assistance for the township, national township and town people's governments for their work". In this way, the rights and obligations would be defined clearly and the ambiguity be eliminated. Moreover, there should be other relevant regulations to make it clear to ensure the villagers committee will be elected and generated totally in accordance with the will of the whole villagers and the whole villagers will have the right to supervise and villagers committee activities and change the member of the villagers committee at any time in accordance with the laws, and in case of no agreement can be reached for the dispute between the villagers committee and government through consultation, the dispute may be submitted to the court (one precondition: the court must be independent from the government. Otherwise the dispute shall be submitted to other independent third party that is under no control of the two parties) for arbitration. Only with such laws, can we really realize village self-governance and guarantee that the villagers committee really represents the villagers' will and interests.

Let's investigate the county and township people's congress. Article 101 of the *Constitution* specifies that "Local people's congresses at their respective levels elect and have the power to recall governors and deputy governors, or mayors and deputy mayors, or heads and deputy heads of counties, districts, townships and towns. Local people's congresses at and above the county level elect, and have the power to recall, presidents of people's courts and chief procurators of people's procuratorates at the corresponding level." and Article 102 "The electoral units and constituencies which elect deputies to local people's congresses at various levels have the power to recall the deputies according to procedures prescribed by law". However, in face of the corruption of the grassroots-level government, manipulation of vicious power and officers' malfeasance, how many officers are replaced through local people's congress? When the things cannot be concealed and covered any more, it is always the superior government step forward to handle the matters and the county and township people's congress becomes "the ear of the deaf". Why? Is it the weak awareness of rights from farmers? It is undeniable that this is a cause, but not the fundamental one. The fundamental reason lies in that the existing system leads to unsmooth expression of farmers' will. If the nature of the above-mentioned villagers committee can be recovered, the issue would be able to be solved.

2. Farmers and their representatives of interests to directly participate in the legislation

The existing agriculture-related legislation is either the results of government issuing forcible order or the experts working behind closed doors. Only few have farmers' and farmers' representatives of interests directly participating in. It is impossible for the laws without direct participation from farmers to receive good observation and maintenance. Moreover, since the law is related with agriculture, if the farmers' direct aspiration cannot be reflected, the law can only be the law of control or exploitation rather than development and the legislation would be unscientific and backward. To regulate people's acts with such kind of laws cannot promote the rule-of-law process and will only make farmers more disappointed with the law.

Our existing legislation procedure sounds good: bringing in a bill—forming a draft—seeking for advice widely—deliberating on and passing the draft—issuing and implementing the law. Two links of the procedure are exaggerated. The first is to bring in a bill. Of today's over 2,000 agriculture-related laws, how many are brought in by farmers? Almost none. The other is to seek for advice widely. The serious formalism makes it basically impossible for farmers to obtain legislation information, or even to learn about the laws years after the issuance. The foregoing dialogue between Chen Dahui and Cao Zhengjie has showed us from one side that the channels for farmers to obtain legal resources are too narrow.

The process for society to promote rural rule-of-law depends mainly on the vast farmers' enthusiasm and belief towards rule-of-law. The direct participation of farmers and farmers' representatives can stimulate such kind of enthusiasm and belief for rule-of-law to the greatest extent, and can put the formulated laws into implementation without discount.

3. Putting into practice the regulations of the Constitution on the government officers' performance evaluation and appointment or dismissal mechanism represents the basic driving force of rural rule-of-law

Here is a dialogue from the interview by Cher Dahui, a journalist of CCTV Half-Hour Economy, to Cao Zhengjie, a farmer from Jiangxi, and Gai Xiaoqi, the former Deputy Director of Rural Development Forum:

"At that time, we received a call from the grassroots-level cadre who said that our agricultural committee compiled a book. The book caused feedback at the lower level, i.e., might affect the stability of the countryside."

"Why didn't they want the book come out? The publishing of the book, especially after the farmers get the book, there will be some consequences. They may not be able to collect some money that shouldn't be collected."

This shows that the root cause that blocks the channels for farmers to obtain legal information lies in the interests of the grassroots-level governmental officers, lies in the existing system. If the administrative officers of each level are really elected and dismissed by the people and people's representatives as stipulated by the constitution, the problems could be solved. Since the *Constitution* has clearly specifies that the administrative, judicial and procuratorial officers of each level are elected and dismissed by the people and people's representatives. Why it cannot be implemented in practices? Why does each officer act only in accordance with the leader's attitude and ignore the people who nourish him/her, and sometimes even fool and persecute the people at all costs? Because only the leader could determine their promotion, dismissal and the interests they can finally receive. Under such mechanism, rule-of-man is extremely promoted and rule-of-law is just slogans and formalism. If farmers cannot create a little restriction to the governmental acts and there exist no basic legal guarantee, there would be no such thing as promoting rule-of-law by the society. Therefore, putting into practice the stipulations of the *Constitution* on the performance evaluation and appointment or dismissal mechanism represents the fundamental driving force of rural rule-of-law.

7.2 APPROACHES TO SOLVE "THREE AGRICULTURE-RELATED PROBLEMS" BY RULE OF LAW

7.2.1 A Fundamental Change in the Government's Ruling Strategy

1. Law-based administration represents a basic requirement of market economy

For a long time, the development of Chinese rural society is enclosed separately not only in urban and rural large society systems, but also within the respective community with the administrative division as the boundary. The community boundary and administration division are of the same structure, and the elements are difficult to flow between different communities. Therefore, the rural communities have to develop their economy depending on their own resources. Because of the differences of resource endowment, historical background and development level, the rural communities featuring close relationship of family, clan and blood tie have showed different development modes and independent economic interests in the economic and social development process. As the representative of community interests and manager of community economy, the county and township governments, even including the village-level organizations, as a matter of course, have the responsibility to organize the community economic construction and promote community economic development. With the reform of "cooking meals separately and delegating power to the lower level of authorities", local governments has changed from the transferring organization responsible for delivering information to both the upper and lower levels into a level of national economic management and subject for organizing local economic activities.[24] Local government has its independent finance, becomes a relatively independent level of government and undertakes the organizers and coordinators of community economy. Meanwhile, local governments, as the subject of local economic activities, have their own pursuits of interests which can only be satisfied during the process of promoting community economic increase. In this way, the pursuits of local interests become the driving force for local governments to promote the economic and social development of the area. The external expression of such driving force evolves into the "local protectionism" always detested by us.

Today, Chinese economic reform, including rural reform, features the basic orientation of market, and the market mechanism represents the most effective and dynamic economic operation mechanism and resource allocation means owned by people by far. However, the market mechanism is far from all-powerful. Even under developed market economy, the market mechanism has its defects that cannot be overcome by itself. These defects are named as "market failure" in western economics. Market failure has provided the fundamental bases for governmental intervention. As a matter of fact, in developed western market economy, governmental intervention has become the "endogenous variable" penetrated into the operation process of market economy. China who is going through the transition from planned economy to market economy needs urgently to restrict, weaken and even return some power and functions to the market, enterprise or society based on clarifying and trimming the original political function system on one side; and strengthen, expand and even increase some functions to practically compensate for the market defects and create a system, policy, social and economic environment favorable for healthy operation and gradual mature of market mechanism.[25] Relatively speaking, the rural market formed on the basis of weak agriculture is more unstable and short of standards, and its resources are more inclined to be short of optimized allocation. Such objective reality requires the government to utilize powerful administrative means rather than just economic means to replace the still rudimentary, incomplete or running failure market mechanism, consciously develop and organize the market, and collect and process the information so as to realize reasonable allocation and effective utilization of resources. For this, the government must realize the transition from the manager role under planned economy to the server role, from the control function that undertakes the whole things of the society to the coordinator role under market economic operation. The law-based administration represents a basic requirement for realizing the change of governmental functions under the background.

The key to law-based administration is to establish an effective mechanism for restricting governmental power. First, it is necessary to define the allocation of power and strengthen the internal control and supervision of public power. The administrative power without expressed term from the laws should not be exercised. Second, to the small and big decisions involving farmers' interests, we shall pay attention to investigation and research and listen widely to the grassroots opinion. Third, whether before, during or after exercising the power, we shall try best to be transparent, encourage farmers to regularly implement law enforcement supervision and safeguard farmers' unblocked channels for supervision. Only with strict official management, can we have democracy and rule-of-law.

Only after possessing the basic awareness of right, can we talk about rule-of-law. Currently, the concept restraining factors of the grassroots-level government are mainly reflected by the legal instrumentalism and lack of law-based administration from the grassroots-level cadres. In rural areas, such factors are reflected by the serious thought of "official standard" and will of leading officials from the grassroots-level cadres. Due to the lack of complete internal supervision system and the awareness of rights and supervision from the "administered" farmers, possibilities have been provided for the abuse of power and ignorance to farmers' interests from the grassroots-level cadres. The function of a system depends mostly on the quality of the law enforcement personnel. The grassroots-level cadre in rural areas, as the most active political subject grasping the public power, represents the implementation personnel of the party and government policies and laws at the grassroots level. Their leading ability, working method and rule-of-law level directly or indirectly affect farmers' recognition and observation to the policies and laws. However, to many grassroots-level cadres, the law constitutes "people-proof tool", and implementing the strategy of ruling the country by law in rural areas means nothing more than utilizing the "tool" of law guaranteed with coercive force to rule farmers. They failed to realize that farmers, as the main part of the masses, represent the first level of subject for rule-of-law. Firstly, the government and its officers are the object of rule-of-law implemented by the Party and the people before they are endowed with the identity of subject of "law-based administration". The relationship between the government and farmers is reflected by the administration and service by the government to the farmers in rule-of-law. Such relationship is interactive. The power must be subject to the governance of the laws, and law-based administration also becomes the most basic requirement of modern society under rule-of-law.[26]

2. Realizing the village self-governance of real sense represents a significant goal of law-based administration in rural areas

The village self-governance is the base of "rural politics" pattern. Since the reform and opening-up, especially since the trial operation of *Villagers Committee Organization Law of the People's Republic of China* in 1987, village self-governance has achieved considerable development from none-existence to existence and from the weak to the strong. It has not only become the starting point and sally port for the vast villages in modern China to construct democratic politics, but also tremendously motivate the vast farmers' enthusiasm and promoted positive change of the agriculture, countryside and farmers. Village self-governance is undoubtedly not only the necessary product of Chinese rural economic system reform and national democratization progress, but also an important expression of rural China walking from single-dimensional economic development to mufti-dimensional development of social politics.[27] However, most of the village self-governance organizations are under strong control of local administration on such aspects as the human resources and funds. Therefore, village self-governance becomes a mere formality and the village self-governance organizations changed from the original representatives of villagers' interests to the governmental agencies. To change such situation and recover the true features of village self-governance, the governments still needs to change their thought, remove the idea of power concentration and establish the concept of rule-of-law.

7.2.2 An Increase of Right Consciousness of the Farmers

The thought of obligation standard still universally exists in rural China. To the national laws, the farmers usually just see the side of coercive force and ignore the side of protection of rights. This has led to a vicious cycle: the stronger the farmers' awareness of obligation and the weaker the farmers' awareness of right is, the harder it would be for farmers to accept the laws from their hearts. Even the laws for the long-term or future interests of the whole society have difficulty in obtaining people's recognition in short period. For example, to raise funds for road repair, run a school, promote family planning and construct spiritual civilization village in accordance with the laws and regulations would sometimes be strongly boycotted by farmers, the final beneficiaries showed in the legislation purpose, and be regarded by farmers as the matters of the government that have no or a little relationship with farmers' direct life,[28] as the overcharge and over-apportion have made the farmers generate distinctive contradiction to the fee collection items. Besides, there are some legal activities involving farmers' own immediate interests that are ignored by farmers themselves. For example, the election for village self-governance—farmers show indifference to the election; the supervision on the use of compensation for land acquisition—farmers think it is reasonable for the villagers committee to use the compensation at will. The persistence from Zhou Yuanlan from Guixi, Jiangxi in claiming for the land acquisition compensation and the unyielding spirit showed by Ding Jianguo in the villagers committee election of Bayi Village, Bayi Town, Changzhi County, Shanxi Province are rare and precious things.

Except for the thought of obligation standard, the weak awareness of private property right from farmers also constitutes the stumbling block for rule-of-law in rural area. The awareness of private property right represents an important item of the whole legal awareness from farmers. Farmers should be aware of not only a kind of "absolute right" over the property already owned by themselves, but also varied kinds of property rights that they would enjoy in their organizations, including the property share, private plot, private hilly land, contracted land and other property rights of the collective organizations. As to the unclear collective property rights formed in history, we should evaluate based on facts the asset share for each stakeholder who have made investments of funds, technology, material objects, labor and the like for the forming and development of the collective properties. In the process, farmers' interests are the most likely to be ignored or infringed. Moreover, once farmers' interests are ignored or infringed, the weak group will meet with the greatest difficulty in seeking for legal and other means of relief and remedy. What's more, the weak group, because of insufficient legal awareness, could not effectively and actively seek for legal assistance and have their rights guaranteed. Therefore, establishing the basic legal awareness represents the most basic requirement to effectively protect their rights for the farmers.

It is obviously incorrect to take the cultivation of farmers' legal awareness as the farmers' business that has nothing to do with the country and society. On the contrary, our country and society shall undertake the obligatory task of forming and improving farmers' legal awareness. The first is to "send the law to the countryside". Currently, Chinese law popularization, though with vigor and vitality in form, brings little effect in essential. According to my memory, in 1982 when the *Constitution* was issued for implementation, all the walls in the villager gathering points in the village were painted with white lime and stipulations of the *Constitution* were copied on the white-painted wall by those with good calligraphy. In their leisure time, the villagers would gather around the wall and discuss about the fundamental law of the country and the illiterate would ask the "scholar" to read the contents to them. Later, some basic laws like the General Principles of Civil Law, criminal law and marriage law have all been posted and published on the wall together with the local rules and regulations valid for the whole village successively. Such phenomenon has disappeared for many years just because of the media evolution. Since 1986, China has successively carried out the first to the forth five-year law popularization, published the books for law popularization one by one and implemented the supervision of law popularization successively. However, the people's legal awareness does not show great progress. The reason lies in the formalism. Farmers actually each got one book for law popularization (with the nature of disguised apportion). However, most of the law popularization books bought with money that could have been spent on more necessary oil and salt were used by the villagers to cover the pickle jars and hadn't ever been read. Some TV programs like "Law Today" and "Net of Justice" have actually stimulated the awakening of awareness of right from some farmers for the reason that they are visualized and close to life. Therefore, China should definitely continue to popularize the laws in rural areas in future. As to how to carry out the popularization, we should listen to the farmers' voice. The second is the judicial publicity. The judicial publicity here is discussed based on the task undertaken by the court for cultivating farmers' legal awareness during the judicial practices in today's rural areas. Our grass-roots courts, especially the detached tribunal in the town, should further improve their announcement system of court session opening while hearing the cases. Most of the courts publish the court session announcement on the wall newspaper column of the court for the auditing and supervision of the vast people. In real practices, the vast farmers do have interest in participating the court session auditing. Strengthening the judicial publicity does play an important role in cultivating the villagers' legal awareness. Finally, we should strive for judicial fairness which is directly related with the awakening and dynamics of villagers' legal awareness. In real practices, such phenomena as judicial unfairness, misuse of law in adjudication, replacing the law with the power, putting individual before the law are the number one killer of people's legal awareness. Since judicial fairness is related with people's reverence to the law and trustworthiness to the court, China must strengthen its work to promote judicial fairness.

7.2.3 An Efficient Supply of Legal Sources in Rural Area

The shortage of legal resources in rural areas has become a serious issue that cannot be avoided or ignored by us to construct a country under rule-of-law. We can catch a glimpse of such phenomenon from the "case of Sun Jin'gen hampering marriage and family".[29] Sun has committed adultery with married woman Lai, an employee from the same plant that he worked in since 1990. On the night of May 4th, 1993, Zhang (Sun's wife) found the flirtation between Sun and Lai. Zhang accused Lai, scratched Lai's face, and threatened to report the flirtation to Lai's husband. Lai felt ashamed and committed suicide through poison on the early morning of next day. On 7th of the same month, after mediation of the township government, Sun Jin'gen compensate Lai's families with RMB 25,000. However, Lai's families, under the excuse that Lai was murdered by Sun Jin'gen, gathered a crowd to make trouble in Sun's house. Local public security organization therefore detained Sun for trial for the suspicion of rape and later obtained a guarantor pending trial for Sun since no substantial evidence was found. However, Lai's families thought that the public security organization was partial to Sun Jin'gen and gathered a crowd to make trouble in Sun's house again. During the process, they also insulted Sun's wife and the younger sister of Sun's wife and beat up multiple policemen who went to settle the disputes. Later, Xiangshan People's Procuratorate filed a public prosecution to Xiangshan People's Court with the charge of hampering marriage and family against the defendant Sun Jin'gen. After a trial, the court, in accordance with Article 79 of *PRC Criminal Law*, and in reference to the stipulation of Article 179, rendered a judgment on August 31, 1993 which judged Sun Jin'gen committed the crime of hampering marriage and family and be sentenced two years of imprisonment. After the pronouncement of the judge, the defendant did not make an appeal. The court reported the case for review in Ningbo Intermediate People's Court in accordance with the law. The latter entered into a decision to affirm the judgement made by Xiangshan People's Court, which was reported to Zhejiang Superior People's Court for review in accordance with the law too. And the latter also affirmed the judgement made by Xiangshan People's Court, which was further reported to the Supreme People's Court for examination and approval. After examination of the case, the Supreme People's Court judged that the defendant Sun Jin'gen undertook no criminal responsibility for Lai's death and the People's Court of the first trial was incorrect in analogy, conviction and measurement of penalty for Sun Jin'gen. After deliberation by the Judicial Committee, the court entered into a criminal judgement on December 27th, 1994 to revoke the previous judge and verdict and announced not guilty for the defendant Sun Jin'gen. The defendant of the case never filed an appeal for the guilty judgment from the court of first instance. The cause and effect relationship that is obviously groundless according to the law actually became the basis for judgment, and was accepted by two levels of superior courts.[30]

Putting aside other factors (for example, the defendant gave up his right to appeal and accepted whatever judgement made by the court), the case shows at least the following three issues. The first is the serious lack of legal knowledge from farmers. Farmers could not basically distinct the boundary between being guilty and not guilty. The defendant thought that Lai has died and died because of their improper men and women relation and therefore he should plead guilty. The second is that the defendant has no conditions to obtain professional legal assistance, i.e., no ability to afford a lawyer or legal assistance from local organizations. The third is that the procurator from the grass-roots People's Procuratorate and the judge from the court shows low professional quality and has no ability to fairly and correctly determine the nature of the case. All of these can be summarized as the lack of legal resources in rural areas.

First, the channels for farmers to acquire legal knowledge are very limited. Law popularization is mostly going through the motions all around our country, not just for the farmers. What I have learned in rural areas shows that farmers' legal knowledge has been improved in recent years and the main channel for them to receive rule-of-law education is the CCTV program of *Law Today*. The program has enormously stimulated the rule-of-law enthusiasm from vast farmers, especially some farmers with certain educational background, especially in the first two years after the launching of the program. After the stimulation of the rule-of-law enthusiasm, some farmers would consciously learn and utilize the laws through other channels, gradually mobilize other farmers to value their own and others' rights and act in accordance with the thinking of rule-of-law. However, the numerous phenomena of judicial unfairness, replacing the law with the power, replacing the law with the individual, putting individual before the law in real life have drastically frustrated their rising enthusiasm for rule-of-law. The farmers' rule-of-law foregoer like Zhou Guangli would also be transformed or hurt by the harsh environment in reality.

Second, the resources on legal service market in rural areas are severely in shortage. China started the trial operation of National Bar Examination since 1986 and changed the examination into judicial examination in 2002. In over a decade, we have not only cultivated but also left unused a group of legal professionals. By 2002, we have nearly 120,000 people with the lawyer qualification and about 30,000 people with the judicial qualification after two years of judicial examination.[31] However, those who actually work on lawyer work account for only over 2/3 and those who join the judicial team from the walks outside the judicial authorities are even rare. The legal talents left unused either want to work as a lawyer in cities, especially the large cities, or do not want to work as a lawyer temporarily because of stable occupation. These people are unwilling to go to the countryside. There are only few lawyers in a county, not to mention in a town. Only quite a few people who have obtained the qualification of law practitioner work in the town legal service offices. The reason lies in that the rural areas are too poor. Today is an era of market economy rather than an era of learning from Lei Feng. Who will voluntarily give up the comfortable environment and good remuneration in urban areas to go to the countryside? Therefore, it seems that one vicious cycle has been formed. The poorer the village is, the less legal talents there are. The legal service resources become increasingly deficient in rural areas and the channels for farmers to seek for legal assistance increasingly narrow.

The third is the quality of the judicial personnel at grassroots level. In most of the towns, only the presiding judge of the court is the judicial officer and others are all acting judicial officers (in other words, temporary workers). As to the judge of the court in the county, they are mostly transferred to civilian work from the troops or transferred from other administrative positions. In recent years, law major graduates from colleges and universities have successively joined the team but are still far from enough. There are still a majority of law major graduates who have not had the luck to join the judicial system. We have currently formed a situation where the unqualified personnel in the judicial team could not be pushed out and the qualified talents have difficulty in getting into the system or exerting influence on the working style and mode of the judicial authority even after they get into the system. More and more low-quality grass-roots judges appeared in recent years have become an important bottleneck for the rule-of-law construction of China. The former President of Xinhua People's Court of Hunan Province was discontented with his successor who amended his original judgment to a case. He went back to his original unit on the first day of the lunar year and smashed the mirror plaque of "taking the people into consideration" sent by the party involved. In an economic case heard by the People's Court of Xincheng District, Hohhot City, the plaintiff requested a property guarantee of RMB 60,000, but the judge froze a property of over RMB 3 million of the defendants during the enforcement process and caused an economic loss of over RMB 780,000 to the party involved. Wang Airu, a farmer from Fuping County of Shaanxi became the judge of the county through improper means. Yao Dinghong from Jiangxian County of Shanxi, a driver with an educational background of primary school level, was promoted successively from the office director to the Deputy President of the county court through illegal means. These low-quality judges have brought about unfavorable influence to the work of the court and directly led to evil consequences of two sides. The first side is the unavoidable misjudged case. Take Shandong court system as an example. Of the 450,000 cases reviewed by the provincial court system in 1998, there are 3,818 with obvious flaws. The other side is the frequent illegal and undisciplined acts from the judge. Take Liaoning court system as an example. According to the statistics in 2000, there are 640 police officers engaged in illegal and undisciplined acts.[32]

The judicial activity has obvious influence on the people's establishment of legal awareness in the district. However, currently the main channel for farmers to receive legal information is the TV media and the town court and judicial system play very little role or even adverse role. The judge and legal workers always weaken the authority of the law in the excuse of flexible handling of a case. A crooked stick will have a crooked shadow. The phenomena that farmers refuse to follow or contend against the law have close relationship with the defects of the grass-roots judicial departments.

Although China is a large country of farmers, farmers are at the lowest level of the society and belong to the greatest weak group. All reform of our rural areas may be summarized as the establishment and safeguarding of farmers' legitimate rights. In recent two decades, the reform and development of the whole rural area are carried out based on the focus of farmers' rights. However, the important task of the time to establish and safeguard farmers' rights is still far from accomplishment. Farmers always witness their legitimate rights being infringed by factors from different aspects, but have difficulty in getting effective legal relief because of economic difficulty or other reasons. To protect the poor farmers from being restricted by economic difficulty, safeguard their right to receive equal legal assistance, guarantee judicial fairness and human rights and realize the constitutional principle of "All people are equal before the law", we need to establish reasonable legal assistance mechanism for farmers and help farmers maintain their own legitimate rights.

Under unsound rule-of-law, it is very difficult to establish sound legal assistance mechanism. For example, of the law breakers that cause the increasingly serious issue of farmers' burden and infringe farmers' rights and interests, most are from the grass-roots level governments. On February 21st, 1993, Ding Zuomin, the hero of the "Ding Zuomin Incident" happened in the local police station of Jiwangchang Township, Lixin County, Anhui Province, was beat up to death by the joint defense personnel instigated by local police station because of his report of farmers' heavy burden.[33] If it was not for the villager collective petition out of intolerance, if it was not for Kong Xiangying, a journalist from Anhui Branch of the Xinhua News Agency who coincidentally encountered the incident and reported it to the Central government out of professional sensitivity and sense of responsibility, we would never know how long the incident would be concealed and covered, not to mention when they would receive legal assistance. Concerning the burden and infringement dispute cases between farmers and the government or local police station of the government, under our currently unsound rule-of-law, the courts have to take into consideration of their own interests while dealing with such kind of cases because of the limitations of existing personnel management system and financial system. Therefore, their efficiency and fairness are usually insufficient, leading to farmers' failure to seek for channels for legal protection. Therefore, under unsound judicial system, the effect of legal assistance is very limited. Under the background of today's rural legal resources, the process of establishing farmers' legal assistance mechanism at current stage covers the logic sequence issue of "assisting the law first and receiving legal assistance later". In other words, we should firstly solve the issue of rural laws and regulations. For example, only by solving such issues as the qualification of administrative litigation subject of the Villagers committee, can we legally solve the dispute of infringement on farmers' rights and interests by the Villagers committee, and therefore enable the assistance organizations to receive the legal instruments for assistance.

The legal assistance mechanism in rural areas needs to comply with Chinese national conditions. As the legal assistance commenced late in China, we are in urgent need of establishing legal assistance mechanism, especially for the greatest weak group. However, where are the sources for the personnel and funds for the assistance? How to carry out the assistance work independently without the influence of administrative intervention? To solve these questions, we need to, based on the reality of China, establish all-dimensional and multi-channel legal assistance mechanism for farmers, improve the existing legal assistance institutions, and based on this, establish special legal assistance institutions for farmers. We need to construct a legal assistance model features the integration of national financial support and social philanthropy. This will not only reflect the national responsibility of legal assistance, but also contribute to solve the issue of restrictions to legal assistance under the circumstance of limited national finance.

NOTES

1. Tian Chengyou, "Practice of Rule of Law in Rural Areas during Social Transition Period," accessed May 12, 2003, http//www.yn148.com.
2. Wen Tiejun et al, "Rural Reconstruction of Chinese Mainland," systemized by Wu Ming, *Open Times* 2 (2003).
3. (British) Locke, *On Government* (Beijing: Commercial Press, 1964), 86.
4. Liang Zhiping, "Rule-of-law: System Construction of Social Transition Period," *Modern China Studies* 2 (2000).
5. Wang Taixian and Ai Ming, "The Concept and Strategy of Rule of Law," (Beijing: China Procuratorate Press, 2001), 252.
6. Information Office of the State Council of PRC: *China's Cause of Human Rights in 2003* white paper.
7. (France) Dugui, *Changes of Public Law: Law and Country* (Shenyang: Liao Hai Publishing House & Chunfeng Literature and Art Publishing House, 1999), 13.
8. Li Zijing, "Miserable Situation Witnessed by Hu Jingtao in Villages: Discovering the Crisis of People's Rebellion Driven by Oppressive Government," accessed January 7, 2004, http://www.peoplemail.com.cn.
9. Liu Haimei, "*Village Self-governance and Law-based Administration*," accessed January 29, 2003, http://www.legaldaily.com.cn.
10. Yang Junkai, "Interpret and Explore Rural Relations During Village Self-governance Process," *Journal of Central China Normal University* 4 (2002).
11. Chen Guidi and Chun Tao, "*The Survey of Chinese Peasants*," (Beijing: People's Literature Publishing House, 2004), 68-71.
12. Chen Guidi and Chun Tao, "*The Survey of Chinese Peasants*," (Beijing: People's Literature Publishing House, 2004),71.
13. Chen Guidi and Chun Tao, "*The Survey of Chinese Peasants*," (Beijing: People's Literature Publishing House, 2004), 56.
14. Lang Peijuan, "Farmers' Issues and Governmental Responsibilities," *Chinese Public Administration* 2 (2001).
15. Cui Binwei, "Never Force Farmers to Do Things against Their Will," *Farmers' Daily*, April 1, 2004.
16. Xu Er'e, "Chinese Agriculture Cannot Rest Easy," accessed April 1, 2004, http://bbs.people.com.cn.
17. Gao Jinying, "Rational Agriculture Enhances French Agriculture Competitiveness," *International Finance News*, March 4, 2003.
18. Liu Jinhong, Duan Qinglin and Dong Minghui, "Research on Social Security System in Rural China," *China Soft Science* 1 (2001).
19. Su Li, "Modernization and Rule-of-law in China of 21st Century," *Study of Law* 1 (1998).
20. Jiang Lishan, "Primary Exploration of Chinese Path of Rule-of-law," *Peking University Law Journal* 4 (1998).
21. Liu Yang, "*The Distance to Well-off Level of Rural Rule-of-law*, " accessed October 3, 2003, http://www.legalinfo.gov.cn,.

22. (British) Friedrich Hayek, *Principles for Order Of Liberty,* trans. Deng Zhenglai (Beijing: SDX Joint Publishing House, 1997), 227.

23. Liu Haimei, "*Village Self-governance and Law-based Administration*," accessed January 29, 2003, http://www.legaldaily.com.cn.

24. Wang Lefu, "Economic Development and Local Government: *A Research on the Pearl River Delta Region*," (Guangzhou: Sun Yat-Sen University Press, 1997), 36.

25. Tang Xinglin and Jin Taijun, "*On the Diversity of Governmental Functions During Market-orientation Process*," *Sun Yat-Sen University Journal*, 1 (2000).

26. Huang Wei and Wei Xin, "On Construction of Rural Rule-of-law," *Administration and Law* 11 (2002).

27. Tang Xinglin, "Governmental Act and Rural Development," Study of Politics 1 (2000).

28. Li Rui, "Rural Rule-of-law Construction and Modern Legal Awareness," *Shandong Social Science* 3 (2000).

29. Chinese Research Institution for Applied Science of Law, Supreme People's Court: People's Court Case Selection.

30. Liang Zhiping, "*Law and Order in Rural Society*," accessed October 26, 2001, http://www.law-thinker.com.

31. Gu Liaohai, "Another Talk About 'Unified Judicial Examination'", Beijing Liaohai Law Office, accessed December 1, 2003, http://www.liaohai.net.

32. Wang Limin, "Low Quality Represents an Important Factor for Judicial Corruption, Low Quality of the Judges from Mainland China is Worrisome," *Hong Kong Commercial Daily*, September 21, 2003.

33. Chen Guidi and Chuntao, *The Survey of Chinese Peasants* (Beijing: People's Literature Publishing House, 2004), 5-19.

Chapter Eight

Legislative Drawbacks of "Three Agriculture-related Problems" and Corresponding Strategies

8.1 AN ANALYSIS OF THE DRAWBACKS IN LEGISLATION CONCERNING "THREE AGRICULTURE-RELATED PROBLEMS"

The rural backwardness certainly has something to do with such objective conditions as the agricultural base of China, but the lagging legislation and insufficient law enforcement efforts constitute the root cause for the issue of rule-of-law. Accelerating the agricultural industrialization would have difficulty to prove effective or even just get the opposite to what we wish without the laws for standardization and with only the uncertain administrative order.

Our agricultural legal system is still far from being sound on the whole. In terms of the development requirements of agriculture and rural economy, the legislation of agriculture is still lagging. Currently, most of agriculture-related legislation are the administrative laws and regulations of agriculture. The civil and commercial legislation related with agriculture reflecting such market economic principles as equality, willingness, compensation of equal value as well as honesty and credibility are still weak and feeble. Some laws in urgent need haven't been formulated. However, in the countries with developed market economy, almost all areas of agricultural activities have laws to follow. Many countries have formulated the basic laws specifying the agricultural policy concept and orientation besides the special agricultural laws and therefore formed relatively complete legal system of agriculture. Japan, as one of the countries with the most complete legal system of agriculture in the world, has established sound legal system of agriculture with the *Basic Law of Agriculture* as the "parent law" and over 200 special agricultural laws as the auxiliary. France has formulated special agricultural code with 1,336 articles covering all areas of agriculture. It is safe to say that no other sector needs so many laws like the sector of agriculture. This is because no other sector utilizes varied kinds of natural resources widely, involves large amount of economic activities including food production, processing, circulation and consumption, or need strong support and protection from the government like the sector of agriculture. In foreign countries, agriculture has become an independent legal department with the nature of both public and private laws. The experience of foreign countries shows that the general law could not replace the special legislation of agriculture. We should treat agriculture as an independent legal department and construct a sound legal system of agriculture based on general legislation.[1]

The education circle also has some constructive opinions on the research of agricultural legislation in recent years which deserve the attention and emphasis from the legislator. For example, in terms of the research of agricultural legislation, Guo Shutian thinks that the guiding thought for modifying *Agricultural Law* should be, firstly, fixate the effective policies and new experience created by the people from practices in the form of law based on the summary of agricultural development achievements and experience after the issuance of *Agricultural Law*; secondly, put forward solutions for the general issues of the agriculture and countryside, which should be standardized in the form of law. Those obsolete wording and regulations should be abolished. As to the principles for modification, he further points out that "the first is to distinct the power of the central and local governments. *Agricultural Law* only specifies the national issues. The second is to define the boundary between *Agricultural Law* and relevant industrial laws already issued. *Agricultural Law* only specifies the overall, fundamental and long-term issues. The third is to define the relationship between the laws and policies. The articles of *Agricultural Law* should be specific and operable. For example, specific regulations should be provided for the issues of the basic status of agriculture, basic operating system of agriculture, land system, farmer cooperative economy organization, farmers' burden, sustainable development strategy of agriculture, promoting agriculture by applying scientific and technological advances, adjusting the industrial structure of agriculture, surplus labor force of agriculture, shifting of governmental functions and the like. As to the legal issues of agricultural investment, experts pointed out that currently the severely insufficient investment to agriculture in China has delayed the process of structural adjustment and affected the structural transformation and upgrade. Currently, the status quo of agricultural input of funds features weakening investment strength to agriculture from the national finance, insufficient investment from farmers and small scale of foreign investment. The root cause of the insufficient investment lies in four contradictions, i.e., the contradictions between the agricultural risk and tendency towards benefits of market economy, between the government investment act and the change of distribution pattern in national revenue, between the inherent characteristics of agricultural investment and the major structure change of agricultural investment, between the motivation of investment subjects' enthusiasm and worsening of investment environment. Giving the above-mentioned root cause, it is suggested a new diversified investment mechanism of agricultural funds should be constructed, systemized and standardized, including the government investment mechanism, credit input mechanism, farmer household input mechanism and foreign investment mechanism. It should be pointed out that the financial investment of government should enter into the orbit of legislation so as to restrict the powers of office in terms of agricultural input, determine the source channels of government agricultural input, and specify the share, field, applicable principles and the like of agricultural input. It is also pointed out that China should standardize the agricultural investment act, include agricultural investment into the orbit of legislation as soon as possible, formulate special laws for agricultural investment and utilize the limited agricultural funds well and flexibly in accordance with the law.[2] In face of the practical and feasible legislation suggestions, the new agricultural law implemented in march of 2003 seems to have failed to carry out the suggestions since many of its regulations are vague, general and difficult to be put into practice, and have left large imaginary space for "rule-of-man" in real practices.

The *Rural Land Contract Law* implemented in March of 2003 was formulated to maintain the agricultural purpose of land and ban non-agricultural construction on farm land; prohibit the change of the nature of land ownership and agricultural purpose of land during the circulation of land contract management right; and define the obligation and responsibility for farmers to contract the land as farming. The original intention to formulate these two articles was obviously to protect the arable land and stabilize agricultural (mainly grain) production since China features large population and small amount of land, and grain represents a great event closely related with national economy and the people's livelihood. From the perspective of theory and phenomenon, such saying is quite reasonable. However, it is out of the tune with the reality in essence. Many people assumed it as a matter of course that Chinese issue means the farmer issue and the farmer issue the land issue, and that the contradiction between the people and land is the main contradiction because of the large population and small land. As a matter of fact, in modern times, the amount of land has no necessary connection with the farmers' wealth. Furthermore, our arable land is not less than that of Japan, South Korea, Taiwan and Hong Kong. Even from the perspective of domestic population growth in recent 30 years, the grain represents no worrisome issue. In this way, the *Land Law* restricts farmers' activities to a designed area or sphere based on the old system with grain as the guiding principle obviously for the purpose of binding farmers to the land and preventing farmers from carrying out non-agricultural production and operation. As a matter of fact, the land use of government and the rich is very casual and the constraint is just for the poor farmers at the early stage of entrepreneurship.[3]

Compared with that of the foreign countries, especially the developed countries, our legislation for the "three agriculture-related problems" is very lagging. The problems of agriculture, rural areas and farmers represent the basic problems for the modernization of each country in the world. To solve the "three agriculture-related problems" is the key to realize agricultural modernization and develop our national economy. According to foreign experience, the development of agriculture, improvement of farmers' income and prosperity of rural economy all cannot be separated from the rule-of-law. USA has issued its *Agricultural Adjustment Act* early in 1933 and provided legal guarantee for efficient supply of agricultural products and reasonable farmers' income. Later, USA revised its agricultural law about once every five years. On May 13, 2003, USA issued new agricultural acts to strengthen farmers' income safety guarantee. Japan and South Korea successively formulated their *Basic Agricultural Law*s in 1960s for the issues of high-speed industrial growth, shrinking agriculture and serious disproportionality between agriculture and industry, and have obviously improved the industrial structure of agriculture, doubly increased the capacity of agricultural production and remarkably enhanced farmers' average income. Just as Japanese experts said, without the *Basic Agricultural Law*, there would be no rapid development of Japanese agriculture since 1960s. In order to enhance agricultural competitiveness on international market and continually increase farmers' income and improve agricultural production conditions, Japan and South Korea successively issued the *Basic Food, Agriculture and Village Law* and *Basic Agriculture and Village Law* in 1999 to strengthened the protection of their own agriculture and promoted overall progress of rural economy and society under the framework of WTO. On the whole, the countries have all achieved obvious effect on promoting and safeguarding agricultural development through agricultural rule-of-law, contained the increasingly serious shrinkage of agriculture caused by industrialization, increased efficient supply of agricultural products, drastically enhanced farmers' income level and gradually narrowed the urban and rural gap.

At the beginning of our reform and opening-up, under the guidance of the series of agricultural and rural policies issued by the Central government, our agricultural and rural economy made great achievements. However, because of the constraints from many aspects like the nature, economy and society, the economic benefit of agriculture is still low and farmers' self-protection ability still weak. Especially with the continual improvement of agricultural marketization, it has become increasingly difficult to coordinate and process the intricate relationship of obligations and rights only through the government. Therefore, while strengthening the policy guidance, we must promote sustainable, stable and coordinated development of agricultural and rural economy and safeguard farmers' legitimate rights and interests through legal means.

Today, our agricultural and rural economy has entered into a new stage of development and encountered many new problems, including the production surplus of agricultural products in our country, slow increase of farmers' income, unreasonable industrial structure and pattern of agriculture, low level of farmers' organization-orientation and low international competitiveness of main agricultural products. Especially after its access to WTO, the agricultural and rural economic development has encountered new challenges. The issuance and implementation of the new *Agricultural Law* has provided necessary legal bases and system foundation for solving the above-mentioned issues. However, we cannot depend only on the basic law, namely the *Agricultural Law*, to solve the "three agriculture-related problems". After the issuance and implementation of the new *Agricultural Law*, we must speed up our formulation and improvement of the supporting laws and construct and improve the legal system of agriculture so that the basic system established by *Agricultural Law* can be more specific and operable.

Most of our existing agricultural laws and regulations particularly put stress on macro-control and policy regulations, and most of the domestic policies for agricultural protection lay emphasis on price protection policies. In accordance with our commitment for access to WTO and the regulations of *Agricultural Agreement*, subsidy would not be allowed for the trade of agricultural products. Therefore, China should turn to improving the production and living infrastructure and market conditions in rural areas as soon as possible, and to support agriculture scientific and technological progress, to improve farmers' quality and enhance other aspects beneficial to strengthening inner competitiveness of agriculture. We should also speed up corresponding legislation and improve our legally system of agriculture. A complete legal system of agriculture should include 16 aspects: the basic agricultural law with overall importance and capacity to guide agriculture economic activities; laws of agriculture economic operation subject; laws of agriculture macro-control; laws of agriculture economic subjects' property rights; laws of agriculture resource development & utilization and environmental protection; laws of agriculture production & management and production safety; laws of agricultural circulation and market transaction; laws of agricultural income distribution and benefit protection; laws of agricultural scientific & technology and education; laws of agricultural disaster relief and insurance; laws for reasonable utilization of rural labor and transfer of surplus labor; laws for promoting sustainable, stable and healthy development of town enterprises; laws of agricultural investment; laws of rural social security; laws for stimulating the prosperity of rural poor areas; and laws for the administrative management and supervision of the state organs (the subject of public power) and the quasi-subject of public power (refers to the enterprise, public institution, social community, folk voluntary association and the like that are authorized by the state organs to exercise specific public power). Some scholars also summarized our legal system of agriculture as including five aspects: legislation related with agricultural input (investment); legislation related with rural contract operation; legislation related with agricultural product circulation; legislation related with agricultural resource protection; and legislation related with protection of farmers' rights and interests.[4]

Our existing legislation related with "three agriculture-related problems" is incomplete and unsound. There is no law to follow for many issues in rural areas. For example, the vacancy of natural disaster prevention and treatment law has led to the result that the agricultural compensation cannot be standardized and can only depend on the reports and comments from the governments and government agencies. The strong nature of public law and lack of pertinence of environmental law has led to increasingly serious damage to environment from agricultural production. The obsolescence and rough outline nature of land law has led to no protection to farmers' land rights and farmland left uncultivated everywhere. Even the *Agricultural Law* recently revised and implemented in 2003 have many issues which mainly include:

8.1.1Problems with Basic Agriculture System

The amendment to *Constitution* of 2004 has clearly put forward the stipulations that involve the rights and interests of each common citizen, especially each farmer, including such aspects as the compensation for land acquisition, private property rights and human right protection. Correspondingly, the *Agricultural Law* should also put emphasis on protecting the land contract right, production &management decision-making right, income distribution right and private property ownership in accordance with the law so that no organization or individual could infringe these rights. Although the existing *Agricultural Law* has strengthened its protection for agriculture in some specific measures, it still fails to fundamentally solve the issues of agricultural backwardness and protection of farmers' interests.

8.1.2 Problems with Land System

It is originally a good thing to implement the *Agricultural Land Contract Law* and new *Agricultural Law* at the same time and make the two cooperate with each other. However, we can see that the two laws still have not solved the fundamental issues and just made some adjustment to specific issues. In accordance with the spirit of the Amendment to Constitution in 2004, the private property should be under the protection of national laws. The varied rights enjoyed by farmers based on the contracted land should be an important and integral part of farmers' private property. No government or any other organization or association could embezzle farmers' land without any payment in accordance with the traditional "supremacy of national and collective interests". To fundamentally solve the problem, it is necessary to specify farmers' farmland ownership. When there is no change for the land ownership of the country and collective, we should determine the scope of collective ownership of land in accordance with the principle of full respect to farmers' willingness. No organization or individual could change the natural village or administrative village determined by legal procedures. We should also specify that the subject exercising the ownership is the cooperative economic organization of natural or administrative village rather than the village self-governance organization, and solve the problem of no distinction between rural administrative organizations and enterprises. In accordance with the principle of separating the "two rights" of ownership and management right, we should specify that the land management right is owned by farmers permanently. In accordance with the principle of "secondary" separation of management right and land use right, if farmers are willing, they would be allowed to transfer the land use right so as to create conditions for expanding management scale. However, the basic management system of family contract operation should not be changed. China should also specify that the land under contract operation by farmers have the functions of both production and social security, and abolish the stipulations prohibiting purchasing of land collectively owned by farmers for non-agricultural operation. The law should allow farmers to reserve their land contract operation right on long-term basis, and encourage and support farmers participating in agriculture industrialized and scale operation as shareholders by means of land contribution and receiving their due earnings in accordance with their stock rights.

8.1.3 Problems with Economic Cooperative of Farmers

The stipulations of Chapter II of *Agricultural Law* obviously cannot fundamentally solve the existing problem of farmers' interests being impaired by the Villagers committee. The administrative function of villagers committee makes the committee impossible to represent villagers' willingness well. On the contrary, it has made the committee the "chief culprit" to infringe villagers' rights. It is extremely urgent to abolish the villagers committee and guide farmers to organize a cooperative organization that actually represents their own willingness. For this, *Agricultural Law* should specify the nature and legal status of the specialized cooperative organization featuring market orientation and integration of production, process and sales so that the organization can become the bridge connecting farmers and the market and enables farmers to receive their due share from the benefits from the added value from the processing and selling links. The law should also define and determine the legal person status of farmer cooperative economy organization—cooperative legal person.

8.1.4 Problems of Farmers' Burden

Premier Wen Jiabao delivered his report on the work of the government on the Second Session of the Tenth National People's Congress and declared to "gradually decrease agricultural tax rate and remove agricultural tax in five years". The news really cheers the people greatly, but also gives people a little melancholy besides the excitement. Why use the words "gradually" and "in five years"? Furthermore, except for the tax, the hateful, unavoidable and unaccountable "apportions" and expenditures for village matters also have perplexed the farmers. The *Agricultural Law* should specify that no organization can collect any fee from farmers forcibly or in disguised form except levying the tax in accordance with the law, and that no tax should be levied on farmers' self-sufficient part of production. The type and rate of agricultural tax shall all be stipulated by law. Any collection of fee from any organization or individual in any form shall be investigated for legal liability except for the funds collected by the cooperative economic organization for village matters, which shall be subject to strict supervision of villager assembly.[5]

To solve the issue of farmers' burden, it is necessary to not only decrease the burden, but also increase the income and subsidy. The "No. 1 Document" issued by the Central Government and State Council in 2004 proposes direct subsidy to grain-growing farmers. Premier Wen Jiabao also stressed in his report on the work of the government on the Second Session of the Tenth National People's Congress that the main grain production area should provide RMB 10 billion for direct subsidy to grain-growing farmers. Jin Renqing, the Minister from the Ministry of Finance gave the follow remarks to direct subsidy: "in brief, direct subsidy to grain-growing farmers means changing the originally indirect subsidy through circulation link to farmers means changing the originally indirect subsidy through circulation link to direct subsidy to farmers. Under the original system, China has played a certain role in protecting grain-growing farmers' benefits through the means of purchasing farmers' surplus grain at the protection price in unlimited manner and providing financial subsidy to the state-owned grain enterprises. However, there also existed outstanding issues under that system. The main reason lies in the overmuch links for subsidy which has led to low efficiency and little direct benefits to farmers. Since the end of 2000, the Ministry of Finance has joined hands with relevant departments to research and explore direct subsidy to grain-growing. The ministry has also guided the nine provinces including Anhui, Jiangxi, Hunan and Hubei to implement pilot reforms of grain-growing subsidy since 2002. For this, Anhui has carried out the pilot work of direct subsidy by integrating the reforms of grain circulation system marketization and rural taxes and fees which achieved much satisfaction from farmers and favorable feedback from society. These pilots have accumulated experience for us to formulate measures for direct subsidy for grain-growing and implement the direct subsidy work well in 2004.[6] We don't hope that these practical, feasible and obviously effective measures just remain at the extremely unstable level of policy. Only after they have been upgraded to the level of legislation, can farmers' interests be practically guaranteed. It is a pity that the current *Agricultural Law* has failed to provide regulations for direct subsidy to grain-growing farmers.

In practices, those governmental officers with strong bureaucratic sense would always say that "we can do nothing about it since Chinese rule-of-law is really unsound" when they want to pass the buck to others in face of issues. Of course such remarks are reasonable to some extent and show the urgency for our legislation. However, after serious contemplation, we will find that our basic system of law has nevertheless been established. The key issue is the serious lagging and overmuch loophole of our existing laws for our social development rather than the absence of law. How to iron out the flaws? It is impracticable to depend on some officers and experts to work behind closed doors or copy the experience from foreign countries. We should "go to the countryside to learn from experience" so as to listen to and inquire about the vast farmers' willingness and voices in large scale. We should ask farmers what issues needs legislation and what kinds of laws are required. Of course, national development needs to take into consideration of the issue of macro-control. We are not demanding the government to implement the legislation for "three agriculture-related problems" totally in accordance with the farmers' willingness. We know that it is impossible. However, it really should be the necessary preparation before the legislation for the "three agriculture-related problems" to take into full consideration of the farmers' actual demand and learn the most concerned and the most hateful items of farmers. Currently, what's in urgent need includes not only the revision and improvement of the existing laws and regulations, including *Agricultural Technology Promotion Law*, *Township Enterprise Law*, *Land Contract Law*, *Land Management Law* and *Agricultural Law* and regulations on agricultural credit, but also the legislation on prevention and treatment of agricultural natural disasters, subsidy for grain-growing farmers, rural social insurance and security, rural infrastructure construction and investment, urbanization construction, guarantee of rights and interests for migrant workers and the like. The administrative policies can only be adjusted and detailed within the scope specified by law.

8.2 STRATEGIES FOR LEGISLATION ADDRESSING "THREE AGRICULTURE-RELATED PROBLEMS"

8.2.1 Constitutionality in Rural Area

We need to substantially modify the articles about agriculture-related problems in the fundamental law and strive to realize rural constitutional government. After another revision in 2004, the existing *Constitution* has provided further stipulations on many aspects including the protection of farmers' land rights, the protection of private property, social security, human right and term of office for township people's congress. This is undoubtedly favorable, but insufficiently beneficial to farmers. We have no necessity to take the stability and step-by-step as excuses and "be afraid to take the next step". Such a situation is obviously unfavorable for realizing rule-of-law in short period.

Of the regulations involving the "three agriculture-related problems" in the constitution, many need further revision and improvement. Take Article 10 of the revised *Constitution* as an example, since it has already regulated the compensation system for land acquisition, why doesn't it further define and determine the farmers' land ownership? Since the state-owned assets from the urban enterprises can be sold and transferred to private ownership, why cannot farmers have complete property right over the land that has always been cultivated by them for a long time? This represents not only an illogical phenomenon, but also a kind of discrimination, a kind of discrimination against farmers, and a kind of discrimination from the country and government. The contract periods of 30 years, 50 years and 70 years specified in *Rural Land Contract Law* are insufficient to safeguard farmers' due rights to their contracted land at all. The villagers committee frequently adjusts the contracted land under different kinds of excuses. The county and township governments may enforce coercive sub-contract for development at any time. The governments can forcibly harrow and destroy the thriving crops on the land and asked farmers to grow other plants actually for the purpose of seeking personal gains but under the excuse of "helping farmers become rich". The root cause of these phenomena lies in that farmers have no complete property rights to the land cultivated by them, i.e., farmers have no ownership. According to the civil law, the owner has the right to deal with his/her property. Therefore, it becomes perfectly justified for the villagers committee to deal with the land at any time. What kind of harm would the endowment of ownership to farmers do to the country? I wonder. On the contrary, after acquiring the farmland ownership, farmers can freely and actively manage the land. This is a good thing to both farmers and the country. Why not do it if it can bring out higher production efficiency and cut down the expenditures for a large group of idlers specialized in entrapping farmers?

Another is the newly-added Article 33 for the issue of "the country respects and protects human rights". The article looks like a general regulation that directs at no specific group. As a matter of fact, it is quite important to farmers since the real problem lies in that farmers' human right conditions are quite worrisome. We need to emphasize the protection of farmers' human rights from the perspectives of both subsistence right and development right. The issues lie in that not many farmers know the definition and contents of human rights and the circumstances when their human rights have been safeguarded or infringed. Although the constitution of a country may be fundamental or abstract, it cannot regard the basic contents and clear scope definition of human rights as superfluous. Currently, many farmers' subsistence rights have been threatened, not to mention the development right. Farmers may have their human rights being infringed by the county and township governments as well as villagers committee on their own land, their salary being deducted by their bosses in the city, and may encounter interrogation on the street which may lead to imprisonment or even death (the blood case of Sun Zhigang has made this point clear to us all) if they happen to be "three without" people: people without ID card, without a residence permit, or without a working permit. It is of great importance for the constitution to specify the contents of human rights. Otherwise some people may think that "the civics' fundamental rights" are exactly the human rights. As a matter of fact, the two mean not the same thing though they do have some overlap.

It is necessary to modify the term of office for local people's congress which is however not the key of the issue. The key is to guarantee the nature of "representative of voters' benefits" of people's congress to exercise effective right of supervision to the state organs. If the two cannot be guaranteed, the simple extension of the representatives' term of office would bring us disasters rather than benefits.

8.2.2 Sustainment or Abolishment of Law of Villagers Committee Organization

We need to take into serious consideration the issue about reserving or abolishing the *Villagers Committee Organization Law* so as to actually realize village self-governance. The existing *Villagers Committee Organization Law* makes it impossible for the villagers committee to fully represent farmers' interests and maintain its administrative nature at the same time as this is in contradiction with village self-governance. Maybe we can abolish the villagers committee and make the town government become the most basic governmental institution. Or we can even reorganize the townships and counties, and take the township as the agency of grass-roots political power.

On the National People's Congress and the Chinese Political Consultative Conference (NPC&CPPCC) of 2004, Ren Yuling, a member of the standing committee of CPPCC and counselor from the State Council, appealed that "the key to alleviate farmers' burden lies in decreasing the number of officers". Farmers' heavy burden has certain connection with the overstaff personnel who are supported by the funds from farmers. Once the number of these people is dropped, farmers' burden would naturally be alleviated. China is now implementing a five-level government system while many countries in the world a three-level government model. The government should guide farmers to establish a variety of autonomous, professional, regional cooperative organizations, to reduce the level of administrative institutions. The so-called reorganization of townships and counties means removing the organization system of the township level and changing it into the village self-governance organization; as well as integrating small scale counties and county-level municipalities and making county government the most basic people's government of China. Where the township does need organizations to perform the governmental functions, agencies would be set.

The reorganization of townships and counties is scientific. Firstly, it totally complies with the requirements of market economy. The market economy asks for "officers stepping back and civics stepping forward" and "small government and large society". In case of bulky governmental organization, wild-running public power and serious corruption, farmers would be easily hurt by varied kinds of unlawful acts. Therefore, the townships of developed countries are all of self-governance. Secondly, it conforms to traditions and conditions of China. Since the ancient time, China has had the tradition of "imperial power does not reach county" and the villages under the county are governed by the families and country gentlemen. Before the reform and opening-up, the people's commune also had only ten to twenty clerks. At that time, the villages were not in chaos. Thirdly, it is beneficial to political power and social stability. The removal of township government can improve the strained relation between cadres and civics, safeguard people's interests and maintain social stability. Lastly, it can tremendously push forward deep-level reform. Currently, the resistance for our village self-governance as well as election and power exercising of village officers comes from the township government to a large extent. Of the institutional reform from the Central government to local government, the one that has the greatest difficulty to be implemented is also the one that is placed at the least significant end, i.e., the reform of township government. Removing the township government will greatly stimulate the reform of political and administrative systems.

8.2.3 Legislation of Property Law in Rural Area

We need to improve the real property right legislation in rural areas and guarantee the realization of farmers' rights. Our legal traditions are basically similar to the continental law system. However, in terms of the basic law of market economy, our civil and commercial laws are very weak. Without the *Civil Code*, to solve the contractual relationship in rural areas with the *Contract Law* seems to be a little far-fetched. Such situation must be changed as soon as possible. What's urgent is to accelerate the legislation for the confirmation and protection of rural land and other property rights. It is not only the base and premise for improving our rural real right laws, but also the key to safeguard varied farmers' rights to endow farmers with the ownership to land. Our *Real Right Law* was implemented in October of 2007 which is obviously a big step forward to the guarantee of rural land right. It is really an encouraging legislative measure. However, we have to admit that the law still is conservative and needs further improvement in terms of sufficient and effective exercising of rural real rights.

8.2.4 Social Security in Rural Area

We need to standardize the legal system of rural labor market and social security, and promote social fairness and productivity development.

Agricultural industrialization and scale operation would break the existing livelihood security pattern from a plot of land. Employment and rural unemployment would emerge successively. The legislation should coordinate the relationship between the employers and employees and promote social fairness while ensuring the efficiency. The free flow of rural surplus labor and social security also urgently need the standardization by legislation.

8.2.5 Construction of Economic Law System in Rural Area

We need to improve the rural economic law system to realize appropriate intervention to rural economy by the state. We should learn from the complete rural economic law system with the agricultural law as the core that has been formed in the developed countries. The forming of agricultural law system cannot be separated from the macro-control of government. An appropriate intervention to rural economy should take into consideration the overall situation of varied regulating measures including the plan, fiscal, tax, finance, price and foreign trade. We also need to construct and improve the agricultural investment legislation; trade legislation for agricultural products and industrialized products required by agriculture; legislation for stimulating moderate concentration and scale operation of land; and legislation for rural credit and scientific & technological promotion so that the government can fully exercise the role of regulator within legal framework.

NOTES

1. 1 Han Jun, "Safeguard and Promote Rural Reform, Development and Stability in Accordance with the Law," from *Collection of Legal System Seminars from the Central Committee of the Communist Party of China* (Beijing: Law Press China, 2001), 113.
2. 2 Ren Dapeng et al, "Research Overview of Agricultural Laws of 2001," *Journal of China Agricultural University* (Social Sciences Edition) 1 (2002).
3. 3 Sun Dawu, "My Opinion on 'Three Agriculture-related Problems'", accessed November 25, 2003, www.sinoliberal.com.
4. 4 Huang Changcai, "WTO Legal Practices and Our Agricultural Issues," *Journal of Nanchang University* (Human Society Edition) 3 (2002).
5. 5 Guo Shutian, "Suggestions for Revising Agricultural Law Concerning Ten Issues," *Rural Cooperative Economic Operation and Management* 3 (2001).
6. 6 Liu Long, "Minister of Finance Jin Renqing: Comprehensive Deployment of Direct Subsidy to Grain Farmers," People's Network, accessed March 6, 2004, http://www.people.com.cn.

Chapter Nine

Judicial Drawbacks of "Three Agriculture-related Problems" and Corresponding Strategies

9.1 AN ANALYSIS OF JUDICIAL DRAWBACKS IN "THREE AGRICULTURE-RELATED PROBLEMS"

Compared with the legislation on "three agriculture-related problems", the judicial and law enforcement supervision of "three agriculture-related problems" are weaker and feeble. The law enforcement subject and act of agricultural administration are far from standardization. Some law enforcement subjects integrate law enforcement and business operation and play the role of both referee and sportsman. The law enforcement departments and personnel abuse their power of law enforcement. A saying that is quite popular in our society goes like this, "to handle an affair, one need to make a law, set an organization, go through one more procedure, and pay one more item of penalty and charge". The applicable agricultural laws cannot be implemented and enforced and the privileged individuals still have the final say for agricultural economic activities. The CCTV *Law Today* reported on May 22, 2003 an event that the township cadres harrowed and destroyed the cornfield in Lianhe Village, Longmiao Town, and Shuyang County, Jiangsu Province and forced the farmers to transfer the land to the county committee office for contract development and planting of flowers. The event exposed the serious disadvantages of insufficient justice and rampant administrative violation of laws. There are still many similar events that haven't been exposed which exist in many places rather than just Shuyang County. Today, the mention of agricultural development would usually lead to "adjusting the structure and enriching the farmers". When delivering his speech during his inspection in

Sichuan, Jiang Zemin opened his remarks with the adjustment of structure. As a matter of fact, that is not what it's all about. We need to be soberly aware of two issues: the first is that the agricultural products of foreign countries are cheaper than ours; the second is that we are now forcing our farmers to produce and have led to the formation of large-area, multiple-species and long-term surplus of agricultural products. Now the macro-control personnel frequently attribute the zero increase of farmers' income to farmers' failure to adjust the structure. However, as to how to adjust the structure, they just become the armchair strategist or build castle in the air. Imagine that you used to produce the rice and now you need to produce fruits. Where could you get the funds? Relevant circulation system in the past also entailed costs which all were paid by farmers. We are really not sure whether the agricultural adjustment is supporting or impairing farmers. What's more, today's structural adjustment in China usually means the call from the superior authority and the stress on typical cases and vanity projects from the lower-level of governments, which always evolves into a kind of torment. The result is always failure rather than success and the farmers are the ultimate victims. As a matter of fact, Chinese farmers are not stupid at all. Instead, they are full of vigor and vitality. What's in shortage is the macro-control policy and legal guarantee for developing such vigor and vitality. [1]

Why are the *Agricultural Law* and *Land Contract Law* a mere scrap of paper in the eyes of the county-level and township-level cadres? Why do the county-level and township-level cadres have the gut to coerce farmers to transfer the land with force? To sum up, "rule-of-man" is making trouble. These grass-roots cadres and departments "attach importance to rule-of-man and make light of rule-of-law". When the law is inconsistent with the leading cadres' requirements, they would rather comply with the leaders' demands. In face of human relationship and the law, they would rather sacrifice the law and reserve human relationship. There exists a popular saying in the society which goes like this, "the black head (legal document) is inferior to the red head (promulgated document of the Party and government administration), the red head inferior to the white head (restricted document of Party and government administration), and the white head inferior to the verbal (direct orders from the leaders)." We always say that farmers' legal awareness is dim and faint. Why is it dim and faint? What is the root cause? That is it. Farmers have been heavily hit by rule-of-man time and time again while seeking for legal protection. How could they have confidence in the law? According to the questionnaire survey conducted by an expert from China Agricultural University (388 samples), about 90% of farmers think it impossible to realize the equality of law application, about 80% of farmers think township cadres fail to act by law, about 25% choose to "bear insult" when their rights and interests are infringed, and the vast farmers show almost complete disappointment over the law. Under such background, when their suffering goes beyond endurance, farmers have no other way but applying for an audience with the higher authorities to appeal for help. I used to interview some farmers appealing for help to higher authorities and ask them why they didn't file a lawsuit. They gave me the surprisingly similar answer: is the law effective? Where can you find Justice Bao (an official from history who is famous for his adherence to principles and upholding of justice) now? We need to turn to the Communist Party now. Isn't the Communist Party a party that works wholeheartedly for the people? Wouldn't the Communist Party uphold the justice for us being treated so unjustly? I feel terribly ashamed because of this as a lawyer and researcher of law. Despair is the greatest sorrow. If farmers still have faith in the tenet of the Communist Party, our Party should try its best not to tear up the last dream of farmers. As a country that is accelerating the construction of socialist rule-of-law and improving the market economic system, how can China allow some people to tread on the law so arbitrarily that our people feel thoroughly disappointed with the law? The effectiveness evaluation and implementation of legislation are closely connected. Without correct and effective implementation and enforcement, even the best law could only be a decoration or even goes to the opposite side of the original intention of the legislation. "Strengthening the administration only through the law will not always lead the villages to order and prosperity", Li Changping sighed with emotion. The reason for his signing also lies in this. "For the issues emerged in rural areas, our habitual practice is strengthening the administration which reminds me of many things. For example, the rural finance becomes increasingly chaotic ever since the emergence of Rural Operation and Management Bureau; and the expenses for compulsory education in rural areas becomes increasingly high and education becomes increasingly inaccessible for children after the emergence of *Law on Compulsory Education*"[2] , said Li. However, after reasonable analysis, we will find that the issue lies not in the legislation but the enforcement.

If the key and difficulty of our rule-of-law construction lie in the judicial link, the priority among priorities and the extremely difficult part would be the judicial in rural areas. The existing judicial difficulty in China is mainly presented by judicial dependence (especially the administrative intervention that remains serious), judicial corruption (lacking necessary and feasible supervision and restriction mechanism), judicial crisis of credibility, lack of judicial seriousness, and shortage of enforcement efforts which "totally break people's heart". All these are especially serious in rural areas.

On September 6, 1999, China Youth News *Freezing Point* published the report *I Seek Justice for Farmers* by Luo Xuhui, one of its journalists. In the report, Luo describes a real story about a farmer from today's northern China. The farmer, Zhou Guangli, comes from Zhouzhuang Village, Yanlou Township, Yanggu County, and Liaocheng City, Shandong Province and is named "the farmer lawyer". He has successively won many cases for local farmers. However, because of this, he also offended the village cadres and encountered many frustrations. For example, in order to avoid the possible revenge, he had to lead a vagabond life in other counties or provinces for three months. He was ever attacked by others: he was once beat by the deputy township leader and other people violently till faint after he sued the illegal penalty from the Family Planning Department on behalf of a farmer. Zhou went to reason with the township government the next day, but the township leader refused to acknowledge the whole thing. He reported the case to local police station in the township, but the local police station rejected the case at the excuse of insufficient evidence. However, Zhou still has faith in the law and court, and therefore gave vent to his grievance through his own way (a legal way of course): he asked for several hundred sets of publicity materials *Civilians Can Sue Officials* from the Administrative Litigation Tribunal of the court, posted the materials on outstanding places of the villages in Yangzhuang Township and left his name and address on each set of the materials. We can see from this the significance of the law in a farmer's heart. However, finally there was a case that not only destroyed Zhou's confidence and embarrassed the people's court upholding justice for farmers. In May, 1995, Sipeng Township Government, Yanggu County, under the excuse that some villagers from Xuezhuang Village had committed the crimes of disrupting public service, producing forged and fake commodity, having more than one child, illegal occupation of land for house building etc., pushed over more than 60 houses with bulldozers and looted the house appliances and clothes of the villagers. In March, 1996, Xue Yuling and other seven villagers whose houses were demolished turned to Zhou Guangli for help in filing a lawsuit against the township government and asked if they could win the case. Zhou told the villagers that those who have committed crime deserve punishment or even imprisonment, but the township government definitely had no right to pull down the villagers' houses. Therefore, the township governments would have to compensate the villagers and the villagers could definitely win the case. Zhou prepared and submitted the complaint to the county court and pleaded for revoking the specific administrative act by the defendant-Sipeng Township Government that has infringed the plaintiffs' property right, returning the looted property and paying RMB 360,000 for compensation. However, the case which is sure to win according to Zhou could not be filed with the court. By the end of May, 1996, Yanggu county court asked for instructions from the Party Committee and the People's Congress of the county. According to *China Youth News*, the court thought that the case involved the overall situation of the county and reported the case to relevant leaders of the Party committee. The related leaders paid great attention to the case, but instructed that the court might consider not accepting the case. On the other hand, some agents' ad item, in accordance with Article 42 of *Administrative Procedural Law*, i.e., "the court shall file the case for trial or give a decision of no acceptance in seven days", urged the court many times and appealed for help from the intermediate court. Some even appealed for help from the provincial TV station. The leaders from the intermediate court also called or personally visited the court to urge the court to take actions. The county court fell into dilemma: on one hand, the court should file the case for trial in accordance with the law. Nevertheless, if the case was filed, the township government would lose the lawsuit as the act of the township government had no legal ground. Furthermore, such kind of act happened not only in Sipeng Township. Although the result of judgment would be beneficial for standardizing the acts of township governments in future, the chain reaction it created would exert great influence on the work of Sipeng Township or even the whole county. For this, the county leaders considered the court should not file the case. On the other hand, non-acceptance for the case means that the litigation right of the party involved has been deprived of. If the decision of "non-acceptance" is issued, the plaintiff might make appeal to the higher court or ask for help from the superior authority in accordance with relevant procedures. Then not only the court should undertake the responsibility of slackness in law enforcement, but also relevant personnel would be called to account for the misjudged case. The whole process would then affect the work of the county and produced huge social influence beyond calculation. In the end, the dispute needs to be settled by litigation. The dilemma of the court reflects an issue of universal relevance for our grass-roots judicial work which has profound historical reasons. It is undoubtedly of great significance for promoting legalization in the vast Chinese rural society to solve the issue.[3] "What's worrisome to the world is no law under resolute enforcement rather than no law", said Heng Kuan in his *Discourses on Salt and Iron* from Han Dynasty. If there is no law, we can make law. However, there would be inconceivable results if there is law which is not enforced.[4]

The causes for the judicial barriers in rural areas mainly include the following:

9.1.1 Non-independence of Judicial Work

First, the administrative is superior to the judicial or the judicial is subject to the administrative. Our judicial system still has no sufficient capability to overcome the unwarranted intervention beyond the law. If the administration would not recognize the consequence resulting from the law, it will lead to illegal administration. This is where the value of administrative adjudication lies. Our goal is to restrict the administrative power of the government with the judicial power of the state so as to rectify the results caused by illegal administrative acts of the government through administrative litigation and remedy the rights and interests of the counterpart. Therefore, it is not irredeemable and hopeless for the administrative officers to not act by law. The critical strike lies in that the people's court in charge of the case is in the end subject to the intervention of the government, which therefore closes the last door to safeguard justice.

The situation that the judicial is subject to the administrative remains serious today and is distinctly manifested by the system of case instruction upon request. Why would the grass-roots judicial personnel need to ask for instructions from local government leaders for those cases that should be accepted in accordance with the constitution and other laws? The constitution and other laws are in themselves important and improved policies that have been fixed. To strictly enforce the law means strictly implementing the policies of the ruling party. The judiciary, especially the civil and administrative judiciary, with professional nature needs even more to comply with the constitutional principle of "the judiciary authorities shall exercise their judicial power independently in accordance with the law". This is also the basic principle and goal of our reform of judicial system. However, the reality of our grass-roots judiciary is the judicial always fails to get rid of the improper intervention from varied sides, leading to the result that the dispute could not be settled timely and a series of social issues were triggered. In terms of the issue, the judicial system reform shares similar necessity with the reform of the administrative enforcement systems like the industrial and commercial administration, technical supervision and People's Bank of China. It seems like that the reform of judicial system, especially the reform of the judicial system at the city and county level, has become an important link to maintain stable development of the countryside.

Second, the administrative shows intentional repulsion or disagreement to the law. In China, the enforcement of most laws is realized through governmental acts. Therefore, such intentional repulsion or disagreement would exert great harm and damage to the judicial and directly affect the judicial authority. The administrative officers might know through political study that today's strategy for running a state is rule-of-law, but they may not know that the subject of rule-of-law is the masses and the object is the national affairs undertaken by governmental officers. As a result, they always formulate and enforce some county laws (i.e., local rules) that go against the constitution and other laws, and therefore improperly intervene in the judicial power that should be independently exercised as regulated by the constitution and infringe the farmers' democratic, property and even personal rights. Sometimes the administrative disagrees with the law. One reason lies in that the value orientation of the law is to regulate and govern the public power which naturally has the inclination of being abused. In other words, the power is always trying to break through the regulation and governance of the law. Furthermore, as the grass-roots work is complicated and overloaded, the officers always like to adopt some local measures which are more efficient to deal with some tough nuts. Some of these local measures are exactly opposite to the procedures regulated by the law. Efficiency and fairness are inherently a pair of contradictory and unified value criteria. We should strive for both rather than making the two go against each other. However, the repulsion or ignorance of fairness in rule-of-law resulting from administrative efficiency has led to total disappearance of the judicial authoritativeness in China. The reality has showed us that the real key object that needs legal education is the governmental officer rather than the masses. Realization of Chinese rule-of-law cannot depend on the automatic awakening of the governmental officers' legal awareness. In rural areas, we should fight against the viewpoint that regards the law as the tool for "punishing the unruly people", doubts the rule-of-law or defends the illegal administrative acts by the grass-roots government under the excuse of the so-called national condition that farmers are uneducated.

Today the issue in urgent need of solution is how to build a fair and efficient judicial system that can independently exercise its power in accordance with the law at the vast grass-roots level so as to timely settle different kinds of social conflicts including the conflict between the people and government, and to safeguard social order and realize social justice through the system. It is certain that, under a good system environment, even the feeble and dim awareness of law from some officers cannot lead to serious disaster. Just like Comrade Deng Xiaoping said while summarizing the Cultural Revolution lessons, a good system can prevent the evil people from doing evil things arbitrarily.

According to judicial principles, the courts should all be independent without superior-subordinate relation. All trial organizations and judges are independent entities that utilize their knowledge and experience to deal with specific cases in accordance with the law. This is one of the significant characteristics that distinct the court from the administrative organization and distinct the judge from the public officers of the administrative organizations. However, in China, the existing court has no distinction with the administrative organizations in terms of such characteristic.

In rural areas, the judicial work is realized mainly through the township court, office of justice, police substation and governments, all of which belong to agencies except for the township government as a level of government. The court, as the core of rural judiciary, has no independent will at all. The township government and the county court are the superior of the township court, to which orders can be made. Furthermore, the Party leaders have certain influence. The leadership of the politics and law committee to the personnel and organizations is sufficient to make the township court judges totally obedient.

9.1.2 Judicial Corruption

In a society, there may emerge corruption where there is power. However, the judicial corruption belongs to the most dangerous one as the judiciary represents the last defense line of social justice. If the defense line is broken through, those being hurt would include not only the party involved but also the image of the judicial authorities, dignity of the law and people's confidence in the country. In real life, some people have contempt for the judicial personnel and police officers as these officers mix their official businesses with corruptions of wine and entertainment. "The judicial people who not only extort the plaintiff and defendant, but also pin the blame on the incomplete and unsound legal system" described in the novel *Abandoned City* also discloses the ugliness of the judicial corruption. Yao Xiaohong, the former Vice President from Jiangxian County of Shanxi, is illiterate, roguish and ignorant of law. The President of the court uses an ordinary jeep, but Yao uses a Santana 2000, the driver of which would always sound the horn at the gate of the court. It is said the horn is to "inform" the police officers inside the court to greet Yao. When Yao walks off the car, a police officer should be there with his hand on the roof of the car door to protect Yao from being hurt by the roof of the car door. Cursing at people with mouth, striking people with hands and hitting people with feet are the "conventional actions" of Yao. Investigation shows that during his two years of service, Yao illegally put over one hundred people into detention, most of whom have suffered such means of torture as handcuff applying and beating. Despite being illiterate and just a cadre at the grade of section-chief, Yao was infinitely resourceful with well-connected network of relationship. The investigation into his crimes has failed for four times before achieving substantial progress after multiple times of written instructions from the Central government leaders including Jiang Zemin, Luo Gan and Xiao Yang. However, during the trial of first instance, Yao still managed to move into the wards for high-ranking officials through medical parole, colluded with the people involved at will to form offensive and defensive alliance. We cannot ignore the perniciousness of the judicial corrupt officials at rural grass-roots level like Yao Xiaohong. Judicial corruption had different expressions in rural areas, including the police officers' dissipated life, unruly work style and the corruption of judicial acts like non-acceptance of case that should be accepted for trial, extortion of confession by torture, illegal imprisonment, dealing with the case for special relation, power-for-money deal, perverting the law in making judgment and decisions, and defiance of law etc. All these have played havoc with the image and authority of the judiciary.

In face of the judicial corruption at the grass-roots level, the key to solve the issue is to find way to establish a feasible supervision and check mechanism. However, what's the situation of the existing supervision and check?

Some may wonder whether the independence is contradictory with the supervision and check. As a matter of fact, the two belongs to a unity of contradictions. The independence asks for no illegal interference rather than no supervision or check. The question is: who would implement effective supervision and check to the judiciary in rural areas? The traditional supervision and check in China means mainly the supervision from the people's congress and Chinese People's Political Consultative Conference (CPPCC), from the procuratorial organ (People's Procuratorate), from the masses, and from the media, all of which are quite weak or even nonexistent in rural areas.

First, the channel for local people's congresses to exercise their power is blocked. According to the report of *Southern Urban Daily (Fang Yuan)*, in the regular general election of the year, in face of the fact that the people's congress of Liannan County elect the court President and Chief Procurator through illegal means, the Standing Committee of People's Congress of Qingyuan City and the Electoral Committee of the Provincial Standing Committee jointly declared invalid the election and guided the county people's congress to re-elect the President and the Chief Procurator, thus successfully safeguarding the dignity of the law.[5] "Bad thing" was changed into "good thing". However, we should see that what the standing committee and the election committee of standing committee from Qingyuan City corrected was just an illegal election, i.e., an illegal *Election Measures*. If we don't retrospect on the root cause of the illegal *Election Measures*, and timely correct the measures, it would be difficult to guarantee no emergence of another illegal *Election Measures*. The illegal election of Liannan County derived from the *Measures to Elect Government Agency Leaders at the Same Level on the First Session of the Twelfth People's Congress of Liannan Yao Nationality Autonomous County* ("*Election Measures*") that was against the law at the superior level. Article 2.1 of the "Election Measures" specified that "the presidium should nominate, in accordance with the law, a candidate for the Chairman of Standing Committee of the county people's congress, county magistrate, court president and chief procurator. Single-candidate election would be implemented if there is no candidate jointly nominated by ten representatives. Primary election would be implemented to determine an official candidate before single-candidate election if the number of nominated candidates is larger than the number of candidates that should be elected." What surprises us was that the *Election Measures* that obviously goes against the law at superior level was actually passed on the assembly of the county people's congress and quoted as the basis for election which directly led to the happening of the illegal election. If the drafter of the *Election Measures* had a little common sense of law, there would have been no emergence of the illegal *Election Measures*. If the members of the standing committee of people's congress had a little common sense of law, the illegal *Election Measures* would not have been submitted to the people's congress assembly for deliberation. Further more, if the vast majority of the people's congress members had a little common sense of law and dared to vote in accordance with their will, the illegal *Election Measures* would not have been passed on the assembly. The fact is however quite contrary to the assumption. The people's congress, as the legislative body, showed serious lack of professional knowledge of law, and the institution for people's congress to exercise national power also showed obstruction in the channel for expression of people's will. According to the news, after the illegal election of the court President and Chief Procurator by Liannan People's Congress, the representatives and masses from the county showed much complaints and discussions. It is obvious that the county People's Congress has failed to attach importance to the representatives' opinion. It is because of this that a letter under the signature of "some representatives from Liannan People's Congress" has been sent to the Election Committee Office of the Standing Committee of Guangdong People's Congress. Except for the lack of knowledge reserve, the lack of energy may also the cause for the representatives' failure to normally perform their functions. Since the representatives of the people's congress are not full-time, and their daily work may affect their function to speak for people's livelihood. On the people's congress assembly, some representatives, owing to of insufficient preparation, have no time and ability to thoroughly think over the differences in opinion about the topics for discussion. They usually just listen to the reports, air some opinions, put forward some suggestions in a casual way, and "follow the general trend" while voting for a bill or decision.

The case fully shows that, as the highest organ of "all power belongs to the people", the existing people's congress still has great distance from the requirements of the constitution, law and the masses. Just imagine, how can the people's congress represent people's will well? In face of such election result, how could such people's congress exercise its supervision power well over the president of people's court?

Second, the legal supervision function of procuratorial organ exists in name only. The *Constitution* defines the people's procuratorate as the legal supervision organ, which remains in name only. From the prosecutorial work report delivered by Jia Chunwang, Chief Procurator of Supreme People's Procuratorate on the Second Session of the Tenth People's Congress in 2004, we can clearly see the main work and nature of the people's procuratorate. The main functions of the people's procuratorate include ratification of arrest, public prosecution, demurrer, antecedent trial for investigation of malfeasance case etc., of which, only the demurrer has certain nature of supervision. Legal supervision can be divided into two types: that of broad sense and that of narrow sense. The subject of legal supervision in broad sense includes any individual and organization. It is obviously short of discussion significance to list the procuratorial organ as one of the subjects of legal supervision in broad sense. The legal supervision organ in narrow sense should be the organs that have the right to directly rectify or instruct relevant organs to rectify through certain means the acts of the supervised subjects. In terms of the nature, status and mutual relation of people's court and people's procuratorate, the law specifies that the two organs independently exercise their functions respectively and they are basically of parallel relationship in practice, although the procuratorial organ has legal supervision power over the trial procedures of the adjudication organ. Concerning the business relationship, in the public prosecution case tried by the court as the adjudicator, the procuratorate would appear at the court with the representation of the public prosecutor, and the procuratorate would have the demurrer right in case of any error found in the effective verdict of inferior court. The procuratorate may be regarded as one party involved in the trial procedures (some people disagree to this viewpoint and regard the act of public prosecutor as the judicial act of the State, thus different from other participants in the case. Further discussion may be necessary for the topic), its status cannot be deemed as equal to the court objectively in litigious activities. Otherwise, there would be no circumstances in which the public prosecutor leaves the court in anger or even wrangle with the adjudicatory personnel. It would be too farfetched to say that the procuratorial organ is implementing legal supervision function at the same time in the public prosecution case. Next, let's talk about demurrer. How can the procuratorate exercise the demurrer right? This is really an issue. If we want the procuratorate to fully exercise the demurrer right, we should instruct the court to transfer all relevant cases to the procuratorate for investigation as of their effective date. In this way, it is obvious that the taxpayers would need to support a large group of unnecessary "idlers" since the function can be exercised totally by the parties involved themselves. What's more, there are few cases in which the procuratorate actively propose demurrer in practice. In most of the cases, the parties involved file the application of demurrer first and the procuratorate decides whether to propose demurrer through investigation later.

In rural areas, there is rare "unjust case" or "misjudged case" that has the honor to be favored by the prosecutorial organ with demurrer proposal. The procuratorate usually avoid the increasing number of farmers that appeal for help as if they are the plague, not to mention demurrer for them.

Third, the masses' supervision is feeble and futile. If we want to make the masses' legal supervision effective, we should provide channels for masses' voice to receive reply. Since the existing political system could not satisfy the demand, the masses' supervision remains feeble and futile. Concerning the civilians' unjust treatment, ancient people expected people like Justice Bao (an official from history who is famous for his adherence to principles and upholding of justice) to uphold justice for them. In modern times, the capitalist democratic thought came to a premature end as a result of the stubborn resistance from the feudal survivals, invasion of big powers as well as other domestic strife and foreign aggression. In the years of burning passions of "the great liberator of Chairman Mao" and "the Communist Party loves the people", the individual's self-ego was denied by the people's commune which is large in size and collective in nature, not to mention unjust treatment. At that time, the only unjust treatment was from the landlord and capitalist in the old days, which were under denouncement and punishment in the movement after liberation. In today's China under the rule of law, individual freedom and rights shall receive maximum respect. "All people are equal before the law" is no longer a slogan. If people encounter any unjust treatment, restriction of freedom, infringement of right or unfair treatment, they can turn to the court for help in a society under rule-of-law. However, what can people do in case of judicial corruption? Can they turn to the Communist Party, the government or the people's congress for help? There are varied circumstances in practice, but only a few people have their problems solved through these means. Otherwise there would not have emerged so large groups of people appealing for help from superior authorities. In face of the surging appeal for help from the superior authorities, we should find breakthrough from the system rather than reproach the incompetence of current government excessively. Also, we need to dredge rather than resort to brute force. There may emerge some elites from the large group of people appealing for help from superior authorities in modern society under rule-of-law who explore ways in adversity. Maybe our people should spontaneously form some groups or organizations that have independent status on the political arena of our society and the capability to represent some or a kind of individuals or groups to conduct equal dialogue with the government. When such groups or organizations emerge and become mature, the masses' supervision would become effective. For this, the government should be open, the scholars and media should cry out and all communities of our society should show more understanding and participation.

9.1.3 Crisis with Judicial Reputation

The adjudication method of "barefoot judge" Ma Xiwu is quite popular among the public, especially the farmers. One reason is the role of publicity and the other is that the image of such kind of judge is close to people in real life, easy to warm people's heart and consistent with the interpersonal relationship of Chinese tradition. Today's "iron-face judge" and the rural cadres' "three iron policies" have led to farmers' total disappointment with the grassroots judiciary. In the *Notes Taken Whiling Working in Villages* by Ma Yinlu, the Division Chief of Organization Department, the village Secretary Wang Jianxiao states frankly and honestly:

Qixiu Village, with many issues, is very difficult to manage. What's more, the county and township governments are not practical, making it impossible to manage the village well. For example, after you arrive at our county, the incumbent secretary of the Party Committee of our township declared on the agricultural tax mobilization meeting convened for the whole county that "three iron policies" would be adopted for tax collection. At that time, I didn't know what was in your mind. In fact, I was scared. The slogan of "three iron policies" just sounds like the "three all policies (The policy of burn all, kill all, and loot all) " of the Japanese devils. Some villagers ground their teeth, "No wonder that they call us the unruly people who refuse to pay tax". The following facts also proved that my fear was not superfluous. The cadres stationed at the village drove the police cars and shouted from one end to the other end of the village. Some villagers and children would still cry upon the sight or sound of the police car.[6]

Our existing grass-roots governments have broken their promises to common people. The judicial organs that shouldn't serve but are actually serving for the government have also broken their promises to common people. While visiting the villagers, we heard many complaints: what's the role of the local police station and court? They don't go to catch or manage the robbers and hooligans everywhere since there is no benefit from those things. What they usually do is to catch and manage the gambling, violation of family planning policies, failure to pay tax and "prostitution"[7] . Why? Because they can get money from these. They can impose heavy fine at will, pull down peoples' houses, take away peoples' cows or sheep, or put people into imprisonment. They would complain about the insufficient police strength and funds in face of the difficulty in filing, trial and enforcement of common cases. They can extend the trial of a common debt dispute to a year and enforcement of the judgment to a far distant date. Numerous theft and robbery cases couldn't be solved. The hooligans and other vicious power were not contained or curbed. However, when it comes to the violation of family planning policies, prostitution, gambling and refusal to pay tax, the police would employ all police power and sometimes even recruit street loiterers as hatchet man. As to the violation of family planning policies, farmers from many places reflect a common phenomenon: when there are people who show the inclination of violating the family planning policies, the cadres would pay no attention to it first even after being informed of the inclination. These cadres would intentionally wait for the birth of the children and go to collect heavy fine after the birth of the babies. The farmers' words may be biased to a certain extent, but they also reflect the worrisome situation of the judicial crisis of credibility in the rural areas from a perspective. If we are not vigilant enough to the situation and change the status quo as soon as possible, the issue would become a great obstacle to the rule-of-law construction in China.

In face of the chaotic situation of rural judiciary, Zhou Guangli sent more than 1,200 sets of publicity materials of *Administrative Procedure Law* for the people's Court of Yanggu County in the above-mentioned Zhou Guangli case. The end of the publicity material, that is,"Call up your courage, use the law to protect your legitimate rights and interests and promote the administrative organs to exercise their functions in accordance with the law. The door of People's Court of Yanggu County will always be open for you" is both funny and distressed. It is true that we all want to have our rights and interests safeguarded to the greatest extent. However, it would be difficult to realize such good wish without a good judicial system and environment.

9.2 STRATEGIES FOR JUDICIAL WORK TACKLING "THREE AGRICULTURE-RELATED PROBLEMS"

9.2.1 To Strengthen and Stabilize Judicial Staff in Rural Area

The weak judicial staff in rural areas represents an important factor that restricts rural rule-of-law. On one hand, large group of graduates from the politics and law universities and colleges are blocked outside the door of the judicial organs in China; on the other hand, the judicial personnel at grass-roots level show seriously insufficient quality. The contradiction is related with the self-reproduction in our existing judicial organs as well as the backward education, economic conditions and judicial situation in rural areas. To change such situation as soon as possible, there are three methods:

The first is to realize fairness of civil servants' treatment. The civil servants who have aspiration for the judicial work at grass-roots level are always terrified by the plight of rural areas, especially the backward areas in western China, and usually striving for a position in urban or developed areas. This conforms to the law of market economy. We advocate, but cannot rely on the selfless dedication of others. Many people may ignore a common knowledge issue that causes regional disparity as well as urban and rural difference here. Why peoples' treatments are so different in different areas after the same civil servant examination of national unified standard? I have two friends who both graduated with bachelor degree of law from the same famous school and luckily become the judges of grass-roots courts. However, the annual income of the one in one district of Shenzhen is eight times of that the one in the county-level city of Hubei Province (based on the legitimate income within the scope of their profession). Some people who are unfamiliar with the reality may have doubt on this. However, this is just what the reality is. Speaking of the issue of high salary for a clean government, Huang Sanhe, the NPC representative, President of Guangdong Association of Industry and Commerce and Deputy Mayor of Zhaoqing City sighed, "In remote and mountain areas and in poverty-stricken areas, some cadres with over 30 years of service length and department-chief-level honor also only have a monthly salary of over RMB 1,000. Their life would be really difficult if there is no other income for their families since they have to support their parents and children and pay for their parents' health care and child's education. Under such circumstances, if a rich boss asks these people for help, they will easily show lopsided psychology and conduct deviant behaviors". He also shared some typical cases, in which, graduates from the same college had totally different income after they successfully reached the same level through great efforts since some of them stayed at the provincial city and some went back to mountain areas for constructing their hometown. "The income for the people in poorer areas is lower. In this way, who would be willing to construct the township and village? It would only be difficult to retain talents in these areas".[8]

To realize fairness of civil servants' treatment means to minimize the civil servants' income gap in different districts for the job of same nature and same level so that the judicial staff at grass-roots level, especially in rural areas, can have reliable support and our national distribution of judicial force can be balanced.

The second is to accelerate rural infrastructure and cultural construction. In the circles of economics and sociology, most people advocate township construction. I believe that their wishes are good, i.e., to enable rural areas to get rid of the small farmer life-style of "going to work upon sunrise and stopping work upon sunset" as soon as possible, accelerate rural modernization and promote the fairness of the whole society. The feasibility of the wishes needs further discussion, so there is no need for conclusion here. However, be it small town or new village, construction asks for input and the government shall undertake unshirkable responsibility. Recent years have witnessed innumerable great achievements of "image projects" in many cities, including the garden type development of riverside road, reconstruction of old city, urban landscaping, recreation square etc., all of which have cost too much. I don't mean to say that these projects are unnecessary. What I want to emphasize is that the backwardness of rural infrastructure construction and cultural input have made it difficult to sing the beautiful song of "hopeful field". It is also the wide gap of infrastructure and cultural construction between urban areas and rural areas that make the scholars supporting agriculture "start off with great enthusiasm but return with empty luggage", just as was written in the song. The varied inconvenience and baldness in the countryside make the rule-of-law volunteers in rural areas unable to resist the loneliness in the end.

The third is to strive for stricter access system of judicial qualification. Professor Su Li, based on the fact that some vice-presidents of some grass-roots courts found it difficult to find "Xiucai (one who passed the imperial examination at the county level)" with political tasks, came to a conclusion that "the circumstance that the court excludes law school graduates especially in grass-roots courts as a general situation is non-existent and fictional."[9] I am sure that Professor Su lacks in-depth investigation concerning this issue. At the end of 20th century, it was very difficult to be recruited to any departments supported or half-supported by governmental finance rather than just the court, as these areas are power rent-seeking places. Without effective supervision and check mechanism, the power could expand to the largest extent so that the market supply and demand rule almost cuts no ice here. What is political task? Haven't you heard the saying of "where there is policy, there is strategy"? What I learned is exactly the "opposite side" of what Professor Su saw. The court reported to the superior that it is short of 10 permanent staff and the superior political task requires five law school graduates at least. Five people with professional training would be strictly selected and five well-connected individuals would be arranged (including the armyman transferred to civilian work and people transferred from other departments who don't necessarily need the skills but must have the relation). This was not the worst. Some courts, in face of the political task, favored more well-connected individuals and rejected large group of law school graduates under the excuse and complaint that "graduates are unwilling to come here". The situation has not been improved till today. China must make great efforts to exchange blood of the judicial system and replace the unqualified personnel inside the judicial system with the large amount of law school graduates or unused law talents that have already acquired the qualification of lawyers or passed the judicial examination (refers to those who are not actually practicing law). This will of course touch the vested interests, especially the interests of persons in power. However, the chaos and low quality of the judicial staff will fundamentally harm the long-term interests of all people, including the people with vested interests. After weighing the advantages and disadvantages, we should be very clear about which course to follow.

9.2.2 To Speed Up Judicial Reform in Rural Area

The ultimate goal of our judicial reform should be safeguarding judicial fairness which should include the procedural fairness, substantial fairness and judicial efficiency. Besides, the specific system design should be carried out by focusing on how to ensure and realize judicial fairness.[10]

Due to the insufficient judicial force in rural areas and the resistance of rural traditions to the law, the judicial model of rural areas always falls far behind the judicial reform of China. The model of "being reasonable—being convinced", cadre conciliation authority, connection, human relationship and the like have not only become the main methods for handling disputes in rural areas, but also penetrated inversely into our national judiciary.[11] The weakening of national authority of law has even created the hotbed for breeding the governance of underworld society nature.

Accelerating the judicial reform in rural areas is the pioneer project for accelerating the rule-of-law process in rural areas. We must make the judicial activities in rural areas consistent with orientation of the judicial system and reform of the whole country, and put emphasis on safeguarding the authority of national laws. Recent years have witnessed a tendency of local rule-of-law or rule-of-law localization. This is not only a contradictory proposition, but also a dangerous thing. The uniformity of laws in one country is very important. Appropriate change or adjustment in accordance with the constitution is allowed only under extremely special circumstance. It goes against the idealized conception of rule-of-law modernization to replace the state laws with rural traditions, elders' willingness and indigenous knowledge, or allow these rural elements to "form positive interaction" with the state laws.

The key of the judicial reform in rural areas lies in the reform of trial mode which means to handle cases in strict accordance with the procedural law. In some districts, due to the low quality of the judicial staff, the trial procedures are in severely short of seriousness and the cases are handled completely based on common local knowledge. In the rural court, it is a common phenomenon that the judge rebukes or "educates" the party involved like reproaching his/her own child; and the court investigation process becomes the process for the party involved to read out the "witness testimony". Sometimes, for the convenience of handling cases, the judge may open the court session on the Kang (a heatable brick bed in North China). This should be an unavoidable and temporary change under special circumstance. However, some people regard it as a typical model that deserves promotion. Ma Xiwu's trial mode does have its positive side. However, its value has been exaggerated by some people. This makes the judge don't know what to do. Our reform of trial modes must develop towards modernization and standardization. Of course, it doesn't mean that the reform can be divorced from the masses. It just means that we need to put emphasis on the seriousness and fairness of the trial modes and safeguard substantial fairness with procedural fairness. Since the judiciary lacks procedural fairness, it is also difficult to realize substantial fairness in rural areas. To realize procedural fairness, we must emphasize the following: the first is to strengthen the business training for the judge to ensure that the judge is familiar with the business and can operate the trial procedures proficiently and correctly; the second is to strengthen the judicial seriousness. The randomness of trial procedures constitutes a formidable enemy of judicial fairness. In recent years, the western countries have strongly called for "access to justice" and domestic scholars are also ready to follow suit. It is originally a good thing to pay close attention to international trial theories and practices. However, some people also vigorously advocate early implementation of these theories and practices in China. "To China that implements typical inquisitorial system model, the judicial reform means exactly starting off from the opposite side of such countries as Britain and US and sailing towards them. Only in this way, can we realize the consistent goal of judicial fairness and procedural economy. Therefore, the procedural law should neither stick to the laissez-faire mode nor simply gain on the inquisitorial system. On the contrary, we need to strive for a balance between the individual initiative of the party involved and appropriate level of control of the judge."[12] To strengthen the seriousness of trial procedures and promote procedural fairness in rural areas becomes increasingly important when the issue of procedural fairness turns into terrible obstacle of judicial fairness.

9.2.3 To Strive for Judicial Independence

Recent years have witnessed greater strength of judicial reform in China. The promotion of demurrer trial mode, not-guilty deduction, mode reform of burden of proof have all made Chinese trial procedures more suitable for the demand of market economy and modern civilized society. However, the fundamental issue of judicial independence only witnessed slow progress. This may waste all our efforts for all the achievements of our judicial reform. The key to safeguard judicial independence is to enable judicial procedures to get rid of administrative interference and governance.

Administrative interference to the judiciary is the most serious in rural areas. Since the appropriation from the county court to the township court is extremely limited and most of the working outlay and expenditures of the court come from and depend on the township finance, the judicial organs become the yes-man and "toilet paper" of the administrative organs. A typical example of administrative interference to or dominance over the judiciary is the circumstance in which the government, judicial and police jointly suppress the "unruly people" in many places. The key to realize judicial independence in rural areas is to strive for the independence of funds and personnel of grass-roots courts first. Of course, the independence here is not absolute but relative to the administration. The independence doesn't mean the absence of supervision and check. On the contrary, all activities of the court must be placed under the voters' supervision, and the appropriation budget and final account of all official business organs including the court should be included in the deliberation procedures of the people and people's representatives.

9.2.4 To Promote the Regulated Legal Service Market in Rural Area

Legal workers represent a product for meeting an emergency and compensating for the shortage of legal service personnel during special period in China.

Currently, a large group of professionals with the qualification of lawyers are blocked outside the gate of legal service market and the legal workers from field army still occupy the absolute market of rural legal service. This may be attributed to the factor of benefit distribution to some extent, for example, the lawyers' income in urban areas is much higher than the income of those who undertake the same job in rural areas. However, the root cause of such phenomenon is the gap between the urban and rural areas. consequently, a vicious circle has been constituted on rural legal service market: poverty in rural areas—shortage of legal service resources—non-regular legal service disturbs rural legal service market and frustrates farmers' belief in the law—farmers cannot obtain effective legal assistance—farmers' weaker legal awareness—rampant illegal activities that harm farmers. To solve the problem, we should improve the legal assistance mechanism of the government. To those farmers who cannot obtain regular legal assistance due to financial difficulty, the government shall provide financial support and assistance.

NOTES

1. Li Changping, "The Drawbacks and Strategies for Existing Policies to Solve 'Three Agriculture-related Problems' in China," *Special Zone Economy* 8 (2002).
2. Li Changping, "The Drawbacks and Strategies for Existing Policies to Solve 'Three Agriculture-related Problems' in China," *Special Zone Economy* 8 (2002).
3. Wang Gang, "Zhou Guangli Sues Government Officials—Without End," *Shandong Weekly*, December 23, 1999.
4. Chen Guidi and Chun Tao, *The Survey of Chinese Peasants* (Beijing: People's Literature Publishing House, 2004), 49.
5. Fang Yuan, "Illegal Election Exposes Weak Awareness of Law from Grass-Roots People's Congress," *Southern Urban Daily*, November 26, 2003.
6. Ma Yinlu, *"Apologize to the Farmers," Xinhua Digest* 4 (2003).
7. The Quotation Mark here implies other meaning, i.e., the prostitution caught by many local polices is actually on hearsay evidence or sometimes even confession under torture. The jokes of "virgin prostitution case" from many places around the country have proved this. Please refer to: Zhou Mu and Xiao Fengshi, *"Virgin Prostitution Case" in Gongxian County, Sichuan is Re-tried and Rectified and Deputy Head of Local Police Station Arrested, Chengdu Evening News*, March 9, 2004; Yu Yang and Han Junjie, "Judgment Announced for 'Virgin Prostitution Case' in Dancheng, Henan and Sentence Applied to Four People's Polices," *China Youth News*, January 25, 2003; *Yan Yang,* "Model Significance of the Judgment Result of Hebei 'Virgin Prostitution Case'," *Southern Urban Daily*, September 19, 2003.
8. Yu Ying, "Can Fat Salary Discourage Corruption? Complete and Sound Supervision Mechanism Represents the Sufficient Condition," *Yangcheng Evening News*, March 15, 2003.
9. Su Li, *Sending Law to the Countryside* (Beijing: China University of Political Science and Law Press, 2000), 341.
10. Chen Weidong, "Ten-year Self-criticism of Judicial Reform," *People's Procuratorial Monthly* 3 (2002).
11. (Japan) Mill Takamizawa, *Disputes and Law in Modern China* (Beijing: Law Press of China, 2003), 78.
12. Xu Xin, "Reference from British Civil Judicial Reform," *Law* 5 (2001).

Chapter Ten

Solving "Three Agriculture-related Problems" by Rule of Law and Legal Consciousness of Relative Subjects

10.1 WEAK LEGAL CONSCIOUSNESS OF FARMERS, INCLUDING RURAL CADRES

According to the textbook, legal awareness refers to the sum of people's ideas, views, knowledge and psychology about legal phenomena. In other words, only after understanding the law and acting by law, can one be deemed as having legal awareness. It is the basic requirement for a society under rule-of-law to enable each subject of the society to have basic legal awareness.

The law would become meaningless if there is no contradiction in the society. The law, rule or regulation, judiciary and the like seems to be born for social contradictions and become the necessity for normal operation of the society.[1] However, for a long time, the main channel that Chinese rural areas adopt for solving the contradictions depends not on the judiciary, but the local customs, human relationship, elder authority and "being reasonable-being convinced".[2] This has added an obstructive factor of legal awareness for realizing rule-of-law in rural areas. Some may say that today's farmers in China are definitely not "legally illiterate" without any knowledge of law at all. In daily social life, they have begun to utilize more legal concept and regulations to deal with their disputes. The old viewpoint about Chinese farmers' legal concept and awareness may be inaccurate.[3]

It is true that farmers today cannot be mentioned in the same breath with farmers yesterday. The traditional obligation standard has covered up personal value and severely restricted personal freedom. The high-level planning control of production and strict limit in allocation of living material have made it impossible to obtain, hold, utilize and dispose the limited citizens' property by virtue of right as a concept medium.[4] In 1993, the market economy system was acknowledged and confirmed by the constitution. The market economy means the rule-of-law economy which emphasizes the respect to individual rights and freedom, the principle of "All people are equal before the law" and zero tolerance of individual privilege going beyond the law. Of the respect to individual rights, a very important element is to respect the individual's property right. The change of national system will lead to corresponding change of citizens' ideology. The market economy asks our citizens for stronger legal awareness. Today our market economy is walking towards maturity, but it would be impractical and subjective judgment to deduct that Chinese farmers have also had stronger legal awareness. Only when the farmers begin to resort to legal channels first in case of contradictions or disputes and utilize legal value to evaluate their behavior scale, can the farmers be deemed as having been equipped with stronger legal awareness. However, it is obvious that today's farmers still cannot realize this.

We should tie up legal awareness with the awareness of right at present. In other words, legal awareness refers to the awareness of right. The 2004 Amendment to *Constitution* specifies for the first time that "citizen's legitimate private property shall not be infringed". This has led to greater extension of citizens' rights. We may say that the awareness of property right represents an important part of the whole legal awareness of farmers. Farmers need to be aware of not only their "absolute right" to the property already owned by them, but also different kinds of property rights they enjoy in their organizations, including the property rights of property share of collective organization, private plot, private mountain, contracted land, etc. The weak group of farmers has the greatest difficulty to seek for legal and other means of remedy and relief, and have their rights safeguarded. Therefore, to farmers, to establish basic legal awareness constitutes the most basic requirement to effectively protect their own rights.

Currently, the weak legal awareness of farmers including the rural cadres has become a large obstacle for solving "three agriculture-related problems" through rule-of-law.

10.1.1 Fatal Destruction to Solving "Three Agriculture-related Problems" Resulting from Abuse of Administrative Power

A direct consequence of abusing administrative power is that both officers and common people in rural areas are full of awe to administrative power and regard the law as trifling matter. There are traditional origins for the idea of power supremacy rather than law supremacy. "The old China has left us with more traditions of feudal autocracy and less traditions of democratic legislative system."[5] Chinese farmers have been at the bottom of the society since feudal society and inclined to accept governance and gotten used to submit to power and be "law-abiding people" and "obedient citizens". The feudal autocratic thought of "power means the law or even superior to the law" has taken root in farmers' awareness. Therefore, farmers are ignorant of, unused to and afraid of safeguarding their rights and interests by the law and mistakenly believe that the law represents the matter of the person in power, can only serve for the person in power and is therefore just a tool of power. Farmers expects honest and upright official, but awfully avoid the law and keep away from the law.

Chinese rural areas in which the administrative power has expanded to the greatest extent represent a fertile land for breeding the abuse of power. Since farmers and county and township administrative officers share strong awareness of power and weak awareness of right, the administrative power almost has no restriction and supervision. In rural areas, the administrative officers have the final say and the vast farmers' total obedience to the instructions from levels of authority even endows the administrative power with an absolute authority. The authority of administrative power has not only overshadowed the local authority like the elders' willingness and patriarchal system, but also makes it impossible for state laws to take root and sprout. We can naturally use different channels to help farmers receive such new information as the concept of market economy and rule-of-law. However, in rural areas where the administrative power expands drastically, these concepts would be destroyed by the ruthless reality. The case that Zhou Guangli left his native place to avoid the attack, retaliation and coercion from the administrative power represents a typical example in which the administrative power tried hard to nip the concept of rule-of-law in the bud.

10.1.2 Repulsion of Law by Folk Feeling

Chinese people look forward to "harmony", attach importance to "kind-heartedness" and care about human relationship and face. Therefore, they tend to regard the whole society as a general family and strive to strengthen their family ties.[6] Such thought is especially deeply-rooted in farmers' heart. The thought deserves praise as a kind of moral thought. However, too much abuse of such thought regardless of conditions and situation, would certainly lead to the circumstances in which the law is replaced by the human relationship, the law is perverted because of human relationship or the legal order is replaced by network order of human relationship. Therefore, in case of villager fighting, even in case of injury that may be punished in accordance with the law, as long as the injury is not very serious, farmers would adopt the measure of kindness and relationship and rarely resort to the law for solution.

Folk feeling objectively rejects the law and has bad effect on the rule-of-law construction in rural areas.

10.1.3 Conflict of Folk Norms with the State Laws

As to the contradiction between the traditional customs in rural areas and state laws, some scholars propose to strive for "integration" of state laws and customs. Such viewpoint deserves further discussion. Let's look at Liang Zhiping's analysis of "La Bai rape case". La Bai, a shepherd from Tanggan Township, Tongde County, Hainan Tibetan Autonomous Prefecture, Qinghai Province raped Cai Rangtai (14 years old), a maiden from the same village on September 29, 1981. After the trial, La Bai was sentenced to six months of imprisonment by Tongde County People's Court. After the judgment was announced, Tongde County People's Procuratorate, on the grounds of "too light measurement of penalty", proposed demurrer to the Intermediate People's Court of Hainan Tibetan Autonomous Prefecture. After the trial, the Intermediate People's Court changed La Bai's sentence into three years of imprisonment. After La Bai's sentence, the local masses said that La Bai was treated unjustly since playing with a girl like that is very common and what La Bai did was ordinary on the grassland; and that the girl (Cai Rangtai) was a demon, etc. Many people not only pay no sympathy to the aggrieved person, but also humiliate her and make it difficult for her to get married. The definition of "rape" from official law is quite different from the standard knowledge of local people in the case. Therefore, people find it difficult to understand and accept the judgement made in accordance with the state law, and even put the blame on the aggrieved person and her families, thus adding salt to the injury of the aggrieved person. When the state laws can neither give up its jurisdiction nor totally replace the folk tradition, the inflicter could only gain safety after accepting double sanction. This is obviously unfair to them.[7] However, it perhaps goes against the progressive tide of time to let the state laws to yield to the customs (especially the backward or even fatuous customs), or even let the customs to deny the authority of state laws. In the corner of the countryside that has almost been neglected by modern civilization, there exist too much old thought and customs inconsistent with modern civilization. Although we cannot say that these old thought and customs should be completely "smashed" like "doing away with the four old items" in Mao Zedong years, we are very clear that we absolutely cannot yield to or promote the old thoughts or customs that contradict with our constitution and basic laws or that try to make our constitution and laws a mere scrap of paper. It is the obligatory duty of all communities of our society and government to cultivate the vast farmers' modern thought of rule-of-law.

10. 2 MEASURES FOR INCREASING THE LEGAL CONSCIOUSNESS OF FARMERS INCLUDING CADRES

Improving farmers' legal awareness asks for the coordination and cooperation from multiple parties as well as corresponding material bases and rule-of-law environment. To be specific, rural areas need more education resources, publicity and assistance as well as better demonstration of rule-of-law from the administrative and judicial authorities.

10.2.1 To Strengthen the Popularization of Law to Enlighten the Legal Consciousness of Farmers

Due to the long-term influence of different unfavorable factors, there will be great difficulty for farmers' legal awareness to be awakened by itself and external force is indispensable. Law popularization, education, judicial fairness, administration by law and punishment to illegal acts are all the necessary forces. The publicity of media has been the best channel in the past and will continue to be in future an important channel to improve people's legal awareness. We need to strengthen the publicity of media for rule-of-law.

To the vast farmers, the level of legal awareness directly determines whether the farmers can govern their own daily activities in accordance with the law, or use the weapon of law to protect their own legitimate rights and interests. According to rural traditions, the guiding thought for farmers' activities contains more "rule-by-rites" than "rule-of-law" and has deeply affected farmers' legal awareness. "Rural society is a society under rule-by-rites", and "in rural society, the law has no way of happening", said Fei Xiaotong. Chinese traditional society is full of canons of good manners in contradiction with modern rule-of-law, including the kingship supremacy, idea that power is superior to the law, ethnic supremacy, and thought that human relationship is superior to the law. The traditional society emphasizes the family group and ignores individual rights and interests. "Patriarchal system has shaped Chinese farmers' legal psychology on double meaning: the first is that it organically integrates the coercing of national laws, natural constraint of customary laws and social supervision of moral court and enables the human relationship to replace official laws of our country to some extent; the second is that, under the veil of patriarchal system, farmers automatically removed the possibility of equality between being independent individual and free man and therefore fundamentally deprived farmers' autonomy to contest a lawsuit in the name of individual." According to usual practices, in case of contradictions or disputes, farmers usually invited seniors with high reputation to conciliate or mitigate the contradictions or disputes through human relationship or rites so as to maintain order and stability, which attach importance to being forbearing and conciliatory to each other rather than pursuing clear distinction between right and wrong by means of law.[8] Although after the reform and opening-up, farmers' legal awareness has greatly improved on general, in many rural areas, especially in the districts with backward economy and culture, the awareness of rule by human relationship or rites still determines farmers' method for solving disputes.

To prompt the awakening of farmers' legal awareness need us to continue as always to strengthen law popularization and change the law popularization of formalism into law popularization in essence. The selling out of 1,200 sets of *Manual for Alleviating Farmers' Burden* complied and printed by *Rural Development Symposium* in half a month demonstrates that farmers would favorably receive "sending the law to the countryside" and the laws that protect their legitimate rights and interests rather than simply administer or regulate them. We must fundamentally reform our law popularization work and send the laws and regulations related with farmers' immediate interests to rural areas through means that farmers can accept. CCTV and varied media that publicize rule-of-law have made great contribution to the rule-of-law which will never be forgotten by our people.

10.2.2 To Carry out Administration Work According to Law and Safeguard the Authority of Law

Our grass-roots democracy and rule-of-law construction have encountered numerous problems and outstanding contradictions, core of which lies in the county and township government level rather than the village. The county and township governments have for a long time violated the *Organization Law of Villagers Committee* and distorted normal relationship in rural areas. This has inflicted heavy losses on the gradually awakening legal awareness of farmers. It seems like that we must reform the political regime at the county and township levels. Returning the power to the people represents not only important content of our government system and management mode reform and a key element for our democracy and rule-of-law construction. It is a wise act to cancel the township government and implement township self-governance and merge the county governments of small scale. However, be it the county government or the reserved township government, we have no time to delay. The law-based administration represents not only a key link for promoting rural rule-of-law, but also a typical project for improving farmers' legal awareness. To administer not by the law means that the authority of law has suffered from fundamental trample. If even the government regards the law as trifling matter, how can the common people expect the benefits from the law?

Currently there emerge such phenomena as "renaissance" of village and township schools, "being reasonable—being convinced" dispute settlement mechanism, attacking national organs of political power and appealing for help in Beijing when farmers are seeking for channels to solve problems. These are not voluntary acts of the farmers, which were forced by abnormal expansion of administrative power and lack of legal authority. By reason, the cost for farmers to choose non-legal channel is much higher than the expenditure of legal channel. However, in practice, farmers "feel puzzled in face of rule-of-law". The government and its agencies implement illegal administration and openly defy the law. Farmers can only seek for the second best and choose the non-legal channels when encountering failure to solve problems through legal channel. If there is alternative, who would be willing to choose the more difficult path of appealing for help from superior authorities? The fact that farmers choose non-legal channels demonstrates farmers' insufficient legal awareness. However, the root cause of farmers' insufficient legal awareness lies in farmers' disappointment with the legal remedy channel. Therefore, the key to strengthen farmers' legal awareness depends on law-based administration and safeguarding the authority of law.

10.2.3 To Practice Self-governance of Villagers and Awaken the Right Consciousness of Farmers

The development of village self-governance has spreading effect. In Chinese double democratic system, the village self-governance at rural grass-roots level enables millions of farmers to exercise the right of being master by establishing strict procedures. Along with the development of direct election of Villagers committee, farmers begin to pay attention to and care for the direct election of county and township people's congress. The social democracy stimulated by village self-governance has especially exerted increasing pressure to the legality of state political power. For example, many farmers start to wonder why the township head could not be produced through direct election since the village head is directly elected by villagers. The spreading effect of village self-governance has started to stimulate direct election of township head in China, and made the vast farmers fully realize their own value. The old obligation standard is also being gradually replaced by the standard of right when the farmers are exercising the right of village self-governance. The standard of right represents an ideological basis of today's rule-of-law. The strengthening of farmers' awareness of right will certainly stimulate the whole process of rule-of-law in rural areas.

10.3 ORIENTATION OF FARMERS AND CADRES IN TERMS OF LEGAL CONSCIOUSNESS

In practice, the legal awareness that different citizens shall have are also different with different focuses:

10.3.1 Consciousness of Cadres in Rural Area

It is no doubt that rural development cannot be separated from the support and guidance of the government. The issue is that under market economy, the traditional government intervention, especially the extreme example of keeping everything in the administers' own hand, always gets rural areas in trouble. The reasons include the easy breeding of corruption and arbitrary order without the knowledge about market order. Therefore, people cannot help wondering whether the vast countryside needs a regulator or server. The answer is obvious. However, the large amount of cases in different places shows that the county and township governments are the governor and regulator of farmers. What's more, since we still cannot apply effective constraint to the abuse of power by the administrative organs (especially the grass-roots administrative organs in villages), the large amount of cases in which farmers' rights and interest are infringed in practice have become inevitable. There exist between farmers and the county and township governments many kinds of legal relationships and indeed a kind of administering-and-administered relationship. Such administrative relationship is mainly represented by the correction and punishment by the government to the illegal activities of the subjects being administered, and the function of the government is realized through such specific functional departments as the public security, tax administration and land authorities. The laws for regulating such kind of legal relation are mostly peremptory norms. The civil legal relationship here is mainly represented by the property and contractual relations between the government and the farmers as equal subjects. The laws for regulating such kind of legal relation are mostly optional norms. The economic legal relationship here refers to the relation between the government as one party of subject for the national economic regulation goal and the subject being regulated, and is mainly represented by governmental regulation over market behaviors, national direct investment for establishment of enterprises as well as different kind of economic leverages like planning, finance and taxation, price and banking used by the government to regulate national economy. Such function of the government is also realized through relevant functional departments. From whichever legal relationship, it is impossible to find any legal basis for the government to directly intervene in or even control farmers. Of the above-mentioned three main relationships, the legal relationship of economy represents the main relation. With the gradual deepening of the transition from planned economy to market economy, there emerge more and more norms of advocacy nature in terms of economic laws and regulations. In other words, the government increasingly guide, encourage and promote the rapid, stable and coordinated development of the whole national economy through different regulating measures rather than forcibly intervene in or even monopolize or govern everything.[9] Therefore, while dealing with the relationship between the government and farmers, the legal awareness emphasized currently mainly refers to the service awareness of the government which is mainly represented by providing the public with public necessities, including standardizing the market behavior, sweeping away the market obstacle, carrying out infrastructure construction, providing the public with social security, etc. This is the basic requirement of market economy and the demand for constructing a country under rule-of-law.

The government service awareness requests the government to thoroughly change its identify of owner and administer and its direct intervention and governance to farmers' bodies, properties and objects. In the past, the villagers committee head was always appointed by the superior government so as to guarantee the absolute control power of the government to farmers. If such practice is feasible under highly planned economy, it would only lead the rural social development to dead end under market economy.

10.3.2 Awareness of Rural Judicial Organs as Neutral Referee

Lord Denning, a famous British judge of contemporary era has repeatedly expounded his position during his career of judge that: The constitution does not allow interests of State to influence our judgments: God forbid it should! We must not regard political consequences; how formidable soever they might be: if rebellion was the certain consequence, we are bound to say 'fiat justitia, ruat caelum'.[10] The judge's professional integrity and spirit of neutral referee is quite different from that of the judges in our country, as our judges have not basically gotten rid of the administrative control. Therefore, our judges could not have the boldness and vision. They would have surrendered before the collapse of heaven. Therefore, the land for the survival of the judges' neutral awareness of complete meaning is the real independence of the judiciary and mainly the judicial independence from the administrative at present.

Of course, when I am mentioning that we still do not have the land for the survival of the judges' neutral awareness of complete meaning, I do not mean to say that our judges could attempt and accomplish nothing. As a matter of fact, our judges face a good development opportunity, i.e., the transition period of our society since the transition period of a society can always create a group of "heroes", i.e., those who walk before the times. Over the many years of judicial reform, Professor He Weifang has "lost his voice" because of his shooting for judicial reform,[11] and it's about time to see some improvements. It would not be enough with only the scholars' shooting for judicial reform. The key lies in the practitioners' acts for our judicial reform. If the judges can totally separate their personal gains from professional activities, it would not be difficult for them to cultivate their neutral awareness.

The judges' neutral role has great significance to the rule-of-law construction in rural areas and is directly related with the position of the judges and laws in the heart of the vast farmers and rural cadres. In rural areas, the establishment of the authority of law is mainly represented by the judges' fair judgment to specific cases. Only when the judges deal with the case in strict accordance with the law, can the public adopts judicial remedy as the final effective means of remedy for disputes. This will unconsciously influence the cultivation of farmers' and rural cadres' legal awareness.

10.3.3 Right Consciousness of Farmers

The highly planned regulation in the production sector and strict supply limit in the living sector under planned economy make it almost unnecessary for the use the right as a concept media to obtain, hold, utilize and process the peoples' property.[12] At that time, peoples' awareness of right represents "reactionary" thought. However, currently, the market economic system has been acknowledged and confirmed by the constitution. The market economy is exactly the rule-of-law economy which needs to emphasize the respect to individuals' rights and freedom, principle of "All people are equal before the law" and zero tolerance of individual privilege going beyond the law. Concerning the respect to individuals' rights, a very important element is the respect to individuals' property right.

It is in urgent need to establish and emphasize farmers' right of private property which constitutes an important item of the whole legal awareness of farmers besides farmers' right of the person and political liberty and rights. Farmers should be aware of not only a kind of "absolute right" over the property already owned by themselves, but also varied kinds of property rights that they would enjoy in their organizations, including the property share, private plot, private hilly land, contracted land and other property rights of the collective organizations. As to the unclear collective property rights formed in history, we should evaluate based on facts the asset share for each stakeholder who have made investments of funds, technology, material objects, labor and the like for the forming and development of the collective properties. However, in reality, due to varied reasons, farmers do not have strong willingness to strive for their rights and even think that they do not enjoy corresponding rights at first. Therefore, establishing the basic legal awareness represents the most basic requirement to effectively protect their rights for the farmers.

NOTES

1. (France) Rene David, *Major Legal System in the World Today* (Shanghai: Shanghai Translation Publishing House, 1984), 486-7.

2. (Japan) Mill Takamizawa, *Disputes and Law in Modern China* (Beijing: Law Press of China, 2003), 4.

3. Zhang Xiaojin, "Research of Chinese Rural Areas: Exchange and Communication," *Socialism Study* 4 (1998).

4. Chen Su, *T ravel with Economic System Reform: Continual Improvement of Citizens' Property Protection Mechanism;* from Zheng Chengsi et al, *Chinese Civil Affairs and Social Power Situation* (Beijing: Kunlun Press, 2001), 140.

5. *Selected Works of Deng Xiaoping* (Beijing: People's Publishing House, 1994), 332.

6. Xu Zhangrun, "Liang Shuming's Discussion about Chinese Attitude towards Life and Legal Life," *Peking University Law Journal* 6 (1988).

7. Liang Zhiping, "Law and Order in Rural Society," accessed October 26, 2001, http://www.law-thinker.com.

8. Lu Mingwei, "On Construction of Legal Assistance Mechanism in Rural Areas," accessed December 6, 2002, http://www.chinareform.org.cn/.

9. Qi Duojun, "Characteristics and New Development of Micro-Control Legislation," *Politics and Law* 1 (2002).

10. He Bing, "Let the Justice be Realized Even in Face of the Collapse of Heaven," *Southern Weekly*, April 9, 2004.

11. Xiao Han, "Sorrow of Chinese Rule-of-law—Re-discussion about He Weifang," accessed December 3, 2001, http://www.law-thinker.com.

12. Chen Su, *Travel with Economic System Reform: Continual Improvement of Citizens' Property Protection Mechanism;* from Zheng Chengsi et al, *Chinese Civil Affairs and Social Power Situation* (Beijing: Kunlun Press, 2001), 140.

Chapter Eleven

Solving "Three Agriculture-related Problems" by Rule of Law and Constitutionality in Rural Area

11.1 THE EMERGENCE OF CONSTITUTIONALITY IN RURAL AREA

11.1.1 The Dual Household System between Urban and Rural Area

It is an important expression of rule-of-law society to safeguard the citizens' right of habitation and freedom to migrate. On that account, the *Common Programme* and the 1954 *Constitution* both expressly stipulate that the PRC citizens have the right of habitation and freedom to migrate. However, the following dual household registration system for urban and rural areas ruthlessly deprived farmers of their right of habitation and freedom to migrate in rural areas. The legal provisions still sleep soundly on the wonderful land of China today.

The *Household Registration Rules of the People's Republic of China* (the "Rules") was issued in January, 1958. It standardizes the national registration system of the whole country, specifies the migrating approval system and settlement according to certificate system, and provides restrictive covenants on household migration. In principle, farmers migrating from rural areas to urban areas and from small city to large city are all subject to strict limitation. Therefore, the household system of new China finally introduces the function of strictly restricting the migration of rural population to urban areas and the dual household registration system for urban and rural areas is finally formed. It is no doubt that relevant articles of the Rules obviously contradict with the 1954 *Constitution* and belongs to the stipulation that seriously violate the constitution.

In 1960s, China successively formulated a series of written and non-written auxiliary systems that are matched with the household system and inclined to urban areas in terms of interests and the household system started to comprehensively permeate all sectors of our social life. The supply of consumer goods, production materials, education, employment, housing, labor insurance and other social welfare are all based on the nature of household registration. The registration function of household changed into the function of interest's allocation and became another obstacle to preventing rural population from entering into urban areas. In the meantime, to guarantee the basic living necessities of all people, the government put forward the regulation that the team of people's commune shall not establish an enterprise under normal circumstances. Therefore, farmers are limited in rural areas and could only grow crops. The household registration and management system with dual and different structures for urban and rural areas is thus solidified.

In this way, the focus of household registration system and the attachment of such fourteen systems as residence, grain supply, subsidiary foodstuff and fuel supply, production material supply, employment, medical insurance, pension insurance, labor protection, marriage and childbearing etc. jointly constitute a system barrier for maintaining the special dual structure for urban and rural areas in China. The urban people could enjoy better livelihood welfare and the employment opportunity allocated by the administrative, while farmers were constrained to the land and actually had no national treatment equal to that for urban residents. Thus, two different identify systems and unequal social groups were formed.

During the "Great Cultural Revolution", the household registration system inherited the past framework and further strengthened its auxiliary restricting functions. In face of the reality, the 1975 *Constitution*, 1978 *Constitution* and applicable 1982 *Constitution* officially revoked the stipulation on citizens' freedom to migrate. Because of this, it seems that the household registration system begins to obtain legality without the suspicion of violating the constitution.

After the "Great Cultural Revolution", the household registration system under the cover of legality became even stricter. The State Council approved and forwarded the *Regulations for Handling Household Migration by Ministry of Public Security* in November, 1977 and requested that the people without household registration in cities and towns should be mobilized back to rural areas within several years. The government also emphasized that "strict control of city and town population represents an important policy of the Party during socialism period", and officially put forward strict control over the "change from 'agricultural to non-agricultural' status" for the first time.

Since the reform and opening-up, especially after 1990s, with the acceleration of industrialization and urbanization, to comply with the requirements of market economy, China has accelerated its reform of household registration system, adopted the policy of continual relaxation of "change from 'agricultural to non-agricultural' status" and promoted such polices as "blueprint household register". All these have weakened the restriction over farmers' freedom to migrate and right of habitation in cities.

Although today's household registration system has been improved to a certain extent and today is no longer the period in which the dual system constitutes the most serious harm, the dual household registration system hasn't been fundamentally shaken due to the historical inertia and high complexity of practical problems. Furthermore, the path dependence of system has made the relationship of interests extremely complicated. Therefore, it is very difficult to radically reform our household registration system. In other words, the dual household registration system for urban and rural areas would exist stubbornly for a long time. As a result, farmers still have a long path and little hope to successively strive for the right of habitation and freedom to migrate equal to that of urban residents. The dual household registration system for urban and rural areas would not easily collapse like the "Berlin wall".

In other countries of the world, separated regulation for urban and rural areas only involves administration organization system, division of areas under administration as well as complication of governmental organizations and functions and has no relationship with citizens' identity. Urban residents or farmers represent only a symbol of profession or place of residence. There is no identification control or migrating barrier at administrative level. In contemporary China, a dual society featuring urban and rural separation has been gradually formed based on the administration organization system featuring separate administration for urban and rural areas. The core of such social system is the rigid household registration system featuring obligatory classification. Under such household registration system, an "identification chasm" has been created between farmers and urban residents. More than that, the agricultural and non-agricultural status also implies a series of inequalities of opportunity and treatment. The inequalities of these systems include the inequalities related with residence, grain supply, subsidiary foodstuff and fuel supply, production material supply, employment, medical insurance, pension insurance, labor protection, marriage and childbearing, etc.[1] Concrete analysis shows that the differences concerning right of equality are represented by the following:

1. In terms of economic right of equality, farmers undertake economic obligations quite out of proportion to their economic strength. From the

scissors differential in the 1950s to today's market economy system implemented during our reform and opening-up period, the income gap between urban and rural areas still shows a tendency of increasingly widening except for the income of quite a few villages. It is no doubt that there are varied reasons for the income gap, but the infringement of farmers' economic right of equality definitely constitutes one of the reasons.

First, during the circulation of market economic commodities, farmers' economic right of equality shows no equal treatment since many new agricultural products have been purchased at low price because of national control over price and the right of trade freedom has been deprived (for example, the unified purchase of tobacco and cotton). At present, our agriculture is still at the stage of transition from traditional to modern agriculture and from individual farmer household production to collective production and features extremely unbalanced level of production in different areas. According to the statistics of State Statistics Bureau, just in the year of 1995, the domestic urea price has increased by 50% over the previous year, the farm chemical price by 18% and agricultural film price by 31%; but the price increase of agricultural products is quite low.[2] However, it is under the circumstance of low productivity that farmers still undertake heavy burden of taxation and varied fees. In some places, the IOU notes obtained after a year of painstaking efforts are exactly a kind of sarcasm to farmers' economic right of equality.

Rural development plays an essential role in the agricultural country. In face of agricultural situation of extremely unbalanced traditional productivity, we should provide more protection policies to farmers in our market competition. According to statistics, the accumulative supply from farmers to our country through the "scissors differential" of agricultural products from 1952 to 1986 add up to RMB 582.374 billion and the agricultural taxes paid by farmers add up to RMB 104.438 billion. The total of the two equals RMB 686.812 billion, accounting for about 18.5% of the value created by farmers. After yearly increase of the amount, the "scissors differential" of agricultural products reached RMB 67 billion in 1994. This and the taxes paid by the agriculture sector and township enterprises have directly or indirectly provided an annual accumulative fund of RMB 100 billion for our country.[3] Over several decades, the agriculture has injected large number of funds for our national development and become investment founder of our national assets. However, the return on investment is quite disproportionate and decreases each year. Our agriculture couldn't obtain its due development opportunity under the mechanism of unequal investment and allocation and could only maintain its survival under heavy burdens as time passes, not to mention to change from traditional agriculture into modern agriculture.

Second, farmers also face varied unequal consumption and social insurance besides the unequal competition, heavy tax burden and high fees. For example, the rural calls and electricity are more expensive than the urban calls and electricity respectively; urban residents have enjoyed "high employment rate, better welfare and more subsidy" for a long time; our country provides urban residents with varied social security up to RMB billions or trillions each year; urban employees enjoy retirement insurance, subsistence allowances and many other social welfare, but only a few impoverished people in rural areas enjoy a little social relief. In face of their insecure old age life, many rural people have to bring up sons to provide for their old age. This has further increased farmers' burden and worsened rural poverty. Under market economy, the essence for constructing socialism lies in realizing collective prosperity and preventing polarization of the poor and rich. However, our existing practices push farmers, the majority of our people, to poverty. Today, with the social development, it has become imperative for us to alleviate the burdens on farmers and seek for real economic equality.

2. In terms of equal political right, farmers lack political rights such as the right to be elected and freedom of association. After becoming the masters of their own affairs, whether the farmers can enjoy equal status in the political life in China and jointly wield the political power of our people's democratic state together with other political entities constitute an important standard to measure the real equality of politics. In real life, farmers rarely get involved in politics. This is attributed to some state laws and regulations to a great extent. For example, the *Election Law* of 1953 has different stipulations for the number of people represented by each urban or rural representative, i.e., the number of people represented by rural representative and urban representative of autonomous prefecture or county is 4 ∶ 1, that by rural representative and urban representative of province or autonomous region is 5:1, and that by rural representative and urban representative of country 8:1. It is not until 1995 that the new *Election Law* changed the proportion of number of people represented by rural representative and urban representative in each level of people's representative election to 4 ∶ 1.

According to the representative constituent of all previous national people's congresses （NPC）, the First NPC includes 63 farmer representatives, accounting for 5.14%; the Second NPC includes 67, accounting for 5.46%; the Third 209, accounting for 6.87%; the Fourth 662, accounting for 29.4%; the Fifth 720, accounting for 20.9%; the Sixth 348, accounting for 11.7%; (the Seventh includes 23% of farmer and worker representatives); the Eighth 280, accounting for 9.4%; the Ninth 240, accounting for 8%, and the Tenth 251, accounting for 11.89% (of 2,985 representatives in total). According to the person in authority, the representatives with real identity of farmer account for no more than 5% in any of previous national people's congresses. These facts show that: in terms of the number of representatives in national people's congress, farmers with its population base of 80% of all Chinese population have only obtained inappropriate seats, therefore farmers' realization of rights and protection of interests have naturally encountered some problems. In political life, there emerge the lack of farmers' voice and frequent incidents of defrauding and harming farmers. We can all imagine the difficulty for solving the problem of farmers' burden. It is true that, due to their own factors and cultural factors, farmers still cannot fully exercise their democratic rights well. However, as the cornerstone of our national democratic dictatorship, farmers shall receive corresponding attention and enjoy the political status equal to that of the working class under whatever circumstances. This is the requirement for the essence of socialism.

Compared with other members of our society, farmers feature large population but have no mass organizations. We always hear about the labor union, Women's Federation and Communist Youth League, but farmer association has become a thing of the history and has been forgotten by people. Without the protection of some mass organizations, it would be more difficult for farmers to contend against with the harm from different illegal powers. Just as Marx points out, the billions of individual farmers that cannot represent themselves or protect their own class interests in their own name but have someone else to represent them, and their representative certainly would also be their master, the superior authority and the governmental power without restriction. Due to the lack of mass organization, farmers have no way of knowing the basic principles and methods of organization and cannot use the organization to solve the village and inter-village public affairs. This has led to the reality that Chinese farmers can only expect their local magistrates to "rule for people" and difficulties arise in calling for and implementing the right of equality for farmers.

3. In terms of equal social right, farmers lack such social rights as the employment right, right to education and right to social security. The dual social structure has led to the fact that farmers are always in a position of inequality in terms of the power and function of social life and regarded as the second-class citizen. In a country with a tradition emphasizing agriculture of long standing, today's farmers are named the "countryside folk and peasant worker" which is full of discrimination. In today's urban areas, the work that urban residents have the greatest unwillingness, that are the cheapest, that harms the social status to the greatest extent and that are the most dangerous, dirty or painstaking are always exclusive belong to farmers. The people who repair the shoes, work as the babysitter, work at the construction site under the blazing sun, peddle, sell the vegetable, clean the toilet, pick up the rubbish, carry the human excrement and risk their life in work are basically the farmers. Farmers have become a symbol of identity rather than a profession. The *Constitution* has explicitly stipulated that citizens shall enjoy the right to work, but farmers have limited employment because of their "identity". In some areas, in case of slow pace of economic development, farmers would immediately become the object rejected by the employment market. For example, the *Temporary Provisions for Trans-Provincial Em-*

ployment of Rural Labor issued by the Ministry of Labor in November, 1994 set varied requirements to restrict employment of farmers in different provinces. Some areas even deprived farmers of their equality rights of employment and labor by means of policies and regulations. For example, Shanghai adopted the employment policy of "urban residents first and rural residents next, people from Shanghai first and people from elsewhere next". Qingdao specifies that migrant labor should not account for more than 14% of the total employees, and that the migrant labor should pay RMB 50 each person. Some farmers could not be recognized as workers even after years of service like other workers. The circumstances in which permanent workers bully and oppress temporary workers and urban temporary workers bully and oppress rural migrant workers in cities are quite common. The rural migrant workers have neither labor subsidy nor statutory labor time. The burdensome physical labor or harsh working environment has seriously affected their health and taken away their youth and life too early.

The State has no responsibility for farmers' "labor protection" or medical fees. After the production team is disassembled, the State has no ability to provide farmers with medical insurance, care for the elderly and other welfare services. After being attacked by a disease, the ordinary farmers would usually be pushed out of the hospital, or could only stay quietly waiting for death. Such phenomena are quite common in China. Statistics show that 70% of farmer patients could not receive medical treatment and 68% could not be hospitalized as required because of their inability to pay medical fees. Owing to the institutional discrimination, the poor needs to pay more money for treating a disease in China. The inequality in front of death has demonstrated a kind of structural ridiculousness and inhumanity in a concentrated manner.

Although we are now facing severe employment situation like reform of large and medium-sized state-owned enterprises as well as redirection of laid-off workers from state organs, the equal right to employment reflects the equal protection of the State to citizens' right to exist in terms of right to work. The unequal regulations on farmers' equal employment undoubtedly classify farmers as the "second-class citizens", and represent a kind of "legal" infringement or "institutional discrimination". "The equality we shall have as human beings is the environmental equality rather than individual equality. It represents the equality of conditions—status, treatment and opportunity."[4] The remarks from Mortimer tell us that the discrimination against farmer workers artificially strengthens the identity color of urban residents and villagers and represents a kind of damage to the right of equality in essence. Tocqueville once said that "the heaviest burden of different forms imposed on farmers by feudal system has been canceled or alleviated undoubtedly; but people could not really understand why other burdens replacing the previous burdens could be much heavier. Farmers do not need to undertake all the suffering of their ancestors, but have to endure much more pain that has never been heard by their ancestors before."

Except for the partiality of employment policies to urban residents, the vast farmers also face inequality of education. Rural children, though being the flowers of PRC like urban children, can only receive education in humid and shabby thatched cottage. For a long time, tens of billions of educational appropriations from the State have almost been utilized in urban areas, and the vast rural areas could only manage their education with their own strength. Since 1995, the national finance has canceled the educational appropriation of RMB 31.5 for each middle school student and RMB 22.5 for each primary school student, source of which was changed "3 withholds and 5 levies (3 withholds, the public accumulated fund, public welfare fund and administrative fee; 5 levies, education surtax, family planning fee, civil military training fee, civil administrative alimony and civil transportation construction fee). The rural teaching body is also worrisome. Those well-educated teachers with strong teaching capability are arranged in urban areas. However, the teachers in rural areas are insufficient not only in quantity but also in quality. Under such school conditions, farmers' children still need to pay painful price to cross higher threshold to enter a higher school. The bad teaching conditions and farmers' restraining factors have forced some farmers' children to stay away or drop out from school.

11.1.2 Rural Area---A Neglected Area by Constitutionalism and Rule of Law

Chinese rural areas have long been "a neglected area" of the constitutionalism and rule-of-law. Our relevant research has been for a long period carried out basically through the superior or so-called mainstream academic discourse like "urban areas" and "western learning". Under such discourse paradigm, we have ignored the right of speech of farmers as the weak group which has been submerged in the so-called sea of modern voice. Under such academic atmosphere, scholars follow the fashion of harangue about some high, refined and advanced theories and get used to consciously or subconsciously arrange different social classes as the stairs of evolution theory one after another. According to the stairs theory and the inherent "citizens' prejudice" and "genius awareness" design of some cities, the rural society represents a farmers' society, and farmers are small self-sufficient producers who are selfish, stupid, ignorant and out-of-order. Therefore, many people despise rural areas and farmers from their hearts. They think that farmers, as the obstacles to Chinese modernization, have hindered the progress of our history and therefore could only live in rural areas and engage in agricultural activities for generations. The folk customs and folk laws of rural areas are sufficient for the operation of rural areas. In other words, the rural areas are too backward to need the laws. In their mind, the terms mentioned frequently by the literati such as freedom, equality, democracy and fairness cannot arouse the interest of farmers. Therefore, when the intellectuals are discussing about how to "arrange" a way out for farmers, they would usually ignore the issue of farmers' basic right, i.e., right to survive, just the same as that of urban residents. The requirements "from subsistence to dignity" have always been "naturally" excluded from the discussion in a system absent of constitutionality. Let's take the definition of land right as an example. Some scholars think that since the land has become farmers' social security, it cannot be handled as means of production by the market. Although the thought has indeed taken into account farmers' interests, it regards a kind of institutional discrimination that has been implemented for several decades as a perfectly justified background factor. In other words, the government only provides social security for urban residents, whereas the farmers, as the "second-class population", could only get support in case of old age and disasters from the existing contracted land rather than enjoy the social security equal to that of urban residents. As to whether the contracted land can guarantee that farmers' living standard reaches the urban residents' "lowest security level", no one cares. Besides, the existing relationship between farmers and the land is just of "quasi-private" type since farmers have never actually acquired the absolute property right of land. Therefore, farmers usually cannot effectively safeguard the most basic rights and interests of their own when their right to the contracted land is infringed by autocratic power. The land system after the "movement of cooperative transformation" represents a reverse of the land system in China since Qin Dynasty, and the land system arrangement at the initial stage of reform and opening-up represents only an expedient reverse adjustment. Only with the guarantee of constitutionality, can farmers have the basic rights to safeguard their personal dignity, including the right to land. Thus, under the so-called urban "discourse hegemony", farmers are naturally excluded from the constitutionalism and rule-of-law. We can even say that farmers are considered as the obstacles to Chinese constitutionalism and rule-of-law.

In the jurisprudence circle, the localization theory of rule-of-law resource is a representative of the academic point of view. It is true that the theory has expanded our horizon of knowledge, increased our "localization knowledge", caused our attention to rural rule-of-law and deepened our understanding to the particularity of Chinese rule-of-law. However, such argument also always makes us excessively addicted to the emphasis on the particularity of Chinese rule-of-law and relativity of rule-of-law, but neglecting the promotion of the universality value of rule-of-law itself. The relativism of rule-of-law has obviously deceived our horizon and provided us with one-sided rather than complete knowledge. Due to the strong tendency of relativism and avoidance of today's practical problems in China, the people who advocate the localization theory of rule-of-law resource cannot improve their own viewpoints to a higher level in accordance with their internal logic and provide real support and argument for rule-of-law resource localization from a higher starting point. As a result, when discussing about the rule-of-law, they would put more emphasis on local bizarre customs and overlook the issue of state power. Metaphorically, they are just like those who have failed to realize the relationship between well-programmed software and its supporting system. They think that their software can also operate and function well without DOS or Windows, or even regard their own software as the operating system itself. In reality, how many people have rejected the universal thing as they regard the special thing as universal and universal thing as special?

In brief, we believe that it is necessary to emphasize appropriate release of the universality value of rule-of-law in rural areas or in the process of solving "three agriculture-related problems". For example, we should not only vigorously promote such values as justice and fairness in urban areas, but also make these values deeply rooted in Chinese rural areas. However, this definitely does not mean to obliterate the Chinese context of rule-of-law. The primary of solving "three agriculture-related problems" by rule-of-law represents the rule of constitution in rural areas. In order to realize rule-of-constitution in rural areas, we must review whether the existing legal systems related with "three agriculture-related problems" go against the constitutional spirit. All legal systems that go against the constitutional spirit should be nullified as soon as possible. Obviously, the existing dual household registration system for urban and rural areas and the dozens of affiliating systems derived from it not only contradict with the existing constitutional principle of "All people are equal before the law", but also deviate from the universality requirement of rule-of-law. Therefore, they should be canceled. However, without the review system of unconstitutionality, the above-mentioned legalized institutional discrimination would continue to exist in an imposing manner and farmers' constitutional rights would not be able to be actually realized. This will continue to aggravate the poverty and backwardness in rural areas and make the "three agriculture-related problems" more complicated. We should not forget that, in today's Chinese society, farmers constitute a great majority of the citizens, and their constitutional and legal rights should obviously not be discriminated or neglected. Furthermore, the reality has showed us that: when farmers' rights are infringed and the remedy and relief of public power is not timely or impossible, farmers would adopt the measure of remedy by themselves. This also constitutes the reason for the frequent occurrence of cases like Wang Binyu Incident. Obviously, it is incompatible between the farmers' measures of remedy by themselves for solving conflict of interests and the harmonious society pursued by us. Therefore, it constitutes our top priority to eliminate the varied discriminatory systems to farmers in order to realize rule-of-constitution in rural areas.

11.2 SURVEY OF RURAL CONSTITUTIONALISM

11.2.1 Connotation of Rural Constitutionalism

Rural constitutionalism shall include the following three levels of implications: (1) to safeguard farmers' rights by modifying and improving the constitutional stipulations; (2) to crystallize, institutionalize and actualize the existing constitutional articles and spirit, nullify all legal systems discriminatory to farmers and practically implement the equality principle of the constitution; (3) to follow the idea of "limited government", standardize the public power activity of the grass-roots government and prevent the infringement to farmers' private right by the grass-roots government.

According to the first level of implication, the agriculture-related problems in the constitution need substantial modification so as to strengthen the guarantee of farmers' rights and realize rural constitutionalism. After revision in 2004, the existing constitution has made further stipulations on such aspects as the protection of farmers' land right, private property right, social security, human right and term of office for township people's congress. This is obviously favorable for, but insufficient to, the farmers. The author thinks that it is totally unnecessary for us to take stability and step-by-step mode as the excuse to hinder bold and resolute reform. Such situation is obviously unfavorable for realizing rule-of-law as soon as possible.

Apart from what is discussed in 8.2.1, it is necessary to recover the rights of habitation and freedom to migrate in the constitution which is logical and a symbol of socialist civilization and progress. It is historical error to nullify relevant articles in the constitution because of some historical factors. Now since we have the conditions to recover the rights, we should recover them through legal procedures.

According to the second level of implication, we should stick to the equality of citizens' rights and obligations as stipulated by the constitution for both farmers and urban residents, and gradually implement the policy of urban and rural unification in terms of such aspects as the health, medical care, employment, social security, market access and other public finance expenditures so as to finally realize urban and rural integration. As we all know, the de facto identity of second-class citizens for farmers is caused by not only the residue of the traditional culture, but also the series of legal systems like the household registration system since the establishment of new China. As a matter of fact, a dual society based on different identities has been formed in Chinese urban and rural areas. In such a society, the means to adjust the relationship between people and people is the identity rather than the market price; and the condition for the initial allocation of varied interest and resources is the identity instead of the equal subject required by market economy. Therefore, the universality and rule-of-law and equality principle of the constitution have completely failed to be reflected. Just imagine, in a society under rule-of-law, the law has become people's standard of behavior. But if our legal system is unfair in itself, to regulate people's behavior through such legal system would only lead to more inequalities. Some people say that the greatest inequality of a society is the inequality of system arrangement. From my point of view, it means that the fairness of system establishment procedures and the equity brought about by the game between relevant interest subjects during the system establishment procedures, which represents the basic conditions for our society to create the opportunity equality for individuals of our society. Only based on this, can we create the conditions and provide equal opportunity for everyone. Under the existing system environment, where is the equal opportunity for farmers to participate in the game? In my opinion, the key of whether farmers can participate in the game lies in the willingness of the government. In the big power of farmers, the grass-roots government making direct contact with farmers should directly serve the farmers. Such direct relationship between the government and farmers needs to be defined by certain rules. Under the system of planned economy, the government implements planned administration of prescriptive nature and the relationship between the government and farmers represents a kind of "order—obey" relation. Under the market economy, farmers play the dominant role of equality in the economy and the relationship between the government and farmers shall represent a kind of "rule—observe" relation. Such "rule" shall be the rule jointly formulated by the government and farmers and such "observe" shall be the joint "observance" of the government and farmers. However, in real life, on one hand, the government still gets used to give administrative orders and command the farmers rather than realizes the change from "order—obey" to "rule—observe" relation. On the other hand, the government gets used to formulate the rule unilaterally and unused to observe the self-restraint rules. This has led to the reality that in face of the concerns related with farmers' own immediate interests, farmers lack the channel to participate in the formulation of game rule through systems and the "coercive force" to request the government to observe the rules as well. As a result, in Chinese society featuring lack of democratic politics, farmers' voice was suppressed. They not only lack the channel for appealing, but also have no spokesperson for their interests. Hence, because of the daily increasing unfairness of system, farmers' rights lose the reliance on systems. Therefore, we need to practically implement the constitutional rights enjoyed by farmers like the right to vote and improve local system of people's congress so that farmers can actually participate in and discuss the government and political affairs and farmers' interests can be properly reflected in the system design process. This is obviously the precondition and basis for realizing system fairness. Therefore, it is also quite significant to practically enable farmers to participate in the interest game of the system reform in the future process of urban and rural integration and the system reform for such aspects as education, medical care, employment, social security, market access and other public finance expenditures. In view of the fact that farmers lack the channel for appealing, we can even design and add relevant systems to provide convenience for the expression of farmers' interests, such as the hearing. In a word, the rural constitutionalism aims at exploding the social relationship based on identity and constructing a kind of social relationship based on contractual equality spirit.

According to the third level of implication, the grass-roots government should change its governmental functions and realize the transformation from an all-round government of administration type to a limited government of service type. In other words, the exercising of public power by the government should be subject to effective standardization and restriction so as to prevent farmers' rights from being infringed by public power. Under market economy, the main functions of governmental include providing public goods and safeguarding social justice and fairness. During the transformation period of our society, the governmental function generally shows the tendency of "offside" and "defect side". On one side, the government plays "offside", shows high on "active administration" and infringes farmers' "passive liberty". The government needs to "do certain things and refrain from doing other things" and the governmental administration can be classified into "active administration" and "passive administration". The "active administration" of grass-roots government may hinder farmers' "passive liberty". For example, the "active administrations" in the form of "abuse of power for public gains" like the development of collective economy, adjustment of agricultural structure and vigorous promotion of vanity projects are quite popular currently. They have severely intervened in farmers' production life and infringed farmers' basic rights and freedom. Farmers, as the PRC citizens, should reasonably enjoy the basic rights and freedom like the freedom of speech, right of personal liberty, property right and right to life which would naturally be enjoyed by farmers if the government does not intervene. The "passive liberty" naturally enjoyed by farmers would only be harmed in case of governmental intervention. The "active administration" of the government represents exactly "offside" and doing things that should not have been done. To safeguard farmers' "passive freedom", the government could only adopt "passive administration" and "refrain from doing other things" so as to avoid disturbance to residents and enable citizens to rehabilitate as well as live and work in peace and contentment. On the other side, the government cannot play "defect side", or attempt and accomplish nothing by means of "passive administration". On the contrary, it needs to "do something" for "active administration" and provide public goods. In modern society, the division of labor becomes more and more specific and people's demand to the government higher and higher. Farmers not only expect no intervention from the government to their normal production life but also yearn for necessary public service and security from the government. This represents farmers' "active liberty". Correspondingly, the government should implement "active administration" and "do something" to compensate for the governmental "defect side". The scope of governmental "active administration" mainly includes providing the public services and facilities like public facility construction, employment, social security, education, science and technology, culture, health and sports, and offering security and creating conditions for farmers' public life and activities. However, when the government showed "offside" and "defect side", farmers' income increase has dropped in successive years and their personal and property rights suffered from unprecedented infringement from some grass-roots violent administrations. The violent administration of the grass-roots government, especially from the township, has created the shocking phenomena of "grass-roots violent administration". Some townships, under the "pressure type system", abuse their power and apply violence administration to farmers in order to accomplish the tasks of target management responsibility system that are usually transmitted from the superior level of government and added at each level of the government.[5] In face of the unprecedented violent administration that severely infringes farmers' personal and property rights, a mainstream view is to criticize some cadres of the Party and government for their rude style and simple working procedure. As a matter of fact, this represents typical illegal and criminal activities and should be brought to justice and punished seriously. In brief, the grass-roots government should practically implement law-based administration and set the target of constructing a limited government that implements neither "offside" nor "defect side", and the exercising of power by the government should be subject to strict standardization and restriction of the law. This represents the third level of implication of rural constitutionalism.

The above may be called the "triple door" of rural constitutionalism. To sum up, rural constitutionalism means the actual implementation of the constitution in rural areas and improvement of farmers-related constitutional and legal rights. One may say that safeguarding farmers' constitutional and legal rights constitutes both the starting point and end result of rural constitutionalism.

11.2.2 Significance of Rural Constitutionalism

1. Rural constitutionalism is conducive to breaking down the system foundation of urban and rural dual structure

With the equality principle of the constitution as the highest philosophy, the system of rural constitutionalism aims at constructing a system framework featuring urban and rural integration. Obviously, it is necessary to destroy the system foundation of existing urban and rural dual structure, mainly the household registration system and its affiliated systems, while constructing the system framework of urban and rural integration. Without destroying the old system, it would be impossible for China to provide living space and foothold for new system. The author thinks that the system reform or creation from "dual structure" to "single structure" obviously has sufficient legal bases and legality. What's puzzling is that the urban and rural dual system suspected of violating the constitution still steadfastly stands on its ground. It is no doubt that after over half a century development, the old system has been attached with a large group of people with vested interests. The people with vested interests in urban areas defend the system on which they rely for existence by instinct. This is also the root cause for the absence of fundamental change to the urban and rural dual system since the reform and opening-up. It's worth noting that the vast farmers, as the victims of old system, have increasingly fallen into the historical vortex without system safeguard. Their psychological need for realizing system reform or creation is so strong. But we have to admit that their voice is so low and weak. In front of the mighty discourse hegemony from urban areas, the farmers' voice can barely be heard. Under such circumstance, we put forward rural constitutionalism to strive for farmers' right of speech and farmers' right protection by the current political ruler since only the government can provide the most effective assistance to them. Therefore, we also call for that the government seek for the system reform of the greatest extent actively, say goodbye to the old system bravely and strive to construct a system framework for urban and rural integration. We also believe that the current government that advocates the "new people-centered principle" can do something and make a difference in this regard so as to stimulate the realization of rural constitutionalism.

2. Rural constitutionalism is conducive to safeguarding farmers' right of equality and freedom and realizing social justice

The core and essence of rural constitutionalism lies in advocating the realization of rural right of equality and freedom as well as the liberation of "modern farmer slaves". We know that the foothold for breaking down the urban and rural dual structure lies in providing for farmers the system safeguard equal to that of urban residents, return the rights and freedom that should be enjoyed by farmers as PRC citizens to farmers and endow farmers with real "national treatment". Just imagine, if the legal system of a country is unequal in itself, would the country have justice? The author thinks that the equal and indiscriminate protection to citizens' rights and freedom by the law constitutes a precondition for realizing social justice. Only under a fair system environment in which everyone has equal right to participate in the society, can the justice be a possible thing.

3. Rural constitutionalism represents the basic channel for constructing a harmonious rural society

On one hand, it is necessary to implement and enforce the constitutional stipulations one by one in rural areas so that farmers can actually enjoy the rights endowed by the constitution. Only when farmers can obtain real and actual interests by exercising their rights, can they live and work in peace and contentment and the harmonious society be realized. On the other hand, under the framework of rural constitutionalism, the relationship between the government and farmers, among the farmers and between urban and rural residents may form a stable, balanced and coordinated pattern to construct a stable social safety valve and stimulate the construction of harmonious society.

11.3 POSSIBILITY AND PROBLEMS WITH RURAL CONSTITUTIONALISM

11.3.1 Possibility of Rural Constitutionalism

Chinese farmers who have been rolled in the market economic wave for over decades are not absent in the promotion of ruling the country by law in today's China. After the trials and hardships of reform and opening-up, farmers have acquired increasingly stronger awareness of right and better concept about democratic legislative system. All these have provided probability for implementing and realizing rural constitutionalism. This seems to offer us a kind of feeling that "Every cloud has a silver lining".

1. Vigorous legal right safeguarding movements by farmers show full awakening of farmers' awareness of right and legal awareness

The "road map" of Chinese farmers' right safeguarding movements has fully demonstrated this. According to scholars' research, Chinese farmers' right safeguarding movements have generally gone through three stages. Before 1992， most of the farmers' contentions may be generally summarized as the "daily resistance" form called by western scholars as the "weapon of the weak ". Such resistance, with individual as the unit of action, requires no planning or mutual coordination and uses the strategy of concealing. With no head-on confrontation with the authority as the characteristic, the resistance represents a kind of "opportunism" contention involving direct personal interests. From 1992 to 1998, farmers' contention may be summarized as "contention-by-law" or "legal revolt" and characterized using the Central government policy to confront the grass-roots government and regarding the superior as the appealing object. Protesters firmly believe that the subject to solve the problems is the superior and do not confront their object of complaint directly. Such contention, in an open, quasi-institutionalized or half-institutionalized form, mainly adopts the channel of appealing for help from superior authorities and uses the authority of the appealing superior government to confront the grass-roots cadres' acts "perverting the law". It is usually based on the background of specific "event" and mainly represents a kind of contention involving specific collective interests. Since 1998, farmers' contention has actually entered into a stage of "organized contention" or "contention through the law". Such contention takes the spokesperson of farmers' interests with clear political belief as the core and establishes relatively stable network of social motivation through varied means. The contenders take other farmers as their appealing objects. They firmly believe that the subject to solve the problems is the farmers including and led by themselves. The contenders directly challenge their opponents, i.e., regard the county and township government as their contending objects. Such contention represents a kind of political contention aiming at declaring and establishing the abstract "legitimate rights and interests" or "citizens' rights" of the social group of farmers. To be specific, we can reach a summary of the following characteristics:

First, farmers' right safeguarding activities have showed many remarkable changes in terms of form. The changes generally reveal an important feature: although appealing for help from superior authorities still represents one of the most important forms of farmers' contention, it has showed new features and functions. What deserves more attention is the new and more active modes and means for contention, mainly including publicizing, forcing a concession, demonstration, and sitting quietly as a form of protest, etc. Therefore, farmers' right safeguarding modes and means have showed the tendency of diversification.

Second, contemporary farmers' right safeguarding movements have set their goal with very clear nature of politics and developed from the contention for resource rights and interests to that for political rights and interests. This is mainly expressed by two aspects: Firstly, the contending contents have public character. Currently the main issues of contention include "alleviating farmers' burden and fighting corrupt officials", "protect farmers' land property", "making village affairs more transparent", "democratic financial management", etc. Since the issues all involve relevant regulations of central government documents and state laws and policies and are all quite serious and ubiquitous in today's rural areas, it is very easy to determine the justification and legitimacy of the right safeguarding farmers' acts. Secondly, since the above-mentioned issues are generally caused by the administrative acts of the public authorities, the objects of the contention-through-the-law are mainly the grass-roots party and government organs of township and village organizations. Such moves that utilize state laws to boycott the lowest political power of the country to realize the goal of farmers' right safeguarding represents a kind of political acts. Therefore, its politic nature represents a remarkable characteristic of the contention-through-the-law by contemporary farmers, whose acts have clear purpose, i.e., safeguarding varied legitimate rights and interests of farmers endowed by the policies of the Central government and the laws of the state.

Third, another remarkable characteristic of current right safeguarding movements by farmers is clear nature of organization. The right safeguarding farmers coordinate and plan their acts by establishing stable organizational networks for mutual contact. In the central region of China, during the contention, farmers directly name their contention organizations as the "burden alleviation team", "burden alleviation committee", "supervision team for burden alleviation", "right safeguarding association for burden alleviation", etc. In some districts, farmers are even preparing for establishing a farmer association of political nature.

The diversification of the right safeguarding means and contents as well as the organization-oriented trend of the movements shows that Chinese farmer' right safeguarding movements have become increasingly rational and reasonable. Chinese farmers are no longer the objects at the mercy of other people and have already known how to better protect their own legitimate rights. If the citizens' awareness of right represents an important feature of modern society under rule-of-law, the awakening of farmers' awareness of right has provided Chinese democratic politics and constitutional China with indispensable bases and conditions.

2. Successful demonstration of village self-governance system has strengthened farmers' idea about democratic legislative system and consciousness of self-independence and opened a new chapter for constitutional China

Firstly, the implementation of village self-governance system has strengthened farmers' idea about democratic legislative system. The democratic election process at village level represents not only a practice process of democracy, but also a democratic education, learning and training process for farmers and grass-roots cadres. It has played very important role for strengthening farmers' and village cadres' democratic awareness, legal sense and democratic capability. It is a naked fact that we now have obviously more appealing events related with the election of villagers committee. This shows that democratic election in rural areas still encounters considerable resistance and there still exists the circumstances in which farmers' democratic rights are infringed on one hand; and that farmers' democratic awareness and legal sense are increasingly strengthening. In China where rural population takes up a vast majority, there would be no democratization for the whole country without rural democratization. Only when Chinese farmers all acquire the democratic consciousness and awareness and get used to the democratic procedures and methods, would Chinese democracy be equipped with solid foundation. Our village self-governance is exactly building the foundation. It represents a social practice of both democracy and law. The process to promote village self-governance in the vast countryside is also the process to implement and enforce the *Villagers Committee Organization Law*. As to the general election held in rural areas, the bases come from the law and the whole set of actions like the formulation, operation and determination of the procedures from the regulations of the *Villagers Committee Organization Law* about the villagers' election procedures and standards. Some districts also take the *Villagers Committee Organization Law* as the weapon for holding several times of election or declaring the election result as illegal. While implementing the village self-governance practice, the broad masses of the people have known, mastered and utilized the law and realized the due rights and obligations of a villager and even the citizen of a country. This would undoubtedly strengthen the villagers' legal sense and make for the legal and modernization construction of the country.

Secondly, farmers' independent consciousness has become stronger and stronger. What's more, in real practice, with the implementation of village self-governance system and development of rural economy, villagers increasingly demand the exercising of the self-governance and autonomous rights regulated by the law, and there emerge more and more resistance to the simple administrative order and direct intervention from township government to internal affairs of Villagers committee. The relationship between township and village has actually gone through soundless change. In 1998, as the elected people was not the person "decided at the higher level but not officially announced", the election result of villagers committee from a village of Huangmei, Hubei was denied by the Town Party Committee and Town Government under the excuse that the election went against legal procedures. The denial was boycotted by the whole villagers in a united manner, leading to paralysis of the whole village work. Some villagers also appealed to the higher authority and requested the higher authority to acknowledge the election result. After three years of stalemate, the Town Government had to agree to another new election and accept the corresponding election result although the newly-elected people were still the same as those from the last election. To this, the Town Party Secretary said with deep feeling that the present were different from the past as at present order and suppression do not work and only compromise and consultation can solve the problems.

Thirdly, the implementation of village self-governance system has stimulated the development of grass-roots political power and national democracy. "Since it is possible to elect the village officers, why is it impossible to elect the township head?", some villagers and rural cadres began to ask the township cadres reprovingly after the implementation of democratic election in villages. Farmers requested further expansion of township political power. For this, some rural areas also began to explore the modes and methods to strengthen and improve township democratic election. From the end of 1997 to the beginning of 1998, Buyun Township from Sichuan and Dapeng Town from Shenzhen initiated the first precedent of direction election of township and town heads (the election result of Dapeng town head was acknowledged and affirmed by the town people's congress in the end), and the candidates of the town and township heads also carried out their publicity and campaign speech in the whole township and town. Although there are only a few townships that implement direct election of township head at present, the direct election of these township heads shows that rural grass-roots democracy has already begun its expansion from village democracy to township democracy, from the democracy of grass-roots organization to that of the national regime organization, and from the democracy of social self-governance to that of national politics. This obviously represents another result full of historical significance brought about by village democracy. Although the village self-governance, simply as a kind of "grass-roots democracy", has many issues and drawbacks, we still have sufficient confidence and courage to continue the great cause of grass-roots democracy. Village self-governance represents a kind of "grass-roots democracy". It means that the democracy of village self-governance, rooted in rural society, has strong local flavor and roughness and imperfections, and therefore should be investigated and analyzed under the specific social environment of rural areas. Although villagers committee is not a kind of statutory regime organization in China, and the village democracy represents also no more than a kind of village self-governance democracy, or social democracy, the implementation of village self-governance and villagers committee election would definitely exert influence on the whole social political system and democratic construction of the country as the villagers committee undertakes the organization and management function of grass-roots community and is consciously and unconsciously deemed as the foundation of national political power rather than being a pure social organization from the beginning. It is exactly because of this that the implementation of villagers committee has not only triggered various change of the power structure of rural grass-roots community and promoted varied change of national political power and system. For example, the adjustment and reform of Party and government relationship, rural relationship and the like has also promoted the democracy of the Party organization and provided a kind of exploratory solution for the fundamental issues of national political system reform like improving the leading mode and method of the Party and strengthening the leading power and authority legality of the Party. If by far, our national political system reform represents no more than an institutional reform or a kind of adjustment and re-allocation of the power within the political system or state institution, village democratic election has for the first time touched the source issue of public power—the leaders' legitimate power can only come from the public's authorization and recognition. What's more, this represents exactly the real starting point of all political democracy. It is no doubt that this has given profound enlightenment to the ongoing reform of national political system. When we pay attention to the issues related with the adjustment of state power structure and power distribution, the first issue that should be solved would be the source and legality issue of the power. When people work on promoting the reform of native political system from the high-level authority of the country in a top-down manner, village self-governance and democratic election may become a reform channel in a down-top manner for promoting our political system reform and national democracy that is comprehensive, long-lasting and profound though with low risk, small vibration and gradualness.

In brief, the achievements of our village self-governance practice deserve full recognition. The implementation of village self-governance has actually endowed millions of farmers the right of democratic autonomy, changed the social political environment of rural areas, substantially improved farmers' and rural cadres' democratic awareness and quality, triggered positive social change of rural society, played greater and greater role of active promotion to the democratic politics and constitutionalism construction of the whole country, and demonstrated the strong vitality of grass-roots democracy in rural areas.

11.3.2 Problems with Rural Constitutionalism

It is true that Chinese farmers' right safeguarding movements and village self-governance have both showed us the flame of hope for rural constitutionalism. However, there exists really doubt over whether the flame can really realize the myth of "a single spark can start a prairie fire". From the author's opinion, the dilemma of our rural constitutionalism is mainly represented by two types of path dependence:

The first is the path dependence of cultural tradition. In Chinese cultural traditions, it is the version of "the law would not change if the heaven does not change" over the period of more than two thousand years since the prosperity of Confucianism that farmers are deemed as the base persons. Furthermore, the household registration system and its affiliated systems after the founding of China have fixated such culture in the form of law. In other words, the cultural tradition that looks down upon farmers has, as a matter of fact, received system guarantee and the discriminatory culture therefore changed into artificially discriminatory system. The cultural tradition has been fixated and handed down to today's generation. As everyone knows, the college entrance examination system (similar to the imperial examination in ancient times) recovered in the latter half of 1970s has been and is still the main channel for the vast majority of farmers to change their status. Although there are more than one million of college graduates encounter failure of employment each year, many farmers' children are still willing to "float" on urban areas with the identity of college graduate. According to analysis from the perspective of economics, the rate of output of the whole education investment is too low, which is obviously abnormal in the developing country of China. The farmers' children refuse to return to their native places after graduating from their colleges or even facing unemployment, and the rational requirement of social aspect is the unwillingness to return to the traditional historical positioning of "base person" and being "in the wild". They would rather float in the city and be "in the wild" of another sense. It is undeniable that some responsible scholars do advocate determining farmers' identity from the perspective of modern civil politics. However, in general, the cultural tradition that farmers are deemed as the "base person" of Confucianism sense has never showed any change. For example, in real life, we would always hear people using such abusive expression of "why do you act like a farmer?" which is full of contempt.

At the beginning of the appearance of "three agriculture-related problems", some people used such phrases as "peasant worker rush" and "exiled person" to define the identity for the farmers that leave their land. The historical inheritance of "gentleman within the city (in urban areas) and base person in the wild (in rural areas)" is quite obstinate. After entering into the 21st century, there still emerge some circumstances in which farmers are illegally detained and fined by the authorities (for settlement of issue) in urban areas frequently. Sun Zhigang Case represents only a typical case of disgusting conduct that attracts social attention. All these demonstrate that the recognition of farmers' identity has a traditional prerequisite: the distinction between "within the city" and "in the wild". Some urban intellectuals' statement about how to control, manage and plan the floating population from rural areas represents in itself a kind of discrimination to farmers. It regards farmers as the barrier to modernization and the part that needs "planning and controlling". The most typical "statement" of this kind comes from an article from the *Reading* in October, 2003. The author of the article thinks that the reasons that Sun Zhigang was beaten to death lies probably in that he looks more like a farmer (exiled person). "In the criminal records of today's big cities in China, more than 50% are related with floating population. However, the rate has risen to 80% in Guangzhou. This is the background for Sun Zhigang Case in Guangzhou"[6] , wrote the author. Regardless of the accuracy of his data and just according to the author's expression and perspective, it is neither precise academic discussion nor immoral statement to simply utilize the number of floating population to imply the negative effect caused by farmers' entering into the city without any discussion about the varied discrimination suffered by farmers in urban areas. Whether the reason for a farmer to commit a crime in urban areas (especially such important cases as abduction and injury to death) is of causal relationship with the unfair treatment directly received by him, we should never avoid the varied discrimination measures taken by the urban system and residents against the farmers—not to mention the common and frequent circumstances in which the labor contractor of construction site and construction company deducts or delays the payment of farmers' salary with evil intention. As a matter of fact, the discrimination against farmers comes from the urban residents' psychic of being superior to farmers and a kind of thought deeply rooted in their minds that farmer workers are "people of a lower social status" which represents modern reflection of traditional culture. The traditional culture of discrimination against farmers has some inertia in itself and could not be fundamentally eliminated in short period. This represents exactly a dilemma for rural constitutionalism.

The second is the historical path dependence of system. The diachronic relevance of system is namely the historical path dependence. In general terms, it means that the formation of a kind of (or a series of) new systems would more or less be affected by the legacy system and have some imprints of the old system. Since the legacy system, especially the informal system (such as the customs, habits, moral idea and belief), may unconsciously "embed into" the new decision-makers' sphere of consciousness and therefore affect their choice behaviors, the forming of a kind of new dynamic strategy is affected by the dynamic interaction of the decision by the participants from different areas rather than being chosen by random entirely during the transitional period of system. It can be seen that the system environment formed in history has led to the path dependence of system and the reasons for the path dependence may be divided into two levels: the first is the objective social and historical conditions and the limited reason from the dominant power of system change; the second is the positive trade fees and benefit factor.

According to the analysis on the root cause for the long time existence of urban and rural system arrangement from the perspective of diachronic relevance, although the corresponding system arrangement formed in compliance with the industrialized overtaking strategy represents an inevitable choice under the historical conditions and has once greatly accelerated our industrialization process and stimulated our economic take-off, the varied urban and rural division systems like the industrial system of urban and rural division, investment and financing system, market system, household registration system and social welfare system have increasingly become a severe obstacle to further development of our urban and rural areas as well as our economy and society with the continual progress of industrialization. It can be said the greater the negative effect of an inefficient system is, the stronger the power of institutional innovation would be. However, whether the new system could replace the old one depends not only on the net earning that may be produced by the new system (the Pareto of the whole society has improved), but also on the difficulty for re-adjusting the interests pattern. If the change of new system would change and harm the interests pattern of the beneficiary (such as the urban residents) under the old system, the people with vested interests would also maintain the old system through varied means even though the ongoing system change could enable the whole society realize Pareto improvement. This undoubtedly increases the difficulty of system change. It can not only interpret the long-term existence of the inefficient system before reform, but also partly explain the great difficulty in the series system reforms for urban and rural division since 1979.

Besides, in accordance with the analysis on the urban and rural system evolution from the perspective of synchronic relevance, the little progress of the urban and rural system reform since 1979 has two root causes. Firstly, the historical path dependence (diachronic relevance) of the series of systems has strengthened the "durability" of the institutional system. Secondly, the synchronic relevance among the series of systems has strengthened the "sluggishness" of the institutional system and therefore led to the fact that "the integral system arrangement of Pareto sub-optimum would continue to show its durability and stability because of the complementarity of all system elements". The system linkage and complementarity can be both Pareto and non-Pareto improvement. What's more, the system synchronic relevance of non-Pareto improvement is generally represented by the fact that the emergence of certain system linkage has created rent opportunities for some participants and worsened the situation of other people; the rent under the existing system linkage may become the reason for the people with vested interests to boycott the emergence of the new systems that threaten their rent opportunities because of technical innovation and knowledge progress.

An investigation into the evolution process of our urban and rural division systems since reform and opening-up shows that it is exactly the system synchronic relevance of non-Pareto improvement among the varied urban and rural division systems based on the household registration system that has strengthened the sluggishness and durability of the inefficient systems. The investment and financing system, employment system, financial and taxation system, social security benefit system, farmland system and the like featuring urban and rural division and based on household registration system are not irrelevant and share mutual cross-domain "embedding" among themselves. For example, it seems like that the household registration system and farmland system are only limited to the domain of farmers or rural areas, and social security benefit system the domain of urban areas as it is the urban residents' monopolization. However, as a matter of fact, the system domains that seem to be irrelevant share mutual cross-domain dependence. The existence of the household registration system that restricts farmers' entering into cities makes it possible for the high security and high welfare system as well as employment system enjoyed exclusively by urban residents to continue, or in other words, the synchronic relevance between the old household registration system and social security welfare system has formed the system complementarity of different domains. The same analysis may be applied to the relevance complementarity among the other systems. The household registration system has restricted large amount of surplus labor from rural areas within the countryside, prevented urban areas and population from expansion and made it possible for promoting the investment and financing system partial to cities; the investment and financing system partial to cities and unfair financial and taxation system have further strengthened urban residents' high security and high welfare system, thus forming the system complementarity; the household registration system and welfare system partial to cities restricted the large population of farmers within the countryside and on the limited land, leading to the reality that the farmland system reform has great difficulty to jump out of the weird circle of "exercising the social security function—dividing equally the land—fragmenting the land" from beginning to end. Of course, such kind of system compliance has only strengthened the sluggishness of the old system rather than improved its efficiency since the system complementarity of such kind has, although created rent opportunities for urban residents, worsen farmers' situation. Of the system relevance, the strongest one is the synchronic relevance between the household registration system and the varied social welfare system and employment system enjoyed exclusively by urban residents. Originally, under the household registration system featuring urban and rural isolation, since farmers have witnessed the greatest loss and urban residents the greatest benefit, farmers should naturally become an active promoter of the system reform. However, farmers are always in the dry tree without the "right of speech" in the system game between the farmers that take up the vast majority and the urban residents that take up the minority; and since urban residents have obtained huge benefits from the series of system arrangements, they would naturally become an opponent to the system change. This has undoubtedly strengthened the durability and sluggishness of the series of system arrangements and increased the difficulty for urban and rural system change. For example, including migrating freedom into the constitution would encounter the obstacles from the "developed districts that can participate in capital gain sharing". This is possible. Some people that have favored and even actively participated in the reform at the initial stage of reform have become the people with vested interests. When the reform needs to further solve the deep-seated problems, some people and districts may become the resistance for continual reform the other way around in order to safeguard the local or personal interests. Of course, we don't want to see such circumstances which are however unavoidable. The essence of reform lies in the adjustment of interests. We cannot prevent the loss of some interests of individual interest groups during the increase of overall interests of our society.

To sum up, it is easy for us to understand the great difficulty for breaking down the urban and rural dual system and realizing rural constitutionalism. We also have to admit that the task is truly "as difficult as climbing to the sky". Such as it is, we should see the positive factors like the strengthening of Chinese farmers' awareness of right and concept about democratic legislative system, and should take full advantage of such positive factor to seek for the system change of the greatest extent and realize rural constitutionalism.

11.4 REALIZATION OF RURAL CONSTITUTIONALISM

Since rural constitutionalism involves many specific problems, the factors affecting the realization of rural constitutionalism are also varied and complicated. The following will specifically analyze the main issues that have revealed themselves in rural areas and affected the realization of rural constitutionalism.

11.4.1 Problems with Land Ownership in Rural Area

The core of the "three agriculture-related problems" lies in the farmer problem and the key of farmer problem lies in the land problem. Therefore, within the framework of rural constitutionalism, the land system is unavoidable.

1. The protection deficiency of the existing land system to farmers' land rights and interests

A few years ago, some village cadres were distressed by large area of desolated rural land abandoned by farmers. However, people begin to be troubled by the daily increasing events of "fighting for paddy field and land" by farmers. The change from farmers' "abandoning the paddy field" to "fighting for the paddy field and land" has undoubtedly showed that actual effect has been realized after the series of policies for farmers' assistance and benefits introduced by the central and local governments since the reform of taxation expenses and exemption of agricultural taxes. However, on the other hand, this has, in itself, demonstrated that the land property right relationship in rural areas is still unclear and unstable and there still exist "disputes" about the right and interests relationship for farmers.

Legally, the collectively-owned land is owned by the farmers' collective and contractually operated by households. Farmers enjoy the contracting, operating and beneficiary rights of the land in accordance with the law, and the property right and contracting relationship of rural land is quite clear. After the first round of contracting, China has explicitly declared that the land contract period would be extended for another 30 years. The *Rural Land Contract Law* further specifies that the party awarding the contract shall not take back or adjust farmers' contract land; any organization or individual shall not deprive farmers of their land contract right or illegally limit farmers' land contract right, or adopt any measures of gender discrimination; the contractor legally enjoys the rights to utilize and benefit from the contract land , to transfer the contracted operation right of the land, to voluntarily organize production and operation, and to dispose of the products; contractors also have the right to obtain corresponding compensation; to apply for arbitration or file a lawsuit to the court for the acts that infringe their contracting rights and interests in accordance with the law; to request the people infringing their rights to bear civil liability and even criminal liability, etc. For this, the State has not only endowed farmers with long-term rural land use right but also protect the long-term stability of rural land contracting relationship in the form of law.

However, according to practice, farmers' land contracting relationship is not stable and their land rights and interests have also been infringed by varied parties. Some districts only go through formalities in the second round of land contracting extension and have failed to clarify the land contracting ownership and put into practice the operating warrant. Some districts make "slight adjustment once a year and great adjustment every three years" to the land. Some districts take back the contracted land from the farmers under the excuses of leaving land uncultivated, failure to pay tax and the like. Some districts merge the land in the name of scale operation and even carry out forceful transfer. Some districts acquire farmers' land in large amount and implement the compensation inappropriately. All these have severely damaged farmers' land contracting rights and interests, caused farmers' dissatisfaction and even group events, and brought about unfavorable influence on the economic development and social stability in rural areas.

2. The two categories and three types of plans for rural land legislation reform and evaluation for the plans

In face of the reality that farmers' land rights and interests are frequently infringed, some scholars have proposed some opinions for solving relevant issues from the perspective of rural land legislation reform which can be generally divided into two categories and three types. The first category of opinions locates the issue at the level of land ownership. These people think poorly of the existing rural land collective ownership system and advocate thorough reform to further simplify the ownership subjects and clarify the rural land property right. The category of opinions can be further divided into two types.

The first asks for the implementation of rural land nationalization. These people usually summarize the problems of rural areas, agriculture and rural land as the "middle impedance" of village collective, and think that the problem of rural land lies in the village organization that utilizes the collective ownership to arbitrarily adjust the land. Therefore, they advocate the implementation of land nationalization and long-term utilization of the land by farmers. Some of these people also propose to deal with the contractors' land usage right in accordance with the real right principle so that farmers can obtain more practical benefits and guarantees.

The second advocate rural land privatization in future. These people trust neither the village community nor nationalization. In this regard, people like Yang Xiaokai and Zhou Qiren have put forward some direct opinions, and some other people propose to promote rural land privatization step by step and district by district under positive national intervention.

The second category represents the plan of "transformation to property rights". These people's basic opinion may be expressed by Chi Fulin's remarks that "there exists great deviation between the rural land system arrangement in real life and the regulations of written laws and policies as well as the Central government policies". In other words, these people do not generally negate the existing system framework of rural land property right. The key issue of rural land system lies in that the policies are inappropriately implemented firstly and need the development towards more clear-cut rural land legislation secondly. Therefore, it is necessary to clarity the existing rural land system, especially the land property right system through appropriate rural land legislation so as to establish a fair and stable rural land system.

The plan advocates that the key of reform lies in the existing rural land system framework and taking full advantage of the "household contract system of collective land". The key is to enable farmers to actually own long-term and safeguarded land use right and the main channel to stimulate the capitalization, property right transformation and legalization of "farmers' long-term land use right" and make the right one of our basic state policies. The categories of opinions, as a matter of fact, ask for both national intervention to rural land and limitation to the land property right and rural land adjustment of village collective.

The first type of opinion shows clear expression and good intention. However, it neither specifies the way the village community could adopt to "arbitrarily" adjust the land, nor pays much attention to whether the land property right nationalization equals to complete elimination of the land control role of the village collective. What's more, if the problem of rural land, problem of rural areas and social problem of China as a whole are not separated, attention should at least be paid to that the self-governance framework of grass-roots society and land nationalization may belong to two different politics administration orientations and therefore might have some contradictions. Such advocacy has obviously ignored such possible contradictions.

Compared with the above-mentioned opinion of state ownership, the third type of opinion features no drastic change to the existing framework of collective ownership. It therefore strengthens farmer households' exclusive control rather than national control over the land. In other words, it takes the protection of farmers' land use right instead of strengthening of governmental control over land as the starting point of legislation and legislation reform. While compared with the foregoing opinion of privatization, it proposes to strengthen farmer households' control over land, but do not expect farmer households' arbitrary control of land which may lead to the change from free transfer to arbitrary loss to rural land and cause instability of rural society in the end.

From the author's opinion, although the second advocacy is criticized for the reason that it takes into little consideration of two factors: first, the reform shall have the precondition of corresponding basic social system; second, the rural land system reform has the requirement of gradual nature and continuity, it can usually find theoretical bases from the explanations of economics about the clarification of property right system and maximization of productivity effect and economic benefit. Therefore, the author agrees with the advocacy. It's worth noting that the first two opinions obviously include a common judgment: the greatest issue of rural land property right lies in the link of village community; and the key of reform is to get rid of the unnecessary links. However, it would not be completely appropriate to attribute the land adjustment issue to the village collective. Zhang Xiaozhi once analyzed and said that in a pattern where the power structure determines the land property right relationship, it is unavoidable to have the issue of overmuch intervention power of the government to the village collective and rural land. Therefore, the key of rural land property right reform lies in preventing the intervention of the village collective and government to farmers' land so that the land property right won't fall into unstable condition and farmers' land rights and interests won't be illegally infringed. For this purpose, the author thinks that the privatization of rural land represents the route we must take owing to the following factors:

First, the existing two-level ownership makes the land property right fall into instability and farmers' land rights and interests lack the expectation of certainty. On the contrary, the privatization of rural land and endowment of land ownership to farmers would make the property right relationship clear, contribute to the formation of stable land property right relationship, effectively prevent the intervention and infringement of public power and provide farmers with the expectation of certainty.

Second, the two-level ownership hinders land transfer and goes against the realization of maximum land efficiency. While under the circumstance of land privatization, land transfer would become easy as farmers enjoy complete decision-making power and would contribute to the intensive benefit produced by scale operation and improve the competitiveness of Chinese agriculture.

Third, the two-level ownership has, as a matter of fact, restricted farmers on the land and hindered the circulation of rural labor, thus realizing the so-called political objective of maintaining social stability. While under the circumstance of rural land privatization, farmers enjoy the right to dispose of the land and may decide for themselves the way to deal with the land, thus realizing the rights of freedom for migration and residence.

Fourth, the deadliest thing lies in that the two-level ownership endows the village collective and government with power and therefore leads to cadres' abuse of power. This is especially true under the circumstance of strong and arbitrary village power when farmers' land rights and interests are usually illegally infringed. While under the circumstance of land privatization, farmers' land property right would receive sufficient legal safeguard and judicial remedy and have the capability to effectively resist the infringement of public power.

3. Land privatization and realization of rural constitutionalism

As the land represents both farmers' source of survival and base of development, it should be an integral part of rural constitutionalism and the base for realizing rural constitutionalism to endow farmers with the land property right. In modern society, the property right, right to life and right of freedom are collectively named as the three basic rights for citizens. The land ownership represents not only the most basic property right for farmers but also the base of other social political rights like the rights to exist and vote. To most farmers, the land represents not only their most basic means of production, but also the most basic and main living security. Protecting farmers' land right also means the most basic, direct, concrete and practical protection to farmers' rights and interests.

Some people say that the free trade of land use right like that in Hong Kong would be sufficient for relevant protection. However, the author could not agree to it without giving serious thought. Our government has several times of bad records involving infringement of the private ownership of land. Even though the government practices one hundred percent private ownership of land, people would doubt whether it will change its decision and infringe the property right of the land again. If the government only permit the use right of private ownership in a half-hearted manner, people would be more anxious and apprehensive. In order to change its image of opportunist, the government must verify the credibility of its commitment with acts. Complete privatization and free trade of land represents a kind of hostage mechanism. Only when the civilians enjoy complete private ownership and have no financial dependence on the government, and the government has financial dependence on the owners of private property, can it be possible to actually restrict the rulers' opportunistic behaviors and thus construct a long-term mechanism under which farmers' private ownership of land can effectively restrict the public power.

Endowment of land property right to farmers may provide the expectation of stability for farmers' land operation and stimulate the development of agricultural and rural economy. With the development of our society and economy, farmers' migration and land transfer become inevitable. However, under the existing conditions, the essence of rural land transfer lies in the transfer and exchange of the contractual right of land. The right-belonging relationship for contractual operation of land is clear but without effective protection. Therefore, it is impossible to provide preconditions for land transfer and scale operation or guarantee the security of rights and interests for the two parties of deal.

To ensure that farmers can enjoy the land ownership and rural constitutionalism be realized, the existing constitution may take into consideration the following amendments:

First, to remove the stipulations on land property right in Article 8 of the constitution through legislative procedures and establish the land privatization system, thus realizing the change of rural land from "quasi-private ownership" to "absolute ownership".

Second, the constitutional amendment about land privatization may specify that the privatized land be transferred and circulated like securities in proportion on the premise that minimum amount for the agriculture of narrow sense has been defined. Securities-like circulation would make it possible to transfer farmers' assets to cities, i.e., to realize replacing transfer.

11.4.2 Self-governance of Villagers

1. Main expressions of the issues of village self-governance

(1) Bad relationship between village self-governance organizations and township

Party and government organs. According to the research on village self-governance as well as the media exposure of some events, the township party and government organs and villagers committee have the issue of uncoordinated work and show the tendency of "excessive administrative intervention" and "excessive self-governance intervention". The so-called "excessive administrative intervention" means that the administrative power of the government outmatches the self-governance power of the village, and the township government regards the villagers committee as its subordinate administrative organization, manage the villagers committee through the traditional control method and arbitrarily intervene in the micro-operation of village self-governance. Some township Party committees and governments directly enact orders and instructions to the villagers committee, intervene in the matters within the self-governance scope of villagers committee, and change the decision made by the villagers committee and villager representative assembly. Some township leading bodies ignore the *Villagers Committee Organization Law* and directly replace the villagers committee members, leading to farmers' dissatisfaction and complaints. A very few township Party and government leaders still make every endeavor to manipulate and control the villager election secretly to include their favorite people and exclude their disliked people with villagers' support in the villagers committee under the excuse for the smoothness of work. Some other township leaders pay no attention to and have no contact with the villagers committee. They name their act as respect to village self-governance which, as a matter of fact, represents a denial to the existence of villagers committee and a measure of indifference to the committee. These acts of the township government have not only led to appearance without reality of the village self-governance but also strained the relationship between the country and rural society (farmers) that is already uncoordinated at first. Some villagers committees also regard themselves as an affiliation to the township government, undertake heavy administrative functions and responsibilities and consciously and forcefully accept the intervention from the township government, leading to shrinkage of their own self-governance function. The so-called "excessive expansion of self-governance" means that the village self-governance has gone beyond the law, constituted challenge to the grass-roots government, disturbed the legitimate and essential state affairs of the country, and restrained and weakened the penetration and control of national power to rural areas. The villagers committee cadres from some districts have distorted the meaning of village self-governance.

They think that they are elected by and working for villagers and the township Party and government organs have no right to replace them or intervene in the matters of self-governance. Therefore, they refuse to accept the guidance and assistance from the township leaders. Some of them even lead villagers to run counter to the township government with drastic emotion of confrontation.

(2) Vague power boundary between the villagers committee and village Party branch.

The division and cooperation of Party and government power constitutes an issue that has been difficult to be solved for a long time at different levels of organizations in China, and a difficult issue for the current village self-governance. Main expressions of the issue include: the power boundary between the village Party branch and village self-governance organization is unclear; the responsibility specification is too abstract and scope lacks specific definition. This has led to the "two-handed saw state" between the Party branch and villagers committee within the public power system and for the functional division.

In the village, the two issues that need to be clearly distinguished are the adherence to the Party leadership and inappropriate intervention of the village Party branch. In real practice, the decision of the villagers committee and even the villager assembly necessarily needs the consent from the village Party branch. This makes it difficult to actually implement the power enjoyed by the village self-governance organization in accordance with the law. Some cadres from the villagers committee think that since they are elected by thousands of masses and have the support of the masses, they have strong masses foundation than the Party branch secretary appointed by superior organization or elected by a few Party members.

Therefore, they are unwilling to submit to the leadership of the Party branch. Some of them even ignore the Party branch and go their own way. This has shaken the core status of the Party branch and decreased the rallying and cohesion power of rural grass-roots community. Collision of the two authorities weakens each other and may possibly lead to the "authority vacuum" within local scope and highly possible to create readily exploitable loopholes for the non-standard participation by the non-official authority, thus threatening the modernization process of rural areas.[7] It is a difficult issue that should be solved for village self-governance to coordinate the relationship between the villagers committee and village Party branch.

(3) Ineffective implementation of democratic election in some areas.

In some districts, the implementation of democratic election of villagers committee cadres could not realize the democracy in its real sense. Canvass and bribery for election still exists in some rural areas. Some villagers sell their voters at the price of RMB 1, 5 or higher. Some villagers committee election also shows the phenomenon of fighting for voters: some villagers committee members promise benefits to voters before the election; some form a partnership to canvass the villagers to become a villagers committee member; some villagers committee cadres are "competent" just because of their large family and strong influence instead of the common expectation from the majority of villagers. These are all common phenomena in the election of rural villagers committee. Secondly, the democratic decision, supervision and management carried out on the basis of democracy become a mere formality. The villagers' representative conference or villager assemblies exist in name only without any real value. Some democratic decisions, especially the decisions concerning inter-village relationship, represent the notification or recognition of villagers committee decisions. It would be difficult for the villagers' representative conference or villager assembly to deny or change the decision which is even though wrong. The *Articles of Association for Villager Self-governance* in some districts become a mere scrap of paper since the villagers committee cadres or village Party branch secretary has the final say for the village matters, while the villagers have no chance to have a say, and even have no channel to tell their complaints. The democratic fund management team and village matters supervision team established autonomously by villagers become a mere formality for supervising village matters and finance and play no due role for restricting the fund spending of the villagers committee. On the contrary, they have led to farmers' financial burden in the village and caused many farmers' complaints and villagers committee's distrust.

Village election disputes arise frequently in the practice of village self-governance. The disputes could be divided into two types: the first is the disputes about election qualification. In accordance with the stipulations of the *Villagers Committee Organization Law*, the subjects that enjoy the right to vote are the "villagers" from the village where the election is held. Thus, the disputes about election qualification are represented by the disputes over the villager identity. The second is the disputes about the election effectiveness, i.e., the disputes over the election subjects and about the effectiveness of the ongoing or completed election. In some districts, there even emerge villagers' mass brawls or large-scale conflict or bloody incident. The media have occasionally reported such kind of election disputes in recent years. The existence of such phenomena has severely hindered the smooth operation and healthy promotion of village self-governance.

(1) System improvements of village self-governance to standardize the relationship between village self-governance and township administration.

Firstly, it is necessary to accurately position the relationship between the two. The *Villagers Committee Organization Law* specifies that the villagers committee is neither the grass-roots regime organization of the country nor the agency of the government. It, as a kind of innovative structure from rural social reform, represents a legally independent populace autonomous organization and independent "legal person forerunner" with autonomous power.

The relationship between the village government and villagers committee is the guiding-being guided type rather than the administrative subjection type of leading-being led.

Secondly, to divide the jurisdiction of "township government" and "village self-governance" reasonably through legal regulations, define the boundary for complete permeation of government and the boundary for exercising village self-governance power, and realize the butt joint and coordinated operation of the two powers on the pathway of rule-of-law. The law shall define explicit, specific and operable regulations in accordance with local reality and actively explore varied village self-governance forms based on compliance with the spirit of village self-governance.

Thirdly, to adjust and reconstruct the relationship between the State and the rural society and change the traditional form of social integration. It can be accepted as a feasible channel to ease the tension between the administration power and the self-governance by breaking down the long-term mode of social administration by the State by means of market and democratic mechanisms. It is the basic function of the country and government to serve the society under market economy. On one hand, the township government must walk out of the shadow of planned economy; change the functions and social control modes. It should change the rural community management from direct control to indirect regulation and from control-orientation to service-orientation. Besides, the township government should, based on the respect to village self-governance power, utilize such means as the law, economy and education more frequently to effectively manage rural society, provide service to farmers and reestablish the legality authority of the State. On the other hand, it is necessary to take full advantage of the village self-governance function so that farmers can really enjoy the autonomous right and consciously perform their legal duty. This can not only reflect the meaning of village self-governance, but also effectively implement the power of state's will.

(2) To coordinate the relationship between the villagers committee and village Party branch.

The *Constitution* has specified the leader status of Chinese Communist in national life. In the national system reform, the direction of the Central Party Committee and the State Council is clear, that is, to separate the Party and the government. To solve the issue of race for power between the two, it is necessary to actively explore the modes and approaches for the village self-governance to both play the core leading role of Party branch and reflect the self-governance function of villagers committee. For this end, it is suggested that the joint committee system of party branch and villagers committee, cross appointment system of two committees, two-way communication and appraisal system, training system to the village cadres, etc. to be established. To be specific, (1) to establish and maintain the political authority and leading nucleus of the village Party branch which is the premise for dealing with the relationship between the two correctly. Only after full play of the leading nucleus role of the Party organization, can we deal with the varied complex contradictions of village self-governance correctly and lead billions of farmers to strive for rural modernization. If the Party branch has no sufficient authority to coordinate varied kinds of contradictions, generic contradictions may be intensified and led to turmoil of rural society. Practice has proved that it represents a successful experience for Chinese Communist to transform rural traditional society to agglomerate billions of farmers through the grass-roots organization of the Party. (2) to further improve the *Villagers*

Committee Organization Law and define the power boundary between the village Party branch and villagers committee by means of implementing rules so that the two can perform their own functions respectively and cooperate with each other. In terms of function and power, the Party organization should pay its attention to the leadership of ideology, politics, line, principles and policies. In terms of the village matters, the Party organization should focus on the leading role for proposing, demonstrating and deciding relevant regulations so that the Party branch could really become the backbone for the ideological and economic work of our village. It is inadvisable for the Party branch secretary to directly take charge of administrative matters or assume the office of the director for the village economic cooperation association. However, the Party branch shall promote the rules and regulations stipulation for financial management and supervise the financial work of villagers committee through rules, regulations and systems. The Party branch shall have the right to correct the financial management issues. The villagers committee, as a working organization, shall comply with the Party leadership and establish a system of regular and timely report to the Party organization so that the villagers committee and village Party branch can strengthen communication and exchange and cooperate well with each other.

(3) To construct a unified dispute settlement mechanism for villager election.

The dispute of villager election means the disputes among relevant subjects of the villager election and caused by the substantial and procedural problems in the election process of the villagers committee and other relevant organizations. The villager election disputes have affected the realization of villagers' right to vote and severely restricted the development of village self-governance cause. We should construct and improve the settlement mechanism of administrative power for villager election disputes, settlement mechanism of judicial power and settlement mechanism of legislative power respectively and strengthen the coordination of these mechanisms to form a unified system so as to promote the settlement of villager election disputes, safeguard the realization of villagers' right to vote and stimulate the development of village self-governance cause.

Through the empirical investigation of the villager election practices and relevant literature review, we find that the villager election disputes have the following characteristics: firstly, in terms of the dispute subjects, the villager election disputes mainly emerge among the villager as the voter, villagers committee candidate and national organization related with the villager election which mainly includes the grass-roots people's congress and people's government. In accordance with the stipulations of the *Villagers Committee Organization Law*, different levels of the standing committee of local people's congress above the county level and local people's congress shall safeguard the implementation of the *Villagers Committee Organization Law* within their administrative district. And the township, National Township and town people's government shall provide guidance for the village self-governance work.[8] "However, in accordance with the functions of local people's congress and its standing committee, the regulation of different levels of people's congress and the standing committee of people's congress at or above the county level on the village self-governance cause is mainly implemented by formulating normative documents. They usually don't intervene in the villager voting process directly and therefore would not get involved in the villager voting disputes with other subjects. Therefore, the national organizations that may get involved in and become the subjects of the villager election disputes are mainly the grass-roots people's government. Because of the difference of the involving subjects, the villager election disputes may be classified into two types: the first type is the disputes between the grass-roots people's government and the villagers as voters or candidates. For example, the disputes emerged when the grass-roots people's government appoints or designates the villagers committee members without an election. The other type is the disputes between such equal subjects as the villagers and candidates. Generally speaking, there exist rare election disputes between the villagers as voters as the voters could express their own willingness through institutionalized election procedures. Some villagers and candidates may have disputes because of the candidates' illegal acts, and the candidates may even have disputes because of the interests of being elected. Therefore, the villager election disputes between the equal subjects are mainly the disputes between some villagers and candidates and between the candidates and candidates."[9]

The settlement mechanism of any dispute shall be an intrinsically unified and coordinated supporting system rather than an isolated one. The same is true for the settlement mechanism of villager election disputes. We should, based on respective improvement of the administrative settlement mechanism of villager election disputes, settlement mechanism of judicial power and settlement mechanism of legislative power, strengthen the coordination of the three dispute settlement mechanisms during operation so that the three could form an intrinsically unified and coordinated system, promote effective settlement of the villager election disputes in China and contribute to safeguarding the realization of villagers' voting right and stimulating the development of village self-governance cause.

(4) To improve the village cadres' and villagers' quality and awareness of democratic participation.

Firstly, Chinese farmers have relatively backward democratic awareness for the reasons like the historical accumulation of feudal autocracy traditions, backward economy, incomplete and unsound democratic legislative system, etc. Secondly, Chinese farmers lack independent individual consciousness and self-management ability. They have strong dependent and political psychology since they usually rely on the country, government and superiors, and place hopes on the feudal "honest and upright officials". They also have strong group consciousness which often overwhelm and cover the initiative and creativity of the individuals as the social subjects. As a result, the democratic rights endowed to farmers by the law have been replaced by some traditional organizations in practice.[10] Because of such situation, in real life, there emerges a strange theory which holds that since Chinese farmers lack the democratic concept and self-governance spirit, and have neither the motivation for autonomous participation nor the knowledge, technique or experience for democratic participation, there would be no good result for implementing democratic self-governance. The one that governs the ideology is the so-called "elite" theory which usually holds that people are of different levels and farmers are at the lowest level. "To achieve success and expected result, the advanced modern systems must rely on the modern personality and quality of the people utilizing them. In whatever country, only when its people can synchronize with varied economic development of modernization in terms of the psychology, attitude and acts, could the country really realize its modernization." Such idea, although having certain reason from appearance, is however ridiculous. Just as criticized by a sage, "The idea can match the concept from the idiot in the old tale who actually said that he would never enter the water before he learned swimming. If people could only sit back and wait for freedom before becoming wise and kind under enslavement state, they might have to wait forever." It is no doubt that the village self-governance system must be rode and controlled by people with certain modern thinking and democratic quality. Without modern people, it would be very difficult to normally implement the democracy. However, democracy has never been any luxury, foreign goods, and castle in the air or inborn character. Rather, it is a kind of instinctive choice and reasonable demand for the people based on self-concern.[11] To the general public, the spirit of democratic self-governance can be cultivated and democracy is earned by struggle. Only through meaningful civic participation, could democracy be really carried forward. If we want farmers to learn the democratic knowledge and experience, we have to enable them to participate in the practice of democratic management and personally experience and practice the benefits of democracy. Since the village cadres are the village leaders directly living in the masses that have great influence on the villager masses and social morality, their politics, ideology and style would directly affect their image in the villagers' heart and development of the whole village. Therefore, special attention should be paid to this. While implementing the political, ideological and style education among the village cadres, special attention should be paid to the two existing issues of tendency: the first is the officers' nonfeasance issue and the other the issue of honesty self-control. Since the village cadres come from the villagers and are elected by the villagers, they should be responsible for the villagers, establish the ideology of serving the people, get rid of the mentality of small-farm agriculture and bureaucratic airs, take a broad and long-term view, make the right decision, put into practice the "four democratic items" and lead the villagers to develop the economy and stride forward to the moderately prosperous society.

Since the village self-governance represents a kind of extensive practice for hundreds of millions of farmers to directly exercise democratic rights, it has become an important part of democratic politics and one of the main indicators for measuring the political development level of a country for farmers to generally and equally participate in the politics. This is especially true for China with a vast majority of farmers. If farmers cannot become the democratic politics subjects of Chinese society, Chinese political development would be abnormal and democracy would descend to a few people's privilege.[12] It's worth noting that the modern democratic politics and required political participation should be the conscious, ordered and reasonable political acts of the subjects. However, our villagers could not consciously participate in the village self-governance currently because of their weak enthusiasm and awareness for political participation and low cultural quality, especially the low politics cultural quality. Therefore, we should, first of all, vigorously develop the scientific, educational and cultural cause and generally enhance farmers' science and politics cultural quality so that farmers could become modernized civics. We should meanwhile promote the update and reform of farmers' view of values and guide farmers to establish the view of values that conforms to the requirements of socialist market economy and overall progress of the society. Besides, we should guide farmers to correctly deal with the individual-community-country relationship, enable them to recognize that national prosperity and collective development represent reliable guarantee for increasing farmers' interests, and improve their consciousness to safeguard the public authority and public interests of the society so as to remove the varied irrational factors that intervene in village self-governance.

To sum up, we should enable farmers to actually become the "rational actors". Next, we should carry out a large amount of publicity and guidance work to propagandize the knowledge related with the *Constitution*, *Villagers Committee Organization Law* and village self-governance so that farmers could realize their position, rights and obligations in the village, actively participate in the construction of the "four democratic items" and understand that village self-governance represents a business of their own and great event closely related with their interests. "Since the construction of democratic politics means to provide people with equal opportunities, people regard democratic politics as their own business and could actively participate in the democratic politics. People's enthusiasm for politics is especially high and strong for those matters directly related with their own economic interests." Therefore, the villagers committee should expand the channel for villagers' democratic participation, develop the rural self-governance organization and mass organization, improve the social organization system of rural society. We should, through the practice of village self-governance, enable farmers to generally accept the basic democratic training, cultivate the democratic awareness and habits, and master the operational skills of self-governance to further enhance their political participation ability so that farmers could gradually become the mature and rational subjects of village self-governance.[13]

11.4.3 Problems with Reform of Township System

Under the framework of rural constitutionalism, it represents an important task to find way to effectively standardize the public power activities of the grass-roots government. Therefore, it is of great significance to discuss the township system reform.

1. Disadvantages and analysis of existing township regime

Since the founding of China, the arrangement of the rural grass-roots regime has gone through many times of change. The first *Constitution* passed in September, 1954 specifies that Chinese rural grass-roots regime includes the township, ethnic township and town. The organizational system of township regime has been officially established since then. However, shortly after that, the township regime system was once canceled in over two decades after 1958 and replaced by the people's commune system of "integration of government administration with commune management" because of the implementation of People Commune System and ten years of the Cultural Revolution turmoil. The constitution amended in 1982 re-established the township as Chinese rural grass-roots regime. From 1980s on, with the change from planned economy to market economy system in China and the development of rural democratic legislative system, disadvantages with the township regime organizations have been continuously exposed which has severely hindered the development of rural society and economy as well as the grass-roots democratic legislative system process. Therefore, further improvement is quite necessary. To sum up, the disadvantages of existing township regime include the two aspects of internal and external part:

(1) Disadvantages of internal structure.

The internal structure of existing township regime has many disadvantages. Firstly, the Party and government are integrated and the power structure unreasonable. The power structure for most of the existing township regime is a kind of centralized Party leadership; the responsibility system of township head remains in name only, and the functions of township people's congress has been severely empty. There exist the phenomena like substituting the government with the Party and unreasonable grass-roots regime system. Secondly, the township government bodies are overstaffed and financial deficit very serious. Currently most of the townships are with "eating finance" or even "begging finance" because of common phenomenon of liabilities.[14] There frequently emerge the phenomena of corresponding arbitrary apportion and charge. Hence, heavy financial burden has been transferred to farmers and farmers suffer a great deal because of daily-increasing burden. Moreover, the township leaders are obedient to the authority rather than the people. Under the existing cadre system, the appointment and removal of township cadres are decided by the superior. Therefore, it naturally becomes the priority issue for township leaders to find way to cater to their superior and realize achievements in their official career. Hence it is not difficult to understand such phenomena as "vanity project", "image project", "deceiving one's superiors and deluding one's subordinates", "false report of figure" and "the higher authorities have policies, the localities have their countermeasures" in most districts. These have led to strained relations between the cadres and masses, damage to national authority and potential crisis of township regime.

(2) The external relationship is uncoordinated.

This is firstly represented by strained relations of townships and villages. Since the implementation of village self-governance in rural areas, the township government and villagers committee are no longer of the leading and obeying relationship. Rather, they are of the guiding and assisting relationship. However, in order to ensure the implementation of the state task, the township governments still universally intervene in the matters within the function scope of the villagers committee to realize their main administrative control to villages. As a result, the relationship between the township government and villagers committee become strained and there frequently emerge the phenomenon of villagers committee director being removed by the township government. This has severely hindered the development of village self-governance system and restricted the growth of village self-governance power. The uncoordinated external relationship is secondly represented by blocked relationship between the county and township and serious "barriers between higher and lower levels or between different departments and regions". Since the setting of the two levels of county and township regimes is in accordance with the principle of "real construction of county regime and imaginary construction of township regime", the township government usually could not perform its functions of a level of regime, and the county government, in order to perform its functions of comprehensive management within its district scope, has established its own vertical control system, set many agencies in townships, dismembered the functions of township government and led to contradictions and friction between the county and township.

The above-mentioned issues of the township regime are caused mainly by two factors: the first is that the existing township political organization system is formed in the era of planned economy and under the highly centralized system. At that time, the administrative intervention was emphasized. Thus an omnipotent government with an unwieldy organization has been formed. However, today when the market economy has been basically established and construction of democracy and law growing rapidly, the originally system could no longer adapt to the requirement of changing situation. At the current stage, to ensure effective operation of market economy and sound progress of the society and adapt to the tide of democratic legal systematization, we need a weak government structure of service, i.e., we need to emphasize the change of governmental functions and roles from micro administration to macro administration and from administer to server. The second is the role of pressure-type system.[15] The township regime, as the grass-roots regime of our rural areas, is located at the base and end of our national regime system. The varied policies, plans and tasks of our country in rural areas need to be implemented by the township government. However, the township government has little public power and few public resources. Under the pressure-type system, in order to accomplish the tasks transmitted from the superior but beyond the capability scope of the township government, the township government has to ask for power from the upper level and funds from the lower level by varied means, or even conceal the true state of affairs from above and below. This can be deemed as an inevitable result for too much intervention of national administrative power in village social matters.[16]

2. Three reform schemes and their appraisal

In recent years, the academic circle of China has carried out heated discussion about township reform and expressed varied points of view. The author summarizes the viewpoints and divided them into the "cancellation theory", "reservation theory" and "self-governance theory". The one who holds the representative viewpoint of "cancellation theory" is Zhao Shukai, a researcher from the Agriculture Department of the Development and Research Center of the State Council. He thinks that "the township government, as the lowest level of regime organization in our national regime structure, is actually an integrated organization of the Party and the government mixed operation at present. From the perspective of external scale, the township government is indeed an enormous organization; while from the perspective of daily performance, the township government has indeed showed some things of 'unruliness'. Therefore, when the power system of the township government itself has already been suspended in midair, it is possible to exploit the situation to reform and directly cancel the township government."[17] The one who holds the representative viewpoint of "reservation theory" is Professor Xu Yong and the Director from China Rural Development Research Center of Central China Normal University. He thinks that "since the 'township government' is the intermediate link between national and social communities that connects the county to the upper level and village to the lower level, it would be difficult for any isolated or individual township reform to realize substantial achievements. Therefore, we should carry out structural reform featuring interlocking of three levels of county, township and village, i.e., realize the system mode change from 'township government and village governance' to 'county government, township agency and village governance', break through the isolating mechanism of 'township government' and 'village governance', and construct an effective village governance system at a low price which features positive interaction between the country and society."[18] The two who hold the representative viewpoint of "self-governance theory" are Dr. Yu Jianrong and Dang Guoying, a researcher from Rural Development and Research Institution of Chinese Academy of Social Sciences. They think that "in the final analysis, the township institutional reform should adopt the path of democratic self-governance and the township self-governance represents a kind of community self-governance that has no relationship of administrative subordination with the superior administrative institution". For this, Dang Guoying proposes to "cancel the village administrative level, transfer the economic functions undertook by the villagers committee and village party branch to the folk economic organization and the public administration function to the township administrative institution, properly downsize the township institution, and implement democratic election, discussion of government affairs and integration of two committees in the township community."[19] Dr. Yu Jianrong proposes to "cancel the township government and establish a self-governance organization; improve and strengthen the agencies of county functional department like the public security, industry and commerce, tax administration, family planning and education; enrich and strengthen the village self-governance organization, develop intermediary organization of community and establish an organization that represents farmers' interests, that is, Farmer Association."[20]

Different people have different views and it is difficult to decide which is right from the above-mentioned experts' views and proposals. The author thinks that the theoretical research and academic debate of real meaning must come back to earth from the heaven. Just as North, the founder of institutional school, pointed out, "once it chooses to go down the original wrong path, the inefficient system would be caught in an 'autolock' state and the original system design would strengthen the stimulation and inertia of the existing system. As a result, it would be very difficult to get free from the system."[21]

Otherwise, "applying the theory to any historical period would be easier than solving one of the easiest simple equation."[22]

The viewpoint of "cancellation theory" has fully realized the disadvantages of existing township system, but canceling the level of township regime is too simple and childish in terms of strategy. It also fails to provide a clear reform plan for future system of township.

The viewpoint of "reservation theory" regards the township as a level of complete entity regime which would cause more serious institutional and people expansion as well as higher administration cost. The reform method would lead to higher administrative level of township grass-roots and more control over rural society, and aggravate the conflict between the country and rural society. Meanwhile, the viewpoint emphasizes "ruling people" in a one-sided way and ignores "government by the people" and "making people rich". Therefore, it represents only a temporary solution rather than permanent cure. Furthermore, it neglects the serious differentiation of urban and rural society.[23] Some scholars from the historic perspective think that the township government still failed to construct a level of complete regime organization at the pre-reform stage featuring extreme expansion of nationalism and political omnipotence and therefore would be even impossible to do this. What's more, the existing configuration of equilibrium between the country and rural society at the township level may be broken down.[24]

The viewpoint of "self-governance theory" is undoubtedly identical with the development direction of democratic politics, although the reform method, tantamount to a social revolution in rural areas, features high level, large cover and great fluctuation and goes against the currently effective political requirements of "maintaining stability is of top priority". However, with the increasingly improved and mature system of village self-governance, the farmers with daily increasing independent consciousness of self-governance and democratic legislative system would not be simply restricted to village self-governance and would definitely further ask for township self-governance. Therefore, township self-governance represents the general trend.

3. Township reform and rural constitutionalism

Township self-governance constitutes an important part of rural constitutionalism. Therefore, the direction of township reform should be building a totally autonomous township regime, accomplishing the change from administration-oriented to service-oriented government, constructing an efficient, honest and democratic law-based government, and trying best to prevent its infringement on farmers' private rights and realize rural constitutionalism.

To realize townships self-governance, suggestions are provided as follows:

First, to make the Party and governmental institutions to retreat from the township completely. Establish a completely autonomous institution of township based on overall popular-election of villagers committee.

Second, to make the political game feasible, the township party agency should only set a special office instead of a committee to manage the village party members in a unified manner. Also, it would be necessary to cancel the setting of village Party branch and make the villagers committee the exclusive institution to exercise the farmers' power of attorney. In other words, no party power should be stronger than the political power in essence. The constitution should explicitly stipulate that those who have no land right in a village shall not take the post of public office. However, the law should encourage the existing township public officers whose parents are in the village to return to their villages (townships) to inherit the land right and participate in the campaign for public office.

Third, the township government officers shall be elected by the village head joint association or specially appointed, i.e., we should change the township governance mode from politics-orientation to company-orientation. During the whole process of transition, we may establish a supervision committee constituted by different levels of people's congress of village as the transitional institution. In order to prevent the recurrence of "good gentry quits and evil gentry joins" in history, the village should construct a "fair criticism congress" to enable the senior people (such as the retired teaching personnel who permanently reside in rural areas and are from rural areas at the very first) to evaluate the administrators' ability and form a kind of public opinion mechanism. The public policy should encourage the intellectuals from rural areas at the very beginning to return to their villages (townships) to participate in the governance and enable them to enjoy the land right in rural areas.

11.4.4 Problems with Farmers' Association

Chinese farmers have always failed to actually exercise the right for freedom of association endowed by the constitution for a long time. This is caused by insufficient system supplies to a large extent. Today, the Chinese farmers edified by modern concept of democratic legislative system increasingly demands the construction of their own institutions or social associations to present their claimed rights and interests. Therefore, in terms of farmers' freedom of association, there emerge the contradiction between the system demand and supply. Solving the contradiction becomes the general trend in order to enable farmers to actually enjoy the right for freedom of association.

We know that one of the main characteristics for civil society is to ask the varied organizations including the farmers' organizations to play an important intermediary agent between the people and government. Accelerating the construction of farmers' organization is very important for forming ordered political participation mechanism. The organized farmers would not only contribute to maintaining farmers' rights and interests and delivering farmers' interest appeal, but also greatly decrease the uncertain factors and reduce the cost for social dialogue and market transactions. The organized right safeguarding and resistance would be more reasonable than those in a state of disunity or rushing into mass action. Currently, under the specific background of our country, the non-organized resistance is more dangerous than the organized one and the unordered power has higher possibility to become out of control. Only the highly organized society can be a society with the highest stability. Therefore, farmers' organization orientation is consistent rather than conflicting with the value pursuit of harmonious society.

As a matter of fact, the condition and opportunity to establish grass-roots farmer association in rural areas have been mature and appropriate. The research cases from the research group of China Institute for Reform and Development show that some districts have strongly cried for establishing grass-roots farmer associations and the government encounters substantially higher pressure for establishing farmer association. According to the questionnaire about Chinese reform from China Institute for Reform and Development, 65.8% of the experts think that the condition and opportunity to establish grass-roots farmer association in rural areas have been mature and appropriate. According to the analysis on the conditions of some districts, it may become a trend for future development of farmers' organizations to establish grass-roots farmer association at the two levels of county and township.

There exist varied forms of farmers' organizations for safeguarding rights, of which, the most typical ones that especially deserve attention include the "representative team", "farmers' right safeguarding association", "farmers' development association" and the like from such places as Hengyang of Hunan, Fuyang of Anhui, Shuyang of Jiangsu. Professor Yu Jianrong from the Rural Development Institute of Chinese Academy of Social Sciences, also a member from the research team of China Institute for Reform and Development, expounded the development trend of farmers' right safeguarding organizations based on tracking investigation and research to farmers' right safeguarding organizations from Hengyang of Hunan. Farmers' right safeguarding organizations are gradually changing from "representative team" (primary form of organization) to "networking" (horizontal integration among organizations) and further to official application to local government for official establishment of "farmer association". During the evolution and development process, there emerge a group of right safeguarding elites and the farmers' organizations also show higher and higher level of systematization and more and more specific targets. Farmers put forward many slogans like "returning four rights to people" (the public autonomous right; production, marketing and operation right, farmer self-governance right, and financial management right) and "cooperating with the government" (no deformation of publicity policies, tough implementation of policies, assistance from all people to a people in plight, removal of corruption and reactionary gang, being united as one for moderate prosperity and permanent loyalty to CPC).

Currently, a vast majority of the right safeguarding activities of these organizations are basically kept within the legal framework and their slogans are usually for propagandizing the Central government policies and protecting some rights and interests that are endowed by the Central government but infringed by the grass-roots government. Hengyang of Hunan has showed no large-scale events since the establishment of farmers' organizations since farmers started to restrict each other, talk with the government in case of any issue and the government also started to communicate with farmers' representatives. The forming of farmers' right safeguarding organizations and rational right safeguarding activities carried by them are now influencing and changing the administration activities of the grass-roots government. In many districts with farmers' right safeguarding organizations, the county and township government started to regard the farmers' right safeguarding representatives as their objects for consultation and dialogue.

The major problem with the existing farmers' right safeguarding organizations is that these organizations haven't obtained the procedural recognition from the civil administration department of the government. Therefore, they are still the "unofficial" organizations without the qualification of "official organization" and even named as the "illegal" organizations. As the governmental department has given up their management duties and failed to provide necessary legal and organizational management training to farmers, a few "appealing representatives" who are with low cultural quality at first lack the necessary awareness of legal protection and systematic thinking about their targets and methods of activity. Some people with radical advocacy try to utilize the situation that farmers' right safeguarding organizations could not be included in normal system management to carry out some normal activities (such as the religious activities) and attempt to lead farmers from "resisting with the law" to "illegal resistance".

Under the foregoing circumstance, with only the methods of restriction and prohibition could only intensify the contradiction. This is obviously conflicting with the pursuit of harmonious society. Therefore, an appropriate method would be adopting education & persuasion, policy guidance and laws & regulations to include the farmers' organizations from the real countryside and farmer workers' habitation in the system framework of social management for the settlement of contradiction and realization of the double effect of stabilizing rural society and stimulating economic development. Currently, we should establish experimental units of grass-roots farmer association in the places with the conditions like Hunan and Anhui. However, during the construction process of farmers' organizations, it is of great necessity to stick to being "non-governmental", "autonomous" and "voluntary". Only in this way, could the farmer associations become the farmers' organizations in real sense. Firstly, we need to stick to the separation between farmer association and the country at the level of system and change the practice of equating farmer association with national regime or quasi-regime organizations in Chinese history so as to maintain the non-governmental nature of farmer association. Secondly, we need to stick to the autonomous nature of farmer associations so that the associations could independently deal with their own businesses. Thirdly, we need to ensure the voluntary nature of farmers' organizations. It should be a legal right rather than obligation for farmers to organize and join in farmer associations, and reasonable quit mechanism must be established. To sum up, in order to make farmer associations become farmers' organizations in real sense, we should, in accordance with the principles and purposes of social organization, enable farmer associations to represent and maintain farmers' interests to the largest extent within the scope of the constitution and other law.

NOTES

1. Guo Shutian and Liu Chunbin, *Unbalanced China—The Past, Present and Future of Urbanization* (Shijiazhuang: Hebei Peoples Publishing House, 1990), 29-75.
2. Yang Yiyong et. al, *Fairness and Efficiency* (Beijing: China Today Press, 1997), 95.
3. Guo Shutian, "Re-discussion About Today's Farmers' Issue,"*Agricultural Economy Issue* 10 (1995).
4. (US) Mortimer J. Adler, *Six Ideas* (Beijing: Tuanjie Press, 1990), 170.
5. Zhou Zuohan and Zhang Yinghong, "Farmers' Free Development and Township System Reform," H*unan Normal University Social Sciences Journal* 4 (2004).
6. Lv Xinyu, "Consciousness of Problems of 'Peasant Worker Rush'," *Reading* 10(2003).
7. Feng Yukui, "Reflection on Correct Settlement of the Contradiction between the 'Two Committees' in Rural Areas," *Socialism Studies*, 1 (2003).
8. Li Kang, *Township Organization of Chinese Rural Community in Social Change (Ningxia Rural Community Research and Investigation)* (Beijing: China Science and Technology Press, 1992).
9. Wang Ying, *New Collectivism: Reorganization of Rural Society* (Beijing: Economic Management Press, 1996), 229-234.
10. Wang Shangyin, "Villagers Dismiss Officers: Village-level Democratic Constriction," *Socialism Studies* 1 (2003).
11. Zhang Xiaojin, "Re-reelection on Village Self-governance of Chinese Rural Areas," *Chinese Book Review* 5 (1998).
12. Peng Zhen, *Selected Works of Pengzhen* (Beijing: People's Publishing House, 1991), 611-13.
13. Du Zanqi, *Culture, Power and Country (North China Villages of 1900-1942)* (Nanjing: Jiangsu People's Publishing House, 1994).
14. According to expert's estimation, China has about 50,000 townships, each of which has a liability of over RMB 4 Million. Therefore, Chinese townships have a total liability of about RMB 220 Billion. Refer to Zhang Qingsong, "*A Liability of Two Hundred Billion Perplexes*

Chinese Townships, Financial Crisis Sows the Seed of Corruption," *China Reform*, June 19, 2001.

15. The so-called "pressure-type" refers to the evaluation system of materialization and administration methods of quantitative task decomposition adopted by a level of political organization to realize the economic catching-up and hit the varied targets transmitted from the superior. To realize the economic catching-up and varied targets, the level of political organizations quantitatively decompose these tasks and targets, transmit them to the organizations and individuals at lower level, instruct these organizations and individuals to accomplish the tasks and hit the targets within specified time, and then implement political and economic rewards and punishments in accordance with the performance of these organizations and individuals. Since some main parts of the tasks and targets adopt the evaluation method of "one-vote veto" system, each level of organizations is operated under the pressure of the evaluation system. — Quoted from Rong Jingben et al., "Investigation and Research Report on the Operational Mechanism of People's Congress System of the Two Levels of County and Township from Xinmi City," *Economic and Social System Comparison* 4 (1997): 83.

16. Yang Jun, "Reconstruction Vision of Township Government," *CPC Sichuan Provincial Party School Journal* 4 (2003).

17. Zhao Shukai, *Township Reform: Self-criticism and Outlook after Investigation to 20 Townships in 10 Provinces (Districts)* (Beijing: China Development Press, 2005).

18. Xu Yong, "County Government, Township Agency and Village Governance: Structural Change of Village Governance," *Jiangsu Social Sciences* 2 (2002).

19. Dang Guoying, "Village Self-governance Would Finally Become Weak and Township Self-governance Shall Be Promoted Quickly," *Southern Rural*, July 21, 2005.

20. Yu Jianrong, "Township Self-governance: Basis and Channel: with the Change of 20th Century Township System as the View," *Strategy and Management* 6 (2002).

21. North, *Structure and Change of Economic History*, trans. Chen Yu and Luo Huaping (Shanghai: Shanghai SDX Joint Publishing House, 1994).

22. Engels, *Selected Work of Marx and Engels* (Beijing: People's Publishing House, 1995), 696.

23. Yang Jun, "Reconstruction Vision of Township Government," *CPC Sichuan Provincial Party School Journal* 4 (2003).

24. Wu Licai, "New Discussion about Township Government," *Open Times*, 5 (2002).

Chapter Twelve

Solving "Three Agriculture-related Problems" by Rule of Law and Improvement of Villagers Committee Election System

12. 1 SURVEY OF ELECTION SYSTEM OF VILLAGERS COMMITTEE

As the most extensive political activities with the largest scale in rural China, the villagers committee election has always followed one distinct value topic: safeguarding and expanding voters' rights and promoting democracy of election. Under the guidance of the value idea, the villagers committee election system has not only inherited other system resources that could be used for reference, but also respected farmers' pioneering spirit, carried out continuous innovation based on practice, gradually formed its own characteristics and become the election system with the highest level of democracy in China currently.

12.1.1 Concept and Nature of Election System of Villagers Committee

Since 1982 when rural village self-governance and villagers committee election were included in the constitution, the villagers committee election system has also become one of the election systems specified by the *Constitution*. Article 111 of the Constitution specifies that "the neighborhood committee or villagers committee by urban and rural areas in accordance with the residents' living area represent the grass-roots mass autonomous organization." Article 2 of *Villagers Committee Organization Law* specifies that "the villagers committee represents a grass-roots mass autonomous organization for farmers' self-governance, self-education and self-service and adopts democratic election, democratic decision, democratic management and democratic supervision. The committee deals with the public affairs and public welfare establishments of the village, settles disputes among the people, provides assistance for safeguarding social security and reports villagers' opinions, requirements and suggestions to the people's government."

As a kind of autonomous organization, the villagers committee is different from local government. Such differences are mainly represented by: firstly, the difference of nature. The villagers committee represents the village autonomous organization and the local government represents the national regime organization. Secondly, the difference of generation method, i.e., the difference of legality source. The villagers committee is generated through direct election by the vast villagers and the local government by different levels of local people's congresses. Thirdly, the difference of power nature and contents. The villagers committee enjoys the village self-governance right of certain scope and the local government enjoys extensive administrative power. Fourthly, the difference of supervision and restriction. The villagers committee shall be responsible and report work to the village council, and local government shall also be responsible and report work to its superior national administrative organization as it is under the leadership of its superior organization in accordance with the administrative subordination relationship except for being responsible to and reporting work to the people's congress of its same level.[1] The villagers committee has no direct "ordering-obeying" administrative subordination relationship with local government and the following legal relationship with the township government: the township government shall provide guidance, support and assistance to the work of villagers committee, but cannot intervene in the matters within the village self-governance scope according to the law; and the villagers committee provides assistance to the work of the township government. The differences between the villagers committee and local government are also represented by such aspects as the organization constituents, working method of the personnel and decision procedures. As the village self-governance organization, the villagers committee has always been the party awarding the contract for land contract operation in practice, implemented the functions of the rural land owner and been the lawsuit subject of rural land disputes because of its role as the representative for the land owner. Therefore, as a kind of autonomous social organization, the villagers committee also has the qualification of civil law subjects.[2] As the standing operating institute of village self-governance system, the villagers committee represents a part of the village self-governance organization system whose members are directly elected by villagers, and has a guidance and assistance relationship with the township government rather than "leading—being led" relationship.

12.1.2 Features of Election System of Villagers committee

Except for the general and common characteristics of election system, the villagers committee election system also has its own unique characteristics, including the nature of selectivity, competitiveness, confidentiality, openness, etc.[3]

1. Selectivity

The nature of selectivity means that, in accordance with the arrangement of the villagers committee election system, the villagers, as the subject of rights, enjoy sufficient right of choice, and therefore can realize their own wills autonomously without interference. The villagers' right of choice runs through the whole process of election, including the voters' right of choice for the presiding organization of election, primary candidate, official candidate, scrutineer, teller, people responsible for counting the voters and final electee; the right to re-elect the villagers committee members within the term of office, etc.

2. Competitiveness

The competitiveness of villagers committee election system is mainly represented by two aspects: the first is the principle of competitive election and the second the campaign regulations.

The *Villagers Committee Organization Law* specifies that the number of candidates shall be more than the number of the people that should be elected. Local villagers committees have materialized the principle of competitive election through their election methods. In general, for the director and deputy director, the number of candidates shall be one more than the people that should be elected; and for the committee members, the number of candidates shall be 1, 2 or 3 more than people that should be elected. This shows that all positions of the villagers committee member shall implement competitive election. Based on multiple candidates, the villagers committee election system allows the candidates to carry out fair and open competition. The introduction of competitive mechanism to election has broken the lifeless state of previous election, made the election alive and enabled the candidates and voters to get in the state of active participation and competition. Direct interaction between the candidates and voters also further animate and brighten the atmosphere of the whole village. The campaign has provided equal opportunity for the candidates to show their ability and strive for success. It contributes to attracting excellent talents to participate in the election and helping the talents stand out on one hand, and enabling voters to make the right judgment about the candidates and rational choice after comparison and making the people with stronger base of public opinion and higher ability to enter into the villagers committee.

3. Confidentiality

The nature of confidentiality of the villagers committee election system means that no one knows about the voting direction in the election, i.e., only the voters know their own voting decisions, including voting for someone rather than the other, affirmative vote, negative vote and abstention vote. This can avoid the voters' concern and enable the voters to express their real wishes. To ensure the confidentiality of the voters' choice, our election system basically requires secret ballot. There is no exception for the villagers committee election system. However, the difference between villagers committee election system and people's congress election system lies in that secret vote writing place is set for further improvement of the principle of secret ballot during the election. Article 14 of the *Villagers Committee Organization Law* specifies that secret vote writing place shall be set during election. The stipulation has fully reflected the principle of secret ballot and protected the voters' right of free choice. Since the village is an "acquaintance society" with complicated interpersonal relationship, if votes are written openly and publicly, voters' will may be easily intervened and affected, as the influence of religion, clan and the like may seize the opportunity to supervise and intervene in voters for their own purposes. This will impose intangible pressure on voters who would have difficulty to express their own will. The setting and utilization of the secret vote writing place can effectively prevent the interference from the family clan and different factions of influence and decrease villagers' worrisome and concern so that villagers can express the will of their own. The innovation of vote writing form represents the unique characteristic of villagers committee election.

4. Openness

Openness represents the guarantee of fairness, ensures the villagers' right to know and contributes to the villagers' supervision of election. Openness runs through the whole process of the villagers committee election: make public the election procedures and specific stipulations so that villagers can know what a legal election is as well as their own rights and obligations; make public the list of voters so as to avoid "registration error" and "registration omission" during voters' registration and ensure each villager's right to vote; make public the number of people that should be elected and candidates' condition to provide guidance for villagers' intention of choice; make public the list and basic conditions of the candidates to avoid internally selected or designated candidates; make public the vote counting and announce the voting result on the spot to avoid "camera bellows" operation, etc. During the villagers committee election, public vote counting is implemented and the announcement of voting result on the spot has great influence on the villagers' mind and the fairness of the election results. To villagers, the legal procedure of public vote counting and announcement of election result on the spot under their own supervision has substantially strengthened their trust on the election. In each election assembly place, public vote counting represents a climax event attracting voters' attention. Voters pay ardent attention to the voting process, expect the voting result and produce a spiritual concern to democracy. Besides, the openness and timeliness of the vote counting and election result contribute to putting an end to such activities as malpractice, fraudulent practice and manipulation of voting result caused by secret vote counting. During the public vote counting process, since the whole process is carried out under villagers' high attention, no township government, election committee or any other people have the possibility to find opportunity or enough courage to apply inappropriate influence on the voting result. In this way, the fairness of voting result can be ensured.

Currently, the set of villagers committee election system is still under development. What's more, there still exists certain distance between the stipulation and actual operation. However, objectively speaking, of the varied election systems in today's China, the villagers committee election system is the one with the highest democratic contents. It has, from the perspective of system arrangement, provided civic participation with necessary channel and space, motivated hundreds of millions of farmers' enthusiasm for participation and avoided the election of formalism. Meanwhile, the procedural fairness of the villagers committee election system has been recognized by varied parties, guided people to pursue procedural legality during election and guaranteed the voting standard and order. The implementation of the election system with unique features has not only produced positive influence on the villagers committee election practice, but also represented valuable resources for the reference of promoting political democracy.

12.1.3 Democratic Tradition in Rural Area and Election System of Villagers Committee

"All legal and system designs are in essence for the purpose of standardizing social operation rules and people's behavioral patterns. However, since such standardization is carried out under certain social and historical environment, it not only regards certain material production methods as the conditions, but also is restricted by social inheritance and actors' way of thinking, mental habits and social relevance."[4] The villagers committee election in rural China based on the *Villagers Committee Organization Law* represents a kind of community self-governance for realizing villagers' self-governance, self-education and self-service in the form of legal documents and from the starting point of reforming the village public power source. However, the villagers committee election is carried out in rural society and would definitely encounter the heritage of traditional rural society which however takes the rural nature of zero democratic awareness as its characteristic.

Democracy refers to people's governance and power and a kind of social administration system under which social members can in general directly or indirectly participate in the decision having influence on all members.[5] The democracy in practice shall take corresponding theoretical system as the support which is generated during the renaissance of western bourgeoisie. The social contract theory thinks that since the humans under natural conditions found so much inconvenience under the state without society or government, they, after consultation, executed a contract and built a society, and released part of the power that originally belongs to individuals to form the public power beyond specific individual.[6] In this way, although the public power enjoyed by the government and country is not specifically commanded by individuals any more, people are still the source of public power. People, in the capability of owner, periodically recycle and award power and the election system is utilized in this sense. Therefore, we may find that the realization of election democracy cannot be separated from the base of two levels: the first is the system framework. In other words, there exists a set of system which may enable the public to realize the status of the sovereign and enjoy public power. The second is the psychological cognition. People actually realize that they are the owner of public power and the cognition has been changed into corresponding way of thinking and behavioral habit. However, when the villagers committee enters into rural China in the form of system framework, there exist no historic traditions agreeing with the set of systems and ideas for continuance. On the contrary, we are faced with a kind of rural social traditions without the consciousness of democracy. Since ancient times, China has neither democratic system nor the thinking of popular sovereignty. On the contrary, the traditional feudal order of importance or seniority in human relationships advocates the hierarchical as well as superiors and inferiors ideas of "Those who work with their brains will rule, those who labor with physical strength are ruled by others" and thinks that those in power are benefiting from the cultivating morality of previous life and those in low position are paying for their evil deeds of previous life. What's more, "the reverence to authority by the people in low position makes these people very obedient to and avoiding the communication with the government and officers".[7]

After the founding of new China, the constitution has explicitly specified the principles of "all men are equal" and "people are the master of their own affairs". These stipulations have radically changed the destiny of Chinese people. However, on the other hand, the system design and theoretical construction of "people are the master of their own affairs" and "popular sovereignty" represent neither the history of Chinese rural society nor people's habitual thought. Up to this day, the democracy and value of western sense is still dissociated from people's behavioral pattern. Real democracy needs the basic premise of the individual-based equality, and recognizes the basic dignity and value enjoyed by social members in the capability of individuals' for participating in public affairs and the "right to be deemed as unique and inviolable" by natural person. The thought has never been our traditions. On the contrary, our traditions reject such thought. The Confucianism representing the mainstream of Chinese traditional sense thinks that there exists the difference between older and younger, between close and distant, and between gentle and simple inside each community and inequality is universal. After the founding of new China, the old social structure and the set of ethical ideas and value systems corresponding with it are "revolutionized" and cleared as the feudal exploitation system and ideology. However, since they are people's thinking and behavioral habits with a history of thousands of years, the shock and impact of nominal revolution and mass movement are naturally limited. The voice and form carried by traditional heritage are hidden in daily life and survive tenaciously. Moreover, when the new China was just founded, there emerged new unequal social structure and ethnic with strong political color under the all-mighty national regime. The social hierarchy divided by class, with mass movement and re-allocation of means of production, became the base of new inequality of rural society. "Inside people's commune, the varied levels of senior and junior cadres who get hold of the means of production and livelihood actually outmatch the common people with strong bureaucratic sense and rigid class stratification among people".[8]

The purpose of election in modern democracy means to elect, through the means of referendum, the people meeting the special requirements who are willing to work for the public in the public authority on behalf of the public. It represents a farewell to the particularism that centering on kinship, human feelings as well as personal likes and dislikes. However, the feature of the standard for interpersonal relationship in rural Chinese society is that of the particularism rather than the election. The interpersonal relationship is divided in accordance with the kinsfolk's identity. While dealing with interpersonal relationship, people usually act in accordance with the "differential pattern"—rounds of wave differences among the people related with oneself and one's social relationship, i.e., the "human relations".

Moreover, in the relatively immobile rural society, "Human relations" and "face" became important media to form a face-to-face acquaintance society. Nobody wants to owe other people a favor or has the courage to rashly "tear up faces". "Courtesy demands reciprocity" has therefore become the basic principle of village society. After the founding of new China, with the land revolution and people's commune movement, the social structure and means of ownership for the means of production in the countryside has showed tremendous change. What's more, after reform and opening-up as well as the establishment of market economy, rural society has showed the phenomenon noticed by scholars that farmers have begun to rationally pursue their own interests and rationalize their interpersonal relationship. However, the rural production modes and living environment shows no essential change and the service system of rural society is imperfect, villagers usually have to rely on their relatives and neighbors to form close blood and geographical relationship in their economic life. Villages are still emerged in the atmosphere of family affection under which people have to notice the principle of priority and guidance of human relations in their communication. The social order, constructed firstly in the field of family affection and secondly the administration, leads to the continuity of the traditional communication rules and logic of rural society.

"All history would be passed on to contemporary era, and contemporary era represents only a continuation of the history, of course, with some changes." The traditional culture has become an element and integral part of social development. The value and purpose accumulated by it has become a kind of collective unconsciousness deeply rooted in each cultural person's consciousness. Although a custom may be changed, its corresponding behavioral pattern would remain for a long time. The influence of rural social history on the reality is inevitable and unavoidable; the influence is based on the premise of certain social time and space. Once new parameters enter rural society, traditional logic would gradually fade out after the change of social settings and behavioral environment. It is in this sense that the principle of secret ballot in the villagers committee election has played important role for democratic election.

12.1.4 Significance of Election System of Villagers Committee

Farmers play a decisive role in Chinese political development. Chinese political development since modern times shows us that the villagers committee election has gradually expanded and improved the vast farmers' scope and level of political participation. Farmers' varied interest relationships are continuously coordinated and political capability is cultivated and trained. These have all stimulated the development of grass-roots democratic politics. In some sense, the villagers committee election would become a cornerstone for the construction and development of Chinese democratic politics.

1. Villagers committee election has stimulated the development of grass-roots democratic politics

China rural areas have started to promote political system reform on a large scale since 1982. Economic basis decides the superstructure. The political system reform in rural areas represents an inevitable requirement after the economic system reform. The promotion of household contract responsibility system with remuneration linked to output has endowed the vast farmers with the decision-making power for production and operation and greatly improved farmers' enthusiasm for production. The highly centralized people's commune system in the past could no longer accommodate the development of productivity. Deng Xiaoping proposed to "delegate power to the grass-roots and people, and to farmers in rural areas." The promotion of villagers committee has enabled farmers to better express their wills and provided more opportunities for farmers to participate in politics. After the trial implementation of *Villagers Committee Organization Law* of 1987, the election of villagers committee has witnessed drastic change. On one hand, the principle of direct election of villagers committee members by farmers has been implemented; on the other hand, the candidates from some places have volunteered their services and public election has been implemented. All these demonstrate that Chinese farmers have walked out of the wrong region of passive and mobilized participation and initiated active and conscious participation in election. Meanwhile, after the voting, voters express their dissatisfaction and complaints through letters for appeal to those acts violating the *Villagers Committee Organization Law* in the election process. This also represents an effective way for farmers' political participation. Farmers' courage to appeal for the illegal acts of the election process demonstrates their improved awareness of political participation.

Although the villagers committee election is carried out at the lowest level of Chinese society, the election could not be deemed as an insignificant variable. In China where farmers take up the vast majority, farmers' level of political participation is directly affecting the development of Chinese democratic politics. The author thinks that the intrinsic base and impetus of rural democracy is the interests and farmers' varied acts are determined and restricted by their interests. Since the reform and opening-up, with the promotion of the household contract responsibility system with remuneration linked to output and development of market economy, farmers have generated stronger sense of identity for individual and family interests. The sense of identity to interests and rights has stimulated farmers' democratic demands and the expansion of farmers' political participation. This represents the main cause for the generation and development of village democracy. "Villagers are participating for the election for economic interests rather than interest in politics or well-meaning understanding for democracy. The level of willingness for their participation depends on the level of interests."[9] Of course we also need to notice that some characteristics of rural areas are also beneficial to villagers' social and political participation. Firstly, the relationship of interests in rural areas is closer, and farmers would pay more attention to the matters in village and therefore may adopt more political participation.

Secondly, the closure of rural society makes farmers restricted by the relatively closed social relationship or even the family kinship formed in a long time. This has strengthened the cohesion of rural society and increased the possibility of villagers' participation. Lastly, the countryside is the district with extremely frequent exchange of information. The communication of varied information may push villagers for more knowledge and attention for public affairs of the community. The generation of democracy is not determined by a single factor. The exterior demonstration effect and vigorous promotion of relevance government departments has played very important role. With increasingly heavy influence on villagers by the outer world, some villagers started to know about relevant policies and other experience and ask for revolution. In the meantime, some grass-roots cadres are also learning and mirroring the experience of other places, and have created new form of democracy suitable for local places and promoted the development of democracy based on consideration for local reality. We may say that the support of national party and government departments have played important role for the development of rural grass-roots democracy.

2. Villagers committee election has promoted the stability of rural society

(1) Farmers have avoided non-system participation through election.

The current non-system political participation is quite commonplace. It represents both a behavior breaking through the existing system regulations and beyond the normal channel. Although farmers have relatively varied participation of relevant system arrangement, they still seek for non-system participation to a certain extent so as to realize their requirement of interests, and such kind of participation becomes more frequent. The main reason for farmers' seeking for non-system participation lies in that farmers lack the channel for them to participate in the solution for the issues of their own interests. The villagers committee has motivated farmers' participation to the greatest extent and the villagers committee election adopted the principles of general election right, equal election right, direct election right and secret ballot (i.e., secret ballot has been adopted and implemented). These principles have fully safeguarded farmers' involvement in the village matters. The villagers committee election can remove those irresponsible village cadres. Meanwhile, continuous democratic participation has great significance for villagers to cultivate the habit to safeguard their own rights and interests through institutionalization and strengthen farmers' confidence in system participation, thus solving the contradictions of rural society before their outburst.

(2) Villagers committee election has strengthened the mobilization capability of village resources and avoided the harmful policies that jeopardize farmers' interests.

The household contract responsibility system with remuneration linked to output has verified farmers' identity and status as the direct taxpayer. Farmers have gradually realized that their own earnings are closely related with the main leaders' administration in their villages except for their own labor, and that the economy of the village collective is also closely related with their own annual bonus when they are working hard on their own contracted land. In order to better safeguard their own interests, farmers have generated the strong desire to show their independent will, participate in the administration of village matters and ask for the right to elect their own "masters". To the village cadres, the villagers' request means better promotion of democracy so that more villagers would be able to participate in the administration of village matters. When deciding some public construction undertakings, the change from decision-making by others to by ourselves has provided guarantee for villagers' interests. Therefore, villagers are more willing to get together to discuss some countermeasures to improve the services for their own production and life so that the countermeasures can take into consideration of the varied interests of all villagers and villagers' dissatisfaction to the decision of village matters can be decreased.

(3) Villagers committee election has effectively restricted the village cadres' misconducts, contained the inclination of elite degradation, and led the people with both ability and political integrity to the leading position.

With further development of rural reform, the old way of designating or recommending elites to govern people is no longer applicable; the mechanism of governance elites asks us to select the capable persons from the diversified elites. The competitive mechanism of villagers committee election has constituted the responsibilities mechanism for village cadres and representatives, and can effectively contain the trend of elite degradation. The competitive mechanism can firstly eliminate the degraded elites and replace them with the responsible and able persons, and secondly restrict the new elites through some rules and regulations to avoid the degradation of the elites. The villagers committee election has led the actually capable person with both ability and political integrity to the leading positions of village matters by establishing competitive mechanism. The villagers committee election law specifies that all villagers over the age of 18 have the right to be elected. This has greatly expanded the scope of the elected elites. Villagers can know about the candidates more comprehensively and thoroughly and choose the elites better through such links as campaign speech and self-introduction. Of course, after the election of the elites who are unqualified, the dismissal procedure may be launched. When the term of office expires, re-election must be carried out to create opportunity for generating new elites. Within the scope of Villagers committee, the incumbent village cadres, if under pressure, would pay more attention to their own images. The solution to issues that may cause collective loss by democratic means has cultivated village representatives' awareness of democracy and responsibility.

12.2 PROBLEMS WITH ELECTION SYSTEM OF VILLAGERS COMMITTEE AND IMPACTING FACTORS

12.2.1 Qualification of Villager Voters

1. Definition of registration scope of voters

Article 12 of the *Villagers Committee Organization Law* specifies that "all villagers over the age of 18, regardless of their ethnic nationality, race, sex, occupation, family background, religious belief, education, property status, length of residence, shall have the right to vote and right to be elected, however, except for those who have been deprived of their political rights in accordance with the law." In accordance with the spirit of the *Villagers Committee Organization Law*, all local villagers over the age of 18, as long as having not been deprived of their political rights, have the right to vote and right to be elected. However, with the development of rural economy and society and reform of population management system, the phenomena of separation between people and household registers in rural community have become increasingly prominent, and villager constituents of local village increasingly complicated, leading to great difficulty for the recognition of voter qualifications.

In practice, most of the places take the household registration as the bases for recognition of villager qualifications. With the development of economy, more and more villagers go into business or provide labor service; the practice of taking the household registration as the bases for recognition of voter qualifications has brought about many difficulties for the general election of villagers committee. There emerged the following three problems in practice:

(1) Varied new situation of household registration management.

For example, the phenomena of separation between people and household register like "empty household register", i.e., household register without people on it; large amount of non-agricultural household register caused by retired people returning to the village. These all make it very difficult to take the household registration as the bases for recognition of villager qualifications.

Many villagers go to other places, mainly the city, to work or do business in slack farming season. Some even live in other places permanently. Although these villagers have their household registered in the countryside, they buy land, build their houses and live in urban areas. Owing to the space and information obstruction, these people have difficulty to timely know about the village matters or directly participate in the public affairs of community. The common practice of varied places is to mobilize these people's families, relatives or friends to ask these people to return to the village to participate in the election through the letter, telegram or telephone. Proxy voting is implemented in some places, while in other places these people would be excluded during voter registration.

*(2) How to safeguard the political rights and interests of floating populatio*n.

On one hand, large amount of rural floating population, because of the lack of close economics tie with their villages or the high cost of election, have failed to participate in the election. On the other hand, in the habitual residence, the rural floating population also has no way to participate in the public political life of the community. Heilongjiang Province specifies that those who have been living in the village for over a year and have been issued with a certificate for voter qualifications by their household registration places shall have the right to vote. Some places also relax the restrictions on voter qualifications and specify that all of the above-mentioned three kinds of people can participate in the villagers committee election activities (which however are not common in current practice). Some places also specify that the above-mentioned three kinds of people with certain qualifications (such as the educational background, professional title, economic strength, performance of village obligations, etc.) shall have the right to vote and right to be elected in the villages. For example, Jilin Province explicitly specifies in the village election measures of the province passed in 2000 that those with the educational background better than junior college, or professional and technical titles over medium-grade or other excellent talents who have volunteered to work and live in rural areas and participate in the campaign for villagers committee members, with consent from the villager congress, can be registered as voters. The ways to determine the voter qualifications all have their own merits. Although it takes the household registration as the recognition standard in strict accordance with relevant regulations of the election system, the first way goes against the realization of the political rights of the floating population and therefore could not reflect the spirit of general election. As a matter of fact, because of the rigid household registration management system, about one hundred million of floating farmers are excluded from the election and other political activities. This actually constitutes great deviation from the principle of general election for villagers to participate in the villagers committee election.

(3) How to overcome the isolation of the village.

Taking the household registration as the bases to determine the villager qualifications would definitely restrict some people who wish to serve villagers and obtain villagers' recognition from entering into villages. Farmers can only choose their own leaders within the limited scope of their villagers. This goes against the intention to change the isolation of villages. Besides, the economic utilization and political exclusion of external population of the village also goes against the integration of external population with the village society. In some economically developed areas, some external villagers who come to work and do business in the villages, after years of accumulation, have realized certain economic strength and popularity and wish to enhance their own social status. These people can also flexibly deal with varied relations and have the quality to be a good villager's committee member. However, they have not had the luck to participate in the election because of their household registration issue. It represents a significant issue in urgent need of solution for village self-governance under the new circumstance to find way to enable external villagers to equally enjoy the grassroots democratic rights and effectively participate in the administration of public affairs and include the floating farmers in the political democracy and society orientation process.

Therefore, when formulating the villagers committee election measures, the provinces, autonomous regions and municipalities directly under the Central government have added some operative contents. For example, Article 13 of *Jilin Villagers Committee Election Measures* specifies that "villagers with the voter qualifications shall be registered as voters in their household registration places. In case of any of the following circumstances, villagers may be registered after verification by the villager election committee. However, relevant organizations shall timely inform the household registration villages so that the household registration villages would not register the villagers as voters again: (1) having been living in their spouses' villages for over a year after marriage whose household registration hasn't been changed; (2) having changed their household registration into the non-agricultural type, but still live in the villages and perform villagers' obligations; (3) other people whose household registration is not in the villages, but who have been living in the villages and performed the villagers' obligations for over three years and who have submitted their application for participation in the election." Article 14 specifies that "those with the educational background better than junior college, or professional and technical titles over medium-grade or other excellent talents who have volunteered to work and live in rural areas and participate in the campaign for villagers committee members, after the discussion and consent from the villager congress, can be registered as voters." Article 15 specifies that "under any of the following circumstances, villagers would not be registered as voters after the verification of the villager election committee: (1) being psychopaths who cannot recognize their own activities; (2) being the villagers with voter qualifications who have failed to return to the villages for voter registration before the announcement of the voter list." The foregoing stipulations also have some problems. For example, for those with their household registered not in the villages can only be registered as voters after over three years of residence in the villages, the period of three years is obviously too long. Article 9.1 of the *Opinions of the Supreme People's Court on Some Issues Concerning the Implementation of the General Principles of the Civil Law of the People's Republic of China*, "the habitual residence refers to the place where citizens have been living for over a year after leaving the original residence" may be applied and the period of over one year of residence in the villages may be adopted. Article 14 obviously constitutes an effective way to solve the issue of low quality of villagers committee members in some villages caused by the loss of large amount of labor, especially the excellent talents. However, detailed rules shall be formulated for close restraint so as to prevent the township government from utilizing the villagers committee as the main channel for the re-position of redundant personnel in organizations under the excuse of optimizing the villagers committee structure, or from taking advantage of the opportunity to manipulate the election. Article 15.1 shall provide explicit stipulation for the intermittent psychopaths. Article 15.2 has restricted the right to vote of the people who permanently live in other places and should therefore be changed into "being the villagers with voter qualifications who live in other places permanently and have failed to return to villages for the voter registration and entrust other villagers to register on behalf of them before the announcement of voter list after receiving the notification of voter registration." Meanwhile, when registering the villagers whose household is not registered in the villages, the following requirements shall be specified: having the housing conditions in the villages, including the houses allocated by the villagers committee, or constructed or bought by themselves through legal procedures; undertaking long-term, stable and rightful occupations in the villages, including the employees of the enterprises established by the villages and excluding the vagrants, beggars or temporary employees. The performed villagers' obligations shall include paying tax, serving in the army, compulsory education, environmental protection, family planning, turning in reserve fund for overall plan, and other public undertakings, etc.

Solutions: (1) to stick to the direction of taking household registration as the bases for recognition of villager qualifications. This is determined by the collective economic system implemented by China in rural areas. (2) to change the situation in which villagers could not effectively exercise their democratic rights and are located at the edge of political democracy and social activities through system innovation. (3) to give full play to the "transmission shaft" function of families between village self-governance and external villagers. (4) to hand over the disputes of villager qualifications to the villagers committee for settlement and give full play to the function of village self-governance.

12.2.2 Qualification of Candidates for Villagers Committee Members

To examine the candidate qualifications, the legislation should also solve the following issues:

1. The capable people in the village have difficulty to become candidates in a "semi-acquaintance society"

The "semi-acquaintance society" is discussed to the relativity of "acquaintance society". In accordance with the *Rural China* written by Fei Xiaotong, "within the scope of natural village, because of the gathering residence of generations, the villagers understand and know well each other and therefore form an 'acquaintance society'".[10] All regimes have strengthened the penetration and control of administrative power to rural society since the 20th century. They divided the residents to different regions for control and "administrative villages" are therefore formed on the natural villages. The administrative villages, as the planned social change, have the same administrative space, but lack the common living space. Therefore, villagers' main activities and communications would naturally concentrate in local natural villages. As a result, although they have provided villagers with the opportunity to know each other, the administrative villages have failed to provide ample public space for villagers to get better acquainted with each other. This kind of administrative villages could only be named as "semi-acquaintance society". In the semi-acquaintance society of villagers committee, there exists certain distance between the village public people and capable people. In some rural election, even when the incumbent villagers committee members are quite unpopular among the villagers, they would become official candidates of the villagers committee with leading percentage of votes obtained during the nomination of "general election". On the contrary, the village capable people recommended by each villager group, although with leading percentage of votes obtained within the scope of local villager group, are unable to enter into the scope of candidates during the voting within the scope of the whole villagers committee.

2. "Those who tries never to offend anybody" from the original villagers committee hold advantage in the candidates

The villagers committee members of some districts are weak in their service ability and low in their educational level. Some are even feeble and sick. However, they leave people with the impression of "one who tries never to offend anybody" with the characteristics of uprightness, honesty and kindness as they do not offense anybody or do not adhere to the principle. Although they have no achievements in their official career that deserve mentioning, such kinds of people have no faults that deserve investigation. They can always be recognized by most of the villagers during the election of candidates. When investigating a mediocre villager-elected director of the village from a county in Jiangxi Province, Xiao Tangbiao found that the reasons for villagers to elect the village director lie in that: "He is a kind person who would not talk nonsense or make a pig of himself and who would do his own work with high enthusiasm. However, with his defect of low ability, he usually could not solve the problem that should have been solved by him and make the decision that should have been made by him." and "Our director respect the masses and would consult and communicate with us in case of any matters."[11]

3. Close relatives enter into candidate list and election organizations at the same time

In China with over 2000 years of history of governance to rural grass-roots society on the base of clan force, the clan force would definitely penetrate into the rural grass-roots election at current stage, and such influence of penetration will exist for a rather long period. To prevent the clan force from controlling the village administration, it is necessary to establish a relative evasion system in rural grass-roots election. For example, the election committee members whose immediate families or collateral relatives within three generations have been elected as candidates shall quit the election committee; the close relatives of the main responsible people of the village party organization shall not be nominated as the candidates of the villagers committee members; in case more than two people of immediate families or collateral relatives within three generations are nominated as candidates, only the one with the most voters would be determined as candidates.

4. Aging of candidates

Affected by the traditional "elder politics", when electing candidates, some villagers would firstly take into consideration the "noble character and high prestige" and "mature wisdom". As a result, the average age of the members of some villagers committees reaches about 50 or 60, and the committee members have remained unchanged for over decades. The consequence is that the leading team severely lacks reserve force and a few villages have showed the fault of leading team, stagnant economy and lifeless society. This has severely affected the long-term stability of rural grass-roots politics and sustainable development of the economy and society.

12.2.3 Problems with Bribery in Election

Bribery refers to the "activities that affect normal election work, and bribe the voters, electors or election working personnel to make these people participate in the election against their own will or cheat in the election with properties or other interests for the purpose of obtaining votes".[12] According to the report from some media, the whole country, regardless of the district or village size, has bribery of different levels. The bribery can take the form of goods and money. The former includes the washing powder, cigarette, blanket, grain and money at the value from RMB 1 to thousands. According to media report, in a village in Hejin City, Shanxi Province with a per capita income less than RMB 1,000, a candidate actually spent over RMB 2,000,000 to bribe villagers at the price of RMB 1,800 per voter. Besides, there are also people who bribe voters through entertaining banquet and party.[13]

Election bribery obviously has its harm. It uses non-forced interests to affect voters' will. Candidates offer interests to the voters to ask voters to vote for them. This goes against the principle of democracy. Although it is non-forced, the election bribery has obvious impact on voters' will. Some people think that it is farmers' low quality and educational level that has led to election bribery, and that farmers have no ability to exercise the democratic power. They hold negative attitude towards the direct election of villagers committee and even the whole village self-governance system. The viewpoint is wrong. It is exactly because of the actual role, realistic value and high "gold content" of the villagers' votes which could affect the election result that bribery appears in election. This obviously represents a great step towards the direction of democratic politics compared with the method of appointing the village head by the township government. The measure is of great significance for stabilizing the countryside, developing rural economy and improving farmers' income. The election bribery is, in essence, accompanied by democratic politics and a by-product of democratic politics. We can neither give up eating for fear of choking nor deny direct election of villagers committee for fear of election bribery. General survey of the countries and districts that implement democratic politics shows that in election there exist different forms and levels of bribery somehow. In Taiwan, China, the bribery in election is so serious that some people are even sentenced because of bribery in election. In the election of municipal people's congress in some districts of China, there also exists the phenomenon of bribery. Therefore, we cannot belittle farmers, think that farmers are of low quality and could not exercise the democratic right, and therefore deny the direct election of villagers committee and even the village self-governance because of the commonplace bribery in direct election of villagers committee. The election bribery issue has severely threatened the whole village self-governance and further construction of socialist democratic politics. We can never treat the election bribery lightly to prevent election bribery from becoming a confirmed habit that is hard to get rid of.

12.2.4 Problems with Removal Procedure

Article 16 of the *Villagers Committees Organization Law* specifies that over one fifth of the villagers with the right to vote can jointly request the removal of villagers committee members on reasonable ground. The villagers committee members who are requested to be removed have the right to bring forward opinions to defend themselves. The villagers committee shall timely convene a villager assembly to vote for the removal request. The removal of villagers committee members shall require over half of the votes from the villagers with the right to vote. However, removal represents a complicated and serious political activity corresponding with the election. The right to remove represents a natural extension and final guarantee of the right to vote. However, just the stipulation is obviously insufficient since the right would produce a series of issues:

1. Asymmetry between the right to vote and the right to remove

In accordance with the regulations about the procedures for general election of villagers committee from Article 14 of *the Villagers Committees Organization Law of the People's Republic of China*, the "double half" principle means that the candidates who have obtained 1/4 of the votes in the affirmative from the villagers with the right to vote would be elected. For example, if a village has 1,000 villagers in total, a candidate with 251 votes in the affirmative would be elected. However, in terms of the removal procedures, in accordance with Article 16 of the *Villagers Committees Organization Law*, a removal would firstly need over 1/5 of the villagers with the right to vote to jointly propose a motion and secondly over half of the votes in the affirmative from the whole villagers with the right to vote. For example, if a village has 1,000 villagers in total, the removal procedures must be launched after the proposal of removal by 201 voters and the removal succeeded after the votes in the affirmative from 501 voters. Compared with the election procedures, the removal procedures are more difficult. However, it is necessary to request over 1/5 of the villagers with the right to vote to propose the removal in order to launch the removal procedures. It represents a very significant political event to launch the removal procedures which must reflect the will of a larger number of villagers. The number of the villagers who jointly propose the removal motion shall reach a certain level, otherwise the removal would be disturbed by the family or clan forces. This is especially true in the villages with some concentrated family forces in which these forces may mutually remove each other by joint forces. This would affect the villagers committee members' working enthusiasm and go against the rural stability. However, the number of the villagers who jointly propose the removal motion shall not be too much, otherwise it would not be easy and suitable to form a joint force and therefore form effective supervision to the unqualified villagers committee cadres. Is it reasonable to set stricter requirements for the removal than for the election? According to the existing *Villagers Committees Organization Law*, to be elected is easier than to be removed. This represents the extension of the habitual logic of "officers are easier to be elected than to be removed", and goes against the strengthening of supervision over the villagers committee members.

2. Whether the township government has the right to remove

Currently, the six provinces, municipalities directly under the Central government or autonomous regions including Beijing, Shanghai, Tianjin, Xinjiang, Hainan and Guangdong have stipulated that the township governments have the right to propose a removal under special circumstances. There are two contradictory views towards the stipulation. The negative view holds that since it has become a common thing for the township governments to arbitrarily replace or remove the village cadres, conferring the township governments the right to propose a removal through legislation is inadvisable since it would undoubtedly legalize the illegal intervention of the township governments. The affirmative view is the opinion that villagers would lack the enthusiasm to propose a motion even under special circumstances since Chinese farmers lack the habit, training and enthusiasm of democracy. If the villagers committee takes the lead in the refusal of the payment of varied payable taxes which is however consistent with the villagers' interests, the villagers would not actively propose a removal motion. Under such circumstance, the township governments shall not refuse to take any further part in the village self-governance and shall have the right to propose a removal. The author agrees with the latter. The township governments only have the right to propose a removal rather than the right of direct replacement. Whether the removal would be effective will be determined by the villager assembly. Therefore, the villagers' right to remove hasn't been infringed.

3. The villagers committee refuses to convene a removal assembly

The party involved cannot play the roles of both athlete and referee. This represents the basic principle of procedural law. The three procedural laws of China have all included and stipulated strict avoidance system in order to ensure the procedural justice. However, Article 16 of the *Villagers Committees Organization Law* specifies that, to the motion proposed by villagers to remove a villager's committee member, "the villagers committee should timely convene a villager assembly to vote for the removal." The stipulation is quite unreasonable since it has violated the basic legal principle and represents the most obvious loophole of the *Villagers Committees Organization Law*. As a matter of fact, it is the varied means that obstruct or even reject the removal procedures rather than the "timely convention of villager assembly to vote for the removal" of the villagers committee that has led to the long-term delaying of the removal procedures in practice. The villagers from Shuixin Village, Chengjiao Township, Lucheng District, and Wenzhou City, Zhejiang Province have spent a year removing the villagers committee members. This represents a typical case, and an important cause is the defect of system design. Therefore Mr. Bai Gang proposed that "we should follow the principle of separation of powers and re-consider who should be responsible for convening the villager assembly or villager representative assembly. This should become an important topic for the legislation reform of village self-governance."[14] A majority of the existing provincial election laws and regulations include corresponding stipulations for the circumstance when the villagers committee refuses to convene villager assemblies which are more complete than the village organization law. The most complete stipulations of this kind are those of Fujian and Jilin provinces which specify not only that the township government has the obligation to convene a villager assembly for the removal proposal, but also that the assembly has to be convened within a month to avoid protraction and improve efficiency. While the provincial elections of some provinces like Beijing have no stipulation for the time limit to convene the villager assembly and therefore provide convenience for the township government to shirk or delay. Some provinces stipulate that the township government shall "guide", "urge" or "assist" the villagers committee for the removal. However, to fulfill its obligations, to what extent should the township government "guide", "urge" or "assist" the villagers committee? It is very difficult to measure. What should the township government do if the villagers committee refuses the "guidance", "urge" or "assistance" from the township government? Without express terms, the villagers' removal right may become impracticable.[15] The essence of village self-governance lies in democratic election, decision, administration and supervision which represent the basic principle for commanding the *Villagers Committees Organization Law*. The new practices created by villagers in reality shall be deemed as effective if they comply with the basic requirements of the democratic election, decision, administration and supervision, and those generally applicable practices shall also be included in the national legislation timely. In practice, there emerges the circumstance under which villagers show distrust to the removal procedures organized by the villagers committee and refuses to participate in the removal assembly. What corresponding regulations should be formulated since the avoidance of the interested party represents a basic requirement to ensure the procedural justice and fairness?

4. Illegal issues for replacing or removing villagers committee members

Article 4 of the *Villagers Committees Organization Law* provides ambiguous stipulations for rural relationship issues and therefore lacks operability. Specifically speaking, the article has failed to list the items that need the guidance, support and assistance from the people's government of the township, ethnic township or town. If the township, ethnic township or town government has failed to perform its duties, how would the villager and villagers committee get the remedy or relief? What items are within the village self-governance scope and shall not be intervened by the township, ethnic township or town government. How would the villager and villagers committee get the remedy or relief if the township, ethnic township or town government intervenes? As no specific legal consequence has been regulated for the illegal activities, the *Villagers Committees Organization Law* has become a "weak law" with weak operability and binding force, and villagers' tendency of political indifference has become more serious. It is the insufficiently specific regulations on rural relationship from the *Villagers Committees Organization Law* that have led to the non-normal state of rural relationship. The township government has usually governed things that couldn't be well governed or shouldn't be governed, but passed the buck for things that should be governed. The illegal replacement and removal of villagers committee members by the township party committee and government represents exactly a prominent problem exposed in village self-governance practices. The cases of this kind can be seen on the newspapers frequently.

12.2.5 Problems with Indifference Attitude in Election

According to relevant research and survey results from contemporary scholars, it would not be difficult for us to find the fact that in the villagers committee election of current stage, although the rural residents from a few district have actively participated in the villagers committee election activities, the villagers from most of the districts in China have showed a kind of attitude featuring indifference, passiveness and non-participation. In the villagers committee election activities, voters are not interested in the election event. They do not know much and don't want to know about the election. They rarely participate in each link of the election and are even unwilling to participate in the voting. They just keep silent or complaint privately even after they have learned about the injustice of the election process and illegal operations of the election organizer. They even take an attitude of "whatever, none of my business" to the unsatisfactory election results.

12.3 SUGGESTIONS FOR COMPLETING ELECTION SYSTEM OF VILLAGERS COMMITTEE

As a form of grass-roots democratic practice by the Party, the villagers committee features profound significance. The germination and development of villagers committee election is, fundamentally speaking, caused by the economic system reform and aligned with the fundamental change of rural economic system. The election of villagers committee also represents a historic change of the political governance system of Chinese rural society and the first grass-roots democratic practice in the most recent five thousand years of history in China. However, since the villagers committee election represents a newly-emerged thing and lacks the reference of historic experience, double and special attention should be paid to the newly-emerged circumstances or issues in the villagers committee election process to ensure active promotion of democratic construction because of the influence of the traditional administration system and series of fundamental adjustments of interests caused by the election. How to make the villagers committee election more reasonable and standard? How to further stimulate the development of grass-roots democratic politics? The answers also deserve our double and special attention.

12.3.1 To Strengthen the Internal Construction of Election System of Villagers Committee

During the villagers committee election process, strengthening the system construction represents a significant requirement to guarantee smooth operation of the process and a basic task of overall and long-term importance.

1. The necessity to strengthen democratic system construction in rural areas

As a systematic and enormous project, the villagers committee election needs the stimulation from the varied supporting coordination. Strengthening the system construction in rural areas represents the groundwork for strengthening the political construction of socialist democracy. The villagers committee represents the grass-roots mass self-governance organization for the vast villagers to legally implement self-governance, self-education and self-development. We have gradually explored from practices the work ideas featuring good implementation of the four links of "democratic election, decision, administration and supervision" as well as further improvement of the three levels of "village, group and household", and basically formed the framework system of village democratic system. This has therefore stimulated continual improvement of the overall quality of villagers committee, made the relations between the Party and the masses and between the cadres and masses closer and promoted the social stability and economic development of rural areas. However, there also exist some issues that could not be ignored: firstly, the democratic system construction at village level is still unbalanced. Secondly, some cadres and masses feature weak legal sense. Some cadres only pursue personal interests and some have failed to take the lead in law-abiding and democratic style and therefore have affected the social stability. In accordance with the situation development and actual requirements, it is necessary and imperative to strengthen the democratic system construction at village level at present and in a future period.

2. Main contents of rural election system construction

Rural election system construction represents a systematic project with extensive contents. The work of the villagers committee involves varied aspects of village matters. This requires our continuous exploration in actual life so as to establish a complete set of sound institutional systems.

(1) Gradually improve the grass-roots democratic election system in rural areas under the basic principles of direct, equal and differential voting as well as secret ballot.

We may say that after years of practices, our villagers committee election has been gradually improved and stepped on the pathway of standardization, institutionalization and democratization. This is mainly represented by the following aspects: (1) "Mass-election" is implemented for nominating the primary candidates so that each legal voter has the nomination right, and official candidates are determined through the means of primary election to all voters based on the "mass election". Before the primary election, it is necessary to carry out qualification examination to the primary candidates. The candidates that don't meet the requirements of election measures shall be disqualified to avoid the appearance of disqualified official candidates. The official candidates determined in this way comply with both the law and popular will. (2) Official candidates carry out equal competition in the election so as to facilitate the voters' right choice. In most districts, the official candidates introduce their own village administration plan and the like to the villagers through public speeches to run for the director of villagers committee. (3) Secret vote filling room has been set so that voters could freely express their own will while filling out the votes without the intervention of religious factors or vicious power from the village.[16]

(2) Gradually popularize the grass-roots democratic decision-making system in rural areas with the villager assembly and villager representative assembly as the main forms.

Democratic decision-making means to set the villager assembly or villager representative assembly in rural areas to study and decide the village matters and issues of public concern so as to make decisions in accordance with the opinions from most people based on relevant laws and regulations.

The generated representatives have extensive representativeness and ability to discuss official businesses, and are integrated with the general election of villagers committee for democracy. The representatives generated and elected by villagers in accordance with the residence zone or villager group, can be reappointed consecutively and replaced or appointed by by-election if necessary. The villager assembly, as the largest-scale assembly of the village with the highest degree of participation, can deliver the villagers' interests and wishes in the most direct and comprehensive way, and therefore represents also the most authoritative and highest organizational form of village self-governance. The village matters are decided either through discussion on the villager assembly or study on the villager representative assembly. The villager representatives, elected and generated by the whole villagers, need to extensively listen to the villagers' opinions and suggestions before the election so as to ensure the scientific and democratic nature of the decisions. Meanwhile, the representatives shall report to the villagers timely the decisions made on the assembly after closing the assembly so that the villagers can timely learn about the village decisions, decide the matters related with their own interests through democratic means and avoid some errors that shouldn't have happened.

(3) Comprehensively promote the democratic administration system at village level by motivating and relying on villagers to jointly administer the village matters and maintain the village order.

This is mainly represented by two aspects: the first is to ensure that villagers can govern the village matters in accordance with the rules and regulations like the local rules and regulations valid for the whole village which intend to fixate the decisions made during the village governance by the villagers and direct villagers' activities into the orbit of standard, procedural and scientific orientation through democratic means. The rules and regulations, formulated by villagers in accordance with local reality, have not only supervised the villagers' activities but also restricted the vast village cadres' activities. Meanwhile, in order to safeguard the implementation of these rules and regulations, the districts have also formulated strict safeguarding system so that villagers can govern the village matters in accordance with the law. The second is that the villagers committee extensively propagandizes the essence of villagers committee election to the villagers so that the vast farmers can throw themselves into the governance activities courageously and righteously. The committee also educates its members so that the members can know their right position. Before the election, most of the villages would distribute some pamphlets, leaflets and the like related with the election to villagers and the villagers committee members also improve their own theoretical level through the propaganda.

(4) Comprehensively promote the democratic supervision featuring such contents as transparency of village administrative affairs and government affairs.

Democratic supervision mainly refers to the supervision of certain forms by the villagers to the village matters and villagers committee members' activities. The transparency of village administrative affairs and government affairs represent the main form of democratic supervision. All the great matters and issues of public concern in the village shall be made public to the villagers. The contents for the transparency of village administrative affairs mainly include the transparency of the village finance, distribution of means of production, quota distribution for family planning, etc. While the transparency of government affairs mainly involves the implementation of the legal policies and regulations of the Party and the State, rules and regulations of the village, etc. These are beneficial for villagers' supervision over the village administrative affairs, elimination of villagers' doubts and close association with the masses. Of course, the contents made public shall be of unified standard to avoid that the practice becomes a mere formality or assumes presentable looks.

3. Rural system construction

Rural system construction is an arduous task. The construction of the four systems of democratic election, decision, administration and supervision has played very important role for safeguarding the stability of rural society. Of all the systems, the villagers committee election system is the one with the most thorough and sound implementation. Therefore, we need to better implement the construction of the other three systems in future, and the implementation of democratic decision, administration and supervision systems would better promote the villagers committee election system and grass-roots democratic development in turn. During the implementation process, we should practically act in accordance with the system, guarantee no formalism in the implementation, vigorously enhance the village cadres' system awareness and improve the cadres' ability to actively implement the systems. Meanwhile, we should strengthen the supervision and examination for the implementation of each system in rural areas. Practice has proved that the system implementation performance and results are all closely related with the powerful examination and supervision. The systems would have difficulty in performing their roles without supervision or with feeble supervision. This requires relevant superior authorities to cultivate and improve their system awareness, promote the grass-roots work, supervise and urge themselves to act by the systems and frequently supervise the grass-roots for timely discovery and rectification of issues. The masses' supervision also represents an important guarantee for the effective implementation of each democratic system in rural areas. As the masses are living at the grass-roots and communicating directly with the village cadres, their supervision is more direct and frequent. We need to change the indifferent attitude towards the masses' opinions so that the masses' supervision could actually control and urge the system implementation effectively.

12.3.2 To Strengthen the External Construction of Election System of Villagers Committee

1. External resistance to villagers committee election

In the villagers committee election, the relationship between the Party branch and villagers committee falls into the category of the issue concerning the relation between the Party and the government. Although after the infancy and development stages, the villagers committee election has started to gradually walk towards the stages of improvement and maturity, the external challenges faced by the villagers committee still represent the issues that we should notice and study.[17]

(1) The influence of the county and township people's election system on the villagers committee election.

Although direct election of township people's representatives has been implemented since 1950s and direct election of county people's representatives has also been put into practice since 1979, the election procedures and technologies could not guarantee the voters' full expression of individual will fundamentally and the elections are just a kind of pro forma elections to a certain extent.

(2) The lagging effect of township system reform.

On one hand, from the perspective of leadership system, the main leaders of the township, mainly appointed by the county committee, also request the village cadres to be obedient and follow directions. Therefore, some township leaders always hold skeptical attitude towards democratic election. Some beneficiaries that are originally appointed by the township leaders also always boycott the villagers committee election. On the other hand, from the perspective of administrative system, the appointed cadres are more determined to implement the tasks for collecting varied fees, agricultural tax, agricultural and forestry specialty product tax and the like assigned by the township leaders, while the village cadres elected by the villagers would take the villagers' perspective, request the township government to administer in accordance with the law and even asks for decision-making democratization of the township government. This constitutes contradictions with the traditional administration structure and methods of the township government.

(3) The influence of the villagers committee and Party branch is also represented by two aspects: the first is the contradiction between the appointment system and election system.

Since the Party branch members are generally appointed and the villagers committee members elected, there emerges the situation in which "people from the superior authorities turn to the branch secretary and villagers turn to the village director". However, the traditional system still upholds the status of the party branch secretary, leading to villagers' frequent complaints. The second is the appearance of the binary decision center. The Party branch represents the traditional center for the decision-making of village administrative affairs, and the villagers committee elected requests exercising of decision-making power in accordance with the law. In case of an issue, the branch secretary says that the Party branch has the right to make the decision since it is the leadership center of the village; while the villagers committee says that it has the right to make the decision based on the *Villagers Committees Organization Law*. This has led to the binary orientation of decision-making.

(4) The administrative guidance has its imperfections.

The villagers committee election lacks systematic and standard policy regulations and the guidance procedures are also not sound and complete. During the guidance, there emerges the phenomenon of low demonstration effect, monopolizing of all issues in the name of guidance, or even wrong guidance resulting from insufficient experience and unclear understanding.

It can be seen that, after the historic development, the villagers committee election is now facing more complicated challenges and issues compared with the already solved issues. We should therefore adopt active measures and methods to make the villagers committee election more standard.

2. Policy choice of villagers committee election

(1) It is necessary to standardize and improve the administrative guidance rules.

Firstly, we need to formulate some necessary guidance rules based on the reality of villagers committee election in some districts. The construction departments of national regime should pay attention to summarizing experience and implementing model demonstration. The revised *Villagers Committees Organization Law* just ambiguously points out that the township government has the right to guide the work of the villagers committee and the villagers committee shall autonomously govern the village matters under the guidance of the township government. The regulation hasn't been well implemented in real life. For this, while implementing the *Villagers Committees Organization Law*, some districts have formulated some rules for the township government to guide the work of villagers committee which have achieved good results. Secondly, we need to standardize the administrative guidance work and improve the administrative guidance level. The administrative guidance work for village self-governance also needs standardization and institutionalization. The administrative guidance mainly includes the policy guidance, overall planning, investigation, examination and supervision and the like, and definitely excludes taking on what ought to be done by the villagers committee.

(2) It is necessary to strengthen the legal construction in rural areas and create good social and legal environment for villagers committee election.

The villagers committee election, as the democratic form of rural grass-roots, must be matched with the corresponding legalization and institutionalization. Influenced by the long history of autocracy, Chinese farmers severely lack the democratic experience and habits and are not good at exercising their already-owned rights. If we don't strengthen the legal consciousness and ideology among the grass-roots cadres and vast farmers and direct village self-governance into the orbit of legalization and institutionalization, the rural society may show the tendencies of "excessive self-governance" and "affiliated administration", and the rural society may show unstable factors which may affect sound development of the grass-roots and even the whole society. The legal construction of rural socialism mainly means conscientious and earnest implementation of the *Villagers Committees Organization Law*. Moreover, we need to firstly strengthen the planning and guidance of legal construction in rural areas, provide clear evaluation indexes for the legal construction status in rural areas and carry out frequent examination and supervision. Secondly, we need to enhance the village cadres' and masses' legal sense so that the village cadres could realize that the cadres' administrative power and business owners' managerial power are limited, and would therefore administer in accordance with the law and accept people's supervision. The vast mass farmers also need to learn about the basic knowledge of law, establish the rights-based concept, cultivate the courage and learn the skills to protect their legitimate rights in accordance with the law, eliminate the situation in which they don't know how to protect their own rights because of their ignorance to the law, and prevent flustered resistance through non-legal means after being driven desperate.

(3) It is necessary to rationalize the varied relations.

In other words, we need to overcome the external resistance of villagers committee election. Firstly, we need to perfect the election system of the county and township people's representatives. The tremendous effect created by villagers committee election in society would definitely expedite the election system reform of county and township people's representatives so that the voters' will be truly reflected in election. Therefore, the election of the county and township people's representatives shall use for reference large amount of repeatedly-proven and successful experience and practices to ensure that voters can freely and fully exercise their own rights and express their own will. Secondly, we need to rationalize the relations between the village and township. The *Villagers Committees Organization Law* has explicit stipulation on the relations between the villagers committee and township government, that is, guidance, support and assistance. Therefore, we need to reform the administrative system of the township to return the rights to people. We need to particularly cut off the connection of economic interests between the township and village to change the situations of "administration of village affairs by the township government" and "management of village finance by the township government" so that the villagers committee could have more rights in itself.[18]

Lastly, we need to rationalize the relation between the Party branch and villagers committee. The law has explicit stipulation that the Party branch represents the leadership center of rural areas which however is the center of political sense and doesn't mean that the Party branch could replace the villagers committee and directly deal with varied village matters. The core roles of Party branch mainly include safeguarding the implementation of the constitution, other laws and the policies of the Party and supervising the work of the villagers committee and village cadres' activities. Meanwhile, the villagers committee itself should also define its own responsibilities, actively and timely solve the issues reasonably required by villagers, and provide cooperation for the work of the Party branch.

3. Enhance Chinese farmers' democratic participation ability

In the process of villagers committee election, villagers' democratic participation ability plays a significant role. The issue of villagers' democratic participation ability represents a comprehensive issue involving such elements as politics, economy, cultural thoughts and social life.

(1) Chinese farmers' democratic participation is mainly reflected by their political participation.

In modern countries, a main turning point for the expansion of political participation is the villagers' involvement in national politics. Chinese political system has provided clear and unobstructed channel for the vast civics' political participation at macro level, and contemporary farmers' institutionalized political participation is mainly reflected by the village self-governance activities featuring democratic election, administration, decision and supervision. Since the promotion of village self-governance, the political participation activities have been attached with great importance by the theoretical circle and the government. The Sixteenth Congress Report of CPC clearly specifies that "we shall perfect the village self-governance and improve the vigorous and energetic village self-governance mechanism led by the village Party organization" and that "the expansion of grass-roots democracy represents the fundamental work for developing socialist democracy". Although China has relatively institutionalized channels for political participation and diversified relevant system settings, farmers are still seeking for non-system participation for realizing their requirements of interests to a great extent. Moreover, such kind of non-system participation by farmers has become more frequent and affected the stability of rural areas. "If farmers acquiesce in and approve the existing social system, they would provide a stable foundation for the system. If farmers actively oppose the system, they would become the carrier of the revolution."[19] Recently, the non-system political participation channels in rural China mainly include: bribery, bypassing the immediate leadership and appealing for help from higher authorities, big-character poster, etc. For example, it is not uncommon to see varied non-system participation in the villagers committee election. The non-system participation channels have severely threatened the construction of rural system, destructed the seriousness of the law and therefore deserve special attention. From the situation of Chinese farmers' political participation, we can see that: (1) Chinese farmers' democratic participation ability is still low. They usually pin their hope on their superior leaders rather than regarding themselves as the subjects of the rights. They also lack the due recognition and resistance capability to varied non-democratic patriarchal systems and ideas. (2) According to the development status of Chinese farmers' democratic participation, there has emerged the contradiction between strong demand and self-repression for democracy. Economic development has made the vast farmers generate the requirements of democracy, but the pernicious influence of feudalism still occupies a space in the vast rural China and has severely hindered the democratic development.

(2) The enhancement of Chinese farmers' democratic participation ability constitutes a powerful impetus for the villagers committee election.

In the villagers committee election, farmers' weak educational background has always been a significant factor affecting election. However, it doesn't mean that farmers deny the democracy. Farmers, even though with inferior family background or even being illiterate or semi-illiterate, would also actively participate in some public affairs of the village for the sake of safeguarding their own legitimate rights and interests or direct involvement in the pursuing of economic interests. There is no necessity to cultivate such participation by education and culture. However, farmers' inferior educational background makes farmers at a disadvantage in the political participation. As farmers lack correct understanding about the constitution and other laws, it has become a significant duty of the vast grass-roots cadres to enhance farmers' educational level, and strengthen and improve their democratic participation ability. We must, with a view to the actual effect of democracy, start from launching and strengthening the democratic mechanism of rural areas to enhance farmers' democratic participation ability. To sum up, we should set about the following tasks:

Firstly, vigorously develop rural economy to enrich the vast farmers and create economic conditions for improving farmers' democratic participation ability. In accordance with the principle of Marxism, economic basis determines the superstructure. Economic development has improved people's living standard and educational level. In order to better maintain their own interests, villagers also have to participate in the villagers committee election to realize their targets. Currently, in rural China, there are still large number of districts featuring underdeveloped productivity and insufficiently-developed commodity economy. Generally speaking, farmers' democratic participation ability in the economically backward districts is relatively low. Only with developed economy and guaranteed life for the vast farmers, can farmers' democratic participation ability be continuously strengthened and enhanced. Meanwhile, economic development would inevitably lead to the circumstance under which farmers are concerned about the village matters and firmly seize their own economic and social rights. With the deepening and strengthening of farmers' understanding about their own rights, the pure economic concept would be enhanced and become a kind of political will.

Secondly, energetically develop the cultural and scientific undertakings in rural areas and improve all farmers' scientific and cultural quality so as to enhance the vast farmers' democratic participation ability.

In general, the cultural and educational level in contemporary rural China is still low as farmers' cultural quality is generally low and the illiterate or semi-illiterate farmers take up a large proportion. Furthermore, the illiterate farmers are usually ignorant of the law and politics. The politically illiterate farmers have little participation awareness or political attitude. Their life is dissociated from the political life. Since modern politics feature complicated and varied contents, to correctly and effectively participate in the political activities, it is necessary for farmers to master certain political knowledge and train the ability to analyze relevant political circumstances. We may say that, in the villagers committee election, the content of science and technology has become higher and higher. The ordinary people have deeply realized that their mastered knowledge is so insufficient for dealing with the complicated situation emerged in the election process, and that they lack the ability to give their due judgment to some circumstances. Quite a few farmers are dissociated from the election under the influence of their insufficient education as the election, competition among voters and the like could not be separated from certain cultural conditions. Just as Lenin said, "there would be no politics and only rumors and prejudices for the illiterate."[20] Meanwhile, the traditional political culture still occupies a deep-rooted position, and the mainstream and foreign political cultures are equally defiant. In this way, the political culture has showed diversified colors in rural life. As the "software" of political system, the political culture is deeply influencing people's political activities with a kind of invisible power. Therefore, it is also necessary and indispensable to master certain cultural knowledge in order to correctly understand the democratic goals and methods and eliminate the feudalism.

To sum up, in order to enable and attract more villagers to actively and effectively participate in the election, a very important task is to mobilize and organize the vast farmers to stand by themselves and act to improve their own democratic quality and ability and strive for their own social rights. We should solve the conflicts of interests and contradictions among villagers through the election and other participation means. Only in this way, can we promote the political development of rural China and lay solid foundation for the development of Chinese democracy.

NOTES

1. Wang Yuming, *Discussion about Election* (Beijing: China University of Political Science and Law Press, 1992), 182.
2. Zhao Cunshou, "Discussion about the Legal Status of Villagers Committee," *Guangxi Political and Legal Cadre Administration College Journal* 12 (1999).
3. Fan Yu, "Characteristics of Villagers Committee Election System," Research on Rural Area in China, http://www.ccrs.org.cn/.
4. Fei Xiaotong, *From the Soil: The Foundations of Chinese Society & The institutions for reproduction* (Beijing: Peking University Press, 1998), 49.
5. Cohen, *Discussion about Democracy* (Beijing: Commercial Press, 1998), 10.
6. Rousseau, *The Social Contract* (Beijing: Commercial Press, 2003), 17.
7. Li Luqu, "Re-thinking over Asian Democracy," *Guizhou Normal University Journal (Social Science Edition)* 4 (2001).
8. Wang Xiaoxia and Le Guoan, "Cultural Evolution of Contemporary Chinese Interpersonal Relationship," *Social Sciences Research* 2 (2001).
9. Lin Chufang, "Towards Political Reform: Official Scholars Submit Chinese Election Report," *Southern Weekend*, February 20, 2003.
10. Fei Xiaotong, *From the Soil: The Foundations of Chinese Society & The institutions for reproduction* (Beijing: Peking University Press, 1998), 36.
11. Ma Junjun, "Law Exploration for Candidate Qualification Issues of Villagers' Committee," *Science of Law*, 1 (2002).
12. Commission of Legislative Affairs of Standing Committee of the National People's Congress: *Textbook for Studying Villagers Committees Organization Law* (Beijing: Chinese Democratic and Legislative System Press, 1998), 40.
13. Liu Jianhua, "A Stupendous Sum of RMB 2,300,000 for the Position of Village Official," *People's Daily*, August 25, 2003.
14. Bai Gang, *Villagers Committee Election: Progress and Challenge* (Beijing: China Society Press, 2001), 157.
15. Ma Junjun, "Law Exploration for Removal Issue of Village Self-governance," *China National School of Administration Journal* 1(2003).
16. Ma Junjun, "Law Exploration for Candidate Qualification Issues of Villagers' Committee," *Science of Law*, 1 (2002).

17. Wang Yu, *Research on Legal Issues of Villager Election,* (Beijing: Peking University Press, 2002), 76.

18. Xu Wenzhou, "Issues and Countermeasures of Existing Villagers Committee election," *Shandong Administration Institute Journal* 5(2004).

19. Cheng Tongshun, *Political Development Research of Rural Areas in Contemporary China* (Tianjin: Tianjin People's Publishing House, 2000), 87.

20. Lenin, *Selected Works of Lenin, Volume I* (Beijing: People's Publishing House, 1972), 693.

Chapter Thirteen

Solving "Three Agriculture-related Problems" by Rule of Law and Improvement of Land System in Rural Area

The land system represents the most basic system of property rights in rural areas. Marxism thinks that the property ownership of land is not only determined by historical course and social system but also closely related with the development of productivity. Currently, the serious "three agriculture-related problems" and further widening gap between urban and rural areas are caused by serious disharmony between the existing land system and rural productivity level and social development stage in the final analysis. Therefore, in order to solve the "three agriculture-related problems", it is necessary to focus on the mainline of clarifying the land property right, deepening the reform of land ownership system and other supporting reforms in rural areas so as to shape a new pattern of economic and social development in rural areas.

13.1 DRAWBACKS OF APPLICABLE LAND OWNERSHIP SYSTEM IN RURAL AREA

Article 74 of the *General Principles of Civil Law* specifies that "the property of the working masses organization is collectively owned by the working masses". The so-called collective ownership of working masses refers to the right to occupy, utilize, benefit from or dispose their own land by the working masses collective in accordance with the law. This kind of land ownership represents neither the ownership by all based on individual ownership nor the ownership by legal person based on shareholding system. It represents a kind of land right system with its own characteristics and the product of agricultural cooperation climax of 1950s. The Tenth Plenary Session of the Eighth People's Congress in 1962 passed a resolution, i.e., the "Sixty Articles of People's Commune" which affirmed the land collective ownership of rural areas. The land collective ownership was further confirmed by the *Constitution* in 1982. Article 10.2 of the *Constitution* specifies that "the land from rural and suburban areas" is owned by the collective except for the land owned by the State in accordance with the law; and the house site, private plot and private hilly land are all owned by the collective." After the implementation of the land contracting management system, the original collective economic organizations in the vast rural areas were disintegrated one after another. Most of the township, town and village farmers' collectives have all been equipped with mere administrative or self-governance functions. Article 8 of the *Land Management Law* specifies that "the collectively-owned land is owned by the village farmers' collective in accordance with the law and shall be operated and managed by the agricultural collective economic organizations or villagers committees like the village agricultural production cooperation. The land that has already been owned by the township, town and farmers' collective economic organizations may be owned by the township, town and farmers' collective." "Farmers' collectively-owned land that has already been owned by more than two agricultural collective economic organizations in the village respectively may be owned by the farmers' collective of each of the agricultural collective economic organizations."

Our land collective ownership system represents the product of specific historical period and the result of successive political movements with historical rationality for its generation. Although the household contract responsibility system with remuneration linked to output has once stimulated the development of our rural economy, the room for efficiency growth of the system has reached extremity. With the development of productivity and continual improvement of market economy, the varied disadvantages of our rural land collective ownership have appeared gradually.

13.1.1 Problems with Collective Land Ownership in Rural Area

The ownership represents a kind of complete right of disposition. All people "have the right to dispose their own property within the scope of the law"[1] . However, the empirical analysis of our land collective ownership shows that it is only a kind of "incomplete ownership" and its incompleteness is specifically represented by ambiguous nature of ownership, empty nature of subjects as well as incomplete powers and functions.

1. Ambiguous nature of ownership

The nature of land collective ownership determines the mode to exercise the ownership right. However, the nature of rural land collective ownership has always been a dispute. One may say that the dispute hasn't been solved theoretically yet. In terms of the dispute, there are three kinds of typical viewpoints: the first thinks that the land collective ownership represents a kind of single ownership enjoyed by the "collective economic organizations";[2] the second thinks that land collective ownership represents a new type of ownership based on which the collective members enjoy the right to occupy, utilize and benefit from the collective property (land), and may exercise the ownership right to the collective land in accordance with the law and principles of equality and willingness;[3] the third thinks that the collective ownership represents the "conjunction of individualization and corporatization", the collective property of "land" shall be owned by the legal person of collective organization, and the collective organization enjoy the stock rights and social rights to the collective property.[4] It is generally accepted that the collective ownership represents a kind of separate ownership form enjoyed by the "collective organization" or "legal person of collective organization".[5] However, some people also think that our collective ownership is essentially a new type of ownership by all which is similar to the traditional one but some updates.

We will not discuss the right and wrong of the dispute for the present time. However, different understanding about the nature of the land ownership would lead to different modes for exercising the ownership right, and correspondingly different propositions and practices like exercising by the representatives, agents and collective members jointly. The modes for exercising farmers' land collective ownership right are disputable theoretically and empty legislatively. As a result, the village and township cadres have become the actual ruler and greatest beneficiary of rural collective land and the ownership of collective land have already turned into emptiness in reality.

The ambiguous nature of ownership has also led to the fuzzy state of the right and obligation relationship between farmers' collective and its members. It seems on the surface that everyone enjoys the ownership, but in reality, the collective members neither know clearly their share of the collective land nor have the capability to exercise the rights through sophisticated institutional framework.

2. Empty nature of subjects

The land ownership is the most important part of the rural land system, and the determination of the ownership subjects represents the precondition and core of the land ownership system. However, currently such defects as the "empty nature and dislocation of subjects" in our land collective ownership system have made it impossible for our existing land system to fully safeguard farmers' immediate interests and hindered the sustainable and stable development of rural areas.

Article 74 of the *General Principles of Civil Law* specifies that "Collectively owned land shall be owned collectively by the village peasants in accordance with the law and shall be worked and managed by village agricultural production cooperatives, other collective agricultural economic organizations or villages' committees. Land already under the ownership of the township (town) peasants' collective economic organizations may be collectively owned by the peasants of the township (town)." While Article 10 of the new *Land Management Law* specifies that "In lands collectively owned by peasants those have been allocated to villagers for collective ownership according to law shall be operated and managed by village collective economic organizations or villagers committee and those have allocated to two or more peasants collective economic organizations of a village , shall be operated and managed jointly by the collective economic organizations of the village or villagers' groups ; and those have allocated to township (town) peasant collectives shall be operated and managed by the rural collective economic organizations of the township (town)". We can see from these that both laws recognize that the subjects of the land collective ownership are the farmers' collective, but have failed to specify the detailed contents of the "farmers' collective" or specific organization forms and operation procedures. As a result, the "farmers' collective" has no capability for direct operation and management, the empty nature of ownership subjects emerges and legal principles of property ownership are violated. The above-mentioned regulations have the following issues:

Firstly, there are only three kinds of juristic subjects: the legal person, natural person and unincorporated entity. "Collective", as a term of politics and economics, is not a legal terminology or concept in itself. Issues emerge and exist when "collective" is used as the subject of village collective land. To use the word directly in laws and regulations would inevitably lead to the difficulty of definition of its nature. If we want to actually take the path of market economy in agriculture, we should also give up the expression way that is left behind by the planned economy and that is unsuitable for the market economy.

Secondly, since the implementation of land contracting management, most of the "collective economic organizations" actually exist in name only. The owners' powers and functions are exercised by some administrative or self-governance organizations without the function of economic budget and accounting. It has led to a kind of administrative orientation of land ownership and management as the collective economic organizations and farmers' collectives are not of one-to-one correspondence. Furthermore, the collective economic organization form has no such basic characteristics as the authority, uniformity and stability that should be possessed by the organization form of ownership subject. Therefore, it can only be expedient for the collective economic organization to exercise the operation and management right of collective land. Moreover, after the disappearance of the system integrating government administration and economic management and featuring "ownership by three levels and based on the group", the township collective economic organizations exist in name only, and the township government has become the subject actually exercising the ownership right. As a level of administrative organization, the township government could not become the owner of the collective land either. Furthermore, the village level of organization represents an agency of the grass-roots regime organization (township) stipulated by the constitution, and the group, as an extension of the village, represents a quasi-administrative organization rather than a pure administrative organization or entity that exercises the ownership right of collective properties. The main body construction mode integrating both ownership right and management right would easily lead to the interference of private rights by public rights and go against the protection of community interests (a prominent expression is that the collective withdraws and retains large amount of money for the village cadres' and community-sponsored teachers' salary and allowance and other social functions rather than non-community functions). The foregoing shows that the organizations that are unqualified for the subjects of collective land ownership right or even inconsistent with the operation and management requirements have actually exercised the power for the collective land ownership, leading to the dislocation of the original legal status of the organizations.

Thirdly, according to the level of legal force, the relationship between the *General Principles of Civil Law* and *Land Management Law* is that between the general law and special law as well as that between the higher-level law and lower-level law. In principle, if the latter conflicts with the former, the latter would become invalid. According to the stipulations of the *Land Management Law*, the subjects of the collective land ownership are the farmers' collective, specifically including the three subjects of township, village and village community that are of inclusion relation with mutually independent and equal statuses. However, the *General Principles of Civil Law* only specifies that the village farmers' collective and township farmers' collective may enjoy the ownership of collective land. There hasn't been any legal or reasonable explanation for the obvious legislation conflict.

The empty nature of the subjects has led to unconcern about the utilization and appreciation of the collective land. What's more, there emerges the dislocation of subjects, and farmers' collectively-owned land become the land owned by the township and cadre groups or by several township and village cadres. Some township and village cadres have become the actual owner of village collective land. They, by virtue of their rights, apportion tasks arbitrarily, increase farmers' burden or even sell the land for their benefits and have therefore led to large amount of land loss.[6]

3. Incomplete powers and functions of ownership

Since the ownership represents one of the most complete and sufficient real rights, its subjects enjoy the right to occupy, utilize, benefit from and finally dispose the property in accordance with the law. However, farmers' ownership of collective land is a kind of ownership under strict restriction. China has strict control over the purpose, circulation and disposal of the land. Compared with the powers and functions of ownership, the powers and functions of farmers' ownership to collective land are incomplete. Farmers' ownership to collective land is unanimously called by some people the "shadow ownership". Some scholars have systematically analyzed our national intervention in farmers' ownership of collective land and reached the conclusion that State "enjoys the final disposal right of land", "enjoys the right to distribute the income from the land", "enjoys the right to choose the land user and regulate the direction of land utilization" and "actually enjoys the earnings from the land". Therefore, "the legal ownership (and nominal ownership) and actual ownership of the rural land are completely inconsistent. The real subject for the ownership of the rural land is the country (different levels of governments). The different levels of governments are just the agents for the subject of the ownership, and the township, village and group collective are the grass-roots agents of the national ownership."[7] It can be seen that farmers' land ownership may be disassembled or hollowed and the subject of right may be dislocated. Of course, the characteristics and status of rural land have determined that the country must have control and regulation over rural land. However, such kind of national administrative power, as a kind of intervention in the rural land ownership as a civil right, should be confined to a reasonable depth and width. Otherwise, such intervention would become a kind of deprivation.

Its specific expressions include: firstly, the final disposal right of collective land is enjoyed by the State, and the transfer of collective land ownership features one-way flow on one hand. The land could not be directly transferred with compensation. It can only be transferred by the State in accordance with the law after being requisitioned by the State. On the other hand, the scope of national land requisition has gone far beyond the scope of "public interests", or even expanded to the scope of all national economic activities. Of the land requisitioned by the State, only a part has been used for the purpose of "public interests" and others for commercial purpose. Since the compensation is very low, some governments requisition the land at a low price and transfer it at a high price for the extra gains from the price difference. There frequently emerges the phenomenon of infringement of farmers' interests. Secondly, there exists no safeguard for the economic interests of farmers' collective ownership. The State has embezzled the transfer earnings of rural collective land. The owner of collective land has lost the transfer right of land. In addition, since the compensation for land requisition is far lower than the trading price on the market, the earnings originally from the collective land have been directed to the State treasury. Thus, some scholars say that "in the land requisition activities, the rural collective economic organizations have made great contribution for the construction of the country"[8] .

13.1.2 Problems with Land Contracting Operation Right in Rural Area

1. The rural land contract features unclear nature and contracting operation right ambiguous nature

In the theoretical circle, there exist two viewpoints concerning the nature of rural land contract, i.e., the viewpoints of administrative contract and civil contract. The theory of administrative contract holds that the establishment of the agricultural contract system with remuneration linked to output has enabled farmers to acquire the land use right through administrative contract executed with the government. The administrative contract has replaced the directive plan and administrative order under the planning system, and took the leading position in terms of the agricultural administration modes of the State.[9] Meanwhile, the theory of civil contract holds that the rural land contract, like the enterprise contracting operation contract, is a kind of bilateral, onerous and consensual contract executed between equal parties.[10] The theoretical dispute also receives corresponding support of legislation. Because of the confusion of administrative and civil relations, the contract has gone beyond the civil rights and obligations between the contract letting party and contractor, and lost its original meaning and become the means for local governments and village cadres to implement overall governance to farmers.

Currently, the debate of the academic circle mainly focuses on the controversy between the theory of real right and theory of creditor's right. Besides the two theories, there are also the theory of labor relation, theory of real right attached by creditor's right, theory of creditor's right attached by real right, theory of (compound) ownership, theory of land perpetual lease (the ownership is the foundation right of land), theory of additional land ownership, theory of social security, etc. In accordance with the civil law theory of continental law system, farmers' land contracting operation right has strong nature of creditor's right. With the continual deepening of rural reform and continuous change of land system, the control from the State and collective to the land contracting operation right has become weaker and weaker with less and less restrictions, and the land contracting period longer and longer.

The stability of varied kinds of land property rights enjoyed by farmers has also become stronger and stronger and showed the tendency of transformation to property right. It is because of this that some scholars' think that the rural land contracting operation right is a kind of creditor's right with the tendency of transformation to property right.[11]

2. The rural land contracting operation right is a kind of incomplete use right

The operation right belongs to the use right in essence, from which, such rights as the right to transfer, rent, capitalization, pledge and dividends may be derived. While the land contracting operation right includes only the right to till the land, part of the right to benefit and a little right of disposal. The incompleteness of the right is prominently represented by the land transfer. The *Opinions on Stabilizing and Improving the Land Contracting Operation Right* issued by the Ministry of Agriculture in 1994 confines the circulation of land contracting operation right within the internal of the collective economic organization. The *Land Management Law* revised in 1998 has relaxed the confinement and restriction to a certain extent. However, it still stipulates that "if a unit or individual outside the collective economic organization intends to contract farmers' collectively-owned land, consent must be sought from two thirds of the members or over two thirds of the villager representatives from the villager assembly and from the township government." The *Rural Land Contract Law* of 2002 also stipulates that "anyone who wants to transfer the land contracting operation right shall seek consent from the party awarding the contract". It can be seen that the lawmaker still tends to confine the contracting operation right within a relatively closed scope. Compared with the real contents of contracting operation right, the utilization right is incomplete. It is just because the contracting operation right belongs to a kind of incomplete utilization right that the arbitrariness in utilization and difficulty in circulation have emerged.[12]

3. Rural land contracting operation right lacks the safeguard of well-established system

The appearance of land contract right represents the result of separation between land ownership and utilization right. Since the rural reform and implementation of family-contract responsibility system, the government has been strengthening and expanding farmers' contracting operation right. However, the government policies for stabilizing the contract relations haven't been well implemented. This is represented by frequent adjustment of land and short contracting period in reality. In the overwhelming majority of districts, periodic land adjustment has become a kind of non-system setting. Such adjustment has severely damaged the stability of land contracting operation right. Our government policies for extending thirty years of land contract period have been implemented only in some districts. The instability of contracting right has greatly reduced the contractor's expectancy. Due to the lack of sense of stability, farmers are unwilling to put long-term investment into the land. Since the land investment improvement is a long-term project with certain risk and farmers are unsure about the future expectation, farmers lack the due stimulation for land investment so that predatory operation has emerged.

Of the two parties of the land contracting operation relationship, the contract letting party, as the land owner, is some kind of policy implementer, usually with certain rights with administrative color. This would easily lead to the result that farmer households' land right would easily be infringed by the contract letting party and the contracting right lacks the ability to compete with the contract letting right. In real life, there frequently emerge the circumstances like arbitrary termination of land contract by the village collective, land resumption from farmers, adjustment of farmers' land by the village collective at any moment, random requisition of farmers' land by the government, illegal sale of village collective land by the village collective, and turning public property into private property. In case of any dispute, farmers, as the weak group, are usually unwilling and dare not safeguard their own rights and interests through legal means.

13.2 IMPROVEMENT OF CIRCULATION SYSTEM OF AGRICULTURE LAND

13.2.1 Significance of Circulation System of Agriculture Land

1. The circulation of rural land utilization right represents not only a necessity but also the corollary of productivity development at current stage

It can be said that the existing household contract responsibility system with remuneration linked to output in China has totally depleted farmers' potential of enthusiasm for production, and the room for the efficiency growth of the system has reached an extremity. The rural areas have continuously adjusted the economic and industrial structure and developed the animal husbandry, fishery, forestry and so on. However, there still emerges the natural "surplus" of Chinese agricultural products which is represented by the difficulty to sell vegetable, fruit, fish, etc. The "natural surplus" of Chinese agricultural products is originated from the surplus labor in rural China. The so-called rural surplus labor refers to the labor exceeding the demand of rural industry. Transferring the part of labor from rural areas would not decrease the current productivity and may, on the contrary, improve the labor efficiency. In other words, the marginal productivity is zero or minus.[13] The transfer of rural surplus labor would definitely lead to the circulation of the utilization right of rural land. Otherwise, if the utilization right of rural land is not allowed for circulation, and farmers working outside the village, i.e., working in the city or doing business outside the village, are not willing to till land in the village, it would only damage the interests of farmers who are forced to be bound on the land and reduce the agricultural productivity effect. Farmers are compelled to abandon the tillage and cultivation. What a sad thing it is to let the fertile farmland lying waste since China originally features prominent contradiction between the large population and scarce farmland resource.

2. Circulation of rural land is beneficial to expanding the collective economy, lightening farmers' burden and increasing farmers' earnings

Marx once pointed out that capital could realize appreciation only in circulation. The same goes with the land resources. Some heavily-indebted villages gathered farmers' uncultivated land for unified development and introduced rich family for development of specialty industry through varied means like leasing management and joint stock partnership. This has not only expanded the village economic strength and defused the village liability, but also lightened farmers' burden and guaranteed normal operation of village organization.

Take the land sub-contract as an example. It has been specified that relevant taxes and sub-contract fees shall be jointly owned by the collective and farmer households in the land circulation. On one hand, farmers' annual net income has been substantially increased. The increase in the economically developed districts is more obvious than that in the under-developed districts. On the other hand, the village and community collective economy has also been expanded. "Corresponding standard for the land sub-contract fees may be formulated in accordance with different land utilization types, land levels and local reality. For the land used for agricultural purpose, the price of average output of the crops in recent years may be calculated and deemed as the sub-contract fee. After land sub-contract, local villagers may get employed in the varied agricultural enterprises operated by the new owners, and may usually get a net income of RMB 15-20 per person per day and learn advanced agricultural technology and managerial experience." According to this, the new owner has actually established a profitable township enterprise for local village or community collective economic or organizations.[14]

3. Circulation of rural land is the requirement for constructing a harmonious society

The setting of each real right system should be able to both guarantee justice and stimulate efficiency and strive for a balance between the justice and efficiency. The design and setting of the ownership system for land as a kind of important object of real right is naturally with no exception. To China in which rural population takes up the vast majority of the total population, full utilization of farmers' collectively-owned land and increase of the economic benefits of land would both stimulate our economic development and keep the goal of social justice and stability.

Only after replacing the pure individual land ownership system or pure social land ownership system with the land ownership system featuring coordination between individual and society, can the system suits the society. Just as Michelson from Australia said, "the ownership is just a kind of monopolistic right rather than an individual right without any interference".[15] Some scholars also summarize the ownership as "a right to exclude all others rather than an absolute right".[16] This involves a compromise and coordination principle, i.e., while exercising their ownership, individuals shall take into consideration the social interests; meanwhile only when individuals have appropriate freedom to exercise their land ownership, could the overall social interests be enhanced. Therefore, some scholars think that such kind of ownership thought featuring coordination between the individual and society represents the mainstream for not only the modern land ownership thought but also the development of land ownership thought in the 21st century.[17] In quite a long period, our rural areas would face the dual tasks of system construction of land property right and land market construction. When the land property right system is neither standard nor stable enough, in order to cultivate and develop the rural land market, we must always respect farmers' position of main market player and decision-making power, and allow farmers to independently choose the modes and objects of land circulation within the scope of the law based on the long-term and guaranteed land contracting operation right endowed to farmers.

The economic construction and promotion of urbanization could not be separated from large amount of land requisitioned from farmers. Currently, the contradiction between farmers' participation in the industrialization with their own land and the national land requisition system is mainly represented in two aspects. Firstly, the State would acquire land from farmers in case of any non-agricultural construction. However, the corresponding compensation is very limited. In recent years, the government has exerted more control over farmers' promotion of industrialization in local villages and implemented the concentration of industrial areas, making it more and more difficult for farmers to share the benefits of industrialization. On the other hand, the increase of land differential rent in developed districts has become more and more obvious and earnings of land rent become more and more. Therefore, the earnings from price differential of land have become an important source of fortune. As a result, neither the collective economic organizations nor farmers support the State to change the collective land to state-owned land through land requisition.

Urban and rural overall development represents an innovation for implementing the circulation of collective land utilization right. We should pay respect to the ownership of collective land and adopt the means of land requisition with caution. Also, we should plan as a whole the construction land in the collective land consistent with the urban planning, land planning and use regulation. Instead of changing the land ownership through the means of land requisition or requisition by purchase, we may just transfer the utilization right of collective land and realize the innovation for the circulation of collective land utilization right. Farmers may rent out the land, become a shareholder or establish a joint venture with the land, and get long-term and stable benefits from the land. Besides, we may also activate the stock of collective land for construction through multiple channels, and actively encourage and lead farmers to establish a cooperation, rent and operate the collective land, and construct and rent standard plants and staff residential buildings so as to get a participation in profit distribution in accordance with the shares at the end of the year. Expanding farmers' collective economic strength and implementing capitalization and transformation to enterprises for the collective land would be beneficial to the overall development of rural economy, mitigating the social contradictions and issues brought about by land requisition and demolishing, and therefore guaranteeing farmers' practical and long-term interests. This would therefore provide a stable way out for the rural economic organizations and vast farmers fundamentally.

13.2.2 Principle of Circulation System of Agriculture Land

1. The principle of willingness

The circulation of rural land utilization right must follow the principle of willingness. This is determined by the development state of productivity and economic development level of the country. Due to the restriction of productivity development level, China could provide very limited employment opportunities. The whole country faces serious employment situation and employment pressure could not be fundamentally relieved in short period. To solve the problem of basic living for the unemployed population in urban areas, the country has provided the basic cost of living allowances for urban residents. However, it has no ability to provide social security for the vast farmers to get prepared for birth, senility, illness and death. Rural land has become the key to success as well as the source of food and cloth for the vast farmers. Farmers can only rely on the rural land and regard the land as the basic means of production and ultimate insurance for survival. When the non-agricultural employment opportunities are still unstable, the overwhelming majority of farmers would still regard the rural land as the "farmland for survival" and the guarantee of non-agricultural unemployment. Therefore, the circulation of rural land in Chinese society must take into consideration the significant issue with economic, political and social meaning, i.e., the way out for the farmers losing their land. We need to promote the industrialization and modernization of agriculture, act according to our ability and fully respect farmers' willingness in the process for realizing scale operation of land. Since the rural land utilization right represents a kind of real right, we could not command or compel for both the joint stock cooperative system and leaseback of rural land. We also have to respect the choice made by farmers as a rational-economic man.

To protect farmers' land contracting right, the Third Plenary Session of the Fifteenth Central Committee pointed out that "the rational circulation of land utilization right should be carried out in accordance with the principles of willingness and compensation. No one can force farmers to transfer the utilization right under any excuse". However, those who are wild about the "two-field system", "leaseback and contract-back" and "joint stock cooperative system of land" are usually the grass-roots cadres and relevant entrepreneurs. The ambiguous definition of rural land rights in the existing rural land system and "circulation" of rural land could bring about large amount of income for different levels of administrative organizations and personnel. Therefore, there exists sufficient motivation for maintaining the existing ambiguous rural land right and "interests group" for "circulation" system of rural land. The vested interests group from local villages (refers to the group benefiting from "circulation" of rural land) have become the largest obstacles for the existing rural land system reform. In face of the policy pressure of the Central government and theoretical pressure of the agricultural economics circle, since direct means of objection or rejection are impossible, defining the land rights for the "circulation" of rural land, or defining the rights after circulation has become the main means to safeguard part of the short-term interests. Varied practices for "circulation" of rural land have been greatly promoted by different levels of local grass-roots governments (of course different from the theoretical circle). Such practices include the two-field system, three-field system, leaseback and contract-back, joint stock cooperative system of farmland. It seems that the "circulation" of agricultural land would lead to concentration of rural land which would bring about high-efficiency agriculture. The "circulation" of rural land has become the main means for rural land system reform. Therefore, "the motivation for village cadres to advocate for land adjustment is complicated and mostly involves the consideration for power and interests. None of the varied practices like the two-field system, contract through public bidding, leaseback and contract-back are simply fishing in the air. These practices have actually brought about interests".[18]

2. The principles of equivalence, compensation and fairness

In accordance with the regulations of the existing *Land Management Law*, the compensation for land requisition is not equivalent. The State has set a maximum limit for the land requisition compensation and such standard has no rationality and equality since it is based on the multiple of production value and takes no consideration for the land type and market factor. The compensation for land requisition paid by the State is just a part of subsidies rather than land rent or price. It is far from being equivalence. The high amount of land earnings is not appreciated because of the change from collective land to state-owned land. It is determined by the land position, natural and geographical conditions as well as the land development level. This is actually a kind of disguised embezzlement to the ownership interests of collective land by the State.

Most of the countries and districts in the world determine the compensation amount in accordance with the market price of land. Some countries and districts also determine the compensation amount in accordance with the future price of land and other indirect losses of the land requisition caused to the land owners. However, our land requisition compensation system is totally statutory. "The land compensation shall be six to ten times of the average output in the previous three years of the farmland before the requisition, the placement subsidy...four to six times, ...However, the total amount of the land compensation and placement subsidy shall not be higher than thirty times of the average output in the previous three years before the requisition to the highest". This represents a kind of policy compensation irrelevant with the market. The land requisition compensation has failed to link up with the market price and the compensation does not equal to the total price of land asset. The government usually acquires the land at a low price of land compensation and transfer the land to the market at a high price. In practice, this part of added-value is very high and actually represents the differential rent of land changing from agricultural land to urban land. For example, for some real estate development, local governments requisition the land from the collective farmers in accordance with the fair price stipulated by the State and sell the land through auction to developers at a price several times or dozens of times higher than the original price. Although they enjoy the utilization right of rural land, farmers could not share the interests from the added value. How can we safeguard farmers' property right?

13.2.3 Problem with Circulation System of Agriculture Land Utilization Right

1. The unbalanced circulation of rural land rights

In China, the state-owned construction land rights could be circulated through market mechanism, but the rural land right is forbidden for circulation through market activities. Furthermore, the circulation of agriculture land within the scope of rural land is just allowed for the circulation of contracting operation right and adjustment to collective land, and the circulation mode is single. Moreover, the circulation of rural land contracting operation right requires the consent from the party awarding the contract of the land. The circulation of the non-agricultural construction land within the scope of rural land refers to the circulation of land utilization right and is allowed only for the share-holding or jointly-owned township enterprises.

The circulation of land within the scope of rural land is also far from equivalent. The circulation of the agriculture land and "four-waste" land refers to the circulation of contracting operation right of rural land, and the circulation of construction land refers to the circulation of utilization right. The circulation modes of agriculture land are different because of the different means for acquiring the land and contents of rights. The contracting operation right for the land acquired through household contract is allowed for subcontract, lease and exchange but not allowed for capital contribution or mortgage. While the contracting operation right of the land contracted through such means as tender, auction and public negotiation is not allowed for capital contribution or mortgage.

2. The incomplete and scattered legislation, lagged management and chaotic circulation

Under the guidance of the principles of the *Constitution*, the NPC Standing Committee has successively formulated seven sets of laws related with rural land rights and circulation. We now have special laws and regulations for the circulation of contract land in rural areas. However, the legislation on the circulation of collective construction land is ambiguous and impractical. To the circulation of the rural land in broad sense, there is no corresponding and complete legislation. In China, the forest land, grass land, farmland and construction land are registered with different departments. The scattered legislation and divided land registration system all go against the circulation of rural land rights. The cadastral management of a country constitutes the foundation for the land right circulation of the country. However, the lagging work of our cadastral management, diversification of the subjects of rural land rights and other factors have led to the unstable state of collective land ownership and other related rights, and affected the legal circulation of land. There have emerged many invisible markets that have failed to reflect the value of land asset and the practices for evasion of law.

3. Further standardization is required for the circulation scope, conditions, procedures, means as well as distribution and utilization of earnings for the rural land

The circulation scope and conditions of rural land are not unified, and procedures and methods not standard. These items would be different based on whether the land is within or beyond the scope or of nonprofit nature. In the trade of rural land, there is no lack of direct circulation of collective land on the invisible trading market of construction land through violation of the land purpose control and agriculture land approval system. The utilization modes with compensation are also not standard as the modes with compensation of first, second and third levels coexist in the first circulation of collective land.

The transfer benefits of rural land are the price transformation of the right holder's right. Only the people with legal or promissory right to the land right have the right to share the benefits. Of the transfer benefits of collective land, the compensation for the non-ground-attachment shall be owned by the collective and collective members. However, in reality, some local governments have participated in the distribution under the excuse of infrastructure investment. To the so-called land "circulation", the main earnings are obtained firstly by the municipal and county land administrative departments and local treasury, and secondly by the township and administrative villages rather than the farmers. Under current circumstance of daily-increasingly tight local finance, the part of income has basically become an important source for narrowing the salary gap and has little relationship with farmers. What constitutes the legal basis for the government to participate in the distribution of the earnings? In the circulation of collective land, in what capacity, by what means and through what channel could the State take away part of the land transfer earnings?

13.2.4 Completion of Circulation System of Agriculture Land

1. The system and methods of rural land right circulation

The difference of legal status between the collective land ownership and the state land ownership constitutes the reason for the blocked circulation of agriculture land use right. As to the legal status of the collective land ownership, the common theory of the academic community holds that, in accordance with the regulations of the *Constitution*, *General Principles of Civil Law* and *Land Management Law*, the collective land ownership has its independence and equal status with the state land ownership. Between the two kinds of land ownership, there exists neither relationship of derivation or subordination nor grade differential. The independence of collective land ownership and equality between the two kinds of land ownership represent the basic principles of the land ownership system. There also exists other different viewpoint which holds that, in accordance with the analysis on current law stipulations and relevant land systems, one can hardly believe that the collective land ownership and state land ownership are of equal legal status and with the same legal protection. The inequality of legal status between the two is embodied by:

Firstly, different land circulation system. In China, no land ownership is allowed for circulation and what is allowed for circulation is the land use right. Moreover, under the circumstances of national requisition of collective land ownership and general nationalization of collective land, the circulation of land ownership only has one direction—the State. Therefore, the land ownership transfer in China is unique and unidirectional. In other words, there exists only the change from collective land ownership to state land ownership rather than circulation between collective ownership or change from state land ownership to collective land ownership. The one-way circulation system of land ownership would definitely lead to gradual expansion of the objects of state land ownership and corresponding shrinkage of the objects of collective land ownership.

Secondly, different way of confirming land ownership right. The confirming of land ownership right refers to the way to determine ownership right of the disputed land. Article 18 of the *Provisions for Confirming the Land Ownership and Utilization Right* issued by the Ministry of Land Management on March 31, 1995 stipulates that, in case of any ownership dispute, if it is impossible to prove that the disputed land is owned by farmers' collective, the land would be deemed as owned by the state. The above-mentioned system belongs to the presumption system of state land ownership. We can see from the above-mentioned stipulations that the lawmaker has adopted policies beneficial to the state land ownership: farmers' collective has to provide proof for their claim to the land ownership; otherwise the land would be regarded as owned by the state. In the dispute of property right, the proof burden principle of "whoever claims for the right shall be responsible for providing proof" should have been applied and the state therefore should also have the corresponding proof burden obligation. Otherwise, people may think that the state is expanding its own land ownership scope through legislation, and the collective land ownership and state land ownership are of unequal legal status.

Thirdly, different public administration system for land. First, different restrictions are applied. The utilization right of collective land is greatly restricted and the utilization method is single. The collective land can only be used for agricultural production, farmers' house site and the construction closely related with the collective like the village enterprises. It cannot enter into the real estate development market with tremendous benefits. The utilization of collective land is restricted by the agricultural policies, farmland protection policies and land management regulations of the state. This represents both the requirement of land socialization and necessity for exercising the public administration power of the country. However, in the real estate development process, the collectively-owned land consistent with the construction land planning and purpose control is not allowed for transfer or transfer of utilization right. However, after the land is requisitioned by the state and changed into national land, it becomes possible and allowable to transfer the land with compensation. This not only goes against the general common sense, but also leads to the deprivation of tremendous benefits that should have been owned by the collective. It is therefore obviously unfair.

Second, different approval systems are implemented. The approval system for land utilization represents a basic system for the land management in China. The utilization of farmers' collectively-owned land for non-agricultural purpose must be approved by the administrative authority in advance in accordance with the law. However, in the approval process, there is no clear specification about the owner's rights of the collective land, and relevant party may directly apply for administrative examination from relevant authority, which neither fully reflected the will and right exercising of the collective land owner, nor paid enough attention to its legal status as the collective land owner.

We should establish a circulation system for the utilization right of rural land the same as that for the state-owned construction land. In China, both the rural land and state-owned construction land belong to the nationalized land of socialism. In terms of the principle of equal rights, theory of separation between property and rights, the development of civil law real right theory, experience of pilot projects for the circulation of rural land rights, the vast farmers' and farm workers' will, rural economic system reform and the like, we should establish the same circulation system and mode for rural land rights as that for the national construction land.

The circulation system of rural land rights should be set to include the circulation of real rights for the land with different nature of ownership or for different purpose in a unified market system and adopt a unified mode for the circulation. For the primary market of land jus in re aliena: the utilization modes with compensation of rural land jus in re aliena include transferring, renting and valuing as capital; for the secondary market of land jus in re aliena: the utilization modes with compensation of rural land jus in re aliena include transferring; and for the third market of land jus in re aliena: the utilization modes with compensation of rural land jus in re aliena include renting, mortgage, etc. The primary market of land jus in re aliena refers to the first circulation of land jus in re aliena, and represents the right transfer between the land owners and users. On the primary market, the rural collective economic organizations transfer the land use right to the land users, and the supplier can only be the land owner. The secondary market of land jus in re aliena refers to the land right transfer between the land users. On the secondary market, the users who have acquired the utilization right of rural collective land with compensation in accordance with the law transfer the remaining period of land use right. On the secondary market, the thing under circulation is the land usufruct; while on the third market, the thing under circulation is the other rights of the usufruct owner.

As to the approach for realizing the circulation of rural land jus in re aliena, the transfer of rural land requires stringent agreement. In case more than two parties want to become the user of the land parcel, bidding, auction or listing may be adopted for the transferring, leasing and valuing as capital contribution for the parcel.

2. To improve the land registration system

The construction of property right system represents the basis for the circulation of construction land. The circulation of non-agricultural construction land of the collective is carried out based on the core contents of collective land property right. Clear property right relationship of land as well as explicit powers and functions are the preconditions for orderly circulation of collective construction land. We can see from the construction process of our state-owned land property right system that the division of land property right boundary is a process for re-defining the different rights of land property right ownership. The continual improvement of land property right system represents the precondition for the reform of land utilization system and the basis for sound and healthy development of land market. In addition, the continual development of land market would in turn stimulate the gradual establishment and improvement of the land property right system. In real life, the loss of land earnings in the land circulation process caused by unclear subjects of property right and incomplete right, and the difficulty of land circulation caused by unstable land contracting right and incomplete utilization right are all closely related with the unclear relationship of property right.[19]

To standardize the circulation of collective construction land, we should strengthen the land registration work, confirm the ownership scope of collective land, clarify the subjects of land property right and safeguard the trade security in accordance with the law. If the property right is unclear, the market mechanism would have difficulty in operation. The necessity to establish a registration system lies in that: firstly, the rural land use right features abstraction. Under the static state, the rural land use right may agree with the state of right in accordance with the dominance relation in appearance. However, with the circulation of rural land use right, change of dynamic debt relation between the parties involved and indirect possession of rural land, the appearance state may have difficulty in reflecting the relation of right and the registration would therefore become the sole standard for determining the right. Secondly, the rural land use right has its value. Owing to the development of modern property right law, the property right has showed the gradual tendency of changing from direct utilization to value conversion. The transferring, capitalization and other means of rural land use right have promoted the value of rural land. When the land gives play to its utilization value and value function, the interests' subjects for occupying and financing for the land are separated and registration is required for publicizing the relationship of right. Only the transaction with the rights being registered can be deemed as the correct transaction of right recognized and protected by the law. Thirdly, the land has its effectiveness of public benefits. The registration system represents an active form for the competent national authority to intervene in the transaction of real right of real estate. Its purpose is to supervise the utilization of real estate and ensure the realization of the social benefits of the real estate. The utilization of rural land, related with the social security of rural areas, represents the core of our national intervention policies for real estate. Therefore, the registration system could not only publicize the static and dynamic states of the utilization right from the perspective of civil law, but also constitute a basic requirement for the State to regulate the rural land order.

As a kind of usufruct, the utilization right of rural land must establish and improve its publicity system and strengthen its credibility.[20] Relevant authorities should register the establishment and circulation of the rural land uses right and expresses the state of the right through certain certificate—the certificate of rural land use right. As the result of the registration by the registration authority, the certificate of rural land use right can cite and demonstrate the utilization right of rural land. However, just as the certificate of real estate that can cite and demonstrate the real estate right could not replace the registration of real estate by the registration authority of real estate, the certificate of rural land use right could not replace the registration of rural land use right. Establishing a registration system for improving the establishment and circulation of rural land use right could not only give full play to the function of property right to prevent and settle disputes and be beneficial to safeguarding the legitimate rights for the people losing their certificates of rural land use right, but also effectively prevent the forging and obliteration of the certificates protect the bona-fide transferee in the circulation of rural land use right, safeguard the transaction order for the circulation of rural land use right, ensure convenient, effective and safe circulation of rural land use right and decrease the transaction fee for the circulation of rural land use right. As to the establishment effectiveness of the rural land use right, the registration effectiveness principle may be adopted in accordance with the separation, formalism and abstraction principles from the German theory of juristic act of real right.[21] A contract may be adopted for establishing the rural land use right and the contract shall be effective as of the establishment of the contract. The rural land use right should be established upon the registration.[22] According to this, the contract for circulation of rural land use right would be effective as of the establishment of the contract and rural land use right be circulated as of the registration.

The registration authority of rural land use right must adhere to the tenet of providing service and convenience for the people, implement diligent and honest administration for the public, establish and improve the registration system of rural land use right and establish an electronic database for the establishment and circulation of rural land use right featuring resource sharing so as to provide convenience for the parties involved in the transaction to search for relevant information. Also, it shall never take the registration as a tool for creating income or seeking for illegitimate income, or increase the cost for circulation of rural land use right.

3. Standards for distributing the benefits from land circulation

The circulation benefits represent the price conversion of the owner's right. Only the party who enjoys statutory or promissory rights to the land can participate in the distribution of the circulation earnings of the land. The circulation earnings from the state-owned agriculture land shall be owned by the state or members who have been utilizing the land permanently. The compensation for the non-ground-attachment from the circulation earnings of the collective land shall be owned by the collective and collective members. However, some local governments have also participated in the distribution of earnings under the excuse of governmental infrastructure investment. What is the legal basis for such practice? By what means, through what channel and in what capacity could the country get a part of the land earnings from the circulation of collective land?

13.3 COMPLETION OF ACQUISITION SYSTEM OF AGRICULTURE LAND

The circulation of rural land use right is closely related with and mutually promoted and restricted by the land requisition system. The establishment and improvement of rural land use right relies on the reform of land requisition system, and reform of land requisition system would in turn stimulate the improvement of rural land rights and establishment of the right circulation system. The Ministry of Land and Resources has carried out pilot projects and researches for the reform of land requisition system by batches in the coastal and hinterland areas, and proposed seeking for alternations for the one-time compensation for requisition of rural collective land. Therefore, the long-term issue of damaging farmers' interests in land requisition may be solved.

The existing land requisition system is generated in the era of planned economy. Under special historical conditions, such land requisition system has played positive role for ensuring the capability of the country to acquire the necessary non-agricultural entrepreneurship and construction land, decreasing the construction land cost and establishing the state ownership of urban land. We may think that such land system is simple, clear and thorough in terms of its role and function to the planned economy. However, when the planned economy system has become the market economy system, and protecting agriculture land and promoting the modernization of agriculture and rural areas have become one of the main tasks today, the requisition system of construction land has exposed its serious inadaptability, and farmers' rights and interests have been seriously infringed. In the era of planned economy, it is an unavoidable choice for the country to exploit the agriculture and accumulate capital for industrial development. However, this constitutes a great unfairness. Moreover, such policy has not only harmed farmers' interests and given rise to social injustice, but also led to low efficiency of urban and industrial land utilization. From the perspective of justice and efficiency, reform of the existing requisition system of rural land constitutes a necessary means to solve the "three agriculture-related problems".

13.3.1 Protection of Farmers' Interests in Land Appropriation Compensation

1. Harm to farmers' interests in land requisition compensation

The current *Land Management Law* specifies that "in case of land requisition, compensation shall be paid in accordance with the original purpose of the requisitioned land. In case of farmland requisition, land compensation, placement compensation as well as the compensation for the ground attachments and immature crops shall be paid." Therefore, Chinese standards for land requisition compensation advocate the compensation in accordance with the original purpose of the requisitioned land for farmers' labor input to the land rather than the capitalization value of the land. In other words, our current land compensation is too low and has great distance from the actual market price.

In most countries and districts of the world, the party requisitioning the land would always pay satisfactory compensation to the land owner. According to the compensation contents of each country and district, there are usually three indispensable items: the compensation for the land and ground construction, attachment and structure based on the market price standard; the compensation for the difficulties caused by the land requisition like the difficulty in replacement, employment and the like; and the compensation for the external dis-economy caused by the land requisition like the compensation for the remnant land, harm to the neighboring land, etc.

Chinese compensation for land is insufficient. Our existing compensation is quite unreasonable and includes only two items:

Compensation for the land and ground construction, attachment and structure: our current land compensation standard represents the product from the era of planned economy. The so-called six to ten times of the average annual output in the previous three years could not reflect the highest level and best purpose of the land. In China, due to the incomplete information of agricultural product market, farmers' low ability to hold the market and lack of government guidance, the utilization of rural land could not always reflect the highest level and best purpose of the land. For example, when the land that could have been grown with cotton has been used for rice farming because of varied factors, measuring the land value in accordance with the rice output would underestimate the potential value of the land, not to mention calculating the compensation in accordance with the six to ten times of the average rice output in the previous years. As to the calculation of compensation for the non-farmland, many districts adopt the standard of half of the compensation for the farmland. This also is a practice without any reasonable base.

Compensation for re-settlement and replacement of the farmers losing the land: in accordance with our current compensation standard for land requisition, the replacement compensation for farmers losing the land equals to four to six times of the average annual output of the land in the previous three years which is obviously very low. As a matter of fact, the re-settlement and replacement for farmers losing their land is divided into two kinds: the first is to provide the social security and medical insurance for the farmers losing all of their land the same as those for the urban residents, and assist and arrange an employment opportunity or provide a one-time compensation to the farmers in view of farmers' weak survival ability in cities; the second is to provide compensation for the farmers who have lost part of their farmland and are not provided with the treatment of changing from "agricultural to non-agricultural" status and social security for their future life since the decrease of their farmland would lead to the decline of their living standard although compensation has been paid for the land itself.

External nature of land requisition: one important item of compensation that has been neglected. Of our current standard for the compensation of land requisition, one item that has been ignored is the compensation for the damage caused by the external dis-economy of land requisition. The external dis-economy of land requisition can include many items like the remnant land (in other words, the requisitioned land may give rise to the division of land, form dis-economic land scale and lead to the loss of land utilization efficiency), and harm to neighboring land (in other words, the new purpose of the requisitioned land may reduce the productivity of the neighboring land. For example, the noise pollution, water pollution, river blockage or raised dust may all reduce the productivity of the crops and increase extra invested cost to the agriculture land).

Only after full consideration for the above-mentioned three factors, the compensation for the ground crops, construction and structure as well as the relocation subsidy, could the compensation for land requisition be deemed as fair. The fair compensation represents another basis for determining whether the exercising of requisition right is legal besides the public purpose. As a matter of fact, even after full consideration for the above-mentioned factors, the party whose land has been requisitioned would still feel unfair as people's evaluation to the lost land is usually higher than the price that people are willing to pay for purchasing the same amount of land on the market. The phenomenon is called the dis-symmetry of value measurement.

2. Low efficiency of land utilization caused by current land requisition system

Under the free price mechanism, the result of land usage competition would lead to the usage change from lower level to higher level and enhance of land earning power. Therefore, the purchase price shall be higher than the existing value of land. However, in the process of exercising land requisition right, the lower level of compensation adopted by the land utilization unit for acquiring the land would not necessarily lead to the land utilization of higher level and the best purpose. On the contrary, it may lead to low efficiency of land utilization and bring about social cost. This is because any unit or individual would, after acquiring the requisitioned land, carry out a cost-profit economic calculation. If the compensation amount for the land requisition is too low, and the investment cost and potential cost are inconsistent, the earnings higher than the paid investment cost would be economic after the land disposal regardless of the potential cost. An inevitable result would be that: the actual demand of land would be higher than the balanced requirement formed based on reasonable requisition price, and extensive utilization of land may be brought about. Since the requisition cost is very low, it would not be a difficult thing for the land utilization units to realize their goal. Even when the land resources are utilized at sub-high efficiency, the land utilization unit could win the profits. Therefore, it is quite difficult to realize the optimization collocation of resources. A good evidence for this is the large amount of the phenomena under which the land is utilized at low efficiency or not utilized at all after being requisitioned.

The underpriced compensation for land requisition has brought about excessive transaction cost for the investors. The negotiation cost caused by the long-term negotiation between the land requisition unit and farmer household, the forcible land requisition by the land requisition unit through legal means after the breakdown of negotiation, the continual appealing for help from higher authority by farmers, and the lawsuit cost constitute the transaction expenses of land requisition. Over-high transaction expenses would exert great influence on the land development.

In many countries, the compensation endowed by the law to the party whose land has been requisitioned is usually higher than the market value of land. This is beneficial to not only guaranteeing that the original living standard of the party whose land has been requisitioned would not be lowered, but also optimizing the collocation of land resources.

13.3.2 Causes for Infringement of Farmers' Interests in Land Appropriation

1. Insecure property relations of rural collective land

Under current land requisition system, the issue of infringement to farmers' interests is an issue of compensation standard for land requisition from appearance. However, at a deeper level, the issue is actually an issue of land property right system. The land ownership, land use right, relationship between the land ownership and land use right as well as the national restriction constitute the basic contents of our property right system of rural land. In accordance with the theory of property right, the land property right can be divided into the guaranteed and rarely guaranteed land property right. "Economically, the absent guarantee of right should be the consequence of three elements: (1) inappropriate quantity of right; (2) insufficient period; (3) insufficient certainty for the exercising of right because of high implementation cost".[23] The inappropriate quantity of right means that the intensity or quantity of the land right obtained by the owner is insufficient for ensuring the exclusiveness of the utilization, sole enjoyment of the benefits and freedom to transferring of the land. The insufficient period means that the horizontal line of time in terms of economy is insufficient for the right holders to be sure of that their investment could be compensated by all the income flux generated by the investment. Certainty is related with the legal commitment and legal implementation ability of the society. According to our current setting of property right system of rural collective land, the land obtained by farmer households-collective and land users-land owners are all short of safeguard.

For example, due to the issue of unclear subjects of land property right, the limited land compensation has been divided and shared by multiple parties. There are actually such seven levels as the Central government, province, municipality, county, township, village and group participated in the distribution of the compensation. The actual compensation finally obtained by the farmers' collective economic organizations is usually much less than the amount paid by the State. For another example, because of the incomplete powers and functions of the property right of rural collective land, the land, in a "virtual property" state completely without price measurement, could not be sold, rented, mortgaged or transferred through other means. The final disposal right of the land is controlled by the State. However, such control is not always an effective complement to the market "malfunction". Once the land requisitioned by the government fails to increase the overall benefits of the society, but only satisfy the interests for several economic subjects, the lack of guarantee for the property right of rural collective land would be showed and reflected.

2. The contradiction between the system requirement and principle of public interests for the land requisition system

According to the general survey of the land requisition system of each country, the public purpose constitutes the single standard for reasonable exercising of land requisition right. Since our current land requisition system is established on the foundation of the public ownership by the State, the law has prohibited the sale of collective land and therefore completely excluded the collective land from the market, and if the enterprises and public institutions have to utilize the collectively-owned land because of investment and construction requirements, it has become necessary to implement relevant regulations for land requisition. "Any entity or individual for construction shall apply for the utilization of state-owned land. The collective land could not be directly sold or transferred. If any construction needs to utilize collective land, the land shall be requisitioned as state-owned land first". This has led to the expansion of land requisition scope, as in accordance with the stipulations on utilization of land with compensation, whatever the nature of the land user is and whether the purpose is for "public interests", the land shall be requisitioned as state-owned land first before being transferred through relevant formalities. As a matter of fact, the principle adopted for the land requisition is the special principle of "system requirement" of the country rather than the principle of "public interests" generally adopted by the international community. The land requisition system of China actually serves for the dual goal of satisfying the requirement of public interests and system demand. Under most circumstances, it mainly serves for satisfying the system demand.

To sum up, the insecure property relations of rural collective land as well as the contradiction between the system requirement and principle of public interests for the land requisition system constitute the root cause for the severe damage to the interests of the rural collective and farmers in the land requisition.

13.3.3 Theoretical Basis of and Measures for Farmers' Interests Protection

1. Legal theory basis for rural land requisition—correct definition of public interests

In China, the requisition right is a power held by the government. However, "all right holders are liable to abuse power. This is a kind of never-changing experience."[24] The expansion nature of administrative power represents one of the intrinsic characteristics of the power itself. In face of beneficial temptation and weak supervision, the expansion desire would become more severe and the abuse of power more unbridled. Therefore, to prevent inappropriate infringement on private right by the national power, each country has established special law to take the purpose of public interests as the sole rightful basis for land requisition and universally acknowledged reason for the country to plea against private ownership. Therefore, the legal theory basis of land requisition system lies in the restriction set by the government on private ownership for the purpose of public interests which represents a kind of legitimate intervention in private right by the public power. More importantly, the clearness of public interests has affected the establishment and completeness of other systems in the land requisition to a great extent. Therefore, the definition of public interests has the value of core meaning to the essence of land requisition.

"Since the public interests are an abstract concept, different people have different opinions about them."[25] There is always no clear definition about the public interests in our community of law (note: the public interests have always been regarded as a conventional concept which has been widely adopted. Some scholars have tried to provide a clear definition about public interests, but the emptiness, fuzziness and expansion nature of public interests still exist). As a result, there emerged boundless expansion of land requisition scope and loss of farmland in practice and formed the black market of land in rural-urban continuum. This has severely damaged the interests of farmers' collective and farmers. Therefore, clarifying the boundary of public interests and standardizing the land requisition activities represent a key element for the reform of land requisition system.

In accordance with the reality of China, the author thinks that we should prescribe a limit to the public interests and divide the public interests into two categories in the land requisition system. The first is the pure public interests, including the national defense equipment and military installations; transportation, water conservancy and energy equipment; education, academy, philanthropy and public health undertakings. The second is the quasi-public interests, including the government and its public buildings; other undertakings held by the government or non-government institutions for the purpose of public interests (note: the quasi-public interests are established as such interests usually involve the discretion factors of the government subject and there might emerge opinions different from the civics'). Only the land requisition activities based on the above-mentioned two categories of public interests could be deemed as legal activities. To the non-public interests construction land, in accordance with the planned purpose and market rule, the utilization right of land could only be obtained through land transaction.

2. Market orientation for the compensation standard of land requisition and natural person orientation of the compensated object

"When the government acquire the ownership or right of possession of the property, it is obviously necessary to pay compensation for the requisitioned property permanently or within a limited period of time."[26] Although it represents a kind of unilateral compulsory act by the government, the national land requisition shall meet two requirements. Otherwise, it would be deemed as illegal or unreasonable. Of the two requirements, the first is that the governmental land requisition must be for the purpose of public interests; and the second, certain compensation must be paid for the land requisition. In accordance with the legal provisions of China, for land requisition, the land utilization unit shall pay certain land compensation, immature crop expenses and replacement subsidies to the party whose land is requisitioned in accordance with the law, and shall appropriately arrange the production and life for the farmers from corresponding unit.

If land is requisitioned for public welfare without compensation paid to the party whose land is requisitioned, it would mean that burdens are applied on small number of specific individuals or groups for public interests. This is unfair. And if compensation is paid, the burden would be undertaken by the public and the party whose land is requisitioned together. This is fair. Just as M · Baessler says, "as a matter of fact, to be precise, the purpose of compensation is to avoid the sacrifice of a person for the social welfare". Compensation shall be paid for land requisition. However, it really constitutes an issue to determine the amount and way of compensation.

In western countries, the compensation standard of land requisition is usually based on the market price of the land. This is reasonable both in theory and in practice. However, in accordance with the law of China, the compensation principle is "appropriate compensation" which is quite ambiguous. Moreover, the compensation is statutory and not based on the market transaction price of the land (namely the market transaction price for the utilization right of the land in China). As a result, the compensation in reality is much lower than the market price. This has severely damaged the legitimate interests of the party whose land is requisitioned (mainly the farmers). The distortion of the land requisition price would always lead to the result that the government officials requisition the land at low price through their power and then transfer the land to the businessman at the market price (usually a little lower than the market price in reality) for the exorbitant profits from collusion between the government and businessmen. Obviously such practice has seriously violated the Pareto optimality principle. It can be seen that we should not only pay compensation for land requisition, but also pay the compensation in accordance with the market price to show rationality.

The compensation for land requisition shall be oriented to the market for the following reasons: firstly, the transfer of rural land may enable farmers to obtain more earnings, but the land requisition has deprived farmers of their obtainable interests. Therefore, compensation shall be paid in accordance with the transfer price on the rural land market. Secondly, because of the great influence of the land requisition on the farmers' production and life, general farmers have difficulty in restoring their living standard before the requisition. Thirdly, as it is impossible to adopt the replacement method for the land requisition (i.e., replace the plot of land with another plot of land as the compensation), and it is necessary to minimize farmers' loss, the principle of "minimum influence on farmers" shall be adopted. The market orientation of land requisition compensation represents exactly a good approach to realize this.

Besides, the compensation subjects shall be oriented to natural person. In accordance with the current law, of the land compensation, the compensation for the ground attachments and subsidies for immature crops shall be owned by farmers and the other compensation of land requisition by the rural collective economic organizations. The land contractor gets the compensation only as a member of the collective. This would easily lead to the disputes between farmers and the collective and among the farmers caused by the distribution of land compensation. Firstly, the land contracting operation right represents a property right independent from the land ownership, and the land contractor a legal subject independent from the land owner instead of just a member of the collective. Secondly, the land requisition would have more influence on the production and life of the land contractor than on that of the collective. Thirdly, the land requisition would constitute different influence on different collective members. Disputes may arise between those whose land is not requisitioned and those whose land is requisitioned for the distribution of compensation. Finally, the collective, as the compensation subject, has actually excluded the farmers and deprived farmers from their participation right and negotiation right. Therefore, our regulations shall specify that the compensation subject shall be the user whose land is requisitioned and the negotiation shall be carried out between the farmers and land users. Although this would lead to higher cost, it may effectively prevent land wastage and corruption issue. Of course, certain part of the total compensation may be withdrawn as collectively-owned earnings for the collective interests. Such part of the total compensation could be even less if the collective has already terminated its investment to the land.

As a matter of fact, the system of "resumption of government land" in Hong Kong is similar to the land requisition system of the mainland and therefore may be used as a reference. In accordance with the *Government Land Resumption Ordinance*, when it resumes the land for public purpose, the government should pay full compensation to the land owner (namely the land tenant). Also, the government may resume the land by purchasing the land. In case an agreement could not be reached, the compensation matters may be transferred to the land arbitration and trial authority (i.e., the court with trial level equivalent to that of local court that is especially responsible for the trial of land ownership disputes) for verdict. The compensation amount is usually calculated in accordance with the open market price on the day the land is resumed by the government of Hong Kong Special Administrative Region.

NOTES

1. Sun Xianzhong, *Contemporary Property Law of Germany* (Beijing: Law Press of China, 1997), 135.

2. Wang Weiguo, *Research on Land Rights in China* (Beijing: China University of Political Science and Law Press, 1997), 114.

3. Han Song, "Essence of Chinese Farmers' Collective Ownership," *Science of Law* 1 (1992).

4. Kong Xiangjun, *Research on New Issues and Corresponding Interpretation of Civil and Commercial Law* (Beijing: People's Court Press, 1996), 378.

5. Tong Rou, *China Civil Law*, P254; Zheng Li and Wang Zuotang: *Science of Civil Law*, P206.

6. Zhou Linbin, *New Theory of Property Law* (Beijing: Peking University Press, 2002), 369.

7. Deng Dacai, "On the Ownership of Rural Land," *Research on Financial and Economic Problems* 2(2000).

8. Finance and Trade Research Institution of Chinese Academy of Social Sciences as well as New York Public Administration Research Institution: *Utilization and Management of Chinese Urban Land* (Beijing: Economics Press, 1992), 62.

9. Wang Ping, "Enlightenment and Comparison of Civil Contract and Administrative Contract," *Wuhan University Journal* 3 (2000): 56-58.

10. Zheng Li and Wang Zuotang, *Science of Civil Law* (Beijing: Peking University Press, 1999), 289-99.

11. Wang Xiaoying, "Land System Change and Transformation of Land Contract Right to Property Right," *China Rural Economy* 1(2000).

12. Gao Fuping, *Land Utilization Right and Real Right for Usufruct* (Beijing: Law Press of China, 2001), 385.

13. Li Tongwen, *Report on People's Livelihood in China* (Beijing: Gold Wall Press, 1998), 52.

14. Fang Huiling, "Research on Joint Stock Cooperative System of Rural Land in Guangdong," *Chinese Rural Economy* 3 (1999):18-21.

15. Wang Liming, *National Ownership Research* (Beijing: Renmin University of China Press, 1991), 113.

16. Law Institute of Shanghai Academy of Social Sciences: *Civil Law*, Knowledge Press, 1981, P78.

17. Liang Huixing, *Research on Chinese Real Right Law* (Beijing: Law Press of China, 1998), 256.

18. Chen Xiwen, "Let Farmers be the Master of Land," *Southern Weekend*, December 1, 2001.

19. Ye Jianping, *Research on Property Right System of Chinese Rural Land* (Beijing: Chinese Agriculture Press, 2000), 47.

20. Wang Liming: *Research on Property Law,* (Beijing: Renmin University of China Press, 2002), 472.

21. Sun Xianzhong, *On Property Right Law* (Beijing: Law Press of China, 2001), 163-64.

22. Liang Huixing, *Recommended Draft for Chinese Property Right Law* (Beijing: Social Sciences Academic Press, 2002), 518.

23. (British) Mitchell Carter, *Chinese Rural Land System Reform of Agricultural Performance and Land System* (Beijing: Peking University Press, 1993).

24. Montesquieu, *On the Spirit of Law* (Vol. I) (Beijing: China Planning Press, 2002), 245.

25. Chen Ruixiong, *New Theory on General Provisions of Civil Law* (Taipei: Taipei Sanming Publishing House, 1982), 913.

26. (USA) Michael. D. Bayles, *Principles of Law* (Beijing: Chinese Encyclopedia Press, 1996), 138.

Chapter Fourteen

Solving "Three Agriculture-related Problems" by Rule of Law and Improvement of Rural Cooperative System

14.1 OVERVIEW OF RURAL COOPERATIVE SYSTEM

14.1.1 Functions and Features of Rural Cooperative System

1. The concept and classification of Cooperative

The word "Cooperative" or "Cooperative Society" is originated from English. However, as to the exact meaning and concept of the word, the legislation in each country has its own definition. Therefore, the specific condition and policy orientation of each country are not the same or more or less different. In face of the situation, the International Cooperative Alliance proposed the definition of cooperative in 1995: cooperative refers to the voluntary association organized by the people who are voluntary to unite for satisfying their own economic, social and cultural requirements and wishes through the enterprises featuring joint ownership and democratic control. The concept has been recognized by the international labor organization in 2002 and affirmed in written by the *Promotion of Cooperatives Recommendation, 2002* passed on the 90th International Labor Conference. However, almost all of the definitions of cooperative by the academic community are around the center of "international standard" but with different emphases and characteristics.

Cooperative may be classified into different types in accordance with different standards. Currently, the main classification approaches in theory include:

1. In accordance with the industrial standard of cooperative, cooperative can be classified into the worker cooperative, consumer cooperative, agricultural cooperative, etc. Of which, the agricultural cooperative includes the supply cooperative, production cooperative and marketing cooperative.
2. In accordance with the behavior content of cooperative, cooperative can be classified into the production cooperative, credit cooperative, consumption cooperative, etc. Of which, the consumption cooperative includes the distribution cooperative for living needs and the supply cooperative for production needs.
3. In accordance with the business scope of cooperative, cooperative can be classified into the comprehensive cooperative and special cooperative. The special cooperative may be a production cooperative, consumption cooperative or credit cooperative; and the business scope of comprehensive cooperative includes two or more than two kinds of the special cooperatives.
4. In accordance with whether a stock is issued, cooperative can be classified into stock cooperative and non-stock cooperative.

2. Development motivation of rural cooperative

Cooperative is a kind of economic system originated from commodity economy and a product of commodity economy development at the market economy stage. Under self-sufficient natural economy conditions, the producers are mainly the farmers and the products are mainly used for family consumption. Only small number of surplus products has been sold in the society for buying other goods required for production and living. Under such circumstance, there exists no space for the survival and development of cooperative. With the development of productivity, social division of labor has become more and more specific, and products more and more in large quantity but single variety. Therefore, only a small part of the products has been used for the producers' own family consumption, and most and even all of the products for sale in order to buy other products for their own production and living. However, at early stage, because of the limited production, the product sale and raw material supply required by the production are all handled by the producers themselves. With the continual expansion of production scale, the supply of raw material and sale of products are constantly increasing and could not be handled totally by the producers themselves. As a result, the producers have to rely on the service from other people of the society. Hence, there emerge more and more middlemen in the society who are responsible for supplying raw materials to the producers and collecting the products generated by the producers to the factory for further processing or for direct sale on the market. However, all of these middlemen are profit-motivated. They gain the maximum price difference (profit) through buying at low price and selling at high price. This is especially true in the period of economic crisis. To prevent the profit from declining, the middlemen would intensify their efforts to raise their supply price and lower their purchasing price, leading to huge loss to the producers. In order to protect their own interests and avoid the exploitation from the middlemen, the producers are forced to organize a cooperative for supply of raw materials and direct sale of their products by themselves. This is the supply and marketing cooperative that provides supply, sale and other relevant services at the earliest time and of the most common occurrence in the market economy countries. Also, in order to avoid the exploitation from the businessman, the consumers organize varied consumer cooperatives. Of course, there are also the credit cooperative, housing cooperative, the cooperative of small producers from handicraft industry and the like besides the consumer cooperative. This constitutes the reason that the cooperatives of many countries in history have developed rapidly in economic crisis. It can be seen from this that, under the market economy, the cooperatives are emerging spontaneously from down to top and prospering with the development of commodity and market economy. The commodity and market economy constitutes the requirements for the generation and development of cooperatives, and the development of cooperatives represents an inevitable result of the commodity and market economy.[1]

Cooperative represents the alliance of weak group. Besides the farmers, there are also such weak groups as the consumers, small producers from handicraft industry and small capitalists. However, most of the cooperatives in many countries are carried out around the center of rural farmers. The agricultural cooperative, as the main component of cooperatives, has basically covered the vast majority of cooperatives (of which, the agricultural supply and marketing cooperative is the most common). The cooperatives formed by other weak groups only take up a tiny minority of the cooperatives. This is mainly determined by the particularity of agricultural production and farmer group. Agriculture, as the industry featuring the principle of "heaven helps those who help themselves", firstly encounters the risk of natural disaster which is very difficult for human force to avoid. People can only avoid the expansion of the damage after the disaster and however do little to prevent or decrease the occurrence of the disaster. Because of the factor as well as the scattered location and seasonal period of agricultural production, farmers' alliance becomes more urgent and possible. Secondly, under market economy, farmers, like other market subjects, need to face the market risk. Compared with the "natural disaster", farmers' own initiative obviously has larger space to make a difference. In view of their own production and marketing interests and based on the guarantee of independent production of products, farmers formed an organization spontaneously and sold their products to the cooperative who was responsible for unified sale or resale after re-processing in accordance with the market demand. In this way, there would be neither grain overstock nor internal cutthroat competition formed by forcing prices down among individual farmers. The cooperative is responsible for unified sale and external negotiation so that the products of all cooperative members could be sold at a good price. After the sale, the cooperative would return the money to the farmers after deducting the costs. If farmers need the seeds, chemical fertilizer, agricultural machinery and other means of production, the cooperative would purchase by batch these goods in a unified way from the producer or wholesaler, and then provide them to the cooperative members. This would obviously reduce the farmer members' production costs. Similarly, if the technical services of agriculture are provided by the cooperative organization or the cooperative as the intermediary, the efficiency would be greatly enhanced and costs decreased. This is the reason that the "market" of cooperative is mainly in rural areas and the root cause for the strong vitality of rural cooperative.

Besides, under the commodity economy, especially under the market economy, farmers, as a kind of weak group, take up a great proportion in terms of both level and quantity. Therefore, although the cooperatives of each country are not confined to the scope of rural agriculture, their main element and center of gravity are placed in the agriculture and rural cooperative. There would be no exception for the cooperative system to be established in China.

3. Features and functions of rural cooperative

The rural cooperatives mentioned herein are geographically located in rural areas. Their features lie in that they are classified by industry. In terms of operation activities, there are production, credit and consumption cooperatives. In terms of operation scope, there are comprehensive and special cooperatives. Of course, another characteristic of rural cooperatives lies in that the cooperative members are mainly farmers.

Except for the several unique features, rural cooperatives also have the general characteristics of all cooperatives, including:

Firstly, the cooperative is a self-governance association independent from the governmental departments and other legal persons and free from the illegal interference from other associations.

Secondly, the cooperative is a voluntary alliance of people which firstly refer to the natural person. However, with the development of legal personality, the law of each country also gradually acknowledges that the legal person may join the cooperative and become qualified cooperative member too.

Meanwhile, the alliance is voluntary. Any people may join or withdraw from the cooperative freely without any compelling or interference.

Thirdly, the property of the cooperative is jointly owned by the cooperative members and democratic management is implemented in the cooperative. The disposal of property and great management matters for the cooperative are usually decided by the means of "one member, one vote". While modern profit-making enterprises usually adopt the principle of "one share, one vote" in accordance with the number of shares. This represents an important difference between the cooperatives for serving their members and enterprises for profit making.

Lastly, the purpose of cooperatives is to satisfy their members' joint economic and social demands. The primary goal for establishing a cooperative is to satisfy its members' economic demands. Therefore, we may say that the cooperative is an economic organization. However, after its establishment, the cooperative serves mainly but not just for its members' economic demands. After gradual development, it also serves for its members' social and cultural demands to certain extent.

To sum up, rural cooperatives have the following features:

(1) Changing of the fierce market competition through horizontal and vertical alliance. The cooperative can change farmers' weak and single-handed state and strengthen farmers' negotiation ability, namely their bargaining capability on the market. From this sense, the cooperative represents a bargaining agent providing assistance for farmers for their bargaining in the fierce market economy. This is the primary and main function of rural cooperative.

(2) Uniting of the scattered farmers' production and provide pre-production, production and post-production information and technical services for farmers to realize large scale of services through concentration and sharing and therefore reduce farmers' expenses for obtaining information and adopting high and new technology.

(3) Carrying out operation activities which is difficult to be implemented by single household or that require high costs through united organization. For example, farmers would jointly utilize the large-scale equipment since the small-scale farmer household usually has insufficient funds to purchase such equipment and their low frequency for utilizing the equipment may lead to uneconomy resulting from frequent idle state of the equipment. The hardware facilities like the irrigation and water conservancy facilities and public roads in rural areas are all similar to such kind of equipment.

(4) Propagating and utilizing science and technology, and realizing spiritual civilization of rural areas by providing assistance for farmers' self-education. Meanwhile, as the representative for the common interests of the cooperative group in certain area, the cooperative has played the role of alliance check and balance, and played a part in striving for social justice,

safeguarding the weak group's rights and interests, and promoting social stability and coordinated development of economy and society between urban and rural areas.[2]

It can be seen that the cooperative has its economic and social characteristics. Firstly, from the economic perspective, it also seeks for economic interests and profits. As a new type of economic organization jointly owned by its members, the cooperative aims at providing transportation and sale, processing, production and living services for its members, forming aggregated scale economy, reducing transaction expenses, enhancing overall competitiveness as well as increasing operation efficiency and members' income and welfare through united access to the market. However, in terms of the economic efficiency, the cooperative aims at obtaining profits and assisting its members to earn money from market transaction by united and joint operation rather than seeking for maximum profits of the cooperative itself, which is different from the general enterprises. The profits from the united and joint operation would be returned to the cooperative members or paid as dividends for share capital in accordance with the volume of business between the cooperative members and the cooperative. Secondly, from the social perspective, the cooperative can help to cultivate its members' spiritual civilization, stimulate the formation of good order of the whole society and therefore realize comprehensive, coordinated and harmonious development of the society. Thus, it can be seen that the dual nature of economy and society of the rural cooperative constitutes the essential feature of the cooperative that distinguishes the cooperative from other market subjects.

14.1.2 Basic Theory of Rural Cooperative Legal System

1. Concept of rural cooperative law

The rural cooperative law refers to the legal norm system for adjusting the social relations generated during the establishment, organization, and operation and termination process of rural cooperative. It represents the summary and abstraction of the cooperation rules generated from the cooperative movements and practices. After the stereotyping and institutionalization of the state will, the rural cooperative law could better guide and standardize the cooperative movements.

In accordance with the legal requirements for the operation of cooperatives and the scope of cooperative law, the objects to be regulated by rural cooperative law shall include:

(1) The internal organizational relationship of cooperative, i.e., the social relations generated among the cooperative, cooperative members and internal institutional framework system of the cooperative.

(2) The economic relations generated by the operation activities of the cooperative, including the property or economic relations generated by the

internal and external operation activities of the enterprise. All the operation activities of the cooperative may be classified into two types: the first type refers to the common business activities like sale and transportation; the second type refers to the business activities directly related with the organization features of the cooperative, including the financing of the cooperative, transactions between the cooperative and cooperative members, etc. The first types, namely the common business activities, are usually regulated by other department laws like the civil law and contract law rather than the cooperative law. Only the second types, namely the business activities, are regulated by the cooperative law.

(3) The control relation between the country and cooperative, namely the administration relation between the country and cooperative in the process of economic management. As one of the market subjects under market economy, the cooperative is also under the control of the country while implementing its varied activities and when the country is performing its economic management functions.

The norms of cooperative may be classified into different types in accordance with different standards. In accordance with different origins of the legal norms, the norms can be classified into the cooperative norm from the constitution, from the cooperative code as well as from other relevant laws and regulations like the civil law, enterprise law and legal interpretation. In accordance with different forms of the legal norms, the norms can be classified into the cooperative norm of narrow sense, namely the cooperative code, and the cooperative norms of broad sense which generally refer to all norms adjusting the cooperative relations. In accordance with different effectiveness of the legal norms, the norms can be classified into the mandatory and discretionary cooperative norms.

2. Legal status of rural cooperative

(1) The rural cooperative represents the legal person of civil subject. Currently, all the countries in the world implementing cooperative legislation has endowed the cooperative with the status of legal person and acknowledged that the cooperative has the legal qualification to carry out the civil activities and undertake the legal liability in its own name.

The legal person can be classified into the public and private legal person in accordance with different establishment goals and legal bases. The former refers to the legal person established in accordance with the public law for accomplishing its public welfare functions and the latter the legal person established for pursuing private goals. In accordance with different establishment foundations, the private legal person can be further divided into the legal person of mass organization and financial group. The former refers to the private legal person that regards the combination of people as the foundation for its establishment, and the latter the private legal person that regards the setting of certain property as the foundation for its establishment. The private legal person can also be further divided into the public-welfare and profit-making legal person in accordance with different goals. The former refers to the legal person established for the interests of most and unspecific people rather than making profits, and the latter established for making profits.

It can be seen that the cooperative belongs to the private legal person and the legal person of mass organization. As it is not established for performing social public functions, the cooperative could not be deemed as a public legal person. Since its establishment foundation is the combination of people, the cooperative belongs to the legal person of mass organization. However, from the perspective of establishment standard, the cooperative belongs to neither public-welfare nor profit-making legal person. Since it is established for the interests of a certain part of specific people, namely its members, rather than the most and unspecific people, the cooperative does not belong to the public-welfare legal person. Although it also carries out certain profit-making activities, the cooperative regards serving its members rather than making profits as its primary purpose. Therefore, it is not a profit-making legal person either. To sum up, according to the above-mentioned types of classifications, the cooperative belong to a third kind of legal person beyond the public-welfare and profit-making legal person. This is determined by the essential attribute of dual nature of both economy and society of the cooperative.

The legal person of cooperative also has its own unique attributes except for the general attributes of legal person required by the law, including the mass character of organization, democracy of management and service purpose which distinguish the cooperative from other enterprise legal persons. These features are usually realized through the cooperative legislation and principle confirmation.

(2) The principles of rural cooperative. The principles of rural cooperative refer to the basic principles confirmed in the form of law and used for guiding the cooperative activities. As the high generalization and abstraction of the legal system of cooperative, the principles play the commanding and guiding role for varied rules and legal norms of cooperative.

At the mention of the cooperative principles, the first one comes to people's mind may be the Rochdale Principles. One may say that the cooperative principles are originally established by the British Rochdale Society of Equitable Pioneers. The Rochdale Principles include: open and voluntary membership; democratic control (one person, one vote); distribution of surplus in proportion to trade; payment of limited interest on capital; political and religious neutrality; cash trading (no credit extended); promotion of education. These principles may be deemed as the cooperative principles with the strongest international influence.

Owing to the ideological difference of different cooperative schools and difference of cooperation thoughts embraced by the legislation of different countries, the cooperative principles haven't been unified in the cooperative legislation of different countries. Owen, the Utopian socialist and great master of cooperative thought holds that the cooperative principles represent joint possession of means of production, equal distribution of labor fruits and implementation of democratic management. Philippe-Joseph-Benjamin Buchez, the main representative of production cooperative school holds that the principles that the production cooperative shall follow include: laborers as members; no employment; goods delivery by day or hour for remuneration of labor in accordance with different people's technical proficiency; as well as withdrawal of certain proportion of reserved funds and establishment of permanent cooperative funds to be collectively owned by the cooperative which shall not be distributed. The principles followed by Rochdale Society of Equitable Pioneers which was established under the enlightenment of the thought from William King from the consumer cooperative school include: funds raising through joint stock; unlimited amount of share capital, no bonus and only stock dividend; democratic management of members and one vote per person; return surplus to the members in accordance with the proportion of goods amount after the withdrawal of reserved funds and public welfare funds; maintain political and religious neutrality; etc. Lenin, the great tutor of the revolution, also points out in his *On Cooperative System* the three basic principles of cooperative: the first is the voluntary principle; the second emphasizes the financial support from the country to the cooperative; the third points out that economic goal of cultural work is the establishment of cooperatives.

In order to promote the unification of the cooperative principles in each country and better guide the implementation and exchange of the cooperative movements in each country, the International Cooperative Alliance, based on certain modification and summary of the Rochdale Principles, proposes six cooperative principles in 1966 so that the cooperative principles could guide varied cooperatives rather than just the consumer cooperative. The "100th Anniversary Representative Assembly of International Co-operative Alliance" held in September of 1995 re-modified the cooperative principles to guide the development of the cooperative movements in 21st century. These principles include:

1. Voluntary and open membership. Co-operatives are voluntary organizations, open to all persons able to use their services and willing to accept the responsibilities of membership, without gender, social, racial, political or religious discrimination.
2. Democratic member control. Co-operatives are democratic organizations controlled by their members, who actively participate in setting

their policies and making decisions. Men and women serving as elected representatives are accountable to the membership. In primary co-operatives, members have equal voting rights (one member, one vote), and co-operatives at other levels are also organized in a democratic manner.

3. Member economic participation. Members contribute equitably to, and democratically control, the capital of their co-operative. At least part of that capital is usually the common property of the co-operative. Members usually receive limited compensation, if any, on capital subscribed as a condition of membership. Members allocate surpluses for any or all of the following purposes: developing their co-operative, possibly by setting up reserves, part of which at least would be indivisible; benefiting members in proportion to their transaction amount with the co-operative; and supporting other activities approved by the membership.
4. Autonomy and independence. Co-operatives are autonomous, self-help organizations controlled by their members. If they enter into agreements with other organizations, including governments, or raise capital from external sources, they do so on terms that ensure democratic control by their members and maintain their co-operative autonomy.
5. Education, training and information. Co-operatives provide education and training for their members, elected representatives, managers, and employees so they can contribute effectively to the development of their co-operatives. They inform the public—particularly young people and opinion leaders—about the nature and benefits of co-operation.
6. Co-operation among Co-operatives. Co-operatives serve their members most effectively and strengthen the co-operative movement by working together through local, national, regional and international structures.
7. Concern for community. Co-operatives work for the sustainable development of their communities through policies approved by their members. Currently, all countries are utilizing or have already utilized these principles to guide the cooperative legislation and practice of their own countries.

3. Basic systems of rural cooperative law

(1) Systems for incorporation and amendment.

These systems mainly include: the requirements for incorporation, including the elements of the initiator, property name and location; convention and rules of procedure for the founding conference of the cooperative; statutory and optional contents of the articles of association for the cooperative as well as the merging, splitting, termination and other systems of the cooperative, including the registration system of the cooperative. One of the statutory contents for registration is the business scope of the cooperative which concerns the legal capacity and disposing capacity scope of the cooperative.

The cooperative legislation of each country usually adopts the statutory principles for the business scope of the cooperative. In other words, they usually directly stipulate the business type of each kind of cooperative in their cooperative laws so as to standardize the implementation of cooperative cause. A controversial issue concerning the establishment of the statutory business type of cooperative is the single and sideline business issue. For this, there are several propositions of cooperative economic theory and legislation: the first is the single business theory which advocates that the operation of cooperative shall be limited to a single business without any other sideline business; the second is the sideline business theory which advocates that the operation of cooperative may focus on a single business and concurrently carry out one or several sideline business(es); the third is the eclecticism which advocates that the operation of cooperative shall be limited to a single business or several businesses according to circumstances.

The reason that the cooperative legislation of each country defines rather than authorizes the cooperative to choose the business scope of the cooperative lies in that the cooperative represents an economic organization featuring members' joint operation and its establishment, existence and extermination are closely related with the public social interests and national macroeconomic policies. Therefore, the countries restrict the legal and disposing capability of each kind of cooperative through the limitation of business scope by legislation so as to avoid any violation to the cooperation purpose.

(2) Membership system of rural cooperative.

The system mainly includes members' admission qualification, rights, obligations, liabilities, and withdrawal from cooperative, including the statutory and voluntary withdrawal.

Members' liability system is a special, controversial and hot topic of cooperative system, for which, different countries have different stipulations. Some countries specify that members have limited liability, while other countries specify that members have unlimited, unlimited remedy, guarantee, limited, dual or other liability for the debt of the cooperative. Theoretically, the cooperative liability shall be optional. The liability pattern stipulated by the cooperative law represents the basis for the general meeting of members to choose and determine the liability of the cooperative in the articles of association of the cooperative. After being recorded by the articles of association and determined by legal procedures, the cooperative liability would become the liability principle for the external activities of the cooperative.

Then, what kind of liability pattern should the law provided for the cooperative? As a matter of fact, currently most countries have stipulated in their cooperative laws that members shall have limited and guarantee liability. Although the liability system of the cooperative may include the unlimited, limited and guarantee liability, the limited and guarantee liability shall be the main pattern of liability.[3]

Internal governance system. The system includes the establishment of inner organizations of the cooperative, including the setting of general meeting of members, board of directors and board of supervisors; allocation and definition of functions, financial management system, post responsibility system, profit distribution system, etc. This represents not only the core of whether the cooperative system can succeed, but also significant embodiment of democratic management and other principles of the cooperative. These systems, quite similar to the corporation law, only have different emphases of goal compared with the corporation law.

14.2 INTERNATIONAL TREND OF RURAL COOPERATIVE LEGAL SYSTEM

14.2.1 International Legislation of Rural Cooperative System

1. Worldwide development of cooperative

As a kind of social-economic system, the cooperative system can be traced back to the period of the Utopian socialist Owen. However, the nearly one century before 1844 can only be deemed as the budding stage of cooperative. The cooperatives at that time only existed in some parts of a few countries with early development of capitalism like Britain and France, and featured simple type.

The first standard cooperative—Rochdale Society of Equitable Pioneers established in 1844 determined the joint declaration for the weak group—the Rochdale Principles which have laid solid foundation for the development of cooperative in the following hundred years. In 1895, cooperatives have emerged in most of the capitalist countries with more types. After the prosperity of cooperative in the major capitalist countries, the International Cooperative Alliance was established in 1895. The establishment of the international organization has practically strengthened the frequent and extensive political, economic, and other exchange and cooperation among the cooperative organizations of all countries, and marked the official inauguration of cooperative movements on the world arena. However, the cooperatives at the stage are mainly concentrated in the relatively developed countries. After World War II, especially in 1960s, the economic and political pattern of the world has showed tremendous change, and both the developed and developing countries have carried out cooperative movements on a large scale. In face of the new circumstance, the International Cooperative Alliance has constantly revised the articles of association for alliance and the cooperative principles have also been updated, developed and improved continuously. Meanwhile, the countries in the world have also established different types of cooperatives suitable for their own national conditions in accordance with local situations. The development characteristics of cooperative at the stage include large quantity, full range, varied types, flexible operation, good development of alliance scope and cooperation level as well as closer exchange and cooperation among the cooperative organizations of all countries.[4] One may say that the cooperative, after worldwide universal development, has become one of the basic economic patterns for developing commercial economy. According to statistics, we now have nearly 3 billion direct beneficiaries of cooperative which account for a half of the total population in the world. The varied cooperatives have provided employment opportunities for 100 million people. The production value of cooperative has taken up certain proportion in many countries. In the developing countries with agriculture as the main industry, the production value of cooperative has already taken up 10-20% of the GNP.

After a general survey of the worldwide agricultural development, we may draw a conclusion that the higher the agricultural modernization and commercialization level of a country is, the more developed the rural cooperative of the country would be. Since the Western Europe and North America are the two largest export areas of agricultural products in the world and their agricultural modernization level and commodity rate are all very high, the rural cooperatives of the two areas are also quite developed. In a majority of European and American countries, most of the farmers are cooperative members. For example, in the Netherlands, a majority of the farmers are the members of at least three to four cooperatives, and more than 60% of the farmers' income is realized through cooperatives. In some countries like Denmark—the exporter of traditional agricultural products, nearly 100% of the farmers have joined a cooperative. In the United States, five of every six farmers have joined two to three purchase and sale cooperatives. The cooperative has controlled 60% of the cereal sale in the whole America and supplied a certain amount of cereals equal to 40% of the gross export volume. In Japan, almost all farmers have joined an agricultural cooperation organization, and 90% of the purchase for means of production and 80% of the sale for agricultural and sideline products are realized through an agricultural cooperation organization.[5]

2. Rural cooperative legislation in various countries of the world

Since the status of cooperative in the economy, especially in the agricultural economy of various countries is so important, various countries have successively established their legislation for the cooperative. However, as to the initiating mode of legislation in different countries, there exist different characteristics of legislative style.

(1) Differences of initiating mode for the legislation of different countries.

In the Western European and North American countries like Britain, America, Germany and France, the cooperatives are mainly established under farmers' initiation and from bottom to top, and then enter into the national legislation under the advocacy of a policy party or other people with great social influence. Therefore, the national legislation mainly generalizes and summarizes the relatively mature cooperative rules, and fixates and reflects the rules in legal form so as to standardize and guide the ongoing and forthcoming cooperative movements. In East Asia, the cooperatives are mostly initiated and organized by the government or some political parties from top to bottom based on the experience of relatively mature cooperative system in the Western Europe and North America and in accordance with the requirements of their own countries. Therefore, in these countries, the cooperative legislation is usually synchronized with the cooperative practices, and the government and outside forces have great influence on the establishment and operation of the cooperative. For example, the Japanese rural cooperatives are prepared and organized by the Japanese government, led by the Ministry of Agriculture, Forestry and Fisheries, and then converted into the organizations run by local people and subsidized by the state.

This kind of situation is caused by both economic and historical and cultural factors. In terms of economy, the western countries have earlier and more mature and developed commercial economy than the East Asian countries. In terms of historical and cultural traditions, the social traditions of western countries have led the civics in these countries to form the habit of establishing social relationship through democratic consultation and covenant. These are all the reasons for the differences.

(2) Differences of legislative style.

Since 1852 when Britain published the first cooperative law—*Industrial Economy Cooperative Law*, the cooperative legislation has realized unprecedented development worldwide and become an important legal category of the legal system in different countries of the world.

The legal standards of cooperative are usually classified, in accordance with the form of these standards, into the cooperative code, separate law of specific cooperative and cooperative-related standard from relevant laws and regulations. And the legislative style of rural cooperative usually refers to the category of the legislative form of cooperative in different countries, i.e., whether the legislation is independent or auxiliary, and whether the legislation is comprehensive or divided by business.

Many countries have established separate legislation for multiple cooperatives and comprehensive legislation for the cooperative cause to enable the cooperative law become the basic law of cooperative. These countries mainly include Britain, America, Germany, etc. Of course, there are some countries without specialized cooperative legislation. These countries only affiliate the cooperative legislation with the civil law, commercial law or other legal system and have no specific standards. A typical example of these countries is France. However, some countries have not only established specialized legislation for the cooperative and formulated the cooperative code as the basic law of the cooperative legal system, but also established special legislation for specific cooperatives. Therefore, their cooperative legal systems, after being greatly enriched and emphasized, are not affiliated to a specific legal branch any more. A typical example of the countries is the post-war Japan.

(3) Main contents of rural cooperative legislation in different countries.

Main contents of the rural cooperative legislation in different countries generally include the following:

Firstly, to endow the rural cooperative with legal status. A common practice of the countries is endowing the rural cooperative with the status of a legal person. However, some countries also allow the existence of a cooperative in unincorporated form and explicitly stipulate the legal status of the cooperative. This represents both the primary content and base of the cooperative legislation. Even in the countries without separate cooperative legislation and with only auxiliary legislation for the cooperative, the legal status of the cooperative constitutes an essential content.

Secondly, to stipulate the inner organizations and operation rules of rural cooperative. The inner organizations, namely the governance structure, of rural cooperative are similar to the corporate governance structure of the enterprises. The cooperatives in Britain and America only set the general meeting of members and council (also named as the board of directors), and no board of supervisors. The council represents both the executing and supervisory agency. However, in the countries implementing continental legal system, the cooperatives usually set the general meeting of members, council and board of supervisors as the decision-making, executing and supervisory agency respectively.

As to the operation rules of rural cooperative, all the countries abide by the basic principles of cooperative, i.e., respect the cooperative as farmers' self-governance economic organization, stick to the principle of democratic management and promote allocation of the surplus in accordance with the transaction volume. To allocate the surplus in accordance with the transaction proportion represents an allocation principle persistently pursued by the cooperative. The cooperative represents the object providing transaction service, and the "transaction volume" the core of the cooperative system. For example, in a purchase and sale cooperative of agricultural products, the cooperative may purchase the agricultural and sideline products at the price similar to that on the market first, and then store, process and sell the products. After deducting the necessary expenses, the value added would be deemed as the surplus of the cooperative which would be returned to the members in accordance with the transaction volume between the members and the cooperative after the withdrawal of public accumulation and distribution of share capital and interests in accordance with legal procedures. Here, the transaction volume represents both the requirement for the members to join the cooperative and the prerequisite for the existence of the cooperative. The allocation of surplus in accordance with the transaction volume also represents an important symbol to distinguish the genuine and sham cooperative. All in all, the purpose is to enable the cooperative to actually become an organization "established, governed and benefited by the people".

Thirdly, to define the status and role of the government in the operation of the cooperative. The governments of different countries usually endow the cooperative with varied kinds of preferential treatments, including the concessions of taxation, credit, etc. Meanwhile, with their development, the cooperatives also gradually extend the industrial chain and connect the agricultural pre-production, production and post-production processes to realize vertical integration; and form comprehensive cooperative economic organization through merging and reorganization of specialized cooperative organizations to realize horizontal integration. This has improved the competitiveness and earning power of the cooperatives themselves and met the demands of fierce market competition. However, it would also inevitably lead to the emergence of such monopoly means as Cartel and Trust in rural agriculture. Hence, the countries also endow the rural cooperative with the special treatment of "monopoly exemption" successively in their anti-monopoly legislation.

14.2.2 New Trends of Rural Cooperative System

1. Disadvantages of traditional cooperative

The classical cooperatives usually refer to the cooperatives before 1970s that abide by the above-mentioned basic principles of cooperative. These cooperatives are suitable for the economic development at that time. They have played great positive role for stabilizing rural economy, improving farmers' income, promoting rural prosperity and realizing harmonious development between urban and rural areas. However, with the development and penetration of market economy as well as the intensifying of market competition, the classical cooperatives can no longer adapt to the economic development well, and have gradually exposed their disadvantages under the original systems which are concretely represented by:

(1) Uneconomical utilization of resources. The implementation of the open membership principle by the classical cooperatives has led to members' joining and withdrawing freely from the cooperative and unstable operation scale of the cooperatives. Meanwhile, as the cooperatives could not organize production on an economical and efficient scale, there frequently emerged overlarge investment of facilities as well as excess supply and production capability, leading to uneconomical utilization of cooperative resources.

(2) Pursuit of short-term benefits. Owing to the limit to the transfer of surplus property right and lack of the secondary market for transferring such right, the flowing of right could not be realized. Members can only share the cash from the cooperative within the period in which they are providing service for the cooperative. Therefore, when choosing the investment items, they would usually select those items with soonest economic returns. This constitutes a suppression to the long-term development of the cooperative.

(3) Weak internal supervision. Classical cooperative has formed inseparable public accumulation. Due to the lack of explicit property right system, with the expansion of the cooperative scale and increase of members, the share of public accumulation would become larger and larger and lead to greater difficulty of members' supervision and management. In case of the management by only a few members, the issue of agent would easily appear. Meanwhile, because of the development of member qualification, there would easily emerge the circumstance under which new members share the benefits from the old members, and the unfairness that the old members who withdraw from the cooperative midway could not share any benefits from the public accumulation.

(4) Blocked financing channel. The funds of classical cooperative mainly come from the share capital paid by the members. However, such share capital is just the qualification share required for the members to join the cooperative and members have no impetus to pay more share capital. This has severely restricted the funds raising capability and scope of the cooperative.

2. New characteristics of emerging cooperative

Since the cooperative represents a product of market economic development, its development should comply with the market economic development. Therefore, from 1980s to 1990s, the development of cooperative showed new favorable turn. The developed countries represented by the United States, under the basic principle of "by the people, under the people and for the people", launched a new generation of cooperative, i.e., the New Generation Cooperatives (NGCs), and therefore brought about a wave of traditional cooperative reform which is still underway today. Many countries are now setting about reforming their cooperative system to adapt to the demand of development situations.[6] The emerging cooperative has the following characteristics:

(1) In terms of members' qualification system. The emerging cooperative has changed the original free access to the cooperative into certain limits for joining and withdrawing from the cooperative.

(2) In terms of management system. The emerging cooperative has changed the one-person-one-vote system of grass-roots cooperative into vote with members' investment. Meanwhile, the council members are not totally elected from members any more. On the contrary, most of the council members are elected from the members and there are also some council members who are not the cooperative members. There also emerges the expert management. Besides, like in the corporate stock system, the cooperative starts to sell preferred stock to the community to increase the funds channel of the cooperative. The preferred stock may effectively bring about stock dividends, although it has interest rate limit and entails no right to vote.

(3) In terms of property right system. The traditional cooperative stipulates that only the members could hold a qualification share which is equivalent and could not be transferred or held by non-members. The new generation cooperatives have canceled such shareholding mode and provided members with two kinds of members' shares, i.e., the transaction share and qualification share, with maximum and minimum limits. The shares could be transferred freely on the market. Such cooperatives also provide shares to non-members. However, the non-member shares entail no right to vote and their rewards also have maximum limit.

(4) In terms of distribution system. Part of the profits from traditional cooperative shall be reserved as inseparable public accumulation. Members would obtain limited rewards for their capital and be allocated with some of the public accumulation in accordance with the transaction amount between the members and the cooperative. While the new cooperatives usually do not reserve any public accumulation which represents a kind of property share with vague property right. They would return all the property of cooperative to members in accordance with the transaction amount, and members' rewards for capital have no limits any more. The cooperatives, without public accumulation, would ask their members to increase their investment in accordance with their proportion of transaction amount if they want to expand their operation scale.

(5) In terms of the orientation of businesses. The emerging cooperatives have changed the main service from producing and selling primary agricultural products to providing value added and increasing profits by manufacture of agricultural products so as to adapt to the intense market competition. Members must provide agricultural products to the cooperative in accordance with the transaction shares held by them. The cooperatives also have strict

requirements for quality. If a member fails to satisfy the quality and quantity requirements, the cooperatives would buy the products for the share from the market and include the expenses in the member's account. Also, members can transfer the right of transaction amount. In other words, such right of transaction amount has its value and negotiability.

The reforms have changed the basic system of traditional cooperative to a great extent. Therefore, some scholars also call the new mode as the "cooperative mode going beyond the classic". Through the reforms, the funds source, utilization efficiency and management system of cooperative have all been greatly improved and farmers' income and cooperative cohesion substantially enhanced.[7] In this way, cooperatives have gained the capability to better adapt to the increasingly developed and intense market competition and maintain their strong vitality in the market competition.

3. Legislative attitude of each country to the emerging cooperatives

In face of the highly effective reform of the cooperative and prosperity of new generation cooperatives, the legislation of the countries (mainly the North American countries) has showed positive response instead of indifference. The countries have actively modified relevant cooperative legislation and standardized the reform measures to ensure smooth operation of the reform and consolidate the reform results. Besides, they have further supported the reform fiscally and financially through financial subsidy and loan; and encouraged the community and other organizations of the community to provide effective support and assistance to the cooperative reform in terms of such soft environment as publicity and education.

To sum up, since the cooperative represents a product of market economic development, it has to develop itself with the development of market economy. Instead of concentrating on a classical mode, the cooperative shall develop itself in accordance with the location and time and improve the cooperative system. Also, the legal system of cooperative shall develop and improve itself along with the development and improvement of cooperative system.

14.3 THEORETICAL AND PRACTICAL BASIS OF RURAL COOPERATIVE SYSTEM IN CHINA

14.3.1 Theoretical Basis of Rural Cooperative Legal System in China

The relationship between the cooperative and "three agriculture-related problems" can be summarized with the viewpoint from the practical scholars represented by Wen Tiejun: the reason for the seriousness of current "three agriculture-related problems" lies in that the rural area lacks not only the science, technology and funds, but also the farmers' self-help organization carrying science, technology and funds, including the economic, cultural and social organization operated under low cost. Increasing farmers' material and spiritual benefits at low cost through certain self-help organization represents a basic channel for solving the "three agriculture-related problems" and realizing the care for people, social harmony and harmony between people and the nature.[8] The self-help organization here refers to the rural cooperative. To be specific:

1. From the perspective of economic function, rural cooperative represents an economic organization for strengthening farmers' competitiveness in market economy.

As mentioned above, after the reform of family-contract responsibility system, in the existing rural economy, the profits brought by the production mode of competing for market by individual household have reached certain limitation and showed the bottleneck effect. As the alliance of weak group, the cooperative aims at increasing the efficiency and decreasing the cost for farmers in the market economy, enhancing farmers' negotiation ability on the market and improving farmers' competitiveness on the market so that farmers can better adapt to the market economy, survive in the game rule of market economy, pinpoint their position in the market economy and benefit from the market economy.

2. From the perspective of social function, rural cooperative also represents a cultural and social organization that improves farmers' spiritual dilemma and provides farmers' spiritual benefits.

Firstly, as we all know, economic basis determines the superstructure. The spiritual demand is always related with the material conditions. The promotion and improvement of rural economy brought by the cooperative can bring about some satisfaction of spiritual demand. This represents the secondary effect of cooperative as an economic organization. Secondly, the cooperative also has its social nature. It can exist as non-economic social organization to satisfy the social, cultural and other demands from its members. This is because, as an organization, the cooperative can better increase the social and cultural information for its members through the scale advantage. Through the collective advantage of people, the cooperative organizes farmers to participate in certain entertainment activities. This has changed the situation of "complete isolation from each other all their lives" for farmers caused by the lack of interests' connection and rationalization of rural interpersonal relationship caused by the infiltration of market economy. The cooperative also makes it possible for farmers to organize certain spiritual and civilized activities to improve their own spiritual life, decrease the operation cost thanks to the scale effect of cooperative and enhance the operation efficiency.

3. From the perspective of policy environment, the establishment of cooperative also represents a demand for improving the two-tier management system that combines unified and decentralized operations in the rural area.

As is known to all, our rural area is currently implementing the two-tier management system that combines unified and decentralized operations and focusing on the household contract responsibility system. However, what we now see and what is actually implemented in rural area is the operation system of household contract responsibility system. This mainly represents the "unified operation" from the "combination of unified and decentralized operations". In other words, farmers are carrying out varied operation activities before, during and after the production by individual household and we rarely see the system of rural "unified operation". This firstly goes against our existing policy system and secondly represents the main cause for the low-efficiency of our existing rural operation system. As a matter of fact, in accordance with the characteristic of agricultural production and operation as well as the analysis of institutional economics, the agricultural production and operation mode featuring combination of unified and decentralized operations represents an optimized production and operation mode for realizing agricultural productivity effect. The specific analysis of system economics will be expounded in the following chapter. We need to change the existing single-tier mode of "decentralized operation without unified operation" and establish cooperatives so as to better realize the two-tier system featuring "combination of unified and decentralized operations" and optimization of agricultural operation system.

14.3.2 Practical Basis of Rural Cooperative System in China

1. Long history of our rural cooperative

(1) The development of cooperative in China before the founding of new China. The development of cooperative in China may be traced back to 1920s-1930s when China was still under the governance of the Republic of China (1912-1949).

The then self-sufficient natural economy of Chinese feudal society had started to collapse, the commercial economy in China had achieved certain development and urbanization and industrialization had all been launched. One may say that the then economic system could be counted as the market economy and farmers' weak position in the market economy had already showed. This constituted the economic condition. With the opening of Chinese gateway and the development of new cultural movements represented by the May 4th Movement, the western classical cooperative thoughts and system were all introduced to China. This constituted the thought and cultural condition. Because of these conditions, the rural cooperative as a kind of farmers' alliance emerged to protect farmers' interests in the market economy. *Jiangcun Village Economy*—a great work from Fei Xiaotong describes the operation conditions of a cooperative organization for Kaixiangong—a village from Jiangsu in that age, including the policy background and financial support of the then government to the cooperative organization, the role and position of the whole cooperative organization in the rural area, farmers' understanding to the cooperative organization, difficulties encountered by the cooperative organization, etc. From the book, we can see some evidences for the development conditions of cooperatives in China before the founding of new China.

Generally speaking, the development of the cooperative in China at that time may be deemed as staying at a filed exploration and experimental stage. It seems that the government had obviously realized the issue and given strong legislative and financial support. However, with the outbreak of the Anti-Japanese War in1937, the whole China was involved in the battlefield of World War II till the victory of the war and end of World War II in 1945. The war is just a comma on the great land of China since it is immediately followed by the war of liberation in China. Therefore, during the period from 1937 to the founding of new China, the war stopped normal development of rural China. It is only after 1949 that the cooperative began its new journey on Chinese land.

Since the Kuomintang government escaped to Taiwan after the war of liberation and brought about series of institutions and systems to Taiwan, the cooperative system in Taiwan after 1949 is developed based on the then existing foundation of 1920s-1930s on the great land of China. Therefore, when researching Taiwanese institutional system of cooperative, modern scholars usually start relevant research from period of 1920s-1930s and always say that "Taiwanese cooperatives have a development history of nearly one century".

(2) The cooperative system in the early days of founding of new China. After the founding of new China in 1949, primary cooperatives of agricultural production have been established all over China in 1950s. The primary cooperatives have modeled themselves on the classical cooperative system principles to different extents. In accordance with the regulations of the *Exemplary Charter of Agricultural Production Cooperative* issued on March 17, 1956, members have the freedom to join or withdraw from a cooperative as well as the right to vote, right to be elected, right to make suggestions, right to supervise, right to utilize the cooperative cause, right to receive the payment of labor and right to participate in the profit allocation of the land and other means of production. Meanwhile, members must perform varied obligations regulated by the Charter. The Exemplary Charter specifies that the primary cooperative would implement democratic management and one-person-one-vote system. The Charter has also provided regulations tallying with the cooperative principles and Chinese national conditions for the man-

agement organization, cooperative funds, cooperative distribution and the like of the primary cooperative. The Exemplary Charter has been implemented in general. This is most importantly represented by the fact that the primary cooperative recognizes the ownership and right to participate in profit allocation to the land and other means of production. However, only partial cooperation has been implemented and farmers could still reserve part of the independent management and sideline businesses besides the limited joint operation. Therefore, such primary cooperative belongs to the cooperative economy in real sense.

However, the development of cooperative has gone through a winding course in China which begins with advanced agricultural production cooperative. In accordance with the *Exemplary Charter of Advance Agricultural Production Cooperative* passed on the Third session of the first National People's Congress on June 30, 1956 (only three months and 13 days after the issuance of the exemplary charter of primary cooperative), Chinese agricultural cooperative has changed into collectivization: (1) "advanced agricultural production cooperative represents the socialist collective economy". Farmers joining the cooperative must change the main means of production like the land, farm animal and large farm tools into those collectively owned by the cooperative, and reserve only the private plot determined by population. (2) the cooperative implements unified management and collective labor. The part of farmer households' operation at the time of primary cooperative has also been canceled and family has become a living unit. (3) the cooperative comprehensively implements "distribution according to work", i.e., distribution by working days. Since the land and other means of production have been collectively owned by the cooperative, there exist no rights to participate in profit allocation any more. This is specified in the Charter and implemented in the practice. People's commune pushes such distortion to the extreme, leading to serious consequence. It is a mistake for China to replace cooperative system with collective system. The reason for China to make such mistake lies mainly in that the decision-making level thinks that there exists necessary connection between collective ownership and socialism, equates cooperative economy with collective economy and even socialism, and therefore regards the cooperative of collective system as the system and organizational form to change small-scale farmer economy and transit to higher form of public ownership. However, according to the proof by facts, it would be ineffective to simply change the ownership of means of production or organizational form of production without great development of social productivity in order to change the small-scale farmer economy. The people's commune that has been existed in rural China for over 20 years has failed not only to move towards the socialism but also to solve the issue of food and clothing for the people. Facts have declared the bankruptcy of the "small-scale farmer transformation theory" of left-leaning principle,[9] and demonstrated that the practice that features confusion of cooperative ownership went against the law of economic development.

(3) The development of rural cooperative in China after reform and opening-up. After the reform and opening-up, people's commune has been disassembled and household responsibility system started to be established. This has provided the possibility and opportunity for China to re-establish a true cooperative system. However, the system of and impact caused by people's commune has also deeply affected farmers. Farmers' impression on cooperative is still the abnormal cooperation system of "Great Leap Forward" and "Communal Pot". Many people associate the little food in hand to eat, low production efficiency and low living standard with the cooperative system. As a result, many farmers still turn pale at the mention of "cooperative" at present. It may be seen that the negative impact of the intensified training type of cooperative before the reform and opening-up still exist to a large extent, and farmers, as the victim of the abnormal cooperative system, still have the reaction of "extremely frightened person". As a result, the establishment of cooperative system of real sense still stays at a stagnation stage.

However, with the deepening of reform and opening-up and further development of market economy, farmers' weak position in the market economy has become more and more outstanding and even more serious. It has become a puzzle for the theoretical and practical circles to solve. As a result, the cooperative system started to re-enter into people's mind. Not a few people of insight have called for the "return" of cooperative system in real sense. Therefore, farmers from not a few places have begun the experiments and practices for the cooperative of real sense under spontaneous organization or advocacy by socially influential scholars and other people. A typical example of the self-organized cooperative is the cooperatives establish by farmers from such coastal districts as Shandong and Jiangsu, and that of the cooperative organized under the influence of certain people is the rural cooperative established under the assistance from the scholars for the "three agriculture-related problems" represented by Wen Tiejun in such places as Lankao.

In accordance with the data of several eastern provinces and municipalities, the standard cooperatives have truly "recovered" the identity union of the cooperative owner and user (patronage), and adopted "Rochdale" as the reference system and voluntary and open membership, democratic management, return of surpluses, limitation on dividend as the basic principles. Therefore, they belong to the cooperatives of classical sense. Moreover, since 1990s, there have also emerged some cooperatives whose principles and forms are different from those of traditional cooperatives in such places as Zhejiang. The cooperatives feature the system arrangement and development trend of "new generation cooperatives".

In general, the establishment of our current rural cooperative system is still at the start-up phase. Most of the farmers' cooperatives feature low level, small scale, low strength, loose structure, irregular management, weak market competitiveness and lack of legal protection. If our economic growth and technical progress after the reform and opening-up have greatly narrowed the gap between China and the developed country, the development of our farmers' cooperative economic organization would be really slow and fall far behind the development pace and requirements of market economic development, and would even be impossible to match the development situation of the cooperative organizations from other countries.

2. The establishment of rural cooperative represents the realistic choice of social development for rural China

As we all know, Chinese reform begins with the rural area which has taken the lead in implementing the household contract responsibility system and breaking through the constraint of planned economy. Therefore, our agricultural productivity has been greatly liberated and agricultural production reaped great harvest for many consecutive years. By 1984, the grain output has reached the peak of 400 billion kilograms and initially solved the issue of food and clothing. In those years, farmers have achieved independence and material benefits and realized great improvement of their life. The gap between urban and rural areas has been narrowed. China has proposed the second step of reform in rural area at that time. However, with the establishment and development of market, farmers' status as weak group has become increasingly obvious in the market economy and the issues of rural area and agriculture also increasingly outstanding. Meanwhile, the gaps between urban and rural areas also become increasingly wide rather than narrow. As a result, there emerge the "three agriculture-related problems" of poor villages, miserable farmers and dangerous agriculture which represent the important issues perplexing successive governments and the primary problem that needs to be solved for realizing a moderately prosperous society.

The existing production mode of single household in rural area represents a kind of relatively traditional work way of intensive cultivation. With the implementation of the household contract responsibility system, the advantages of the production mode have showed up and production efficiency under such mode been greatly enhanced. However, the advantages of such production mode are limited after all. Within several years after the reform and opening-up, such advantages have totally showed up and the production efficiency reached its peak without new breakthrough. As a result, there emerged the bottleneck issue for increasing productivity and farmers' economic conditions can be called as "surplus for basic food and clothing, but insufficient for moderate prosperity". While the urban residents become richer and richer with the deepening of reform and development of market economy, by comparison, the farmers become poorer and poorer and occupy smaller and smaller proportion of social resources. As a result, the gap between urban and rural areas become wider and wider. Therefore, developing rural economy and increasing farmers' income has become an important issue for establishing a moderately prosperous society, realizing comprehensive and coordinated development of urban and rural areas and constructing a harmonious society.

As a matter of fact, when we are saying that villages are really poor and farmers really miserable today, it doesn't mean that today's farmers are poorer or more miserable than those in other historic periods. Today, farmers' poverty and misery mostly refers to the poverty and misery after satisfying the basic food and clothing requirements, the poverty and misery of "short on cash but enough for basic food and clothing", and the poverty and misery with labor intensity much less and living standard much higher than that in the period of people's commune.[10] Therefore, such poverty and misery are based on basic food and clothing and comparative as far as urban residents are concerned. Moreover, with the development and progress of the society, the "Engel's Index" for residents' living consumption should have been decreased continuously, other material enjoyment beyond the basic food and clothing been enriched constantly and taken up increasing proportion in total residents' consumption. However, farmers' life can only stay at the existing bottleneck stage without effective breakthrough. With the development of mass media as well as the convenience and diversification of information exchange, urban residents' increasingly improved living conditions have provided farmers with more understanding and comparison opportunities. Under such circumstance, farmers' feeling of "paleness by comparison" has become more serious and led to their spiritual "misery" which is difficult to be communicated, eased or transferred because of farmers' single household production mode. Of course, such spiritual "misery" also originates from the economic gap as well as the gap between urban and rural areas.

Meanwhile, with the influence of market economy on rural areas, farmers' pursuit for their own interests has become more and more obvious. In order to become rich, farmers started to "show their special prowess like the eight immortals cross the sea in the Chinese myth". Some started to work part-time in urban area, some work on subsidiary businesses, some establish township enterprises in virtue of their advantage as home town of overseas Chinese and other advantages. . . As a result, the "acquaintance society" constructed by the clan relation based on blood relationship as written by Fei Xiaotong showed some change too. Under Chinese traditions, the society regards ethics as the standard. In Fei Xiaotong's words, our society represents a society of differential pattern, in which, each traditional Chinese is surrounded by layers of human relations. Such relations are imposed on each people by blood relationship rather than chosen by people themselves. The "differential pattern" is self-centered. In such pattern, one's relationships with other people are not a straight line on the same plane. Rather, it is like the ripples produced after throwing a pebble into water which spread by circles and become less distinct at further distance. This represents the basic characteristic of Chinese social structure. Such relations still had many expressions in rural China before the reform and opening-up. Therefore, there are always scholars who describe rural China as an "acquaintance society". However, it would be one-sided rather than comprehensive and even incorrect and subjective to describe today's rural China in this way as the differential pattern is now changing with the filtration of market economy into rural economy. The communication and exchange among people are more and more related with interests rather than simple clan ethic relationship. Interests have become an important weight for determining the distance of relationship. As a result, rationality began to enter into varied aspects of farmers' life gradually; official relations showed more milk of human kindness and non-official relations revealed more rationality. Yang Shanhua and Hou Hongrui regard the phenomenon as the rationality of "differential pattern". However, He Xuefeng thinks that the differential pattern in rural China has collapsed, and the role of family, especially the clan system represented by clan regulations has disappeared. Typical examples of such phenomenon include the disassembly of family, rapid fading of traditional customs and rites, extensive existence and relative-orientation of friendship, increasing importance of affinity, selective exchange among relatives, estrangement of fraternity, increasingly serious issue of provision for the aged in rural area, rational consideration for bearing children, division of property and residential place between parents and children, etc. The interpersonal relationship in rural area has been totally rationalized.

The rationalization of interpersonal relationship in rural area has become an indisputable fact. However, the differential pattern hasn't totally disappeared. The traditional ethical thought is affecting farmers' idea and clan relation in rural areas influencing farmers' life more or less. The rationalization of interpersonal relationship would become increasingly extensive and continuously infiltrate and affect farmers' life and production. However, the influence of acquaintance society would not disappear quickly. Therefore, as far as the interpersonal relations are concerned, it is appropriate to describe today's rural area as a semi-acquaintance society, in which, the close relationship among people in an acquaintance society has broken up on one side, but a highly market-oriented "stranger society" with highly refined division of labor hasn't been actually formed on the other hand. In such semi-acquaintance society, the labor of single family has difficulty to resist the market risk and the production relationship among families needs a kind of bond for connection. The cooperative represents exactly an appropriate choice of such bond.

14.4 NECESSITY AND FEASIBILITY OF RURAL COOPERATIVE LEGAL SYSTEM IN CHINA

14.4.1 Necessity of Rural Cooperative Legal System in China

First, establishing cooperative legal system represents an agricultural policy for implementing the two-tier management system featuring combination of unified and decentralized operations which is a good agricultural operating system. However, because of its abstraction, although the "decentralized operation" may be realized through the existing household contract management system, the specific mode of "unified operation" has no existing template for reference. It's no wonder that the "unified operation" of agriculture has always been in blank and chaotic state. Besides, the operation system stays only on the level of policy and has neither specific implementation system nor safeguards of judicial power. As a result, the reasonable two-tier management system featuring combination of unified and decentralized operations stays just on the level of slogan. As a matter of fact, although the two-tier management system that combines unified and decentralized operations has been promoted for years, the system stays mostly on the level of the single-tier operating mode of "household contract responsibility system". Therefore, it is extremely urgent to establish the legal system of rural cooperative in China.

Second, establishing cooperative legal system can guide the cooperative system to be established well. One of the social functions of law is to guide. Since the existing cooperative system is still at an exploration stage, a set of relatively complete laws would undoubtedly become a good guide for establishing the system. Some people may wonder whether this would be contradictory with the hysteresis quality of the law. The answer is negative. It is true that the law, as the superstructure of the society, is established based on the generalization and abstraction of cooperative practices, and then starts to guide the cooperative practices in turn. However, to Chinese current situation, we can't wait for exploration from the beginning and then formulate corresponding legal system after abstraction. Nor can we go against the law to create a set of cooperative legal systems out of nothing. The practice and exploration of our cooperative system, abstraction of cooperative rules as well as foreign and domestic cooperative movements have made the preparatory work for us. What we need to do is to research the existing cooperative systems carefully and then borrow and transfer the essence of these systems in a reserved and creative manner after investigating and analyzing Chinese conditions. This can both help us avoid the unnecessary winding course and overcome the hysteresis issue of law well.

Third, establishing cooperative legal system represents a requirement for standardizing the cooperative system and strengthening the legal safeguard for effective operation of cooperative system. The law, as a kind of social standard, undoubtedly has played certain standardization role for the existing system. The reason that the law represents a kind of effective and common standardization system lies in that a country always provides series of measures for safeguarding effective implementation of the law, which are mainly represented by the safeguard of judicial power to the implementation of law and, without exception, to the cooperative system.

Lastly, establishing cooperative legal system represents a requirement for our legal construction. Our legal construction is to ensure that all social work is implemented effectively and orderly under legal standardization and make the law the basic standard of varied work. The rural cooperative system would become a basic system for the agricultural operation in rural China. Therefore, it would also be necessary to establish a legal system as the basic principles for standardization.

14.4.2 Feasibility of Rural Cooperative Legal System in China

1. Institutional economics analysis for establishing rural cooperative system in China

While researching the system design, the institutional economics mainly researches the expectancy from the subject of the system on the potential profit brought about by the system, the consumption of the system subject's system operating cost as well as their influence on the system subject's choice to the whole system and internal organization of the system. Therefore, the first issue the institutional economics needs to solve is the choice issue of the system, i.e., the issue of whether it is necessary to introduce the whole system. To solve the issue is to research the earnings that could be brought about by the whole system itself for the system subject, the cost required for operating the system as well as whether the system subject can pay the cost and has the willingness to pay such cost for the earnings. As a matter of fact, the issue is to let the system subject weigh the balance of cost and earnings. Of course, as the economic man under market economy, as long as the earnings are higher than the cost, i.e., the operation of a system can bring about earnings for the subject, the system would generally be able to operate. If the operation cost of a system is higher than or equal to the earnings that could be brought about by the system, there would be issue for the operation of the system, and it would be necessary to re-consider the existence or cancellation of the system.

Under the market economy, enterprises represent the most basic activity subject. Enterprises, as a kind of integrated system arrangement, can bring about economies of scale by their scale operation, decrease the transaction cost on market, internalize the external cost and exchange the internal management cost for the transaction cost on market. When the marginal increase of management cost caused by expansion of the enterprise scale is equal to the marginal decrease of the transaction cost on market saved, the enterprises would stop to expand their scale and the enterprise scale and market scale would be in balance.

However, not all production and operation modes are suitable for the integration system of enterprises. The agricultural production and operation represents one of such modes unsuitable for the integration system of enterprises. This is determined by the characteristics of agricultural production itself. The enterprise mode of integration would bring about economies of scale however at the cost of management expenses. The reason for the effective operation of enterprise system lies exactly in that the management expenses are lower than the economies of scale brought about by the operation mode. However, if agricultural production needs to apply such mode, its internal management cost, especially the supervision cost for labor, would be extremely high, and even equal to or higher than the economies of scale brought about by such integrated operation. The reason is that the most basic characteristic of agricultural production is the mingling of natural and economic reproduction. The labor subject of agricultural production is the living animal and plant organisms. The laborer needs to have strong responsibility and love and care for the labor object. The inconsistency among the seasonality of agricultural production, production time of plants and animals as well as people's labor time asks the flexibility and independence of labor employment time from the laborer.[11] Moreover, the agricultural production period is long and production results could be measured only through the terminal products. It would be difficult to implement precise measurement and pay the remuneration for the labor process. Therefore, unified scale operation would definitely bring about large space to loaf on the job for the laborer. This would require large amount of costs for the supervision of the laborers. And the geographical decentralization of agricultural production would definitely increase the difficulty and cost for the supervision too. The risks are unbearable for the agriculture under the dual pressure of natural and market risks. Meanwhile, there also exists the supervision issue for the supervisors themselves, i.e., the supervision over the supervisors to ensure normal operation of the supervision system. This would also require costs. This also represents the institutional economics reason for the rare success of the production cooperative of the agricultural cooperative in the world. Therefore, the agriculture of most countries still implements the operation mode of single farmer household. In this way, farmers have become the surplus claimant of agricultural production. Because of the high consistency of the household members' interests, good coordination, self-discipline and self-supervision become possible and loafing on the job changes into the internal cost of farmer household production. Under such circumstance, the supervision cost for agricultural production and operation becomes zero. The characteristic of agricultural production happens to have provided favorable position for the use of the system arrangement of quasi-integration like cooperative since the cooperative exactly involves no agricultural mid-production. On the contrary, the cooperative mainly provides system arrangement of scale before and after the agricultural production and bring about economies of scale. And the operation cost of the two links, i.e., links before and after production, unlike the agricultural mid-production link, require high supervision cost. This represents exactly the reason why the supply and marketing cooperative is the most successful and influential. Of course, it is not true that the cooperative system plays absolutely no role for the mid-production process of agricultural operation. The system could still play certain role in the supporting links like the technology, information and service. Therefore, the two-tier management system that combines unified and decentralized operations represents the operating mode that is the most suitable for agricultural production. Of course, the "unified operation" is before and after the production and "decentralized operation" during the production. The latter has been implemented by our family contract responsibility system and the former needs to be implemented by establishing rural cooperative system.

After solving the preliminary issue of whether to choose rural cooperative system, the key issue that institutional economics needs to deal with immediately is the property right issue of cooperative. The institutional economics asks for clear property right. Specifically, the clearness of property right for the cooperative system asks for clear definition for the property right system of cooperative. This also includes two aspects: (1) the owner of the property right of the cooperative, i.e., the obligee of the cooperative and the people with the right to benefit from the operation of the cooperative; (2) the issue of who will pay the operating cost for the cooperative in what way. An important reason for the failure of the abnormal cooperative in China before reform and opening-up lies in the failure to make certain the property right system of the cooperative. Such cooperative simply specifies the property of the cooperative established by farmers in a unified manner as collectively-owned rather than clearly defines the connotation of collective which has become an abstract concept. The absence of real obligee has led to the absence of the owner under national guidance and superior instruction, and even to the confusion between collectively-owned and state-owned. Therefore, there existed the understanding confusion and misunderstanding of the cooperative nature for a long time. However, the operating cost of the cooperative is paid by all members in the form of equalitarianism. The non-equivalence of rights and obligations featuring unclear subject of earnings and subject equalization of costs has severely damaged farmers' enthusiasm in the cooperative and determined the destiny that such cooperative could not normally and effectively operate among farmers and could only survive difficultly in virtue of the coercive power of the government. Therefore, the abnormal system has immediately been abandoned after the reform and opening-up.

Therefore, normal operation of the cooperative system requires a clear property right system. The earnings and costs of the cooperative require clear subjects and need to be reflected and distributed among the subjects fairly and reasonably.

2. Analysis on farmers' cooperative ability

Rural cooperative represents a private subject under the market economy and a self-governance organization established by farmers through voluntary manner. It requires the trust and cooperation among farmers through the manner of contract, i.e., farmers' cooperative ability. This represents the subject element required by the cooperative.

As to the issue of farmers' cooperative ability, it is necessary to carry out intensive empirical research for farmers' current situation in rural area. One may say that *China besides the Yellow River* is the most wonderful and salable book that is published recently and related with research and investigation in rural area. Cao Jinqing, the author, spent a year in the rural area of Henan besides the Yellow River. Of the issues that have been researched by him, the one featuring the deepest feeling and thought is the issue of cooperative ability for the farmers besides the Yellow River. Mr. Cao has realized that, even in case of urgent needs for larger and more creative cooperation beyond the traditional scope, small farmers would still act in accordance with traditional manner: restoring the alliance among relatives or the organizational form of patriarchal clan, or introducing the relative principle to the internal of the private or collective enterprises. Therefore, Mr. Cao signed with emotion in the end that Chinese farmers are "good at separation rather than cooperation". He Xuefeng shows more pessimism to farmers' cooperative ability in his *New Rural China.* In the village of Jingmen investigated by him, the patriarchal clan organizations have all been disassembled; most of the road and public welfare establishments in the village received little attention from people; abnormal death of the aged was common and mostly caused by unfilial children. The reason lies in that the law has the difficulty to intervene in such trivial matters as family provision and the originally-existing pressure from public opinion in rural area has already been disintegrated. For example, a cow may be used for the cultivation by three farmer households. However, due to the lack of cooperation, each household needs to raise a cow. As to the so-called large farm implements in the most urgent need of cooperation in traditional Chinese society like the modern mechanical tools, if purchased by single household, the utilization efficiency would be too low and price too high. However, contradictions would always emerge in case of cooperative purchase. As a result, in current village of Jingmen, each household has similar simple farm implements. All or none of the households have or has the large farm implements. The cooperative purchase by several households, even by several blood brothers, is quite rare. In other words, in the village of Jingmen, modern cooperative ability hasn't been established and traditional cooperative way has been disintegrated. Farmers' production and operation are based on the unit of household.[12]

As a matter of fact, with the development and influence of market economy, rural China has changed from a traditional "acquaintance" society with ethics as the base into a "semi-acquaintance" society, the differential pattern has been changed gradually, people's relationship has been comprehensively rationalized, and interests have become an important factor affecting the interpersonal relationship in rural areas. However, such rationalization hasn't reached the level of "civil society" and the influence of traditional ethic clan relationship hasn't completely disappeared. Therefore, such society can only be called as a "semi-acquaintance" society. This has exactly provided good subject elements for establishing the rural cooperative system:

First, the traditional ethic relationship hasn't been completely disintegrated or disappeared. The blood, marriage and geographical relationship as well as the trust among friends still exist within certain scope. In this way, after signing a modern contract, farmers could decrease their transaction costs because of such trust and increase their cooperative profits from other perspectives. This can also explain the secret for the success of Chinese family enterprises to certain extent.

Second, because of the rationalization of interpersonal relationship, although our society hasn't realized the state of western "civil society", people's relationship is all maintained by a contractual manner featuring consultation on the basis of equality. However, with common goal and requirement of interests, the rationalized farmers would completely have the possibility to act and cooperate based on a contract featuring equality so as to realize their interests' goal. Of course, it is just a possibility. To turn the possibility into reality, an impetus is required just like the law of physics—the impact of an external force is required to change an object from static state to state of motion. In terms of this, the author shares the same conclusion of viewpoint with Cao Jingqing: Mr. Cao also advocates introducing the cooperative organizations and principles beyond the traditional to the villages and farmers through external force. He asserted that "the contractual organization established through consultation on the basis of equality represents the most effective and powerful means for the independent small farmers under the contract system to finally get rid of the poverty and backwardness, the invasion and harassment of natural disaster, exploitation and oppression from local corrupt officials and market risks."

However, the "impetus" for our country needs to be stronger since the "shadow" of abnormal cooperative before the reform and opening-up hasn't been completely dropped away and the effect of "extremely frightened person" still exists. This has also demonstrated to certain extent that the establishment of our cooperative system faces greater difficulty and requires more caution. Also, such external force is a reasonable and complete cooperative legal system. In other words, we would guide the establishment of cooperative through legal policies and safeguard the operation of cooperative through the coercive force of law.

3. The support of the existing rural land system and village self-governance system to the establishment of cooperative system

First, since the cooperative ownership is a kind of ownership by all members, and the land, as the primary means of production for agricultural production, is not owned by farmers in our current villages, would the ownership or requirement for clear property right for the cooperative be affected? The answer is negative since as a kind of quasi-integrated operating mode, the cooperative mainly plays its role before and after rather than during the production. It is enough for the existing rural land system to ensure farmers complete ownership to the harvest of the crops. The complete ownership and right to transfer for the land is not indispensable for the operation of the cooperative. Therefore, such worrisome is needless. Second, in accordance with Article 111 of *Constitution*, the villagers committee is a self-governance organization organized by the grass-roots masses from rural areas in nature. However, it has "deteriorated" into the agent of the grass-roots government in actual operation process. Therefore, as a new type of self-governance organization, would the cooperative tread the heel of villagers committee and become deteriorated? We cannot totally deny such possibility. However, would it be like "giving up eating for fear of choking" to give up such system for fear of such future uncertainty? Meanwhile, some people also think that the establishment of rural cooperative would threaten the position and even existence of villagers committee. The argument is too much like shocking statement attracting attention. As a matter of fact, the cooperative and villagers committee basically have "no interference with each other" since the former mainly represents an economic organization (though with certain social functions at the same time) and the latter a political organization from the perspective of labor division. Moreover, the promotion for rural economy and improvement for the construction of rural spiritual civilization of the cooperative may change the existing strained relations between the villagers committee and villagers to a certain extent.

14.5 LEGISLATION OF RURAL COOPERATIVE SYSTEM IN CHINA

14.5.1 Legislation of Rural Cooperative System Before Founding of New China

As mentioned above, the cooperative has realized its primary development in the Republic of China in 1920s-1930s and the then government has also provided high attention and support. On legal aspect, the government issued the *Cooperative Law* on March 1st, 1934 which was put into enforcement in 1935. Besides, the government has also formulated a series of laws and regulations like the *Rules for Enforcing Cooperative Law* in 1935, *Memorandum of Association for Different Levels of County Cooperatives* in 1940, *Measures for Organizing Cooperative Factory* in 1945 and *Measures for Establishing Cooperative Farm* in 1946. The emergence and enforcement of the laws and regulations have provided the basic legal system for the cooperative.

Thereafter, the laws haven't been enforced well because of the war, especially in mainland China. However, the laws have been brought to Taiwan later and become the blueprint and basis for the cooperative legal system in Taiwan. Currently, the whole cooperative legal system in Taiwan is established on the basis of such laws and regulations.

14.5.2 Legislation of Rural Cooperative System at Beginning of New China

After the foundation of new China, in order to reconstruct the rural economic system, re-establish the cooperative system and send the cooperative to the right track in the ruins of war, under Liu Shaoqi's direct leadership and Bo Yibo's presidency, the *Cooperative Law of People's Republic of China (Draft)* was drafted and later discussed and passed on the first representative assembly of national cooperative workers in July of 1950. After that, Liu Shaoqi carefully studied the draft for several times and personally modified more than 40 points of the draft. The draft, with about 10,000 words, includes six chapters and 37 articles in total, including the general provisions and provisions for the grass-roots cooperative, different levels of cooperative associations and registration as well as the supplementary provisions. Liu submitted the draft and *Measures for Registering Cooperatives in People's Republic of China* to the Central government and each department on October 24, 1950. However, because of varied factors, the draft was not officially publicized or enforced in the end. Nevertheless, the draft provided detailed regulations for the specific legal system of cooperative and therefore represents an important literature in the law-making history for the cooperative in

China with great significance and reference value for current theoretical research and legislative improvement of cooperatives.

Thereafter, the *Constitution of the People's Republic of China* formulated on the First Session of the First National People's Congress on September 20, 1954 stipulated that "the cooperative ownership refers to the collective ownership of the working masses", and started since then the history of equating the cooperative economy with the collective economy and confusing the two kinds of economy.

14.5.3 Legislation of Rural Cooperative System in China at Present Stage

Since China is now implementing the "one country, two systems" policy, our existing cooperative legal system has also showed diversification state. There exist regional differences between the legal system in Mainland and that of Hong Kong, Macao and Taiwan.

The cooperative legislation in Taiwan represents an extension of the cooperative legislation of old China. As mentioned above, it directly quotes corresponding cooperative legislation of old China and implements further revision and improvement based on the legislation of old China. A good example is the "items need to be improved for relevant organization issues of credit cooperative" in 1975. Taiwan has now formed relatively complete standardized system of cooperative law, provided suitable legal form for safeguarding smooth operation of rural cooperative system and offered sufficient legal bases for the development of varied kinds of cooperative causes in Taiwan.

The cooperative law currently executed in Hong Kong is the *Cooperative Regulations* revised in the middle of 1980s, which consists of 11 parts and 59 articles in total and aims at regulating the management for the establishment and operation of the cooperative. Basic contents of the *Co-operative Societies Ordinance* include the general provisions, provisions for the registration; responsibility and privilege of the cooperative; members' right and obligation; registration of the property and funds of the cooperative; audit, reference and inquiry; dissolution; compensation and detention; dispute; rules, miscellaneous, etc. When Hong Kong returned to China and became a special administrative region of China in 1997, in accordance with Article 8 of the *Basic Law for Hong Kong Special Administrative Region of People's Republic of China*, "the original laws of Hong Kong, namely the common law, equity law, supplementary legislation and customary law, should be reserved except for those go against the regulations hereunder or those have been revised by the legislative body of Hong Kong Special Administrative Region." Therefore, the status of Hong Kong cooperative cannot be ignored.[13]

As to the cooperative legislation in mainland China after the reform and opening-up, with the reform of economic system, the cooperative economy has been paid more attention and legislation for rural cooperative been placed on the agenda again. As a result, there emerged a series of ministry and commission rules and local regulations like the *Temporary Provisions for Farmer Shareholding Cooperative Enterprises* issued in 1990 by the Ministry of Agriculture. Some provinces and municipalities including Beijing, Shanghai, Chongqing, Shenzhen, Jinan, Wuhan, Hebei, Hubei, Liaoning and Yunnan have issued local rules and regulations successively to guide and promote the development of cooperative economy. We should admit that our cooperative legislation has realized significant achievements. However, the low level of scattered legislation is far from satisfying the development of cooperative economy. It has become an expectation of the masses to introduce a cooperative code. According to the statistics from the Office of Legislative Affairs of the Head Office of National Supply and Marketing Cooperative, since 1995, the Head Office of National Supply and Marketing Cooperative and other authorities have continuously put forward ten times of legislative suggestions in total to the National People's Congress and State Council. Finally, in December of 2003, the Tenth Standing Committee of the National People's Congress listed the *Farmers' Cooperative Economic Organization Law* in its legislative plan and as a legal draft that should be prepared after research and arranged for deliberation at a mature time within its five-year tenure. Thus, Chinese rural cooperative legislation was officially included in the legislative progress.

Of course, introducing a set of cooperative code is not a thing that could be realized overnight. We also need relevant laws and regulations to provide legal support for the development of cooperative system in the process. For example, the *Opinions on Supporting and Promoting the Development of Farmers' Specialized Cooperative Organization* issued by the Ministry of Agriculture on May 15 2005 represents a good legal support of this kind.

14.6 SETTING UP A COOPERATIVE SYSTEM FITTING FOR RURAL AREA IN CHINA

14.6.1 Major Problems in Setting Up of Rural Cooperative Legal System in China

1. Great difficulty to start the establishment of a cooperative legal system

Currently, the development of our cooperative is still at the start-up stage. However, the start-up stage does not begin with "zero". Since the negative impact of the abnormal cooperative history before the reform and opening-up still has deep imprint on many people's mind, many people still have misunderstanding to the real cooperative system. Therefore, in a certain sense, the start-up stage begins with "minus". One important role for establishing cooperative legal system is to guide the establishment of cooperative. However, to start from scratch to establish a cooperative needs a motive power. And in today's China, the motive power needs to be stronger and more powerful. Therefore, the historical mission of cooperative legal system may be described as "there is still a long way to go".

2. Confusion of cooperative system and collective system

This also represents an issue of long history that may be traced back to the *Constitution* of 1954, which defines the cooperative ownership in the following manner: the cooperative ownership refers to the collective ownership by the working masses. Since then, our cooperative ownership and collective ownership have had indissoluble bond. All constitutions after that, including the current constitution, namely the *Constitution* of 1982, have confused the cooperative ownership and collective ownership. Article 8 of the *Constitution* stipulates that the varied forms of cooperative economies like the production, supply and marketing, credit and consumption in rural areas are collectively owned by the socialist labor masses. This goes against the basic characteristic that the cooperative is collectively owned by the members as laborers, and has great harm: to the external, this has interfered with the status of the cooperative as a complete private subject of market economy; to the internal, this has also brought about great disadvantage for internal management of the cooperative. As our collective ownership is related with an abstract collective, there emerge the phenomenon of absence of owners. The collective ownership has become the excuse for the command similar to the superior instruction in the state-owned institutions or has been manipulated by internal management personnel and become a tool for the personnel to seek for personal gains. This has been well verified in the period of people's commune and left us with profound historic lessons. Based on this, the current rural cooperative legislation must clarify the relationship between the two. This would require further revision of our constitution.

14.6.2 Major Problems to be Solved in Setting Up of Rural Cooperative Legal System in China

1. On a macro level, establishing a cooperative legal system suitable for the rural status quo needs to solve the following issues:

(1) It is necessary to make necessary revision to Article 8 of the applicable Constitution which is about the relationship between cooperative ownership and collective ownership so as to provide constitutional bases for the legislation of the cooperative.

(2) Formulate a high-rank cooperative code. The low level, decentralization and mess of existing legislation desperately asks for a set of code with

general validity all around the whole country which shall be a comprehensive basic law so as to determine the common basic cooperative system of varied forms and patterns through legal form. While the specific systems for specific type of specialized cooperative may be determined through legal form when it is necessary and the conditions are mature after formulating corresponding administrative laws and regulations based on the basic law.

(3) While implementing the cooperative legislation, it is necessary to learn the historic lessons of people's commune and "radically reform" the cooperative, i.e., establish a cooperative system of real sense. Of course, this mainly represents the establishment of classical cooperative system. Besides this, we also need to learn the successful experience of new generation cooperatives from the North American countries to avoid the disadvantages brought about by the traditional cooperative or save twists and turns of our cooperative system.

(4) Pay attention to coordinate the relationship between our cooperative law and the cooperative laws of Hong Kong, Macao and Taiwan. Because of the implementation of the "one country, two systems" policy, the legal system difference between mainland China and the three regions would not disappear in short period. However, because of the frequent economic exchange and increasing blending economic life between mainland China and the three regions, relevant economic systems are also converging gradually. Therefore, it is necessary to take into account the factor while formulating relevant laws.

2. From a microscopic point of view, in order to establish a cooperative legal system suitable for the current situation of our rural area, it is necessary to pay attention to solve the following issues:

(1) Establishing the status of a legal person for rural cooperative. According to the above analysis, the cooperative represents a legal body of mass organization from the category of private legal person, and a third type of legal person different from the profit-making or public-welfare legal person. However, since our civil legislation abandons the classification of legal body of mass organization and legal body of financial group and adopts the classification of enterprise legal person and social-organization legal person like the government departments and public institutions, there emerge the difficulty for the registration of cooperative: the cooperative is classified either as the enterprise legal person and therefore couldn't enjoy varied kinds of tax preferences, or as institution legal person and therefore couldn't carry out the profit-making activities or provide the service for its members. Another scenario is that the cooperative has difficulty to be registered. This has led to the result that the cooperative, as a legal subject that could originally have had free access in the market economy and enjoyed varied types of preferential policies, become an "unregistered household" of market economy and couldn't even enjoy the basic "sunshine, rain and dew". This has played a

"red card" for smooth development of cooperative from the source and led to great disadvantage for the development of rural cooperative economic organization.

Therefore, for the cooperative legislation to be implemented, it is necessary to, based on the understanding of the dual nature of economy and society of the cooperative, overcome the disadvantage of the existing classification of legal person and provide reasonable and correct legal orientation for the cooperative so that farmers can have legal status of "legal person" while competing on the market and the cooperative can see the sunshine, rain and dew once more and enjoy its due and deserved treatment.

(2) Establishing the main principles of cooperative. The legislation for the rural cooperative shall adhere to the basic principles of cooperative (mainly the principles established by the International Cooperative Alliance in 1995), highlight its own emphases based on the characteristics of Chinese society, learn from the successful reform experience of the developed countries for the cooperative and deal with well the hysteresis quality of the law to the cooperative system. This section will mainly discuss the three principles of cooperative:

The first is the principle of voluntary membership. As the common principle of the cooperative laws of varied countries and common ground of varied cooperative schools, the principle implies the basic meaning that members' membership is totally determined by the members' individual will and free from any coercion or interference from any external force. However, the principle has its special significance in China as at the beginning of the foundation of new China, our country has forced farmers to join the cooperative through the means of administrative compelling order or pressure from public opinion created in the society, which seriously violated the principle and initiated the abnormality of the cooperative system at that time.

What needs special attention is that the principle of voluntary membership includes the freedom of not only joining but also withdrawing from the cooperative. This is quite important. This represents an important lesson not only from the abnormal cooperative at the beginning of the foundation of new China but also the three years of crisis during 1959-1961. Lin Yifu interprets the crisis from the perspective of the mechanism for the freedom to join and withdraw from the cooperative rather than the perspective of natural disaster or man-made calamity. In his opinion, it is a game to join and withdraw from the cooperative. He interprets the issue from the perspective of game theory: because of the difficulty of agricultural production supervision, the success of agricultural cooperation or collective farm can only depend on certain agreement of "self-implementation" among the cooperative members. Under such agreement, each member undertakes to provide the same effort as that on his own farm. However, such agreement of self-implementation can sustain only under the circumstance of repeated game. If members have the freedom to withdraw from the cooperative, the cooperative would be regarded as possessing the nature of repeated game. However, if the members' freedom to withdraw from the cooperative is deprived, the cooperative would be deemed as possessing the nature of "one-time game". In the movement of people's commune after 1958, members' freedom to withdraw from the cooperative has been deprived. As a result, the agreement of "self-implementation" couldn't sustain any more, and people's enthusiasm for labor and production rate have all greatly decreased. Thus, there emerged a crisis.[14]

Therefore, in understanding the principle of voluntary membership, it is necessary to master the dual meanings of joining the cooperative voluntarily and withdrawing from the cooperative freely.

The second is the democratic principle which represents not only the cornerstone of the cooperative principles of each country but also the marks that distinct the cooperative as an economically democratic organization from other economic organizations.

In traditional cooperatives, in accordance with the democratic principle, the establishment and operation of the internal organizations of the cooperative should conform to the democratic requirements and separate the functions of decision-making, implementation and supervision. In the meantime, it is necessary to request that the generation of cooperative management personnel is based on democratic election and the cooperative members enjoy full rights to elect and to be elected. As to the right to elect, each cooperative member, regardless of his/her gender, ethnic, religious belief and quantity of the cooperative shares held by them, shall have and only have one vote. As to the right to be elected, the cooperative characteristics of self-help, self-governance and self-accountability request that the management personnel can only be elected from the cooperative members. However, with the development of the market economy and increasing demand on the cooperative profitability, we may learn from the practices of new generation cooperatives to permit the linking between members' right to vote and their investment amount under certain conditions and with certain quota limit. Meanwhile, in the cooperatives with certain scale and high level of specialization, it is possible to appropriately introduce specialized cooperative management personnel to enhance the management efficiency and decrease the management cost.

The last principle that deserves emphasis is the principle of distribution self-governance. The principle means that within legal scope, the distribution mode of the cooperative for the cooperative surpluses can be regulated and defined on the general meeting of members and through the articles of association for the cooperative, and that no other organization or individual can interfere or participate in the surplus distribution of the cooperative. This is compatible with the basic principles of "self-organization, self-governance and self-benefiting" for the cooperative. It has also provided more "self-governance" space to the new generation and traditional cooperatives to resolve the difference of whether withdrawing and retaining indivisible public accumulation. The cooperatives may make their independent choices in accordance with their own scale, characteristic, goal and other specific conditions.

(3) Specifying the role of the government in rural cooperative system and the national supporting system for the cooperative. In accordance with the basic principles of "self-organization, self-governance and self-benefiting", the government shall not exert unnecessary or disguised interference to the establishment and operation of the cooperative. It is necessary to lean from the lessons of the people's commune period like the disguised and compulsive demand on laborers' membership through administrative appeal and public opinion pressure. Therefore, to sum up, the governmental role shall be defined as becoming a backstage worker to provide good development environment and varied preferential conditions and a hard-working and friendly server and supporter for the development of the cooperative rather than a rude intervener. The request to the government to provide the "supporter" insurance for the cooperative without interfering in the cooperative matters is also determined by the characteristics of the cooperative itself. The farmers' cooperative economic organization, as a joint self-help organization of weak group, has the possibility and capability to utilize its potential to help the government "realize the development goal of our society, especially eliminate the poverty, create adequate and efficient employment and promote social integration", stimulate the formation of good order in the whole society and become a dependable and effective cooperation assistant of the government. Besides, the cooperative is conducive to the realization of public welfare and fairness goals and would therefore become one important form for constructing a harmonious society. Therefore, the government shall create a supportive and functional environment for the sound and sustainable development of the farmers' cooperative economic organization.

To be specific, what supporting system should China provide for the cooperative? In accordance with the essential nature of cooperative economy and the special relationship between the government and farmers' cooperative economic organization, especially the special feebleness of our farmers' cooperative organization at the current start-up stage, our government should provide necessary preferential policies to the farmers' cooperative economic organization in such aspects as the finance, taxation, loan and price: to establish a cooperative taxation system and implement low or zero tax policies like the exemption of income tax and business tax for the cooperative; to provide low-interest or soft loan; to offer awards and free subsidies like the free subsidies for the operation equipment by the government to the projects invested and developed by the cooperative and consistent with the industrial policies of the State, as well as the awards provided to the cooperative with its operation reaching relevant standards; to supply the means of production at low price or offer price subsidies; to establish special funds for financial support to the development of rural cooperative, mainly used for the cost subsidy, sustainable development and international communication of the cooperative organizations; to exempt the income tax for the social contribution accepted by the cooperative; to legally prohibit any individual or organization from seeking profits or apportions from the rural cooperative; to ensure the priority of the rural cooperative to undertake or participate in the national projects related with agriculture like active invitation to the cooperative for the cooperative to actively participate in and implement the national comprehensive development projects, poverty relief projects, technology promotion projects, environmental and ecological protection projects and the like related with agriculture;[15] to establish an independent operating mechanism of cooperative, through which, the government and cooperative can have the channel for dialogue, the government can have the channel for providing policy and market information freely to the rural cooperative and organize or assist the cooperative professionals to carry out short-term training, and the cooperative can provide timely feedback to the country in terms of the varied information of the cooperative in real practice for the convenience of the national statistics, timely response, macro-control and policy adjustment and inclination; to provide a competitive environment of "monopoly immunity" for the cooperative since it is necessary to strengthen the legal status of the cooperative as an alliance of weak group in the market competition.

(4) Standardizing the governance structure of rural cooperative. Currently, the internal governance structure of our rural cooperative has the issues similar to those of the governance structure of corporate legal person, including the issues of vague property right, integration of society and commune, poor arrangement of internal organization and failure to form effective check and balance system for internal management. Therefore, it is necessary to improve the situation from the following aspects:

First, clarifying the property right system of cooperative and separate the society and commune. It should firstly be specified that the cooperative is owned by its members rather than by an abstract collective, and the governmental department shall no longer exercise the owner's right on behalf of the abstract collective. This represents both the primary and most fundamental step for improving the governance structure of the cooperative.

Second, improving the internal organization structure of cooperative. In accordance with the existing cooperative practices, the cooperatives have basically set up the general meeting of members as the highest authority, council (also named as the "board of directors") as the executing agency and board of supervisors as the supervisory body of the cooperative. However, in real practice, because of the power expansion of the board of directors, the weakening of the general meeting of members and the existence of board of directors in name only, the cooperatives have introduced the independent system of board of directors in the companies from the countries without the common practice of setting up the board of supervisors. This has led to the overlap of the supervisory functions of the board of supervisors and independent board of directors, buck-passing of the supervisory responsibility, waste of more resources and zero or even minus improvement of the internal organization structure. In view of this, the author suggests that, in terms of the internal governance structure, the cooperative may learn from the British and American experience and set no board of supervisors. Under such circumstance, the supervisory function would be directly exercised by the general meeting of members or board of directors. Meanwhile, the cooperative shall explicitly define the function and responsibility of the supervisor so as to check and balance the right and responsibility of the supervisor. Otherwise, there would also emerge the scenario of supervision without urging effect from the supervisor.

It would definitely require a complicated and systematic process to establish a cooperative legal system which also asks for the efforts and cooperation from varied sides. It is even more so to establish a cooperative legal system suitable for our national conditions. Although the process is difficult and arduous, the feasibility and possibility to establish the system has provided us with hope, confidence and enthusiasm. The establishment of the legal system represents not only the legal support for rural cooperative system and integral part of rural rule-of-law, but also an important channel for constructing a harmonious society.

NOTES

1. Xu Gengsheng, "Survival and Development of Cooperative in Advanced Market Economy Countries," *Chinese Supply and Marketing Cooperative Economy* 7 (1994).
2. Niu Ruofeng, "On the Evolution and Development of Cooperative System," accessed January 15, 2005, http://www.econ-stage.net.cn.
3. Qi Duojun, *Chinese Economic Organization Law* (Beijing: China University of Political Science and Law Press, 2003), 154.
4. Tang Min, "On the Inevitability and Essence of Cooperative Evolution," *China Co-Operation Economy* 12 (2004).
5. Pan Jing, "Development of Foreign Rural Cooperative," *Chinese Purchase and Sale Cooperative Economy* 4(2000).
6. Ding Guomin, *Corporate and Business Law* (Beijing: China Yanshi Press, 2007), 334.
7. Guo Hongdong and Qian Cuihong, "Development and Enlightenment of North American New Generation Cooperatives," *Rural Operation and Management* 5 (2004).
8. He Huili and Zhao Xiaofeng, *Report on Overall Conditions of Lankao Farmers' Cooperative*, September 28, 2005.
9. Niu Ruofeng, "On the Progress and Development of Cooperative," accessed January 15, 2005, http://www.econ-stage.net.cn.

10. He Xuefeng, *Rural China in the 21 st Century*, (Nanning: Guangxi Normal University Press, 2003), 36.

11. Xin Deshu, "Institutional Economics Analysis of Agricultural Cooperative," *Jiangxi Agricultural University Journal* 9 (2004).

12. He Xuefeng, *Rural China in the 21 st Century* (Nanning: Guangxi Normal University Press, 2003), 60.

13. Qi Duojun, *Chinese Economic Organization Law* (Beijing: Chinese Politics and Law Press, 2003), 164.

14. Lin Yifu, *System, Technology and Chinese Agricultural Development* (Shanghai: Shanghai SDX Joint Publishing House, 1992), 7.

15. Niu Ruofeng, "On the Evolution and Development of Cooperative System," accessed January 15, 2005, http://www.econ-stage.net.cn.

Chapter Fifteen

Solving "Three Agriculture-related Problems" by Rule of Law and Improvement of Agricultural Industrialization System

15.1 OVERVIEW OF AGRICULTURAL INDUSTRIALIZATION

Agricultural industrialization is another great innovation of rural policy after the household contract responsibility system in the rural area, which complies with the requirement of the new era and conforms to the target of constructing a harmonious society at present stage. Agricultural industrialization will accelerate the process of agricultural modernization in China and better to meet the challenge of the fierce competition after its access into WTO. In addition, the function of agricultural industrialization to the transformation of China's social structure cannot be ignored. The smooth progress of agricultural industrialization will accelerate the integration of the three relatively independent industries in China, thus solving the problem, i.e., the pattern of dual structure between urban and rural areas. From a micro perspective, agricultural industrialization with farmer household as the basis and the impetus is likely to change the status of the stagnant rural economy, thus solving the problem of higher yielding and lower income which has puzzled the household for years.

15.1.1 Background of Agricultural Industrialization

Rural economy is not only to provide people the source of food and clothing. It is not only the economic activity, but also has the function of protecting the ecological environment and the national culture, stabilizing the rural society, and safeguarding the state security. Therefore, the importance of the rural economy can never be neglected. After the founding of New China, the authority has attached great importance to agricultural issues, and has been exploring for a road in accordance with the actual situation of China. In general, strategic structural adjustment of rural grassroots social and economic system has experienced four stages. The first stage is the land reform at the early stage of founding of New China, just the liberation period. By this time the economic model is the government at the county level plus the farmers, and there is no other intermediary structure in between. A household normally constitutes of a single family. Although a small number families take the form of mutual-aid group, a household usually is an independent unit. The system in the second stage is the people's communes. At this stage, the single household is replaced by the people's commune, and the economic model is converted to the government at the county level plus the people's commune. The people's commune is composed of farmers, but the structure of the system is actually the entire government running all the business by means of executive order in the rural production and the business operation activities. It should be said that at this stage the farmer's right of self-disposition has been deprived, and China's economic system has entered the stage of planned economy, in which the government takes an absolute leading role. This structural adjustment destroyed the grass-roots social structure formed at the first stage and brought about many negative influences. The third stage is the two-tier management system that combines unified and decentralized operations proposed after the reform and opening up on the basis of household contract management, which broke the organization of people's commune and enable farmers to regain the subject qualification. However, the system doesn't make the farmers really dominate their production activities, as the dual operation system takes the form of farmers plus the collective, in which the farmers are subject to the collective. As we all know, the so-called collective is formed by administrative means in China. What is the concept of collective? Who occupies the core position in the organization? Through the analysis of the administrative institution in rural area, we can quickly get a hint. Between the county government and the farmers there emerges the township government. Although the people's commune has been repealed, the management mode of the people's commune resurges in a disguised way. By the way, it is worth mentioning that the many of the "three agriculture-related problems" problems, just come up at the township government level. In some places of the township government officials have become the local tyrants of the "new era" who just prey on its people. The fourth stage is the agricultural industrialization at the present stage, which is composed of the entrepreneurs and the farmers. This mode of industrialization cuts off the intermediary link of the township government and connects the county government directly, thus avoiding the unnecessary loss of the intermediate links and helping the flow of information and improvement of efficiency. The structural adjustment of this stage paved the way for the emergence of the economic structure at the next stage. The agricultural and rural grassroots organization structure mode in the western developed countries is just a goal for us to achieve for the next step, in which the farmer household is replaced by entrepreneur stratum in autonomy organization, hence the model in the form of entrepreneur plus the county government. Just as put forward in the report of the 16th National Congress of the CPC, we must push forward the industrialized operation of agriculture, better organize farmers in their access to the market and improve the overall efficiency of agriculture. Agricultural industrialization is not a slogan, but the advanced ideology which will help change the poverty and backwardness situations of the underdeveloped rural areas.

15.1.2 Clarification of the Concept of Agricultural Industrialization

We have been talking about agricultural industrialization, but what kind of concept is it? Quite a few people are not clear. They just have a fuzzy understanding that industrialization is beneficial to the liberation of productive forces, beneficial to the welfare of farmers, which will promote the development of rural economy, and thus it is a production mode totally different from the traditional agriculture. In a word, it is a new thing. However, half knowledge is a dangerous thing. A fuzzy understanding is not good for the concept to become popularized in the rural area. For instance, in some places, the mode of agricultural industrialization is copied from the advanced area. However, in the practice of later days, it is turned out that the copied mode does not work for the development of local agriculture industry and the communication among the parties are not smooth. Consequently, a great loss of resources has been caused, so that the original structure had to be annulled, thus the enthusiasm of the farmer was frustrated. They are only the specific experience limited to some places, but not the understanding from the perspective of industry system. What's more their understanding of industrialization is also relatively simple. In their mind, agricultural industrialization is an integration of production, supply and sale; they are always talking about industrialization in a local region, or even industrialization in a village. This is nothing more than a magnification of small-scale farmer economy, in which production, supply and sale can be accomplished even in a single family. This is not what we advocate of agricultural industrialization with modern management pattern. Therefore, to reveal the essence of agricultural industrialization hidden behind the various models has become the most urgent task.

Throughout the country, agricultural industrialization can take various forms on the surface. However, there is no fundamental difference in nature. From the key elements in the foregoing analysis, we know it generally can be divided into two categories, and the essence of the difference between the two lies in how to understand and deal with the relationship between the farmers, the market and the government. One type of agricultural industrialization emphasizes the role of market and farmers, which believes that the agricultural industrialization should take the market as the guidance, which farmers and other operators enjoy sufficient management autonomy, and dominate their own economic behavior independently. This type of industrialization focuses on freedom of the operators to choose, and the interaction of management behavior and environment. Another type of agricultural industrialization highlights the role of the government. This view argues that China is not a strong agricultural country, but a small farmer economy, which in nature has a conservative and non-market element. In this case, optimized allocation of resources cannot be completed by the market mechanism itself, and the governments become the first choice to solve this problem. The agricultural industrialization lead by the government become the model to overcome the disadvantages of small farmers and market mechanism, and the notions of "localized planning", "specialized production", "enterprise management", "integrated operation", and "organized farmer" were put forward to reconfigure the rural resources and regulate the interest relationship. The demarcation between these two types of agricultural industrialization is the government role in the industrial chain. Accordingly, the former is called "the industrialization of the farmers" and the latter is "industrialization of the government".

In China, the government plays a role in almost every economic activity, intervening the economic activity more or less, and the rationality and efficiency of the intervention decide whether the economic subject can fully play its role. Although China belongs to market economy, in essence it is just at the primary degree of marketization, far behind the western developed countries that have a high level of marketization. Although we are unified in understanding, and are familiar with the concept of market economy, although we understand market economy should be market oriented, there are still many government departments, under the influence of ideology, management mode and conduct code of the planned economy, formulate plenty of economic policies which hinder the development of market economy. It would be an ideal state that the government transcend all other economic body and not seek its own interests. However, this state is hard to come by in China at the current stage. Owing to the policy reform, political reform including fiscal and tax reform is difficult to realize the target goal, the governments at all levels, especially the competent agencies, have their own independent interests. It is not uncommon that different departments struggled with each other for the power and interest. The government agencies' behavior will inevitably be distorted under such motivation, and hard to surpass the other economic subjects. In addition, the bulky local government agencies cannot transmit information in a timely and sufficient way. Consequently, it cannot act like a market in allocating the resources reasonably so as to adjust effectively the variable specific interest at the grass-roots. Some government agencies provide means of production and finance facilities to the farmers in the name of "serving the people". In nature it is a kind of monopoly, which is converting into various fees to be collected from the farmer. As a result, the investment by these government agencies ultimately transforms to be the agriculture cost. This is one of the reasons for the heavy burden of the farmer.

For the above reasons, the government shall not interfere with the microeconomy or participate too much in the benefit distribution between the microscopic economic subjects, so as to guard against the increase of burden of the economic entities. As the so-called "industrialization of the government" focuses on the functions of the government and relies too much on the government's administrative guidance and administrative command means, whereas the government as the representative of state power, occupies a dominant position in the industrial chain, which destroys the equality between the different participants of the market, thus suppressing the subjective initiative of the participants and violating the tenet of constructing the socialist market economy. With the deepening of the marketization in China, the participation of the government in the production and distribution shall decrease relatively, and its function of creating better environment for subjects of market economy and providing security and service function shall be strengthened. In all, the government shall be geared to be a government of service. As a result, the "industrialization of the government" could only exist in a specific period for a certain time. Possibly its effect will be better than the industrialization of the farmer, as the government boasts an advantage of concentrating all the resources to get big jobs done, and establishing an industry framework in a short period. This industrial framework meets the demands of the market of that time and the government role in it is obvious. However, the market is not static, and if the change of market information could not be transmitted to the government in a timely way, the government would not be able to make the corresponding adjustment and the industrialization framework of the government would not keep pace with the ever-changing market. Eventually, the loss from the failure of industrialization of the government will be borne by the farmers, the ultimate sufferer of the industrialization. In order that the farmer can exercise their power effectively, the government shall delegate the power to lower levels, so as to mobilize the enthusiasm and creativity of the various subjects. In this way, the farmers will weather the storms in the economic activities of market competition, meet the challenge and face the opportunity brought about by the market, thus abandoning the thought of small proprietors of farmers and cultivate the market consciousness of farmer, and speed up the pace of agricultural industrialization. After the transition, it does not mean that the government will adopt a "laissez-faire" policy. Instead, the government can still support the reform of countryside and agriculture through amendment to the laws and regulations, adjustment to the systems, and reform of some of financial policies. The delegation of power by the government and the transformation from commanding government to serving government will accelerate the democratic progress in China, and the agricultural modernization will speed up the evolution of China from an agricultural society to an industrial society.

As a major innovation of rural reform after the household contract responsibility system, agricultural industrialization is also for the aim of liberating rural productivity, for the development of rural economy, for the improvement of farmers' income, and for the overall progress of society as a whole. The development of the society is not a single form of development, and the establishment of industrial society does not mean to be heavily dependent on the one-sided development of industry. A modern society should be the integrated modernization of urban and rural areas, rather than the sharp contrast between the prosperous city on the one side and the dismal village on the other side. While the urban residents turn up their noses at the ordinary consumption, most rural residents are yet to get rid of the poverty. Just as said by Li Changping in deep sigh, "the farmers are really bitter, the countryside is really poor, and the agriculture is really in danger". However, there is no use sighing. Currently the most urgent thing for us is to change the present situation of rural area as soon as possible. It is the most crucial step to build a harmonious society. Only after harmony is realized between the urban area and the rural area, can the harmony of society be guaranteed.

15.1.3 Essential Features of Agricultural Industrialization

Agricultural industrialization is not the mere emphasis on one or several of the solidified modes, but should be defined by the substantial contents. First we shall understand that the aim of agricultural industrialization is for the development of rural economy and the improvement of farmers' income. Its ultimate goal is to realize the harmonious development of the society as a whole; meanwhile it shall also avoid the polarization between urban and rural areas, the widening of gap between the rich and the poor, thus guaranteeing the stable, healthy and rapid development of national economy. Next we will, unify our understanding through analyzing of the substantial contents of the agricultural industrialization and singling out those amplified small-scale farmer economy which seems like industrialization.

1. The core position of entrepreneurs in agricultural industrialization

In whichever type of agricultural industrialization, the key factor is the human resources. As entrepreneurs possess the trait of catering to market economy, the entrepreneur's role in the process of agricultural industrialization is outstanding. If there were no several entrepreneurs in an industry, the entity would be supported by the local government by administrative means, and the farmers would be guided through policy or even command in the production. This kind of production mode should not be included in the category of industrialization. Why is the factor of entrepreneurs most important? First of all, we should understand that agricultural industrialization is based on the market and thus is market-oriented, and the entrepreneurs boast the characters required by the market economy. They have the impulsion to make profits, and also has the capability to take risks. In the face of complex and flexible market competition, the entrepreneur's innovation ability will be inspired, including product innovation, market innovation, technology innovation and innovation of business strategy. Those scarce valuable innovative thinking is difficult to appear in the business established by the government, as there is no motivation mechanism in the government supported enterprise, and the loss will either be borne by the government or fall to farmers. On the contrary, the entrepreneurs take a large part of risk for enterprise established by them. They have no other choice but to do his best in enterprise management.

The pioneering and innovating spirit, market insight and coordination ability of entrepreneurs are all indispensable elements for a successful business. They are also needed in agriculture industrialization. To ensure that entrepreneurs play a positive role in the process of industrialization, a good environment for entrepreneurs shall be created in the aspects of system, policies and legislation, and their private property will be protected against illegal infringement, so that they can devote themselves into the operation, and not be beset by other intricate errands. If the property right is not clear, or their private property being infringed arbitrarily, more often than not the enterprises will be killed at the early stage. This kind of environment is not conducive to the long time operation of the enterprise, and will do great harm to the building of a harmonious society.

The entrepreneurs take great responsibility in the process of agricultural industrialization. From this perspective, we will analyze the concept of industrialization again. That is, no matter what the external structure is, the element which really works is the people. From this point, we can put the agricultural industrialization into a formula, namely agricultural industrialization = market + N entrepreneurs + farmers (single farmer household or cooperative households of farmers). This is in line with the agricultural industrialization system of the western developed country, that is, market +

entrepreneurs (joint). The only difference is the element of farmers is missing in the western type. This is because their farmers have been successfully transformed to be entrepreneurs, which is the ideal state that we seek to attain. What we advocate at present stage belongs to the primary stage of agricultural industrialization.

2. Organized enterprise management

Organized enterprise management is an outstanding feature of agricultural industrialization. It is a usual phenomenon that agricultural income does not keep pace with the increase of production. The reason is that, besides some institutional factors, the key factor is that most of the farmers are weak in market sense. They are in lack of consciousness of operators and cannot effectively analyze market information. As all people are profit-oriented, in the absence of a rational guidance, farmers generally choose marketable agricultural products. Consequently, everyone is rushing to grow something in recent years, from planting grain to planting vegetables, from fruits to flowers, from the crab, turtle, shrimp, eel to quail and ostrich etc. The farmers are just using their excellent skills and hardworking sweat, making each product quickly saturated at the market. When supply surpasses the demand, the price drops down, and the farmers are still struggling under the poverty line. It may not be a hard job for the experienced merchant to ride away the rush hour of sales season to arrange the agricultural production. However, for the isolated single farmer household, it is rather difficult. In this case, the government can play the role of macroeconomic control regulator and provide policy guidance to guide the farmer in production. Another solution is to manage the farmers according to the enterprise management system. Its core idea is to manage the agriculture industry with modern enterprise management methods, that is, to create agricultural enterprises according to the current administrative system, to organize farmers, according to the work division of enterprise organization, and to distribute profits according to the distribution of enterprise operation. Through the enterprise management mode, the constraints of the small-scale operating will be broken, and the farmers will actively and orderly merge into the collaboration of production of modern society.

3. Intensive production scale

The status quo of agriculture in China is the low per capita land resources, the serious surplus of rural labor force, and the unbalanced ratio of the input and output of agriculture. One reason for the low agricultural productivity is that farmer's land scale is too small, limiting the progress of production technology, the improvement of product variety, as well as the improvement of organization scale of production. This production and operation capacity is difficult to compete with the farm industry in the developed countries which are dozens or hundreds of times larger than the scale of operation. How to improve the agriculture productivity to achieve ideal effect of input and output? A proved feasible way is to promote the intensive production.

Agricultural industrialization is to carry out intensive production, to innovate and equip the agriculture with industrial means so as to upgrade agricultural productivity. This is also the core of agricultural innovation. For the agriculture to realize industrialization development it is necessary to replace the traditional backward mode of people digging and carrying with modern industrial means in the whole process of the industrialization. From the practice in the country, where the agriculture technology facilities are better, the overall agriculture returns are higher.

15.2 REGULATION OF GOVERNMENT ACTIVITIES IN AGRICULTURAL INDUSTRIALIZATION

In economic activity, the behavior of the government is an indispensable part. Its appropriateness directly affects the efficiency of economic activity. The Chinese special national condition decided the government has a special place in every economic activity, intervening the economic activity more or less.

The aim of political reform undertaken by the Chinese government at present stage is to gradually enable the government to shift from rule of man to rule of law government, from the command type government to service-oriented government, which requires the government to put more energy on macro policy, creating a fair and free competition environment, reducing the interference of micro-economy, and respecting each subject of the market. In the rural areas, it is a common phenomenon that the grass-roots government intervene agriculture by means of executive order. In the transition period, the shift of government function at grassroots levels will be really hard and unsmooth. Whether the policy can be carried out depends on the rationality and feasibility of the system. The direction of the reform is to really make the rural grassroots government serves the masses of farmers, reduce government misuse of public power to violate the interests of the farmers.

As the transition, it does not mean that the government will adopt a "laissez-*fair* e" policy. Instead, the government can still support the reform of countryside and agriculture through amendment to the laws and regulations, adjustment to the systems, and reform of some of financial policies. The government shall do something great in formulating the overall policy, or in a clearer sense, in the macroeconomic control, which shall be beneficial for economic development, and which requires no discrimination against rural areas in terms of infrastructure construction, in supply and distribution system, and in providing production material of pesticide, machinery, petrol-chemical product and power etc. In addition, the various groups in rural areas shall have the right to make choice in their best interests, and the price of agricultural product shall not be meddled for the sake of urban consumption and government revenue.

15.2.1 Necessity of Governmental Macro-control in Agricultural Industrialization

Agricultural industrialization is a kind of management mode under the market economy. Market economy requires the economic activity of the economic subject should be market-oriented and in compliance with the requirements of the market activities, either in the field of production or circulation. Only in this way can the economic subject adapt to the ever-changing market and respond to the market information accurately and quickly, which will make the economic subject take an advantageous position in the fierce market competition. In this process, the self-regulation function of economic subject is reflected by itself in making judgment independently according to the market. That is to say, our government shall find their own position in the market economy. They shall play a service role to economic activity of market subject, instead of meticulous specific guidance, or even the whole thing. with the deepening of the market economy, the government shall also promote the formation of the market economy ideology and make the government behavior more scientific and reasonable, so as to stimulate the initiative and enthusiasm of market subject, and help foster a more active market.

The defects of market mechanism need a moderate government intervention in the agricultural industrialization

To bring the market mechanism into full play in the basic role of effective allocation of social resources, the market shall be in a state of free competition. In this case, the degree of scarcity of various kinds of market factors can be fully reflected, and the price changes can reflect the changes of market supply of the product. However, in reality, the theoretical ideal state will not remain stable and exist for a long time, as the market is changing constantly, with a certain degree of incompleteness, which will limit the function of the market to some degree. The purpose of the government's macroeconomic control is to reduce as far as possible the incompleteness of the market, so as to ensure that the markets really reflect the social and economic fluctuations.

As far as agricultural industrialization is concerned, in fact it is an agricultural operation behavior under the condition of market economy. This behavior is naturally regulated by the market, and shall be in compliance with the laws and regulation and abide by the general rules of games of the market economy. Market is not omnipotent. It will also dysfunction and cause varying degrees of loss and waste of social resources.

In addition, the market mechanism is a kind of benefit drive mechanism, through which social resources are allocated to the good department or industry with high efficiency. However, due to the large investment, slow return and high risk of agriculture, it cannot fully enjoy the social resources if only through spontaneous adjustment. Therefore, with a view to making up for the weak point and make agricultural industrialization develop fully, the government is deemed to do something, that is, through macroeconomic control, preferential policies, perfect supporting facilities, and formulated laws and regulations to guarantee the smooth progress of industrialization, and give full play to the agriculture operation organization and market mechanism for industrialization.

2. The constraint of law in government function

Agriculture is a weak industry which heavily relies on the weather, its risk of investment is increased with long production cycle and strong seasonal feature. What is more, China is a developing agricultural country. Over the years, agriculture has remained in the backward state of natural economy. When it comes to risk resistance, there is not a mature security mechanism, just like the foreign developed country, e.g., agricultural insurance, agricultural subsidy policy etc. All these postnatal deficiencies are added to the inherent constitutional infirmity of agriculture, including tighter supply of agricultural production resources, inadequate infrastructure, closed market information and backward market consciousness of farmers, backward mode of production, etc.

Agricultural industrialization is a great innovation in the rural economy development of China. Although we dare not jump to the conclusion that it is the sole approach to modern agriculture. Neither will we brag this mode of operation will change the backwardness and poverty of rural area in China at present stage. After all, the formation and development of agricultural industrialization cannot be realized without the optimum conditions, and we shall not advocate the unrealistic mode to promote agricultural industrialization. Nevertheless, compared with the primitive natural way of agricultural production, agricultural industrialization mode is advanced and worth experimenting in regions where conditions are relatively mature.

In the industrial chain, agricultural industrialization is a new thing. Also, agriculture is a weak industry, involving several links. The present situation is, those links - the lower reach industries and upper reach industries are administered by different industries and departments, the integrity and functions of agricultural industrialization organization are fragmented and scattered. Given the situation, it is necessary for a shift of the government function and the reform of the existing institutions, so that all those links of upper and lower industries will be administered as a whole, that the efficiency of the government departments will be improved, and its important role of guidance, coordination and regulation will be given full play.

We have been stressing the government should adjust their own position to play its role on economic promotion. In terms of agricultural industrialization, how the government should play its role is quite a problem worthy to be discussed. It is sure that the impetus of agricultural industrialization lies in the micro economic subjects, to be specific, the farmers, the agricultural companies and some agricultural economic cooperative organizations, e.g., cooperative. This vast "locomotive" of agricultural industrialization are just pushing forward by them. The function of government is to serve, to pave the way for, and adjust the relationship between each links of, the "locomotive". Agricultural industrialization as a product of historical progress, can be said to be a revolution of traditional agriculture. In the process of the development and transformation, the interests of various departments, various links, and different subjects of economic interests are involved. It involves the adjustment of the production relations and organizational innovation; involves the construction and coordination of the chain of production, processing and marketing of agricultural products, with agricultural production as the core; involves system reform and function adjustment of related agriculture administrative departments and service departments, to be more practical, ranging from the determining and fostering of leading industry to construction base, covering the small farmer household and big market, the local market, national market and international market. Although the spectacular agricultural revolution originated from the folk, it is needless to say the government is a powerful force which cannot be neglected. Whether it functions properly can directly affect the health development of agricultural industrialization; it will determine whether or not the agricultural industrialization will be out of track, e.g., degraded to be the industrialization of government, and whether or not the agricultural industrialization will go smoothly. Therefore, it is important that the government behavior be regulated through special laws so as to reduce the subjective arbitrariness. Regarding the status of the government in agricultural industrialization, we should be very clear it is not the main body of agricultural industrialization, but just a server. It is the subjects of legislation and law enforcement, subject of administrative management, and subjects of macro regulation and market service. Improper intervention cannot bring about the desired effect. It will also affect the enthusiasm of farmers. In some regions, the agricultural industrialization is the main work of agriculture and rural economy. It is regarded as a perfect way to make political achievements, as it is just the industrialization of agriculture by administrative power according to unified planning, by which the farmers are forced to grow certain crops, and the unqualified enterprises are allowed to be set up. Although this kind of disguised industrialization has met the requirement of production scale, and there are also the so-called leading enterprises emerging, this kind of industrialization drifts away from the actual situation of the rural area, and is likely to cause huge waste of social resources which has already been scarce. At the same time, it shall be pointed out that the governments at all levels and their departments also have their own independent interests. The inconsistency of interests allows them to enjoy the benefit in the exercise of power, but need not take the corresponding risk of decision-making. Therefore, with a view to getting better government performance, the policymakers would rush up to some immature projects which only survive a short period. Even the project fails; they do not have to take the responsibility of decision-making, but just take office in another place for another term. Similarly, their successors may repeat the same story. In such a vicious circle, the farmers are just the ultimate victims, and the foundation of Chinese agriculture is ruined. Such action will surely cause tensions between government and farmers. The prestige of the government is based on people's fear of power abuse, rather than sincerely support on the basis of all the policies of the government. Consequently, the construction of a service-oriented government is particularly urgent to change this situation.

15.2.2 Obviation and Rectification of Government Activities

1. Deviation of government behavior

Some successful example of agricultural industrialization stimulates the interesting of some local governments. However, they are too eager to get succeed in agricultural industrialization for a good performance for promotion. In some places, there are even the practices of forcing farmers to get rich. The government will by executive order promote the project and, regardless whether the farmers accept not, wipe out the crops in the farmers' fields, and force them to plant the so-called "high efficiency" species. However, due to the reasons such as climate, soil, or the market etc., those projects fail, and the farmers inevitably complain a lot. Some local governments even take economic measures to intervene agriculture industrialization, promoting projects arbitrarily. If the farmers or grass-roots collectives do not accept the project, they will be fined, or even be treated as "second-class citizens". Sometimes even though the projects are launched, it may be left unfinished halfway just because of inadequate preparation or technical reasons, thus causing great loss. At the beginning, maybe the local government was with a good intention to serve the people. However, they are just against the objective law, against the wish of the farmers, and are lack of communication with the farmers. Their arbitrary behavior eventually brings the costly consequences. In a country with sound legal system, the occurrence of this phenomenon is difficult to imagine. These only shows that we are still on the stage of rule of man, especially at the grassroots levels, and the rule of law are just staying on the surface. The debate over rule by law and rule by man is distinct in this field. Administration according to law is easier said than done. That's a serious topic, because in some places, there is hardly any legal constraint against administrative power. Therefore, what we need to ponder over is, when the illegal administrative directly deprives the basic rights of citizens to life and freedom, to property, and rights to business operation, who will bear legal responsibility? How to bear?

2. Causes of government deviation in agriculture industrialized operation

Although China has entered the stage of market economy, in essence it just belongs to marketization at the primary stage, far from the high level of marketization.in the western developed countries. Although we are unified in understanding, and are not strange with the concept of market economy which is market-oriented, there are still many government departments, under the ideology, the management mode and the of conduct code of the planned economy, formulate plenty of policies unfavorable to the development of market economy. Whether the government can transcend all other economic bodies and does not seek its own interests, this ideal state is hard to come by in China at present stage. As the policy reform, fiscal and tax reform, political reform is hard to put in place, the governments at all levels, especially the competent agencies, have their own independent interests, it is not uncommon that different departments scramble over the interests. Under such circumstances, the behavior of government agencies will inevitably be distorted under economic motivation, hard to surpassing other economic subjects and realizing justice. In addition, as the local government is redundancy and cumbersome, in which the information cannot be transferred timely and sufficiently, so it cannot allocate the resources like the market, and cannot effectively adjust the diverse and specific interests occurred at the grass-root level. Some government departments provide farmers with production materials and a variety of the so-called "service", including financial, marketing, etc., all with the essence of monopoly, which will be converted into various charges. Therefore, the fixed investment of those departments eventually translates into agricultural costs, lead to rising cost of agriculture and become a source of farmers' burden.

3. Correction of government behavior in agricultural industrialization

From the above analysis we will know the role to be played by the government, that is, the government shall not become a comprehensive control model in the microeconomic, and shall not participate too much in the benefit distribution between the microscopic economic subjects, with a view to preventing the situation of government's revenue increase at the burden of various economic entities. As the so-called "government's industrialization" of the agricultural industrialization focuses on the functions of the government and relies too much on the government's administrative ordinance and administrative command, and the government, on behalf of the public power, is in an absolute advantageous position in the industrial chain. Its strong position breaks the equality between different subjects, suppresses the subjective initiative of the economic subjects in the economic activity, and thus violates the aim of the construction of the socialist market economy. With the deepening of marketization, the situation of government's participation directly in the production or circulation shall be reduced moderately; whereas its function of creating good environment and providing the security and service for the market economy subjects from the system and the structure perspectives will become all the more important. The government's industrialization can only appear in the specific historical period under the specific circumstances. Its effect may be better than the farmer's industrialization for the time being. That is just because of the particularity of the government, i.e., gathering all the resources to get big jobs done. It can rapidly build up industry framework in the short run which adapts to the demand of the market at that time. Under such circumstance, the role played by government is obvious. However, the market is not static. With the change of the market, the changing market information cannot be timely conveyed to the government. Without a corresponding adjustment, the government's industrial structure will be difficult to keep up with the ever-changing market, and the government industrialization will fail. Eventually it is the farmers to bear the loss. The following is a discussion of regulating the behavior of the government in the process of agricultural industrialization.

(1) The system construction for safeguarding of farmers' rights and interests. Protection of rights and interests of farmers has become a major national project of policy makers. In the revised *Agricultural Law*, a chapter is specially laid out named "Protection of the Rights and Interests of Farmers", with 20 articles. However, the enforcement of a new law is often faced with two problems. One is the issue of publicity, namely, for the farmers and the related law enforcement personnel to understand the law, to master and apply it to safeguard the rights and interests of farmers. In terms of publicity, it happens in some regions, the national policy, decree and law cannot be implemented, because some officials believe that their power will be restrained and supervised, thus are reluctant to let their status be challenged. They did not publicize the policy of Central Committee of CPC and the laws of the state. Instead, they took an opposite line to conceal the spirit of the CPC, and treated the document of CPC as banned books. They prohibited publicity of the "banned book" and even searched and confiscated the books in farmer's home. This seriously obstructed the publicity of the spirit of CPC, thus some system shall be constructed to ensure the enforcement of policy will not be hindered. The other is the issue of law enforcement, i.e., while the farmers are safeguarding their rights according to the law, there will be an

independent department to accept the petition of the farmers and make an award of justice. Here the problem lies in that, when the issue to be tackled involves the illegal activities of the government, whether the court will take an independent position and make a fair judgment. It is well known in China that the government and the court are not separate, in particular in the local area. It is quite often that the judicial power is intervened by the administrative power, and the judges even have to make inquiry with the administrative power before making a rule. This situation is the deformity of law, which frustrates the farmers' confidence to safeguard their rights and interests. This is a serious obstruction to the legal system construction of China. As a result, it is particularly important to set up an independent court which has separate interests with the local government, or which belongs to the provincial or the Central government directly.

(2) The completion of government accountability system. When the government interferes with the agricultural industrialization regardless of the situation of local area, how will the government account for it? Only when this problem is solved can the lock on the industrialization operation be fundamentally lifted. Since the power exercised by the government is endowed by the people, then, accordingly, the principle of equality of power and responsibility shall be followed, i.e., the power and the responsibility shall be equal. In this way, the policy makers will think twice when making decisions in the economy field. Premier Wen Jiabao pointed out in his Government Work Report in 2004 that we should institute an accountability system for law enforcement and a mechanism for investigating and prosecuting law enforcement improprieties, and improve and strictly implement a system of administrative compensation that "holds those who exercise power accountable, places them under supervision and compensates those whose rights have been infringed". This creates conditions for the political reform and the government's own construction in China. It also pointed out the direction for the implementation of the administrative accountability system. In April 2004, the State Council promulgated the *Program for Comprehensively Promoting Administration by Law*, which specifies that the administrative body shall adhere to the principle of unification of the power and responsibility, which is the basic principle of administration according to law.[1] In promoting administration according to law and the process of building the socialist rule of law government, one of the important contents is to carry out administrative law enforcement responsibility system, in which the law enforcement responsibility will be defined according to law, law enforcement positions will be set scientifically, and law enforcement procedures will be standardized.

Only a responsible government can get the support of the people; only when the work route from the masses to the masses is carried out can the government work meet the requirements of people's interests. As the government is a special organization made up of people, it will make mistakes inevitably. What is more, as it is a powerful public monopoly organization supported by public power, it is stronger than any other organizations, and also has great destructive power. Therefore, we shall be prudent in the exercise of power. At present stage, a feasible way is to adopt some rules and regulations to regulate the behavior of government administrative personnel. On April 27, 2005, with the promulgation of "*The Civil Servant Law of the People's Republic of China*", administrative accountability was further legalized and standardized, which provided the legal protection for the construction of responsible government in China.

15.3 LEGAL ISSUES OF VARIOUS SUBJECTS IN AGRICULTURAL INDUSTRIALIZATION

Agricultural industrialization is the industrial chain which is connected by each link of the chain. All the link of upper reach and lower reach industries are both relatively independent and closely connected. Therefore, it is necessary to refine the whole process of operation and concretely analyze each link of the agricultural industrialization. It is mentioned before that agricultural industrialization, as a locomotive, needs the interaction of each link to function. If any of the links does not work, the locomotive will not operate properly. We have been always emphasizing that the government should support and serve the agricultural industrialization, and strengthen the safeguard of agricultural industrialization from the legislative perspective, and the first step is to clarify the object protected by the law, determine the nature of each economic entity in the industry and their status as civil subjects in the legal relationship. In a nutshell, the first thing is to have their identification determined before entering the market for fair competition with other market subjects, and to resort to the law with the identity where litigation is necessary.

15.3.1 Qualification of Legal Subjects of Farmer Household in Agricultural Industrialization

It has been proved that farmer household is the most basic and the most active factor in agricultural production and operation. It is also the most important motivation in the agricultural industrialization. What is farmer household? In accordance with the *Rural Land Contract Law*, farmer household is the contractor of the land. Whereas the *General Participles of Civil Law* stipulates that, "Farm household" refers to members of a rural collective economic organization who engage in commodity production under a contract and within the spheres permitted by law. It can be seen that both the stipulation of law and the opinion of the scholar treat the farmer household as one of the economic entities. In addition, this form of economic organization adapted to the development level of productivity in vast rural area in China, with the flexible mode of operation and mode of organization. In a word, it is safe to say farmer household is the most basic production unit in rural area. However, the problems reflect the current situation in rural area in China, including high default rate of agricultural contract, the recurring phenomenon of damaging the interests of farmers, which is a show of the fuzzy or misunderstanding of, or even indifference to, the legal status of farmers. The existence of the problems pushed us to re-examine the legal status of the farmer household, safeguard the property rights and business operation right of farmer household as a civil subject, and make legislative spirit deeply rooted in the hearts of the people.

The farmer household, a term emerges with the rural land reform, reflects the social content of the reform of land and the mode of operation in China. Farmer household, both at home and abroad, as a critical link of the social network and lying at the bottom of the social stratum, bears the social function of economy, politics, culture, etc. At present stage, the farmers engage in business activities in the name of farmer household contract system, which is a blend of political factors and economic factors, and can be said to be a basic feature of organization in China. An analysis of the special organization will help us further understand the legal status of farmer household in rural areas.

We should be clear that, first, the farmer household is a family. It is an organization composed of family members, with kinship rather than a contractual relationship. Second, the farmer household is an organization for agricultural management. At the specific historical period, the policy of two-tier management system that combines unified and decentralized operations enabled the farmers to be separated from the collective management to become the independent operators. Although collective management has not been completely canceled, there is a clear boundary of interest between the collective and the farmers, between different farmers, and between the farmers and other stakeholders of the industrialization chain. In practice, as a critical part of the agricultural industrialization, it is particularly important to determine the legal status of farmers and their property right.

To establish the status of farmer household as an independent legal personality, we should first prove it is an organization. Regarding this point, we shall first take a look at the concept of farmer household in the enacted law, especially the stipulation on property liability. According to Article 29 of the *General Principles of the Civil Law*, "The debts of an individual business or a lease holding farm household shall be secured with the individual s property if the business is operated by an individual and with the family s property if the business is operated by a family", the farmer household is divided into two parts: individual management and family management. However, from the current situation of China's rural area, individual management accounts for only a small portion in the agricultural production. The success of family management in rural reform has proved the suitability of this method in agricultural production. It cannot be denied that farmer household is an organization although there also exists individual management mode.

The organization is different from an individual natural person in that, in law, the homogeneity avails the natural person a kind of universal common personality, while the heterogeneity makes the organization far more complex than a natural person. Professor Jiang Ping points out in his book *Theory of Legal Person System*: groups are distinctive owing to different shape, subordination, nature, function etc., thus the research on group shall have started from the comparison of different legal formation of the group. For the groups of different properties, their legal personalities might be different. At present, groups can be roughly divided into two categories: legal person and non-legal person. As legal person has strict qualitative requirements, the farmer household could only be excluded from the category. Therefore, if we assume that farmer household is an organization, it belongs to non-legal person. Next, we need to make an analysis of the characteristics of the organization.

First of all, as an organization, the first question is stability. The key elements of organization include people, capital and labor. Different organizations have different combinations. Sometimes the people take a dominant role; sometimes the capital takes a dominant role. However, these elements are all needed for an organization's basic composition; the only difference is the proportion of different elements. As far as farmer household is concerned, obviously the people take a dominant role, as the formation of family is based on the feelings of family members; the combination of labor is also obvious, as agricultural cooperation production in the form of family is necessary under existing conditions of rural China. As an organization dominate by element of people, stability is utmost important. It is safe to say that the marriage and family relations regulated by law provided the stability for family organization.

Secondly, from the efficiency brought about by the organization. We have been stressing that farmers itself is a link of a social unit based on kinship, without any commercial purposes. However, from the development history of rural China, the individual farmer household has been playing the role of the agricultural operator. Due to the low level of agricultural productivity, collaboration among the family members has become the best production mode, which fits the development level of the time. However, from the mid-1950s, the people's commune movement made the management function of farmer household basically lost. The guideline of "Yi Da Er Gong" (large in size and collective in nature) provided that the land belongs to the collective, all members work together, and make distributions according to workload. This deprived farmers of the status of economic subjects. Although the policy of "San Zi Yi Bao (plots of land for private use, small free markets, enterprises with sole responsibility for their own profit or loss, and fixing output quotas on a household basis)" still existed and seemed to be based on the farmer household, in fact these economic activities was to maintain the most basic consumption demand of a family, and did not possess the commercial nature. After the implementation of household contract responsibility system, farmers were liberated from the collective, and regained the status of economic subject to sign contract with the collective independently and arrange production activities and conduct business operations according to the business scope of the contract.

Finally, analyzing from the perspective of independent property. To carry out business activities with other economic subjects, the organization shall ensure that it possess the independent property to handle matters related to business activities. This mainly involves the bearing of the debts. According to the stipulation of "*Marriage Law*" of China, the family is the organization with independent property, and the system adopted by the law is the common property in marriage. Family property is totally different from the property system of the business organizations. As the family was not established for the purpose of business operation at the beginning, but an outcome of the feelings interaction of man and woman, thus it has the non-operational feature. While the farmer households' sign contracts with the collective or other economic organizations, its status has been changed. Apart from being a family, it has become a party with equal status to the contract letting party. Under such circumstance, subtle changes have taken place with family property. The independence of the property become utmost important for the safety of the transactions and the performance of the contract. In fact, regarding the question of whether or not the family property is independent, we need not think too much. Since the farmer household is protected by the *Marriage Law*, then the law will protect the property of farmer's family without exception, without asking whether the family property will be used to carry out business activities. In fact, "*Marriage Law*" stipulates the independence of the common property in business operation.

It can be seen from the historical development of legal subject system that, the civil law subject from theory to practice has experienced a process from single subject to multiple subjects. In fact, the doctrines and precedents in Germany, Japan, and Taiwan, China have gradually acknowledged the subject status of some non-legal persons. With the scope of civil subjects enlarged to meet the demand of the development trend of transaction, it is logical that the farmer household with family operation as essence is endowed with the independent legal status of civil subject.

15.3.2 Agriculture Economic Cooperative

This section will mainly discuss the agricultural cooperative economic organization as a link in the chain of agriculture industrialization. It should be noted that some scholars also put the whole agricultural industrialization in the scope of agricultural cooperative economic organization. This does not conflict with what we are discussing here. As what we are going to talk about is an intermediate organization, which associate farmers with circulation market, or which acts as the representative of the interests of farmers to conduct dialogue with the enterprises or company group at an equal foot. Some scholars treat the agricultural economic cooperative organization as agricultural industrialization. In fact, it is an agriculture entity incorporated by the farmer, integrating production, supply and sale, trade, industry and agriculture etc., in which members of the entity make distribution in accordance with the proportion of their investment, whether in fund, or labor, production material data in percentage. This will be detailed in the next section.

1. The necessity of the agricultural economic cooperation organization and the existing problems

According to M. Olson, if an interest group in a society intends to impose some influence to government policies to protect their own interests, some action must be taken. That is the so-called "collective action". For the collective action to become effective, you need an organization to represent the interests of the group members. Within such organization, the group members will effectively communicate and coordinate, and take consistent actions in dealing with others, to enhance the collective bargaining power. In addition, the member of the collective must have the enough incentives to avoid the phenomenon of "free-ride". [2] In China, the farmer belongs to the category of the vulnerable groups, and the main reason is that farmers live in the inconvenient remote area, without good traffic or communication facilities, and lead a simple life of male plowing and female wovening. Since it is a single economic activity, the farmers are lack of collective consciousness and will not take the initiative to seek joint action of collective economic activity. Consequently, the farmers become helpless under the huge market pressure and could only passively accept the unfavorable transactions terms. In the face of the unreasonable agricultural policies formulated by the local government at the support of public power, or in the face of harsh conditions offered by other powerful and mature market players, they had no choice but to accept. As a result, if we are to protect the interests of farmers, we will need to gather these dispersed strengths up to form an organization, thereby getting the equal status in bargaining. In the agricultural industrialization chain, it is for the same purpose to set up agricultural economic organizations. In addition, agricultural economic organizations also have the function of guiding farmers to enter the market in order, thus connecting the thousands of small farmers with the ever-changing market, reducing the blindness of farmers in production and operation, and getting rid of the situation of manipulation of farmers. Through the operation of organization mode, the price of agricultural products will be decided by market mechanism directly. This is also the essential characteristics of market economy. Under the guidance of market rules, a reasonable price can be formed to safeguard the legitimate interests of the farmers.

2. Legal status of agricultural economic organizations

The state has always paid special attention to the rights and interests of farmers. In the *Agriculture Law*, there are stipulations on the establishment of economic organization, "The state encourages farmers to voluntarily organize themselves into various kinds of specialized cooperative economic organizations on the basis of household contractual management. Specialized cooperative economic organizations of farmers shall adhere to the aim of serving their members and in accordance with the principles of voluntary participation， free withdrawal， democratic management and return of the surplus and in accordance with law， engage in agricultural production and operation and provide services within the scope prescribed by their articles of association. Specialized cooperative economic organizations of farmers may take diversified forms and shall be established and registered in accordance with law. no organizations or individuals may infringe upon the property of such organizations or their right of decision-making in management."

From the stipulation of *Agriculture Law*, it can be seen that the state has a positive attitude to the legal status of agricultural economic organizations, and has made relatively explicit demarcation to this kind of economic organization, namely economic organization composed voluntarily on the basis of household contract responsibility system, highlighting the economic principle of freedom and equality between the members in the organization. The property right and the decision-making power in the operation and management have been established by the law for economic organizations organized and registered in accordance with the stipulation of law. However, the simple stipulation of the law shows the inadequacy of the state in legislation of economic organizations. With the advance of agriculture industrialization, and innovation of agricultural economic organization forms and operation mechanism, some problems arising in the course of innovation urgently need to be solved. First is the laggardness of legislation, leading to the vagueness of nature and legal status of farmer's economic cooperative. Second is the great confusion in registration process. In some places, it is registered in the department of agriculture; in other places, it is registered in the administration of industry and commerce (AIC), or in the civil affairs bureau, or departments of science and technology. There are still others do not go through registration process at all. All these situations are detrimental to the healthy development of farmers' cooperative organization. Third is neglect of the characteristics and functions of the farmers' cooperative organization, therefore, how to furnish support from finance, tax, credit to encourage and support the farmers' cooperative organization remains to be studied.

As there is not a law applicable to the whole country regarding the farmers' cooperative organization, great confusion appears regarding the status of the organization. Just as listed above, different departments have different views regarding the registration process. In some places, it is registered with the administrative for industry and commerce (AIC) as a partnership; in other places, it is registered with the civil affairs bureau as a corporation. Therefore, the one registered with the AIC obtains the qualification of legal entity and may get loans in the name of legal entity; however, it may not be entitled to some preferential policies for farmers. For example, some local governments may have promulgated some preferential policies to support the farmers' cooperative, e.g., "the agricultural products sold by the farmers' cooperative shall be regarded as the products produced and sold by the farmers, and shall be exempted from the value added tax". However, the national tax bureau may not agree to these provisions, as they believe the cooperative is a joint-stock enterprise or partnership with independent legal personality, and, according to the relevant provisions of the state, it shall have to pay taxes. Moreover, the opinions of the local government and party committee, cannot serve as the basis of tax reduction or exemption. On the other hand, the farmer cooperative organization registered with the civil affairs administration cannot engage in business activities. Its ability to organize economic activities is greatly reduced, which is against the fundamental purpose of the farmers in participating economic cooperative organization. Therefore, endowing the farmer cooperative organization with the status of legal person, i.e., treating it as the market subject in the market activities, become an urgent problem to be solved at present.

3. Determination of the legal status of the farmers' economic cooperative

If we take a look at the farmers' cooperative organizations in China at present stage, we will find they all have the essential features of legal person. Next we will analyze the status of legal person of the farmers' cooperative organization from the requirements of legal person.

From the basic requirement of legal person, according to the German scholar Karl Larenz's point of view, "the basic characteristics of the legal person, is its separation from the constituent members or function organ of individuals."[3] The reason why a legal person is called legal person is that, fundamentally it is an independent object, namely its existence as an independent social unit, i.e., itself is an independent integrated structure. This is different from what we call “group of majority”. It not only requires the element of people, but also need the element of thing. The existing form of legal person, whether corporate legal person or consortium legal person, are all independent entities combining people and property. The only difference is the former is founded with people as the basic elements, while the latter is based on the property. According to the traditional view of “organization theory”, the cause for establishment of the legal person is that legal person as the “appropriate subject to assume the rights and obligations”, and the degree of appropriateness is that the degree of organization of the group has made it an independent integral structure, so that it can act as an independent party and bear the corresponding legal responsibilities in legal relationship.

From the essence of the legal constitutive requirements, first of all, the establishment of the legal person must have a sustainable legal purpose, just as Mr. Jiang Ping points out: “What the legal person system considers is not the unity of the group formation in the legal perspective, but the purpose for its combination. It is the particular purpose of combination decides the internal and external relationship of group composed of individuals”. [4] To achieve a certain purpose constitutes the fundamental motive force to organize the independent structure. Why do people combine groups? The purpose is to use the group as a tool for realizing their interests. The requirement of sustainability differs from those who are combined for short-term purposes, namely ordinary partnership for civil purposes, which is a kind of organization combined through internal agreements between partners, with loose and unstable relationship of people and property. What is legal purpose? It means compliance with the provisions of the law and non-violation of public social order. A group of people or combination of property for illegal purposes will not be recognized by law. The sustainable legal purpose takes the form of articles of association, objective, scope of business, as well as the purpose of incorporation in the agreement between the members. In this respect, the agricultural cooperative organization obviously contains all the characteristics: the article of association is the basis of its founding, spelling out the purpose of the incorporation, the rights and obligations of each member, and organization of governance. In all, it is totally different from the partnership, which is just based on an agreement.

Second, legal person shall have an independent name. As an independent civil subject to participate in social life, it shall have a corresponding social identity to show its integral existence. The striking difference between different subjects is to grant them a separate name, just like the natural persons’ distinction from each other with different names. Each legal person uses a unique name, namely the social symbol, to conduct social activities and compete with other market subject. In this way the safety of transactions can be secured and the adverse effect of vagueness will be avoided. As we may not be able to understand the internal situation of a group, but we can tell whether the group is independent or not from its name. A unique name is the manifestation of the independent integral structure of the group. It is a symbol of personality and a media for conveying the will of the group in the transaction. Agricultural economic cooperative as a collective concept is the generalization of various kinds of farmers' cooperative organization, embodying the nature of the cooperative organization. Specifically, different kinds of economic organizations all have their own independent names, from which we can tell the organizational type, purpose, scope of business, etc.

Third, a legal person needs to have independent property. The law allows the legal entity to participate in the civil relationship in the name of independent legal person, and then the artificial person shall have independent property which is disposable. Independent property is vital for groups of independent integrity. If a group is only the combination of people, it is a loose group; only with the combination of property, can the group become an integral interest group. In the meantime, the personal property becomes the property to be independently disposed by the group. This combination manifests the relatively independence of people and property. In addition, independent property is the material basis and guarantee for the legal person to carry out activities and realize the goal, which is also so the prerequisite for the counterpart to enter into transactions. As civil legal relationship falls into two categories of property relationships and personal relationships, and the economic activity of groups mainly involves the property relationship, thus the independent property is directly related to the smooth transaction and the capacity to bear civil liability. The property of agricultural cooperative organization generally comes from members of the capital contribution of the members, accumulated capital and government loans, together with a few other funds. These properties constitute the independent disposable property of the cooperative economy organization, which can be independently used to cover the corresponding civil liability, and which the members of organization have no right to refuse. Therefore, agricultural cooperative organizations meet the same requirements as required of the legal person.

Finally, the decision-making mechanism and the representative of the mechanism shall be set up for the legal person. This requires the group of the organ for forming decisions and the organ for expression. Since the law has endowed the group the status of artificial personality, it requires that the independent integral structure possesses the organs of thinking and expression, just like a human body. Brain is the decision-making mechanism in corporate system, and the mouthpiece is the representative system. Through the decision-making mechanism, the opinions of each member of the organization will be collected and summarized into the group will. The function of the organ for forming decisions is to form a group will to guide the legal person's behavior. As for the organ for expression, this is the representative or manager, i.e., a mechanism for performing and expressing the will of the group. One instance is the legal representative of the enterprise, acts on behalf of the enterprise at the authorization of the enterprise. The structure of the agricultural cooperative organization is the same as company, with the general assembly as the highest authority, i.e., the decision-making body, and the board of directors (the board) and the board of supervisors being responsible to the assembly. As for the representative mechanism, it is authorized by the decision-making body as an organ for expression, to act on behalf of economic organization within the scope of the authorization.

From the above analysis of the nature of the agricultural cooperative organization in terms of constitutive requirements of legal person, it can be concluded that agricultural economic cooperative organization has all the characteristics of legal person. It is of great significance to admit its status of legal person. First, it is beneficial to the construction of the organization itself. The granting of status of the legal person means it's founding and operation shall not only comply with the general principles of agricultural economic cooperation organization, but also comply with the provisions of *General Principles of Civil Law* on legal person system, which is conducive to the moulding of independent civil subject with legitimate operating capacity. Second, it is beneficial for economic exchange activities. Once the status of legal person is obtained, it can carry out business activities in its own name independently, obtain a variety of legitimate property rights, participate in the negotiations with other market subject on an equal foot, and sign the contract for a clearer protection by the law, thus avoiding the awkward situation of vague legal status.

Regarding the legal status of the agricultural cooperative organization, many jurists have expressed their views, thus the theory is growing mature in theory. In practice, we can feel the progress of legal system in China. In January, 2005, the obscure legal status of farmer cooperatives was first confirmed in Zhejiang Province, with the promulgation of *Rules of Zhejiang Province on Farmers Cooperatives*, the first regulatory documents in China on farmers' cooperative organizations. The rule stipulates that cooperatives can obtain the status of legal person through registration. The promulgation of local rules and regulations is a positive tentative legislative activity in solving the problem of legal status of farmers' cooperative organizations. In the process of execution, it will inevitably produce unexpected new problems, it will also prompt us to constantly accumulate experience in practice, and promote the promulgation of a national law applicable for the whole country at an early date.

15.3.3 Legal Personality of the Subjects in Agricultural Industrialization

As agricultural industrialization in China takes a diversified and flexible management mode, which is in line with the different development levels in rural China, it has become an ideal approach to change the present situation of China's rural area. However, the diversified management mode of agricultural industrialization throughout the country will easily make people confused. The divergence of understanding will be detrimental to the legal construction, and naturally there exists vacuum space of law. This paper will have a discussion of the model theory and the legal issues involved, based on the analysis of the relationship between internal factors of different management modes of agricultural industrialization. Roughly, it can be divided into three categories, based on which the legal issues involved with different management mode will be analyzed.

1. Determination of legal personality of organization with loose management mode

Loose management mode is the pure transaction of commodities, which could be considered to be the primary stage of agricultural industrialization. The different subjects are connected through buying and selling of goods, with little binding force, and greater freedom. In this relationship, the subject has the independent legal status, and is entitled to bargain over the price of agricultural products and the terms and conditions for transaction. Strictly speaking, this kind of spontaneous coalition could not be called an organization owing to the loose connection and flexible terms and conditions owing to bargaining. It is safe to say that it is just a prototype of organization. According to the requirements of law, an organization shall have the feature of stability, thus the organization with loose management mode cannot meet the requirement and cannot be granted the qualification of legal person. However, does it mean that the law will do nothing regarding problems existing at this stage of agricultural industrialization? Can the law exert its remedy functions for the participants of transactions? In fact, the applicable law is completely adequate to deal with disputes between the subjects, and the transaction parties can have access to the legal relief stipulated by the law. In the agricultural industrialization process, each business body has the independent legal personality in accordance with the law. Although the relationship between each other is not close, each participant can bear its respective business risk independently. It can be said that the regulation of applicable law on the behaviors of each participant guaranteed the smooth operation of the model. On the other hand, however, as it is just a primary model, it is gradually replaced by the other higher level of organization mode.

2. Determination of legal personality of organization with half-loose management mode

Compared with the loose management mode, half-loose management mode has made some progress, with clearer legal relationship between the subjects. The so-called half-loose management organization refers to the cooperation relationship for interests established through contract between the subjects of industrialization on the basis of commodity transaction. With the contract as the link between different parties, the economic subjects shall enjoy the rights and bear the obligations according to the stipulations of the contract. This mode of management takes the form of "company + farmer household", "agricultural economic organization + company", and "wholesale +farmer household" etc., and *Contract Law of the People's Republic of China* is the law regulating their relationship. The contracts between those subjects are concluded through equal negotiation and reciprocity. Each party shall abide by the principle of honest and good faith in performing the obligation, enjoying the right and distributing the profits. In the view of the author, this kind of model is built on the basis of contracts, thus it does not have the qualification of legal person. The main reason is the organization lacks the stability. As in this model, the dominant power is the company and wholesalers, and the farmers or agricultural economic organizations are at a passive position. Usually the companies and wholesalers signed the product purchase contract with the farmer household in the previous year according to their demand. As the signed contract belongs to the purchase contract which the contract parties may bargain over the price and other contract terms. However, only through the contract will not make them an integrated organization, and they just belong to a temporary coalition. Since after the completion of the contract, they are free as to whether to extend the contract or find a new cooperative partner. Under such circumstance, it is impossible for them to form an integrated organization to carry out business activities. Neither is it feasible for the half-loose management organization to have an independent name and independent property, each belonging to the respective transaction party. As a result, although this kind of industrialization mode has made some progress, it still does not meet the legal requirements for legal person. Therefore, there is no need to spend extra legislation cost on the issue of legal person of this kind of organization. Where necessary, it can be regulated through minor amendment to *Contract Law*.

3. Determination of legal personality of organization with close management mode

With the development of agricultural industrialization, in some places where conditions are mature there appeared a kind of organization which is integrated with the link of property right. Within the organization, the enterprise and the farmer household are combined closely to be a unity through the joint interests. This type of organization pattern plays a more and more important role in the process of agricultural industrialization. In fact, such a closely-knitted group is a new enterprise group composed of farmer household and enterprises owing to joint interests, generally in the form of share cooperation, i.e., the farmers and the original enterprise respectively make contribution of investment by means of production material, technology, capital, labor force etc., and participate in daily production and business operations, with each subject bearing the risks and enjoying the profits according to the proportion of his investment. This kind of organization has already formed a unified structure. Within the structure the farmers and the original enterprise have a joint interest. As a result, they will pay more attention to the overall operation of the organization, not limiting to only one or two fields which they were familiar with. This is totally different from the loose management mode and the half-loose management mode. For instance, in the loose management mode, the farmers can bargain over the price of the products with the enterprise on site, which is just like the ordinary transaction. The half-loose management mode is based on the contract, and the obligation of the farmer household is to perform his duties stipulated in the contract. When it comes to the delivery of product, as long as the farmers provide the contract goods, they can get the payment according to the contract. Therefore, the two modes have one thing in common. That is, the farmers will be OK if they complete their share of work, and they need not care about the operation of other economic bodies. On the other hand, in the close management mode, as the participants are closely-knitted, and the activities of all parties directly influence the efficiency of the whole organization, and the efficiency of the organization in turn influence the interest of each member of the organization. In this way, each participant will, apart from doing well the work of each own, also pay attention to the work of others in the organization. Hence the coordination between each party is strengthened, and the cooperation makes it possible for the new enterprise to compete in the market as an independent subject.

Here, we will make an analysis of the issue of legal person of the organization of close management mode from the requirements of law regarding the legal person. First is the sustainable legal purpose. The close management mode organization is with a clear purpose, that is, with the agricultural production as the key business. While at the incorporation stage, the farmer household and the former enterprise may formulate rules of management and articles of association to specify the scope of business of the company, and make clear the rights and obligation of each party. Within the organization, each member enjoys the right and bears the obligations according to the share of investment. In this way, the interest of each party is connected with the interest of the enterprise, and all the parties jointly form a unity with permanent interest rather than temporary interest. Second, legal person shall have an independent name. This is a basic requirement for the close management organization. Independent name implies the status of the market subject, through which the other market subject may understand the identity of the organization, so as to improve efficiency and reduce transaction risk. Third, a legal person needs to have independent property. While illustrating this organization mode in the previous paragraph, the capital element is already mentioned. The farmer and the enterprise investors input the production materials, fund, technology, and labor forces in exchange for the share, which represents the rights and duties of the investor in the new enterprise. The invested capitals are all transformed into the independent assets of the new enterprise. Last, the decision-making mechanism and the representative of the mechanism shall be set up for the legal person. It is imaginable for the independent organization to operate without the decision-making mechanism and the representative of the mechanism. It is a necessity to establish the decision-making mechanism and the representative mechanism according to the requirements enterprise law and company law of China. From the above analysis, it can be seen that the close management mode basically meets the requirements for legal person. Consequently, the law confirms its legal status so that it can participate the market activities and develop healthily within the sphere of law.

15.4 LEGAL ISSUES OF OPERATIONAL ACTIVITIES IN AGRICULTURAL INDUSTRIALIZATION

While the agricultural industrialization brings vitality to rural area in China, we should also keep a sharp insight into the hidden flaws under the disguise of aura; otherwise the dark side will encroach on the fruits of industrialization and discourage the confidence of the people in agricultural industrialization if not addressed early. The legal loopholes will also bring damage to the normal order of the market in China, which is not conducive to the construction of a harmonious society. This chapter will concentrate on the legal analysis of contract, the most common issue in the agricultural industrialization management, to explore the solution to the problem. At the same time, a tentative analysis will be made on the legal issues involving the special kind of agricultural industrialization, manor economy pattern.

15.4.1 Legal Issues Concerning Contract in Agricultural Industrialization

In the process of agricultural industrialization at present stage, according to the actual development level in rural area, the half-loose management mode, the transition from junior to senior stage, accounts for a large share. The connection between them is based on the contract. As the contract may take various forms and the powers are unbalanced between the contracting parties, or owing to dishonest behaviors, many legal problems arise regarding the performance of contract.

1. The problems existing in the contract in the agricultural industrialization

First let us have a look at the various types of contract which may appear in the agricultural industrialization, which mainly include sales contract, the contract of transportation, lease contract, employment contract etc. All those contracts have something in common: (1) they belong to some link of the agricultural industrialization, or run throughout the industry chain; (2) such contracts are almost all about vulnerable industries - agriculture related products as object, with long production cycle, strong seasonality, high storage requirements etc. All these elements are the focus of the contract. In order to protect the rights and interests of both parties and prevent the risks and disputes, the contract in the industrialization process generally takes the written form, and the reciprocal rights and obligations are spelt out for the contracting parties; (3) this kind of contract, especially the contract signed with individual farmer household, usually involves small amount of value with longer performance period; (4) such contracts tend to be influenced by national policy, especially the national agricultural policy. Some contracts may be even with the characteristics of the administrative contract.

Although a great variety of contract forms are available in the process of agricultural industrialization, it does not mean there are not any problems in contents, the most serious being the default of contract. Default behavior can be basically divided into two categories: one is the breach from the purchaser, that is, when the contract price is much higher than the current market price, the purchaser with a view to reducing loss, refuses to perform its obligation of purchaser. The other is the default by the vendor, i.e., when the market price are higher than the contract price, the farmer with a view to increasing income, would find fault with the contract. In addition, the non-standard order has seriously hurt the enthusiasm of farmers. This includes: one, the order from unknown source. Such orders are usually published on illegal publications, which were mailed to the farmer household, selling seeds and seedlings all in the name of product buy-back. After the farmers remit the fund for the seeds and seedlings, they get no response. The second is the contract drafted by one party, similar to the format contract, the contract drafting party takes all advantage of the favorable terms and conditions to it, and the farmers signed the contract without negotiation. Once disputes arise, the farmers will have greater difficulty in fighting for their own interests. The third is the order with the deposit. Some seeds companies singed the seeds selling contract with the farmers on the terms of deposit and collect the deposit from farmers at the excuse of farmers' breaching of contract. On surface it is for the prevention against farmers breaching of contract, in fact it is a trap to the farmers. The fourth is the idealistic order. In some place the planting or breeding business may bring good economic returns, but in other place, the same project may meet the fate of failure. This is because different natural conditions and production levels. The fifth is the oral agreement. There is not any written record regarding this kind of order. Once market changes and litigation arises, there is not any evidence to support the claim.[5]

2. Solution to the problem of contract breach in agricultural industrialization

Contract as a critical adhesive between different subjects, is of vital significance for the development of agricultural industrialization. The improvement of the contract law system not only helps to standardize the behaviors of market subjects, safeguard the normal operation of agricultural industrialization, but also help promote a fair, free and safe market order, and promote the construction of socialist harmonious society. In signing and performance of contract, we should pay attention to the following questions.

(1) Although the agricultural cooperation movement involves a great variety of contracts, generally they are all included in the Contract Law of the People's Republic of China. When making a contract, the general principles of the Contract Law shall be complied with, including equal legal status of contracting parties, a party may not impose its will to the other side; principle of free will, any unit or individual may not illegally interfere in the freedom of contracting parties; the principle of fairness, i.e., the reciprocity of rights and obligation of contracting parties; the principle of honesty and good faith in exercise of right and performance of obligations; together with the principle of legality, that is, the parties shall abide by the laws, administrative regulations, respect social morality, and shall not disrupt social and economic order or do harm to public interests etc.

Here it is necessary to expound further the equal legal status of the contracting parties in combination with agricultural industrialization. It has been discussed that the farmer belongs to the vulnerable groups in society, and the agriculture belongs to the weak industry. In the contract negotiations with other strong economic counterpart, as a weak party, although it is vested the equal status by the law, the equality in form cannot cover inequality de facto. In addition, agriculture belongs to the high risk industry. However, even if in face of unfair contract, as long as it can meet the basic requirements of living, the farmers are also likely to accept the unfair terms and conditions of the contract. In order to change the weak strength of the scattered individual farmers, it is necessary to establish the farmer cooperative economy organization or agricultural industry association, so as to pull the power of the farmers together and to represent the interests of the farmers (which have been discussed in the previous chapter). In this way, the strength can be concentrated on the negotiation table to fight for the interests of farmers. The agricultural industry association can also provide legal aid to farmers. As a result, the contract signed by both parties under the condition of equilibrium will be reasonable in the allocation of rights and obligations.

After the contract is signed, if any party fails to perform its obligations as agreed in the contract, the law shall impose harsh sanctions on the defaulter. If the farmers breach the contract, their liability could not be exempted just because of their weak legal consciousness, otherwise it will bring a lot of negative effects to transaction security. In order to reduce the phenomenon of farmers' default, it is necessary to the carry out legal education in rural areas to enhance the farmers' legal consciousness. If the agricultural enterprise (company) breaches the contract, punishment shall be imposed in accordance with the provisions of the law. In addition, it is necessary to set up an enterprise credit rating institution, and lower the credit rating of default enterprise (company), so as to make it exposed to the society. This mechanism will urge the enterprise (company) to carry out operation honestly, earnestly fulfill its obligations and reduce the situation of damaging the interest of the farmers.

(2) In the agricultural industrialization contract, the subject matter is agricultural products. Usually the farmers' contract obligation is to grow crops or breed animals according to the requirements of the contract. This obligation is closely associated with unpredictable nature situation. With the current low level agricultural productivity in China, and the condition of the low content of science and technology, the farmers will be helpless in front of natural disasters; this will directly lead to default of contract performance. Due to the particularity of the contract, the characteristics of agricultural production and agricultural products shall be fully considered before signing of the contract. That is, the factors of force majeure shall be included in the contract for both parties to bear the risks caused by force majeure, and considering that the farmer is a weak party, the enterprise (company) can bear more risks, so as to protect the farmers' production enthusiasm, and protect the basic rights and interests of farmers.

15.4.2 Discussion over the Manor Model as a Close Relationship Model

In agricultural industrialization, the more mature and advanced operating mode is the close management mode, in which all the subjects are integrated through the link of property right. This mode can strengthen the sense of identity of the subjects, so that they can put their own interests and the overall interests together. Manor economic model is one of the typical representatives, on which people have set great hopes as a solution to the problems in rural area for many years. The manor economy does possess these advantages. For instance, it can gather and guide the social surplus funds to invest in agriculture and thus can greatly promote the development of agriculture. Its basic connotation lies in the land development mode of integrated planning, unified operation and management: land developers (large and medium-sized enterprises or the company) by buying land ownership (in China is the land use right) of a certain area of land, and the land are divided into several equal parts (units) accordingly. Merchants and funds can be invited through the sale of land interest certificate or beneficiary certificate of shares to the public. Under this economic mode, the farmer household may make investment in the form of land use right and/or labor force and become the investor of the company (enterprise), or participate in the daily operation of the company (enterprise), and enjoy the right equally according to the proportion of shareholding, such as right to election, supervision, right to profit distribution etc. The status of the participant will really bring the farmers a sense of business owners and inspire their enthusiasm in the production.

However, after all, the manor economy is still at the growth stage in China and there are many drawbacks. The loopholes of law in the field give some unscrupulous businessmen the opportunity to "cry up wine and sell vinegar", and engaged in the illegal fund-raising activities; some developers do not have the basic conditions for agriculture development, such as capital, technology and management skill, and just totally rely on commercial hype to attract investors. Therefore, it is particularly urgent to formulated relevant laws and regulations to clean up the sham of passing off fish eyes for pearls, and create a good external environment for agricultural industrialization development.

Regarding the financing problem of manor economy, some scholars consider it illegal fund-raising. Their arguments being that, since the recognized ways of fund-raising mainly include two categories: one is the investment, i.e., setting up limited liability company or joint stock limited company; the other is investment in securities, i.e., the purchase of stocks and bonds or other securities. Except that, whether to raise fund publicly or to issue bonds to the public, shall have the prior approval of relevant department. Any activities of fund-raising directly to the public without the approval from China Securities Regulatory Commission, the People's Bank of China, or the State Planning Commission fall into the illegal fund raising.[6]

Regarding the issue of illegal fund-raising, the author holds that it should be treated more objectively and fairly. it shall not be inferred as illegal just because of similar stipulations of the rules and regulations. We all know that things are developing constantly. If we come to a standstill just because some negative factors, then the development of new things will be greatly hindered. As for the issue of illegal fund-raising, can we also have a look at both sides of the coin? Concerning the fund-raising in folks, the Chinese government usually adopts a prohibitive policy on the excuse that there is no security for the fund and the fund-raiser may even disappear with the fund on purpose. As a result, to safeguard the order of financial market, the folk fund-raising should be banned.

Similar problems of fund-raising also exist in manor economy, in which the land resources are divided into small units, and bonds or beneficiary certificates are issued to investors. What the investor buys is not the land itself, but rather a certificate representing the income from the land. In this way, the fixed and materialized land resources are converted to a certificate of land profit which can be circulated. In a certain sense, this kind of bonds or beneficiary certificate has the characteristics of modern securities. Therefore, it is advisable that it be regulated from the perspective of securities, instead of prohibition totally through administrative decree.

If the manor economy is to be included in the sphere of securities law, then the Sangong Principle, i.e., openness, justice, and fairness shall be manifested in the manor economy. The fund-raising activities in manor economy have different purposes. It may be used as a means of swindling and cheating; it may also be used for both honest operations to promote the development of industrialization. The Sanggong principles of securities law are just in time to regulate this purpose. As long as the information is fully disclosed, the investors will decide whether to buy or not. Whether it is the selling of land, or issuance of bond, as long as the investor makes decision on the basis of the full information, the government shall not interfere with the transaction, regardless of what great risk is involved in the transaction. This is the basic theory of security law. [7] What the government needs to do is to construct a mechanism of information disclosure, rather than interference through administrative means.

Regarding the question of whether the company (enterprise) is entitled to carry out the manor economic activities, the author proposes examination and approval system be strictly followed. Developing of manor economy mainly involves two issues. One is the financing from the society, the other is the transfer of land use right or land operation right. Relevant government departments (mainly related to the department of agriculture and forestry and the land planning department) shall make responds as soon as possible, work out the corresponding administrative measures and examination and approval procedures, strictly enforce the land management policy and strategy of land utilization, and avoid various kinds of illegal activities. The manor economy will develop steadily and orderly through strict examination and approval procedure. [8]

NOTES

1. Liu Xinyan, "Administrative Accountability: Why Focus on People in Charge?" *People's Daily,* Oct. 30, 2006.

2. Zhao Kai, *Studies of the Development of Chinese Agricultural Economic Cooperation Organization* (Beijing: China Agriculture Press, 2004), 45.

3. (DE) Karl Larenz, *The General Theory of German Civil Law*, trans. Wang Xiaoye (Beijing: Law Press of China, 2003), 186.

4. Jiang Ping and Long Weiqiu, "Studies of Legal Nature and its Basic Structure," *China Jurisprudence* 2(1998).

5. Zhao Kai, *Studies of the Development of Chinese Agricultural Economic Cooperation Organization* (Beijing: China Agriculture Press, 2004), 92.

6. Wang Xinglv and Wang Dongchuan, "Legal Thinking Manor Economy," *China Jurisprudence* 1(1999).

7. Zhu Jinqing, *Securities Law* (Beijing: Peking University Press, 2004), 26.

8. Wenjun Sun and Chang-wen Zhao, "The 'Manor economy': A New Mode of Agricultural Industrialization," *Rural Economy* 3(1999).

Chapter Sixteen

Solving "Three Agriculture-related Problems" by Rule of Law and Completion of Social Security System in Rural Area

16.1 OVERVIEW OF SOCIAL SECURITY IN RURAL AREA

Social security in rural area is a concept of Chinese characteristics. As when it comes to the social security in rural area, we can read between the lines that there is also "social security in urban area", which fully embodies the characteristics of China's urban and rural dual social structure, a rare situation in the other places of the world. In other countries, especially in Western Europe, owing to the establishment of the civil society and the city-state, the agriculture, rural areas and farmers account for only a small portion in the whole society. In terms of social security, there is not any big gap between the rural area and the urban area.

16.1.1 Basic Contents of Social Security

The so-called social security refers to the welfare system established by the State within the scope of the whole society to overcome the old age, illness, disability, unemployment, birth, death and other risks of adverse effects in life, to ensure the basic survival needs of the social members. William Beveridge, Father of the Welfare State, points out in his *Social Insurance and Allied Services* that the social security includes social insurance, national assistance and voluntary insurance.

Generally speaking, due to the influence of the "welfare state", the content of the social security in western country is rather rich, which basically covers the various needs "from cradle to grave", "from fetus to heaven", such as old age, birth, unemployment, work injury, disability, and family allowances, child allowances and housing allowances and other benefits. After the 1970s, owing to the influence of oil crisis and an ageing population, the social security fund is hard to make ends meet, and there was a big cut on social security programs. From 1973 to 1981, the fiscal deficit of British government increased from 3.9 billion pounds to 12 billion pounds, debt increased from 37.5 billion pounds in 1973 to 110.8 billion pounds at the end of 1981.

On April 12, 1986, the Fourth Session of Sixth National People's Congress adopted the *Seventh Five-year Plan of People's Republic of China On National Economic and Social Development*, which expanded the concept of social security into four aspects: social insurance, social relief, social welfare and special care and placement. Among them, the special care and placement system is a special content of China. It is a general term of the preferential treatment and national relief. It refers to a special treatment system for the personnel (and his family) who sacrifices himself for the interest and safety of the country and the people. Although the contents of social security vary from country to country, basically they include three aspects: social insurance, social relief and social welfare.

16.1.2 Emergence and Development of Social Security

The term "social security" appears in the *Social Security Act* (1935) in the United States, but Britain is the birthplace of social security. The legislation of social security can be traced back to the *Elizabethan Poor Law* (1601) promulgated by the British government, also known as *Poor Law*.

At the time of the 16th century, with the expansion of British shipping and the development of foreign trade, the British wool textile industry was becoming more and more prosperous. The nobles and the landlord, with a view to enlarging the production of wool, expelled the farmers and the temple servants from the feudal land and public land, enclosed large areas of land into pastures. The farmers and the temple servants were deprived of land and were forced to leave their hometown, exile. Some of them entered the city to become industrial workers or craftsmen, others become vagrants or refugees.

At the same time in the city, along with the continuous development of productive forces, the machine mass production quickly replaced manual production and reduced the demand for labor force in the new industry. Meanwhile, a large number of backward manual mills went bankruptcy due to failure in the competition with the machine production, leading to the unemployment of craftsmen. Once the laid-off workers and the vagrants' refugees became extremely poor, they began to commit a series of illegal activities, including theft and robbery, which affected the social stability and shook the feudal rule of the British Emperor.

To alleviate the increasingly serious political crisis and maintain social stability, Queen Elizabeth I of England, on the basis of the original folk remedy, enacted the *Poor Law* in 1601, also called *Old Poor Law*. In 1834, the bourgeoisie who has mastered the state power, according to the needs of the situation, made some changes to the old poor law, and passed *Amendments to Poor Law*, namely the *New Poor Law*. The *Poor law* is regarded as the first social security law in the real sense, just because it put forward the state responsibility of social relief for the first time in the world, namely, social relief is a right of the nationals, whereas providing social relief is the obligation of the state. Social relief is no longer a charity, a mercy, or a gift. State responsibility is the distinction between the social relief in the modern sense and the previous relief in the folks.

After the social security system is established in the UK, France, Germany and other western European countries successively set up their own social security system. Since then, the social security systems were established throughout the world, and have been gradually completed ever since.

In Germany, the world's first social insurance law, the *Health Insurance of Workers Law of 1883* promulgated by Bismarck regime, together with the *Accident Insurance Law of 1884*, and the *Old Age and Invalidity Insurance Law of 1889*, marking the formal establishment of modern social insurance system. The *British National Insurance Act (1911)* is the world's first comprehensive social insurance law.

The world's first comprehensive social security law as mentioned before is the *Social Security Act (1935)* in the United States, which is inseparable from the specific historical environment at that time. In 1929, the economic crisis which spread all over the western capitalist countries was originated in the United States. On October 24, the New York stock market was in a panic. The banks went bankruptcy, the factories were closed and the workers became unemployed. The financial markets were on the brink of collapse, and the whole society was in chaos. At the influence of the liberal capitalism ideology, the Hoover government advocated autonomic recovery of the economic crisis and would not intervene in the economy, which incurred widespread criticism and strong opposition of the entire society, hence his resignation in 1935 before the end of the presidency.

After Roosevelt took office, he adopted the Keynesian Theory of the state economic intervention and began to establish the social security system, to stimulate people's social needs and promote the comprehensive recovery of economy. The *Social Security Act* was just issued in this context soon after President Roosevelt's assumption of office.

The earliest socialist security system was originated in in the Soviet Union. During the period of Wartime Communism from the summer of 1918 to 1921, the Soviet Union issued the first social security law of socialist country, the *Social Security Rules of Laborer*.

After the Second World War, capitalism witnessed rapid economic development. The enormous growth of the material wealth provides powerful support for the completion of the social security system. The social program in the capitalist countries has achieved great development and basically covers all the basic needs of live. In 1942, the famous British social security expert Beveridge published his *Social Insurance and Allied Services*, is a typical representative of the "welfare state" theory.

However, good time does not last for long. When it comes to the 1970s, the outbreaks of the two oil crises have led to the full-blown recession of capitalist economy. Meanwhile, with the intensifying of the aging problem, the problem becomes more outstanding with the fund-raising for social security, and the national treasury cannot afford such a heavy burden. For instance, the ratio of total public expenditure and GNP in Sweden was 44.8% in 1970, 52.6% in 1976, and 67% in 1980.

In analyzing the deep reasons of economic recession, the governments of some countries are of the opinion that the high levels of social security system caused the reduction of consumption and inadequate demand lowered the work enthusiasm and economic efficiency. As a result, the capitalist countries, under the hypothesis that the level of social security should be compatible with the level of economic development, reduced the scope and level of social security, and introduced the personal responsibility of social security system, which emphasizes on the sense of individual self-insurance besides the social security and employer liability.

16.1.3 Background of Social Security in Rural Area

The issue of social security in China rural area is a major and serious problem related to the national economy, people's livelihood, social stability and social justice. It is not formed in a day or two, and cannot be solved in a short while. When talking about the social security problems in rural area, it is not adequate to be confined in this issue. We shall jump out of the issue itself and go directly to the source of the problem, namely, the three agriculture-related problems of agriculture, farmer and rural area, just because the lack of social security is also one reason of the "three agriculture-related problems".

Rural social security is intimately involved with the "three agriculture-related problems". Just like the iconic poster of Su Mingjuan "big eyes" in the Hope Project, it not only enriched her own frustrations and hardships, but also reflected the backwardness of rural education. Rural social security is a microcosm of the entire problem of "three agriculture-related problems". If the problem of "three agriculture-related problems" is a chess game, the rural social security is probably some of the pieces, or a few steps in the game. The small game of the rural social security shall rely on the strategy of the whole game. Therefore, the issue of rural social security must be put in the grand strategy of "three agriculture-related problems" for overall consideration. Consequently, to study earnestly and explore the cause and effect of "three agriculture-related problems" undoubtedly has important significance.

Just as the saying goes, Rome was not built in a day. The "three agriculture-related problems" has a long history. It is the result of the long-term economic policy and political development in China for many years. Since the Opium War in 1840, China, as a "farmer country" with farmers accounting for the majority of population, suffered multiple exploitation and oppression by feudalism, imperialism and bureaucrat capitalism. Even worse, with successive years of war, disasters, the self-sufficient natural economy was destroyed, the broad masses of the people lived a miserable life, and the rural economy was even worse.

During the period of early new-democratic revolution war, the cities were basically occupied by the bureaucratic landlords and warlord compradors; whereas the communist forces, represented by Mao Zedong, Chen Duxiu, Deng Zhongxia etc., carried out the revolutionary struggle in the remote rural areas. They organized the masses, established revolutionary base areas, and adopted the strategy of from rural areas to the cities and seizure of power through armed forces. The urban area and the rural area have long been in a state of hostility and separation, which has aggravated the closeness and isolation of each other. From the Agrarian Revolutionary War to the Anti-Japanese War to the Liberation War, although the rural life was much better than in the period ruled by Kuomintang reactionary, the rural economy was still depressed and agricultural development was still difficult due to the destruction of war, influence of disasters and revolutionary consumption. The high burden of the farmers and the destitution of the agricultural economy all caused great influence on the "three agriculture-related problems" in the days to come. For instance, during the Agrarian Revolutionary War period, the taxes of farmers amounted to 10% ~ 20% of total agricultural output; in some place, the figure even reached 25%. That did not include the social burden of transportation, rescue, reconnaissance, comfort and other civilian war service burden as well as the burden of common land of the Red Army, cultivation and harvest on the land for the families of revolutionary martyrs and servicemen.

During the Anti-Japanese War, the burden of commerce was generally lower than agriculture. According to investigation of the Shensi-Kansu-Ningsia border region, from 1944 to 1945, the proportion of burden and income of businessman was 5.5% ~ 12% for large business; 4.3% ~ 11% for medium-sized business, and 1.6% ~ 8.3% for small businesses; whereas in the same period, the proportion of burden and income was 3% ~ 5% for poor farmers, 6% ~ 8% for middle farmers, 7% ~ 10% for middle-up farmers, 9% ~ 13% for rich farmer, and 20% ~ 30% for the landlord.

During the period of Liberation War, in his Speech in Tianjin in April 1949, Liu Shaoqi said, "the government fiscal is too difficult, and the farmers take the highest burden. They are required to contribute grains, they will send family member join the army, they themselves act as coolie to support the frontline, they also have to help the families of revolutionary martyrs and servicemen, in addition, they need to pay educational expenses, etc. Your burden is lighter than the farmers, so they complain that workers, businessmen, capitalists are leading a better life. The complaint is commonplace". From those remarks, it can be seen that, compared with the city and the working class, the vast rural area and poor farmers made greater contribution for the victory of the new democratic revolution, which the Party, the government and the people of the whole country shall never forget.

The Second Plenary Session of the Seventh Central Committee of the C. P. C. held in March 1949 marks the shift of the main work of the Party and the State from rural areas to cities. After the founding of new China, the devastated country needed to be rebuilt, and the Party and the country faced the historical problem of recovery and development of the national economy to consolidate the newborn regime in the soonest period. Due to the specific domestic and international environment, China did not get rid of the influence of the former Soviet Union, but instead, took the approach of agricultural supporting industry and gave priority to the development of heavy industry.

In order to provide industrial capital accumulation, China carried out cooperative movement in rural area and adopted the policy of monopolized operation of agricultural products. In the urban area, the system of planned accommodation was adopted in resource allocation, which took advantage of the "price scissors (by holding down purchasing price of agricultural products, increasing sales price of industrial products)" between agricultural products and industrial products to inhibit the farmers' living consumption and production inputs, so as to grab as much as possible the agricultural surplus to input into the industry, to serve the country's industrialization strategy. Under the guidance of the policy, the State lowered the price of the grain and raises the prices of industrial products (gauze, etc.) for three times in January, April, and July of 1951 respectively.

At that time, in order to effectively solve the problem of urban unemployment, and reduce grain consumption for export in exchange for heavy industry equipment, the State adopted a series of administrative measures: (1) to carry out the agricultural cooperative movement in the rural areas so as to bind the broad masses of farmers in rural areas; (2) to establish the urban and rural household registration systems, so as to cut off the natural channel between urban area and rural area, and forbid the farmers to flow to the cities; (3) to enjoin the local county government from recommending farmers to work in the cities; to prohibit the farmers to find job in the cities; to stipulate that the vagrant farmers do not belong to unemployed personnel and are not entitled to the food subsidies; to forbid the city enterprise to recruit farmer workers, etc.; (4) to organize the unemployed person to go back to rural area, thus creating the reverse flow of labor force between urban areas and rural areas. The movement of educated youth going to the countryside which later spread over the country and influenced generations of Chinese was originated from this thought. The only difference is that the latter was not only an economic policies or measures, but also mingled with more ideology factors of political reform.

During the period of founding of new China to the reform and opening up, the series of policies and measures adopted by Chinese government for realizing of industrialization strategy have produced profound influence on the economy and politics, agriculture and industry, state planning and market in China: (1) agricultural cooperation and monopolized operation (unified purchase and sale) hampered the agricultural accumulation and investment, hit the enthusiasm of farmers, and reduced the efficiency of agricultural labor; (2) it contributed to the formation of the planned economy system, and limited the development of urban and rural market economy; (3) it caused the imbalance development of heavy industry, light industry and agriculture; (4) it resulted in the formation of urban and rural dual economic and social structure, expanded the difference between urban and rural areas, and caused social injustice; (5) it aggravated the problems of agriculture, rural areas and farmers, which became a serious obstacle to the further development of society, economy and politics in China in the new period.

According to statistics, during the 29 years before the reform and opening up (1950 ~ 1978), the government, through levying direct and indirect system, obtained from rural area "direct tax" of 97.8 billion yuan, "indirect tax" of 510 billion yuan. From1952 to 1978, the ratio of industrial output growth rate and agricultural output growth rate was as high as 4.2:1.

Since the reform and opening-up, especially in the mid-1980s, with the establishment of the two-tier management system that combines unified and decentralized operations, China has basically completed the original capital accumulation stage of industrialization with agriculture supporting industry, and entered the period of paying equal attention to agriculture and industry. By rights, it was high time for the government to make change to the former system of supporting industry with agriculture through extraction of agriculture surplus. However, due to long-term practice of the rigid bureaucracy and the reasons of interests, the out of date policy has not been changed, but rather, it shows a tendency to be strengthened.

For the 16 years from 1979 to 1994, the government through the "direct tax" got revenue of 175.5 billion yuan from the farmers, and through the "indirect tax" got revenue of about 1.5 trillion yuan. Meanwhile, the proportion of finance support to agriculture in the whole national financial expenditure was declining. In 1984, the finance support to agriculture accounted for 9.1%, which fell to 8.3% in 1985, and 7.9% in 1986, and has been remained at the low level since then. The proportion of investment in agricultural infrastructure construction to the total investment was also declining. In 1983, the proportion was 6%, which fell to 5% in 1984, 3.3% in 1985 and 3% in 1986, 3.1% in 1987, and 3% in 1988. In 1988, the absolute amount of investment on agricultural infrastructure construction was 4.746 billion yuan, 12.7% less than 5.434 billion yuan, the figure of 1978.

The gap between the industry and agriculture has been widened. From 1952 to 1990, China's industry had grown for more than 65 times, and agriculture had increased by 3 times only, with the growth ratio up to 21:1. The farmers' income growth was slow, the gaps between the rich and the poor, and between the east and the west were increasingly widening. In 1990 ~ 2001, the growth rate of annual per capita net income of farmers was 4.48%, which is only half of the 1980s. Whereas the urban per capita disposable income increased 110.15%, with average annual growth of 7%. In the same period, the proportion of the gross domestic production of the 12 east coast provinces and municipalities increased from 47.9% to 66.1%, while the proportion of the central and western regions fell to 52.1% from 33.9%.

The tension between the cadres and masses are growing, and mass incidents emerge frequently, which seriously affected the stability of rural society. Just as Li Changping (the Secretary of the Party Committee of Qipan Township, Jianli County, and Hubei Province) put it, "the farmers are really hard, the rural areas are really in poverty and the agriculture is really dangerous". It was high time for special attention and reflection of the society from all walks of life.

If, after the founding of new China, the adoption the policy of agriculture supporting industry and the separation of the urban and the rural is owing to the various practical need and the restriction of objective conditions, then, after the completion of primitive accumulation for the industrialization, there has been no effective measures taken to change the situation of imbalance between agriculture and industry, losing the opportunities to solve the problem of agriculture, countryside and farmers, and causing the historical debt of the "three agriculture-related problems" piling up. This is unforgivable, because it is not a natural disaster, but a man-made one.

16.1.4 Present Status of Social Security in Rural Area Perplexed by "Three Agriculture-related Problems"

The dual structure in China with agriculture supporting industry, emphasizing industry and belittling agriculture directly affected the national investment in agriculture, rural areas and farmers, caused to the backwardness of establishment and development of rural social security system, which lagged far behind the city social security system, and does not keep pace with the development level of rural economy. For quite a long time, compared with the urban social security, the rural social security appears to have been quietly lying in the corner that is forgotten by people.

At the preliminary stage of the founding of New China, as a result of the exploitation and oppression of the imperial powers, the landlords and the Kuomintang reactionary aristocracy, and the destruction of war and natural disaster, the nation economy was in depression, and a large number of people were displaced from their homes. In order to recover the national economy, stabilize the daily life of the masses, the Government Administration Council of that time issued *Instructions on Production and Disaster Relief* in December 1949, and convened the General Conference of Relief of Chinese People in April 1950, and carried out different relief work in urban areas and rural areas. In the countryside, in addition to the land reform, concerning the poor and the refugees, the governments at various levels took the measures of distributing relief fund and relief materials, organizing villagers cooperative and assistance as well as tax reduction and exemption etc., and thus, to a great extent, solved the farmer's survival problems. Relief for this period included the regular relief and temporary relief, which is arbitrary and passive, and lack of institutional guarantee.

In the mid-1950s, the cooperative movement was gradually implemented in the countryside, and there are great changes in the form of social relief. On June 30, 1956, the First Session of the Third National People's Congress passed *Model Terms of Articles of Association of Advanced Agricultural Production Cooperatives*, which confirmed for the first time that "Five-Guarantees" system be practiced in the countryside, namely, guarantee of eating, wearing, fuel, education (of children), and funeral. In nature, Five-Guarantees is a system of providing welfare relief by all the members to the old, the weak, the widowed, the handicapped member of the village who has no or has lost the working ability. Its principle is "the collective to provide support, the state and the society to provide relief".

Usually, the determination of Five-Guarantees shall follow the following 5 steps: (1) applications to be made by the villager himself or to be nominated by the villagers group; (2) to be reviewed by the villagers committee; (3) to be reported to the people's governments of townships for approval; (4) to be issued the certificate of "Five-Guarantees" after approval.

Once the recipient of the Five-Guarantees has the obligor of maintenance in the law, or get the resource of living or come of the age of 16, the treatment of Five-Guarantees will be ceased with the confirmation of the villagers committee and the approval of the township government.

The standard of Five-Guarantees shall not be lower than the average living standard of the local area, which shall be specified by the local township government. The fund and material for Five-Guarantees shall be allocated from the surplus of the village and the township fiscal budget; where there is collective project, the fees shall be drawn from the revenue or profits of the collective enterprise. After the reform of agricultural taxes and fees, the fund for Five-Guarantees mainly come from the State treasury, and the deficit is to be made up from the agricultural tax; the local governments at various levels of the disaster area or poor area, while allocating the disaster relief, shall give priority to the recipients of the Five-Guarantees and guarantee their living.

The recipients of Five-Guarantees are supported through concentrated system and dispersed system. In the place where conditions are mature, nursing houses are established for concentrated nursing. Nursing houses take the rule of joining voluntarily and leaving freely. Besides the daily nursing service, health care, education assistance, the nursing houses also develop animal husbandry and sidelines for extra income, which are used for better development of the nursing house.

Regarding the dispersed system, the township people's government, the rural collective economic organizations, and the recipients of Five-Guarantees shall sign a supporting or education agreement, which will legalize and systemize their respective rights and obligations. For the recipient with the entrusting principals, the supporting and education agreement shall be signed between the rural collective economic organizations, the entrusting principals, and the recipients of Five-Guarantees. In this way, the rights and obligations of respective parties are consolidated in the legal forms, so as to ensure the smooth enforcement of the supporting work. The personal property of the recipient of Five-Guarantees may be used (but cannot be disposed) by the individual owner during life time. After the death of the recipient of Five-Guarantees, his heritage shall be inherited by the rural collective economic organization. Regarding those who ceased the five-guarantee agreement due to resumed working ability, regained obligor of maintenance, or coming of age 16, the personal property shall belong to the individual owner and be inherited by the inheritor according to the law.

With the deepening of the cooperation, especially during the Great Leap Forward in 1958, cooperative medical care system and health epidemic prevention station were set up in many of the people's commune. In November 1959, a session of the national rural health conference was convened in Jishan County, Shanxi Province. In the conference, the experience of health cooperatives in Shensi-Kansu-Ningsia border region and the experience of

Gaoping, County, and Shanxi Province were summarized and disseminated around the country. Since then, the rural grassroots medical and health system was set up and began to develop gradually.

However, at the early stage of medical and health system, there was serious shortage of medicine and health care workers in rural areas. During the three years of natural disasters from 1959 to 1961, due to food shortages and disease, plenty of rural residents died abnormally. Although the rural cooperative medical system did its share of work, the situation was not improved fundamentally. After all, the root cause of the three years of natural disasters did not lie in the medical and health system, but in the serious food shortage caused by the wrong guideline in agriculture policy. If the food was not adequate to solve the basic issue of survival, there would be no use to have a perfect medical system and sophisticated medical skills. After all, the medical service would buy no beef.

In 1965, Mao Zedong made the June 26 Instruction of "Putting the focus of the medical and health work in rural areas", and the hard situation of rural medical had a great change. In 1968, Yao Wenyuan recommended to Mao Zedong two reports (*Orientation of Medical Education from the Growth of Barefoot Doctors in Jiangzhen Township* and cooperative medical report in Leyuan Commune, Changyang County, Hubei Province), which won Mao Zedong's appreciation and support, and were published in the *People's Daily* and other major media successively, causing a great social influence. Since then, the cooperative medical care system and the system of "barefoot doctors" in the countryside have been widely promoted in the rural areas.

Cooperative medical system is to make contribution jointly by the people's commune, the production brigade and the villager individuals, with all the people bearing the risk. Thus in a sense it is a system of mutual assistance whereby the minority sick person is helped by the majority healthy person. The "barefoot doctors" were just selected from farmers to provide medical service after simple medical training. Those "barefoot doctors" would engage in studying and attending the patient at the same time, engage in agricultural production and medical service concurrently. They would take tours to visit the patients in field, on the land, or at home. They can both provide the villagers with medical care of ordinary illness, while at the same time carry on agricultural production. They lowered the running cost of the professional medical service system, solved the problem of hard situation in the rural areas and safeguarded farmers' health.

By 1975, the number of "barefoot doctors" across the country had reached over 1.3 million, health workers and birth attendants reached 3.6 million. By the late 1970s, cooperative medical care system had been established in over 90% of the villages in China. In 1984, life expectancy of people in the country with per capita GNP over $11000 was 75 years old; life expectancy of the 99 developing countries with per capita GNP of $1720 was

59 years old. Whereas, in 1982, while the per capita GNP is less than $300 in China, the average life expectancy was as high as 68 years old, which is at least 15 years longer than the people of similar income in foreign countries. This was regarded as a wonder of the world. In May 1974, at the 27th World Health Assembly in Geneva, the health care experience introduced by the Chinese delegation aroused the interest of the World Health Organization and the third world countries. The UN Women's and Children's Foundation even pointed out in 1980 ~ 1981 Annual Report that China's system of "barefoot doctors" set a good example for the majority of developing countries to improve the level of medical and health care.

It should be noted that, from the mid-1950s to the end of 1970s, the popularization of the Five-Guarantees and the cooperative medical care system in China were inseparable with the weakening of family function and the growth of the collective economy. With the gradual deepening of the cooperative movement, the traditional function of family as a minimum production units and social life in the past greatly abated, which was replaced by the cooperative as the basic unit of social economy. Only with the development of rural collective economy, the collective welfare based on the cooperative could have a chance to exist and develop. Although this kind of collective welfare system made certain contribution for the stability of rural area and farmers' health, in general it was at the lower level. As in the cooperative economy, it was the same regardless of more contribution or less contribution, which greatly hit the laborer's enthusiasm and caused low labor efficiency. In some place there was not enough financial support for social security, making the collective welfare, especially the cooperative medical care system, an empty shell, and the positive role of cooperative medical care were also discounted.

After the reform and opening up, especially in the mid-1980s, the two-tier management system with household contract management as main body was fully established in the rural areas. The family, not like in the period of "Yi Da Er Gong" (large in size and collective in nature, the family does not possess production materials, but only small amount of consumption materials), began to regain important means of production such as land, farming machines etc., and once again become a basic unit of production and consumption in the social structure. In striking contrast, the cooperative organizations began to collapse, and the cooperative economy became weaker and weaker. Due to lack of strong support of the economic foundation, the collective welfare based on the cooperative economy also tends to decline. In the mid-1980s, the cooperative medical care systems failed to keep up with the pace of reform and opening up and were dismantled. As can be seen from the figure, in the late 1970s, cooperation medical care system was adopted in over 90% of the villages; but in 1989, the proportion was only 4.8%.

Along with the advancement of the economic system reform in China, the market economy develops continuously. In the countryside, the contradiction between the increasing demand for health service and a lack of supply of medical service and the shortage of farmers' purchasing power has been intensified. In 1993, the "poverty-stricken family owing to health problem" account for 26.4% of the total number of poor families in China, by the turn of the century, the proportion rose up to 45.1%. In view of this situation, the state and the government began to attach great importance to the reconstruction of cooperative medical care system in the countryside. The pilot work has been carried out in quite a few places. In spite of this, the reconstruction of the rural cooperative medical work is still slow, and the population participating in cooperative medical care system accounts for only one tenth of the rural population, far below the proportion at the peak period.

Different from the situation of the cooperative medical care system, China began exploration work of setting up social security system at the grassroots level in rural area in the late 1980. On April 12, 1986, the Sixth Sessions of the Fourth National People's Congress adopted the *Seventh Five-year Plan on National Economic and Social Development of the People's Republic of China*, which clearly put forward for the first time: "to build the prototype of social security system with Chinese characteristics in a systematic manner". In October the same year, the Ministry of Civil Affairs held the Symposium of National Rural Grassroots Social Security Work in Zhangjiagang City, Jiangsu Province, marks the starting of rural grassroots social security work in theory and in practice. According to the *National Economic and Social Development of the Ninth Five-year Plan and the Outline of the Long-Term Target for the Year 2010* adopted on March 17, 1996 by the Fourth Session of Eighth National People's Congress, by the end of the 20th century, a multi-level social security system combining social insurance, social relief, social welfare and special care and placement, social mutual assistance and personal savings shall be preliminarily established, and the relatively complete social security system shall be set up by 2010. As early as 1991, China began the pilot work of rural social endowment insurance in the economic developed areas. Shandong was the first province in this regard. In January 1992, the Ministry of Civil Affairs, on the basis of summing up the experience of difference places, formulated the *Basic Plan of Rural Social Endowment Insurance at Country Level (Temporary)* for reference in implementation around the country. The main contents of the plan include:

(1) starting from the reality of rural area, with a view to safeguard the basic life of the old, a unified social insurance system will be adopted for rural residents and the fund shall mainly come from the individual, with the collective providing subsidies and the state providing policy guidance;

(2) the age for paying premium is from 20 to 60, the age beginning to receive old pension is 60; the individual account will be set up, the individual payment and collective subsidies will be recorded under the personal name;

(3) the guarantee period for old pension is 10 years, if the beneficiary dies prior to the expiration of the 10 years, the balance can be inherited; if the beneficiary live beyond the 10-year limitation, he is still entitled to the old pension until death.

(4) the value preservation and appreciation for the fund will mainly from the buying of treasury bonds and bank interests. It cannot be used for direct investment; the old pension adopts the 3-tier management system at the county, township and village levels; with features of low standards, wide coverage, and multi-levels.

The Report dated November 8, 2002 of the Sixteenth National Congress of Communist Party of China (CPC), and the *Decision of the Central Committee of the Communist Party of China on Improving the Socialist Market Economic System* adopted on Third Plenary Session of the 16th Central Committee of CPC on October 14, 2003 points out, the rural minimum living security system shall be in places where conditions allow. At present, the pilot work of the system is being gradually carried out. In addition, the effective development of poverty alleviation has greatly promoted the establishment and improvement of the rural social security system.

Generally speaking, great achievements have been made with the rural social security system construction in China. However, the rural social security is basically at the low level of social assistance and special care and placement. In summary, it has the following characteristics:

(1) The low levels.

On the one hand, at present stage, the rural social security mainly covers the low level security of disaster relief, Five-Guarantees, the social insurance and social welfare such as pension, medical care etc., which are still at the pilot stage, far from being a unified and complete system; on the other hand, the amount of social security payment is at low level, inadequate to maintain the basic survival needs of the farmers.

(2) The small scope.

At present, the endowment insurance and cooperative medical care in rural area cover only about 10% of the population. The Five-Guarantees, special care and placement, and disaster relief are addressed to only a small number of special groups, most farmers being excluded from the social security system.

(3) Confused systems.

Except the Five-Guarantees system and the special care and placement system, most welfare projects were not systemized, for which there is no unified policy arrangement, and basically it is decided by the local governments.

(4) Low effectiveness.

There are few laws, but more regulations and rules on rural social security; more local legislation, but few legislations of the Central government.

(5) Thin hierarchy.

Apart from the basic rural security, there is few supplemental security; basically, it is the government security, with few commercial security and inadequate private participation. In addition, compared with the urban social security, the rural social security is extremely backward.

Since the promulgation of the *Rules of the People's Republic of China on Labor Insurance* in 1951, the old pension, medical treatment, worker's compensation, unemployment and other social insurance system and urban minimum living security system have been gradually established in urban areas, whereas the agriculture, rural areas and farmers who/which have made a great contribution and sacrifice to/for industrialization and urbanization of the nation, cannot enjoy a relatively complete social security, just like the urban residents. It is very unfair for farmers. We shall increase investment in rural social security to narrow the gap between the urban areas and the rural areas, so that the broad masses of farmers can get the national treatment with fairness and justice.

16.1.5 Construction of Harmonic Socialist Society and Social Security System in Rural Area

On September 19, 2004, the *Decision of the Central Committee of the Communist Party of China on Strengthening the Construction of the Party's Governing Capacity* adopted by the Fourth Plenary Session of the 16th National Congress of Communist Party of China formally put forward the new proposition of building a harmonious socialist society. On February 19, 2005, President Hu Jintao, at the seminar for provincial leaders to improve the ability of building a harmonious socialist society, pointed out that the socialist harmonious society is a society of democracy, of fairness and justice, a society ruled by the law, a society of honesty and friendliness, a society of vitality, stability and order, a society of harmony between human and nature. Democracy means the socialist democracy is advocated, rule by the law means the basic strategy of rule of law can be implemented; fairness and justice, means the various social interest relationship can be coordinated, and the contradictions among the people and other social contradictions can be handled correctly, social justice and equity can be safeguarded and realized; honesty and friendliness means honest and trustworthy, equality, fraternity, all the people get along well with each other and help each other; vibrant means respecting the creativity which is helpful for the progress of society, the creation movement is supported and the creative achievement is appreciated; stability and order means there is a sound social organization mechanism, complete social management, good social order, the people live and work in peace and contentment, and the society maintains stable and united; and harmony between human and nature means scientific production, affluent life, and favorable ecological environment. Building a harmonious socialist society is a great strategy put forward with the deep understanding of the new situation, new characteristics in China in the new period of reform and opening up. It sets the goals for the establishment and promotion of rural social security system.

First of all, from above analysis of the plight of agriculture, rural areas and farmers in China, and the present situation of the rural social security, we can see that the largest problem is the disharmony between the urban and the rural, disharmony between the industrial and the agriculture, and disharmony between the east and the west. China has been engaged in the reform and opening-up undertaking for more than a decade, and has made remarkable achievements. However, the gaps between the urban and rural areas, between the industry and the agriculture, between the east and the west have been widened constantly, with conflict being continuously deepened and the society becoming more and more turbulent. Regarding the above problems, the social security is a mechanism to regulate the social distribution, narrow the gap between the rich and the poor, and reverse the social imbalances. Therefore, we must increase investment in "three agriculture-related problems" and set up rural social security system of various levels and various standards so as to turn the situation around.

Second, the fairness and justice connotation of socialist harmonious society requires the rural social security system be established and promoted. Agriculture, rural areas and farmers have made great contribution to the industrialization and the socialist modernization in China, but the farmers cannot live like the urban residents and equally enjoy the benefits of the modern social security: the urban residents can enjoy abundant benefits, whereas in rural area a unified social security system has not been established yet. This is extremely unfair for them. Farmers in the process of modernization are not destined to be the victims, and they should also be the beneficiaries. We can no longer ignore the interests of farmers.

Again, the harmony of human and nature demands that we should establish and complete the rural social security system. With the continuous development of economy, the traditional extensive economic growth pattern has caused negative impact on human beings: resources shortage, serious pollution, frequent disasters, and recurring disease epidemic. In recent years of the mad cow disease, foot and mouth disease, avian flu, SARS and influenza are all the consequence of serious imbalance between human and nature, which not only seriously blows the global economic development, but also endangers the survival of mankind, and which has become a difficult problem faced by the mankind. Although the establishment of rural social security system cannot necessarily ease the contradiction between man and nature, its medical insurance and social relief can effectively alleviate the disease threat to humanity, and ensure the basic survival needs of the farmers.

Finally, the establishment of rural social security system is also the important guarantee of building a harmonious socialist society. Just as the saying goes, the Empire, long divided, must unite; long united, must divide. Did you ever know what the reason is behind? The five thousand years of civilization in China has already indicated that the Chinese problem is the problem of farmers, and the Chinese revolution is the revolution of farmers. It was so in the past, it is the same at present, and remains the same in the foreseeable future. Who really understands the farmers, who will understand China; who is supported by the farmers, who can have the world. From the current situation in China, if agriculture thrives, everything will be smooth; if the farmers are rich, the state will be rich; if the rural area is stable, the country will be stable. The establishment of rural social security system is an important means to guarantee the stability of "three agriculture-related problems". It is an inseparable part of harmonious socialist society. Without the stability of the "three agriculture-related problems", the socialist harmonious society will become empty talk.

16.2 SOCIAL SECURITY FUNCTION OF LAND IS BEING QUESTIONED

China's problem is the issue of farmers, and the farmers' problem is land problem. In the majestic, vigorous, and endless miles of historical tide, the land problem has been extended for thousands of years. So far, it is still an unsolvable problem. Now, the land is magically endowed with "the function of social security". This view was widespread and has great influence. Its advocates even include the "celebrities" and "expert" in the related field. Their theoretical bases are as following:

(1) while the State confers the land use right to farmers, it also assigns the responsibilities of social security for farmers. The farmers will live on the land and shall not depend on the State anymore.

(2) China is a country with too many more people and fewer land, the income from the land could only meet the basic needs of the people, its

function of basic maintenance is far greater than the function of making fortune;

(3) the land can also provide insurance functions such as pension, unemployment, thus doing a great job for the stability of the countryside.

16.2.1 To Pierce the Veil of Social Security Function of Land

What is the land? According to the views of Marxist political economics, the land is one of the most basic factors of production. Of course, the land can also be used as a means of livelihood, but in essence its function is mainly reflected in the production, so it is the focus of our discussion. Farmers operation of land is to get more output with fewer investments, thus to enjoy the increase of value brought by the land. For instance, if 30 *Jin* (one Jin equals to half a kilogram) is sowed in one mu of land, we can get a good harvest of 800 *Jin*. After deducting the cost of chemical fertilizers, pesticides, agricultural, taxes, fees and other costs, we can still have a profit of several hundred yuan. However, if the output cannot cover the cost, no one will operate the land. In recent years, the income from farming has dropped dramatically, so that in many regions, especially in the eastern coastal area, many farmers left the land unattended. Therefore, the land is not mysterious. It is only a kind of production material. When it is profitable, people would flock to it; when the income from the land cannot cover the cost, people would quit it. No one would live and die with the land just because it is the production material, unless there is no other choice. From this point of view, the farming of the farmers is just the same as the working of the workers, and there is no essential difference. The farmers earn a life in the land, and the workers earn a life in the factory. The farmers are entitled to the right use right, but not the land ownership; the worker are the proletariat who do not possess any production material. If the farmers cannot earn money from operating the land, they can quit the land; if the worker cannot make a living from the factory, they can resign. From this sense, farming and workmanship are all means for make a living, is there any difference in essence?

As one kind of production material, if the land possesses the security function, then in essence the "security function" is the value-added function of the land. Some scholars insisted on the so-called "security function" of land, in fact, their meaning is that the net output of the land can provide financial or material support for the guarantee of farmers. Isn't that part of the production function of the land? If the land cannot make the ends meet, or even goes to zero, then the farmer's basic living will be influenced, what security can the land provide for the farmer? Thus, the value-added function of the land is untrue. It is just a disguise. In essence, it is the production function. Apart from this function, there is no other new function affiliated with the land.

If the land had the security function, by the same logic, does "work", another means of making a living, also possess the security function? Because, according to the above analysis, both the land and work are means of making living, both are sources of income. Although their appearances are different, essentially they are the same. If the land had the security function, the work should also have the security function. But in fact, the security function of work is not as beautiful as logical reasoning: the farmer may come across difficulty in farming; workers will also have their trouble in work. Workers may have difficulty in supporting a whole family even though they have a job, otherwise there will be not so many poor people and shanty area in the cities. Even worse, a sword of Damocles is being hung above the head of the workers. That is, unemployment may happen at any time. If the worker lost his job, where is the workers' security? Similarly, the "security function" of work is also junk and slick. In fact, the so-called "security function" is actually "reliance". You have something to rely on when your work is smooth; but if you meet difficulties in work or are laid off, you have nothing to rely on. It is just because of the precarious critical defect in the security function of "work" that the State and the society take great trouble and spend huge amount in setting up the old pension, medical care, worker's compensation, maternity and minimum living standard and other welfare systems.

Compared with the "security function" of "work", the "security function" of land is also vulnerable and exists in name only. Farming is an industry heavily dependent on the climate. Even though the wheat ear is long, the kernel is completely filled, and the rice is golden and the crops are prosperous, there is no security before the harvest. Only when the green crops have become the golden grain and entered the barn of the farmers, can we say to have a good harvest. Otherwise, everything is only a "duck" at the mouth, which may slip away at any time. The author also comes from the farmer families, and fully understands the influence of climate on the crops. The deepest impression is in the middle of 1994, when the wheat harvest season comes, everyone is ready to enjoy the pleasure of harvest. However, a heavy rain of seven days extinguished the hopes of the farmers who had toiled on the land for half a year. The wheat all germinated or get mouldy, making the output of that year even less than half of the average yield. Even worse, the harvested wheat is black and thin, hard to sell, hard to eat, most of which could only be used for pigs fodde at last. In that year, if the farmers had no surplus grain from previous years, they would have trouble in getting enough food. Let alone the security function of the land.

What will it be like in case of a good harvest? Even though the production is increased, production does not equal to income. Examples are not few that the grain cannot be sold out. In history, especially in 1984 and 1996, the bumper crop harvest led to the drastic increase of total grain output. However, the excitement of farmers once again fell into the "ice": the grain could not sell out, production is not income! In my mind, the price of rice was as low as twenty cents a *Jin* (500g). If the output was at 500 kg per *mu*, the total income would be 200 yuan per *mu*. There are six people in my family, with a total land of five or six *mu* (including residential land), except for some small pieces of land used to plant some fruits and vegetables, oil seed rape, soybean etc., the other land was used for growing of wheat. With a total area of around 5 *mu* of wheat, the income was about 1000 yuan. The per capita income was less than RMB 200 for half a year. This happened in North Jiangsu Province where economic conditions are relatively better. If it was in the western mountain areas, it would be even worse. Similar examples are countless. Therefore, it can be seen that good harvest is not necessarily a security.

Actually, agriculture has been an industry of deficit since the middle of the 20th century, the farmers with per capita cash income below the average line has been up to 70%, and the farmers' income with zero growth or negative growth has reached about 50%.[1]

The data from a survey into the rural household in 2002 shows the per capita net income of Chinese farmers is RMB 2366.40 in 2001, whereas the per capita expenditure is RMB 2779.96, with a deficit of per capita RMB 413.20. To be more specific, the per capita net incomes were RMB 3232.75, RMB 2163.52 and RMB 1662.71 for the rural areas in the eastern, central and western parts respectively, whereas the expenditures were RMB 3355.51, RMB 2646.96 and RMB 2185.14 respectively, with deficits of per capita RMB 122.76, RMB 483.44 and RMB 522.43 respectively.[2] While the agricultural yields kept a continued depression, the prices of fertilizer, seeds, pesticides, feed and other means of agricultural production and light industrial products were soaring, which greatly increased the cost of agriculture, and reduced the agricultural profits.

Through the above analysis it can be seen that, at present time, whether good climate or flood drought, farmers farming is basically hard to make ends meet. In this case, how can the land provide guarantee to the farmers? What kind of guarantee can it provide? The opinion on the security function of land is really asking for the moon.

16.2.2 Malfunction of Government and Market

Government also noticed the problems of agriculture, and thus formulated a series of systems, including the protective purchase price for grain. The government's intention is good, but in fact the effect of the implementation has backfired. Since the implementation of the protective system for grain purchase price, the government protective price has seldom been higher than the market price. Instead, for most of the years, the government protective prices were far below the market prices. The Farmers had no choice, but sell the grain on the market with a relatively better price (still very low price).

When it comes to the role of government in the rural economy, it is often the case that the government not only failed to help the farmers, but often go to the opposite side. Of course, the government's intentions were good. After Deng Xiaoping made his southern inspection tour in 1992, China entered into a period of comprehensively establishing the socialist market economy. Many development zones were set up in different regions, and stirred up a wave of investment. With the increase of investment, the demand for labor surged. In 1992, 46 million migrant workers were attracted into the city, in 1993, the total number of migrant worker reached 60 million, in 1994 ~ 95, the number is 70 ~ 80 million. Formerly, those migrant workers were self-sufficient, and now they have become the commodity grain consumers, with an annual demand of 60 billion *Jin* (500g), which greatly stimulated the demand of food.[3] At the same time, on January 1, 1994, the exchange rate of RMB was depreciated by 57%, resulting in the original importer in southeast coastal areas also turned to hoard food in the domestic market.

The above two factors greatly pushed up the domestic market prices of the grain, leading to a short supply of grain despite of good harvest in China for consecutive years. Therefore, the government successively raised the grain purchase price in 1994 and 1996, up to 105%. At the same time, the household contract responsibility system was confirmed to remain unchanged for 30 years. These policy and measures greatly stimulated the food production, making the total grain output achieved the goal of 1 trillion *jin* in 1996, four years in advance of the schedule. All these caused the second large backlog of grain in 1996 since reform and opening up in China, and the farmers' revenue from the grain declined significantly, serious harming the farmers' enthusiasm of grain production and economic interests.

It should be noted that, previously in order to alleviate the situation of grain shortage in the grain market, the government imported a large quantity of food, with a total of 300 million tons from 1995 to 1996. This not only greatly brought down the domestic food prices, but also drove up the international market. In 2000, the production of soybean in China was 15 million tons, but by then, China's soybean imports from abroad has been as high as 12 million tons, accounting for 80% of total soybean output in 2000. We can imagine the influence of such a huge amount of imported soybean on China market and Chinese farmers. In my mind, there is no other country that is so "generosity" in protecting the interest of the farmers. Generous to others is indifference to its own people!

When supply exceeds demand, the farmers will be hurt by the low prices. This is understandable. However, when the grain is in short supply, it is still hard for farmers to get profits. This vicious cycle it is caused by the agricultural policy in China, I think. As the saying goes, "to the country, people is all-important, to the people, foodstuff is all-important". China is a big country with a population of one billion three hundred million, so the food issue is the most important issue for any country. Therefore, the country must guarantee the stability of grain markets, and avoid social unrest owing to short supplies.

When supply exceeds demand, the country will take some remedial measures to protect the interests of the farmers, so that the initiative of the farmer will not be hurt and cut off production drastically. When the grain is in short supply, the country would raise grain prices to stimulate the grain production; while at the same time import great amount of grain from abroad to maintain the stability of the domestic market. In short, the stability of the market and safety of grain is the basic starting point and end-result of all the agricultural policy in China, while the interests of the farmers are in the secondary consideration. I do not think, this may also explain the status quo why the farmers will not die of hunger, nor will they become rich from farming on the land. From a deeper understanding, the vicious circle is also caused by the inherent contradiction between the planned economy and market economy in the fields of agriculture and industry and commerce, in rural areas and urban areas: agricultural sector in China is still a deep imprint of planned economy. Although on the surface the farmers obtained autonomy in operation, the scattered vulnerable, small farmer economy cannot adapt to the ever-changing market economy, and the government is still in a dominant position in the field of agriculture. What kind of crops will the farmers grow? How many crops to grow? And how to grow? These questions are decided by the government. In particular, the grain purchase price and sale price is not spontaneously formed by the market. As a result, for more than a decade after the reform and opening-up, the agriculture, rural areas and farmers were still largely free from the market economy. The market function does not work in the face of "three agriculture-related problems". Meanwhile, the government planned economy played a leading role and had profound influence on "three agriculture-related problems", but it is doomed to be a failure by the historical experience, whether in the past or at present. The dual failures of government and market resulted in the unequal status of the farmers in the bargaining of grain transaction and the defeat in the commercial battle of market economy. So far, the so-called security function of the land is just like the colorful bubbles, which cannot get rid of the fate of bubble burst after moment of fantasy.

16.2.3 Security Function of Land Does Not Equal to "Social Security"

Since production function of land is weakened, and the security function is strengthened, then, according to the logic of some people, it's exactly the evidence of the welfare function of the land. This view is wrong. The production function of land is the production function; it will not change to the welfare function just because of the weakening of production functions. Can it be said that the land with production capacity of 1000 *jin* per mu represents the production function of the land, while the land with production capacity of 300 *jin* per mu represents the social security of the land? Similarly, can it be said the job with salary of RMB 3000 represents the production function, while the job with salary of RMB 500 yuan represents the social security function? The weakening of production function does not mean the strengthening of the social security function, but instead, the decrease of social security function, which means the decrease of supporting capacity of the land to the social security system. In fact, the "security function" claimed by the scholars should be called life supporting or reliance function, which belongs to the sphere of production function even though the production capacity is weakened, and which is quite different from the social security function in normal sense.

As mentioned earlier, the so-called social security is the social welfare system established within the scope of the whole society by the State to overcome the adverse effects on people's life brought about by old age, illness, disability, unemployment, birth, death and other survival risks, and to ensure the basic survival needs of the social members. In short, "any public measures taken according to the relevant laws and policies to tackle the risk of the society and provide its members with security, can be called social security".[4]

As can be seen from the definition, social security is a self-contained social system; it is completely independent from the land, workshop, equipment and other material wealth creation system. The establishment of social security is not based on the existence of any production materials: its existence does not rely on the land as the premise. Nor does it rely on plant, equipment, or other production factors. Otherwise we will jump to the absurd conclusion of losing of productive resources such as land, plant and equipment is equal to losing of social security. Farmers can enjoy social security as long as they are farming on the land, workers can enjoy social security even though they do not have land. When farmers lost land, or worker get unemployed, they can still enjoy social security. This is the relative independence between social security and production material.

For the people to live in the world, there are four protection levels, or four safety nets: the first is the income from farming or working to meet the material and cultural needs of life; the second is the personal or family deposit or insurance; the third is the supplementary insurance provided by the enterprises, for-profit organizations, or insurance applicant themselves according to their own economic strength and security demand; the fourth is the integrated arrangement by the society, i.e., parts of material wealth created by farming and working are stored and put together, which will be paid in case of old age, disease, unemployment or other risks to meet the basic survival needs of the people. The forth level of protection for human survival is the social security in normal sense. The so-called "land security function" just belongs to the first protection level, which in fact is one of the forms of production function, rather than social security.

16.2.4 Land Household Contracting Is Not a Blessing of the State to the Farmer

Some scholars claim that since the State has allowed the farmers to occupy the land in the name of the all-round responsibility system, its responsibilities of the social security for farmers is exempted.[5] I think that this view is purely the academic cognition of individualism, for which there is no legal basis.

First of all, let the farmers occupies the land use right is not a free gift to the farmers. In 1952, the completed land reform allowed the land to be possessed by the farmers. This is signified in the 1954 *Constitution*, of which Article 8 states that the farmers land ownership and other means of production are protected in accordance with the law. Later, when it came to the cooperative movement, the personal ownership of land was gradually replaced by the collective ownership of cooperatives. The farmers no longer enjoyed the land ownership, but enjoyed the membership in the cooperative. In 1978, the land reform was initiated in the rural areas, and the farmers were allowed to contract the cooperative land collectively in the name of household. This can be said to be partly resumption of the rights of the farmers to the land. The mention of partly resumption was just because after the all-round responsibility system, the land was still owned by the collective, and the farmers did not resume the ownership of land, but just the right to use the land. Thus it can be seen that formerly the land belongs to the farmers and the State allows the farmers to use the land does not mean a gift of the State, but just partly resumption of the former land system. Therefore, it is a wrong belief that the State shall be exempted from the society security responsibility to the farmers because the farmers enjoy a gift of using the land by contracting system.

Second, the administrative obligation of the State to provide the farmers with social security shall not be exempted, even though the land use rights are bestowed to the farmers. Clause 4 of Article 14 of the *Constitution* stipulates, "The state shall establish and complete the society security system in compliance with the economy development", and Clause 1 of Article 45 stipulates that citizens of the People's Republic of China have the right to material assistance from the state and society when they are old, ill or disabled. The State develops social insurance, social relief and medical and health services that are required for citizens to enjoy this right. Article 3 of

Labor Law spells out the laborer right to the social insurance and welfare. Article 70 provides that the State shall develop social insurance undertakings, establish a social insurance system, and set up social insurance funds so that laborers may receive assistance and compensations under such circumstances as old age, illness, work-related injury, unemployment and childbearing.

It can be seen that both the constitution and general law provide the farmers' right to enjoy social security and the obligation of the State to provide social security for farmers. This obligation of the State will not be exempted by conferring farmers land contract right, unless otherwise provided for in the future. The claim that farmers waived social security right in exchange for the land use right is groundless. It is a kind of evasion of State responsibility and indifference to the rights and interests of farmers.

16.3 CONSTRUCTION OF SOCIAL SECURITY SYSTEM IN RURAL AREA

16.3.1 Construction of Minimum Living Security System for Rural Residents

Whether it is urban residents or rural residents, as long as they are the citizens of the People's Republic of China, they should equally enjoy the right to social security. We could not create injustice or privileges on the ground of difference on household registration. Otherwise it will be against the ideology of modern constitutionalism. Urban and rural residents shall enjoy the equal national treatment. It is the same in terms of social security.

At present, the city residents can enjoy a relatively perfect social security service, whereas the rural social security not only lags far behind the urban social security, it also cannot keep pace with the economic development level of the rural area. Construction of rural social security system is a long-term and complicated process. If this process is compared to the long march of twenty-five thousand *li*, the first step is to build the minimum living security system for rural residents, so I think. The reasons are as follows:

1. China is fully capable of establishing a minimum living security system for rural residents

As we all know, social security includes social insurance, social welfare, social relief and special care and placement. Among them, social relief is the lowest level of social security, which concerns the survival issue. The social welfare is the highest level of social security, which seeks for the comfort and ease of life. As an indispensable part of social relief, the system of minimum living security system for rural residents is for the most vulnerable groups of the society who are struggling for survival. The problem to be solved is the fundamental issue of survival or death.

It has been nearly 30 years since the reform and opening-up, China's economic construction has made remarkable achievements, and people's living standards have improved greatly. Generally, China has entered a transition period from being adequately fed and clad to being fairly well-off. The people living on the brink of survival are few, and the problem to solve is the basic issues of food and clothing. Therefore, the cost of manpower, material and financial resources will be limited. Comparatively, it will be easier for the State and society to solve this problem.

According to the fifth national population census in 2000, China's population reached 1.29533 billion, among which, the rural population accounts for 63.91%, or 827.85 million people. According to the estimation of the National Bureau of Statistics, by the end of 2002, the number of people below the absolute poverty line, i.e., with per capita annual net income of less than RMB 627 yuan is 28.2 million people in rural areas, accounting for 2.2% of the total population, and 3.4% of the rural population. Their average annual per capita income was RMB 531 yuan. If the difference between real income and poverty line is to made up, the State will have to pay 2.7072 billion yuan a year. In 2003, the poverty line was adjusted to the average annual per captia income of 637 yuan, and the population below the poverty line reached $29 million. Even if the population below the absolute poverty line is calculated at 30 million, the supplementary fund will be 3.2 billion to make up the gap. Compared to the central fiscal avenue of 2.639647 trillion yuan in 2004, this figure is a drop in the bucket. Besides, the rural minimum living security funds mainly come from the local government, and are not all borne by the Central government, thus the 3.2 billion minimum living security funds can be resolved anyway. In addition, the recipients of the rural minimum living security funds overlap to a large degree with the traditional recipients of civil administrative relief, e.g., the households in hardships, needy households and households of Five-Guarantees etc. As a result, the construction of rural minimum living security system will not greatly increase the financial burden, and is completely within the range of affordable.

2. The urgency to build rural minimum living security

Rural minimum living security system is for the most vulnerable groups of the society who are struggling for survival. The problem to be solved is the fundamental issue of survival or death. Is there anything urgent than saving the people's life? Some officials in the local government neglect the life and dignity of the poor people. They either did not include the minimum living security fund in the financial budget, or they just use it as a shop sign. That means even though they include the minimum security fund in the budget, they would spend less or would not use the fund at all on the minimum security. It is no exaggeration that those officials are "murdering people in cold blood". If a government cannot even solve the survival problem of the people, it is a government of incompetence. If the governments have the ability to solve the problem but just turns a blind eye to the survival issue of the masses of poor people, the government is a delinquent one!

Of course, there exist some difficulties in some relatively backward economic region in raising funds for rural minimum living fund, however, they are not unsolvable problems. As long as the local government fully understand the importance and urgency of rural minimum living fund, and take less consideration of individual utilitarian, then, I think, the rural minimum living fund can be solved absolutely. For about 30 years after reform and opening-up, the GDP in China have expanded several times, high buildings sprung up one after another, highways came out one after another. Can't we even solve the problem of food and clothing of the people? Of course we can. Even though the funds are unavailable, we should also reduce other unnecessary spending, and make enough money to solve the survival problem of the poor; besides, according to the current economic strength, is it a hard job? If we cut an image project, the fund saved will be adequate for rural minimum living security for several years.

Some people might say, China is still a developing country, its economic strength is limited, and we should put the fund in economic development. I think, the view is an excuse. Absolute excuse even though it seems grandiose. When there is problem with survival, what is the use talking about development? What is the purpose for development? Eventually it is for the living of the masses. Therefore, survival is the premise of development, and development is for a better life. If we talk about development without thinking of survival, it will be putting the cart before the horse.

Some people are overly optimistic and place the problem of survival on development. They hold that once the economy develops, the survival problems can be solved. This may be not sure. America is one of the richest in the world, with its IBM, Bill Gates, and even several space tourisms. However, there are still many people wandering about the streets, too! Is that the America's economic power not strong enough to let them live a decent and dignified life? Do those people like wandering about the streets instead of leading a happy life?

In recent years, the new generation of the CPC Central Committee with Hu Jintao as the core put forward the grand conception of building a harmonious socialist society. This is a brilliant decision, which will open a new chapter for the great undertaking of Chinese rejuvenation. However, if the survival problem remains an issue, how can we build a harmonious society? It is sheer nonsense talking about harmonization while a person remains hungry, and talking about stability while people cannot afford medical fees! In recent years, the gap between the urban and rural areas continued to be widened the relationship between the masses and the cadres are deteriorating, which is the embodiment of social imbalances. Therefore, it is top priority to build minimum living security system for rural residents and to solve the problem of the survival of farmers as soon as possible.

3. The building of minimum living security system is the demand of rule of law in rural area

People with a slight understanding of social security all know, there exist a series of defects in the traditional social relief, such as narrow scope of relief, low standard; lack of unified standards in the choice of recipients, leading to duplicate relief; irregular and casual relief; low level of the stipulation on relief, with administrative rules as the highest; some are just local policies, varies from place to place and year to year, lacking of legal effect, stability and regularity. To build the system of minimum living security for rural residents is to integrate and sort out the traditional rural relief system according to the principles of openness, fairness, impartiality and fully embody the spirit of rule of law, earnestly safeguard the farmer's right to exist, and guarantee the harmony and stability of rural area.

With the development of social economy, the improvement of living standards and the advancement of rule of law in China, the masses of people, including the farmers, are awakening with the rights consciousness. They are no longer contented with the verbal provisions of the law on right, and begin to pursue the specific and practical right to survive. As far as the farmers are concerned, they hope their right to survive is not just a slogan, but a practical right of getting material support from the State and society when they are in trouble and obtaining the social guarantee to lead a dignified life when they are in trouble. To ensure the right to survive of the poor farmers, the State and society shall provide a public product to make them free from worries about their survival. Otherwise, the lack of rural minimum living security will not only highlight the government's dereliction of duty and omission, but also render the 29 million poor farmers' right to exist empty talk. As to maintaining social justice, narrowing the gap between the urban and rural areas, and promoting equality and justice, all become impossible.

At present, the rural social security is uneven in different places in China, with some places developing fast and some places just so so. Among the reasons, I think some people put too much stresses on the difference of economic development level and neglect the fundamental flaws in the system. In my opinion, besides the differences in economic strength, the more important reason is the different understanding of rural social security of the local governments at different places. If the leaders of local government have a good understanding, the social security work will go smoothly. Otherwise, without the support of party leaders and government leaders, even a clever woman cannot cook a meal without rice. This is the actual situation of rural social security mechanism; it is also the crux of the problem. We cannot importune every leader fully understand the importance of the rural social security. Even if the present leaders have strong support for rural social security, how about the next leaders? Who can guarantee that they will act like the present leaders? Even though they pay no attention to, or take no actions regarding rural social security, they will not get any adverse consequences. This is a typical of rule of man.

The rural social security work can't rely on the joys and sorrows of the leaders, as there will be thunder and rain. Who can guarantee there will be clear blue skies every day? Therefore, in my opinion, the rural social security should be consolidated by means of law, whereby it will not be changed with the change of leaders. Neither will it be changed with the expiration of the government term of office. That is to implement the rural social security under the rule of law. Rural minimum living security system is just one means of rule of law, whereby every government and every official will be bound by law in promoting the work of rural minimum living security. Of course, this is not only the issue of rural social security itself, but also involves the process of political system reform.

16.3.2 Design of Minimum Living Security System for Rural Residents

1. The principle of rural minimum living security system

(1) The principle of urban and rural areas integration.

Principle of urban and rural areas integration of minimum living security does not mean ignoring the economic difference and income gap between urban and rural areas and adopting exactly the same level of security and payment standards, but the integration of urban and rural minimal living security at the central and provincial levels on the basis of the same law, while at the same time allowing different security and payment standards according to the different economic development level and residential income, e.g., the different poverty lines and different financing modes between urban and rural areas. The integration here is at the preliminary stage, and to be more specifically, the integration of the personality and dignity, rather than integration of poverty line or financing mode, etc. The integration of urban and rural minimum living security system is the first step to bridge the gap between urban and rural areas. It is conducive to the gradual change of the dual economic and social structure between the urban and rural areas, and finally the complete reunification of the urban and rural minimum living security from ideology and essence.

Good examples have been set up in Shanghai, Guangdong, Zhejiang and other regions in this respect and achievements have been made. On August

15, 2001, *Measure for Minimum Living Security in Zhejiang Province* was issued by Zhejiang People's Government by Decree No. 131, which stipulated that the integrated minimum living security between urban and rural areas be implemented since October 1, 2001. So far, over 500 thousand people have been included in the scope of minimum living security system, and good economic and social benefits have been achieved.

(2) The principle of ensuring basic life.

The nature of minimum living security system determines that the standard of security shall be limited to the guarantee of basic need for life, and cannot be too high. Otherwise, it will deviate from the nature of the system of survival relief and because serious financial burden to the government at all levels on the one hand; on the other hand, if the standard of minimum living security is too high, it will also breed a phenomenon of laziness, which is not conducive to social fairness and efficiency. Of course, the relief standard cannot be too low, otherwise there will be no significance and the purpose of ensuring minimum living standard cannot be realized. The standard of minimum living security, I believe, should be carefully set on the basis of scientific survey into the level of economic development, residents' income level, financial capacity and price index etc. It shall be formulated in the principle of opening low and going high, i.e., at the beginning the standard can be lower, which can be improved gradually according to the actual conditions. The situation of opening high and going low shall be avoided. If we start with a high standard, there will be no room for maneuver. Therefore, we shall be prudent at the beginning. Currently, there are different views on the standard of China's poverty line (the reference standard of minimum living security). In my opinion, these arguments are unnecessary. The crux of the problem is not whether the poverty line is high or low, but how high the poverty line can reflect the actual situation and can be most feasible. If we really have economic strengths, it may be raised at any time according to the actual situation; but if the fund is limited, it will not make sense even we set the standard too high. As a result, it is advisable the minimum living security be set for the purpose of ensuring the basic life, which can be adjusted according to the actual situation. There is no need to reach the goal in one step.

(3) The principle of openness, fairness and justice (three-fair principle).

The three-fair principles require the operation of rural minimum living security system shall be transparent and in compliance with the law. Openness means the standard of minimum living security, the recipients of the minimum living security, and the amount of relief shall be disclosed to the public, and the black box operation shall be rejected. Fairness and justice means as long as the per capita income of the family members is below the local poverty line, they shall have the right to apply for the minimum living security and obtain the corresponding remedy. We could not say turkey to one and bazzard to another. To this end, a social supervision mechanism shall be introduced in the designing of substantial and procedure content of the rural minimum living security system, any blind spots in the supervision procedure shall be rejected, so as to ensure the substantive justice and procedural justice of the minimum living security system. The implementation of three-fair principles, I believe, can be combined with the transparency of government affairs, so that the related party and the news media have sufficient participation and supervision. Regarding this point, there will be elaboration in the next pages.

(4) The principle of combing state security, social support and personal relief.

Chinese citizens enjoy the right to get material assistance from the State and society in case of old age, disease or losing working capacity. As part of the social relief, the rural minimum living security is different from the social insurance. Its fund is mainly provided by the government, and the recipient is not required to pay any fees. It is the legal obligation of the government to guarantee a steady supply of the funds required for the minimum living security. However, it does not exclude other financing channels for minimum living security. Government, in providing the fund for minimum living security, should also actively encourage and support the social strength from all walks of life to make donation enthusiastically, and carry out mutual support movement, so as to fully carry forward the spirit of solidarity and mutual assistance, and make the recipients of rural minimum living security become rich at an early date.

China is a country with philanthropic and benevolent tradition, and with overseas Chinese almost in all corners of the world, we shall pay special attention to social donations, and other charitable welfare assistance in expanding the financing channels of rural minimum living security. Only in this way can the rural minimum living security work can be carried out effectively.

For example, for the six years from 1996 to 2001, the donation of fund and goods amounted to over RMB 11.6 billion, which solved the problem of 320 million victims and poor people. Especially in 1996, flood disasters visited Hunan, Hebei and some other provinces, and the country launched a social donation to raise relief funds and goods of 1.58 billion yuan. Catastrophic floods occurred in China in 1998, Tianjin and other 12 provinces organized fundraising and received fund of 3.515 billion yuan, and nearly a hundred million pieces of clothes and other goods, RBM 3.744 billion in value, totaling RBM 7.259 billion, which greatly exceeded the expenditure from central and local government on disaster relief, and fully demonstrate the great force of social mutual aid. In 2002, the country received a donation of RMB 1.11 billion, and clothing, quilt and other goods of 230 million pieces, which benefited 35.181 million people.[6]

In terms of social donation, the government departments shall do a good job in system design to increase the transparency of work, and make the work of all links under the supervision of parties from all walks of life, especially under the supervision of the donor. This work is indispensable, as far as the political environment and the people's credit are concerned, there is a widespread suspicion and mistrust from the donors, who worry that their hard-won donations will be put into the private pockets, rather than the hands of recipients. A few years ago, there was a scandal that the welfare charity fund was embezzled, which was a great blow to the donation undertakings of the society. Therefore, the relevant departments shall learn a lesson from the past, and block the loopholes of corruption in system design.

In addition, the local government shall encourage and support the recipients with the working capability to participate in the work relief, such as carry out concurrent business or working out etc. They can never foster a parasitic thought of reliance and receiving. The local government and its subordinate departments shall formulate the supporting policies to help ease the burden of the recipient of minimum living security and increase their income, such as reduction or exemption of pooling fund, tuition fees, reduction of working attendance etc. and provide them with more opportunities to earn money.

2. The substantial framework of rural minimum living security system

In 1996, the Ministry of Civil Affairs issued the *Opinion on Accelerating the Construction of Rural Social Security System*, which requires the minimum living security system be established as a key work. From 1996 to 2004, the minimum living security system was established in 1206 counties (cities), 4.964 million villagers from 2.386 million households enjoyed the minimum living security, among which: Five-Guarantees of 320,000 households, accounting for 13.4%; needy households of 1.431 million, accounting for 60%; and other 636,000 households, accounting for 26.7% of total.[7]

To be specific, in August 2001, Zhejiang Province issued the *Measure on Minimum Living Security in Zhejiang Province*; in early 2004, Fujian Province promulgated the *Implementation Rules for Minimum Living Security System for Rural Residents in Fujian Province*; in October 2004, Liaoning Province issued *Interim Measures for Minimum Living Security for Rural Residents in Liaoning Province*. Apart from that, rules and regulations on minimum living security were also issued in Beijing, Guangdong, Shanghai, Hebei and other provinces, and minimum living security systems were also established in those provinces. Although those systems vary from each other, they basically include the following basic elements:

(1) Recipient of minimum living security.

In general, every member of the household whose per capita annual income is lower than the rural minimum living security standard may apply for minimum living security, and should be included in the category of social security, unless otherwise specified.

Take Zhejiang Province as an example, the following persons are excluded from the category of minimum living security: household members with working capability refuses the job offer without any reasonable cause and does not stand on their own feet; household possessing idle productive facilities or unproductive facilities (not including housing and other basic necessities), with discounted per capita value over 6 times of the standard of the local minimum living security; family living standard obviously higher than the standard of the local minimum living security standard.

In Liaoning Province, household with the following circumstances cannot enjoy minimum security: building house, purchase commercial housing or decorating house with high standard within the last 3 years; buying top grade of unnecessities (specific value limits to be decided by local area); household with a non-operational vehicles; household with telephone or mobile phone, and monthly total costs in excess of 80% of the standard of local minimum living security; household with high value of collection or securities investment; household with children attending selected school, with children studying abroad on their own expense, or with children attending school with charges during the period of compulsory education; household in difficult situation owing to the behavior of gambling, drug use, illegal marriage, or illegal adoption, which has not yet been corrected; household with members visiting the catering and entertainment places frequently.

Taken together, the recipients of the rural minimum living security shall include the old, the weak, the sick and the youth beyond the statutory working age, who are mainly the traditional recipients of Five-Guarantees. These people shall be included into the category of minimum living security system, and the security enjoyed by them shall be a certain percentage higher than the full amount of minimum living security, so that their lives will not be lower than the general living standard of local residents. In this respect, reference can be made to the practice in Fujian province. The second groups include residents within the statutory working age, which lost work capability owing to sickness or handicap; the third group includes healthy residents within the statutory working age, who are under the bad living environment and lack of fund resources. Among them, the former two groups are the most vulnerable, who shall be the key groups for relief, just as the group for special care and placement; The last group of people has the working ability, thus their relief should be combined with poverty alleviation and development assistance, so that they can support themselves eventually.

In respects of determination of family income, usually it is based on the monetary income and physical income of the applicant family for the first 12 months prior to application, but not including the fees for special care and replacement, government subsidies, funeral expenses, relief pensions, economic compensation, bonuses for honor, non-consuming part of personal injury compensation, etc., which shall be specified by the local government.

(2) Standards of minimum living security.

The current standards of rural minimum living security are formulated by the civil affairs department of the people's government, jointly with the finance, statistics, commodity price departments, with reference to the factors of local economic conditions, resident income, governmental financial capability etc., which will be publicized and enforced with approval by the government at the same level and filing with the government at higher level. The central and provincial governments generally do not make specific provisions, with the exception of Fujian Province, which makes it clear that the minimum living security shall not below the standard of per capita annual income of RMB 1000.

Due to the serious unbalance of regional economic development in China, there is great difference between the standards of minimum living security in different areas, ranging from RMB 500-600 to 3000-4000. On January 1, 2005, Shenzhen set up a unified standard of monthly income of RMB 344, i.e., annually 4128, for the urban and rural minimum living security in its six districts, ranking highest in the country. In 2003, each recipient got a monthly income of RMB 58 yuan. In 2004, the amount was increased to 65 yuan; in the first half of 2005, the amount rose to 70 yuan.[8]

From the actual situation across the country, generally the standards of minimum living security are higher than the national absolute poverty line of RMB 637. This on one side shows that China's absolute poverty line is too low; on the other hand, it also reflects the rural minimum living security is not just for the lowest need of survival, but also focuses on the basic needs of living, including food, clothing, housing, and fuel etc. In regions where recipient of Five-Guarantees are included in the minimum living security system, the security standard for households of Five-Guarantees are higher than that of the minimum standard. In some places, the Five-Guarantees recipients are entitled to a certain percentage higher than the full amount of minimum living security; in other places, the recipients of Five-Guarantees may get the matching fund and policy apart from the full amount of minimum living security. As a result, the living standards of the recipient of Five-Guarantees are higher than the ordinary people of minimum living security.

It is a valuable exploration to include the Five-Guarantees in the scope of minimum living security and integrate the two systems, which saves the resources for public services in rural areas, reduces the operation cost of the system, and increases the degree of integration and standardization of the rural relief system, and finally, are conducive to the progress of legalization.

In general, the minimum living security systems in most areas are formulated in accordance with the principle of starting with low standard, and rising with the tide, so that the basic need can be guaranteed, and the laziness thought can be prevented. This prudent method is of great feasibility in practice. At the same time, in principle the dynamic management mode is adopted for the minimum living security system, which will be adjusted from time to time, usually once a year, by the competent authority according to the price index.

(3) Financing mode.

At present, the rural minimum living security fund is basically afforded by the local treasury according to the principle of "hoe one's own potatoes ", which shall be listed in the annual budget of the local government. Under such circumstance, although such a system is like "every miller draws water to his own mill", its disadvantages are also obvious: the economic developed regions have no difficulties in raising the fund with a high standard owing to the economic strength and fewer people in need of minimum living security; but the vast Midwest areas are in great need of minimum living security and have great difficulty in raising fund owing to low economic level and living standard, and large number of people in need. Consequently, in some poorer places, the minimum living security funds are either not included in the financial budget, or even if they are listed in the financial budget, they will not be affected, thus forming a vicious circle. The fundamental reason for this problem is that in China, the different economic development levels in different areas and the principle of self-sufficiency and fluctuating along with the market change are emphasized too much in the rural minimum living security system, whereas the integration and relevancy of the system has not been understood from the overall perspective.

As far as the fund-raising for rural minimum living security is concerned, it shall be borne by the three levels of fiscal treasury of city, district/county and township, with the exception of central and provincial subsidies. The proportion between the county/district and township shall be fixed by the county/district government. In principle, the proportion borne by the township government shall not exceed 30%; for the township with relatively developed collective economy, the proportion can be raised moderately, but not more than 50%. The village collective organization shall not afford the minimum living security in principle, with the exception of villages with developed economy like South of Jiangsu Province, which can afford a certain proportion. The government of city having jurisdictions over districts is responsible for formulating the proportion of two-level fiscal burden between the city and its county/district: in regions with strong county economy, such as the National 100 Top Counties, the city treasury may take a smaller burden; whereas in regions with poor county economy, such as state-level poor counties, the city treasury can take a larger burden.

The specific proportion shall be fixed by the municipal civil affairs department, together with the finance, statistics, commodity price departments, in reference to the factors including the per capita income, gross national product (GNP), fiscal capacity etc. Governments at various levels should set up a special account for the minimum living security for the special purpose, thus preventing corruption and embezzlement.

In principle, the provincial treasury will not give financial support to the minimum living security of cities with GNP over a certain amount, but will provide fiscal support to the counties with per capita GDP lower than a certain level. The funding subsidy from the province and the city allocated fund shall be at a direct proportion. Otherwise, some city may reduce the allocated fund to the poor county in the excuse of provincial fiscal subsidies. Provincial subsidies shall be directly allocated to the special account of the county, rather than to the city municipal treasury, which will reduce the intermediate links, and improve the efficiency of fund use.

The economically developed provinces, such as Beijing, Tianjin, Shanghai, Jiangsu, Zhejiang, Guangdong, Fujian and other coastal provinces shall raise funds for minimum living security by themselves, and the Central government basically does not provide financial support. In contrast, the Central government must furnish strong support of funds for minimum living security to the economy backward western provinces and the northeast old industrial base, so as to solve the problems of fund-raising in these regions. The fund from Central government can be allocated to the provincial special fiscal account, or be directly allocated to the county special fiscal account, and in direct proportion to the local minimum living security fund.

Although the minimum living security funds are borne by the three levels of treasury, i.e., the city, the county and the township. However, the author prefers the transfer payment by the Central and provincial treasury of the funds from city and the county. This system is essential, because the provincial fiscal transfer payment is the key approach to narrow the gap between different cities and the Central fiscal transfer payment is an important measure to narrow the gap between different provinces.

In addition, the rural minimum living security as well as the whole society security system are not only for the equality of qualifications between different subjects, but also the equality of outcome. As a means of economic control, the rural minimum living security is to narrow the gap of polarization in society, and relocate the fortune of the whole society so as to meet the basic demand of a few groups in hardship. Consequently, a strong regulation and control will be required of the State in deploying the public resources, and transfer payment is an important means.

It is the pity that a coordinated and unified transfer payment system has not been completed between the Central government and the provincial government. This will be the goal of our effort in the future, which will be of great significance in narrowing the gap between different areas, maintaining the balanced development and promoting the harmony of society. It is believed that by establishing a scientific, reasonable and operational fiscal transfer payment system at the central and provincial level, through which the central and provincial treasury provide finance support for rural minimum living security in the poor cities and counties, the dual goals of solving financial difficulties and reduce regional disparities, will surely be achieved.

3. The procedure framework of rural minimum living security

There is a bad habit of stressing substantial and belittling procedure in China, but the principles of openness, fairness, justice demands that we must pay full attention to procedural justice in practice. In the process of carrying out the work of rural minimum living security, the government has noticed the defects of the traditional system and has attached great importance to the procedure work, which is of great significance to maintain fairness and justice, and ensure the efficient and smooth operation of the system.

(1) The legal subject and its rights and obligations.

The subjects of rural minimum living security are basically divided into examining and approval party, applicant and supervising party. Governments at various levels shall assume the overall responsibility for minimum living security. The civil affairs departments of the people's governments at or above the county level shall be responsible for management of rural minimum living security work within their respective administrative areas. Finance, statistics, prices, auditing, labor and social security, and personnel departments shall, within the scope of their respective duties, coordinate with and give assistance with the civil affairs departments to carry out the rural minimum living security work. County (city, district) and township (town) people's government, as the examining and approval authority, shall be responsible for the specific examining and approval work of the rural minimum living security in the local area, and the villagers committees, as the villagers' autonomous management organization, is commissioned by the examining and approval authority, to carry out the relevant management and service work.

The examining and approval party is empowered with all the statutory functions and powers, and have the right to exercise their functions and powers in accordance with the law. They should also bear the adverse consequences resulting from illegal administrative activity or nonfeasance. If the behavior violates the criminal law, they shall also bear the criminal responsibility. The examining and approval party must ensure transparency of the administration activity according to law, safeguard the right to know and the right to participate of the relevant parties. As the applicant for the minimum living security, all the persons in the agricultural household register and other persons meeting the requirements prescribed by the law shall have the right to make application, which shall be filed by the examining and approval party. The applicant shall ensure all the documents submitted be genuine and effective, otherwise he shall bear the legal liability for behavior of cheating, forgery, misrepresentation, lying, etc. Regarding the decision made by the examining and approval party concerning the applicant, the applicant shall have the right to raise objection, to apply for administrative reconsideration or institute an administrative lawsuit. The auditing, the supervision, the public social organizations and individuals constitute the supervising party, who shall have the right to supervise and inspect the rural minimum living security work and the behaviors of the various legal subjects within his scope of power, and bring forward comments and suggestions, or to lodge complaint according to the law.

(2) Operating procedures.

Any household with family member's per capita income below the local minimum living standard of the local rural area shall have the right to apply for minimum living security. The principal applicant of each household shall submit the application to the township government through the village committee, together with the household register, ID card etc., and retrieve and file the *Application for Approval of Minimum Living Security of Rural Residents*, with details of the name, age, sex, relationship, employer, family main property, area of land, income, labor force etc. of the principal applicant and the family members.

After receiving the application and proof document of the applicant's, the township (town) government shall verify the information of the applicant at the assistance of the village committee and convene the village committees for democratic appraisal, the result of which and the name list shall be posted in public place for not less than 5 days. Upon expiration of the publicity period, the township (town) government shall give opinion on publicity and investigation, and shall submit the name list of qualified applicants to the civil affairs department of the county (city, district) for approval, whereupon the result shall be delivered to the applicant by mail or by courier of the village committee. For the unqualified applicant, the name list and the reasons for not being qualified shall be posted and the result shall be delivered to the applicant through mail or by courier of the village committee. The applicant may, within 15 days file a petition for administrative review or litigation. The township (town) government must complete investigation and verification within 15 days from the date of receipt of the petition, and sign out verification opinion. The civil affairs department of the county (city, district) shall, within 20 working days as of the application date complete the examining and approval work, and notify the township (town) government and the village committee of the result of examination and approval. The village committee shall post the name of the petitioner, the decision made, and the amount to be made up, and be subject to the supervision and examination of the social from all walks of life. The applicant may, within 15 days after the receipt of final approval, apply for administrative review or lodge a suit.

It is worth mentioning that in the rural minimum living security work, we shall make full use of the advantage of the existing system in China, which is the villager autonomy organization network across the whole country. According to the statistics, by the end of 2004, there had been 80,017 residents committees, and 625,147 villagers committees. Villagers' autonomous organizations cover all the villagers and are familiar with the most families, with good geographical advantages and humanistic contact, which are beneficial to the rural work. In the minimum living security work, the villagers' autonomous organizations have the convenience of verifying and investigating the information of the applicant, and carry out a dynamic tracking management of the minimum living security households, which greatly saves the operating costs and public resources, improves operational efficiency, and effectively alleviates the pressure of the fund shortage. Otherwise, if the township (town) government or the ministry of civil affairs at or above the county level were to conduct the door to door verifying and investigation work, it would be time-consuming and greatly reduce the work efficiency, thus increasing the operating costs of the whole system, which would be detrimental to solve the financing problem of the rural minimum living security. Therefore, in the work of rural minimum living security, especially in the case of investigation and verification and other basic information collection, the village committee shall act as the main body, and the governing authority may carry out the random inspection or regular inspection biannually.

NOTES

1. Wen Tiejun, "Reflection on the 'Three Agriculture-related Problems' Over the Century", *Reading* 12 (1999), 71.
2. Xi Meikong and Yang Qizhi, "Questioning the Social Security Function of Rural Land," China Land 1(2004).
3. Wen Tiejun, "Reflection on the 'Three Agriculture-related Problems' Over the Century," *Reading* 12(1999), 75-76.
4. Wei Xinwu, *Social Security Century Looking Back*, (Beijing: China Social Sciences Press, 2003), 2.
5. Wen Tiejun, "Reflection on the 'Three Agriculture-related Problems' Over the Century", *Reading* 12(1999), 113, 166.

6. Li Kang, “The Chinese Civil Affairs Development Report, 2002-2003: Perfect Social Assistance and Social Welfare”, accessed July 16, 2003, http://www.china.com.cn/.

7. The Ministry of Civil Affairs “The 2004 Statistics Bulletin of the Civilian Career Development”, accessed April 8, 2005.

8. Tang Jun, “The Implementation of Urban and Rural Subsistence Allowances System in China, accessed September 10, 2005, http://www.globalview.cn.

Chapter Seventeen

Solving "Three Agriculture-related Problems" by Rule of Law and Protection of Rights of Migrant Workers

Migrant workers can be said to be the extension of "three agriculture issues". Along with the economic system transformation from the planned economy to the market economy, a large number of rural surplus labor forces were liberated from the land, and flocked to the cities for urban construction. Although they lived in the cities, working in cities, or doing business in the cities, and their life seems to be no difference with the urban residents, they have never been admitted by the city. Their identities of farmer have become the shackles of them forever in the urban-rural dual structure of the household registration management system.

Are they rural residents? Or urban residents? The existing system cannot give an answer. The emergence of "migrant workers" group proves the deficiencies of the existing system. They are marginalized by the institutional system and excluded from the vested interests. They have made huge contribution for the urban construction, but they cannot enjoy a fair and reasonable treatment, or even being discriminated, and their basic rights and interests cannot be guaranteed.

China is an agricultural country. Among the 1.3 billion population more than 900 million are farmers, with large number of migrant workers. According to statistics, as of May 2005, the number of rural migrant workers has been about 120 million, among which about 100 million works in the city, and the number of migrant workers flowing between the provinces is about 60 million.[1] Therefore, the problems of migrant workers, and the rights and interests of migrant workers are closely related to the overall rights and interests of Chinese citizens, related to the harmonious development between the urban and rural areas, and related to the harmony and stability of the society, which is an integral part of constructing the socialist harmonious society.

Regarding the issues migrant workers, they are mainly divided into two categories: the first is the social problems brought by the migrant workers; the second involves the safeguarding of migrant workers' rights and interests. The author believes that the existence of the second problem is just outcome of the first problem. Therefore, in describing the problems of rural migrant workers, the author only refers to the second problem of migrant workers, i.e., the safeguarding of their rights and interests. If it involves the social problems brought by the migrant workers, it will be specified. The term "migrant workers" does not carry any discrimination connotation in this paper, which is only for the convenience of writing.

17.1 PRESENT STATUS OF PROTECTION OF MIGRANT WORKERS

17.1.1 Problems with Politic Rights

There have been obvious deficiencies in the system for the migrant workers to exercise the right to vote and right to be voted, to participate in the democratic political activity, and manage the community affairs.

Article 34 of *The Constitution of the People's Republic of China* stipulates, all citizens of the People's Republic of China who have reached the age of 18 have the right to vote and stand for election, regardless of ethnic status, race, sex, occupation, family background, religious belief, education, property status or length of residence, except persons deprived of political rights according to law. It can be seen that the right to vote and to be voted is the citizen's basic constitutional rights. It is the channel for the citizen to participate in national political life, and also the means for the citizen to make claim and deliver opinions. However, in real life, due to the limitation of household register system, the migrant workers cannot fully exercise their rights to vote and the right to be voted.[2]

The identifying of qualification of the voters shall be conducted at the place of household registration. Although it is stipulated in the *Provisions of the Standing Committee of the National People's Congress for the Direct Election of Deputies to People's Congress at or Below the County Level* by the Standing Committee of NPC in 1983 that voters who have actually moved out to live in other places may take part in the election in the electoral districts of their present places of residence after obtaining the qualification certificate of voters in their original electoral districts, the procedure for the migrant worker to obtain the voter qualification certificate of the original electoral districts is relatively complex and the cost is high, which has increased the burden of the migrant workers so that they will not exercise the right to vote.

As a result of long exclusion from the urban life, the migrant farmer workers' access to information is relatively single. During the election, if the electoral units do not do a good job in publicity of the operation mechanism of electoral system or the procedure for obtaining of voters qualification, the migrant workers will not understand their rights vested by the law. Quite often than not they will lose the opportunity to exercise the right to vote and the right to be voted. This kind of unconscious abstention of right is an abnormal state of right, which compared to the voluntary abstention in the state of full understanding, shows the drawbacks of the existing democratic institutions.

The election of delegate of people's congress is directly related to formulation of national and local systems, related to the question of whether the rights and interests of the voters have been taken into consideration in the decision making of the state and local affairs, and related to the smooth communication between the State and the citizens. The lack of the right to vote and the right to be voted can be said to be one of the important reasons for the migrant workers' marginalization. Having no spokesman and defender of their own interests, the migrant workers have lost the most effective political basis and system guaranteed for their own interests.

The marginalization of system has increased their sense of loss in the identity, which is detrimental for them to merge into the society, and also affects the actual effect of the government management. In explaining the widespread discrimination policy of agriculture and rural areas in the developing countries in the process of economic development, the development economics theory is usually divided into two main schools of views. One is represented by Lipton and Bates, who attempted to find the answer from the political structure in the developing world. In their view, the reason why agriculture is discriminated against in the process of development is that the city class has a strong influence on politics, whereas the farmers are lack of political influence owing to disperse distribution and high communication cost in collective action, and the free lift phenomenon resulting from the small share of the individual farmer's products in total agricultural output. The other is represented by Olson, who explains that phenomenon of large number and weak political power of farmers with the theory of Quantitative paradox.[3]

17.1.2 Problems with Labor Rights and Interests

The safeguard of labor rights and interests of migrant workers is the most vulnerable and hardest part in the safeguard of rights and interests of migrant farmers. Article 3 of *Labor Law* provides that the laborers shall have the right to be employed on an equal basis, chose occupations, obtaining remunerations for labor, take rests, have holidays and leaves, receive labor safety and sanitation protection, get training in professional skills, enjoy social insurance and welfare treatment, and submit applications for settlement of labor disputes, and other labor rights stipulated by law. However, in real life, the status of migrant workers is vague. Although they engaged in the work of workers, they are not treated as workers. A large number of jobs shut the door for them, or raise the threshold for them. They could only take the most dirty and tiring work that the urban residents are not willing to do. They often work overtime, but only get low labor remuneration. Even so, they often encounter difficulties in getting payment from the employers. They overdraw their own youth and energy for city construction, but do not enjoy the social security. They cannot afford the medical fees for serious disease or injury. The safety measures were not implemented for them so that they often succumb to occupational disease or become victims of occupational injury. In general, the existing security level for the rights and interests of migrant workers is very poor. The main problems are as follows:

1. The right to choose a career is restricted

The migrant workers' right to choose occupations is restricted by the labor market division system and local employment protection policies.

The existing labor market is artificially divided into two areas: labor market and talent market. Labor market is managed by the labor department, and talent market is managed by the personnel department. Artificial segmentation directly affects the remuneration of different occupations. According to the statistics of Labor Bureau of Beijing City, in Beijing, the number of industries and professions which limited the use of migrant workers increased from 14 in 1996 to 32 in 1997; in 1997, migrant workers were also excluded from the profession of shop assistants; in 1998, 8 industries limited the use of migrant workers; and the professions which limited the use of migrant workers included 4 large categories, 12 middle classes, 35 small classes, and 103 fine class in 1999. Besides the restrictions on the industry and the profession, there are also quotas and certificate management in Beijing City to control the number of migrant workers. Workers doing business in Beijing shall obtain "Temporary Residence Permits" and "Migrant Workers Employment Permit"; in particular, the migrant workers who engage in the household service shall apply for Household Service Permit for Migrant Workers in Beijing. As far as Temporary Residence Permits is concerned, it can be divided into the three categories of A, B, C according to the duration of stay, working records and performance in Beijing etc.[4] Owing to the policy of strict control, a high threshold has been set up for migrant workers. Therefore, both the employer and the migrant workers face high cost in recruitment or job selection. This actually limited their right to choose an occupation freely. As a result, they can only take up the most dirty and hardest job which the urban residents will not choose, mainly in the high labor intensity areas of construction, mining, chemical industry, and textile industry, focusing on foreign-funded enterprises and private enterprises.

2. Right to get work payment is hard to be realized

This problem mainly displays in the three aspects: same occupation with different payment, overtime work without payment and delayed payment.

Delayed payment is an outstanding proof that the rights and interests of migrant workers are not guaranteed. According to the incomplete statistics of National Federation of Trade Unions, by mid-November 2004, the delayed wages of national rural migrant workers totaled about 100 billion yuan. Since December 2003, Beijing Youth Legal Aid and Research Centre issued 8000 copies of questionnaires in eight provinces nationwide on status of migrant workers' rights and interests, involving 17 typical cases of right safeguard by migrant workers. According to the survey, 48.1% of migrant workers have had the experience of working without getting payment. Among them, 30.6% defaulted payment ranges from 100 yuan to 1000 yuan, 15.7% from 1000 yuan to 5000 yuan, 1.6% more than 5000 yuan.[5] In addition, it is very common for migrant workers to work overtime without overtime payment as stipulated in the labor law. It can be said that the wage is the sole source of income of migrant workers who leave their hometown to work in the strange city, and default payment is adding insult to injury for migrant workers. In order to retrieve the payment, it is no wonder they often go to extremes, even at the price of their own lives, to call attention of the society to their rights and interests.

3. Social security right is hard to be realized

Article 70 of Labor Law of China stipulates that the State shall develop social insurance undertakings, establish a social insurance system, and set up social insurance funds so that the laborers may receive assistance and compensations under such circumstances as old age, illness, work-related injury, unemployment and child bearing. The social insurance undertakings are run by the State in accordance with the stipulation of the law. It imposes a special fund, which will be used for providing the basic needs of life to workers who temporarily or permanently lose working ability. It is a return to the social wealth creators, which is utmost important for guaranteeing of citizens' survival and development, and maintaining of social stability. It is a social security for the all workers. However, the *Provisional Regulations on Collection and Payment of Social Insurance Premiums* stipulates the collection and payment scope of basic pensions: State-owned enterprises, collectively owned enterprises in cities and towns, enterprises with foreign investment, privately owned enterprises in cities and towns and other enterprises in cities and towns as well as their staff and workers, and institutions managed as enterprise as well as their staff and workers. In this way, only the urban residents can enjoy the social insurance. Consequently, if the employer only pays the insurance premium for its staff of urban residents, it is in compliance with the stipulation of the law. This actually excluded the right of the migrant workers in the implementation of law.[6]

At present stage, the percentage of insurance rate of migrant workers is relatively low. Except the employment injury insurance, the insurance rate for old pension is only 15%; the medical care insurance is about 10%, and the unemployment insurance and maternity insurance seemed have nothing to do with the migrant workers.[7] According to the statistics, the various benefits of migrant workers in Shanghai are only one fifth of the local urban resident workers, the gap mainly lying in the difference in social security; 33.5% of migrant workers in cities have had the experience of unemployment, among which 30% of migrant farmer workers has ever been unemployed for over half a year. After unemployed, migrant workers mostly depend on their past savings or loans from friends and relatives; after fell into illness, 59.3% of the migrant workers would not spend money on visiting doctors, the other 40% visiting doctors spend 885.46 yuan on average, and their employers would just share 72.3 yuan for them, less than 1/12 of the actual treatment costs.[8] Therefore, for the vast majority of migrant workers, they have to bear most of the risks occurring in the process of work, or rely on their past savings or rely on loans from relatives and friends. Their rights to survival and development cannot be guaranteed. In 2003, when "SARS" was in the high-risk period, a large number of migrant workers returned their hometown, and resulting in the spread of "SARS" from city to the countryside, an important reason is that the migrant workers cannot get social security in the city.

4. Lack of labor protection measures

Article 4 of *The Law of the People's Republic of China on Prevention and Control of Occupational Diseases* stipulates that, the workers enjoy the right to occupational health protection. The employer shall create the working environment and conditions that conform to the national norms for occupational health and requirements for public health and take measures to ensure that the workers receive occupational health protection.

For this end, the *Law on Prevention and Control of Occupational Diseases* also endows the workers 11 kinds of rights, including right to know, right to training, right for special security and right for damages etc. However, in the practical work, the employers always take advantages of the weak consciousness of migrant worker in self-protection, and do not take the necessary measures or provide them with the necessary products for health and sanitary protection. Nor did the employers give the migrant worker necessary advice or explanation, thus seriously damaged their physical and mental health. According to the survey of relevant departments, by 2005, there have been 16 million enterprises involving the poisonous and harmful work, and there are over 200 million people under the threat of occupational disease, among which most are migrant workers. So far, there have been 590,000 cases of reported pneumoconiosis patients, with an increase rate of 10,000 case each year, accounting for 80% of the total number of new occupational diseases.[9] The victims of coal mine accident total over 6000 people each year, most of whom are migrant workers.

5. Exploitation of illegal intermediaries

The migrant workers work in the city mainly through introduction of town fellows or friends and relatives. Their channel of employment is relatively small. Therefore, some illegal intermediaries take advantage of information monopolization to cheat the migrant workers with false information, or to increase the service fees or increase the items for collecting fees, thus infringing the interests of the migrant workers.[10]

There are many reasons for the infringement of the rights and interests of migrant workers, among which there are institutional causes, causes of the employer, and causes of the migrant workers themselves. From the institutional perspective, the local government's attention is mainly focused on the impact of the migrant worker on the local economic order, and thus the policy tends to strengthen management of the migrant workers to prevent the negative impact and thus neglect the protection of the interest of the group, which is mainly shown in three aspects: in the legislation, the economic and administrative punishment takes a dominant position and the necessary service and protection of interest is not adequate; the legal norms are too general and there is a lack of specific operational procedures; in the law enforcement: there is no corresponding supervision mechanism, and the law cannot be implemented; in the judicial aspects: the approach of legal relief is relatively narrow. At present, the migrant workers have not yet been included in the *Rules on Legal Aid* as target of aiding. This does not accord with national conditions of China. As a social vulnerable group, migrant workers deserve a special protection system. According to the survey, the cost for the migrant workers to safe guard their rights are quite high. Take an example of recovering delayed payment; the costs of recovering often exceed the amount of unpaid wages. Therefore, on the choice of approach to legal relief, the migrant workers seemed helpless, as they couldn't afford the legal fees for safeguarding their interests. Consequently, they had to resort to kidnap, stirring up trouble, plundering property, or even self-immolation and other extreme behaviors. From the perspective of employers, as the main body of market economy, they are always in pursuit of profit, and seek to reduce costs and increase output. On the one hand, they increase the workload of the laborers; on the other hand, they put the worker's wages in arrears as a management strategy of reducing enterprise cost. As far as the enterprise is concerned, providing workers with basic social security, providing reasonable labor treatment, providing a decent working condition, will all increase the cost of the enterprise. In a period of unsound social system and bad money driving out good money, the enterprise would choose to keep the market competitiveness at the cost of the rights and interests in workers.

According to the survey conducted by China Committee of Trade Union of Light Industry and Textile, China Federation of Finance & Commerce, the daily work time of migrant workers is 12 hours. In some cottage industry enterprises, the work time may reach 16 hours. A general survey in Guangdong also shows that 52.4% of migrant workers work more than 8 hours. In addition, there is a universal problem of employing migrant workers without signing labor contract. According to statistics, in 2004 the average rate of labor contract signing was 57.1%, and the figure in the private enterprises was only 30.5%.[11] In addition, even if the employer signed the labor contracts with migrant workers, the contract text was not standard, with large number of void clauses and overbearing clauses. Consequently, even if the employers conducted some illegal activities in recruitment, they could escape the punishment through the non-standard labor contract. From the perspective of the migrant workers themselves, migrant workers flew frequently, and the employers were reluctant to invest more fund on them, and tended to increase the working efficiency through increased workload rather than through professional training. Meanwhile, the education level of the migrant workers constrained their use of legal resources. Through the survey, we can see that the education level of most migrant workers is below the high school level, which limits their use of resources, and also limits their development space.

As the migrant workers do not know the rights endowed by the law, and have no knowledge of the approach and procedure for claiming rights, they can't really enjoy the rights endowed by laws. Of course, this also is consistent with the mode of right protection in China, wherein rights protection is usually vested by the state from top to bottom, quite different from the western mode of from bottom to top through continuous struggle. As far as most migrant workers are concerned, they are weak in right consciousness, and with low enthusiasm in right protection, and on the contrary, rely too heavily on the state policy and state protection.

17.1.3 Problems with Cultural and Educational Rights

1. Lack of vocational and technical training

Most migrant workers only completed the nine-year compulsory education. Their vocational skill is low and cannot meet the requirements of modern production, which largely limits their development space in cities, and suppresses their right consciousness. We all had known that migrant workers shall receive some vocational training if they are to be competent in a job. However, from the actual situation, the training received by the migrant workers is mainly provided by the employer, the content of which is relatively simple and is limited to the specific job, thus neglecting the education of occupational safety. Migrant workers usually engaged in the dirty, bitter and tiresome work, which always have safe hazards. The lack of safety education is an important cause of frequent accidents. Although there are various vocational skills training in the society, they are mainly created for local new workers and are basically not open to migrant workers. For the few training institutions which are open to migrant workers, their operation is not standard and the training level is low, lacking of coordinated and unified management. In a word, the further education of migrant workers is not free of worry.

2. Difficulty in children's education

The problem of children's education is another instance of marginalization of migrant workers by the city. At present stage, the education system in urban area is the region segmentation system based on the household registration management system. For migrant workers' children to enter the local public school, they need to pay extra fee, the school selection fee and other fees in the name of donation, which is a heavy burden for migrant workers. In Shanghai, if the migrant workers' children need to study in public schools, they need to pay extra fee of about 1200 yuan in addition to the normal charging items.[12] In addition, even if some migrant workers spent big money sending children to public schools, their children are often looked down upon by the students and the parents of urban residents, or even by the teachers, which is harmful for the healthy growth of children's psychology. This circumstance has given birth to the migrant children schools, a solution outside the State education system. The migrant children schools are mainly operated by the migrant workers themselves with low tuition fees, and are well received by the migrant workers. For this reason, the State Education Commission formulated the *Interim Measures for Schooling of Migrant Children and Adolescents* in 1998, in which the qualification of the migrant children schools is accepted. However, there are still many problems with the operation of migrant children school. The school facilities are simple and crude, mostly located in the leased workshop, warehouse, or residential houses in urban-rural continuum, which are unsafe and with poor health condition; most teachers have not gone through the formal certification procedure, which is hard to ensure the teaching quality. This kind of teaching environment is not conducive to the healthy growth of migrant workers' children, and they are embarrassingly forced to receive the nine-year compulsory education outside the urban and rural education system.

17.1.4 Problems with Basic Living Standard

1. Absence of responsibility in the leftover family

When the young migrant workers go to the cities, the old, the young and the sick are left behind. In many families, it is very common that grandparents live together with grandchildren. Sometimes an old man has to take care of two to three children at the same time. These people belong to the vulnerable groups in society. With weak self-protection ability, how could they take care of the others? For the family in the rural area with family security as the main reliance, adult child is the pillar of life. If the adult child is not at home, there would be no security for those people. In recent years, there have been reports on the tragedy of grandparents and grandchildren died of starvation at home, which exposed the seriousness of the problem. It might be considered highly irresponsible behavior to leave the parents and children at home for the purpose of earning money in the cities. However, the migrant workers are in a dilemma between getting rid of poverty through working out and bearing family responsibility at home. How can they keep a balance? Why do the urban residents can work without worries and enjoy the social security, while the migrant workers have so much to care?

2. Poor living conditions

In the survey concerning the migrant workers, a problem of great concern is the rent in the cities. For migrant workers, they are out of the welfare housing distribution system or government subsidy system to buy the commercial property. They live in the rent house or in the simple collective dormitory provided by the factory, or build simple shelter with the recycled materials. In case of a rent house, it is quite often that several people or even dozens of villagers or relatives crowded in a room because of high rent. As far as the simple dormitory is concerned, the conditions are really simple, crowded and dirty, with no ventilation facilities, which is of great harm to migrant worker's health. In recent years, the project of migrant workers' community has been launched in some cities with the fund of the government for leasing dormitory to the migrant workers through unified management. There has been no obviously effect, largely due to the low willing of the migrant workers to afford the additional charge of the rent.

17.2 CAUSES OF PROBLEMS WITH MIGRANT WORKERS

There are many reasons for the poor conditions of migrant workers' rights, which are mainly focused on the four aspects.

17.2.1 Causes of Problems with Migrant Workers

Before 1978, the government's strategy of giving priority for heavy industry changed the urban and rural economic relations into a part of the planning and control, thus blocking the flow of labor between the rural and urban areas. Compared with the light industry, the heavy industry was capital intensive, with weak capacity of labor force. The implementation of heavy industry priority strategy meant sacrifice of many employment opportunities. As a result, Chinese government had to make corresponding arrangements for employment issues. To further control labor outflow of the rural areas, and ensure full employment and other welfare of urban residents, the *hukou* (household) system arouse at the right moment. From the experience of last decades, the household registration system has indeed shown its power in restricting the flow of population between the urban and rural areas. Since the 1960s, the blind flow of rural population has been ceased. The practice of the household registration system also provided the outlet for the government to discharge surplus urban population to rural area in time of economic trouble. For instance, in the early 1960s, when the food supply in the cities was worsened, 26 million urban were returned to the rural area. During the "Cultural Revolution" Period, about 30 million migrated to the rural areas from the urban areas. The migration of population at the scale of moderately developed countries from urban to rural area were impossible in a country of market mechanism with population spontaneous adjustment system.[13]

Today, however, the environment for the dual structure division of the household registration system has been changed. That means the shortage economy period has been passed, and the industrial structure is constantly going through adjustment and upgrade, resulting in the lack of a large number of labor force in the second and third industries, and the need to seek rural surplus labor to force supply and replenishment. However, the existing system of urban and rural dual structure has greatly hindered the satisfaction of this need; this is the root cause why the rights and interests of migrant workers are not guaranteed.

17.2.2 Incoordinate Relationship between Employers and Employees

The tension between the capital and labor has been evolved into the contradiction between the employers and the employees. The capital, in pursuit of profit maximization, will do everything to squeeze the labor, which includes, on the one hand, extending the labor time to increase the output; on the other hand, lowering the standards of labor and social security and deducting the remuneration to save costs. From the perspective of the employer, the pursuit of profit is understandable, as every rational person will seek to maximize their own interests. They will not take the initiative to improve the working conditions of employees, or voluntarily take into consideration the interests of employees, which is the moral demands for them, and on which the society shall not have too high expectations. Due to the unclear social status of migrant workers, and their dispersed strength and the weak consciousness of right and interests, an unbalanced pattern is formed into the confrontation between the capital and the labor force, in which the labor force is too weak to confront the capital and thus their interests will easily be succumbed to the expansion of the capital.

17.2.3 Incoordinate Relationship between Public Investment and Private Investment

All along, the migrant workers are regarded as social vagrants and thus are discriminated by the urban residents. When people meet the migrant workers with dust all over, they will look down upon them and avoid them. In their mind, the migrant workers are dirty, unhygienic, smart, and unreasonable. Not only that, in the eyes of urban residents, migrant workers are also the dangerous scoundrel who disturb the social order and the culprits who take away the job opportunities of the local people.

It can be said that the crime problems of migrant workers in cities are very serious. According to the survey in large and medium-sized cities, the proportion of criminal cases committed by the migrant workers rose from 30% in the 80s to 50%.[14] The downgrade of social order and the increase of unemployment put the government under great pressure. As the government is indirectly elected by the local residents, it needs to be responsible for the local voters. Therefore, catering for the psychology of residents, and strictly controlling over the migrant workers to prevent them from bringing the negative effects on the city, constitutes an effective way of taking responsibility. As a result, the local governments would wear colored glasses in the management of migrant workers, i.e., being service oriented for local residents and control oriented for migrant workers. Meanwhile, the dispersed strength of the migrant workers and the difficulty in the exercise of voting rights also limited their ability to make defense for themselves, so that they had to accept the difference in local governments to their rights.

In March 2003, the university graduate Sun Zhigang, 27, was tortured to death in Guangzhou Asylum. The cause was that he did not have a temporary residence permit. The tragedy caused by the internment and repatriation system aroused quite a stir in society, which directly led to annulment of *Measure for the Internment and Repatriation of Urban Vagrant and Beggars* which has been in force for 21 years. However, if we give it a second thought, we will find the reasons behind the events, is largely due to the government's long time discrimination against migrant workers and disregard of their rights.

In addition, the local governments have all kinds of performance appraisal index, and the ability of the investment promotion and capital introduction is as an important index for examination and assessment of the government performance. If the security work for the right of migrant workers is strengthened, it will certainly increase the labor costs of enterprises, which will frustrate the investment enthusiasm of the enterprises in the local area. When the security levels across the country are not unified, how can the local government protect the interests in the migrant workers at the expense of local taxation interests and government economic performance?

17.2.4 Incoordinate Relationship between Different Regions

Imbalance between regions is an important factor affecting the safeguard level of migrant workers' rights and interests. The urban structure of China is not reasonable, with inadequate number of small and medium-sized cities, resulting in the rural surplus labor force flocked to a small number of large cities, which are mainly concentrated in the following cities: Beijing-Tianjin-Hebei urban agglomerations, the Pearl River Delta with Guangzhou- Shenzhen-Zhuhai as the core, the Yangtze River Delta with Shanghai- Nanjing-Hangzhou as the core, and Liaoning Urban Agglomeration with Shenyang - Dalian as the core, Jiaodong Urban Agglomeration with Jinan- Yantai- Qingdao as the core, the urban agglomerations of Yangtze river middle reaches with Wuhan-Changsha-Hengyang as the core, as well as the urban agglomerations with Chengdu - Chongqing as the core.[15] The influx of rural surplus labor force has brought a sharp rise in the population and a heavy environmental pressure and burden with employment in the area, which makes the local government hard to keep up with the management, let alone the security of the rights and interests in migrant workers.

17.3 MEASURES FOR PROTECTION OF BASIC RIGHTS AND INTERESTS OF MIGRANT WORKERS

17.3.1 To Break Up the Dual System between Urban Area and Rural Area Is the Fundamental Measure to Protect the Rights and Interests of Migrant Workers

Constructing the socialism harmonious society should include two aspects: the first is to reflect the essential demand of socialism, i.e., the liberation of productive forces, the development of the productive forces, elimination of exploitation and oppression, and finally achieve common prosperity; the second is to achieve the overall social harmony and progress in an all-round way.

The socialist harmonious society should be a society of economic and social coordinated development. In order to realize the overall harmonization of socialist society, economic development is the premise. Comrade Deng Xiaoping once pointed out that "Poverty is not socialism", "Development is the absolute principle". Without the development of economy, the development of the society is just like water without source. Development is not, however, the ultimate goal of socialism. Indeed, the ultimate goal of socialism is to realize the communist society, with no oppression, no exploitation, no gap between the rich and the poor. If there is no overall progress of society, no harmony of all members of the society, no social development along with the economic development, the ultimate degree of economic development will also be limited.

It can be said that in a society with wide gap between the rich and the poor, it is impossible to achieve the long-term stable development of social economy. Therefore, the existing urban and rural segmentation system in China conflicts with the requirements of the socialist harmonious society.

In addition, the harmonious society of socialism must be a society which pays close attention to individual social fairness and justice. This kind of fairness is not only embodied in the fair distribution, but also in the fair opportunities for development. In the society, all the citizens, regardless of origin or profession, shall have a fair development opportunities and should be treated fairly by law. Amartya Sen has pointed out, that poverty is not just the deprivation of income, it is also the deprivation of ability.[16] When the poor people are unable to exercise some basic functions, it is an absolute deprivation. For migrant workers, it is these differences in identity constraints their development. This kind of deprivation from the source is the root of all their problems.

Therefore, breaking the urban-rural binary partition system and promoting the coordinated development of urban and rural areas to give migrant workers equal opportunities for development and strengthen the protection for legitimate rights and interests of migrant workers, is not only the requirement of economic development, but also the requirement of building a harmonious socialist society, which embodies the most basic care of socialist harmonious society to the individual person.

To fix the various kind of inharmonious relationship and improve the situation of rights and interests security of migrant workers, the first thing to do is to have a comprehensive and correct understanding of the social group of migrant workers.

First of all, the farmer working in the cities is the objective demand of the national economic development. It is also the effective way to solve the problem of overpopulation with few lands, to improve the level of farmers' income, and to alleviate the gap between the rich and the poor.

As the average area of cultivated land is small in China, there emerged the agricultural surplus labor with the promotion of agricultural mechanization. According to China *Statistical Yearbook (2001)*, the population of China in 2000 is 1.265 billion, and the rural population is 807 million, among which the rural labor force is 498 million. However, according to the study of research group of the Ministry of Agriculture etc., the reasonable demand for labor force is only around 150 million at the current level of productivity. This means that in the labor force of 498 million, nearly 350 million is in surplus. In addition, if analyzed from the proportion of the industrial structure, China has entered the intermediate stage of industrialization. In 2001, for example, industrial production value occupied a larger proportion of 51.1%, and the third industry reached 33.6%, whereas the agriculture industry accounted for only 15.2%. Obviously, it is not reasonable to attract 50% of the workforce to the 15.2% output value, which is not conducive to the increase of farmers' income and the promotion of their living conditions.

What's more, with the rapid development of the second and third industries, objectively more labor force is demanded. Just like the manufacturing and service industries, many of them are labor-intensive industries. Obviously the local population of urban residents are inadequate to meet the demand. At present, in the second and the third industries in China, the proportion of labor force transferred from agriculture industry is rather high. In the service industry, the proportion is over 50%; in the manufacturing industry, the proportion is over 60%; and in the construction industry, the proportion is about 80%.

Under these circumstances, we can see the farmer migrant workers are not the "blind flow of people" in nature, but the result of the economic development and urban construction. They play an important role in accelerating the urbanization process and economic development. It can be said that the emergence of migrant worker tide is the efflorescence of industry structure adjustment and the farmers spontaneously pursuit of better life in the process of deepening socialist market economy. The farmers did not migrate to the cities owing to the pressure of living, but at the drive for the comparative advantage between the urban and the rural areas, between industry and agriculture. They are not blind flow, but a regular and reasonable flow from inland to coast area, from countryside to city, from underdeveloped areas to developed areas, from low-income career to high-income career. For the migrant workers, the flow is a process of enhancement of the social economic status.[17]

China is an agricultural country, the issues of agriculture, rural areas and farmers have been the top issues relating to the overall development level and national stability and unity. So far, the farmers' income increase in China is not optimistic. For the seven years from 1997 to 2003, the annual increase rate of net income of farmers was at 4%, while at the same period, the increase rate of urban residents was at 8%. The income gap between the urban and the rural residents was widening. Besides, relying solely on agriculture would often result in the phenomenon of "more production with less income". If the fund provision for seed and fertilizer was deducted in advance for the cultivation of the next year, the disposable per capita net income would be fewer. [18] Under such circumstance, if the migrant workers went out to work, they could not only bring a more stable income to the family and help the farmers get out of poverty, but also accumulated the fund for further development of rural areas. Sichuan is a populous provinces and major agricultural province, with rural surplus labor force of more than 1300 million, accounting for one third of the whole province labor force. In 2000, 4.6 million of Sichuan migrant worker went out to work in the cities, and remitted total income of RMB 21 billion through the post offices and the banks all over the countries. The labor service has become one major source of income of migrant workers. Considerable labor income and a large number of modern farmer entrepreneurs have become the important material base and the talent guarantee for economic and social sustainable development of rural areas in Sichuan Province, which is of great significance to mitigate the situation of imbalanced economic development between different regions.[19]

Therefore, we should not avoid the coming of migrant worker's tide, or even hinder the farmer migrant workers, but should face the reality and the development trend boldly, and actively steer it to the direction of standardization and normalization. Safeguarding the legitimate rights and interests in migrant workers, solving the various social problems brought about by the migrant worker's tide, and cancelling the limitations on farmer migrant workers gradually, so as to bring the positive role of migrant workers into play and overcome their negative effects, is a win-win choice either to the countryside or to the city.

Second, the cities shall bear an unshirkable responsibility for migrant workers' high crime rate.

Migrant workers have been wandering on the edge of the city. Although they work and live in the city, they are not accepted by the city and do not have the psychological identity of urban residents. Although they are physically in the city, they mainly stay with the town fellows and form a rural society in the city, with geographic and kinship relationship as the link. The indifference to the city makes their social circle completely isolated from the city, and hard to form the necessary communication and interaction with the urban residents. The difference in identity causes them to lose their behavior standards, as they have been separated from the bondage of the acquaintance society; they have lost the education of normal ethical culture and the supervision of public opinion. Meanwhile, as they have not been merged into the track of urban social management and education, they finally step towards the life of crime in the face of the temptation of materialistic world.

Further, as their basic rights are not guaranteed, and their labor remuneration, living environment and development space fall far behind with that of the urban residents, this will easily lead to the psychological imbalance of migrant workers. The sense of superiority and the repelling attitude of urban residents towards migrant workers has exacerbated this psychological imbalance, which easily lead the migrant workers to stand on the opposite side of city. In the new generation of migrant workers, this conflict is especially prominent. These groups of people are mostly born in the 1980s. They have experienced the baptism of modern media and communication technology. They have a strong desire to pursue a new life, but will produce in psychology a sense of discrimination and deprivation, and thus produce antagonistic behavior easily.

In the criminal cases involving the migrant workers, some crimes committed against the employers owing to the conflicts between the workers and the employer, in particular in the cases of disputes over unpaid wages. The extreme behaviors conducted by the migrant workers for unpaid wages were in fact the last resort. An example at hand is case of Wang Binyu in Gansu Province involving unpaid wage. Wang Binyu started to work in the cities since 17, and consecutively worked in Tianshui, Lanzhou in GansuProvince and Zhongwei, Yinchuan, Shizuishan, Zhongning in Ningxia Autonomous Region etc. He led a hard and humiliated life. In May 2005, his father was wounded on the leg, and Wang Binyu was in great need of money. He came to the boss for the unpaid wage of RMB 5000, but only got 50 yuan. Then he lodged the complaints to the labor department and the courts respectively, but all in vain. Finally, Wang Binyu went back to the home of the boss for the unpaid sum, but was insulted and beat up by the boss. Under extreme despair and anger, Wang Binyu killed four people and seriously wounded 1 person. After that, he cleaned the blood in the river and voluntarily surrendered himself to the public security bureau. On June 29, 2005, Wang Binyu was sentenced to death by Ningxia Shizuishan Intermediate People's

Court.[20] Wang Binyu was not ignorant of law, and his behavior of surrender shows that he originally did not want to do harm to the society. However, while his rights and interests could not be safeguarded, and all the doors were shut to him, how much can we expect him to keep rational? On January 8, 2002, migrant workers Yin Yong etc. from Sichuan Province climbed up the tower crane on the construction site, demanding the unpaid wages from the building contractor. Yin Yong claimed that the boss owed them more than one million. On the tower crane of over 40 meters high, Yin Yong and his fellows found a strong point to fix themselves on the long arm of tower crane. They stayed on the crane for 7 hours against the strong winds in the winter. This is the famous "Claiming Salary on Tower Crane" in Shenzhen. Migrant worker Liu Jiaxing from Sichuan is the head of the migrant workers group. After the irrational incident, he on behalf of the migrant workers participated in the negotiation with the contractor and the government department. "We have no other choice. We just wanted to draw enough attention. If we had other way, who would act like this?" It can be seen that, even in the eyes of Sichuan migrant workers; this kind of behavior was unreasonable. It was the last choice. Therefore, while we blame the legal consciousness of migrant workers, we should also have some retrospection whether the employer and the government has done all things necessary. The unpaid wages are all hard-earned money, or even a lifeline, of migrant workers. However, the channel of litigation cannot ensure that migrant workers recover their own wages smoothly. On the contrary, the lengthy arbitration proceedings and litigation procedure are easily to bring down the weak party of the migrant workers themselves.

Third, there is a supplementary relationship between the migrant workers and the urban residents concerning occupation selection.

The influx of migrant workers has brought great impact on the privileges of urban residents, caused the dissatisfaction and resistance of the urban residents. Especially at the present stage of state-owned enterprise reform and industrial structure adjustment, as the urban employees are under severe pressure of unemployment, they have a misunderstanding that the migrant workers have taken away the working opportunities and thus attributed the responsibility to the migrant workers.

The development history of world city shows that in all countries in the world there exist the phenomenon of original urban residents and government officials rejecting and limiting foreign laborers in the process of urbanization. This kind of phenomenon was originated from a wrong hypothesis in labor employment market, i.e., fixed total demand for labor force. According to this hypothesis, the scale of employment is a fixed amount, and employment has become "a game of one party benefiting from the damage to the other party", meaning providing employment opportunity for one person will cause another person out of work. However, this hypothesis is not reasonable. Employment scale is not always fixed. On the contrary, in a sense, the urban labor employment increases with the increase of the demand. Working in the cities is not like farming in rural area. The farming is a singular activity, and could only feed a fixed number of people; whereas the urban workers from groups of networks between each other, and creates the value which can be circulated, therefore it can support more people.[21] When the farmers migrate to the cities and become the labor force in the cities, their price is lower than that of the urban residents, which is helpful for the expansion of production and increase of employment. Migrant workers themselves will need products and services from others; farmer entrepreneur will set up factories and run shops in the city, which will absorb some of the laid-off workers, providing them with the "re-employment" jobs. At the same time, migrant workers pay various taxes and fees, which will be used by the government to support the re-employment project. Therefore, migrant workers working in the city will, to a certain extent, help expansion of employment in the cities.[22]

In addition, we also need to see that the jobs taken by the migrant workers are always the hardest, the dirtiest and tiresome in the city. The technical requirements for those jobs are not high, mostly the physical labor, such as mining, textile, construction, etc., which are not favored by the urban residents. Therefore, migrant rural labor force, to a large extent, filled the working space left by the urban residents. It is a kind of "supplementary relationship" rather than "replacement relationship".

In 1997, Nanjing launched a massive movement of repelling migrant workers as an important step of re-employment project. The repelling work went on smoothly and 4000 vacancies were ready from light industry, metallurgy, machinery, chemical industry, textile and other departments. However, only 1000 local people would like to fill the gap, and several months later, many of them took French leave. A tannery was in need of 20 people to act as the tannage workers. However, owing to the bad work environment and the repelling smell, none of the laid-off workers would take up the job after the migrant workers were repelled. A Woolen mill in Nanjing ever made a vacancy for over 100 machinists, but only 49 local workers made applications. According to the survey into the enterprises in Nanjing City, as for the hard, dirty and tiresome work, even the laid-off workers are not willing to do, and eventually the migrant workers were called back.[23] In the long term "big-pot" distribution system and "iron rice bowl" system of the Maoist era, the urban workers developed a habit of passiveness and reliance and the thoughts of "wait, rely and demand". They will not participate in the rival for new job after being laid off, but rely on the government to solve the problem. They are choosy about the jobs and will not take up the inferior dirty or hard works. These are all bad habits of the planning economy, which cannot meet the requirements of the market economy. On the contrary, most of the migrant workers are hardworking and meet the demand of the market, which is conducive to the change of ideology of urban workers in recruitment and employment. As a result, the migrant workers work in cities will not hinder the employment of urban residents, but will promote the latter to some extent.

On the contrary, in recent years, with the emerging of city community economy, the employment space of the migrant workers has been squeezed by the social services industry with the domestic service and goods delivery as the main bodies, with the enterprise management and capital monopoly advantages. The standard management of business activities in the plan of the building also makes small business or small trades hard to survive. In addition, with the upgrade of the industrial structure, the capital and technology intensive industries are enhanced, which is unfavorable for the expansion of employment space of migrant workers. Therefore, it can be seen that in the contradiction of employment, the migrant workers are at a disadvantageous position, rather than the labor force of the urban residents. In the face of such inequality of employment opportunities, what reasons do we have to condemn the migrant workers?

17.3.2 The Principles to Follow for Protection of Rights and Interests of Migrant Workers

1. The road of guarantee in accordance with the law to be taken

From the above analysis, we can see that the legislation on the protection of migrant workers' rights and interests is rather weak at present stage. Not only are there few laws specially addressing the protection of migrant workers' rights and interests, but also the existing laws are contradictory and conflicting, which greatly weakened effectiveness of security. It can be said that the law is the last line of defense of social justice, especially for the social vulnerable groups like migrant workers. Only the security provided with the legal means is the most fundamental and most stable.

2. The urbanization process is irreversible

The problems of migrant workers come with the urbanization process. However, this does not mean that the urbanization road that we are taking is wrong. So to speak, the migrant worker problems are not caused by the urbanization, but by the legal status and the government management level which do not keep pace with the urbanization process.

3. The step by step policy shall be taken in the opening of the city

The segmentation of urban and rural areas is a historical problem. This problem needs to be resolved, but cannot be accomplished overnight. The integration of migrant workers into the city is a gradual and step by step process and both sides will need a certain coordination and adaptation period. Completely open in a rush will not only be detrimental to social stability, but also hinder the process of urbanization ultimately.

17.3.3 Specific System for Protection of Rights and Interests of Migrant Workers

1. The transition from the management government to the service-oriented government, and the coordination between the government and migrant workers

In the democratic civilized society, the legitimacy of government power is derived from the authorization of citizens, thus the government should exercise their power properly, and submit itself to the supervision of the public. It shall not only ensure the country's stability and unity and social order, but also actively safeguard citizens' legal rights, and provide service for citizens. However, just because of the local protectionism of the government and the preconceived discriminatory attitude towards migrant workers, the governments generally adopted the controlling policy on the issue of migrant workers and pay little attention to the protection of rights and interests of migrant workers.

In the eyes of the government, the migrant workers are only the object of the obligations, rather than subject of the rights and interests. This led to the low protection level of the migrant workers, who even become the victims of public power. Therefore, in order to safeguard the farmer workers' rights and interests, the government role transformation is required from the "administrator" to the "servant", which are mainly embodied in:

(1) to establish a regular employment information reporting system and provide employment information to migrant workers, so as to avoid the blind flow of migrant workers and improve the efficiency of labor resource allocation;

(2) to unify the labor market and strengthen the management of the professional intermediary market;

(3) to strengthen the overall planning and comprehensive management of vocational and technical training market, and to provide various levels of continuing education opportunities to migrant workers;

(4) to strengthen the education of migrant workers on safety production, and to supervise the employers in legitimate use of the workers;

(5) to cancel the restriction on migrant workers, including the temporary residence permits, and to put an end to the various kinds of unreasonable fees for migrant workers;

(6) to establish a sound administrative procedures, and exercise the power of government in accordance with the law;

(7) to set up a responsibility system, and to supervise the illegal administrative activities.

2. The migrant workers should be included in the social security system

It is reported that in Zhejiang Province there are over 30000 migrant workers quitted the social security system, and in parts of Guangdong Province, the cancellation rate of migrant workers has reached more than 95%. Form the latest statistics from the Ministry of Labour and Social Security, the coverage of social security programs of migrant workers is only about 15%. Why do migrant workers quit the social security system? The reason is that the social security system was originally tailored for urban residents. However, the migrant workers have their own particularity. Migrant workers have the characteristics of short-term and fluidity. They not only flow between different units, but also flow between different regions. In addition, after they sell their labor to the city, they finally go back to the countryside. However, the existing social security system provides a fixed number of years for paying premium. For instance, the applicable old pension system specifies that the minimum years for premium payment are 15 years for the applicant to be entitled to the monthly old pension. This is not easy for migrant workers who flow frequently. Besides, the current social security accounts are difficult to match or settle account between the urban area and the rural area, between different regions, or even between different units, and each unit as a whole is separated and has different policy, which makes the migrant workers lose confidence in the social security system.

The characteristics of migrant workers have set a higher requirement for the design of social security system. Some experts have proposed a classified social security be established for migrant workers, which will distinguish between stable employment and unstable employment respectively. Regarding the migrant workers of stable employment, they can be incorporated into the current urban social security system, including all the social insurance for urban residents, such as old pension, medical, unemployment, work injury, etc. Meanwhile, the current system of old pension and medical insurance can be reformed to facilitate the migrant workers of stable employment to enjoy the same rights as the urban residents. For migrant workers of unstable employment, a transitional way can be adopted, in which the transitional individual account will be set up instead of the social pooling, and the social security for the individual migrant workers will be credited to the personal account directly, except for the industrial injury and unemployment insurance, which will follow the stipulations of the applicable regulations.[24]

3. To break the enterprise trade union system and establish the modern trade union organizations based on the community and industry

Among the industrial workers, the power of the migrant workers is particularly weak. Under such circumstances, there is a serious imbalance between the capital and the workers, and the status of internal trade union organizations is in an embarrassed position, which makes it hard to safeguard the rights and interests of migrant workers. Therefore, the modern trade union organizations based on the community and industry rather than the internal structure of the enterprise can overcome the barriers of the capital and organize well the migrant workers to protect their rights and interests.

To cancel the restriction of public schools on children of migrant workers so as to admit the migrant children into the local normal education system, so that they can equally enjoy the local education resources.

The existence of migrant children school, to a certain extent, can alleviate the pressure on the migrant children's education, but this man-made prior segmentation can hinder the contact between the migrant children and children of residents of similar age, which is not conducive to their integration into the city.

Migrant workers should be brought into the community management system, so that they will be gradually integrated into the city, participate in the political and culture life of the city, and find their own entities.

NOTES

1. Liu Sheng, "The High Threshold of Social Security Excludes Migrant Workers with Medical Insurance Rate at 10%," *China Youth Daily*, August 11, 2005.
2. Jiang Yue Etc., "The Status Quo and Countermeasure Study of Foreign Women's Rights and Interests," *Xiamen University Law Review 8th Volume* (Xiamen: Xiamen University Press, 2004), 313.
3. Zhao Yong, *The Strategy of Benign Interaction Between Urban and Rural Areas* (Beijing: The Commercial Press, 2004), 192-193.
4. Zhao Yong, *The Strategy of Benign Interaction Between Urban and Rural Areas* (Beijing: The Commercial Press, 2004), 192-93.
5. Song Zhenyuan, "The Cost for Peasant Workers to Safeguard Rights: Deferred Payment of RMB100 Billion, Cost for Retrieving Amounting to RMB300 Billion," *China Youth Daily*, June 9, 2005.
6. Gao Jindeng and Li Lintai, "Thinking of Migrant Workers Social Security Issues," *Journal of Guangxi Management Cadre Institute of Politics and Law* 1(2004).
7. Liu Sheng, "The High Threshold of Social Security Excludes Migrant Workers with Medical Insurance Rate at 10%," *China Youth Daily*, August 11, 2005.
8. Lixiong Yang: "'Move to the City', or 'Back Home'? Migrant Workers Social Security Policy Path Choice," *Journal of Social Science of Hunan Normal University*, 2(2004).
9. Cao Xia, "'New Killer'" Occupational Disease of Migrant Workers," accessed July 25, 2005, http://www.jjrbncb.com.
10. Han Zhiquan, "The Rich Coal and Mine the Dead," accessed July 21, 2004, http://www.southcn.com.
11. Zhang Zhenghai, "Build a Harmonious Society to Solve the Problems of Rural Migrant Workers," accessed July 12, 2005, http://www.cqyl.org.cn.
12. Yu Hong and Ding Chengcheng, *China's Migrant Workers to Investigate* (Beijing: Kunlun Press, 2004), 176.

13. Zhao Yong, *The Strategy of Benign Interaction between Urban and Rural Areas* (Beijing: The Commercial Press, 2004), 189-92.

14. Yu Hong and Ding Chengcheng, *China's Migrant Workers to Investigate* (Beijing: Kunlun Press,2004), 163.

15. ——— *China's Migrant Workers to Investigate* (Beijing: Kunlun Press, 2004), 23.

16. Zhang Xiaoshan, "The Theory of Problem in Thinking," *Journal of China National School of Administration*1 (2004).

17. Yu Hong and Ding Chengcheng, *China's Migrant Workers to Investigate* (Beijing: Kunlun Press, 2004), 38.

18. Liu Shuduo, "Chen, A Rural Hot Difficult Problem," *China Economic Times*, February 10, 2004.

19. Yu Hong and Ding Chengcheng, *China's Migrant Workers to Investigate* (Beijing: Kunlun Press, 2004), 38.

20. Zhang Yaoyao, "Wang Binyu Case A Second Trial Yesterday," *Southern Metropolis Daily*, September 30, 2005.

21. Zhiyong Mao, Tan Yifei and Zhou Hucheng, "Scholars Series interview on Wu Si (II): The Slums Can't be Swept," *South Rural Newspaper*, July 19, 2005.

22. Zhao Yong, *The Strategy of Benign Interaction Between Urban and Rural Areas*," (Beijing: Commercial Press, 2004), 208-09.

23. Yu Hong and Ding Chengcheng, *China's Migrant Workers to Investigate* (Beijing: Kunlun Press, 2004), 301.

24. Liu Sheng, "Why Migrant Workers Surrender Insurance, Social Security in China Faces Test of "Immigration", *China Youth Daily*, October 22, 2005.

Chapter Eighteen

Summary, Prospect and Acknowledgment

18.1 SUMMARY OF THE BOOK

Under the grand project of "three agriculture-related problems", there left a great many subjects for further study, among which "solving the problems of agriculture, rural areas and farmers by rule of law" is an important topic which the scholars have failed to conduct systematic research. It involves a fundamental issue of whether the cause of reform and opening up in China will go smoothly. In addition to the experience from field trip, a lot of materials inspiration of thoughts in the writing of the book came from the existing documents and related reports. With these early achievements with sharp ideas and detailed and reliable raw materials, my vision and thought were expanded.

The book, with the rule of law as the guideline, with the study of the specific issues of "agriculture, rural areas and farmers" as the main theme, with raising questions and finding solutions to the problem as the main research method, puts forward the proposition of "solving the problems of agriculture, rural areas and farmers" by rule of law. The concept of the rule of law itself is statecraft; "agriculture, rural areas and farmers" is a kind of phenomenon, a problem. The proposition was meant to govern the "three agriculture-related problems" in accordance with the law.

This book is innovative in the following aspects:

(1) To comprehensively treat solving the "three agriculture-related problems" as a systematic project

"Three agriculture-related problems" itself is a multidimensional problem, which cannot be solved in a short period. Although the previous approaches addressed the specific problems, but they unavoidably had one-sidedness. For the same problem, there would be a variety of solutions from different aspects, some solutions were even completely contradictory, which facilitated us in the all-round grasp of the issue but also left us a problem of trade-off and comprehensive judgment. The "three agriculture-related problems" must be treated as a systematic project to govern comprehensively. The analysis of the book on "three agriculture-related problems" does not just stay on the surface, but pay more attention to its cause and origin, with a view to solving the problem fundamentally.

(2) The "three agriculture-related problems" shall be incorporated in the sphere of the rule of law

According to the grim reality of "three agriculture-related problems", all walks of life have given a variety of approaches from different perspectives: the construction of rural democratic politics, the property rights, especially the reform of the farmland property right, the urban and rural co-ordination etc. All these are good solutions to solve "three agriculture-related problems". However, the implementation of good policy needs the protection of law so that the various controlling measures will be systematized and standardized. Only in this way can we get rid of the bottleneck of short-term effect. Moreover, the rule of law is inseparable from both the rural spiritual civilization construction and meeting the requirements of the WTO. The practice of rule of law in rural China and the successful experience of foreign countries in tackling the "three agriculture-related problems" have proved that solving the "three agriculture-related problems" by rule of law is feasible.

(3) A tentative analysis has been made concerning the target, principles，implementation steps and contents of the system of solving the "three agriculture-related problems" by rule of law

The striking problems of the "three agriculture-related problems" include instability of rural society, backwardness of agricultural industry, inequality between the urban areas and the rural areas, as well as the weak protection of farmers' rights. Correspondingly, the solutions to the problem of "agriculture, rural areas and farmers" should be pertinent. The order, efficiency, fairness and justice of the rule of law happen to coincide with the target of "three agriculture-related problems" solution plan. The principle of solving the problem of "agriculture, rural areas and farmers" by rule of law is the basic norm for realizing the above target. It shall follow the principles of supreme authority of the state law, safeguarding farmers' equal rights, right to appeal, and principle of integrated governance and so on. Solving the "three agriculture-related problems" by rule of law cannot be accomplished overnight. It should follow a path of separated administration, coordinated development and integrated development of the urban areas and rural areas. From a macro view, the content of solving the "three agriculture-related problems" by rule of law shall include the complete legislation, the standard judicial and administrative procedure, the healthy rural legal service market and the promotion of the legal awareness of related people.

(4) Concrete analysis has been made on the mode and approach for implementation of solving the "three agriculture-related problems" by rule of law

As rule of man is deeply rooted in the countryside in China of a long time, and the cost of time is too high for the evolution of social ruling in the traditional way, the realization of solving the "three agriculture-related problems" by rule of law is inseparable from the support of the government. However, the government driving will be efficient just at the initial stage. With the further development of the rule of law in terms of the "three agriculture-related problems", the government drive will in turn become the resistance, which shall be replaced by the social drive. As a result, the implementation of the rule of law in terms of "three agriculture-related problems" will need the fundamental shift of the statecraft, namely the rule of law in the real sense, the strengthening of farmers' rights consciousness, and the supply of the rural legal resources in place.

(5) Bold analysis on some sensitive issues

The author realizes that the root of the "three agriculture-related problems" is not in the grass-roots, but in the Central government and the whole system. He points out that the local grassroots public security, procuratorate, court and the administration are not in a position of check and balance, but a kind of "cooperative relationship" based on the common interest, which has greatly endangered the right of farmers and the rule of law in the grass-root level. He also realizes that the system of appointment or dismissal of cadres in rural area is the direct cause of law breaking in administration. Appointment and removal of grassroots cadres depends on the higher leader, who usually behaves arbitrarily and does not follow the legal procedures. As a result, administrative offense is rampant and cannot be supervised and controlled effectively.

(6) Regarding the relationship between the state law and the folk law in a modern society, the author makes it clear that rule of law could only be confined to the state law rather than the folk law, thus upholding the absolute authority of the state law.

However, reflection and reform shall be made on the formation, implementation method and evaluation system of state law. That is to say, the rule of law in terms of "three agriculture-related problems" shall be established on the basis of democratic politics.

18.2 PROSPECT OF THE STUDY

After the topic was chosen, I felt great responsibility. The "three agriculture-related problems" is a fashionable and sensitive topic, and the first step is troublesome. In the process of surveying and data collecting, I always got very emotional about the status of the farmers. Although it is a kind of involuntary show, it will more or less affect the rational thinking of the book. In addition, as I got too close with the reality, while my theoretical knowledge is underdeveloped, the theoretical depth of the book needs to be tapped. Owing to the limit of space and time, some specific contents could only be scratched on the surface, such as the construction of small town, income increase and burden alleviation of farmers, rural tax reform and so on. In the study to be continued, in addition to pondering over systematic theory of rule of law in terms of "three agriculture-related problems", more attention will be focused on the specific issues:

(1) The rule of law in terms of "three agriculture-related problems" and the rural urbanization construction

The existing legal system of rural land and the problem in rural urbanization; the legal analysis of the negative effect of pan administration on rural urbanization; the household registration system and the problems in rural urbanization.

(2) The rule of law in terms of "three agriculture-related problems" and income increase and burden alleviation of farmers

The legal obstacles to farmers' income increase; the legal countermeasures for farmers' income increasing and burden alleviating.

This research on this topic is of great significance and prospect under the market economy. The "three agriculture-related problems" involves the deeper issues of China's political system reform, the exploration into its root cause and the research on its development tendency in China are still in its infancy. There will be more scholars with a keen eye to observe and analyze the problem of "three agriculture-related problems", and put forward the fundamental solution to the problems. The analysis from the perspective of the rule of law has more theoretical and practical significance.

18.3 ACKNOWLEDGMENT

The main part of the book is my doctoral dissertation. Therefore, I wish to take this opportunity to express heartfelt thanks to my mentor, Professor Qi Duojun, whose intelligence, erudition and scholarly pursuits are my life-long goals. As the "three agriculture-related problems" changes with the development of time, and there will be always new contents springing up, after I completed the dissertation defense, my mentor suggested that I need not have the book published too early, but put it off two years, with more thinking, modification and polishing, so that the book can furnish a governance model more effective and more durable. The teacher's rigorous and highly social responsibility is admirable.

My graduate students have made a substantial contribution in the following chapters: Liao Cailin (Chapter 11), Zhang Shuikun (Chapter 12), Yang Ying (Chapter 13), Chen Xianying (Chapter 14), Huang Biao (Chapter 15), Wei Xing (Chapter 16), and Huang Yunjing (Chapter 17). In the publication of the manuscript, my sincere gratitude is expressed for their hard work.

Bibliography

1. (USSR) Andrew J Grad, *Japan's Land and Peasants*, World Affairs Press, 1957.
2. Aristotle, *Political Science*, The Commercial Company, 1965.
3. Aviam Soifer, *Law and the Company We Keep*, Cambridge, Harvard University Press,1995.
4. A. Maunder, *Agriculture and Governments in an Interdependent World*, Darmouth, 1989.
5. (UK) Bakunin, *Statism and Anarchy (Photocopy)*, China University of Political Science and Law Press, 2003.
6. (USA) Barrington Moore, *Social Origins of Dictatorship and Democracy*, Huaxia Publishing House, 1987.
7. (USA) Bodenheimer, *Jurisprudence: The Philosophy and Method of Law*, China University of Political Science and Law Press, 1999.
8. Bo Qingjiu, *Local Government and Self-Governance (2nd ed.)*, Wu-Nan Book Company, 1993.
9. Cao Jinqing, *Changes of Society and Culture in Contemporary Village Located in Northern Zhejiang,* Shanghai Far East Publishers, 1995.
10. Cao Jinqing, *China Along the Yellow River: A Scholar's Observation and Consideration on Rural Society*, Shanghai Literature and Art Publishing House, 2000.
11. Chen Guidi and ChunTao, *The Survey of Chinese Peasants*, People's Literature Publishing House, 2004.
12. Chen Jiyuan and Hu Biliang, *Village Economy and Village Culture in Contemporary China*, Shangxi Economic Publishing House, 1996.
13. Chen Xinyong et al, *Social Support System in China*, Yunnan People's Publishing House, 1997.
14. Claude Aubert, *Rural China, 1985-1990: Are the Reforms Really Bogging Down?* The Chinese University of Hong Kong, 1991.
15. Christopher Jessel, *The Law of the Manor*, Barry Rose Law Publishers Ltd., 1998.
16. (France) Condorcet, *The Sketch for a Historical Picture of the Progress of the Human Mind*, SDX Joint Publishing House, 1998.
17. Dai Yanhui, *Rural Politics in Taiwan in the Qing Dynasty*, Linking Publishing Company, 1979.
18. David Bevan, *Peasants and Governments: An Economic Analysis*, Clarendon Press, 1989.
19. David Dixon, *Law in Policing: Legal Regulation and Police Practices*, Oxford: Clarendon Press, 1997.
20. Dong Xiangfei, *Local Self-Governance and Government*, Wu-Nan Book Company, 1983.
21. Donnald Curtis, *Beyond Government: Organizations for Common Benefit*,Macmillan, 1991.

22. Duanmu Mei et al, *Social Issues in the Process of French Modernization: Peasants Women Education*, China Social Sciences Press, 2001.
23. (France) Duguit, *Changes of Public Law Law and State*, Liaohai Publishing House, Chunfeng Literature and Art Publishing House, 1999.
24. (USA) Dworkin, *Law's Empire*, Encyclopedia of China Publishing House, 1996.
25. (USA) Edward H. Levi, *An Introduction to Legal Reasoning*, China University of Political Science and Law Press, 2002.
26. Ehrmann, *Comparative Legal Cultures*, SDX Joint Publishing Company, 1990.
27. (USA) Ehrmann, *Comparative Legal Cultures*, SDX Joint Publishing Company, 1990.
28. Ehrmann, *Comparative Legal Cultures*, SDX Joint Publishing Company, 1990.
29. (USA) Ely, Morehouse, *Elements of Land Economics*, The Commercial Company, 1982.
30. Francis G. Snyder, *Law of the Common Agricultural Policy*, London, Sweet & Maxwell, 1985.
31. Fang Jiangshan, *Non-institution Political Participation*, People Press, 2000.
32. Fei Xiaotong, *From the Soil: the Foundations of Chinese Society*, SDX Joint Publishing Company, 1985.
33. Fei Xiaotong, *From the Soil: The Foundations of Chinese Society &The Institutions for Reproduction*, Peking University Press, 1998.
34. Fu Yulin, *Researches on Rural Law Services at the Basic Level*, China University of Political Science and Law Press, 2006.
35. Gao Qicai, *A Theory of Chinese Customary Law*, Hunan People's Publishing House, 1995.
36. (India) Ghatak, *Development Economics,* The Commercial Press, 1989.
37. Gilbert Rozman, *The Modernization of China,* Jiangsu People's Publishing House, 1988.
38. Gong Benxin, *Teahouse For Jurists Part II*, Shandong People's publishing House, 2003.
39. Gong Pixiang, *Legal Philosophy and Modernization of Legal System*, Nanjing Normal University Press, 1998.
40. Gu Yikang, *Research on the question of "Three Agricultures": Theoretical Analyses of Experience at the Forefront of Rural Reform*, China Agriculture Science & technology Press, 2003.
41. Guo Daohui, *Epochal Call for Law*, China Legal Publishing House, 1998.
42. Guo Shutian et al, *Imbalance in China*, Hebei People's Publishing House, 1990.
43. Guo Xiaoming and Zhao Changwe, *In the Name of Farmers Cooperation*, The Chinese University of Hong Kong. Hong Kong Institute of Asia-Pacific Studies, 2000.
44. Han Mingmo, *Rural Sociology*, Peking University Press, 2001.
45. (UK) Hart, *The Concept of Law*, Encyclopedia of China Publishing House, 1996.
46. He Qinglian, *The Pitfalls of Modernization-Social and Economic Issues in Contemporary China,* China Today Press, 1998.
47. He Weifang, *The Concept and System of Judicature*, China University of Political Science and Law, 1998.
48. He Weifang, *The Detailed Rule of Law*, Law Press, 2002.
49. He Xuefeng, *Rural China in the 21th century*, Guangxi Normal University Press, 2003.
50. Huang Zongzhi, *The Peasant Economy and Social Change in North China*, Zhonghua Book Company, 1986.
51. Huang Zongzhi, *Small Rural Households in Yangtze River Delta and Rural Development*, Zhonghua Book Company, 1992.
52. JinYaoji, *From Tradition to Modernity*, Guangzhou Culture Publishing House, 1989.
53. John King Fairbank. *The United States and China*. The Commercial Press, 1987.
54. J Oi, *State and Peasant in Contemporary China*, University of California Press, 1989.
55. (UK) Katherine Barnard, *EU Employment Law*, trans. Fu Xin, Guo Jie, China Legal Publishing House, 2005.
56. (Austria) Kelsen, *General Theory of Law and State,* Encyclopedia of China Publishing House, 1996.
57. L.Alexander Norsworthy, *Rural Development, Natural Resources and the Environment: Lessons of Experience in Eastern Europe and Central Asia*, The World Bank Washington, DC, 2000.

58. Legal Popularity Office of Ministry of Justice, *Compilation of Rule of Law Lectures in the Central Committee of the CPC*, Law Press of China, 2001.
59. Liao Weidong and Wang Wanshan, *Research on Sustainable Development of Chinese Rural Economy under the Background of Economic Globalization*, Jiangxi People's Publishing House, 2002.
60. Liang Shuming, *The Substance of Chinese Culture,* Xuelin Press, 1984.
61. Liang Zhiping, *Cultural Interpretation of Law*, SDX Joint Publishing House, 1994.
62. Liang Zhiping, *Customary Law in Qing Dynasty: Society and State*, China University of Political Science and Law Press, 1996.
63. Liang Zhiping, *Searching for Harmony in Natural Order: Study on Chinese Traditional Legal Culture*, China University of Political Science and Law, 1997.
64. Li Buyun, *Moving towards Rule of Law*, Hunan People's Publishing House, 1998.
65. Li Changping, *I Told the Truth to Premier,* Guangming Daily Press, 2002.
66. Li Long, *A Theory of Rule of Law,* Wuhan University Press, 1997.
67. Lin Yusheng, *Creative Transformation of Chinese Tradition,* SDX Joint Publishing Company, 1996.
68. Lin Yusheng, *Creative Transformation of Chinese tradition*, SDX Joint Publishing Company, 1988.
69. Liu Zuoxiang, *Theories on Legal Culture*, The Commercial Press, 1999.
70. Lu Fuying, *Village Governance in the Process of Peasants' Differentiation*, South Press, 2000.
71. Lu Xueyi, *A Theory of "Three Agricultures": Study on Agriculture, Villages and Peasants in Contemporary China*, Social Sciences Academic Press, 2002.
72. Luther Tweeten, *Japanese and American Agriculture: Tradition and Progress in Conflict*, Westview Press, 1993.
73. Luo Haocai, *Balance Theory of Modern Administrative Law*, Peking University Press, 1997.
74. Lv Laiming, *Land Moves towards the Market-a New Theory of Landed Estate Law*, Guizhou People's Publishing House, 1995.
75. (UK) Malinowski, *Crime: Society and Culture*, Guangxi Normal University Press, 2003.
76. Max Weber, *On Law in Economy and Society*, Encyclopedia of China Publishing House, 1998.
77. Ma Yinlu, *Apologize to the Farmers*, Northwest University Press, 2002.
78. (Japan) Mill Takamizawa, *Disputes and Law in Modern China*, Law Press, 2003.
79. Min Qi, *Political Culture in Chin,* Yunnan People's Publishing House, 1989.
80. (USA) Munroe Smith, *The Development of European Law*, China University of Political Science and Law Press, 1999.
81. Nicholas Herbert-Young, *Law, Police and Development in the Rural Environment*, University of Wales Press, Cardiff, 1999.
82. Prasenjit Duara, *Culture, Power and the State*, Jiangsu People' Publishing House, 1995.
83. Qian Hang and Xie Weiyang, *Tradition and Transformation: Clan Forms of Taihe Village in Jiangxi*, Shanghai Academy of Social Sciences Press, 1995.
84. Qi Duojun, *The Basic Theory of Economic Law (3rd ed.)*, Wuhan University Press, 2000.
85. Qi Duojun, *Economic Law,* Wuhan University Press, 1998.
86. Qi Duojun, *Legislative View of Enterprise in Market Economy*, Wuhan University Press, 2000.
87. Qi Duojun, *Economic Law Forum (Vol. 1-8)*, China Fangzheng Press, 1999-2003.
88. Qi Duojun, *Characteristics and New Development of Micro-Control Legislation*, Political Science and Law, No.1, 2002.
89. Qi Duojun, *On Power*. Chinese Journal of Law, No.1, 2001.
90. Qi Duojun, *Three Phases of the Market Economy's Development and its Legal Protection System*, Law Science, No.2, 1999.
91. Qi Duojun, *On System of Legal Guarantees for Contemporary Market Economy*, China Legal Science, No.5, 1994.
92. Qi Duojun, *WTO: Market Internationalization and New Development of International Regulation*, Journal of Central South University (Social Science Edition), No.4, 2003.

93. Qin Hui, *Peasants in China: Historical Reflection and Realistic Choice*, Henan People's Publishing House, 2003.
94. (France) Rene David, *Major Legal System in the World Today*, Shanghai Translation Publishing House, 1984.
95. Research Center for Rural Economy, Research Office for Contemporary Agricultural History, *Study on Ideas of "Three Agricultures" in CPC*, China Agriculture Press, 2002.
96. Richard Falk, *Law in an Emerging Global Village: A Post-Westphalian Perspective*, Transnational Publishers, Inc. 1998.
97. Robert D. Gray, *Democratic Theory and Post-Communist Change*, Prentice-Hall, 1995.
98. (Germany) Roif Stoter, *German Economic Administrative Law*, China University of Political Science and Law Press, 1999.
99. (USA) Roger Cotterrell, *The Sociology of Law: An Introduction*, Huaxia Publishing House, 1989.
100. Roger Cotterrell, *The Sociology of Law: An Introduction*, Huaxia Publishing House, 1989.
101. Rousseau, *The Social Contract,* The Commercial Company, 2nd ed., 1980.
102. S. A. Olanrewaju, *Rural Development Problems in Nigeria*, Avebury, 1992.
103. (Germany) Savigny, *On the Contemporary Mission of Legislation and Law*, China Legal Publishing House, 2001.
104. Scott Rozelle and Li Jianzhong, *Economic Behavior of Village Cadres in China's Economic Reform*, Economy and Management Publishing House, 1992.
105. Shi Taifeng, *Legislation on Capitalist Market Economy*, Party School of the Central Committee of CPC Press, 1994.
106. Shi Weimin and Liu Zhizhu, *Normative Election*, China Social Sciences Press, 2003.
107. (USA) Steven J. Burton, *An Introduction to Law and Legal Reasoning*, China University of Political Science and Law Press, 1998.
108. (USA) Stephen Holmes, *The Cost of Rights–Why Liberty Depends on Taxes*, Peking University Press, 2004.
109. Su Li, *Rule of Law and its Local Resources*, China University of Political Science and Law Press, 1996.
110. Su Li, *Sending Law to the Countryside*, China University of Political Science and Law Press, 2000.
111. Su Yongqin, *The State Coercion in Private Autonomy*, China Legal Publishing House, 2005.
112. Sun Youhai, *Research on Land Circulating System*, China Land Press, 2001.
113. (Japan) Tanase Takashio, *Dispute Resolution and the Judicial System*, China University of Political Science and Law Press, 1994.
114. Tian Chengyou, *Traditional Culture and Modernization of Rule of Law*, Guizhou People's Publishing House, 1999.
115. Unger, R, *Law in Modern Society*, China University of Political Science and Law, 1994.
116. (Germany) Utz Schliesky, *Economic Law*, Trans. Yu Wenguang, Law Press of China, 2006.
117. Wang Chunguang, *Social Change in Rural China*, Yunnan People's Publishing House, 1996.
118. Wang Cunxue and Luo Yousheng, *The Basic Issues of Rural Economic Law in China*, Law Press of China, 1998.
119. Wang Feng, *Investigation and Consideration on "Three Agricultural" Issues*, China Agriculture Press, 2002.
120. Wang Huning, *Family Culture in Contemporary China's Village-An Exploration of Chinese Social Modernization*, Shanghai People's Publishing House, 1991.
121. Wang Jiafu and Liu Hainian (eds.), *Rule of Law-Build a socialist country under rule of law*, Social Sciences Academic Press, 1997.
122. Wang Mingming and Wang Sifu, *Order. Justice and Authority in Rural Society*, China University of Political Science and Law Press, 1997.
123. Wang Mingming, *The Course of Community,* Tianjin People's Publishing House, 1997.
124. Wang Mingming, *Social Anthropology and China Studies*, SDX Joint Publishing Company, 1997.

125. Wang Mingming, *Culture and Power in Villages*, SDX Joint Publishing Company, 1997.
126. Wang Taixian and Ai Ming, *Concept and Strategy of Rule of Law*, China Procuratorate Press, 2001.
127. Wang Tonghui and Fei Xiaotong, *Social Organizations of Hualan Yao Nationality,* Jiangsu People's Publishing House, 1988.
128. Wang Weiguo, *Research on Land Rights in China*, China University of Political Science and Law Press, 1997.
129. Wang Yaxin and Liang Zhiping(eds.), *Civil Trial and Civil Contract in the Ming and Qing Dynasties*, Law Press, 1998.
130. Wang Ying, She Xiaoye and Sun Yaobing, *Min-class Society-Reform and Mass Organizations in China*, China Reform Press, 1993.
131. Wang Yongfei and Liu Jinguo, *Theory of Rule of Law in Process of Anti-Corruption*, Higher Education Press, 2003.
132. Wang Zhongtian, *Village Politics: Investigation and Consideration on Chinese Villager's Self-Governance*, Jiangxi People's Publishing House, 1999.
133. Wang Zhuo and Xu Bang, *Rural Land Property Rights System in China*, Economy and Management Publishing House, 1996.
134. Wei Qiong, *The Development of Western Economy*, Peking University Press, 2006.
135. Wen Fengwen, *Modern Society and Development of Land Ownership Theory*, Wu-Nan Book Company, 1984
136. Wu Yi, *Experience of Villager's Self-Governance in Rural Society*, Huazhong Normal University Press. 2002.
137. Wu Yi, *Changes of the Village Governance's Authority and Order–the Expression of the Shuang Village Located in Eastern Sichuan in the 20th Century*, China Social Sciences Press. 2002.
138. Xie Hui and Chen Jinzhao, *Customary Law (Vol.1)*, Shandong People's Publishing House, 2002.
139. Xu Yong, *Unbalanced Politics in China: Comparison of Urban and Rural Areas*, Central Radio & TV University Press, 1992.
140. Xu Yong, *Villager's Self-Governance in Rural China*, Huazhong Normal University Press, 1997.
141. Xu Jingyong, *Research on Rural Economic Reform in China*, China Financial Publishing House, 2001.
142. Yu Jianrong, *Yue Village Politics-the Change of China Rural Political Structure in Transitional Era*, The Commercial Press, 2001.
143. Yujiro Hayami, *Japanese Agriculture Under Siege: The Political Economy of Agricultural Policies*, Macmillan Press, 1988.
144. Yin Tian, *French Property Law*, Law Press, 1998.
145. Yu Yuhe, *A Comparative Study of the "Rule by Rite" in China and "Rule by Law" in West*. Tianjin Normal University Doctoral Dissertations, Master and Doctor's Dissertations Database in Fangzheng, Collection Number y371134.
146. Zhang Jimin, *Datasets of Tibetan Tribe's Custom Law in Qinghai*, Qinghai People's Publishing House, 1993.
147. Zhang Jimin, *The Research on Tibetan Tribe's Custom Law Series (All Three Volumes)*, Qinghai People Publishing House, Sept., 2002.
148. Zhang Qianfan, *Market Economy and Legal Regulation*, China Legal Publishing House, 1998.
149. Zhang Xiaojian, *Study on Employment and Mobility of Rural Labour in China*, China Labour Publishing House, 1999.
150. Zhang Wenxian, *Modern Western Legal Philosophy*, Jilin University Press, 1987.
151. Zhao Zhenjiang, *Sociology of Law*, Peking University Press, 1998.
152. Zheng Yongliu, *A Preliminary Study on Road to Development of Rural Law in Contemporary China*, Shanghai Academy of Social Sciences Press, 1991.
153. Zheng Yongliu et al, *Legal Consciousness of Peasants and Development of Rural Law*, Wuhan Publishing House, 1993.

154. Zheng Yongliu, *Four Chapters of Rule of Law-Sources of Britain and Germany. International Standards and China Issues*, China Renmin University Press, 2002.
155. Zhou Xiaohong, *Tradition and Change-Jiangsu and Zhejiang Peasants' Social Psychology and its Evolution Since Modern Times*. SDX Joint Publishing Company, 1998.
156. Zhou Yangshan, *Liberty and Authority*, San Min Book Co. Ltd., 1991.
157. Zhu Jingwen, *Framework and methods of Comparative Sociology of Law*, China Renmin University Press, 2001.
158. Zhu Qiuxia, *The Reform of Rural Land System in China Mainland*, Zhengzhong Book Company, 1995.
159. Zhu Zhiwen and Lei Xingchang, *Study on "Three Agricultural" Issues in Western Development*, Gansu People's Publishing House, 2002.

www.ingramcontent.com/pod-product-compliance
Ingram Content Group UK Ltd.
Pitfield, Milton Keynes, MK11 3LW, UK
UKHW041129071026
15587UKWH00009B/299

9 780761 869207